Public Management
in Global Perspective

Salvatore Schiavo-Campo is an international consultant with experience in leading roles in over fifty countries. A former senior official of the World Bank, Asian Development Bank, and International Monetary Fund, he was previously Professor and Chairman of Economics at University of Massachusetts, Boston. He holds a Ph.D. in Economics and an M.A. in International Affairs from Columbia University and an LL.D. from the Università di Palermo, and has published extensively in international economics and public management, including the classic *Perspectives of Economic Development* (with Hans Singer) and the recent *Managing Government Expenditure.*

Hazel M. McFerson is Associate Professor of Public and International Affairs and Associate of the Institute for Conflict Analysis and Resolution at George Mason University, and previously taught at the University of the South Pacific in Fiji and the University of Asia and Pacific in Manila. She has received several awards, including a Fulbright, and holds a Ph.D. from Brandeis University, an M.A. from the Fletcher School of Law and Diplomacy, Tufts University, and a B.A. from University of Massachusetts, Boston. Her latest books are *Mixed Blessing: The Impact of American Colonial Policy on the Philippines,* and *Blacks and Asians: Crossings, Conflict and Commonalities.*

Public Management in Global Perspective

Salvatore Schiavo-Campo and Hazel M. McFerson

M.E.Sharpe
Armonk, New York
London, England

Library of Congress Cataloging-in-Publication Data

Schiavo-Campo, Salvatore.
  Public management in global perspective / by Salvatore Schiavo-Campo and
Hazel M. McFerson.
    p. cm.
  Includes bibliographical references and index.
  ISBN-13: 978-0-7656-1726-2 (pbk. : alk. paper)
  1. Public administration. 2. Public administration—United States. 3. State, The.
4. Globalization—Political aspects. I. McFerson, Hazel M. II. Title.
  JF1351.S345 2008
  351—dc22   2007022835

Printed in the United States of America

The paper used in this publication meets the minimum requirements of
American National Standard for Information Sciences
Permanence of Paper for Printed Library Materials,
ANSI Z 39.48-1984.

∞

BM (p)   10   9   8   7   6   5   4   3   2   1

Contents

List of Boxes,
Tables, and Figures

BOXES

TABLES

FIGURES

Preface and Introduction

OBJECTIVES, SCOPE, AND LIMITATIONS OF THE BOOK

It is a shopworn cliché that the world is increasingly interdependent and likely to become even more so in future years. Cliché or not, the reality of globalization suggests that public administration students and public managers would be best served by some understanding of other administrative cultures and decision systems in addition to their own, grounded on cross-cutting universals as well as actual international experience. Consequently, this volume has three aims: combine the conceptual foundations of public administration with nonparochial coverage of the United States and other major countries' systems, and with the lessons of international experience; meet the concerns of both academics and public officials; and move past the sterile dichotomy of "new public management" and "traditional public administration" to a fusion of the best elements of each. Accordingly, our target audience is threefold: students of public administration, mid- and high-level practitioners, and academics.

We were also interested in expanding the public administration discussion in three critical directions. Although most current treatments of the field do include some discussion of accountability, they rarely elaborate on the overall governance context—articulated around the four pillars of accountability, transparency, rule of law, and participation. Also largely missing is an adequate consideration of institutions—in the Coase-North-Williamson sense of "rules of the game" rather than the descriptive meaning of the older German literature. Finally, the rich and complex influence of social capital on public management is given here far more prominence than is usually the case.

It would not be possible to write a book that is internationally versatile as well as responsive to the concerns of both academics and public practitioners, *and* incorporates the governance and institutional dimension, without making deliberate sacrifices in coverage. We limited ourselves in a number of ways. Although the book starts with a recapitulation of the historical and cultural roots of the fundamental concepts of government and public administration, the standard discussion of political theories and management approaches is kept to a minimum, and the important but elusive subject of organizational effectiveness is not addressed at all—except indirectly through the discussion of each topic. We also eschewed the lengthy dissection of practical problems typical of the technical public management manuals, in favor of a readable synthesis of options and solutions. (Some of the more technical topics are discussed in Appendices to the various chapters.) Finally, instead of the exhaustive description of the country's structures and practices that is found in purely "national" treatments of public administration, each chapter contains a synopsis of the key administrative features in the United States, and a large number of illustrations and micro-case studies of other countries worldwide. Thus, this book can usefully be complemented by selected readings that address some of the issues that could not be covered here.

STRUCTURE

After an introductory chapter providing an overview of the main themes subtending the entire book, Part I covers the functions and organization of government around the world and in the United States beginning with a recapitulation of the common roots of public administration in ancient Greece, China, and India and an explanation of the major roles of government, and proceeding in turn to a discussion of the regulatory and policy-making functions, the organizational architecture of central government, the geographic articulation of state power and responsibilities, and the issues of decentralization. Part II deals with the core of public administration: managing government financial resources, managing government personnel, managing public procurement, and managing for results by fostering a stronger orientation to performance. Part III moves beyond the internal workings of the administrative apparatus to examine the major facets of the interface between government and the citizens. It covers the "four pillars" of governance, by discussing in turn accountability, participation and social capital, transparency (including the role of the media and the contribution of information technology), and the rule of law. The concluding Part IV consists of two brief chapters, on the major administrative reforms in developed countries over the last two decades, and on improving administration by combining into "principled pragmatism" the "new public management" emphasis on results and performance with the imperative to preserve the traditional requirements of integrity and due process.

Within each chapter, the general concepts and principles are first explained, and reference is made to relevant international experience. Where appropriate, subsections of a chapter touch on the special issues relevant to developing countries or transition economies. While these subsections are fully integrated into the chapter discussion, readers wishing to skip them can easily do so without losing the continuity of the argument. One important caveat is necessary upfront, to avoid having to repeat it over and over in the text. The distinction between "developed" and "developing" countries entails a major oversimplification, as there are obvious and substantial differences within both categories—Japan is hardly Canada, and Nepal is very different from Paraguay. The same is true of "transition economies," a category that encompasses countries as diverse as Vietnam and Moldova. The reader is asked to make allowances for the sweeping generalizations that are inevitably associated with such broad categories. Nevertheless, owing to the close linkages between a country's income level and the modalities of public management, the differences between "developed," "developing," and "transition" countries are significantly greater than the variance within each group. Generalizations are possible and meaningful.

Detailed references and endnotes are kept to a minimum, as we wanted to avoid the feel of pedantry and the discontinuity that are generated by a vast number of endnotes and detailed references. For each section, of course, there is a clear attribution of credit to the main sources used, although in many cases credit for specific points cannot be assigned to individual authors, as their contributions were amalgamated and synthesized in this book in an entirely personal way and under our responsibility for any error or misunderstanding. One caveat: the necessary delay between writing and publishing makes it impossible for all data and information to be current. Whenever possible, the information was updated. In any case, the latest version of the manuscript was carefully reviewed to make sure that the discussion and conclusions remained valid as of late 2007.

Most chapters include a next-to-last section on the situation in the United States. It was possible to keep those sections fairly short, as most of the principles and issues relevant also to the

United States are addressed in the preceding sections of the chapter. Nevertheless, readers wishing greater detail on certain topics in the United States are advised to peruse some of the excellent books focusing entirely on American public administration. Conversely, readers from other countries may wish to skip the U.S. sections altogether in favor of readings directly pertinent to their own country.

Most chapters conclude with a short section on general directions for improvement. These sections in no way pretend to offer an agenda for reform, as any such agenda must be specific to a time and place. They are only intended as pointers to the more frequent problems and opportunities for improvement and are to be viewed as elements of reflection more than suggestions—and certainly not as prescriptions. (These sections can also serve to recall some of the key issues addressed in the chapter.)

The chapters are also framed by a very brief section at the start, noting what is to be expected from the chapter, and a list of discussion questions at the end. The discussion questions are deliberately open-ended, have no clear-cut or implied right-or-wrong answer, and are meant to serve as trigger of the brainstorming and genuine discussion that are essential to reveal the richness and complexity of the issue at hand.

ACKNOWLEDGMENTS

We owe much to many. Our first debt of gratitude goes to Pachampet S. A. Sundaram, Schiavo-Campo's co-author of an earlier publication covering many of these issues, as well as to the Asian Development Bank, which provided the enabling environment that made that book possible and gave kind permission to use material from it.[1]

The next largest debt is owed to Trevor Robinson, president of IBIS Consulting, who took the time and trouble of reviewing the entire manuscript—some chapters more than once—and whose wealth of knowledge and experience saved us from numerous errors and made for wiser conclusions.

Parts of this book have been improved by contributions by several colleagues—mainly Robert F. Beschel of the World Bank for chapters 4 and 14; Frederic Bouder and Janos Bertok of the OECD for chapters 14 and 15; Giulio de Tommaso of the World Bank for chapter 7; Helena Ireen Baylon of the Asian Development Bank for chapter 5; Marilyn Pizarro and Clay Wescott, also of the ADB, for chapter 13; and Daniel Tommasi, the foremost expert in applied budgeting active today, for chapter 6.

Extensive and valuable criticism and comments were offered by professors Richard Batley of the University of Birmingham International School of Public Policy; Alain Billon of the Ecole Nationale d'Administration; Peter Larmour of the Australian National University; Jon Quah of Oxford University; Art Stevenson, director of the Commonwealth Association for Public Administration; Young-Pyoung Kim, president of the Korean Institute of Public Administration; as well as Tony Hughes, Bruce Knapman, Anne-Marie Leroy, Terry Morrison, and Paul Oquist.

Among the many others who commented on selected chapters are Eveline Herfkens, UN Executive Coordinator for the Millennium Development Goals; Constantine Michalopoulos; Dolores Bonifacio of the Philippines Civil Service Commission; and professors Brack Brown and Min Wang of George Mason University. Tommie Porter and Mara Schiavocampo gave us the benefit of their professional expertise in commenting, respectively, on the chapter on information technology and on the role of the media in governance.

Finally, our thanks go to Harry Briggs for his warm encouragement, Elizabeth Granda for editorial direction, Angela Piliouras for production guidance, Jerry Altobelli for able copy editing, Jesse Sanchez for the elegent cover design, and Jean Mooney for the thorough indexing.

This book is in every respect a joint effort, with each of us reviewing, editing and contributing in some measure to the entire book. However, our respective expertise and interests led to McFerson being primarily responsible for chapter 2 and much of Part III (as well as the U.S. sections and the ancillary material, e.g., discussion questions), and Schiavo-Campo primarily responsible for the remainder.

NOTE

1. Schiavo-Campo and Sundaram (2000), Asian Development Bank. The views expressed in the publication are those of the authors and do not necessarily represent those of the Asian Development Bank, or its Board of Directors or the governments the Directors represent. For more information on development in Asia and the Pacific, see www.adb.org. Portions of that publication are incorporated throughout this book, but, as appropriate, they are credited to the primary sources rather than to the ADB publication itself.

Public Management
in Global Perspective

CHAPTER 1

Public Administration in the Century of Interdependence

> The times are changing, and we along with them.
> —*Ovid, 8 C.E.*

WHAT TO EXPECT

Any discussion of the administration of the "public thing"—the ancient Roman *res publica,* from which "republic" is derived—must be predicated on the existence of some government legitimacy and some measure of legal and political accountability. The issue of the appropriate relationship between "policy" and "administration" is an old one. On the one hand, the policy question of "what" is to be done is different from the management question of "how" it is to be done. The distinction between the quality of the management instruments and the goals that they are meant to achieve is important. One can explain how to sharpen a knife without discussing whether it is to be used for peeling apples or chopping onions. Thus, this book discusses public administration issues mainly in their instrumental aspects. On the other hand, excessively hard boundaries between "policy" and "implementation" eventually lead to both unrealistic policies and bad implementation. Therefore, wherever appropriate, the discussion will shade into public policy issues and the interaction between public policy and public management.

But make no mistake—whatever the right mix of the "what" and the "how," allowing public administration to be relegated to the backseat by the sexier issues of public policy invariably blows back to destroy the policy itself. A strategy paper without a roadmap is a paper, not a strategy; a decision without implementation is a wish, not a decision; a law without enforcement is a pantomime, not a law. Organized government, no matter how representative and democratic it may be, is utterly impotent without the instruments to carry out its will. This is the broad canvas of this book—tinted by the major trends of our time, from globalization to the resurgence of ethnicity and religion and the risk of regression to an apolar international system.

This overview chapter describes the main contemporary trends influencing public management in the United States and elsewhere in the world. The institutional and cultural context of public management is outlined next—including the all-important concept of governance—and the chapter concludes with setting out criteria for assessing and improving public administration. The basic themes and concepts introduced in this overview are embedded in the discussion of the various dimensions of public administration presented in the subsequent chapters.

THE MAJOR INFLUENCES ON ADMINISTRATION IN THE TWENTY-FIRST CENTURY

Globalization: A Smaller Planet, Spinning Faster

Asking the Right Question

In late 2007, an internet search for "globalization" showed about 27 million entries (growing at the rate of about one million every three months). Yet, interdependence among individuals, among groups, among nations, has always been a reality—indeed, it has been the basis for the evolution of organized human society. Moreover, the increase in interdependence is not new. From as far back as the fourteenth century, global interdependence has been increasing because of the continuing reduction in "economic distance"—the cost of transferring goods, services, labor, capital, and information from one place to another—due to improvements in transport technology, tariff cuts, creation of international institutions, telecommunications and informatics, among other reasons. With that said, the acceleration witnessed in the last two decades has been spectacular. Thus, "globalization" is more than just a catchy term for an old phenomenon. There may be no difference in overall impact between, say, the invention of the railroad and that of the computer. However, the difference in degree and speed of impact is so vast as to constitute in effect a new phenomenon—particularly as it coincided with the rapid liberalization of external financial transactions that took place in most major countries. In Thomas Friedman's expression, globalization has made the world flat (Friedman, 2005).

And so, let's be clear about the key question. The genuine core of the globalization debate is not the continuing decrease in economic distance, per se, but the valid concern that in recent years economic distance has been shrinking faster than can be reasonably managed by the international system—let alone by an individual country. The foremost consequence of this disconnect between an integrated world economy and an un-integrated world political system is the lack of a functioning mechanism to address the problems of individuals, groups and countries on the losing end of the process.

Globalization and Public Administration

Globalization has an impact on most dimensions of public administration in most countries, and constrains the ability of national governments to act independently. Gone are the days when major decisions on the extent and manner of state intervention could be taken in isolation. The new reality is the imperative of considering the impact of those decisions on the outside world and the blowback from it. This reality cuts two ways. On the one hand, there is a new constraint on many governments' ability to sustain inefficient economic policies; on the other hand, the implementation of government's independent social policies and redistributive objectives is hampered as well.

Globalization is also changing the role of government by introducing a new source of insecurity at the same time as it has raised efficiency (particularly in North America but to an increasing extent in Europe as well). Not long ago, in most developed countries economic security was found largely in the workplace. With the employers' market and sources of input supply fairly predictable, it was possible to provide employees with reasonable assurances of employment security and post-employment benefits. As markets have become globalized, and plants, input supply and jobs increasingly outsourced, uncertainty has increased substantially for both the employers and the employees. The employers have accordingly passed through much of that uncertainty to their employees, by larger, more frequent and less predictable layoffs, and by shedding as much as possible the cost of health insurance and retirement benefits. Individuals are thus coming to look more and more to the government for the economic security they used to enjoy in the private workplace. Conversely, in developing countries, people at the receiving end of the outsourced jobs are relying more and more on the private sector for gainful employment and rapid advancement. This trend is still at the beginning and its impact in different areas of administration cannot yet be clearly defined, but it will heavily influence the role of government and the modalities of public administration for the foreseeable future.

Stopping the Tide?

Thus, the economic and social benefits from globalization can be immense, but the costs and risks can be high as well, and *the distribution of costs and risks among individuals, groups and countries is different from the distribution of benefits*. Globalization also has an impact on the concentration of economic power between and within countries. The answer to this problem is not a retreat into national isolation or a weakening of international rules—quite the opposite. It is as impossible to reverse the globalization process as it would be to make television or the internet disappear. Indeed, efforts at reversing globalization may even be counterproductive, because they divert attention from the need to counteract the possible negative impact of the globalization tendency on income distribution and effective competition. The analytical and operational challenge is to strengthen the international and regional management of the process, primarily to (1) slow down the external transmission of destructive developments in any one country; (2) prevent overreaction; and (3) protect vulnerable groups and countries from carrying the brunt of the adjustment and being left farther and farther behind.

Finally, it is well to remember that globalization is a two-way channel, making it much easier to transmit internationally both positive and negative changes. For example, not only jobs and technology have been globalized, but crime as well. A recent book (Naim, 2006) provides analysis and illustrations of the new phenomenon of drug traffickers and other organized criminals operating globally—see Box 1.1.

Decentralization: A Double Squeeze on Central Government

Gone, too, are the days when central administration had the virtual monopoly of state power. As economic distance between any two areas is reduced, the space for the center naturally shrinks. Globally, the nation-state occupies the center, and the reduction in economic distance from the rest of the world has meant a loss in effective national administrative autonomy. But central governments have been squeezed from below as well. The greater mobility of persons and goods and the ease of communication and information flows have brought several public activities within effective reach of local government. Combined with a stronger civil society and a more assertive population, these developments have led to pressures on the center to "download" onto local government both authority and resources.

As an overall trend, internal decentralization may be as unstoppable as globalization. At the same time, however, decentralization of certain functions generates the need for greater centralization of other functions (or for stronger central supervision). Moreover, the need to meet the challenges of globalization is itself a factor making for centralization of state power. The vector resulting from the contrasting forces of centralization and decentralization will of course differ in different countries. In the United States, the post-9/11 perception of major threats to national security

BOX 1.1

The Seamy Underbelly of Globalization

The last decade has seen a mushrooming of international networks of illicit activities. These comprise more than the "traditional" smuggling and drug trafficking, and include transport of illegal migrants, trade in women and children for prostitution (up to and including slavery), money laundering, pirated movies and counterfeit software, trade in human organs and endangered animals, weapons—anything on which profitable international trade has been made possible by the extraordinary advances in information and communications technology. It is estimated that the total value of "production" by these crime networks is as high as 10 percent of the world economy.

These crime networks are extremely efficient—flat, decentralized, fluid, and adaptable. They navigate in the interstices of the international system, are interconnected, and can form, mutate, merge, split, and recombine very quickly to adapt to changes in the "market." These networks are already distorting global trade and financial flows and are increasingly capable of capturing small and weak states. There is also considerable crossover between the criminal and the terrorist networks. (Concerning the latter, it is critical to make a distinction between groups with a legitimate or at least definable political agenda and those whose sole goal is to destroy and create instability.)

Because of the global reach of the new crime networks, it is extremely difficult for any single country to counteract them effectively, and an effective response would have to be equally global. Ideally, this would call for the creation of a truly multilateral public entity with the mandate, autonomy, and resources to meet this new challenge. A partial move in this direction has been made by the European Union, where since 1999 the judicial authorities in one country may order an arrest based on a warrant issued in another European country and may also seize evidence requested by judges in another country and transmit it to them. Even in Europe, however, national governments have balked at further integration of their criminal justice systems.

At a minimum, far better and systematic communication is needed between national security agencies and the international police organization INTERPOL. Considering the difficulties in communicating even between security agencies of the same country (e.g., the well-known "territorial" mentality of the FBI and other police agencies in the United States), this will not be easy. However, the increased effectiveness of international law enforcement and the genuine improvement in national security all around will be well worth the cost of the effort.

Source: Partly based and adapted from Naim (2006) and *The Economist,* "Charlemagne," September 30, 2006.

and the push to combat and reverse what some view as an erosion of basic values have enabled a recentralization of power in the federal government. Only time and the political choices of the American people will tell whether this signals a new trend or is a temporary blip—with a return to the long-term trend toward decentralization as soon as the largely fabricated sense of insecurity wanes. In Europe, by contrast, there has been a voluntary uploading of substantial powers from the component member-states to the European Union as a supranational entity. (But in Europe, too, a backlash has been evident in recent years.)

Hence, instead of arguing about decentralization or centralization, in the current context it is more useful to ask:

- which functions are suitable for greater decentralization (and which are not);
- what is needed to make decentralization of the suitable functions effective; and
- what modifications in central government role are necessary to protect the country and vulnerable groups from the risks and costs of decentralization.

The reader can see the close parallel between globalization and decentralization. Like globalization, decentralization carries a potential for large overall benefits as well as risks and losses for the more vulnerable areas and groups. The management of decentralization within a country therefore calls for strong national action, just as the management of globalization requires strong international action.

Moreover, the intermediate administrative space is shrinking internally as well as internationally. Until the middle of the twentieth century, the intermediate level of government (the "state" in federal systems such as the United States' or the "province" in unitary systems such as France's) typically enjoyed a double monopoly position: as sole interpreter of government policy vis-à-vis local governments and as sole provider of information and of upward feedback to the center. Economic distance has contracted *within* countries as well, and this state of affairs has been changing. (Countries wracked by civil conflict or prolonged malgovernance are a major exception, with internal economic distance growing sharply in the last two decades.)

In future years, decentralization may primarily entail a leapfrogging of some administrative powers and resources from the central to the lowest level of local government, bypassing the intermediate level of government, *plus* a further devolution of powers to local government from the intermediate level itself. In addition, confronted with the erosion of their autonomy vis-à-vis the global market and external entities, national governments are likely to "repossess" responsibilities and resources previously assigned to the provinces.

On all these counts, the traditional role of the intermediate levels of government administration may be substantially reduced. This does not necessarily mean a reduction in their influence, however; their role may remain just as important, but will have to evolve away from direction and control toward facilitation and technical assistance. As noted, these trends will manifest themselves differently in federal states such as the United States, Canada, or India than in unitary states such as China, France, or Spain.

The International Political Environment

It is well known that the end of the Cold War (conventionally dated from the fall of the Berlin Wall in October 1989) and the disappearance of the Soviet Union at the end of 1991 have caused fundamental changes in international politics. These changes have three important implications for the role of government and for public administration in the United States and elsewhere.

New Countries, New Systems

The end of the Cold War opened the door to a massive transformation in Eastern Europe, in the former Soviet Union and, indirectly, in the centrally planned economies of Asia. These diverse countries are frequently lumped together under the designation of "transition countries." The common designation is useful insofar as moving toward greater reliance on the market mechanism and a streamlined role of the state require adjustments of a similar sort. However, the common designation can be misleading because, in addition to the substantial diversity among these countries, the structural challenges are very different.

The maximum degree of systemic transformation has been faced by the newly independent countries that were the component "republics" of the former Soviet Union.[1] Radical changes in economy and society have occurred in the past, for example, in China during the last century. And new states have emerged throughout history, too—for example, many of the former colonies of western powers, or some components of the former Austro-Hungarian empire destroyed by World War I. But never before has history witnessed a complete reversal of the economic system at the same time as the coming into existence of brand new political entities. The enormity of the double challenge of nation-building and economic transformation in many of the countries of the former USSR is still insufficiently understood and recognized. Certainly, the governance and administrative transition is far from complete on either front, as shown by the resurgent authoritarianism in Russia and the fragility of institutions in countries such as Ukraine after the victory of democratic forces in the 2004 presidential elections.

In central and eastern Europe, the command economy also gave way to a market economy, but this happened in nation-states that had been in existence for generations or centuries. The transformation challenge was massive, certainly, but was confined to the economic and political system. Although the transition is still uneven between different countries, at the beginning of the twenty-first century virtually all central and eastern European countries are now market economies with representative governance.

The circumstances of the Southeast Asian centrally planned economies of Vietnam, Cambodia, and Laos are very different. These countries are also in transition, in the direction of greater reliance on the market mechanism, some reduction in state intervention, and external openness, but more in an evolutionary way and within the same national as well as political parameters. And China, with its spectacular economic growth record of the past generation, horrendous environmental problems and continuing repressive political regime, is in a category by itself.

The Dark Side of Ethnicity

Since 1990, ethnic conflict and narrow-based nationalisms—never absent—were given a new lease on life. As is well known, these past seventeen years have been stained by murderous internecine conflict (sometimes spontaneous, more commonly manufactured or fomented for power purposes), ranging from the genocide of one million Tutsis and moderate Hutus in Rwanda in just three months in 1994 to "ethnic cleansing" in the former Yugoslavia, spasmodic brutality in Aceh and other parts of Indonesia, systematic repression and mass murder in Darfur (in the west of Sudan), and many other tragedies. Indeed, there is plenty of evidence that ethnicity trumps even religion as a source of conflict. In Darfur, for example, the local African (and Muslim) population has been systematically oppressed and repressed by a central government in Khartoum dominated by an Arab (and Muslim) elite. Or, recall the many Hutu priests and nuns who actively cooperated in the genocide of Catholic Tutsis—their own parishioners. These conflicts revalidated at the end of the century the prediction made at its beginning by African-American political scientist W. E. B. DuBois that this would be the dominant question of the twentieth century.[2] Who knows—it may even remain the dominant question for a good part of this century.

For public administration, the implications of the ethnic factor concern mainly the need for extreme caution when introducing into multiethnic countries "contractual" and performance management practices developed in homogeneous societies, as well as the design of decentralization. Decentralization, long viewed as a "technical" issue (albeit one of high order) must in future years be carefully weighed in light of the new centrifugal and fragmentation risks in many countries. (This is one of the themes of chapter 5.) Of the many breakups of countries witnessed in the 1990s, only one (Czechoslovakia) occurred peacefully. The argument is two-edged, of course—in some circumstances, only genuine decentralization can prevent ethnic tensions from eventually erupting into overt conflict, as appears to be the case in Iraq.

Similar issues apply to long-neglected caste minorities and low-status social groups in certain countries, such as the *Dalits* in India (formerly called "untouchables") or the *Burakumin* in Japan. Albeit of the same ethnicity, religion, and language as the majority population, these groups have been treated in all respects as oppressed ethnic minorities and find themselves in the same predicament.

In the United States, of course, the racial and ethnic question has been central to political discourse and government policy ever since the first African slave was brought into the country. In contemporary times, this question has coalesced around the issue of "affirmative action." Subsequent chapters will examine the implications of this issue for various areas of public administration, from government contracting to personnel management. At this stage, we only wish to underline that the semantic fog, ambiguous evidence, and deliberately misleading arguments brought up in the "affirmative action" debate in recent years are a major reason why it has not proven possible in America to build a social consensus on the appropriate handling of ethnic differences. It is not possible to find good answers to bad questions, which have unfortunately dominated the debate.

The Disappearing Peace Dividend

The Numbers. The end of the Cold War also changed the perspective on "national security" and therefore on military expenditure—not only for the great powers but for most countries. All estimates of military expenditure must be taken with a pound of salt—transparency is pretty good in some countries, while in other countries much military expenditure is hidden under the rug of civilian spending. In addition, there are difficult methodological issues, such as the valuation of the services of soldiers. However, the available figures do show very clear trends.

Expressed in constant 1995 prices (thus accounting for inflation), world military expenditure fell in real terms by one third from 1989 to 1992, from the equivalent of US$1.7 trillion to $1.1 trillion, and the trend continued after the dissolution of the Soviet Union. Overall, world military expenditure was cut in half between 1989 and 1998. Because of the substantial economic growth during the 1990s, in relative terms the peace dividend was even more pronounced, with military spending absorbing almost 6 percent of world Gross Domestic Product (GDP) in 1989 and less than 2 percent in 1998. (The GDP is the standard measure of the value of total annual production.)

The United States shared in this decline, from $373 billion in military spending in 1989 to $251 billion in 1998—from 5.6 percent to 3.1 percent of GDP—a decline that indirectly permitted an increase in expenditure on education and health care even while a fiscal surplus was being achieved. During the first years of this century this trend has been reversed, with military spending up sharply to about $500 billion in 2005—more than 6 percent of GDP—as a result of the military response to the complicity of the Taliban regime in the 9/11 attack[3] and, to a far greater extent, the cost of the war in Iraq.

As of December 2006, the Central Intelligence Agency estimates that total world military expenditure is back up to more than one trillion dollars per year, with the five highest spenders being the United States ($518 billion), China ($81 billion), France ($45 billion), Japan ($44 billion—surprisingly for a country with a pacifist constitution), and the United Kingdom ($43 billion). The next five highest-spending countries are, in order, Germany, Italy, South Korea, India, and Saudi Arabia.[4] We hope there is no need to underline that high placement on this list is not enviable and should not be a source of national pride.

The Issues. Unfortunately, the reduction in military spending in the 1990s did not correlate with diminished conflict. This was partly due to the reemergence of ethnic hostility, noted earlier, and to "labor-intensive" localized conflicts—cheap but highly efficient producers of human suffering. Labor-intensive conflict (i.e., relying on lots of manpower armed with simple and basic weapons) is not to be confused with "low-intensity" conflict. The Rwandan genocide, for example, was heavily "labor intensive," using a lot of people armed with sticks and machetes, and yet managed to massacre a million people in three months—a rate twice as fast as the Nazi-driven Holocaust with its advanced killing technology.

In addition, the logic of globalization has also entailed the formation of trans-border networks of financial support for internal conflict, sometimes involving diaspora groups (e.g., Ireland or Sri Lanka) and sometimes the drug trade (e.g., Burma or Colombia). The manipulation of trans-border trade and external support has further contributed to the erosion of central government authority and to the growth in transnational organized crime, as illustrated earlier in Box 1.1.

An extended discussion of the implications of military spending would not be appropriate in this book. However, some general considerations are useful to frame the issue.

First, there is no necessary connection between military expenditure and the security of the nation or of its people. It is often argued that military unpreparedness invites attack. This may be true. However, the opposite can be true as well. The Greek historian Thucydides identified 2,500 years ago what later came to be called the "security dilemma": "What made war inevitable was the growth of Athenian power and the fear which this caused in Sparta."[5]

When actions by one state to enhance its security through higher military spending are seen by another state as threatening, they may lead the latter to take countermeasures, and the higher military spending actually diminishes security for both states. It is not really a paradox that the safest and most secure country in Central America is Costa Rica, which for over fifty years has had no army or other military apparatus. Consistent with the security dilemma, such knowledgeable observers as Costa Rican president and 1989 Nobel Peace laureate Oscar Arias explained to one of the authors that Costa Rica has greater security precisely because it has no army.[6] Or, concerning internal security, consider the sad reality that in much of Africa the worst threat to the African citizen is the African soldier.

Second, in countries where a military apparatus is considered justified on grounds of genuine national security, it does not necessarily follow that *increases* in military expenditure bring about an improvement in security. The relationship of military spending to national security, to the extent that it exists, is far more complex. It depends on many things, including the composition of military expenditure, the extent of wasteful spending, the suitability of military hardware, and motivational factors. For example, the huge military and security apparatus of the Shah of Iran in the late 1970s gave the regime no protection against a determined civil upheaval. (Even his personal guard, "The Immortals," melted away, giving rise to the joke that their name was explained by their ability to avoid danger.)

Third, in cases where it is determined that (1) a military apparatus is necessary; (2) the overall amount of military spending is appropriate; (3) its composition is suitable; and (4) there is limited waste, the "opportunity cost" of the expenditure must still be reckoned with. Opportunity cost is the economist's measure of cost (i.e., the goods or services that could have been produced by the same resources—the opportunities lost). Military spending inevitably crowds out civilian expenditure, and/or requires tax increases, and/or destabilizes the public finances. This is particularly unfortunate in poor countries, which still spend about fifty cents on the military for every government dollar they spend on health and education. The ensuing adverse impact on development and on long-term poverty reduction ranks as a fundamental consideration in the debate on the appropriateness of military expenditure.[7] Returning to the example of Costa Rica, that country's respectable economic performance for fifty years and excellent human development indicators are unquestionably related to the higher level of government expenditure on basic social services permitted by not having to spend the money for military purposes.

But the economic and social cost of military expenditure is also substantial in rich countries like the United States. Thus, aside from a judgment on the Iraq War, it is a matter of simple arithmetic that the money spent on the war could have helped fix the future financial problems of the social security system, or provided health insurance for the forty-seven million Americans currently not covered, or extended financial aid to practically all college students in the country, or paid off the public debt, or gone to any number of other worthy purposes.

In a democracy, it is for the people to decide through their political system whether certain expenditures are "worth it." In doing so, it is always essential to imagine what "it" could be. The political issue is how to balance the benefits from military spending—however they may be defined—against the benefits that would otherwise accrue from spending the same money for other purposes or improving the health of the economy.

HOW SHOULD GOVERNMENT ACT?

The Governance Context

Government administration has traditionally been viewed with jaundiced and hypercritical eyes—sometimes with good reason, sometimes not. Let's first underline that problems of excessive red tape, lack of responsiveness, fraud, waste, and abuse can exist in *all* very large organizations, whether public or private, and are certainly not limited to government bureaucracies. This is not a theoretical presumption—it is an empirical reality. No government bureaucrat in developed countries has ever managed to buy $16,000 umbrella stands with shareholders' money, as former Tyco CEO Dennis Koslovsky did; or "borrow" tens of millions of dollars from his company and then have the loans "forgiven," as Adelphia's John Rigas did; or receive a severance payment of $210 million, as Robert Nardelli did when Home Depot fired him in 2007. But then, too, no corrupt corporate CEO has ever succeeded in turning an entire country into a kleptocracy and keeping it an economic basket case despite huge natural riches, as did Mobutu Sese Seko, the former dictator of Zaire (now Democratic Republic of Congo); or to steal billions of dollars from the public treasury, as former Philippines' strongman Ferdinand Marcos was proud to acknowledge; or run an entire country into the ground, as president Robert Mugabe has done to Zimbabwe. So, the operative concepts are the size of the organization, the concentration of power, and weak accountability mechanisms—not whether the organization is public or private.

There are four criteria by which to judge whether government administration is good, bad, or indifferent—and the same criteria provide essential guidance for any effort to improve public administration for the benefit of the population. These criteria are subsumed in the term "good governance."

Figure 1.1   **The "Temple" of Good Governance**

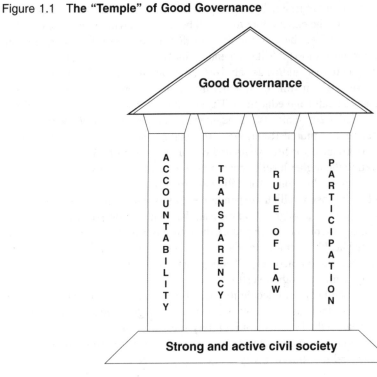

The Four Pillars of Governance

"Governance" is the manner in which state power is exercised—as distinct from the purposes for which state power is exercised. It has to do with the quality of the process, not the quality of the outcomes. It is quite possible for bad and arbitrary decision-making processes to occasionally produce good decisions, and for bad decisions to sometimes come out of good and fair systems. In the long run, however, just like democracy, good governance tends to produce good decisions and bad governance leads to bad decisions. *Sustainability* is the issue. Even when an apparently sound decision is produced in arbitrary and authoritarian ways, it cannot command the active support of the public and is thus much more likely to be ineffective or reversed. If you are concerned only with the quality of each decision and not with the process of decision making, eventually you will get—and you will deserve—bad decisions.

Good governance rests on four pillars—accountability, transparency, predictability (through the rule of law), and participation—supported by the foundation of a strong civil society. Accountability means the capacity to call public officials to task for their actions; transparency entails the low-cost access to relevant information; predictability results primarily from laws and regulations that are clear, known in advance, and uniformly and effectively enforced; and participation is needed to supply reliable information and provide a reality check for government action. These are simply represented in Figure 1.1.

It is clear that each of the four pillars is related to and instrumental in supporting the other three. For example, accountability is hollow in the face of administrative secrecy and is meaningless without predictable consequences. Furthermore, all governance concepts are universal in application but relative in nature. Accountability is a must everywhere but does not become operational until one defines accountability "of whom," "for what," and "to whom." Transparency can be problematic when it infringes on necessary confidentiality or privacy; full predictability of inefficiency or corruption is not a great advantage; and, of course, it is impossible to provide for participation by everybody in everything. The relevance of these concepts to the various aspects of public administration will be brought out throughout this book. A few general implications for public management are provided here.

Predictability of government action and consistent application of laws and rules is needed by civil servants to plan for the provision of services and by the private sector as a signpost to guide its own production, marketing, and investment decisions. *Transparency* of government information is a must for an informed executive branch, legislature, and public at large—normally through the filter of competent legislative staff and capable and independent public media. (It is essential not only that information be provided, but that it be relevant and in understandable form.) Concerning *participation,* the sound formulation of public policies and programs requires participation by concerned public employees and by other stakeholders; the achievement of operational efficiency requires participation by external entities; and the monitoring of access to and quality of public services requires feedback by users of the services. Finally, *accountability* is essential for the use of public money and the results of spending it, and for government action in general.

Accountability Is Key

Although all four pillars of governance are interrelated, accountability is at the center and under-pins most of the discussion in this book. Through overuse, the term "accountability" has acquired mantra-like qualities (and has no exact translation in many languages). It is therefore helpful to unbundle it at the outset. Effective accountability has two components: (1) answerability and (2) consequences. First, answerability (the original meaning of the word "responsibility") is the requirement for public officials to respond periodically to questions concerning how they used their authority, where the resources went, and what was achieved with them. A robust dialogue matters more than any bean counting or mechanistic checking of results. Second, there is a need for predictable and meaningful consequences (not necessarily punitive; not necessarily mon-etary; not necessarily individual). Third, because government must account both for the use of its authority and of public resources and the results, internal administrative accountability must be complemented by external accountability through feedback from service users and the citizenry. (External accountability is also often referred to as "social accountability.") Strengthening external accountability is especially necessary in the context of initiatives for greater decentralization or for managerial autonomy, when new checks and balances are required to ensure that access to and quality of public services is not compromised as a result of the initiative, especially for the poorer areas or segments of the population.

Governance and Democracy

In this book, we cannot delve into the meaning of "democracy." The reader is referred to Dahl (1998) and to an excellent recent book by John Dunn (2006), who traces the development of democracy from ancient Greece and sees its contemporary evolution in terms of the tension between efficiency and equity—with equity generally losing. For now, simply note that the term "democracy" is amenable to different definitions.[8]

Good governance, with robust accountability, transparency, and respect for the rule of law, is possible in formally "undemocratic" regimes. By the same token, there are many examples of badly mismanaged formal democracies. To address this paradox, one is tempted to argue that good governance is only *sustainable* in democratic systems. This is true, but only in the very long run—and, as John Maynard Keynes said, "in the long run, we are all dead." No wonder that, faced with a choice between good public management and greater democratic openness, many peoples and some countries have opted for the former. The real answer to the paradox lies in the critical distinction between formal democracy and government legitimacy, which rests on the voluntary consent of the people based on their acceptance of the validity of the laws and actions of their government.

Democracy (as a *process* of government) and legitimacy (as an *attribute* of government) are not coterminous. Legitimacy is indeed conferred by elections and other formal democratic processes, but may also be conferred in other ways. Fortunately, the facts come to the rescue: throughout history, the instances of well-governed authoritarian states are few, and those of well-governed totalitarian states are nonexistent. Whether conceptually coterminous or not and however they may be defined, democratic processes do tend to go hand in hand with good governance, and the absence of democratic processes does eventually erode government legitimacy.

Corruption and Public Management: A Preview

The phenomenon of corruption should not be viewed in isolation, but as part and parcel of the broader issue of governance and effective public management. Hence, the international recognition in the late 1990s of the serious problem of corruption was a logical outgrowth of the understanding of the link between governance and development at the beginning of the decade. Corruption has occurred from the earliest of time in all societies and virtually every aspect of public administration can be a source of corruption—tax administration, debt management, customs, ill-designed privatizations, and large procurements and major public works projects.[9] Chapter 14 is largely dedicated to this issue.

Definitions of corruption can be extremely long-winded. The simplest definition is also the most powerful: *corruption is the misuse of public or private office for personal gain.* "Misuse" (unlike "abuse") covers both sins of commission (i.e., taking illegal actions) and sins of omission (i.e., looking the other way). The inclusion of the term "private" in the definition of corruption underlines the fact that there cannot be a bribe received without a bribe given. Much corruption is externally generated, and attention needs to be paid to the corruptor as well as the corrupted, and to "imported corruption" as well as the homegrown variety. The United States was a pioneer among developed countries in prohibiting bribe-giving by U.S. corporations through the passage of the Foreign Corrupt Practices Act in 1989.

Well into the twentieth century in the United States and other developed countries (and until a few years ago in poor countries), corruption was tolerated as useful ("grease for the machine"), inevitable ("the way the system works") or routine ("everybody does it"). In recent years, views have changed dramatically, and for good reason. Even aside from moral and legal considerations, there is solid evidence that corruption harms administrative effectiveness, distorts resource allocation away from the more efficient to the more dishonest, and especially hurts poor and vulnerable groups. During the last ten years, this well-established consensus has been translated into actual policies of international organizations and governments around the world.[10]

The Institutional and Cultural Context

Although the governance principles are universal, their implementation is country-specific. Administrative systems and procedures must be solidly grounded in the economic, social, and cultural realities of the specific country.

The New Meaning of "Institutions"

Particularly important to determine such applicability is an evaluation of the country's institutional framework and of the availability of relevant and reliable data and sufficient skills. Traditionally, the term "institution" has been used as a synonym for organization, but institutions should be understood in their contemporary meaning as the *basic rules* of behavior and are different from the organizations that function under the rules. For example, a football game may be played well or badly depending on the talent of the players and the game plan, but so long as the same rules apply, it is still a game of football.

The challenge of assessing the institutional landscape of a country or of an organization is complicated by the reality that the majority of norms by which society runs are informal norms (including informal incentives or penalties), which are typically not visible to the outside observer. This explains the well-known paradox of so many countries where the formal laws, administrative systems, and processes appear sound and coherent, while in reality government efficiency is poor, corruption is endemic, and public services are badly inadequate. Indeed, informality is predominant in some countries, with the informal economy supplying more goods and services than the government but at a high cost in terms of efficiency, equity, and development.[11] The norms, or rules, are distinct from the organizations that function under them.[12] Because the total stock of rules comprises both formal and informal rules, many technical "improvements" have failed because they were in conflict with the less-visible informal rules and incentives. This is especially true in very small countries and in multiethnic societies.

To use a mundane example, where the family is the principal social unit and custom calls for the main meal to take place at midday, the implementation of "flextime" working arrangements is difficult. Or, a performance bonus scheme for civil servants may appear to be well designed but fail to produce improvements if it is inconsistent with an informal social rule that managers should use their power to help members of their own ethnic or regional group. Indeed, under these circumstances, the "reform" may lead managers to manipulate the performance pay system in the interest of "their" people and thus lead to more conflict and a less-efficient system.

This leads to four basic points:

- A design failure to take into account key informal rules is likely to lead to a failure of the administrative reform itself. However, it is very difficult for outsiders to be aware of these informal rules—this is a major argument for local "ownership" and participation in the design and implementation of reforms.
- Durable institutional change takes a long time (a result of what Douglass North [1991] called "path dependence"). The expression "rapid institutional change" is an oxymoron, except possibly as a result of a political revolution.
- Government departments and organizations can be merged, restructured, and created, but no change in behavior (and hence in administrative outcomes) will result unless the basic rules, procedures, and incentives change as well. An example of the need for rules, procedures, and incentives to change in order for behavior to change is the 2005 creation of the new National Intelligence Directorate in the United States. This directorate, superimposed onto the Central Intelligence Agency and the various other intelligence bodies, has accomplished little to improve the provision of good security information to policy makers. The reason is that such improvement cannot occur without a concomitant change in the rules of behavior of the various agencies, which in turn would require a change in the framework of rewards and penalties.

- Institutional development can be defined as a move from a less to a more efficient set of basic rules and procedures and can be measured by the reduction in "transaction costs." Think of transaction costs as the total costs of doing business (i.e., all costs aside from out-of-pocket expenditure that are associated with the time and opportunities lost in concluding the transaction in question). For example, simplifying an unnecessarily complex government regulation reduces the cost of compliance without adverse effects.

A Question of Culture

In many countries (especially in developing countries where the experience of colonization froze in its tracks the normal pattern of cultural change and adaptation), the nature and exercise of government authority is explained more by cultural factors, including the role of gender and ethnicity, than by formal legal and administrative rules. The multiple roles played in many developing countries by government leaders—in business, tribal chiefly roles, and the churches—explain why the machinery of government works differently from its formal design and why ethnic and kinship loyalties often predominate over formal responsibilities.

While cultural factors do make a major difference in how governments are run and how the public sector is managed, recognizing their importance must not lead to immobility or relativism. First, cultural factors do not explain why some countries succeed in crafting effective impersonal institutions alongside kinship and ascriptive criteria, while other countries in the same cultural matrix do not. In East Asia, for example, Confucian values are alleged to constrain economic efficiency and development by emphasizing paternalism, and family loyalty has been used to justify personalism and nepotism in public transactions (see chapter 2). But the "Confucian values" explanation does not account for the different record of success of different Asian countries in the same tradition. The experience of Singapore and, more recently, Korea shows that strong political leaders with broad legitimacy can move society away from ascriptive standards and establish an efficient and responsive public administration based on merit criteria. (Whatever may be said about its governance model, Singapore has also been admirably uncompromising in its intolerance of ethnic intolerance.)

Second, there is a temptation to use cultural specificities as a justification for more mundane objectives, such as trade protectionism. The difficult but critical challenge is therefore to differentiate between those cultural values that are genuine and positive from those that are code words used as cover for vested interests. In the case of East Asia, there are unquestionably cultural values that have fostered economic and social progress—primarily, an attitude of cooperation between the public and private sectors and a propensity for hard work. "Asian values," however, have also been used to justify the cronyism and closed circles of influence and privilege that eventually led to the financial crisis of 1997–1999. Since then, references to "Asian values" to justify practices inimical to good governance have been conspicuously absent.

Third, culture should not be confused with mere habits of individual conformity with others' behavior—when everyone does something only because they expect everyone else to do the same or, conversely, when nobody obeys a particular rule because they do not expect that anyone else will. In these cases, more often than not, it turns out that each individual would be better off if everyone were to cease their dysfunctional behavior or began to obey a rule designed for the benefit of all. For example, it would be better for each person in a group if everyone lined up in an orderly line to get on a bus with plenty of seats than if everyone had to push and shove to do so. In these cases, the ingrained dysfunctional habits can be made to change almost overnight if appropriate material or moral incentives and disincentives are applied fairly and uniformly.

ASSESSING AND IMPROVING PUBLIC ADMINISTRATION

Beyond Dichotomies

The field of public administration has been sown with false dichotomies that have made clear debate and sensible solutions difficult. While the more egregious instances appear to have run their course, these false dichotomies still interfere with the clarity of thought on efficient public management that is essential regardless of one's political views and predilections. Here are the major ones.

Public versus Private

In a nutshell, the conventional wisdom of the late 1960s and 1970s held that government action was inherently superior to the private sector, and that countries could expect to make progress only through public ownership and management of major industrial enterprises. The demonstrated failure of this approach was succeeded in the 1980s by its converse: far from being the *solution,* government was seen in many countries as the *problem.* (A major corollary was the belief that private management practices can and should be applied to public administration. This is not always the case, as discussed at length in subsequent chapters.) The 1990s have witnessed the plain but fundamental recognition that both "public" and "private" sectors in a society behave within the same set of institutional parameters: the operational concepts are power, size, competition, and accountability and not ownership per se. The public versus private dichotomy will continue to be trotted out every now and then, but serious observers have no doubt that government can be part of the solution, or part of the problem, or both—depending on what it is asked to do, how its activities are supported and monitored, how it is held accountable and, of course, who happens to be in charge at the time.

Efficiency versus Control

Measures to give more autonomy to public managers (or to devolve authority to lower government levels) are often resisted from fear of losing necessary central control. Conversely, advocates of those measures tend to precisely view the loosening of central control as one of the advantages of delegation. These opposing viewpoints reflect the same false dichotomy. A plethora of detailed controls is inimical both to operational efficiency and to robust control, but disregarding the need to introduce more effective control in a context of delegation of authority makes managerial autonomy survive only until the first major scandal.

The alleged trade-off between efficiency and control is especially damaging in the fight against corruption. When confronted with a new anti-corruption stance by the political leadership, the reflexive tendency of the bureaucracy is to buy cover by introducing a variety of new controls or by applying more literally and rigidly the controls that do exist. (This is more prevalent in government than in large private corporations because public and media scrutiny tends to focus more on government activity.) This tendency is understandable, particularly in countries where public administration has been demonized and trust in civil servants has eroded. Yet, as explained in chapter 9, such tightening up protects against minor misappropriations at the much higher cost of clogging up the operational channels and does nothing to prevent large-scale corruption to boot. (As the Minister of Public Works of a certain country once told one of the authors: "Don't be naive: the bigger the theft, the easier the theft.") As noted, there is no contradiction between efficiency and control, so long as the control mechanism itself is efficient.

Unfortunately, the consequences for the civil servant are asymmetrical. There is no visible result—and thus no reward—from acting selectively to protect public resources while enabling efficient operations, but severe personal consequences are likely in the event that something goes wrong. It is rational for civil servants to act to protect themselves even when they are well aware of the adverse impact on efficiency. There is no easy solution to this dilemma, but a greater degree of public trust in civil servants would help, as would strong political and managerial support combined with swift and severe penalties for demonstrated malfeasance, as opposed to penalizing honest mistakes or discouraging the flexibility needed to enable operational efficiency.

Results versus Process

Chapter 10 will examine at length the question of performance, its measurement, and its management. Suffice to note here that "performance" is a relative and culture-specific concept. Government employees are considered "well-performing" if they stick to the letter of the rules—in a system where rule compliance is the dominant goal; if they account precisely for every cent of public money—in a system where protection of resources is the dominant goal; if they obey without question a superior's instructions—in a strictly hierarchical system; if they compete vigorously for individual influence and resources—in a system where such competition is viewed positively; if they cooperate harmoniously for group influence—in a system where conflict is discouraged; and so on.

This is not at all to say that all "performance" notions are equally efficient, but only to recognize that there *are* different notions. Administrative cultures evolve in response to concrete problems and incentive structures. Even when an administrative culture has become badly dysfunctional, it is still necessary to understand its roots to improve it in a durable way. In the United States, the most recent illustration is the debate on the restructuring of the intelligence agencies. Without understanding the roots of the administrative "culture" of the Central Intelligence Agency, the Federal Bureau of Investigation, and the National Security Agency, among others, it is difficult to devise ways to improve performance in, for example, the sharing of relevant security information. Overall, while process is meaningless without reference to results, an exclusive focus on results without understanding the different norms of due process is not sustainable. Thus, holding to the false results/process dichotomy makes it less likely that public performance will actually be improved in a lasting manner.

Public Administration versus Public Management

The reader will have noticed that we use the terms "management" and "administration" interchangeably. Much has been made of an alleged distinction between the two terms, and a substantial literature on the "new public management" has emerged. "Management" has a more dynamic, "with it" ring, but all major dictionaries list management and administration as synonyms.

There is some merit in the broad distinction between the traditional paradigm of government behavior—usually associated with public "administration"—and a new paradigm of "management." Traditionally, public service was defined by the two P's of probity and propriety, while recent contributions have rightly emphasized the two different P's of policy and performance.[13] Again, common sense and reality suggest that no contradiction exists. On the one hand, procedures are not ends in themselves but means to results. On the other hand, a results orientation without respect for due process will not only destroy the process but eventually produce bad results as well. This view is echoed to some extent by Michael Macaulay and Alan Lawton, who consider unsustainable the distinction between "virtue" and "competence," as the public administrator cannot be competent without being ethical.[14]

The new synthesis of public administration/management for the twenty-first century should therefore include all four P's: Policy, Performance, Probity, and Propriety. Like the legs of a chair, all four are necessary to assure the soundness and durability of the administrative system, as explained further in the next and last section of this chapter.

Administrative Effectiveness: From Three to Four Es

Whatever the decision on the appropriate role of the state, the role must be performed well. As discussed more fully in chapter 10, the classic "Three E's" of public administration are Economy, Efficiency, and Effectiveness. *Economy* refers to the acquisition of goods and services of a given quality at lowest cost and on a timely basis. (Economy is the main criterion of efficient government procurement—see chapter 9.) The criterion of *efficiency* entails production at the lowest possible *unit* cost (for a given quality). It subsumes therefore the criterion of economy, as production efficiency cannot be achieved unless, among other things, the inputs are procured at lowest cost. Finally, *effectiveness* refers to the extent to which the ultimate objectives of the activity are achieved. For example, in a vaccination program, the criterion of economy calls for purchasing quality vaccine at lowest cost and on a timely basis; the criterion of efficiency calls for performing the maximum number of vaccinations given the resources available; and the criterion of effectiveness entails the highest reduction of the disease.

Can we then conclude that a public management system that operates economically, efficiently and effectively, is necessarily a good system? No, for two reasons. First, as noted earlier, due process must be respected or the legitimacy and credibility of government will be impaired over time. Second, someone must look out for the long term and for the needs of the poor and the marginalized. Thus, a fourth "E" must be added to the mix: *Equity*—consistent with the position first stated in the United States by President Andrew Jackson in the 1830s, that the welfare of society must be assessed by looking at the conditions of the base, not of the top.[15] Unless a government takes into fair consideration the circumstances and needs of the poorer and disadvantaged groups in society, the most "efficient" system will not be fair and—to be practical about it—will not be sustainable. This is because it will produce cumulative internal tensions, and eventually the withdrawal of that voluntary cooperation by the citizens which is the glue of good governance. In the short run, there may be a conflict between efficiency objectives and equity objectives; in the long run, there is none.

Hence, in the course of the difficult adjustments of public administration imposed by the new global context, technological trends, and widespread changes being introduced in the United States, it is imperative to keep in sight both the requirement of *serving* the public well and the requirement of *preserving* the cultural, ecological and social capital of the country. As in the motto of some police departments in the United States, the job of public administrators is "to serve and protect." This is the central theme of this book. However, before moving on to these heavy issues, let's conclude this overview with a touch of levity—but do keep in mind that it is caricature, not reality, which applies to all large organizations, whether governmental or private.

BOX 1.2

Administratium: New Chemical Element Discovered

The heaviest known chemical element was recently discovered at a major research university. The element, named *Administratium*, has no protons or electrons. It has one neutron, 80 assistant neutrons, 20 vice neutrons and 120 assistant vice neutrons, giving it an atomic mass of 221 particles—which is held together by the continuous exchange of particles called morons. Since it has no electrons, *Administratium* is inert. However, it interacts with productive reactions, and causes them to be completed in about ten times the time normally required. The element tends to concentrate at certain points such as governments, large corporations, and international agencies, and can usually be found in the newest and best-appointed facilities.

Administratium has a half-life of three or four years, at which time it does not continue to decay, but undergoes reorganization and reform. In this process, assistant neutrons, vice neutrons, and assistant vice neutrons instantly exchange places. Studies have shown that the mass of *Administratium* actually increases after each reorganization.

Caution must be exercised when in contact with this element, as its behavior can be highly contagious, is toxic at any level of concentration, and can easily destroy productive reactions when it is allowed to accumulate. Attempts have been made to determine how the damage from *Administratium* can be controlled and its growth limited, but results so far are not encouraging.

Source: Anonymous, circa 1996.

NOTES

1. The Baltic states of Estonia, Latvia and Lithuania have known periods of independence in the past, as also have Georgia, Armenia and, of course, Russia itself. The remaining nine former Soviet Republics were never independent states.

2. The context was of course very different, and so was the concern. Du Bois stated that "The problem of the twentieth century is the problem of the color line" ("The Freedmen's Bureau," *Atlantic Monthly,* 87, 1901), whereas most contemporary conflicts have had an ethnic rather than racial dimension. His insight remains relevant, however.

3. The Taliban regime not only hosted but was thoroughly commingled with al Qaeda, with the Taliban leader Mullah Omar having married one of Osama bin Laden's daughters.

4. See the *CIA.Factbook* (www.cia.gov/cia/publications/factbook) which, incidentally, is a superb source of international information on a large number of topics. On military spending in general, as well as other topics related to international security, see the Stockholm International Peace Research Institute (www.sipri.org).

5. See *The History of the Peloponnesian War,* 431 B.C.E. Translated by Richard Crawley. www.etext. library.adelaide.edu.au/mirror/classics.mit.edu/Thucydides/pelopwar.html. For a contemporary elaboration of the security dilemma, see Herz (1959).

6. During attendance at the World Conference on Market Economy, Democracy and Development, Seoul, Korea, February 1999.

7. This is the recognition that led the international development institutions to focus their attention on military expenditure. From the mid-1990s, decisions on the level and composition of aid have increasingly been influenced by considerations of the crowding-out impact of military expenditure on development expenditure in the recipient countries.

8. Including the tongue-in-cheek definition by Benjamin Franklin: "Democracy is two wolves and a lamb voting on what to have for dinner." Franklin added: "Liberty is a well-armed lamb contesting the vote." (Quoted by Bill Moyers in a January 26, 2007, address to the Media Reform Conference.)

9. See Tanzi and Schuknect (1997).

10. A remarkable, indeed historic, convergence of actions and policies has occurred in this area. The World Bank enacted an official policy against corruption in September 1997. Other multilateral development banks (MDBs) followed suit rapidly. The anti-corruption policy of the Asian Development Bank was approved in July 1998, and anti-corruption cooperation among the MDBs has been strengthened since then. At the same time, the International Monetary Fund (IMF) promulgated the Code for Fiscal Transparency, and the Organization for Economic Cooperation and Development (OECD—the "developed countries' club") succeeded in negotiating in December 1997 a landmark convention against bribe-giving, which entered into force in February 1999. The convention made the bribing of foreign officials a crime at par with national laws concerning bribery of national officials—in all member countries of the OECD. Although most of the implementation lies ahead, and corruption will of course never disappear, for the first time in contemporary history there is a concrete opportunity to reduce substantially "the cancer of corruption." (See *Building an Equitable World*. Annual Meeting Address by World Bank President James Wolfensohn in Prague, September 26, 2000.)

11. See, for the case of Peru, de Soto (1989).

12. See, among others, North (1991), Sachs and Williamson (1985).

13. Stewart and Hansom (1988).

14. "From Virtue to Competence: Changing the Principles of Public Service," *Public Administration Review*, vol. 66, September–October, 2006.

15. This was reaffirmed by George W. Bush's statement in the 2005 State of the Union speech that a society is judged on how it treats the poor and the vulnerable. Regrettably, the statement was utterly at odds with the actual social and budgetary policies of his administration.

PART I

GOVERNMENT FUNCTIONS AND ORGANIZATION

C H A P T E R 2

■———————————————————————■

The Genesis and Roles of Government

> A government will not endure long if the administration of it remains on the shoulders
> of a single individual; it is well, then, to confide this to the charge of the many, for thus it
> will be sustained by the many.
> —*Nicoló Macchiavelli*[1]

WHAT TO EXPECT

As noted in chapter 1, there is a necessary distinction between policy ("*what* is to be done") and administration ("*how* it is to be done"), but this distinction must not become a firewall, on penalty of producing both bad policy and unrealistic implementation. Moreover, public managers do not act in a vacuum and public administration practices have historical roots in political ideas, some of which are still influential today. Thus, although public administration is inherently instrumental, it cannot be viewed clearly without some light from basic political science concepts, and a brief look back to the genesis of these concepts is important to understand the business of government in contemporary times. In keeping with the international theme of this book, such a look back is not limited to the standard "western" views of government but also must scan the main views evolved in other cultures. The chapter then sets out the rationale for government intervention and suggests a set of decision criteria. Finally, the crucial issue of the distribution of costs and benefits of government intervention is raised, with the general conclusion that sustainability and legitimacy of government intervention require that a policy that is generally advantageous include specific mechanisms to compensate those who are likely to lose from its implementation. Because of the conceptual and general nature of the subject, there is no concluding section of directions of improvement.

WHY ANY GOVERNMENT? THE ROOTS OF POLITICAL FUNDAMENTALS IN DIFFERENT CULTURES

How did unrelated individual human beings become members of a formal group—a state—and surrender to the state some of their individual freedom of action while accepting to carry out its orders in certain areas? What are the key differences between a "state" and other groupings of individuals, such as a bridge club or a hunting party? What is the proper nature of the relationship between the state and the citizens? By what justification does a government prohibit or demand certain behaviors by the citizens? What is the best form of government, the highest attribute of governmental leadership, the wisest exercise of state power? The answers to these and other core political questions have shaped the earliest of civilizations—from ancient Egypt, Sumeria, China, Babylon and India, to the Greeks and Romans, precolonial African states such as Mali and Songhai, American kingdoms such as the Inca and Maya, and so on.

Thinkers have continued to grapple with these same basic questions from as far back as the Chinese Confucius, the Hindus Ashoka and Kautilya (*The Arthashastra*), and the Greek Aristotle, in the fifth and fourth centuries BCE. These questions were later pondered by the Arab Averrhoes (Ibn Roshd) in medieval times, the English Thomas Hobbes (*Leviathan*) in the sixteenth century, the German Max Weber in the nineteenth century, the American John Rawls in contemporary times, and so many others. Naturally, thinking has evolved, and the conceptual emphasis has shifted to fit the changing circumstances of the times. Perhaps the most salient evolution has been toward analyzing the links between government and economic growth and, with the rapid material progress in the West, the replacement of the traditional focus on state survival with a concern for an equitable, more humane, and just society.

The importance of these concepts for understanding public management anywhere in the world needs no elaboration. Moreover, as we face the problem of failed states in the twenty-first century and its implications for international stability, terrorism, and other issues, the definition of the "good" modalities of government rule assumes greater global and cross-cultural significance. While it is obviously not possible here to examine all the major conceptual contributions—not even in telegraphic fashion—the following selection should illustrate the common principles and diverse forms of public administration in today's world.

Aristotle

The Greek philosopher Aristotle (384–322 BCE), the father of "western" political thought, researched and classified 158 political constitutions. His views on the nature and origins of the state, explained in his *Politics*,[2] are heavily influenced by the small and homogenous context of his native Athens and the other city-states in classical Greece. The focus is thus on the city-state, or *polis*—a small, homogeneous, and stable entity, the "natural order" in which man, "by nature a political animal," realizes perfection. The state, which is a community established to pursue some common good, is as essential for the survival of mankind as are marriage and procreation. Without the state, man is a "tribeless, lawless, heartless one." Almost 2,000 years later, Thomas Hobbes was to echo this view in his statement in *Leviathan* that outside the organized state, human life is "nasty, brutish, and short."[3]

There is a link between the family and the state, but not a complete parallel. Relations between man and woman are primary: "there must be a union of those who cannot exist without each other that the race may continue."[4] The first institution is therefore the family—"the association established by nature for the supply of men's everyday wants."[5] Next is the establishment of households, which expand into villages, and the state comes into existence when several villages unite in a single self-sufficient community to meet the necessities for "a good life."

Societies are hierarchical and reflect the two basic forms of human association: between man and woman, and between master and slave. "By nature," some members of society are destined to be rulers and others slaves. Although there is an obvious distinction between women and slaves insofar as slaves are not free, in Aristotle's view women and slaves are similar, as "there is no natural ruler among them":

> Of household management . . . there are three parts—one is the rule of a master over slaves, . . . another of a father, and the third of a husband. A husband and father . . . rules over wife

and children, both free, but the rule differs, the rule over his children being of a royal, over his wife a constitutional rule. For although there may be exceptions to the order of nature, the male is by nature fitter for command than the female, just as the elder and full-grown is superior to the younger and more immature. (*Politics*, I.7)

Leaving aside Aristotle's views on the "natural" subordination of women and on slavery, quite unacceptable today but which reflected the near-unanimous thinking of the day,[6] the core of his concept of government is expressed as follows (*Politics*, III.7):

> . . . government, which is the supreme authority in states, must be in the hands of one, . . . a few, or . . . many. The true forms of government, therefore, are those in which the one, or the few, or the many, govern with a view to the common interest; but governments which rule with a view to the private interest . . . are perversions. . . . [We call] forms of government in which one rules . . . kingship or royalty; that in which more than one, but not many, rule, aristocracy; . . . when the citizens at large administer the state for the common interest, the government is called by the generic name—a constitutional government. [Aristocracy] is the best . . . because the few have at heart the best interests of the state and of the citizens. [Emphasis added]

Although aristocracy is, in his view, the best form of government, Aristotle sees clearly that any form of government can be perverted:

> . . . the perversions are as follows: of royalty, tyranny; of aristocracy, oligarchy; of consti-tutional government, democracy. For tyranny is a kind of monarchy which has in view the interest of the monarch only; oligarchy has in view the interest of the wealthy; democracy, of the needy: none of them the common good of all. (*Politics*, III.7)

Note that in this view "aristocracy" means literally and only "rule by the best," and is different from oligarchy (rule by the few) or hereditary nobility. Left partly unanswered, therefore, is the question of how "the best" rulers are to be selected—*and by whom*. If "the best" are selected by the population in an accepted and transparent manner and for a defined period of time, Aristotle's "aristocracy" comes close to the ideal representative democracy of most democratic systems of today—the ruling few are selected by the many *because* they are perceived as the best and can be kicked out if they do not pursue the common good.

If instead "the best" are selected on the basis of the intensity of their political participation and worth of their contribution, Aristotle's "aristocracy" comes close to the New England–style "town meeting," where policy is made by those who choose to dedicate their time and effort to participating in town affairs.[7] In that sense, his model may still be very relevant to small towns—as indeed is consistent with his focus on small city-states. Ancient Athens had only about 30,000 free male citizens at its peak, and Aristotle's teacher Plato put at just 5,000 the optimal population of a city-state. Plato, too, considered the best rulers to be those who had riches and a much better life outside government and participated reluctantly for the sake of the common good rather than for the sake of power.[8] But if instead "the best" are really not the best individuals at all, but merely those chosen by the happenstance of wealth or "noble" birth aristocracy becomes oligarchy—still rule by the few, but not the best (indeed, more likely the worst).

Despite his general preference for "government by the best," Aristotle saw clearly that the risks of the "perversions" of tyranny and oligarchy far outweigh those of democracy. In a passage as fresh and relevant in today's political climate as twenty-four centuries ago, he notes: "The middle class is least likely to shrink from rule . . . Those who have too much of the goods of fortune, strength, wealth, friends and the like, are neither willing nor able to submit to authority [while] the very poor are too downtrodden" (*Politics*, 4.6).

Finally, there is the basic conundrum of how to define the "common good." Even in the narrowest definition of the common good as simply the survival of the state, one must specify the period of time over which the probability of such survival can be assessed—since nothing lasts forever. If one complicates the definition by adding dimensions of the common good beyond survival of the state (e.g., entitlement to the Jeffersonian "pursuit of happiness"), it becomes difficult indeed to judge whether the rulers are acting for the common good. To sum up, in the Aristotelian vision the best ruler is the citizen-politician (in the mode of the classic film *Mr. Smith Goes to Washington*) and the best administrator is a respected member of the community who chooses to volunteer his best effort, for a limited time, to pursuing the common interest.[9]

Confucius

The Moral Value System and the Political Order

The Chinese philosopher Confucius (K'ung Fu Tzu, 551–479 B.C.E.) lived in a chaotic period in China and the context of war and turbulence heavily influenced his views of the state (as, much later, Hobbes was similarly affected by the historical experience of bloody internecine warfare in England).

Confucius' views, as recorded by his disciples in the *Analects*, are rooted in the concept of the "Superior Man," who embodies ethical conduct and moral example. The ruler is the "Son of Heaven," who derives his authority and legitimacy from a divinely inspired "Mandate of Heaven." This notion, which continues to have vital force in today's China, entails the possibility that Heaven may withdraw its mandate in the event of persistent misrule. Because persistent misrule is manifested in bad political and economic outcomes and thus dissatisfaction of the people, a revolution can be successful only if the ruler has lost the Mandate of Heaven, and the success of the revolution itself is proof of the unfitness of the ruler to continue in power. (Mencius, Confucius' main disciple, even argued that it is acceptable to kill a ruler who ignores the people's needs and rules harshly.) Hence, Confucius in effect justifies the right to rule by the same fundamental concept of the "common good" that was accented at about the same time by Aristotle on the other side of the planet, although the very different context and circumstances led to a very different prescription for the desirable form of government.

Even though the right to rule is grounded on legitimacy, that is, the consent of the governed, the Confucian view does not admit formal democracy, as the structure and order of the government must parallel the hierarchical and unitary structure of the Universe. As Dao Minh Chau (1996) cogently put it, the Confucian conception is "government of the people and for the people, but not by the people."[10]

In Confucianism, the parallel between the family and the state is complete. The family is a patriarchy, with clear and rigid hierarchy—and so is the state: ". . . the prince is prince, and the minister is minister . . . the father is father, and the son is son. . . . every man has his place and stays in it.[11] . . . Persons being cultivated, their families [are] regulated . . . families being regulated, states [are] rightly governed . . . states being rightly governed, the whole kingdom [is] made tranquil and happy."[12]

The Way of Jen ("humanity" or "love") is a central Confucian concept revolving around filial piety. Filial piety is the stem from which grows all virtue. The moral reasoning is as follows:

We receive our bodies . . . from our parents, and we must not presume to injure or wound them. This is the beginning of filial piety. When we have established our character by the practice of the [filial] course, so as to make our name famous in future ages and thereby glorify our parents, this is the end [culmination] of filial piety. It commences with the service of parents; it proceeds to the service of the ruler; the establishment of character completes it. . . . The root of the kingdom is in the State; the root of the State is in the family; the root of the family [and of the kingdom] is in the person of its Head.[13]

Thus, filial piety and adherence to one's place in the social structure are not only moral precepts but also requirements to preserve one's assets and justify one's status. They permeate all aspects of politics and government:

When the Princes' riches and nobility do not leave their persons, then they are able to preserve . . . their land and grain, and secure the harmony of their people and men in office. . . . When a prince's personal conduct is correct, his government is effective without the issuing of orders. If his personal conduct is not correct, he may issue orders, but they will not be followed. . . . When the High Ministers and Great Officers do not presume to wear robes other than those appointed by the laws of the ancient kings, nor to speak words other than those sanctioned by their speech, nor to exhibit conduct other than that exemplified by their virtuous ways . . . [they] can then preserve their ancestral temples. . . . The Common People [must be] careful of their conduct and economical in their expenditure in order to nourish their parents.[14]

It follows from these precepts that the basic Confucian principles of public administration are order, unity, harmony, and sustainability. However, the contemporary concepts of efficiency and effectiveness also have clear Confucian roots: "The Master said that [the first excellent thing] is when the person in authority is beneficent without great expenditure . . . makes more beneficial to the people the things from which they naturally derive benefit."

The top public administrators in the Confucian system—the "Mandarins"—are by definition an elite corps with sharply defined rights and responsibilities who could be appointed to office anywhere in the land (as in the contemporary practice of many countries of rotating senior civil servants to other jobs or regions). It is a meritocratic elite, insofar as it requires learning and dutifulness of service commensurate with high status, but an elite that can, through time, degrade into privileged caste. Such a syndrome is not of merely historical interest. As we shall see in chapter 8, the debate on the proper role of an elite executive service is alive and well not only in China, but in today's France as well as Japan.

The End of Filial Piety?

Although the weight of Confucian values on government administration and economic behavior in contemporary China and other East Asian countries has been much exaggerated by some writers, they have been influential through contemporary times. For example, the corruption that was endemic to the *chaebol* industrial conglomerates in South Korea and which contributed to the 1997–1999 Asian financial crisis was partly related to the "all-in-the-family" Confucian mind-set.

Also, those who marvel at China's stupendous savings rates of today (which have underpinned the spectacular economic growth of the past twenty-five years and indirectly contribute to keeping mortgage interest rates low in the United States, by increasing liquidity through Chinese purchases of American bonds) should recall the Confucian principles of "careful conduct and economic expenditure" quoted earlier. Those who are rightly concerned at the extreme—and growing—inequality of income in modern China, particularly between the rural very poor and the urban very rich, are entitled by cultural history to speculate on the scenario of a repetition of the many peasant revolts in Chinese history—and the ensuing loss of the "Communist" government's Mandate of Heaven.

In the last twenty years, a new scenario has emerged, under which Confucian values may be overthrown by the irresistible forces of supply and demand—manifested in this case through the changing ratio of young to old people. The "one-child" policy instituted by China in the mid-1980s has been successful (largely through repressive methods and brutal practices) in cutting the natural growth rate of the population. This has now produced a relative scarcity of children and abundance of old people. In turn, in a crude but real sense, the demographic shift has increased the value of children and diminished the value (and status) of old people. Certain problems are emerging in China, such as neglect of old parents by their families and mushrooming of nursing homes that were unknown throughout Chinese history and are antithetical to any notion of filial piety. (Even casual visitors to China observe the spoiling of the family's "little princes.") As the two current generations of grandparents and parents die, the ratio of young to old people will stabilize. However, it will not return to the numerical preponderance of the young in earlier Chinese history, either because the one-child policy will continue or because rising incomes will cut the birth rate (as it has happened in most other countries)—or both. It is quite possible, therefore, that the respect and care for the elderly will never regain the traditional high level prescribed by that bedrock of the Confucian value system—filial piety—with far-reaching repercussions for China's society, economy, and politics.

Buddha

Buddhism was founded in Nepal about 590 BCE by the Hindu prince Siddhartha Gautama, who became the "Buddha" (The Enlightened One). It is very difficult to try and summarize the impact of Buddha's philosophy on political concepts, partly because it shades into and becomes religion. The Buddha devoted his life to understanding the source of the suffering he saw around him and discovering a way out of it. Because he saw suffering and unhappiness as stemming from frustration, and frustration coming in turn from unfulfilled desire, he pointed the way out of misery as progressively divesting oneself of all desire: nonattachment is the best of all human states.

The foundation of Buddhism is the Four Noble Truths. First, all life is suffering—birth, aging, illness, death, union with the unpleasant, separation from the pleasant, inability to get what one wants—everything that is subject to clinging causes suffering. Thus, second, the root cause of suffering is desire and, third, the cessation of suffering entails the cessation of desire. And finally, the way to the cessation of desire and suffering is through eight steps forming the Noble Eightfold Path.[15]

Buddhism views compassion for one's fellow man as one of the highest of virtues: "If Buddha finds a man suffering . . . he feels compassion and shares the burden with him." Among the best known verses in the *Dhammapada*, a collection of the Buddha's essential teachings, is: "Do no evil; . . . cultivate good; . . . purify your mind."[16]

Finally, and related to the root Hindu belief in reincarnation, Buddhism prohibits killing of any living being and prescribes respect for all life—including, of course, human life—consistent with the fifth step in the Noble Eightfold Path, which prescribes living in a way that does no harm to oneself or others.

Because of the mainly spiritual nature of Buddhism, its influence on the vision of government and the mode of public administration is much less direct than in the case of Confucius or Aristotle. However, one can extract from the basic tenets of Buddhism the following generalizations—some conducive to effective public administrations, others less so.

First, the doctrine of nonattachment is not such as to encourage proactive citizens' participation in politics and administration. Other things being equal, the counterweight of a vibrant civil society to government power may tend to be weaker in devoutly Buddhist countries. Second, the respect for human life militates against using violence to cope with conflict—except during times of extreme stress, when the "nonviolent" Buddhist is capable of atrocities (Cambodia under the Khmer Rouge) as extreme as those occasionally perpetrated by the presumably "peaceful" Malay, the "submissive" Muslim, or the "charitable" Christian (for example, the Inquisition). Third, the Buddhist dislike for tension and confrontation can lead to lowest common denominator "consensus" modes of administrative decisionmaking conducive to sustainability but dysfunctional when urgent action is required and major changes are to be managed. Finally, the precept of compassion leads to great discomfort with inequalities of any sort and to an emphasis in public administration on equal provision and access to public services by the entire population. These are very broad generalizations, of course, and even if correct are frequently honored in the breach. However, as general tendencies, they are consistent with the thrust of Buddhist thought.

Ashoka

The wide reach of Buddhism is illustrated by its dramatic influence on the rule of the great Hindu king Ashoka (268–232 BCE), the third and greatest of the Mauryan Hindu rulers. Disgusted with the carnage of his latest victorious battle and under the influence of Buddhist thought, Ashoka turned away from further military slaughter and conquest and focused his attention on administering his kingdom well.

Ashoka's *Rock Edicts*, carved onto stone pillars or on polished cliff walls in today's Indian state of Orissa, translate Buddhist principles into administrative practices and instructions, including, most significantly, that of "moderation in [government] spending." One edict in particular embodies notions of government responsiveness, accountability, open debate, service orientation, and transparency that remain guideposts in public administration today. It is worth quoting at some length:

> In the past, state business was not transacted nor were reports delivered to the king at all hours. But now I have given this order, that at any time, whether I am eating, in the women's quarters, the bed chamber, the chariot, the palanquin, in the park or wherever, reporters are to be posted with instructions to *report to me the affairs of the people* so that I might attend to these affairs wherever I am. And whatever I orally order in connection with donations or proclamations, or when urgent business presses itself on the Mahamatras, *if disagreement or debate arises in the Council, then it must be reported to me immediately*. This is what I have ordered. . . . *I consider the welfare of all to be my duty*, [and] *the root of this is . . . prompt dispatch of business*. There is no better work than promoting the welfare of all the people and whatever efforts I . . . owe to all . . . to assure their happiness in this life, and attain heaven in the next.[17] [Emphasis added]

LEGITIMACY AND THE NATURE OF ELITES

Moving on to more recent ideas, underlying each of these concepts of the state are three types of what the German political scientist Max Weber (1864–1920) termed "legitimacy," or the lawful basis by which people obey their government's orders and abide by its rules.[18] These are traditional, charismatic, and bureaucratic legitimacy.

Traditional legitimacy refers to the authority of the "eternal yesterday" (i.e., of the mores sanctified through ancient recognition and orientation to conform)—in other words, citizens' compliance by force of values and ingrained customs, as evidenced, for example, in tribal entities. *Charismatic legitimacy* is "the authority of the extraordinary and personal gift of grace (charisma), the absolutely personal devotion and personal confidence in revelation, heroism, or other qualities of individual leader . . . ," as accorded to the elected warlord, the "plebiscitarian" ruler, the great demagogue, or the political party leader. Finally, the "modern" concept of *bureaucratic legitimacy* rests on people's acceptance of the validity of the laws, and belief in the functional competence of government administrators based on rational rules. From this notion, Weber derived a definition of the state that is still the most commonly accepted today: ". . . a human community that successfully claims the monopoly of the legitimate use of physical force within a given territory."

The prevailing nature of legitimacy in a state is also connected to the profile of the elite that administers state power—the "governing elite," as contrasted with the (nongoverning) economic and intellectual elite. Understanding the nature of the governing elite is the key to understanding the state and the modalities of public administration. This is, in part because of the need to counteract the generic tendency of any elite (whether a state, political party, or private corporation) toward preserving its own power rather than furthering the original goals of the group. This tendency was termed by German sociologist Robert Michels (1876–1936) the "Iron Law of Oligarchy"[19] (i.e., that large organizations eventually develop leadership that produces ". . . domination of the elected over the electors, of the mandatories over the mandators, of the delegates over the delega-tors"). Translating this tendency in contemporary terms, it implies an unstable "principal-agent" relationship, by which eventually the agent no longer acts in the interest of the owner. (We prefer, however, the colloquial and pithy "Big outfits are run in the interest of those who run them"—which may be called "Trevor Robinson's Law,"[20] after the name of the English management consultant who first stated it.)

Helpful to further flesh out these concepts is a typology of rulers developed by the Italian economist Vilfredo Pareto (1848–1923), who placed the basic aspirations of different people in six classes, all present but unevenly distributed across the population.[21] The most relevant categories for understanding government elites are Class I—the instinct for innovation—and Class II—the tendency to conservation. Class I types are "foxes," who rule by guile and are calculating, mate-rialistic, and creative. Class II types are "lions," who rule by command and are regulation-bound, idealistic, and conservative.

Pareto claimed that social stability requires a balanced number of Class I and Class II people in the governing elite. Optimistically, he also believed in a natural tendency toward such balance through the exit and entry of different types of people into the governing elite. Stretching Pareto's views to a contemporary frame, recall our argument in chapter 1 that sound governance and good service to the public calls for a fusion of "public administration" and "public management"—not a lurch from one to the other.

Finally, the contemporary distinction between "power elite" and "functional elite" also helps to understand public administration the world over. In 1956, C. Wright Mills coined the term "power elite" to connote the American ruling group of the day, composed of business, government, and military leaders bound together by a shared social background and the interchange (circulation) of leading personnel among the three sectors.[22] In contrast, a functional elite is a new managerial class, primarily rule-oriented and with status and behavior based on hierarchical positions and responsibilities in the organization rather than on individual personality, social class, or informal networks.[23]

HOW BIG "SHOULD" GOVERNMENT BE?

The articulation in practice of all of these basic concepts has depended on myriad choices made by people and their governments over the centuries in response to different challenges, resulting (among other things) in vast differences in the function and, thus, the size of government in different countries. Therefore, it is clear that there is no such thing as an "optimal" size of government valid everywhere. A useful signpost can, however, be provided by the range of *actual* government sizes around the world, as measured by government activity as percentage of the country's Gross Domestic Product (GDP—the value of all goods and services produced in one year).[24]

At the beginning of this century, central government worldwide accounted for an average of about one third of GDP. This fraction has increased somewhat during the last twenty-five years, with general government (i.e., all levels of government, central, provincial, municipal) accounting for between 40 and 50 percent. The average masks substantial regional differences—mainly a significant expansion of central government in industrial countries combined with some contraction in the rest of the world. Central government expenditure rose in the rich countries (i.e., the members of the Organization for Economic Cooperation and Development—OECD) from one third of GDP in 1980 to about 40 percent in 2000. In the rest of the world, it fell from over 28 percent of GDP to less than 26 percent. What is of greater concern for poor countries is that the entirety of this decline was accounted for by public investment expenditures, which fell in relative terms by more than one third, to just 4 percent of GDP.

In developed countries, the increase in government size came about largely in continental European countries, which generally reaffirmed their commitment to an extensive system of social protection. A few rich countries (notably New Zealand and, to a lesser extent, Ireland and the Netherlands) showed a significant shrinkage of government, and the others remained at about the same relative levels. Major regional and country differences exist in the rest of the world as well. In the United States, expenditure by the federal government grew from under 10 percent of GDP in 1940 to about 22 percent by 1990, declined to about 18 percent by 2000, and increased again in the last few years back to over 20 percent. Particularly striking has been the expansion in government spending in the last seven years, with expenditure estimated to reach $2.8 trillion in 2007 (in current dollars).

In any event, as noted, the size of government cannot be assessed in isolation from the population preferences concerning the role of the state and of the effectiveness of government action. A very small government can still be too large if it is inefficient and wasteful and a large government can still justify further expansion if it has demonstrated its effectiveness and the citizens wish it to undertake additional tasks.

Also, the increase in central government over the last two decades was accompanied by a considerable improvement in the global fiscal situation. The overall fiscal deficit declined almost across the board (from 4.9 percent to 3.8 percent of GDP in rich countries and from 3.9 percent to 2.6 percent of GDP in the rest of the world), giving to the nongovernment sector greater financial room to maneuver and reducing pressure on interest rates. In the United States, by contrast, recent years have seen the opposite trend. The federal fiscal accounts have deteriorated from a surplus of

$236 billion in fiscal year 2000 to a deficit estimated at $244 billion in 2007, producing a cumulative fiscal deficit of over $1.6 trillion during the last seven years.

Clearly, if sensible answers are to be given to the question of whether a country's government is too big, too small, or just right, broad generalizations must give way to a country-specific and detailed analysis. What is beyond question is that throughout the world government is large enough to be a major positive influence on the economy if it is effective and a major economic drag if it is not. The *effectiveness* of public administration is therefore a relevant subject everywhere, and its improvement is a major challenge in all countries. Of course, given the particular level of government spending consistent with population preferences and administrative effectiveness, taxes must be collected to finance that spending. As any Economics 101 student knows, "there is no such thing as a free lunch." In any event, beyond crude inferences from proxy measures such as the overall size of government, a framework is needed to justify government intervention and help decide whether and how it should take place on any particular issue.

THE CONCEPTUAL JUSTIFICATIONS FOR GOVERNMENT INTERVENTION

There is a diversity of reasons for government action—defense, law and order, equity, social stability, or other public interest as may be decided by the population of a country in the exercise of its sovereignty through its representative organs of governance. However, three general requirements for government intervention can be stated:

- the public interest to be served should be specific and well demonstrated;
- the cost to the community (or specific groups) must be explicitly considered; and
- the process of deciding whether and how government intervenes should be transparent and accountable.

Echoing the ancient requirement that government must pursue the "common good," under the early twentieth century theory of the public interest two conceptual justifications for government are advanced: public goods and natural monopolies.

Public Goods

A first key justification for government action is the classic concept of "public goods." In brief, the free market mechanism works to allocate resources to their best uses because the forces of supply and demand in a *competitive* market yield a price that corresponds to the real cost of resources. That price acts as a "signal" for private profit-seeking producers to shift resources accordingly, and in so doing they also pursue the common interest of efficient production.[25] The market mechanism, however, fails in respect to certain goods and services that are "nonrival" and "nonexcludable." "Nonrival" means that anyone's consumption of the good or service does not reduce the amount available for others. "Nonexcludable" means that nobody can be prevented from consuming the good once it is made available to anybody. The classic example is clean air—nonrival because everyone can breathe as much of it as needed regardless of how many others are breathing it; nonexcludable because it is impossible to split it up and charge for individual consumption. There is no private incentive to "produce" clean air (i.e., prevent air pollution) because the costs of doing so cannot be recovered through the market. Therefore, preventing air pollution and producing the socially-desirable amount of other public goods and services requires government intervention—whether to produce the public service itself, provide subsidies or tax advantages, or regulation—to correct the failure of the market mechanism.

Natural Monopolies

A second key justification for government intervention is the existence of "natural monopolies" (i.e., goods or services where the economies of large-scale production are so high as to prevent any competitor from entering the market once the first company has begun production in large enough amounts). As natural monopolies are completely insulated from competition, they also systematically underproduce in order to keep prices at the profit-maximization level—and stifle technical progress to boot. Government direct production, or—preferably—regulation of price and access or a breakup of the monopoly company are needed to approximate the outcome of a competitive market.

The Dynamic Nature of Government Intervention

Note first that, conceptually, the objective of government intervention is not to supplant the market mechanism but to remedy its failures and thereby achieve the same outcomes that a well-functioning competitive market would yield. Second, it is important to recognize the dynamic nature of these concepts. A good or service that has the characteristics of a public good or of a natural monopoly may become suitable for the market mechanism as a result of technical or institutional changes, thus rendering government intervention unnecessary. For example, cost reductions through technological improvements have introduced competition and weakened the natural monopoly element of telecommunications, and thus the justification for direct government ownership. A single huge telephone company for the entire United States was appropriate in the 1950s but would be unthinkable today; correspondingly, pervasive government regulation of telephone services was a necessity then, but is largely an undesirable hindrance today. Major changes can turn a public good into a private one.

The opposite is also true, however. Change works both ways, and *new* public goods can emerge to justify a new government role that did not previously exist (e.g., internet security). Also, to the extent that the benefits and costs of globalization spill beyond national frontiers and are accelerated by the new information and communication technology, new *international* public goods have emerged (e.g., reversing global warming, preventing international epidemics, preserving world cultural heritage, protecting global financial stability, and so on) with the ensuing need of *international* public action to protect these goods.[26] In between, there are *regional* public goods as well, e.g., the use of a river basin common to several countries such as the Mekong in Indochina, for which there is a symmetrical case in favor of regional public action.[27]

A PRACTICAL FRAMEWORK TO FACILITATE DECISIONS ON GOVERNMENT INTERVENTION

A Decision Tree for Government Intervention

The two conceptual justifications for intervention are not enough to decide whether or not government intervention is justified in a particular case. The distinction between public and private goods can be fuzzy, and market imperfections may or may not be sufficiently serious to require government intervention. The boundary between the functions best left to private action and the

Figure 2.1   **"Decision Tree" for Government Intervention**

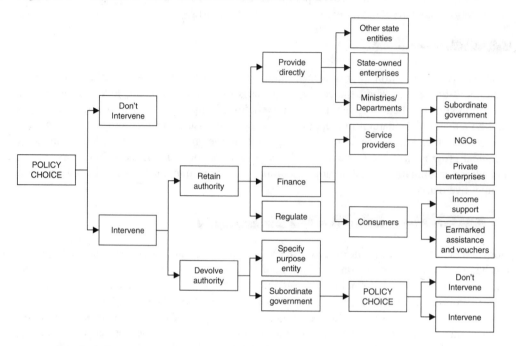

functions to be entrusted to the government will have to be drawn by the citizens of each country in accordance with their circumstances and preferences. However, the hierarchy of decisions depicted in Figure 2.1 can help clarify the choices and their sequence.

How often should decisions on government roles be revisited? Clearly, life does not begin anew every day and most government programs are intended to continue indefinitely. Thus, for example, the "zero-based budgeting" approach of the late 1970s in the United States, which called for yearly reviews of every major government program from the ground up, was quickly abandoned as impractical and of little benefit. It is helpful, however, to introduce in the enabling legislation for major new government programs a "sunset" provision—the automatic termination of the program in the absence of a specific decision to extend it. As a general rule, it is prudent to load the cards heavily in favor of the termination of programs and organizations, as there is a strong inertia for public organizations to survive way past any useful purpose. (For example, it may be advisable to require a qualified majority vote for extending the life of a program/organization beyond the specified sunset date.) It is also desirable to avoid "open-ended" entitlements or commitments, the cost of which in future years cannot be anticipated with precision. A major recent violation of this principle in the United States is the "prescription drug" legislation passed in 2004.

The Worm in the Apple: Whose Ox Is Being Gored?

The major problem with this decision-tree scheme (and similar approaches) is that it assumes away the impact on different groups of any one of the decisions depicted in it. (As argued earlier, the same difficulty was sidestepped by Aristotle in his advocacy of the "common good.") It is an axiom of economics and politics—indeed, of organized group life in general—that most group decisions entail both winners and losers, however good they may be for the group as a whole.

Thus, overall efficiency of government is an important criterion, but it is certainly not the only one and is not even the main criterion in most political environments. The question of whether a particular activity is appropriate to the domain of the state or a certain service suitable for private delivery will be answered differently by different interest groups and individuals (and often by the same individual if the question is phrased differently, as pollsters have demonstrated). The essence of a good political system is not to make the inherent conflicts of interest disappear, which is impossible, but to *manage* them in a peaceful manner and through a process which society as a whole believes fair and effective. This will usually require a departure from a purely "technocratic" application of decision criteria to determine the role of government.

In this context, one must emphasize the distinction between majority, unanimity, and consensus. Beyond arithmetic majority rule, sustainable legitimacy requires providing guarantees for the rights of minority groups and systematic opportunities for minority opinions to be heard. Unanimity is obviously an impossible decision-rule, and undesirable because it would lead to either paralysis of decisionmaking or active repression of minority views, but *"consensus" does not require unanimity*. Consensus entails that no significant segment of society is so strongly opposed to the decisions as to diminish its willing continued cooperation with the system as a whole and thus in time erode the system's legitimacy. Therefore, the design of administrative changes that affect large groups of citizens must always incorporate meaningful consultation of those concerned, and implementation of the changes should be mindful of their legitimate interests.

Nevertheless, if it is not applied ideologically or mechanically, the approach shown earlier in Figure 2.1 can be a useful starting point to clarify the public/private boundaries in specific instances.

Let "Winners" Be Winners and "Losers" Be Content

As mentioned, every government decision entails winners and losers. Repeat: *every* government decision entails winners and losers. However, a functioning democracy must have provisions for the protection of minorities' rights, and the survival of the state requires its continued legitimacy (i.e., the consent of the governed). Thus, the losing individuals or groups may be willing to accept an adverse decision both because they believe it to be for the common good—although contrary to their personal material interest—*and* because they expect to be on the winning side in some future instance. If sizeable groups in society instead come to the conclusion that they will always and systematically be on the losing side, their adherence to the state will weaken and, in time, may threaten the common prosperity and survival of the state. *Sustainability* of the government decision-making process is key. Let's elaborate.

A well-known principle of economics is that a situation cannot be improved upon if it is impossible to make somebody better off without causing someone else to lose—the so-called "Pareto optimum," from the same Vilfredo Pareto who developed the typology of ruling elites. Conversely, an economic state of affairs is suboptimal, and a change is economically desirable, if it is *possible* to produce gains for the winners without making anyone else worse off (i.e., if it produces a *net* gain). Economists (at least, the narrow-minded ones) are therefore satisfied if the change *permits* the losers to be fully compensated while still producing gains for others—*whether or not the compensation actually takes place*.

Policy makers and public managers, however, cannot be satisfied so easily, for the losers will only accept actual, not potential, compensation. As the quip has it: "If I eat two chickens and you eat none, on average we've eaten one each." Indeed, the fact that compensation is made possible by the benefits of the policy, yet is not provided, will make the losers feel even worse about the change. The worse they feel, the more they will fight the change, even though it would have benefits for society as a whole; and the more often they lose, the weaker will become their allegiance to the common rules and institutions.

The classic, but still very much current, example is foreign trade liberalization.[28] Except in special and unusual circumstances, freer trade provides overall benefits for both the exporting and the importing countries taken as a whole.[29] This simple proposition has been proven and demonstrated by centuries of experience and by economic theory, just about as solidly as the "theory" of evolution. Yet, it is not only rational but also appropriate for the potential losers from a trade liberalization measure to oppose it strongly if they do not believe that a sufficient part of the national gain will be dedicated to compensating them for their losses in some appropriate manner. Ideally, compensation should provide a mix of *relevant* training and other measures to enable those affected to shift to more competitive jobs or economic activities, complemented by income-maintenance provisions adequate to cushion the transition.[30] If adequate compensation in the appropriate forms does not occur, the outcomes are obvious and inevitable: either the trade liberalization measure will not be enacted—foregoing the benefit for the country as a whole; or the resentment of the losers will erode their allegiance to the state, and thus its legitimacy.

The heuristic implication of this argument is not that policy changes should be avoided—quite the contrary. The enactment of a new policy is facilitated if it embodies adequate provisions for compensating the prospective losers, and if the public administration is nimble enough to deliver the gains from the policy while providing the offsetting compensation efficiently and in a sustainable manner.

A CONCLUDING WORD

The core functions of government are to protect the safety of the citizens, defend the territory of the state, make and enforce the laws and rules, assure public order, enable a favorable and stable economic environment, foster competitive markets, and protect the physical environment. Some would argue for additional functions, but there is little argument about the above functions. There is plenty of argument, however, about *how* far government should go in each of these roles and how it should exercise them, because different groups benefit from government exercise of those functions to very different degrees. Politics is a system to make choices on the allocation of benefits and costs among different individuals and groups in society—underpinned by some notion of the common good—and public administration is the machinery for operationalizing those choices, delivering the benefits and minimizing the costs. Thus, in everything that follows in this book, the "technical" nature of the discussion should not be allowed to obscure the fundamentally political nature of the compact by which citizens surrender some freedom of individual action in exchange for certain protections and services which can only be provided on a collective basis. This compact gives the citizens a moral and political entitlement to having their government provide such protection and services in the most efficient and effective fashion—and this is the subject of the remainder of this book.

QUESTIONS FOR DISCUSSION

1. "Representative democracy with free periodic elections is the only form of legitimate government." Discuss.
2. "A strong leader is always necessary to prevent civil strife and enforce the rules." Discuss.
3. Is there a difference, in practice and over time, between oligarchy and aristocracy?

4. Are there key similarities among the views of the state expressed by Confucius, the ancient Greeks, and contemporary political theories?

5. "A government is too small to be effective if it accounts for less than 20 percent of national economic activity and suffocates the private sector if it accounts for more than 40 percent of economic activity." Discuss.

6. Name the basic functions of government in developed countries in contemporary times. Would this list be longer or shorter or different in developing countries?

7. If there is a clear social need that is not met by the private sector, does government have a political and moral responsibility to act to meet that need?

8. If it can be demonstrated that a particular change in policy carries benefits for society as a whole that are greater than its overall costs, should government always make that change?

APPENDIX 2.1. THE BASIC TERMS[31]

Although most readers will be familiar with the basic concepts of state and government, they may find the brief recapitulation below a convenient reference.

The State

A state is an association of individuals in a defined territory that is supreme over all other associations and individuals residing in the same territory and has the monopoly of the legitimate use of physical force. This monopoly of coercive power is one of the key attributes of *sovereignty*, and its exercise can be delegated by the state to other entities but only on its own terms. The state operates through the medium of an organized government.

The Government

Government is the totality of structures and organizational arrangements to exercise the sovereign authority of the state. Government comprises three distinct organs, each with an assigned role essential to the exercise of sovereign power: the legislature, to make the laws; the executive, to implement the laws and run the administration; and the judiciary, to interpret the law and adjudicate disputes. In turn, the legislature can consist of one "chamber" (unicameral) or two chambers (bicameral); in the latter case, there is a "lower house" and an "upper house" (often called "Senate") with both concurrent and separate responsibilities. The judiciary can function on the basis of "common law" (the weight of accumulated judicial precedents), codified law, or usually a combination of the two.

Central (or National) Government

There are various levels of government within a state, depending on the geographic scope and authority. Central (or national) government exercises the main attributes of state sovereignty and is superior to all other levels of government.

Subnational Government

Below the central government level there are usually at least two other levels of government: the intermediate level (the "province" in unitary states and the "state" in federal systems—see below) and the municipal level. Other levels can also exist, such as county government, district government, and, at the lowest level, village government.

General Government

In public administration, the term "general government" subsumes all levels of government in a country from the central to the lowest formal level of government. (Village government is included in general government only if it is part of the formal structure.)

The Public Sector

The public sector is defined as general government plus all financial and nonfinancial entities that are majority-owned by the state. Public enterprises, known also as state enterprises or parastatals, are corporations of which 50 percent or more is owned by the government. Government therefore controls their policy and activities, but they are supposed to be autonomous in their day-to-day operations. Public enterprises as a group are sometimes referred to as the "parastatal sector."

The Constitution

Definition and Amendments

A constitution is the basic set of rules prescribing the institutions and procedures of government—"the highest law of the land." Constitutions may be written (e.g., France, the United States) or unwritten (e.g., the United Kingdom). Written constitutions are found not only in democratic systems but also in countries under authoritarian rule. In the latter, however, enforcement of constitutional provisions is weak or discretionary. Thus, the mere existence of a formal written constitution does not necessarily imply the existence and good functioning of democratic institutions. Unenforced law is no law at all.

The constitution is preeminent over all other laws and regulations. The supremacy of the constitution is maintained by the power of judicial review. In most countries, it is generally accepted that it is the sole prerogative of the courts to decide what the law means. The special high status of the constitution is also ensured through its relative inflexibility as compared with ordinary laws and by special provisions for amending it. Constitutions may be classified as "flexible" or "rigid" according to how easily they can be amended. At the flexible extreme, the constitution may be amended by a simple majority vote of the legislature. At the rigid extreme is, for example, the U.S. Constitution, which can be amended only by two-thirds majorities in both houses of Congress and then approval by three fourths of the states.

Regardless of the formal amending process, the constitutions of some countries have been amended less than twenty times in a century, while the constitutions of others have been amended as many as eighty times over the last fifty years, and in nondemocratic countries, as noted, the constitution is rarely amended but is routinely disregarded by the government.

The constitution is supplemented by framework rules enacted by the legislature on fundamental matters such as the electoral system, delimitation of constituencies, organization of the judiciary, and the establishment of the civil service—framework rules often called "organic laws." The constitutions are also supplemented and altered by the interpretations of the highest court, usually called "Constitutional Court" (as in Europe) or "Supreme Court" (as in the United States), through the principle of *stare decisis* (i.e., respect for earlier decisions of the Court).

Aside from formal law, the constitution is also supplemented and altered through usage and convention by a whole collection of rules, which, though not necessarily part of formal law, are accepted by society as binding. These rules (e.g., those on the functioning of the cabinet system) regulate the political institutions and form a part of the overall institutional framework of government.

Hierarchy of Laws

Under the supremacy of the constitution, there are four levels of legislation. In hierarchical order, these are:

- Enabling acts (or organic acts), which create an agency, define its powers, and establish its jurisdiction;
- Authorization statutes create programs or instruct agencies to undertake certain responsibilities;
- Appropriation statutes provide funds, and prescribe or prohibit certain actions; and
- Administrative regulations are promulgated by the agency itself in pursuance of its responsibilities and within its proper authority as determined above.

Understanding the Roots of Public Administration

To understand a country's public administration "culture" and behavior, it is important to know the underlying constitutional and legal provisions and the tradition of enforcement. As noted, the workings of the political system and its flexibility depend not only on the provisions of the written constitution but also on the country's track record of respect for the rule of law.

As explained in the text of this chapter, it is also necessary to look at the political history of a country. For example, countries with a British system of parliamentary government, civil service, and local government have evolved differently from countries that have followed the strong unitary French political tradition. Without knowledge of those different roots, it is difficult to arrive at a sound assessment of the administrative system and its rationale, and hence risky to try and change it for the better. Even when an administrative culture has become inefficient, it is necessary to understand its roots in order to improve it in a lasting way.

In former colonies, the evolution of government has also varied according to the degree and modes of colonial control and to the ideological predilections of the early post-independence leaders. In former British colonies, for example, where the principle of "indirect rule" was followed, colonial authority was largely limited to the central government and left intact the traditional forms of local government, which thus persisted after independence. Instead, many newly independent countries kept the forms of central government but changed its orientation toward a central planning ideology which disempowered or coopted traditional local government.

Forms of Government

The form of government is prescribed in the constitution. In a *republic* the head of state is elected for specified periods; in a *monarchy* the head of state is hereditary and usually for life; in a *constitutional monarchy*, the monarch has no executive powers. In addition, forms of government vary according to the distribution of powers among levels of government, and, within the central government itself, among the different organs of state. Based on the distribution of governmental powers within the country, governments can be classified as federal or unitary, and parliamentary or presidential.

Federal Government

In a federal constitution, the powers of government are divided between the government for the whole country ("federal") and government for parts of the country (state or province) in such a way that each level of government is legally independent within its own sphere, has its own powers, and generally exercises them without interference from the other levels of government. In a few federal countries, the provinces may adopt their own constitution to define in detail the nature and functions of provincial institutions, provided that it does not conflict with the national constitution (which, as noted, is preeminent over all other laws in the state's territory).

Examples of federal constitution are those of the United States, Canada, Australia, and India. Some countries (for example, Canada and India) permit the central government to exercise limited control over the provincial governments and also to veto provincial bills, disallow provincial acts, and appoint the provincial governors. In other countries (for example, the United States), most state government actions cannot be countermanded unless they are explicitly in conflict with federal laws or the constitution.

In some countries, such as the United States, the independent status of the provinces (or states) has been preserved by the federal government and the courts. (The principle of *subsidiarity*—namely, that all powers should be exercised by the lowest possible level of government—is reflected in the U.S. Constitution, leaving to the states all powers that are not expressly assigned to the federal government.) In other countries, the control of the federal government over the provincial governments has gradually become so great as to render the provinces *de facto* administrative agencies of central government. This has arisen partly from the forces of centralization and partly from the dependence of the provinces on the federal government for financial assistance. In practice, these "quasifederal" countries operate in a manner similar to unitary governments with a substantial measure of legal decentralization.

It is important to compare the formal constitution with the actual practice of government, and always risky to assume that official political arrangements correspond to country realities. In many countries with unrepresentative governance, the formal constitution is just a piece of paper to be observed or not entirely at the discretion of the political executive. For example, the Soviet constitution of 1936 was a model statement of sound principles of government and basic individual rights, but was a purely cosmetic document with no actual relevance. Even then, in periods of transition, the existence of formal basic documents can sometimes be put to good use. To stay with the example of the Soviet Union, its adherence to the Helsinki Declaration of human rights, even though intended to be a meaningless public relations gesture, was used later to good effect by dissident groups (e.g., the Helsinki Monitoring Group) demanding that the Soviet government abide by the principles which it had officially accepted.

Unitary Government

In a unitary constitution, the national legislature is the supreme lawmaking body in the country. It may permit subordinate legislative bodies but has the right to overrule them. As in federal governments, unitary governments also include a variety of possible arrangements and degrees of decentralization. A government that is unitary and highly centralized on paper may be almost federal in practice. Broadly, unitary governments may be classified into two groups—the "Westminster style" countries influenced by the British tradition and the "Napoleonic style" countries influenced by the French model. In some countries (Italy, Spain, Sri Lanka), new arrangements have emerged whereby the regions under a unitary government are granted substantial degrees of autonomy.

Parliamentary System

In a parliamentary system, such as the United Kingdom, Italy, and the Netherlands, the executive branch of government is selected by a majority of members of the legislature and loses office when it no longer enjoys majority support, as shown by a formal vote of "no confidence." Members of the executive are normally selected from among the elected members of the legislature; the prime minister is the leader of government and usually (but not necessarily) the leader of the largest party in the legislature. The council of ministers is the organ composed of all executive members of government with an assigned portfolio of responsibilities. The cabinet may be identical to the council of ministers, or a subset of ministers holding the most important portfolios, and a "kitchen cabinet" is an informal group of the most influential political leaders to advise the prime minister on major decisions.

Because the executive is the creature of the legislative majority, in a parliamentary system proposals by the executive are normally approved by the legislature. Legislative rejection of an important proposal—such as the annual budget—is equivalent to a vote of no confidence and thus leads to the resignation of the government. In India, this is done through the device of a motion to cut a nominal one rupee from the government budget; passage of the "one-rupee-cut" motion signifies no confidence in the government. (There is an old joke about a new member of parliament who, listening to the heated debate on the "one-rupee cut" in the budget, volunteered to resolve the problem by paying the rupee himself.) If a new governing majority cannot be assembled from among the members of the sitting legislature, new parliamentary elections ensue. (The decision to dissolve parliament is normally reserved to the head of state, the only real power of an office that has become largely ceremonial.) Regular elections are prescribed in the constitution, normally at prescribed times, but not always. In the United Kingdom, for example, the ruling party can call for new elections at any time within its six-year mandate.

Presidential System

In a presidential system, executive power is vested in a president elected (directly or indirectly) by the entire electorate for a specified term of office and his or her position is therefore independent of the legislature. The president is empowered to nominate all ministers and other higher officers of government. Presidential systems vary widely. In some cases, such as in the United States, the appointment of cabinet members and other high officials requires the consent of the legislature; in the Russian Federation, only the presidential nominee for prime minister needs to be approved by the legislature; in other presidential systems, the prime minister and all other executive officers are appointed directly by the president. In presidential systems, the executive officers of government do not have to be (and usually are not) members of the legislature, and owe loyalty to the president.

France has a "cohabitation" model of a popularly elected president with substantial powers (especially in defense and foreign affairs) and a prime minister elected by the legislature, in which the president's party may or may not have the majority. A similar system exists in Sri Lanka, with an "executive president" and a prime minister elected by parliament.

Checks and Balances

Common to all forms of government—federal, unitary, parliamentary, or presidential—are constitutional provisions for checks and balances on executive authority from both the legislative and judicial organs of government. Such checks and balances are essential to complement the political account-ability of both the executive and the members of the legislature, which cannot be provided only through the periodic elections. In most countries, members of the judiciary are appointed for life, not elected, and can only be removed for cause and through special processes in order to insulate them from political pressures and passions of the moment. These issues, as well as the variety of organizational arrangements for central and local government, are examined in the subsequent chapters.

NOTES

1. *Discourses on the First Ten Books of Titus Livius*, I.ix., Niccolo Machiavelli, 1531.

2. *Politics*. Written 350 B.C.E. Translated by Benjamin Jowett. Available at http://classics.mit.edu//Aristotle/politics.html.

3. Thomas Hobbes, *Leviathan* (1660).

4. Aristotle, I.II.

5. Ibid.

6. Indeed, less than 150 years ago slavery was considered a "natural" institution in much of the United States, and women were not given basic political rights until the twentieth century.

7. It is also close to the "caucus" mode of selection of presidential candidates in certain state primaries (e.g., Iowa), where only those who take the trouble to attend and participate in the debate for a significant period of time get to express their choice of candidate.

8. *The Republic*, written 360 B.C.E. Translated by Benjamin Jowett. Available at http://classics.mit.edu/Plato/republic.html.

9. This model is close to the administrative practice in the first forty years of the United States, when men of means would volunteer for a brief spell of public service as a civil duty (see chapter 8). For a recent excellent account of the evolution of democracy from Athenian times, see John Dunn's *Democracy: A History*. New York: Atlantic Monthly Press, 2006.

10. "Administrative Concepts in Confucianism and Their Influence on Development in Confucian Countries," *Asian Journal of Public Administration*, vol. 18, no. 1, June 1996.

11. Confucius. *The Analects*. XII.11. The Classical Library, 2001. Available at www.classicallibrary.org/confucius/index.htm.

12. Confucius. *The Great Learning*, circa 500 B.C.E. Translated by James Legge, 1893. www.sacred-texts.com/cfu/conf2.htm.

13. "The Classic of Filial Piety." Xiao Jing [Hsiao Ching] From: *The Sacred Books of the East: The Texts of Confucianism*, vol. III, part I: *The Shu King, The Religious Portions of the Shih King, The Hsiao King*. Translated by James Legge, 2nd edition, Oxford: Clarendon Press, 1899, pp. 465–488. Available at www.chinapage.com/confucius/xiaojing-be.html.

14. *Analects*, 1.13.

15. The Noble Eightfold Path entails the Right Viewpoint (realizing the Four Noble Truths), Right Intention (commitment to mental and moral growth), Right Speech (speaking in nonhurtful, not exaggerated, truthful ways), Right Actions (avoiding harmful action), Right Lifestyle (living in a way that does no harm to oneself or others), Right Effort (efforts to improve), Right Mindfulness (ability to see things clearly for what they are), and Right Meditation (concentration in higher states of consciousness).

16. Coincidentally, then, Google's motto—"Don't be evil"—is consistent with the Buddhist spirit, so long as it continues to be practiced, of course...

17. Indian History Sourcebook: Ashoka, King of Behar: *The Rock Edicts*, c. 257 B.C.E. "The Prompt Dispatch of Business." www.fordham.edu/halsall/india/ashoka-edicts.html.

18. Max M. Weber. 1919. *Politics as a Vocation*. Extracts at www.mdx.ac.uk/www/study/xWeb.htm.

19. Michels (1998).

20. Personal communication.

21. Pareto, *The Mind and Society*, ed. Arthur Livingston, translated by Andrew Bongiomo, 1935. (The book was originally published twenty years earlier in Italian, as the *Trattato di Sociologia Generale* [Treatise on General Sociology].)

22. C. Wright Mills. *The Power Elite*. New York: Oxford Press, 1956.

23. See, for example, Brint (1984).

24. It has been shown that this measure is closely correlated with other measures of government size, such as the percentage of population (or of total employment) accounted for by government employment, or government taxes as percentage of national income, and is thus a fairly accurate way to rank countries by size of government.

25. This mechanism was termed the "invisible hand" of the market by Adam Smith in his *The Wealth of Nations*, considered the first seminal work of modern economics.

26. For a good treatment of international public goods, see Kaul, Grunberg, and Stern (1999).

27. See Ferroni (2001).

28. At the time of writing, the "Doha Round" of trade liberalization was comatose and perhaps fatally wounded by resurgent protectionist interests in the largest countries, both developed and developing. Whether in agriculture, with large U.S. agricultural corporations defending their vast subsidies from the American taxpayers and European farmers hanging on to the indirect subsidies provided by the tariffs on imported farm products, or in the areas of trade interest to China, India and Brazil, an unwillingness to make reciprocal concessions looks likely to lead to failure of the trade negotiations, despite the large potential of trade liberalization for stimulating economic growth throughout the world and reducing poverty in developing countries.

29. For one among the multitude of references and demonstrations of this, see Schiavo-Campo (1978).

30. In the United States, such compensation goes under the name of "trade adjustment assistance" program, managed by the Labor Department, but the funding has generally been grossly inadequate. Moreover, trade adjustment assistance has been one of the twenty-two federal programs rated "ineffective" by the White House Office of Management and Budget (out of the 112 programs it evaluated). The insufficiency and ineffectiveness of the compensation mechanism has contributed to the persisting suspicion of free trade in America. The appropriate policy response to this justified suspicion is not protectionism, but a transparent, participatory, adequate, effective, and credible system for compensating the losers from free trade while making the economy as a whole better off.

31. For a full discussion see, among others, Finer (1949) and Wheare (1966).

CHAPTER 3

Setting and Enforcing
Government Regulations

Ill-made legal shoes pinch the citizen's foot.
—*Chinese proverb*

WHAT TO EXPECT

In the decision tree shown in the preceding chapter, if it is determined that there is a good enough reason for government intervention in a specific activity, the next question is whether to choose direct government involvement or indirect government influence through regulating the activity. The provision of any public service has three key components: setting the rules and standards, financing, and actual delivery. The government roles in service financing and service delivery are the subject of Part II; the role of government as rule-maker and standard-setter is discussed here. This chapter reviews the justifications for government regulation and its evolution in recent times and then discusses the approaches to streamlining and improving the regulatory framework. The subject of regulation is complex and extremely varied and this chapter is only a brief synthesis and introduction. Although each subsequent chapter does touch on the main regulatory aspects of the topics under discussion in it, the reader interested in a specific aspect of government regulation should delve into the extensive literature on the subject.[1]

This chapter is the first to include a section on the situation in the United States and to conclude with suggested general directions for reform and improvement.

THE GENERAL CONTEXT

Regulation, Legitimacy, and Incentives

Why do most people obey government rules? In totalitarian states such as North Korea, people follow the rules because indoctrination from the cradle has made them psychologically unable to conceive doing otherwise.[2] There and in similar regimes elsewhere, the fear of "extreme" state sanction is another obvious motivating factor. In a legitimate state, instead, most citizens follow the rules set by the proper authorities because they accept the validity of the underlying social purpose, and expect that everyone else will follow them too. Compliance is largely voluntary and rule violation is the exception. Indeed, the rules can only be enforced effectively if most people obey them voluntarily. For example, it would be extremely difficult to enforce the rule against running red lights if most drivers refused to stop at red lights.

There is an ethical dimension to rule compliance as well. A core precept in the moral construct of nineteenth-century German philosopher Immanuel Kant states that one should behave "as if [his behavior] could form the basis of a universal rule." For example, stealing is immoral because a society could not possibly survive if everyone constantly stole from everyone else.

Rules and customs are not static, of course. It is certainly true that some formal rules and customs outlive their utility, yet people keep obeying them out of habit. But most rules that are widely seen as unreasonable or have lost their purpose tend to fall by the wayside, either by being formally abrogated or by being progressively ignored by everyone. To stay with the traffic analogy, applying a 40-mile-per-hour speed limit to a six-lane expressway would only lead to universal violation of the speed limit and thus a lack of enforcement.

Consider next that the behavior of each citizen is partly influenced by the relevant incentives and partly by the behavior of others—the de facto community norms. Let's take a real-life illustration. A friend of the authors, a learned and respectable gentleman who always cleans up after his dog when in the vicinity of his high-end townhouse complex in Washington DC, never does so when walking the animal near his second home in a Caribbean beach resort town. The explanation is simple: this behavior is tolerated there, but not in his Washington neighborhood. Same man; same dog; *different context*. Therefore, in addition to the legitimacy of the rules themselves, effective enforcement must ensure that the cost of complying with the rules is significantly lower than the costs of violating them (either in terms of money or of social disapproval or both). As we will see in chapter 14, Singapore, one of the most corrupt places on earth in the early 1950s, became in a few years one of the cleanest through an intelligent and resolute application of sanctions and rewards.

Culture, Habit, and Rule Avoidance

A society's "culture" is the totality of shared behavior patterns, arts, beliefs, and institutions—the outgrowth of generations of common values and experience. Culture has a huge influence on citizens' propensity to comply with the rules of the game or to refuse to abide by them, and on public policy and the structure and modalities of public sector management. It takes a long time for ingrained cultural norms to change. But *culture should never be confused with habit*. Often, what look like rooted cultural patterns turn out to simply be conformity of all individuals to what they expect others to do. In logic, there is a fallacy termed the "fallacy of composition," whereby behavior that is useful for a single person is useless if all persons behave the same way. (At a crowded ball game, if you stand up, you will see the game better; if everybody stands up, few people will see any better.) The converse is also true. Behavior that would make everyone better off if everyone followed it would make an individual worse off if he alone followed it. It is unreasonable to expect someone to be the only person in a group who abides by the rules. "I would really rather be a good citizen, but there is a difference between good citizen and sucker, and I refuse to be the only sucker in Manila," a businessman in the Philippines told the authors.

Of course, "everybody does it" is the classic excuse of the rule-breaker. But if the excuse is stood on its head, it points the way to improving compliance. When everybody *doesn't* do it, one can then expect that most people will begin to abide by the rules. A swift, adequate, and well-publicized change in penalties or rewards can sometimes cause alleged "deep-rooted and ancient cultural habits" to change overnight. What happened at the Palermo (Italy) symphony concerts in the 1950s, described in Box 3.1, is only an illustration of the possibilities for improving rule compliance for the benefit of everyone, as well as of the crucial difference between culture and mere habit.

BOX 3.1

The Great Cultural Revolution at the Palermo Symphony

In the early 1950s, classical music concerts at the Teatro Biondo in Palermo, Italy, scheduled to start at 8:30 p.m., didn't begin till 9 p.m. or so. Patrons would trickle in around 8:30, but most did not show up for a while longer. Everyone complained, chuckling about "Sicilian time," bemoaning this "cultural trait," shaking their heads at the impossibility of changing this "deep-rooted custom" in less than a generation or two.

Herbert von Karajan, the great German conductor, came to Palermo for a special two-day guest conductor engagement. At 8:30 there were perhaps 100 people in the sold-out theater. He ordered the doors to the concert hall closed and to be kept closed for the entire performance of Beethoven's Pastoral Symphony, leaving a couple thousand latecomers milling about in the lobby and spilling onto Via Roma, fuming in anger and disbelief.

The next day there were wrathful resolutions by the *Amici della Musica* (Friends of Music) club ("never invite another German guest conductor"), editorials in the city newspapers ("intolerable arrogance by a visitor to our ancient city"), and even a small demonstration in front of city hall—the mayor proclaiming his solidarity. Everyone was indignant—"*who does he think he is?*" was the expression on every pair of upper middle-class Palermitan lips.

At the next performance of the Palermo Symphony Orchestra, everyone was in their seats at 8:25. From then on, classical concerts in Palermo began at 8:30 on the dot. The "deep-rooted custom" had vanished, the Great Cultural Revolution had succeeded overnight, and, incidentally, everyone was happier that way. . .

Postscript: Gradually, concert starting times in Palermo slipped again (though not as badly as before), proving that—like toilet training—even the most successful "cultural revolution" needs periodic reinforcement to take firm root.

THE CONCEPTUAL BASIS OF REGULATION

The Notion of the Public Interest

As discussed in chapter 2, the basis of government regulation in contemporary economics rests on the "public interest" theory of the English economist Arthur Pigou and on the notions of "public goods" and "natural monopolies." On the one hand, the conventional theory has been expanded by some who argue that the imperfections of the market mechanism are especially bad in poor countries and thus more government regulation is called for.[3] However, that argument fails to take into proper account the substantial imperfections of *government* in poor countries—and thus the likelihood that expanding regulation might only lead to more arbitrariness and bribery rather than correcting market imperfections. On the other hand, the conventional theory of regulation has been criticized in three ways.

Contemporary Critiques

The first criticism argues that failures in the market mechanism are self-correcting (i.e., the unfettered functioning of the market would itself lead to remedying problems of quality, safety, exploitation, etc.). For example, a producer of unsafe drugs would eventually be pushed out of business by competitors producing safer medicines. The problem is that while the market corrects itself at its leisurely pace, large numbers of people become sick or die. Moreover, the argument itself is not valid, owing to imperfect information: the culprit can easily incorporate in another state under a different name and go through the same profit-maximizing and people-killing process over and over again.

The second criticism has a bit more force. With robust government protection of property and contractual rights, an efficient judicial system can remedy the imperfections of the market system without any government regulation.[4] For example, the CEO of a company that knowingly distributes unsafe drugs could be put out of business by consumer lawsuits and perhaps end up as an involuntary guest of the government for a few years. Unfortunately, things are different in real life—in all countries, legal proceedings are expensive; in most countries the judicial process is slow; and in many countries justice is not blind, with court decisions tending to favor the rich and powerful.

Most applicable is the third criticism of the traditional approach to regulation, namely, the risk that powerful business interests can "capture" the regulatory process (either through political contributions or by wining-and-dining-and-golfing the politicians and bureaucrats in charge) and twist the process to their own benefit rather than to the common good. (We will provide many such real-life examples throughout the book.) To stay with the analogy of drugs, the U.S. regulation prohibiting the importation of lower-priced drugs from Canada (*Canada!*), allegedly to protect public health, can only be understood as a way to protect the profits of American drug manufacturers—see Box 3.2.

THE BENEFITS AND COSTS OF REGULATION

All of this produces no clear-cut (and wrong) answers, but should leave us with a healthy sense of skepticism and a *propensity to scrutinize* the specific arguments for and against specific regulations. Although effective regulation to achieve a specified public interest is an essential function of government everywhere, there is plenty of room for differences in scope and content of government regulations in different countries and at different times. In sum, a good regulatory system supports national economic activity, development, public safety, and equity in many ways, but excessive regulation—especially when unclear and arbitrarily enforced—raises transaction costs for the economy as a whole, generates various risks, including corruption, and is especially bad for the poor. To decide on the net advantage of a particular regulation, its expected benefits must be weighed against its estimated costs—never closing one's eyes to either the benefit or the cost side.

The Benefits of Regulation

Government regulation is essential for defining and protecting property rights and important to foster competition, correct market failures, protect public safety, and promote sound social and environmental policies. Moreover, clear and good rules:

* provide predictability and consistency for those outside as well as inside the government;
* reduce the scope for arbitrary behavior;

- enhance the likelihood of orderly and efficient transactions;
- help legislators and citizens alike in holding the agencies accountable;
- provide the basis for legislative oversight and consistent audit practices; and
- help to convey fairness and consistency to the citizens, if the process of rulemaking is regular, open, and participatory.

The Costs of Regulation

In countries with unrepresentative regimes or weak accountability mechanisms, a complex and opaque regulatory framework is the largest single source of corruption—where every single "stop" in the regulatory process is also an opportunity for the "regulator" to extort a bribe. In addition to the risk of corruption inherent in excessive and opaque regulation, the cost of regulation has four other main components:

- costs to the government of administering the regulation—in the United States, such costs increased more than five times between 1970 and 2000;
- administrative and paperwork costs for businesses and citizens—in developed countries, this cost is estimated at almost 2 percent of GDP;
- indirect costs to the economy, in the form of reduced transparency, slower innovation, and lower investment; and
- especially heavy costs for the poor and for those without "connections."

The Quality of Regulation

In general, and all other things being equal, the quality of regulation is inversely related to the volume of regulation. This is largely because, without an improvement in regulatory capacity, enforcement becomes more and more difficult the more rules there are to be enforced. But the effectiveness of enforcement is also a function of the appropriateness of the rules themselves. Unrealistic regulations, petty nuisance rules, and either trivial or draconian penalties lead to weak enforcement, widespread evasion, and reliance on "informal" transactions. On the other hand, when it is difficult for individual users to obtain adequate information about the quality of the service (e.g., in health care), the government must itself establish uniform standards, especially when it finances the provision of the service. Next, the standards must be monitored adequately, either by the government itself or by contracting out the monitoring function to private entities.

SOURCES AND TYPES OF REGULATION

Sources of Regulations

Regulations are promulgated by different governmental entities. Legislative delegation of regulatory powers to central government administrative agencies is an accepted feature of most countries' public administration. But regulation is a major activity of provincial and local governments as well, either under their own authority or through the delegated administration of national programs. Indeed, it is subnational regulations that affect most activities of daily importance to the citizen—licenses, land use, building codes, and so on. A case that received wide attention in 2005 was the "taking" by the city of New London, Connecticut, of private

BOX 3.2

Importing Cheaper Drugs from Canada

Many Americans, especially senior citizens on fixed incomes, are faced with the choice of buying medicine or food and other necessities. Drug prices in Canada are one third of the prices in the United States, where drug prices are the highest in the world. Soaring U.S. prescription drug costs and the growth of the Internet have fueled cross-border drug sales in recent years. Close to two million Americans rely on Canadian supplies, and a U.S. Department of Heath and Human Services study estimated that more than 12 million pre-scriptions for American patients were filled by Canadian pharmacies in 2003 alone, for a total of $700 million in sales, and even larger figures in 2004, 2005 and 2006. "Canada Pharmacy" is a licensed online service, accredited by the Canadian International Pharmacy Association and approved by the College of Pharmacists of British Columbia. It ensures through physical inspection and other means that all participating pharmacies are fully licensed, follow specific guidelines, and dispense only branded medications.

State government in Illinois, Minnesota, New Hampshire, North Dakota, and Wisconsin and cities such as Springfield, Massachusetts have set up programs to help cash-strapped residents buy their medicines from Canada. Polls uniformly find that three out of four Americans support legal changes that would allow them unre-stricted access to Canadian drugs. Not surprisingly, the American drug companies are strongly opposed to unrestricted imports of Canadian drugs cutting into their profits and some, such as Pfizer and GlaxoSmithKline, have retaliated by refusing to supply Canadian pharmacies and wholesalers that serve American consumers.

The Bush administration, through the Federal Drug Administration, has sided with the pharmaceutical companies and firmly resisted legalizing medicine imports from Canada. The argument, as made by then-acting FDA Commis-sioner Lester M. Crawford, is that "continuing to illegally import unapproved drugs . . . is putting at risk the health of patients who are expecting to improve their health." Moreover, reportedly under pressure from the U.S. government, the Canadian government announced in 2005 that it was drafting legislation to restrict bulk exports of Canadian drugs, allegedly from a concern that such exports could cause domestic pharmaceutical shortages.

It took a dive in the popularity of President Bush to finally persuade the U.S. Senate in July 2006 to approve a proposal to de facto allow Canadian drugs into the country by forbidding customs and border security officers from stopping persons bringing medicines if they have a doctor's prescription.

Sources: Various news reports, but see in particular Amanda Gardner, "Canada Drug Export Ban Could Change Rx Landscape in U.S." *HealthDay News*, July 1, 2005.

BOX 3.3

What Is Public Use? "Taking" Private Property in
New London, Connecticut

The well-established doctrine of "eminent domain" permits a government to take
private property for fair compensation when necessary for "public use" and in
the United States it is endorsed in the Fifth Amendment (". . . *nor shall property
be taken for public use, without just compensation*."). Echoing Aristotle's ancient
dilemma of defining the "common good" that gives legitimacy to the state, the
meaning of "public use" has recently been at the center of a major dispute in New
London, Connecticut. In 1998, the pharmaceutical company Pfizer announced that
it would build a global research facility near the Fort Trumbull neighborhood. Just
two months later, New London's city council approved the plan of the New London
Development Corporation (NLDC), a private nonprofit, to redevelop ninety acres
of Fort Trumbull in order to "complement the facility that Pfizer was planning to
build, create jobs, increase tax and other revenues . . . and 'build momentum' for
the revitalization of the rest of the city." The plan called for the expropriation of a
number of private homes. Several home owners sued, and the case ended up in the
U.S. Supreme Court, which in 2005 sided with the city (and thus with the NLDC
and, indirectly, Pfizer) in *KELO et al. v. City of New London et al.* In June 2006 the
New London City Council voted to evict the residents of the houses in question.

Public reaction has been resoundingly negative. John Harwood noted: ". . . Americans overall cite 'private-property rights' as the current legal issue they care most
about, topping parental notification for minors, abortions or state right-to-die laws."
The issue is whether the term "public use" can be stretched to justify government
seizure of homes and businesses for private development and higher tax revenues,
whereas eminent domain has traditionally been invoked to build highways or other
public works. What makes the issue resonate with the public is that Fort Trumbull is
no slum. The human faces include that of Susette Kelo, with her "little pink house"
on the water; the Dery family, living in the house their grandfather built in 1895;
and others. Yet, the issue is hardly new. Such battles have long been a staple of U.S.
westward expansion. In the 19th century, farmers, railroads, and ranchers competed
for the opportunity to exploit rural resources, and the line between "public" and
"private" interest was blurry. Today, the dispute has moved to the cities, focusing
on stadiums, office parks, and shopping centers. A study by the property-rights
advocate Institute for Justice found some 10,000 cases just between 1998 and 2002
of local governments in forty-one states using or threatening to use eminent domain
to transfer properties from one private owner to another.

The Supreme Court KELO decision is most certainly not the end of the issue.
Within a few weeks of the decision, Alabama, Delaware, and Texas passed bills
with huge bipartisan support to limit seizures of property for private development;
by early 2007 almost all states had passed or were considering similar legislation,

and making its way through Congress was a Private Property Rights Protection Act to deny federal funding to any jurisdiction that seizes private property for other than traditional eminent domain purposes. This cascade of opposition has alarmed proponents of revitalization of urban areas, such as the National League of Cities, who are beginning to fight back. Stay tuned.

Sources: Various, but see especially John Harwood, "Poll Shows Division on Court Pick," *Wall Street Journal,* July 15, 2005, and John Broder, *New York Times,* February 21, 2006.

property to assign it to other private individuals for development and the ensuing increase in tax revenue—see Box 3.3.

Central government regulatory power may be administered by the concerned government department itself or delegated to specialized agencies. entities. (The last section of this chapter gives a partial list of the permanent regulatory bodies in the United States and their purposes.) The monitoring of compliance with regulations can also be done directly by the government or contracted out to private entities, although great care is needed lest the presumed efficiency advantages are nullified by loss of accountability and reduction in service quality. (Contracting out, or outsourcing, is discussed in chapter 11.)

Types of Regulations

There are three broad categories of regulations:

- Economic regulations that directly affect the market, such as rules on pricing, competition, market entry or exit, employment, contract enforcement, and access to credit;
- social regulations to protect public interests, such as the environment, health, safety, and so on (e.g., health warnings on cigarettes); and
- administrative regulations, through which governments collect information on a variety of subjects and intervene in individual cases under specified criteria.

There is also a hierarchy of regulations, from those prescribed in legal statutes to administrative rules, and other tools, as Box 3.4 describes.

Economic Regulation Around the World

Social, health, environmental safety, and other regulations are too diverse to be discussed in any detail here. Economic regulation has a somewhat narrower focus and is especially relevant to an assessment of a country's competitiveness and enabling environment for productive activity. Included here is a summary of the main aspects of economic regulation, on which the World Bank conducts large-scale annual surveys of some 150 countries—beginning in 2004 (World Bank, 2004).[5] Three broad findings of the study were that (1) business regulation varies very widely around the world, (2) heavier regulation of economic activity generally produces bad outcomes, and (3) rich countries regulate business in a more consistent manner

---

BOX 3.4

A Hierarchy of Rules

Administrative law comprises the legal instruments governing the administration of the public sector at all levels, including public enterprises. The government's powers of regulation derive from these legislative statutes, and thus indirectly from the people themselves. Therefore, *administrative regulations* enacted under the delegated powers of a statute carry the force of law so long as the ministry or agency that issued them had such authority and followed the prescribed legal process. In addition, many countries (e.g., the United States, South Korea) have enacted laws providing for public consultation prior to issue of these regulations.

Consistent with the agency's statutory authority, *orders and licenses* are used in the course of an agency's performance of its duties, often through front-line employees. Orders are statements about the rights, duties, or legal status of those over whom the agency has jurisdiction. Service providers and government regulators issue an order every time they act on a claim or respond to a request for service. Licenses are a form of order, authorizing specific actions or granting permissions. Orders and licenses are part of the ongoing administrative function of *adjudication* of rights or conflicts, which occurs whenever a public agency makes a decision regarding an individual or organization's rights, duties, or status under the law.

Finally, there are *contracts* (discussed in chapter 9) and *interjurisdictional agreements,* which are quasi-contractual understandings between two or more governmental units to share or exchange services and information.

---

than poor countries. Selected dimensions of economic regulation are listed in Table 3.1.[6] (More specific findings are summarized later, in Table 3.3, when comparing U.S. regulatory flexibility to other countries.)

All cross-country comparisons must be taken with a pound of salt. Local realities are rarely fully reflected in broad country indicators. As just one example, the average time to get approval to start a business in Tunisia is only five days—among the shortest in the world. However, the reality is that very few businessmen bother applying for a Tunisian business license unless they are first "connected" to a partner in the ruling elite. Otherwise, their chance of approval is slim or nonexistent, whereas such connection will produce speedy action by the bureaucracy. This is hardly proof of "regulatory effectiveness." More illuminating than cross-country comparisons are comparisons of regulations in the same country at different times. Other things being equal, it is legitimate to conclude that an improvement in the indicator does reflect a genuine improvement in the underlying regulatory effectiveness. Thus, when repeated, such worldwide surveys create positive incentives for countries to do better. Image is money.

It is important not to assume that lighter regulation and greater regulatory flexibility are necessarily good things. Societies make choices concerning the balance between reward and

Table 3.1

Major Dimensions of Economic Regulation in Various Countries

Area of Regulation				
Starting a business	Hiring and firing	Enforcing contracts	Getting credit	Closing a business
Number of procedures	Differentiated procedures for hiring part-timers	Number of procedures	No. of public credit-reporting agencies	Number of years
Number of days required	Flexible conditions of employment	Number of days required	No. of public credit-reporting agencies	Cost (% of assets)
Average total cost (in US$)	Ease of firing for redundancy	Average total cost (in US$)	Protection of lender rights	Priority of claims respected
Cost (in % of per capita income)	Ease of firing procedures; notice & severance	Cost (in % of per capita income)	Protection of borrower rights	Goals of insolvency met

Source: World Bank (2004).

uncertainty, effort and leisure, and efficiency and equity, and these choices are translated into different regulatory action. Particularly in the area of employment conditions, the trade-offs between these various objectives are adjudicated differently in different countries, allowing no judgment of which regulatory choice is "better" or "worse," provided that those choices are made through a democratic process. For example, Europeans generally place more emphasis than Americans on family and leisure: the government-mandated minimum vacation of four or five weeks per year (compared to the standard two weeks for Americans) is what those societies find desirable—even at a cost in terms of lower salaries and reduced job mobility. In general, however, in areas of economic regulation other than employment, such as business licensing and contract enforcement, the *initial* presumption is that lighter regulation and greater flexibility are generally desirable.

In any case, to take into account nuances of country context and differences in social choices is one thing; to justify extravagant regulatory inefficiencies is another. For example, there is room to argue whether government should mandate uniform overtime compensation, but there is no room to justify the five months and eleven administrative procedures required in Indonesia to start a business; or the sum equal to five times per capita income that must be deposited in Burkina Faso as minimum capital; or the nineteen separate steps and four years required in Guatemala to have a contract enforced; or the ten years it takes in Brazil to conclude bankruptcy proceedings; or the 38 percent of assets that are soaked up by bankruptcy proceedings in Venezuela. These outcomes are due in part to weak administrative and judicial institutions, but in large measure also to the unnecessary thicket of government rules. Moreover, weak administrative and judicial capacity should logically be a reason to simplify the regulatory framework as much as possible, in order to give the rules a chance to be enforced efficiently and fairly. Box 3.5 gives a flavor of the frustrating, inefficient, and corrupting itinerary imposed on producers (and thus indirectly on consumers and society as a whole) by the suffocating regulatory environment in many countries.

BOX 3.5

Vignettes in Frustration

In Indonesia, Teuku wants to open a clothing factory—he has a business plan, machinery, potential employees, and customers lined up. "All" he has to do is register his company. He gets the extensive forms required, fills them out, and has them notarized; proves he is a resident and has no criminal record; requests a tax number, applies for a license, deposits the minimum capital requirement, publishes the articles of association, pays a stamp fee, and registers at the ministry of justice. At several of these steps, he has to pay a "facilitation fee" to the government employee in charge. After almost six months of effort and bribes, he becomes legally entitled to make clothes—but in the meantime his customers have gone somewhere else.

In Panama, one of Carmen's employees often doesn't show up, makes very expensive mistakes, and antagonizes customers. She has identified another person, far more reliable and efficient, who is eager for the job. However, to hire him and replace the non-performing employee, she would need to assemble a detailed paper trail of misbehavior, obtain approval from the union, and pay five months' severance pay. She prefers not to bother; the guy stays on, and the more qualified applicant stays unemployed.

Juan, a trader in Guatemala, has a customer who refuses to honor his contract to pay for merchandise delivered. If Juan sues her, it will take heavy legal costs and four years to have the contract enforced by the court. He decides to forget the whole thing and to deal in the future only with customers he knows personally or to demand payment in advance. His business stagnates, and new potential clients have no access to the merchandise.

In Ethiopia, Genet needs a loan to employ more workers and expand her successful business. However, she has no "connections," government regulations prevent her from using certain company assets as collateral, and the bank knows that if she defaults on the debt, regulations adverse to creditors would make it difficult to recover the money. She doesn't get the loan; her business stays small and the additional jobs are not created.

In India, Avik's company is no longer profitable and he needs to go out of business. Faced with a ten-year process to go through formal bankruptcy and undergo huge hassles and personal losses in the meantime, he sells company assets, takes the money, and skips the country—leaving the workers, creditors, shareholders, and the government tax agency with nothing.

Source: Condensed and adapted from World Bank (2004) by permission.

RESOLVING REGULATORY CONFLICTS

Vertical and Horizontal Conflicts

A first potential conflict is a "vertical" one between national regulations and the actions (or preferences) of decentralized government bodies. Minimum national standards are needed in areas like environmental protection, use of natural resources, health and safety, international obligations (e.g., the European Union rules), and protection of minorities. Such national standards may well conflict with the needs of devolution and local autonomy or may be inconsistent with the ability of local government to enforce national standards when funds to do so are not provided centrally (the so-called "unfunded mandates"). A well-publicized example of a vertical conflict in the United States is the assertion by the federal Justice Department of authority to prosecute sellers and consumers of medical marijuana even when the state concerned has declared the activity legal—see Box 3.6.

A second potential conflict is "horizontal," between national regulations and specific national government entities. Such horizontal conflict occurs most often in the area of personnel management, including rights and obligations of civil servants, privacy and integrity protection, and affirmative action. In countries that have moved toward managerial flexibility based on contractual relationships (e.g., New Zealand) a conflict has arisen between the traditional principles of equality of treatment of government employees and the differentiated treatment of employees in different agencies. The desire of a government agency manager to be free to hire and fire and promote employees at her discretion conflicts with the requirement that all government employees should be subject to the same treatment regardless of the specific agency where they happen to work. Horizontal conflict is also endemic between the essential provisions for accountability and transparency of public administration and the reluctance of individual agencies to disclose the bases of their decisions or invest time in adequately informing the public (this problem will be addressed in chapter 12).

Judicial Review of Regulatory Actions

In addition to disclosure by public agencies of their regulatory actions under information laws, external checks are needed to ensure accountability. In most countries, judicial review is the main forum for challenging administrative actions and seeking redress. Judicial review typically covers the following issues, in order: whether the agency or the ministry violated constitutional provisions or statutory obligations; failed to adhere to procedural requirements; abused its discretion; or acted without substantial evidence. Challengers of the agency's actions may seek criminal prosecution, money damages, or injunctive relief. In some countries, the individual employees may be held liable (and not only the agency); other countries, such as India, provide for challenging administrative actions in consumer courts. In general, in the many countries where the judicial system is generally weak or corrupt and powerful political executives can refuse with impunity to abide by court orders, the effectiveness of judicial protection against administrative arbitrariness is minimal. Conversely, when honest professional bureaucrats are buffeted by political pressures, judicial pronouncements can enable them to take the right course of action, while at the same time affording relief to the citizen.

THE EVOLUTION OF GOVERNMENT REGULATION

Different Countries, Different Problems

Even where the formal regulatory framework appears substantially sound, the underlying reality often differs. The extent of legislative oversight of executive action may be uneven in depth and

BOX 3.6

Should Sick Americans Be Allowed to Use Pot if It Is Medically Necessary?

California and ten other states have legalized limited use of marijuana for patients, under a doctor's care and subject to certain provisions. After California's referendum passed in 1996, "cannabis clubs" sprung up across the state to provide marijuana to patients, but were eventually shut down by the state's attorney general. In 2001, the Supreme Court ruled that anyone distributing medical marijuana could be subject to federal prosecution despite claims that their activity was a "medical activity." Left open was the broader issue of whether the marijuana users themselves can be subject to prosecution even when they do so with a doctor's prescription, are using it to ease chronic pain, and the practice is legal under state law. Which level of government should decide—state or federal?

The U.S. Supreme Court ruled in June 2005 (*Gonzales v. Raich*) that federal authorities may prosecute sick people who use marijuana. The case concerned Diane Monson, who had degenerative spine disease and grew marijuana plants in her backyard, and Angel Raich, who suffered from scoliosis, a brain tumor, chronic nausea, fatigue, and pain—which could only be alleviated by smoking pot. The first judicial decision held that these purely local activities belong to the state jurisdiction and are beyond the reach of federal power. A federal appeals court concurred, concluding that since the medical marijuana was neither bought nor sold, its use is "noncommercial" and therefore not subject to federal authority. But the U.S. Justice Department argued successfully at the Supreme Court that homegrown marijuana does affect interstate commerce, because garden production would have an impact on "overall production" of marijuana, much of it imported across American borders by drug gangs.

Justice John Paul Stevens, writing for the 6–3 Supreme Court majority, noted that if Congress wished, it could change the law to allow medical use of marijuana. Therefore, as CNN's Jeffrey Toobin said, "If medical marijuana advocates want to get their views successfully presented, they have to go to Congress; they can't go to the states, because it's really the federal government that's in charge here." The case will have vast repercussions on other vertical regulatory conflicts between the states and the federal government, each fought on the same old ground—the interpretation of the federal power to regulate "interstate commerce"—but newly shaped by the peculiarities of the specific situation.

Sources: Various news reports, but see especially Gina Holland, "Court Rules Against Pot for Sick People," *Associated Press,* June 6, 2005.

quality; the organization of the judiciary varies, depending on the country's administrative tradition; and formal regulations coexist with customary rules (which often prevail).

In *developing countries,* the most frequent problem is weak capacity to enforce government regulations. In addition, enforcement is largely dependent on power relationships, there is collusion between the regulators and the regulated, and the rule-making process itself is opaque and discretionary. Combined with the excessive number of regulations, many of which are archaic and unnecessary, this state of affairs may produce the worst of both worlds: a regulatory framework that hinders economic activity, individual freedom and social equity, without achieving any of the benefits it purports to provide.

In *developed countries,* such as the United States and in Europe, the key issue is the cost of enforcing the regulations and the distribution of the benefits and costs of regulation among different groups. Also prevalent, especially in East Asia, are cozy relationships between the regulator and the operator, which restrict not only competition but accountability as well. A case in point is the formal privatization of telecommunications, where the original public sector operator has often succeeded in retaining de facto the power to license new operators and fix tariffs. Similar conflicts of interest are seen in civil aviation and utilities.

Regulatory Inflation

Inter-country differences notwithstanding, the twentieth century has seen a vast expansion of government regulation. Much of this expansion has been justified by a consensus on an expanded role for government itself—much has not. The French Council of State (which rules on the legality and propriety of administrative and legal proposals) calls the explosion of rules in the second half of the twentieth century a "regulatory hemorrhage." In France between 1960 and 2000, the annual production of laws and decrees increased by about one third. Australia saw a doubling of subordinate legislation between 1982 and 1990. In India, the Commission on Administrative Law estimated the number of Central Acts in force in 1998 at around 2,500, and felt that fully half of them could safely be repealed. And in the United States, the comprehensive Code of Federal Regulations swelled from 54,834 pages in 1970 to over 138,000 pages in 1995.

The trend is not much different in other countries, both developed and developing. In addition to national regulations, there is the mass of provincial and municipal orders, decisions by independent administrative authorities and tribunals, and government circulars—not to mention the regulations of international bodies (e.g., the European Commission or the World Trade Organization) with which countries and companies also must comply. Not only is there a plethora of regulations, but they change so quickly that citizens (and sometimes the front-line government employees) don't know their current content.

There are at least five nonexclusive explanations for such regulatory inflation, only the first of which is valid and acceptable:

* appropriate government response to genuine emerging problems and concerns;
* sheer bureaucratic momentum (illustrated in the well-known "law" by the English humorist C. Northcote Parkinson, by which "work expands according to time allotted"—Parkinson, 1958);
* influence of vested interests looking for special advantages;
* political response to exaggerated fears by a segment of the population; and
* "defensive" administrative strategies, mainly for public relations purposes—vulgarly called "CYA" strategies. (There are many examples in the bureaucratic response to the terrorist attacks—from airport security confiscating old ladies' cuticle scissors to rainbow-colored

systems "alerting" citizens that something bad might possibly happen somewhere in the world at some undefined future time—or not.)

Whatever the explanations, there is no question that, overall, government regulation around the world is now far in excess of what is *justified* by legitimate public purposes or what is *enforceable* given the limited administrative capacities.

Beyond the sheer volume of regulations in many countries is their haphazardness and inconsistency, exposing the citizens to the discretion of petty officials. For example, the cost of red tape and bribery for an exporter in Bangladesh can be more than three times the cost of setting up the business. (World Bank, 1996.) The "red tape" problem is aggravated by lack of transparency and of citizens' access to information on the regulations and on the procedures for dispute resolution. Indeed, as noted earlier, the single most important source of corruption the world over is a complex, opaque, and overlapping regulatory framework. Accordingly, the strongest single anti-corruption measure is regulatory simplification and streamlining.

DEREGULATION

All Deliberate Speed

The previous examples should make clear that there is a strong case for streamlining and reducing the regulatory framework in most countries, particularly poor countries. However, the earlier rush to regulate should not now be succeeded by a rush to deregulate; pell-mell deregulation is risky, unnecessary and just as mindless as the earlier haste to regulate.

A variety of well-publicized efforts at deregulation or regulatory simplification have been undertaken in many countries. Regulations are hardy weeds, however—partly because most of them serve specific interests and partly because they generate the employment of regulators, who are understandably unhappy at the prospect of losing the basis of their jobs. It is certainly true that these efforts have significantly reduced government regulation below what it *would have been* in their absence. It is doubtful, however, that deregulation efforts have so far made much of a dent in the volume of regulation overall—with the signal exception of a few countries (Australia, Brazil, New Zealand, Iceland, the United Kingdom, and the Scandinavian countries). Box 3.7 contains some illustrations of these efforts.

Ingredients of Successful Deregulation

The ingredients of successful deregulation are generally:[7]

*   unequivocal support from the top political leadership;
*   no interference during the process;
*   tough penalties for officials who do not comply;
*   defined time limit for action;
*   professional skills of the office in charge; and
*   broad credibility with officials and the public.

Improving the Functioning of Existing Regulations

Aside from reducing the overall volume of regulation, a number of improvements can be made to the existing rules. The cost of the rules can be lessened and their enforcement strengthened by:

BOX 3.7

Some Examples of Deregulation Efforts Around the World

Many countries have established specialized offices at ministerial level for streamlining regulation across the government. These include, among others:

- The Office of Regulatory Affairs in Canada
- The Deregulation Unit in the U.K. Cabinet Office
- The Office of Information and Regulatory Affairs in the U.S. Office of the President
- The Economic Deregulation Board in Mexico
- Japan's Administrative Reform Committee (advising the Prime Minister)

Such offices are most effective if they are independent, enjoy horizontal authority across government agencies, have the right expertise, are able to take the initiative, and are linked to centers of oversight and political authority (OECD, 1997c).

In addition, regulatory reviews have taken place from time to time. Some have had substantial results; others have been largely cosmetic, or their recommendations have been frustrated by powerful vested interests. There are several examples of comparative success in deregulation:

- In 1988, a "deregulation czar" was appointed in Mexico, reporting directly to the President, operating to revise, or abolish within forty-five days, a rule regarding which it received a complaint.
- Brazil's Federal Deregulation Commission managed to revoke 112,000 of the 127,000 decrees written since the beginning of the republic.
- Turkey completed a codification program that eliminated 1,600 laws and consolidated 12,000 others.
- India's Commission for Review of Administrative Law recommended in 1998 the repeal of more than half the central laws and changes in many regulations.
- The United States has introduced sunset clauses and given Congress the authority to veto any new regulation. Also, the National Performance Review has resulted in the drastic reduction and simplification of many manuals.
- The U.K. Deregulation and Contracting Act makes it possible to reduce the burden imposed by provisions of different Acts through a consultative process of notification.
- The Malaysian government took initiatives to issue composite licenses for business and investment, extend their period of validity, establish one-stop licensing centers, and abolish certain licenses.

- reviewing each rule to assure maximum clarity;
- reviewing each rule to simplify it as much as possible while preserving its purpose;
- reviewing actual enforcement, removing unnecessary bottlenecks, and providing additional resources on a selective basis;
- making affirmative outreach efforts to disseminate and explain the regulations to the individuals and groups directly affected; and
- enlisting the public's cooperation in rule enforcement, insofar as possible and as it may be appropriate.

Streamlining the Regulatory Framework

In general, the approach to regulatory reform should follow four broad criteria:

- As previously stated, a *scalpel, not a hatchet* is needed. One must consider the original purpose of each rule and anticipate the reasonable consequences of removing it.
- The review should embody a zero-based mind-set, by which the burden of proof is placed onto those who argue for retaining a given rule rather than on those who favor removing it.
- A large part of such burden of proof should be to demonstrate that the regulation can be effectively enforced given the country's administrative and judicial capacity.
- Maximum feasible feedback from those affected by the rule or its removal is especially necessary when the rule is old or was enacted without sufficient participation and consultation in the first place.

For economic deregulation in particular, the main criteria are to:

- focus deregulation on competitive markets—deregulating in uncompetitive markets carries severe risks because an unfettered private monopoly is much worse for society than a well-regulated one;
- enhance government protection of property rights (including creditors' rights), which lowers the cost of doing business by making it unnecessary for individuals and firms to recur to more expensive defensive strategies;
- minimize recourse to formal court intervention, as delays and inefficiencies in the judicial system are a constraint to equity and efficiency in most countries;[8] and
- focus also on the regulators rather than only on the regulations and ascertain whether their function is still necessary.

A major example of the last point in continental Europe and Latin America is the role of the "notaries," legal professionals at par with lawyers, whose personal intervention is legally required for most business transactions, at a cost way out of proportion to the value added. A professional and trustworthy functionary to verify the identity of the parties to a transaction and certify business documents was a necessity in the Middle Ages, but is an expensive anachronism today. Naturally, the tens of thousands of notaries active today are strenuously opposed to any reform that would put them out of business by turning notarization of documents and signatures into a simple routine, performed at low cost by a large number of licensed persons—as in the United States. This is understandable. Yet, the single step of taking professional notaries out of the regulatory loop would bring vast efficiency improvements, and at no cost to society other than the literal "stroke of the pen."

Related to the last point, would-be deregulators should never forget that deleting unnecessarily regulations has an impact on those employed in administering them. This is certainly not an excuse for tolerating intrusive and inefficient rules, but it is a reason why effective deregulation initiatives must be mindful of the employment impact, and therefore either prepare to do battle with the employees concerned or discuss measures to cushion the impact, or both. Nonetheless, in general the political calculus is likely to favor deregulation, as it mobilizes the support of the much larger number of people who are adversely affected by the inefficient rules.

Preventing the Introduction of New Inefficient Regulations

Efforts to improve the functioning of appropriate regulations and to eliminate inappropriate rules will not produce lasting improvements in regulatory effectiveness without putting in place new procedures to vet proposed new regulations and prevent the adoption of unsound ones. As a ship collects barnacles during its voyages, unnecessary or harmful new rules are likely to stick to the administrative apparatus as time goes by because the operation of vested interests leads to a systematic bias in favor of introducing new government rules.

The costs and benefits from a new rule are likely to affect different groups, and then over different time periods. Therefore, the decision on whether to enact a new regulation always has a political dimension. "Regulatory impact assessments," introduced in the early 1980s in the United States, Canada, and United Kingdom and now adopted by most other developed countries, allow evaluation of the impact of a regulatory measure before enacting it. Such assessments can be very complex and costly and can also be misused as a deliberate tactic to obstruct new regulation that may be otherwise appropriate. First, however, the costs of regulatory impact assessments can be contained by focusing the assessment only on the major components of expected costs and benefits and keeping the methodology simple. Second, that these assessments may be misused to delay or frustrate necessary regulations should lead to measures to prevent such misuse and not to abandon the practice altogether.

Starting from the principle that the burden of proof rests on those who advocate introduction of a new government regulation, much can be achieved by employing a "double sense" criterion: economic sense, to identify in general terms the probable costs and benefits of the rule, and common sense, through a reality check with a representative sample of knowledgeable stakeholders. Recall, in particular, that the existence of a government regulation always carries the risk that those administering it may use it to extract bribes or other illicit favors. Common sense can go a long way toward recognizing that motivation in a proposed new rule. For example, new regulations were introduced in Italy in the 1960s requiring that rubber dinghies used for seaside vacations carry flares and other equipment more suited to a cruise ship. The alleged rationale was marine safety, but it did not take Italian vacationers long to conclude that the real reason was to provide an artificial captive market for producers of that equipment.

FEDERAL REGULATION IN THE UNITED STATES

Roots and Expansion

Because the states have all the powers that the Constitution does not specifically reserve for the federal government, most of the regulatory function of government in the United States is exercised at state and local government level, from building codes to business rules, driver licenses, and so on. These are obviously too diverse to be summarized here.

At federal level, the authority to issue regulations binding on lower levels of government stems mainly from the interstate commerce clause of the Constitution (Art. 1, Section 8: "Congress shall have Power . . . to regulate Commerce . . . among the several States"). Pursuant to that clause, several federal departments issue regulations in their area of competence (e.g., the inspection service of the Department of Agriculture) and a number of regulatory agencies have been established as part of the federal government apparatus but run autonomously.

The regulatory function has expanded substantially since 1787, from minimal to covering most economic and social activities. Regulations on health and safety were established at the end of the nineteenth century following the uproar over congested and dangerous conditions in "sweatshop" factories and later expanded by concerns about workers' welfare in general and prohibition of child labor. Scandals about stock market manipulations sparked the introduction of securities' market regulations in 1929; the health impact of unsafe drugs and foodstuffs impelled the establishment of the Food and Drug Administration; the concern with environmental damage led to environmental protection regulations in the 1970s; the plunder of company assets by some CEOs led to new legislation on corporate governance; and so on. Two factors are evident in this evolution. First, the expansion in U.S. government regulation has been impelled, in part, by an evolving popular consensus on an expanded role of government. Second, it often took major scandals or problems coming to the surface before new regulations were enacted.

Current Regulatory Activity

The enlargement of federal regulatory activity has been impressive (or depressing, depending on political viewpoint). In mid-2005, there were 1,181 regulatory entities of the federal government. The vast majority—839—are in the executive branch, but 79 agencies belong to Congress, 45 to the judiciary, and 218 are assorted boards, commissions, and committees. The sheer number of regulatory bodies sounds enormous and fit only for a hatchet, but every one of these entities was set up for a purpose, and benefits somebody, somewhere. The proper approach, as argued earlier, is to weigh the costs of the regulation to the community (or to a group of individuals) against the benefits to a group of individuals (or to the community as a whole). This approach requires a careful agency-by-agency analysis.

Moreover, as noted, much regulatory power is not in federal hands, but in the many regulatory agencies in the fifty states and the thousands of counties and municipalities in their respective spheres of authority. Many of those agencies use their power competently to administer sensible rules. But those who worry about cumbersome federal rules or unresponsive federal offices should worry much more about local government regulations. In New York City, for example, the completely valid social purpose of protecting poor tenants against arbitrary action and landlord harassment has been perverted into a byzantine farrago of inconsistent housing rules, administered with stupefying incompetence by agencies such as the department of Housing Preservation and Development (better known among the New York cognoscenti as the department of Housing Perdition and Destruction).

Table 3.2 illustrates the diversity of federal regulatory agencies in the United States by listing a few of the better-known ones.

Economic Regulation: Where in the World Does the United States Stand?

As noted earlier, the health, safety, environmental, and other social-purpose regulations number in the tens of thousands, and no generalization or comparison with other countries is possible.

Table 3.2

Some Federal Regulatory Entities in the United States

Entity	Year founded	Mandate
Animal Plant Health Inspection Service (APHIS)	1977	Protects and promotes U.S. agricultural health, administers the Animal Welfare Act, and carries out wildlife management.
Federal Communications Commission (FCC)	1934	Regulates interstate and international communications by radio, TV, wire, satellite and cable.
Federal Power Commission (FPC)	1920	Regulates interstate power distribution— succeeded by FERC, below.
Federal Energy Regulatory Commission (FERC)	1978	Regulates the interstate transmission of natural gas, oil, and electricity, as well as gas and hydropower projects.
Environmental Protection Agency (EPA)	1970	Develops and enforces regulations that implement environmental laws.
Securities and Exchange Commission (SEC)	1929	Regulates U.S. stock and other securities markets.
Occupational Safety and Health Administration (OSHA)	1970	Sets safety and health standards in the workplace.
National Transportation Safety Board (NTSB)	1967	Investigates all civil aviation accidents and significant accidents in other modes.
National Highway Traffic Safety (NTHS)	1970	Sets standards to save lives, prevent injuries and reduce economic costs of traffic crashes.
Interstate Commerce Commission (ICC)	1887	Regulates commerce between the States, and broad related powers.
Administration on Developmental Disabilities (ADD)	2000	Implements the Disabilities Assistance and Bill of Rights Act.
Food and Drug Administration (FDA)	1906	Regulates the marketing of food and pharmaceuticals.

Source: Various U.S. government websites.

However, *economic* regulation is focused on fewer measures, and we can compare the United States with other countries. Table 3.3 shows the placement of the United States compared with the OECD group of developed countries and with the world as a whole, on a number of key economic regulations and restrictions. (See the note to the table for an explanation of the indicators.)

Where the United States does comparatively "best" is in the area of employment conditions, especially the ease of firing employees. While this appears to be a perverse sort of advantage, employers do tend to *hire* people more easily if they know they can let them go with equal ease. This is unquestionably a major reason why the United States has a significantly lower unemployment rate than Europe. Good employment conditions don't do a lot of good for those who are not employed. On the other hand, Europe also has much more generous provisions for unemployed workers. Consider also that the much greater flexibility in conditions of employment in the United States (with an index of 29, compared to the developed countries' average of 50 and the world

Table 3.3

Selected Economic Regulations, U.S. and Other Countries, 2003–4

Area of regulation	U.S.	OECD average	WORLD average	Least "flexible"	Most "flexible"
Starting a Business					
Number of procedures	5	7	10	19 (Belarus)	2 (Australia, Canada)
Time (days)	4	24	52	215 (Congo)	2 (Australia)
Cost (% pcY)	0.6	11	85	1,297 (Sierra Leone)	0.2 (New Zealand)
Labor Rigidity					
Flexibility in hiring	33	50	52	81 (Panama)	17 (China)
Employment conditions	29	50	70	95 (Bolivia)	25 (Denmark)
Flexibility in firing	5	28	41	74 (Angola)	4 (Papua New Guinea)
Enforcing Contracts					
Number of procedures	17	17	27	55 (Puerto Rico)	11 (Australia)
Time (days)	365	231	357	1,460 (Guatemala)	7 (Tunisia)
Cost (% pcY)	0.4	8.9	44	520 (Malawi)	0.3 (Jordan)
Closing a Business					
Time (years)	3.0	2.1	3.5	11.3 (India)	0.4 (Ireland)
Cost (% assets)	4.0	9.8	14.3	38.0 (Venezuela)	1.0 (Finland, Holland, Singapore)
Percent goals satisfaction	88	76	49	8 (Angola, Togo, others)	99 (Finland, Norway, Singapore)

Source: Extracted and adapted from World Bank (2004).

Note: some indices are self-explanatory, e.g., the number of individual steps required to start a business or to enforce a contract, or the time expended, or the cost. (The cost is expressed in relative terms, as a percentage of per capita national income in the country in question.) Other indices are on a scale of 0–100. The ratings in the labor flexibility area fall in this category, as well as the percentage of "satisfaction" of the goals of insolvency procedures. The methodology, although not without weaknesses, is by far the best that one can elaborate, and perhaps the best feature of the study is that the primary information was obtained from a number of experts in each country rather than from armchair calculations.

average of 70) results from an absence of government regulation of such matters as maximum overtime or minimum annual leave.

But remember the importance of different choices made by different countries. As mentioned earlier, Europeans are astonished to hear that an American worker has just ten working days' paid vacation time in a year, or that an employee can be fired after twenty or thirty years of service with two weeks' notice and without much justification (if any). Americans are equally incredulous that a European employee can have as much as two months paid annual vacation and six months' maternity leave at full pay and another six months at half pay—by law. By contrast, the extent of government regulation of the workweek in many East Asian countries in practice means little in a social milieu like Japan, where an employee wouldn't even think of going home before his boss—regardless of the hour.

Thus, it is important to be especially wary of normative conclusions in the area of employment regulation: it is in this area that the issue of winners and losers is most relevant and where different cultures and social choices produce different outcomes—all more or less suitable to their respective contexts. On balance, we personally consider that in this respect Europe should become more like the United States, and the United States more like Europe. Unfortunately, it appears that the two systems are moving further apart, with protections for workers' rights eroding rapidly in the United States and unwarranted employment rigidities in Europe showing no sign of improvement.

A Look in the Crystal Ball

The next big issue in the United States is likely to be whether to introduce federal regulation to protect the privacy of personal data, especially financial records. In contrast with Europe, where all countries have strict privacy laws and national data protection offices, the United States lacks a unified national set of standards and protections. As Eric Dash has noted (*New York Times,* August 7, 2005), the underlying reason is that "privacy" is viewed as a citizen right in Europe, but as an economic commodity in the United States. Thus, the probability of new federal e-privacy rules is mainly a function of whether the ability of hackers to get to private information grows faster than the capacity of the system to keep them out. Historically, as mentioned, large expansions of federal regulation occurred only in response to crises or major scandals. Some significant leakages of personal financial data occurred in 2004, 2005, and 2006; a couple more big problems of this sort are likely to spark a move for federal regulation.

Whether or not e-privacy will be the next big issue, the reach of the regulatory powers of the federal government is certain to remain a central topic of debate, and may expand or contract in future years depending largely on Supreme Court decisions. For example, in 1995 and 2000, the Supreme Court set new limits to the authority of Congress to intervene in "non-commercial" interstate matters. In 2005, the Court went the other way and upheld the power of the U.S. Justice Department to prosecute users of medical marijuana (as described earlier in Box 3.5).

However, while an expansion of federal regulation would almost certainly entail an expansion in total government regulation in the United States, the opposite is not true: shrinking *federal* regulatory authority might simply lead to a corresponding expansion of regulation by state and local governments. Strictly speaking, therefore, the Supreme Court decisions will affect more the distribution of regulatory authority between federal and state governments, and the uniformity of American citizens' treatment in different states, than the extent of *overall* government regulation in the country. That will be determined through the political process by future congresses, presidents, governors, state legislatures, county councils, and mayors all over the country.

GENERAL DIRECTIONS OF IMPROVEMENT

Government regulation is essential for defining and protecting property rights and is important to foster competition, correct market failures, protect public safety, and promote sound social and environmental policies. Moreover, clear and effective regulations have the benefits of:

- providing predictability and consistency for those outside as well as inside the government;
- reducing the scope for arbitrary behavior;
- enhancing the likelihood of orderly and efficient transactions;
- helping legislators and citizens alike in holding government agencies accountable;
- providing the basis for legislative oversight and consistent audit practices; and
- helping to convey fairness and consistency to the citizens, if the process of rulemaking is regular, open, and participatory.

All regulations carry costs—to the government for enforcing them and to the private sector for complying with them. These costs are justified for essential regulations, but not for obsolete, intrusive, or unimportant ones, which also produce indirect costs in the form of reduced transparency and slower innovation and investment. Moreover, inessential regulations carry especially heavy costs for the poor and for persons without "connections." Thus, a regulatory impact assessment is advisable for regulations with presumptively broad reach. Such an assessment need be neither complex nor costly. A lot can be achieved by employing the "double sense" criterion: economic sense, to identify in general terms the probable cost and their distribution, and common sense—as achieved with the help of a representative sample of concerned stakeholders.

In countries with unrepresentative regimes or weak accountability mechanisms, a complex and opaque regulatory framework is the largest single source of corruption—where every single stop in the regulatory process is also an opportunity for the "regulator" to extort a bribe. The burden of proof therefore lies heavily on to the proponents of new rules or the opponents of simplification of the existing rules. Clarification of the rules instead carries no burden of proof at all: the more clarity the better.

Most developing countries have an additional special burden in this respect, as they inherited from the former colonial authorities regulations that are not only likely to be obsolete but were designed in the first place for control and exploitation rather than for protection of the local public interest. Many more regulations promulgated after independence were then superimposed onto these rules. A related major issue in most developing countries is the lax and erratic regulatory enforcement.

Most countries would therefore benefit from a two-pronged effort at regulatory reform by: extensive pruning of the welter of regulation; and building the capacity for robust, nondiscriminatory, and predictable enforcement of the key regulations—particularly the regulations that protect competition, public safety and health, the environment, and land use.

QUESTIONS FOR DISCUSSION

1. Can a strong government enforce the laws and the rules whether or not most citizens comply voluntarily?
2. In the specific context of government regulation, what's the difference between "culture" and "habit"?
3. What right does some government bureaucrat in Washington or Sacramento have to tell you what to do and not to do, and who gave him that right?
4. Pick one of the two following statements and make a credible argument for it:
    a. "Just as the road to hell is paved with good intentions, most well-meant government interference with private markets ends up doing harm to society."
    b. "Because individuals have a short-term perspective, without extensive government regulation society would suffer substantial harm in the long run."
5. In Europe, it's hard to be fired and hard to be hired. In the United States, it's easy to be fired and easy to be hired. As a person with a lifetime of work opportunities and uncertainties ahead of you (and aside from all other preferences and considerations), where would you rather be?
6. How would you define the difference between a costly but necessary regulation and one that is simple and inefficient?
7. Is a clear and unnecessary government rule worse than a necessary and ambiguous rule?
8. Are mandatory annual motor vehicle inspections mainly a device to create business for licensed mechanics?
9. Mandatory building codes are much stricter in Chicago and New York City than in most U.S. cities. Moreover, in some states (e.g., West Virginia) although there is a mandatory building code, state law leaves it to the individual counties and municipalities whether or not to conduct inspections—and most of them do not.[9] Why the difference?
10. Does the government have a legitimate interest in regulating the internet? If yes, what legitimate interest would that be?

NOTES

1. This chapter draws in part from the articles by Bradburd (1992); Cooper and Newland (1997); OECD (1997b); World Bank (1997b, 2004), country profiles, Commonwealth Secretariat (1995a). Also see Perry (1999); OECD (1997e); Self (1972); Starling (1998); Fesler and Kettl (1991); Commonwealth Secretariat (1997b); World Bank (2006).

2. When freed from the ingrained habit of following government command, people become literally lost and unable to function in a new environment where they are allowed—indeed, expected—to reach their own decisions in most activities. The psychological dimension of the transition from a command economy is enormous and has been generally underestimated in studies of countries in transition. Thus, inattention to the psychological blinders of people living in the former Soviet Union produced major policy mistakes and prediction errors that still echo in authoritarian post-Soviet Russia fifteen years later.

3. See, for example, Stiglitz (1989).

4. The argument is associated with Nobel Prize winner Ronald Coase (1960) and is at the center of much of the "new institutional economics" briefly described in chapter 1.

5. This World Bank study is occasionally inattentive to the fundamental issue of the internal distribution of regulatory costs and benefits and oblivious of the core issue of societal choices concerning the balance between reward and uncertainty, effort and leisure, and efficiency and equity. However, it is the best global study of economic regulation. The reader interested in economic regulation around the world is urged to consult it.

6. For an explanation of the implications of each dimension, see World Bank, *Doing Business 2004: Understanding Regulation*. Washington, DC, 2004.

7. World Bank (1997b).

8. For example, the Singapore Registry of Companies and Businesses allowed businesses to make minor corrections by lodging a statutory declaration instead of going through the courts.

9. Chas Minor, personal communication.

CHAPTER 4

Policy-making Machinery and the Organization of Central Government

> We tend to meet difficult situations by reorganizing, which gives the illusion of progress while only creating confusion and demoralization.
> —*Petronius Arbiter, 66* C.E.[1]

> Mrs. Schwimmer is suing me because I made her dental bridge as I felt it and not to fit her ridiculous mouth . . . I can't work to order like a common tradesman . . . I find it beautiful. She claims she can't chew. What do I care whether she can chew or not!
> —*Woody Allen, 1976*[2]

WHAT TO EXPECT

Although the job of the administrative apparatus is to implement policy and not to make it, its major roles are also to advise, support, and facilitate the making of policy. Next come the many aspects of implementing government policy—fleshing out the standards and norms, delivering public goods and services, and elaborating the most efficient partnership and division of labor between the public and private sectors. None of these tasks can be performed efficiently unless the organizational architecture of central government is sound. Because it is difficult to implement bad policy decisions well, the chapter starts by summarizing the main criteria for good policy making and then describes the various types of mechanisms in different countries for supporting the central government policy makers. The principles for distributing the work of government are discussed next, along with the criteria for organizing ministries and departments in central government, the patterns of international experience, and the key issues of horizontal coordination within government between ministries and agencies. The sections summarizing the current state of affairs in the United States and suggesting general directions of improvement conclude the chapter. (These same issues with respect to subnational and local government are treated in chapter 5.)

Note that although rules and experience can help, none of the decisions on the organizational structure of government should be interpreted as purely technical. The organization of government must also respond to the need for making room for influential figures of the governing party, giving political payback and distribution of the fruits of office, pacifying important constituencies, and so on. Moreover, the choice of ministers and agency heads can be a deliberate signal of the importance the government attaches to a particular function. The readers should therefore frame their understanding of the following issues in their inherently political context.

CENTRAL MECHANISMS TO SUPPORT POLICY MAKING[3]

Proper administrative support is essential for good policy making. Such support consists of sifting out of the countless claims for political attention those important few that merit the consideration of political leaders; assuring the provision of relevant information to the policy makers; regulating the "traffic" flow; disseminating the policies that have been decided; monitoring their implementation; and reporting back to the decision makers. These roles are performed differently in different systems of government. In a presidential system, the policy-making support function is usually performed by an "office of the president." The core issue in this case is a proper balance of power and responsibility between the office of the president and the heads of the government departments. When the power shifts too much to the president's office, policy implementation and interdepartmental cooperation suffer; when the president's office is too weak, a unified view of overall government policy is jeopardized. In a parliamentary system, support to policy making is normally provided by a secretariat to the "cabinet" (either coterminous with the "council of ministers," or a subset of the council of ministers), which is the primary policy-making body. The core issue in this case is the proper balance between expeditious decision-making and "ownership" of the decisions. If the cabinet is too small, those excluded do not feel they share in the collective responsibility; if the cabinet is too large, reaching decisions is slow and the policy outcome may be diluted.

Criteria of Good Policy Decisions

Good policy decisions normally meet four criteria, loosely related to the four governance pillars of accountability, transparency, rule of law and participation previewed in chapter 1:

- *Discipline* requires policy decisions to be internally consistent, financially realistic, and capable of being implemented. (For example, large new expenditures or tax cuts without regard to their affordability violate this principle.)
- *Stability* in decision making and avoiding frequent policy reversals have been shown to be important for investment and economic activity.
- *Transparency* of policy-making procedures is equally important. While the deliberations themselves should normally be confidential to permit free internal debate, the *process* by which decisions are taken must be clear, explicit, and public.
- *Selectivity* should guide the process of policy making (i.e., the attention of policy makers should be systematically channeled to decisions that warrant such attention, as the capacity to decide is the scarcest government resource of all and should not be wasted on trivial matters).

The Tasks of the Policy-Making Support Mechanism

Accordingly, an effective policy support mechanism must foster policy discipline, stability, and clarity and filter out the unimportant. Specifically, a good mechanism—whether cabinet secretariat, president's office, or other such group—needs to perform the following five tasks well.

Early Provision of Relevant Information

The policy support unit must prepare the agendas for meetings of the policy makers and circulate them sufficiently in advance and with the (few) key documents essential for informed debate and eventual decision.

Adequate Consultation

The support unit is responsible for ensuring that all government entities with a stake in the issue at hand are adequately consulted in advance. Not only is advance consultation necessary to channel relevant expertise and viewpoints into the policy-making process, but it also helps generate "ownership" by those who will be responsible for implementing the policy. On special occasions, it may be necessary to restrict the circle of participants to accelerate the decision and prevent leaks, but the procedure should normally favor the largest practicable consultation of stakeholders.

Contestability

The most severe danger to good policy making arises when "consensus" becomes acquiescence to the conventional wisdom of the moment. (In recent U.S. experience, the intelligence debacle that produced the myth of "weapons of mass destruction" in Iraq is a classic illustration of the disastrous impact of "group-think" on the policy-making process.) It is always difficult for lower-ranking officials to speak up when confronted with the different views of their bosses, especially when they sense that the policy decision has been preordained. It is therefore critical to put in place procedures to assure, not just allow, dissenting voices and contrary information to emerge early in the debate. This requires systematically asking questions such as: "How do we know and from whom do we know it?"; "What else is likely to happen?"; "And then, what do we do?" For this—a "designated tire-kicker" or similar mechanism can be useful. (In the Vatican process of recognizing sainthood, this essential function is performed by a "devil's advocate.")

Recording and Dissemination

A policy that is not properly communicated to the government administrative apparatus cannot be properly implemented. It is the job of the policy support unit to record the decisions accurately and disseminate them to those concerned. Practice varies in different countries on how far to go in recording the reasons and arguments behind the decision. In the United Kingdom, the Cabinet conclusions—not "decisions"—are expected to include enough of the discussion and the reasoning to make clear to those charged with implementing them what needs to be done and why.

Monitoring Policy Implementation

President Harry Truman is reputed to have said on leaving office in 1953 after the election of General Dwight Eisenhower: "Wait till the General sits here and orders something to be done, and nothing happens." Taking a decision is no assurance that it will be executed, particularly when diverse vested interests are at stake. In itself, a policy paper is not a policy, it is a paper. At least on a selective basis, the support unit should monitor the implementation of policy decisions by those responsible and report back to the policy makers any major problems requiring their intervention.

International Practice in Policy Support Mechanisms

With minor variants, all policy-support mechanisms around the world fit one of the four archetypes described in Box 4.1—"weak secretariat," "strong secretariat," "watchdog secretariat," and "top cop"—each evolving organically from the type of government system and the political culture of the country, and its size and complexity.

BOX 4.1

Archetypes of Policy Support Mechanisms

Weak Secretariat. Weak secretariats perform "pure" logistical and facilitation functions. They receive and distribute papers for consideration of Cabinet, assemble agendas on a first-come, first-served basis and record and relay Cabinet decisions. Weak secretariats have no proposal-sifting role, do not serve as gatekeeper, have a very small staff, and are typical of small countries with a substantial degree of ex ante policy cohesion. An example is the Singapore Cabinet Office.

Strong Secretariat. A strong secretariat is not only responsible to ensure the smooth functioning of cabinet meetings, but also has a major gatekeeping role in determining what items to be placed on the agenda and in briefing the prime minister on technical aspects or proposals and options for alternative solutions. An example is the U.K. Cabinet Office, well-staffed but with personnel seconded from the various ministries rather than assigned permanently to the cabinet office—assuring that the technical concerns of the various sectors are well reflected. (The prime minister has his own small staff to advise him on the big picture and on political considerations.)

"Watchdog" Secretariat. In addition to the normal functions of a "strong" cabinet office, these policy support units also have the legal responsibility of advising the government on legislative procedures and constitutional issues and other substantive duties. The main illustration is the General Secretariat of Government in France, which drafts the cabinet agenda for a full six months in advance and only permits fully vetted and agreed proposals to be presented to cabinet. (Different cover colors denote different stages of completeness and staff agreement on a proposal; when a policy proposal is considered by the General Secretariat to be "ripe" for cabinet discussion, it is given a blue cover. Asking "Do you have a 'blue'?" is the best way to defuse a claim by a bureaucratic opponent that a policy proposal is pretty much already agreed at technical level.) Watchdog-type offices are present only in large countries and have both a sizeable staff of their own as well as a much larger group staff (more than 5,000 in France), either seconded from ministries or attached to the prime minister's office.

"Top Cop" Office. The best example of this strongest of policy support units is the Office of the President in the United States, which coordinates policy, recommends all senior appointments, formulates budget proposals, and so on—with staff and resources as vast as its responsibilities. (The Office of the President is described in greater detail in the concluding section of this chapter.)

THE ORGANIZATIONAL STRUCTURE OF CENTRAL GOVERNMENT

In buildings, American architect Louis Sullivan said in 1896, form follows function.[4] The same is true of the organizational architecture of government. Institutional functions come first, and the organization must be adapted to implement them. The temptation to design government structures to look neat and "logical," regardless of whether they suit actual needs, leads to the absurdity of the Woody Allen quote at the beginning of this chapter. And "reorganization" should not consist of just moving organizational boxes around or, worse, be used as a device to avoid confronting real problems—as was perceptively diagnosed over 2,000 years ago by the Roman commentator Petronius in the other quote at the top of the chapter. Consider the contemporary example of the Department of Homeland Security (DHS) in the United States. Confronted with the substantive problem of lack of focus, cooperation and accountability in the ramshackle assemblage of the twenty-two different federal agencies that were merged in 2002 into the new DHS, the "solution" was to contract a public relations firm to "rebrand" the department and give it a new typeface, color scheme, employee lapel pins, and new seal designed to "convey 'strength' and 'gravitas.'"[5] Petronius must be chuckling in his ancient grave.

If the government is to be able to fulfill its compact with the citizens to deliver protection and services efficiently and effectively, its organizational structure should be tailored to the size and complexity of the country, the nature of the political system, and the policy objectives and priorities. However, some general guidance is applicable to all countries based on a number of principles developed through the centuries to shape the structure of government—principles this chapter will summarize.

But first, some definitions. A "ministry" is a first-level unit headed by a high-ranking political appointee known as a minister. In some countries (e.g., the United States, the United Kingdom, and most British Commonwealth countries), this primary unit is called a "department" and its head a "secretary." In most other countries, the term "department" refers instead to a subdivision of a ministry, and departments are in turn usually divided into divisions, branches, and sections—in descending hierarchical order. The term "agency" normally refers to an entity of government that is attached to ministries and is created for special government purposes, and the term "executive agency" refers to an entity that is part of the government but is run independently of any ministry and has full operational autonomy.

Principles for Distributing the Work of Government

The general objective of good organizational design is to distribute responsibilities in a manner that is both efficient and clear, with a minimum of duplication and overlapping, so that each administrative unit is properly subject to legal and political controls and can be made accountable for its activities. In addition, the organizational scheme should encourage managerial flexibility and responsiveness to policies and new development. In this light, there are four principles for distributing the work of government: the area covered, the clients served, the process employed, and the function performed.

The *Area Principle* is no longer used as a general basis for allocating central government responsibilities, except in the case of a ministry focused on a defined region for political reasons (e.g., the former Secretary for Northern Ireland in the United Kingdom), or of an agency addressing specific needs of a region (e.g., the Tennessee Valley Authority in the United States).

The *Client Principle* applies to entities charged with the problems of specific client groups (e.g., the Department for Veterans Affairs in the United States). It, too, is not used as a general criterion for division of labor among ministries. However, within ministries the work is often subdivided according to specialized needs of clients. For example, a ministry of social welfare may have divisions focusing on the needs of specific client groups such as the handicapped, or another ministry may have a unit to deal with specified minorities (e.g., the Bureau of Indian Affairs in the U.S. Interior Department).

The *Process Principle* rests on the advantages of concentrating specialized skills and techniques and is applicable to "technical" organizations (e.g., ministries for water resources or information technology) normally staffed largely by engineers and other professionals. Process-based departments are found more often in local government than in central government, where it is more common to subordinate process units to a broader functional structure (e.g., locating the information technology in a ministry of scientific research).

The *Function Principle* (setting up different ministries for education, health, defense, and so on) is the dominant criterion of first-level organization in most governments. Wilson (1989) identifies four groupings of function-based government organizations that depend on the degree to which their outputs and outcomes can be assessed. (Outputs are the goods or services produced [e.g., the number of vaccinations performed]; outcomes are the purposes which the outputs are meant to achieve [e.g., disease reduction]—see chapter 10.) These groupings are:

- production organizations, where both outputs and outcomes can be observed (e.g., the Internal Revenue Service);
- procedural organizations, where the outputs can be observed but not the outcomes (e.g., armed forces during peace time, employment agencies);
- craft organizations, where outputs are not easily observed but outcomes can be evaluated (e.g., the Federal Bureau of Investigation); and
- coping organizations where neither outputs nor outcomes can be observed (e.g., the diplomatic service).

These groupings are not of academic interest only, but are important to determine the scope of administrative accountability and the mechanisms to put in place to monitor and improve the performance of different government entities—the central topic of chapter 10.

Criteria for Allocating Government Functions

Within the function principle of organization, there are four criteria for efficient allocation of tasks: non-fragmentation, homogeneity, non-overlap, and span of control.

Non-fragmentation

Non-fragmentation means that all responsibility for a specific purpose should be placed in a single unit. The criterion relates to both purpose and place, the latter coming into play in the case of fragmentation among levels of government and among agencies in the same area. The criterion of non-fragmentation cannot be followed consistently, since to unify responsibility for one major function will often lead to fragmenting responsibility for another function (Oakerson, 1989). For example, a comprehensive attack on drug abuse would cut across a number of other functions associated with education, law enforcement, public assistance, and health. The dilemma is this: On the one hand, if the ministry of education is responsible for drug abuse education, the health ministry for drug treatment, the interior ministry for drug enforcement, and so on, the fight against drug abuse is fragmented and thus ineffective. On the other hand, to set up a separate department for all aspects of drug abuse leads to the fragmentation of a host of *other* government programs in education, health, and law enforcement. This dilemma cannot be resolved, but it must be recognized and managed in practical ways. To stay with the drug abuse example, the solution adopted in the United States was to create a "drug czar" office to coordinate the anti-drug activities of the government departments without taking over authority in their various areas of activity. (That this solution has been largely ineffective in this particular example is not the point here.)

Homogeneity

The criterion of homogeneity prescribes that no administrative unit should perform heterogeneous functions or serve competing purposes. In reality, it is an aspect of the criterion of non-fragmentation and is listed separately here only to be consistent with most of the literature on the subject.

Non-overlap

The criterion of non-overlap implies that two or more ministries or departments should not be given the same authority to act in the same circumstances. While fragmentation divides authority, jurisdictional overlap creates redundant authority and dilutes accountability, with each entity enabled to point fingers at the other. Fragmentation makes government ineffective, while overlap makes government unaccountable. Once again, some measure of overlap of authority between different ministries is inevitable in the real world—the objective is to keep it to a realistic minimum and to foster coordination.

Span of Control

This criterion calls for manageable organizational size. If each ministry is very small, the resulting large number of ministries will lead to problems of inter-ministerial coordination and a risk of incoherent overall government policy. If ministries are very large, intra-ministerial coordination problems will emerge, with the risk of inefficient and unaccountable implementation. Some organizational theorists have argued for systematically grouping functions in such a way as to produce departments of roughly equal size. This is pretty silly advice, as in the real world political and other factors are intrinsically opposed to such tidy patterns—which leads to the final point.

Balancing the Criteria

None of these criteria can be fully applied without affecting the application of the others, and a reasonable balance is called for. In any event, the criteria can only be general guidelines, as the organizational structure of government is by definition heavily influenced by political considerations. Different decisions will be made in different countries, or at different times, depending on the importance of the function at hand, the degree of central control which is considered desirable, and the interplay with powerful private interests. Thus, for example, exporters' interests are usually served by separating foreign trade from other ministries in order to focus policy and administrative attention on exports—and, conversely, the existence of such a separate ministry may be an indication of the political weight of exporters in the country. Or, the health care establishment may push for outsourcing the function of public health monitoring out of the ministry of health. Obviously, there can be no blueprint on how these political dynamics will work in different countries. However, gross violations of these organizational criteria raise red flags that the media and civil society are well advised to investigate, and international practice does provide some useful benchmarks.

International Practice

General Considerations

The number and designation of ministries vary across countries. For example, there may be one single ministry for infrastructure, as in Algeria until the 1990s, while most countries have chosen to constitute separate ministries for different infrastructure like roads, ports, water supply and sewerage, and railways. Some countries have a comprehensive ministry for industry. Others, such as India, have, in addition to a central ministry for industry, separate ministries for steel, mining, heavy industry, small scale industry, petrochemicals, fertilizers, and food processing. Some countries combine industry and trade and others create super-ministries to coordinate all economic work of government. The establishment of ministries is often a signaling device for policy emphases (e.g., ministries for women or for minorities or for environment).

The importance of the finance and planning ministries and their relative power varies in different countries. Countries also vary in where they locate cross-cutting theme areas like women's development, public assistance and welfare, environment, foreign trade, housing, local government, and consumer rights. Specific subjects like civil aviation, standards, information technology, and statistics often migrate over time from one ministry to another with no apparent logic. Most often, the underlying reason is the need to accommodate a well-connected politician or government official.

The number of ministers depends also on political considerations, which may dictate appointing additional ministers for the sake of party balancing. Also, certain functions of government may acquire new importance due to international developments, advance of technology, external aid, or domestic concerns—as is the case with the environment, women's development, minority affairs, control of major diseases, information technology, and communications. There is a temptation, whenever a new function emerges, to entrust it to a newly created ministry or autonomous agency (see Box 4.2).

Proliferation of central government organizations means confusion for the public and complexity for the political executive (Self, 1972). Some countries (e.g., the United Kingdom) have avoided this temptation, preferring instead to create new units under the existing ministries or hive off functions to non-ministerial bodies. Elsewhere, there has been a move to reduce and reorganize the ministries and departments by merger and consolidation. In federal countries, the reduction in the number of central ministries often represents a downward shift of functions to provinces. (A similar downloading to subnational levels of government is noticeable in recent years in unitary countries as well, including France and in several Latin American countries.) Therefore, it may be misleading to look only at changes in the size of central government without considering what happens to subnational levels of government.

Current International Patterns

International practices on the number of central ministries vary widely. For example, in large unitary Japan there are only eleven ministries and almost all public administration is conducted by their internal units or by attached agencies. Progressively, all the freestanding agencies have

BOX 4.2

Mushrooming of Government in Bangladesh

From independence in 1971 to the mid-1990s, the government of Bangladesh more than doubled the number of central government bodies. The number of ministries increased from 21 to 35; the number of departments and directorates from 109 to 221; and public employment grew from about 450,000 in 1971 to over one million (i.e., at a rate of over 3 percent per year, compared to the population growth rate of 2.5 percent). In the last ten years the situation has worsened further.

In part, new ministries, divisions, and departments have been created to meet genuine emerging needs, such as environmental concerns and women's issues. But the state has also intruded more and more into commercial economic activities. Moreover, the growth of government has often been stimulated by partisan political considerations rather than by an expanded role of the state. The "winner take all" style of Bangladeshi politics until the military intervention of 2006 led to an increase in ministries to accommodate intraparty interest groups, more high-level official positions, and more jobs to be dispensed by party leaders for patronage reasons. Aside from the negative budgetary impact, this expansion has stretched the implementation capacity of the administration, compounded coordination problems, and exacerbated regulatory intrusiveness. Even worse, it has also created vested interests that have consistently blocked efforts at rationalization and reform.

Source: World Bank (1996).

been subsumed within the ministries, leaving only a few regulatory agencies outside the system. By contrast, federal Australia has twenty-three departments (ministries), seventy-six government bodies with some measure of independence, and fourteen statutory authorities. Despite its larger size, the United States has only fifteen federal government departments (almost half of which were created within the last fifty years), under which a number of specialized offices are subsumed, and fifty-six government agencies with varying degrees of autonomy. In the countries influenced by the British administrative tradition, the ministries are organized on hierarchical lines, with the "permanent secretary" (a career civil servant) at the top and responsible directly to the minister, a number of deputy secretaries and undersecretaries, divisions, sections, and at the lowest level, an army of administrative assistants and secretarial staff. (Sometimes, semantic differences cause protocol problems, as on the occasion when a very young Indian "undersecretary" [the lowest professional administrative rung in India] found to his embarrassment that he had been given precedence at an international conference over an American "assistant secretary" [the responsible authority for a major function of federal government]). Superimposed on this system are the staff advisers and technical employees whose advice is fitted into the hierarchical decision-making process.

Table 4.1 shows the average number of central government ministries in the various regions of the world. Overall, the average number of central government ministries is sixteen, ranging from

Table 4.1

Central Government Ministries Around the World: Number and Size
(Various years, turn of the century)

Countries in:	Average number of ministries	Average population (thousands)	Population per ministry (thousands)	Central government employment (thousands)	Average number of employees per ministry
Africa (Sub-Saharan)	19	13,942	926	1,046	71,000
Asia	20	123,951	4,696	1,069	51,000
Eastern Europe & Ex-USSR	15	17,813	747	1,264	73,000
Latin America & Caribbean	15	17,142	1,169	2,275	192,000
Middle East & North Africa	20	14,992	643	1,390	62,000
Pacific Islands	10	587	44	5.4	360
Developed Countries	14	37,286	3,022	1,658	132,000
World	16	32,245	1,607	2,015	135,000

Original sources: Various country embassies and consular offices; internet government websites; World Bank and Asian Development Bank desk officers and field representatives. For details on the approximately 150 individual countries, see ADB (2000), Appendix III.

Note that the figures for average population per ministry and employees per ministry do not match the ratios, because the mean numbers of ministries in countries in each region are unweighted by either population or government employment.

ten in the small Pacific countries to twenty in the bloated governments of the Middle East and North Africa. Within each region, intercountry variation is larger. The average number of ministries ranges from ten to twenty-eight in countries of Sub-Saharan Africa, from eleven to twenty-seven in Latin America, and from six to sixteen in the Pacific. The largest variation is in Asia, from a low of seven ministries to a high of eighty-five, with South Asia generally on the high side and East Asia on the low side. The lowest intercountry differences are found in Eastern Europe and the developed countries, most of which cluster around fifteen ministries. Obviously, the number of central government ministries tends to be greater in the larger countries and in centralized unitary states. However, there is very strong evidence of administrative economies of scale: neither the number of ministries nor their size increases in proportion to the size of the country. The two extremes are the Cook Islands in the Pacific, where each ministry serves on average just over 1,000 citizens, and—not surprisingly—China, with 43 million people per central ministry.

Does the Number of Ministries Really Matter?

The number of ministries certainly matters in the calculation of political leaders, who are interested in political accommodation, or of rulers who award cabinet posts to personal followers. But the issue is important for effective government as well. On the one hand, having too many ministries adds to overhead costs of government on account of the staff and infrastructure connected with each. Moreover, each ministry seeks to find new work, fueling the bureaucratic pressure for expansion. Next, problems are created when several ministries perform similar functions and tread on each other's toes. Finally, it is harder to have a good dialogue and coordination among too many players. On the other hand, a reasonable span of management control as well as effective accountability would be jeopardized if the ministries are too large because there are too few of them. Also, reducing the number of ministries in and of itself may not produce efficiency or cost reduction. Indeed, the consolidation of ministries might even lead to the erosion of checks and balances, as occurred in South Korea before the restoration of democracy in the 1990s. This is because, in authoritarian states, in the absence of external contestability some overlap among ministries can provide a minimum of internal competition to spur efficient performance and generate debate.

Nevertheless, in the last two decades a number of countries have succeeded in reducing the number of ministries and agencies. In Singapore, the Committee on Reorganization of Ministries led in streamlining government, by transferring to one ministry closely related functions in various ministries, and improving central coordination of activities. In 1999, South Korea adopted a Government Organization Act, which produced a smaller but more efficient and responsive central government apparatus. The Japanese government—where the number of ministries has traditionally been small—is in the midst of transferring many functions to the private sector. In Australia, the number of cabinet departments was first reduced from 28 to 18 in 1987, then to 14 in 1996. And Italy, traditionally known for dropsical government, reduced in 1999 the number of central government ministries to 11, the lowest in Europe. However, the number has crept up since then and there is still little sign of major improvements in administrative efficiency (see Box 4.3).

In the countries in transition of Central and Eastern Europe and the former Soviet Union, reorganization of the ministerial structure was part of the restructuring away from central planning of both the economic and political systems. In the organization of economies in transition, it has been a massive challenge to determine how to:

- phase out government organizations unsuited to the new market-oriented economic system;
- restructure organizations whose rationale has changed radically (e.g., a ministry of finance, from its limited role in a centrally planned system as merely the state's accountant and paymaster to the leading entity for financial management);
- create from scratch organs that can address the new functions of government (e.g., protecting private property rights);
- avoid incoherence between the new organizations and the persisting old institutions during the transition.

To comprehend the enormity magnitude of the reorganization required, consider that many separate ministries had to be merged, and others fundamentally restructured for their new mandate (e.g., reorienting the ministry of interior from political control of the citizens to maintenance of law and order); ministries of education and culture were turned upside down, shedding their propaganda function and moving to design and implement a thorough reformulation of school curricula; and ministries of finance and planning had to be reorganized and restaffed to exercise their new functions of public financial management (see chapter 6). All this requires nothing less than a replacement of most of the high officials, staff retrenchment and redeployment on a large scale, and a gigantic retraining program—including a psychological shift from a wait-for-orders passive attitude to the active mind-set required of civil servants in a market-oriented economy.

An Ideal Central Government Structure?

General Considerations

Based on the experience across countries, is it possible to suggest an appropriate number of central government ministries? On the methodological side, in order for the experience of other countries

BOX 4.3

Central Government in Italy: From Obese to Lean to Overweight

The Italian state has 20 regions, divided into about 100 provinces, each headed by a "prefect" appointed by and responsible to the central government. Five regions—Sardinia, Sicily, Trentino-Alto Adige, Valle d' Aosta, and Friuli-Venezia Giulia—have special autonomy. The establishment of regional governments has brought some decentralization to the national governmental machinery.

Several legislative decisions were made in the 1970s and 1980s in the direction of government reorganization, but none were implemented. Delay and procrastination also affected the implementation of other important administrative reform measures, including some prescribed in the Constitution itself. It took the peaceful upheaval of the Italian political system, triggered in the early 1990s by a remarkable group of activist prosecutors investigating the scandals of *"tangentopoli"* ("Bribe City"), to eventually make all those paper plans a political and administrative reality.

The number of central ministries in Italy, which had peaked in the 1980s at 22, was gradually reduced to 18. Combined with the many autonomous government agencies, it was still one of the heaviest central government structures in Europe. In 1999, Italy formulated a far-reaching reorganization of the apparatus of central government—more than thirty years after the 1968 law that had first prescribed it. Indeed, this was the first general ministerial reorganization since 1853—*before* the unification of Italy in 1860. As a result of the 1999 reorganization, the Italian central government was reduced to only 11 ministries and 10 autonomous agencies. At the same time, the prime minister's office was streamlined to strengthen its policy coordination and guidance function, and the powerful provincial prefectures were to be transformed into more modest de-concentrated government offices. The reorganization brought the number of ministries in Italy below the 14 central ministries of France and the United Kingdom—the two countries most comparable to Italy in terms of level of development and of economic, geographic, and demographic size, and the structure of central government in Italy compared favorably in simplicity and organizational logic to that of other European countries. Since then, however, due to a combination of the usual reasons—patronage and political coalition-building—the number of central ministries has crept up again to 13 in 2006, in addition to a new department for policy implementation, a department for public administration, and the autonomous agencies.

Beyond the reorganization, the more difficult challenge is the institutional one of transforming the actual behavior of government entities—and of their employees—toward a genuine public service orientation. As all other massive behavioral change, this challenge will require concrete improvements in the framework of incentives (penalties as well as rewards) and the systematic provision of more "voice" to the users of public services. So far, despite substantial progress, Italy still deserves some of its erstwhile reputation for administrative unresponsiveness and inefficiency. This was compounded under the Berlusconi government in power through early 2006 by a return of political corruption partway to the levels of the 1980s, although in different forms and, of course, with different "beneficiaries."

to be useful, the comparison must be between countries of similar size and political structure. For example, a federal state will by definition have a smaller *central* government than a unitary state—other things being equal—but this says nothing in itself about overall government effectiveness. Also, it is important to verify that a streamlined ministerial structure does not hide segmentation and weak coordination *within* ministries—with similar adverse implications for government efficiency. Conceptually, too, each country has to flow with its administrative traditions and political realities.

Still, the extremes are easy to spot. Countries like India, with eighty-five central ministries (despite its federal structure), suffer major problems of internal coordination, waste, and bureaucratic vested interests. Overly complex and mushrooming ministerial structures are neither good economics nor good politics. It is true that the existence of many central government organizations is in part due to the need for managing coalitions in a plural society and thus for political and social sustainability. However, political goals can be pursued in ways other than creating yet another inefficient government organization. In practice, the burden of proof should rest on whether creating a separate ministry is really necessary, especially if the objective is inherently transitory, as in the case of fleeting political party alliances. It is a lot easier to create a new organization than to disband an existing one. Thus, a good practical answer to the problem of political balancing is to appoint ministers without thereby creating a ministry.

The Apostles' Principle

Clearly, there is no pat answer to the question of "ideal" government architecture. However, a list of core government functions can be made, and country experience and historical trends do yield a general guideline that we call the Apostles' Principle: *"Twelve is enough."* The twelve ministries sufficient to carry out the typical government functions and meeting a reasonable balance among the four criteria for allocating government functions would be:

- finance and planning (including economic forecasting and trade and aid policies);
- foreign affairs (including external trade framework agreements but not trade policies);
- information and communications (including information technology);
- interior (including local government oversight, in unitary-government countries);
- law and justice (including prisons);
- human resources (covering education, culture, sports, science, and technology other than informatics);
- health and population (including family planning and youth issues);
- human settlements and environment (covering urban and rural development, housing and related service infrastructure, agriculture, water resources, and environment);
- energy, industry, and mining;
- labor and social welfare (covering employment regulation, socially and economically disadvantaged groups, women, and social welfare);
- infrastructure (including roads, rail, ports, and all other physical infrastructure); and
- defense (if and where needed—as previously mentioned, the few countries in the world without armed forces, such as Costa Rica, enjoy typically greater national security than their neighbors).

In any event, as emphasized repeatedly, the principal challenge is not to define this or that ideal number of central government organizations, but to identify the core tasks of government in the specific country, establish reasonably coherent structures to perform these tasks and, most importantly, put in place the rules and the monetary and nonmonetary incentives that will induce good performance by public managers and employees—all subjects discussed in Part II.

COORDINATION AND MANAGEMENT ISSUES IN CENTRAL GOVERNMENT[6]

Common Problems

Assuming the organizational structure of government is sound, a central question is how to weave a coherent overall policy out of the separate actions of the component entities of government—each with its "turf," institutional concerns, and personal agendas of its leaders. Except in the smallest countries, policy coordination is a major and constant challenge. This challenge can be met, in some part, by a well-functioning apparatus for support to policy making, as discussed earlier. But weak policy coordination is usually due to one or more of the following broader and interrelated factors:

- lack of trust between senior policy makers;
- unclear definition of organizational roles;
- conflicting agenda of line ministries and lack of communication among them;
- the presence of parallel groups (often shady and unaccountable) influencing policy from outside the formal government; and
- the absence of an enabling environment for open debate on policy options.

Coordination problems affect to some extent every government, as manifested mainly in internal policy conflicts, inconsistencies, abrupt reversals in policy, and evident waste of resources in duplicating or overlapping expenditure programs. However, such problems have proven especially serious in developing countries, owing to the more fluid political landscape. Paradoxically, "coordination" is easier in authoritarian regimes and is guaranteed in totalitarian regimes. Of course, coordination and coherence in a policy designed for optimal repression of the citizenry and to serve only the interests of the rulers is not a great blessing.

When regimes change, attention must be paid to the resulting power vacuum—an obvious lesson, but often disregarded. In the transition countries of Eastern Europe and the former USSR, the abolition of the Communist party at the beginning of the 1990s removed the central apparatus for decision making and coordination of the various ministries. For a decade, the resulting institutional vacuum produced overlapping responsibilities, multiple accountability, incoherent policy, and a vast "underground government." In the Ukraine of 1992, for example, the number of central government bodies was over 110, responsibilities overlapped, and lines of accountability were utterly confused (World Bank, 1997b). Much has changed since then, especially in Eastern European countries that became members of the European Union and as a result of EU requirements for accession: countries such as Poland, Czech Republic, Hungary, Romania, and Bulgaria have streamlined government and built functioning coordination mechanisms.

Some Recurrent Themes

First, assuring coordination only at the top levels of government is not sufficient: much policy making, most coordination, and all implementation occur below the top level and within ministries, departments, or individual offices. Unless the concerned government officials with different technical expertise and diverse legitimate views work well together, the best coordination at presidential or cabinet level is an edifice built on sand. Indeed, the important objective is not how to foster "coordination," which implies the reconciliation of diverse actions and must usually be imposed, but *cooperation,* which entails a continuous association for a common purpose and must usually be induced. As former U.S. Agency for International Development deputy head Joe Wheeler used to say: "Organizations do not make policy; people do"[7]

Second, appropriate cooperation mechanisms should be encouraged. The longest and best-structured meetings are often not as productive of joint action as a quick face-to-face exchange by the proverbial water cooler. Indeed, now that office water coolers are a quaint anachronism and office "public spaces" have been paved over with internal e-mail, the adverse impact on genuine cooperation from loss of direct personal interaction has partly outweighed the positive impact of the spectacular increase in intragovernmental communications. We do not at all imply a preference for old technology. The preference is for *appropriate* technology. Many issues can be better resolved by a 5-minute chat rather than a 30-minute exchange of e-mails, replies, rebuttals, and rejoinders. The face-to-face encounter also has a better potential of building reciprocal trust and social capital—see chapter 12.

Third, the challenge of government coordination raises important issues for staffing and recruitment. The advantages of staff continuity—institutional memory, expertise, dedication—must be combined with the need for contestability. As mentioned earlier, few things are as damaging to good policy making as "group-think." Everyone falls into line sooner or later. Thus, unless the circle of government decision makers is constantly replenished with new individuals who can ask the irritating but essential questions "Why?" "How do we know?" and "What happens then?" it is unlikely that inconsistencies among different policies will be identified and remedied. A major implication of this is that good coordination and cooperation cannot be entirely accomplished by sticking exclusively to the inner circle of government interlocutors. Particularly when implementation problems are at issue, it is essential to systematically get reality checks from the employees "in the trenches," from the users of the service, and from the private sector.

The Role of Elite Agencies

Although policy coordination from the top is insufficient, it is nonetheless necessary. In most countries, "core" ministries have acted as "elite agencies" to assure inter-ministerial coordination in both formulation and implementation of government policy. Normally, these are the ministry in charge of taxation and public expenditure—the ministry of finance—and the ministry in charge of economic planning. The role of the finance ministry in top-level policy coordination has been profound because of its decisive say on taxation, expenditure, public services, and especially on arbitrating expenditure cuts in times of austerity.

Aside from France, where the ministry of finance and economy has the central economic policy and coordinating role, the best-known examples of elite agencies are found in Asia. In Japan, for more than fifty years the Ministry of Finance has controlled the entire fiscal and financial apparatus, and until very recently the Ministry of International Trade and Industry (MITI) has had the dominant influence on investment patterns throughout the economy—the reason why the Japanese economy used to be referred to as "Japan, Inc." In Korea, the Economic Planning Board is a "super-ministry" with control over both public finance and economic planning. In Thailand, the so-called "Gang of Four"—composed of the Ministry of Finance, the Budget Bureau in the Prime Minister's office, the Central Bank, and the National Economic and Social Development

Board—used to regularly consult each other in budget preparation, control of inflation, and other economic policies. In Indonesia, the Ministry of Finance now cooperates closely with the planning agency Bappenas in defining the country's short- and long-term policy priorities underpinning the budget, and assuring coordination with the line ministries. And in Malaysia, a similar role is played by the Prime Minister's Department.

THE SITUATION IN THE UNITED STATES

The organizational structure of the federal government reflects the genesis of American independence and the particularities of the U.S. Constitution—especially the "power of the purse" given to Congress and the articulation of responsibilities between the central government and the states—the guiding principle being that all government powers belongs to the states except those explicitly assigned to the federal government. The basic foundations of the U.S. federal system are certainly well-known to the American reader, but are very quickly recapitulated here for the sake of comprehensiveness, before moving to describing the structure of the executive branch.

The Separation of Powers Doctrine and the Three Branches of Government

The separation of powers doctrine is traced to Charles-Louis de Secondat, Baron of Montesquieu (1689–1755), in his *L'Esprit des Lois* (The Spirit of the Laws, 1748).[8] Based on the conceptual premise and historical evidence that *all* concentration of government power is dangerous, the doctrine seeks to safeguard liberty through separating the power of government into three separate and co-equal branches: the legislative, to make the laws; the executive, to implement the laws; and the judiciary, to judge disputes under the laws and to interpret the Constitution. Concomitant with the doctrine of separation of powers is the essential principle of "checks and balances," with each of the three branches serving as a check on the power of the other two. The first three articles of the U.S. Constitution closely follow the separation of powers doctrine in establishing the legislative, executive, and judicial branches of the government of the United States. Progressively through the last two centuries, the separation of powers has been somewhat blurred in the United States by the attribution of certain legislative, regulatory, and quasi-judicial functions to executive branch agencies. However, the doctrine and the principle of checks and balances remains the backbone of the political system in the United States, as well as in most other countries with representative governance and government legitimacy.

The Legislative Branch

Congress makes all the federal laws (consistent with the Constitution), and is composed of the Senate and the House of Representatives. The Senate has two members from each state (currently 100) who serve for six-year terms, and the members of the House of Representatives (currently 435) represent "districts" defined in proportion to population and serve two-year terms. Therefore, every two years, the entire House and one third of the Senate is elected. The idea was to provide continuity through the Senate and responsiveness to the electorate through the House of Representatives. Unfortunately, a number of recent developments have reduced the intended rotation of members of the House to a minimum, with almost all incumbents routinely reelected. These developments cannot be summarized here, but particularly worrisome is the fact that most House electoral districts are increasingly "gerrymandered" (deliberately designed to favor the party in power in the state legislature). Gerrymandering has been practiced for a long time, but has reached a new high in recent years through the use of sophisticated voter-identification techniques and computerization. As a result, in most cases, instead of the voters selecting their representatives, the representatives in effect select the voters—hardly what the Constitution intended or what basic democracy requires. Of all reforms of the political infrastructure in the United States that do not require a constitutional amendment, the single most important one is to take away from the state legislatures the power to define federal electoral district boundaries, and assign the task to the judiciary or to an impartial body—as is already done in a few states.

The Judicial Branch

The federal judiciary oversees the court system of the United States, interprets the Constitution, and pronounces on the constitutionality of laws passed by Congress. The highest court is the U.S. Supreme Court, composed of nine judges—"justices," one of whom is designated as Chief Justice. All justices are nominated by the president and confirmed by the Senate through its power to "advise and consent" (power which also applies to most major executive appointments). The justices serve for life and decisions of the Supreme Court are final and binding upon the executive.

The Executive Branch

The general duty of the executive is to "take care that the laws are faithfully executed." The head of the executive branch (and the head of state of the United States of America) is the president, who among other things has the power to approve laws passed by the legislature. However, his disapproval of a law ("veto") can be overturned, and the law becomes effective without his signature if it is confirmed by at least a two-thirds vote of the legislature. The executive branch also includes the vice president, the members of the cabinet, and all officials and employees of the federal government except those serving the Congress and the judiciary. The cabinet is made up of the heads of the fifteen major departments of the government and is supposed to provide collegial advice to the president on policy issues. The role of cabinet as a collective deliberative body has substantially diminished over the past century, and policy has increasingly originated in the Office of the President—see below.

The Executive Branch

Because public administration is, by definition, mainly the business of the executive branch, the main elements of its current structure are described below. Following the order of the earlier discussion in this chapter, we review first the support mechanisms for policy making, then the main government departments. The full chart of organization of the U.S. government is reproduced in Figure 4.1.

The Office of the President

Among the types of support units for policy making in presidential systems around the world, the Office of the President in the United States is the largest and most powerful. It wasn't always so. Indeed, during most of American history, the president had only a couple of personal assistants and a secretary. Practically all federal employees were located in the various departments. It was not until the twentieth century, especially under the presidencies of Franklin D. Roosevelt, John

Figure 4.1 The Government of the United States

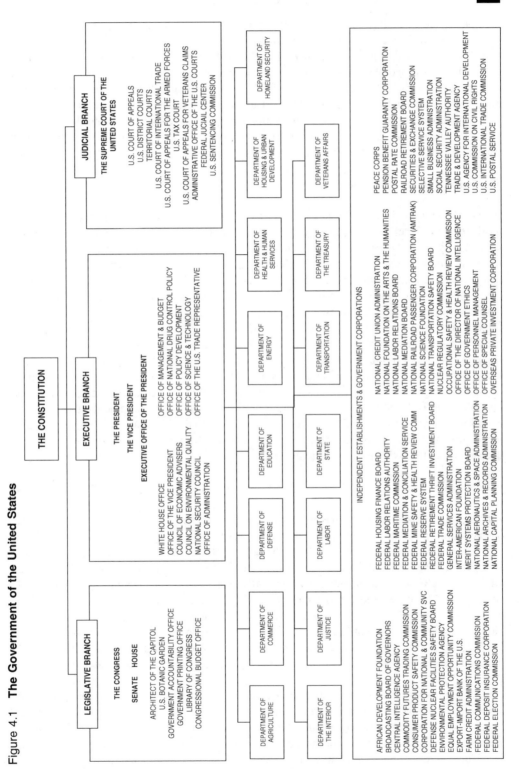

F. Kennedy, and Ronald Reagan, that the White House staff progressively expanded to its present size of over 4,000—and so did its power. In particular, the Office of Management and Budget (OMB) evaluates budget proposals from the individual line departments and consolidates them into a unified budget proposal presented to Congress, and the Office of Personnel Management (OPM) screens candidacies for appointments to federal office, including all senior appointments down three or four levels in the bureaucracy. Thus, in addition to its influence in many other areas (e.g., on foreign policy through the office of the National Security Advisor), the White House staff has top management authority for both the money and the personnel of the entire federal government. Box 4.4 shows the structure of the Office of the President as of mid-2006.

The Cabinet-level Departments

In parallel with the growth in size and importance of the White House staff, the effective authority of the cabinet as a collective body representing the executive as a whole has diminished significantly since the 1930s, as noted. Individual line departments, of course, are responsible for most policy making, and for all implementation in their areas of competence. Individual department secretaries can have great influence, depending largely on their stature and public credibility, as well as personal rapport with the president. As listed in Table 4.2 (see p. 90), there are fifteen regular "cabinet-level" departments of the federal government. Of these, the original three were the Department of State, to handle foreign relations; the Treasury Department, to address economic and financial issues; and the War Department (renamed Defense Department in 1947), all created in 1789 within a few weeks of each other. The most recent is the Department of Homeland Security, established in 2002. (The many regulatory agencies of the federal government were discussed in chapter 3.) Within each department, the principal operating unit is the bureau. These operating units are so important in practice that the entire executive branch in the United States may be literally called a "bureaucracy." In some departments, the top levels of management are almost only a purely formal superstructure and most decisions are effectively made at bureau level.

A Concluding Word

Although the cabinet, as noted, has little authority as such, the system does provide substantial countervailing power to the White House. Formally, such countervailing power resides in the organizational infrastructure of Congress—which mainly includes, in addition to the staff of congressional committees and of individual members of the House and Senate, the Congressional Budget Office and the General Accountability Office. Also, meaningful contestability is inherent in the congressional legal power to subpoena members of the executive branch to testify and to schedule hearings and inquiries on particular issues. In practice, the countervailing power of Congress is very weak when the House of Representatives and/or the Senate are controlled by the same party to which the president belongs and of which he is the titular head—whichever party happens to be in power. Moreover, "executive privilege," i.e., the protection of confidential advice given to the President by his staff, can be invoked to refuse to appear in response to a congressional subpoena or provide documents requested by Congress. In this case, the independent federal judiciary remains as the only constitutional restraint over the executive. Without such restraints, the U.S. presidential system could too easily turn into an authoritarian "*caudillo*" regime such as the ones punctuating the history of Latin American countries, most of which, at independence, essentially copied the U.S. Constitution as their own. This demonstrates once again that the same formal structures and

BOX 4.4

Structure of the Executive Office of the President

The Executive Office of the President, under the direct authority of the President, includes the following councils and offices, listed here in alphabetical order:

- Council of Economic Advisers
- Council on Environmental Quality
- Domestic Policy Council
- Homeland Security Council
- National Economic Council
- National Security Council
- Office of Administration
- Office of Faith-Based and Community Initiatives
- Office of Management and Budget
- Office of National AIDS Policy
- Office of National Drug Control Policy
- Office of Science & Technology
- Office of the United States Trade Representative
- President's Critical Infrastructure Protection Board
- President's Foreign Intelligence Advisory Board
- USA Freedom Corps
- White House Military Office

Although there is no formal hierarchy of offices, as each is responsible directly to the president, in practice the most important are the Office of Management and Budget, with the lead on all budgetary and organizational matters; the National Security Council, with responsibility for all foreign policy; and the Office of U.S. Trade Representative, on issues relating to foreign trade and trade negotiations. The most recent entity is the Homeland Security Council. The Council of Economic Advisers, set up by President Kennedy and very influential in the formulation of economic policy through the 1970s, has lost its primacy since then. The influence of the other offices waxes and wanes largely according to the importance attached to the subject by the different presidents, and also partly as a function of the personality of their leaders.

legal organizations can produce very different outcomes when the institutional foundations and shared rules of the game are lacking.

Aside from formal countervailing power, regardless of which party controls the formal governmental institutions, America's active media and vital civil society serve to provide a regular check on the abuse of federal government power—if not on each specific instance and in the short run, certainly over time. (And then, of course, there are the periodic elections.)

Table 4.2

Cabinet-level Departments and Dates of Establishment

Department	Date Established
Agriculture	1889
Commerce	1903/1913
Defense*	1947
Education**	1979
Energy	1977
Health and Human Services**	1980
Homeland Security	2002
Housing and Urban Development	1965
Interior	1849
Justice	1870
Labor	1913
State	1789
Transportation	1966/1967
Treasury	1789
Veterans Affairs	1930

Note: Responsibility for the important area of foreign trade was fragmented among different agencies until the 1970s. In 1916, Congress set up the U.S. Tariff Commission as an independent, quasi-judicial agency to investigate dumping cases, conduct studies, and recommend on foreign trade policy. The agency was renamed International Trade Commission in 1974, redesignated in 1979 as the Office of the U.S. Trade Representative by President Carter. Under President George W. Bush, cabinet rank has been accorded to the U.S. Trade Representative, as well as the Administrator of the Environmental Protection Agency, the Director of the Office of Management and Budget, the Director of National Drug Control Policy, and the Director of National Intelligence.

*Prior to 1947, the department was named War Department, one of the three original ones founded in 1789.

**The Department of Health, Education and Welfare was created under President Eisenhower in 1953, and was reshaped and renamed Health and Human Services following the creation in 1979 of the separate Department of Education. (To understand the late date of the establishment of the Department of Education, recall that in the American federal system responsibility for most public education rests with the states and local government, particularly the counties.)

GENERAL DIRECTIONS OF IMPROVEMENT

As noted at the outset, the policy support function and the organizational architecture of government are influenced by politics and depend on country characteristics. Few recommendations can be advanced in such an area. However, certain general considerations are pertinent.

First, of the key principles of good policy formulation, probably the least observed in most countries is the principle of discipline. Promulgating policies that are dead on arrival because they are unrealistic devalues the policy-making process and reduces the impact of the leadership. It is essential, therefore, to introduce concrete provisions for greater discipline in policy formulation—primarily a requirement that no proposal can be presented for leadership approval unless it is both fully costed and consistent with other legislation and rules.

For this, if the government does not possess a strong technical mechanism to support and facilitate good policy making, its creation is absolute priority. As we keep emphasizing, it is possible that bad implementation can turn a sound policy decision into a bad outcome, but the best implementation cannot turn a bad policy into a good one, nor resolve incoherence between different policies. Almost all developed countries have a technical mechanism to support good policy making, but many developing countries—including some comparatively well-governed countries—do not. Such technical mechanism assists the political leadership to take major policy decisions by:

- providing timely notice of the policy items likely to come before the political leadership;
- ensuring prior consultation of all agencies and ministries with a major stake in a given issue;
- providing supporting analysis and consideration of options;
- recording and disseminating decisions; and
- monitoring implementation of the decisions and follow up.

On the assignment of governmental responsibilities, by and large developing countries are internally more heterogeneous than developed countries and their independence is more recent. Therefore, while the function principle rightly dominates the organization of central government in developed countries, much of the developing world could usefully consider the value of ministries serving a particularly important geographic area or clientele.

Also, there is a potential trade-off between coordination and accountability: a larger number of ministries makes coordination more difficult but facilitates the placement of responsibility. In developing countries, weak accountability is more of a problem than loose coordination of government decisions. To that extent, special care should be taken to assure clear assignment of responsibility and rules for accountability, whatever the number of ministries may be. Nevertheless, although the specific number of ministries depends largely on country size, goals, and circumstances, most developing countries of average size can get by with many fewer than twenty ministries, and the very small countries with fewer than ten.

Next, although it may be necessary to appoint new ministers to satisfy certain important constituencies or to signal the importance of a specific policy objective, this should be limited to the minimum demonstrably necessary, and the natural tendency to then create a ministry around the new minister must be resisted. Mindful of the reality that it is much easier to create a new organization than to disband an obsolete one, adequate procedures must be put in place to build a technical and legislative obstacle course that can be navigated successfully only when the case for creating a new ministry is overwhelming.

Finally, it is healthy to always beware of the illusion of change through "reorganization." Reshuffling organizational boxes, splitting up ministries, swapping top managers' duties, and merging different departments accomplishes nothing in itself but the creation of new titles and plaques for office doors. In the words of former House Speaker Newt Gingrich, "Real change needs real change."[9]

QUESTIONS FOR DISCUSSION

1. Pick one of the two following statements and make a credible argument for it:
   a. "There must be a very sharp division of responsibilities between policy, which is to be decided by the duly elected politicians, and administration, which is to be carried out by hired civil servants."
   b. "Because policy and administration are two sides of the same coin, they must be decided and carried out as a joint responsibility of the politician and the civil servant."
2. Which of the four criteria of good policy formulation (discipline, stability, transparency, selectivity) do you believe is especially important?
3. "If a government department is too big, it cannot be controlled; if it is too small, it cannot be effective." Which is worse? Discuss.

4. Who cares if a government has ten ministries or fifty, so long as a strong central authority exists to assure that they coordinate their work?

5. In the United States, how can one reconcile the constitutional doctrine of checks and balances with the doctrine of separation of powers?

6. In recent years, the practice has arisen in the United States of presidential "signing statements," whereby the president, when approving a law passed by Congress, adds his own statement of interpretation or reservation. Are such signing statements consistent with the doctrine of separation of powers? In practice, what difference does it make?

7. Pick one of the following two statements, and make a credible argument for it:

   a. "When Congress investigates excessively and constantly second-guesses the actions of the executive branch, coherent government action is impossible."

   b. "When Congress fails to exercise its oversight responsibility, government action becomes arbitrary and unaccountable."

NOTES

1. Gaius Petronius (~27–66 C.E.), author of the *Satyricon,* was the unofficial judge of Roman elegance and good taste (*arbiter elegantiarum*) in Emperor Nero's time.

2. "If the Impressionists Had Been Dentists: A Fantasy Exploring the Transposition of Temperament," in *Without Feathers.* New York: Warner Books.

3. This section relies in part on Beschel and Manning (2000).

4. Sullivan, Louis H. "The Tall Office Building Artistically Considered." *Lippincott's Magazine,* March 1896.

5. As reported by Susan B. Glasser and Michael Grunwald in the *Washington Post,* December 22, 2005.

6. This section has drawn partly on World Bank (1997a); Commonwealth Secretariat (1997); country reports; and OECD (1997).

7. Personal communication (1981).

8. Cohler, Miller, and Stone (1989).

9. On NBC's Meet the Press, December 16, 2006.

CHAPTER 5

Decentralization and the Organizational Architecture of Subnational Government

> "Unity to be real must stand strain without breaking."
> —*Gandhi*

WHAT TO EXPECT

Below the central (national) government in all countries are the subnational government entities, with varying legal and administrative powers and resources. Most countries have levels of subnational government: upper intermediate—provinces or states; lower intermediate—counties or districts; upper local—cities and municipalities; and villages or area committees at the lowest local level. In this chapter, we simplify the classification to "central," "intermediate," and "lower" levels of government; use "subnational government" to refer to all layers of government below the central level; and denote as "local government" all units that provide direct services to citizens. After describing how the powers and standing of subnational governments are largely determined by the country's history and its political structure, the chapter sets out the different approaches to subdividing a country's territory and then proceeds to discussing decentralization.

Decentralization is neither menace nor panacea, and can have both advantages and disadvantages that are mirror images of each other. For example, decentralization improves overall governance where local governments are more accountable, but is likely to damage it in a country where local governments are more corrupt and less accountable than central government. After dealing with issues of vertical coordination among the different levels of government, the chapter moves to discussing the problems of administration in local government and the management of cities—with special attention to the complex problems of megacities and large metropolitan areas. Some general observations on state and local government in the United States conclude the chapter, which is then rounded out by the customary section on general directions for improvement.

STRUCTURE OF SUBNATIONAL GOVERNMENT

The geographic articulation of the power of the state varies according to the nature of the political system. In most unitary systems of government, intermediate government entities exercise authority under the principle of *ultra vires* ("beyond the powers"): their powers are specifically delegated to them by the central government, which can override their decisions.[1] In most federal systems, as in the United States, intermediate governments operate under the principle of *general competence,* by which they are entitled to exercise all powers that are not explicitly reserved to the national government. (However, this principle is not necessarily applied also to local government below the intermediate government level, as will be explained.)

Local government units are generally the constitutional creation and responsibility of the intermediate level of government (the province or state) in both unitary and federal systems. Thus, central governments normally do not have direct control over municipal and other local governments, although—as in the United States—they can choose to administer national programs through them. Moreover, municipal and other local governments often have only the authorities expressly granted to them by the province or state.

The powers of the intermediate level of government depend mainly on whether the country is a federal or unitary state. As for local government, its powers show considerable variety around the world, depending on history, customary forms of local administration, and the nature of post-independence leadership. At one end of the autonomy spectrum are fully autonomous local governments, controlled by elected representatives and provided with sufficient resources to exercise their responsibilities. At the other end of the spectrum are local government units that are mere creatures of the central government, which appoints and dismisses their leaders and can change their functions and cancel their actions at will—devoid of authority, deprived of resources, and virtually incapable of responding to the local communities. Most local governments around the world are situated somewhere in between those two extremes. In general, as can be expected, local governments have greater autonomy in federal systems and less autonomy in unitary states. In particular, their powers are mainly explained by the history of the country.

The Weight of History

The structure and standing of local government are largely determined by a country's history. In some countries (e.g., Italy with its city-states), the local government units were sovereign for centuries, long before the country in its present form was constituted in 1860, and the local habits of government and administration were well-rooted. In general, developed countries have a long historical experience of gradual evolution of internal spatial change along with economic development.

By contrast, ex-colonial developing countries have spatial divisions that were defined largely on the basis of the economic interests of the former colonizing power. Especially in Africa, colonialism imposed artificial boundaries—set externally by the scramble for colonial territory among western powers and internally by the objectives of resource exploitation and of colonial control. Among other problems, this has generated special difficulties for establishing links among economic activities and ethnic groups in the post-independence period and has been inimical to nation building. After independence, experience diverged in different regions.

In Africa, the urban elites who had acted as intermediaries for the former colonial powers typically tended to dominate the political landscape in the post-colonial era. Even in countries where the original post-independence leaders were replaced by military coups and other means, the urban orientation persisted and economic policies carried a strong pro-industry, pro-city bias. Moreover, the centralization of political and economic power was intensified by the central-planning paradigm prevalent in the 1960s and 1970s, with the consequence that subnational government remained very weak throughout most of Africa.

Of course, there are exceptions. There were no local intermediary elites in the former Portuguese settler colonies of Angola and Mozambique, where virtually every formal job was filled by Portuguese. When they departed suddenly in 1975 following the revolution in Portugal that deposed the dictatorship of Antonio Salazar, they left behind not a local elite but a total administrative vacuum. Similarly, at independence in 1960, the former Belgian Congo had a grand total of three indigenous university graduates, as the Belgians fully expected to be able to continue controlling the territory by less direct means. Instead, the result was thirty years of kleptocracy and fifteen years of exceedingly violent chaos and civil conflict. (It is just conceivable that the elections of 2006 may signal the beginning of the end of the great Congolese tragedy, which extends all the way back to the extraordinarily brutal private colonial regime of Belgian King Leopold II in the late 1800s.)[2]

There are positive exceptions, as well. Thus, although Tanzania's President Julius Nyerere was himself educated first at Makerere University in Uganda (then a first-rate institution, viewed by the Imperial College in London as its equal in quality) and then at the University of Edinburgh, where he earned a master's degree (only the second African leader to obtain a degree outside Africa), his policies were deliberately inclusive of the countryside, with substantial autonomy given to local governments.[3] It is also plausible that such policies, as well as his insistence on Kiswahili as the national language, were a key factor of his success in turning Tanzania from a patchwork of ethnic groups into a nation—a signal African exception in this respect. Nevertheless, in general, post-independence policies in African countries had a strong anti-rural and centralizing bias.

By contrast, in many Asian countries, independence led to the emergence of political leadership from the more populated rural areas and an ensuing shift in the composition of the legislative and executive branches of government. Some political theorists in the 1960s also fueled rural fears about the adverse terms of trade for agricultural products, identified rural life with tradition and genuine nationalism, and created the myth of the "parasitic" role of cities. Consequently, while in these Asian countries the intermediate levels of subnational government acquired greater responsibility and authority, economic policies were slanted toward rural interests and the central cities suffered from neglect. This ideology—originally positive—found its extreme perverted expression in the murderous pathology of the Khmer Rouge regime in Cambodia under Pol Pot from 1975 to 1979. The regime viewed the capital of Phnom Penh as "The Great Whore by the Mekong River" and forcibly emptied it, systematically butchering well over a million people—15 percent of the population, equivalent in America to 40 million—including virtually all educated individuals.

Aside from the applicability of these generalizations, the central message of this discussion is the need to delve into the history of the specific country if one wishes to understand why subnational levels of government have greater or lesser powers.

APPROACHES TO DEFINING SUBNATIONAL TERRITORIES[4]

Physical Approach

The intuitive approach to dividing the national territory is on the basis of the natural properties and physical features of regions within the country. Although the term "region" means different things in geography than in public administration, administrative boundaries are often drawn on the basis of physical geography—especially when coping with such matters as water supply, land drainage, erosion control, irrigation, soil or wildlife conservation, forest development, recreation, and waste disposal. In the United Kingdom, for example, each of ten water authorities is responsible in its area for the entire range of functions connected with water usage—conservation, distribution, sewerage and disposal, land drainage, pollution control, and recreation—and the geographic boundaries of each authority are determined by the natural water catchment areas. Another example of an administrative structure based on geographical features is the Tennessee Valley Authority in the United States, probably the best-known instance of a multipurpose development authority based on a watershed area.

Physical geography can also offer an appropriate basis for economic and social planning, especially if the lives of the inhabitants are tied closely to the exploitation of natural resources—for example, in the case of tribal people living in a specific forest area.[5] When the natural characteristics are dominant, as in the case of a valley or a defined coastal area or a mountain range, geography can provide a good basis for administrative divisions. However, space is a continuum and any division of it is inherently arbitrary. Therefore, physical criteria must be complemented by other criteria.

Functional/Efficiency Approach

This approach matches administrative area to function by identifying the government functions and the associated institutions, and on that basis delimiting the geographic boundaries within which the government functions are to be performed. In this approach, the hierarchy of geographic areas corresponds to the scale of operations necessary for the optimum performance of the general government. Here, too, there are difficulties. Aside from the problem that the different functions may produce overlapping boundaries, it is impossible to objectively restrict the "natural" geographic area of certain broad functions, such as health, housing, or the environment. The functional assignment remains a main point of reference, but it too needs to be complemented by other considerations.

A variant of the functional approach is the "efficiency approach" aimed at achieving the highest efficiency (lowest unit cost given the quality) in government service provision. This approach tends to produce large jurisdictions with large populations, permitting local governments to (1) widen their range of activity to serve more people; (2) benefit from a larger tax base; and (3) optimize their workloads. The efficiency approach is most appropriate for local public services such as urban planning, housing, water, sewerage, and transportation. However, unlike these services, whose output is quantifiable, meaningful objective criteria for measuring the "output" of services of teachers, social workers, and policemen are harder to define (see chapter 10), and setting appropriate geographic boundaries is correspondingly difficult.

Moreover, although many western European countries (notably Denmark, Germany, Britain, and Sweden) have reduced the number of their municipalities through mergers, there is no conclusive evidence that operating in larger jurisdictions is always and necessarily more efficient than operating in smaller ones. Scale economies constantly change with changes in technology and the mix of government functions. Also, exploiting scale economies does not necessarily require an administrative entity of "optimum" size. Scale economies can also be achieved by joint service agreements and by "uploading" the execution of a variety of local services to provincial (state) governments.

Management Approach

This approach corresponds roughly to the "span of control" criterion for central government organization (discussed in chapter 4). The aim is to divide state territory into "manageable" parts by drawing area boundaries according to how the flow of government work can best be handled. The number and location of field offices are decided based on an optimum span of control by headquarters or are based on the workload appropriate for a field office. This approach is more appropriate for deconcentration and delegation, rather than for political decentralization or for the constitution of local government units. Nevertheless, in the assignment of responsibilities to subnational government entities, management constraints are as much a reality as are geographic and technical considerations.

Community Approach

The community approach prescribes that internal government boundaries should correspond to the areas whose inhabitants manifest common needs and interdependence. This approach involves identifying urban centers and their "natural" hinterlands, with the interdependence between city and hinterland indicated mainly by the number of regional inhabitants employed in the city's banks, shops, schools, hospitals, newspapers, and so on. Sometimes also known as the "central town" concept, the approach has been applied notably in Belgium, Germany, Sweden, and France, where strong links were built between the various urban centers and the corresponding hinterlands.

The community approach is useful for the design of effective land-use plans, traffic management, highway development, and public transport. If done well, the identification of subnational government boundaries on this basis would not only "internalize" the costs and benefits of local government, but also produce a more equitable distribution of government services in the (interdependent) community. The community approach can therefore be very useful when it grows organically from the bottom up, and is limited to recognizing current realities and supporting them. When instead it is misapplied as systematic top-down government attempts at creating regional "growth poles" from scratch (as in the development approach of the French economist François Perroux, popular in the 1950s),[6] it is likely to lead only to substantial waste. The message is simple: do take into account the existing interdependence between city and surrounding area, but do not try to manufacture it by government policy.

Social/Ethnic Approach

The territorial structure of government may include socially distinct regions based on history, ethnicity, culture, religion, language, or some combination of these. The social/ethnic approach is especially useful when, during the process of unification of a country, some of the constituent areas continue to experience a sense of separate identity that cannot be overlooked in the new constitutional and administrative system. Conversely, when faced with centrifugal tendencies, redrawing subnational boundaries to reflect ethnic identities may become necessary for the survival of the unified state. Changing the boundaries of the provinces (states) of a federal country is more difficult than changing regional boundaries within unitary states because the provinces in federal countries are usually protected by constitutional guarantees. However, when provincial boundaries in a federation are the artificial creation of an external power (normally through colonial experience or war), restructuring a federation may be easier. Iraq offers the most dramatic contemporary manifestation of this problem. For centuries constituted of different provinces within the vast Ottoman Empire, "Iraq" was an artificial creation of British colonialism in 1920 and was kept together after independence mainly by repression from successive central governments in Baghdad. After the American invasion in 2003 and the fall of the thuggish Saddam Hussein regime, the country faced the extremely delicate challenge of accommodating within a single state the previously repressed aspirations of the three very different Kurdish, Sunni, and Shi'a communities (all three in turn segmented among different sects, tribes, or clans). As of the end of 2007, the eventual outcome of this challenge was in doubt, but none of the likely scenarios were pleasant to contemplate.

DECENTRALIZATION: THE GEOGRAPHIC
ARTICULATION OF STATE POWER

In the 1980s and 1990s, there was a strong decentralization trend in Europe and Latin America, and a variety of initiatives in that direction have been taken in many other countries as well. Decentralization of central power and authority to subnational entities can be important for political stability, effective service delivery, and equity. However, when ill-designed or inappropriate to country circumstances, decentralization can also carry serious risks. In developed countries, decentralization has been an organic outcome of long social evolution over decades, but in recently-independent developing countries hasty decentralization carries risks.

The dictionary definition of decentralization is "the removal of certain centralized powers or control to various areas, usually the area where operations take place" (Webster, 2002). However, the term is associated with a wide range of meanings. Moreover, the term has been abused to apply to very different phenomena; for example, the dispersal of functions to organizations outside the government apparatus, various forms of alternative service delivery, and even privatization. Here we use the generic term decentralization to refer to the varying degrees of dispersing functions and authority along the formal structure of government (i.e., the geographic articulation of state power and activity).

Dimensions of decentralization include the geographic, functional, administrative, political, and fiscal. Degrees of decentralization include deconcentration, delegation, and devolution.

Dimensions of Decentralization

Geographic Decentralization

Geographic decentralization entails dividing the territory of a state into smaller areas and distributing powers among them. Examples are the provinces and districts of Zambia; the departments and communes of France; the counties and districts of England; the states, counties, and municipalities of the United States; the regions and districts of Scotland; and the provinces, autonomous regions, counties, municipalities, people's communes, and production brigades of the People's Republic of China; and so on.

Functional Decentralization

Functional decentralization is the distribution of state authority and responsibility among different functional entities of government. It involves determining the type, amount, and mix of government services and creating the entities to deliver them. Accordingly, subnational government entities may be regional offices of the central ministries, service districts, autonomous agencies, or local units of government. The geographic and functional dimensions of decentralization are, in practice, intertwined.

Administrative Decentralization

The degree of administrative decentralization is largely a function of the political structure of the state. A federal constitution by definition entails more decentralized administrative arrangements than a unitary system. The correspondence is not perfect, however. It is possible for a unitary state to assign substantial powers to provincial governments, as in Papua New Guinea.

Conversely, some federal constitutions provide for the exercise of significant central power over subnational governments. In Canada, for example, the federal government may disallow provincial laws, and appoints lieutenants-governor and important officials of the judiciary. In India, extensive powers are conferred on the federal government, including the power to replace elected state leaders in unusual situations and redraw states' boundaries. The conditions attached to federal spending also influence the extent of real local power. Thus in the United States, the growth in federal spending on grant-aided programs means that state and local governments are required to abide by certain conditions under close federal supervision, and thus lose some de facto autonomy.

Political Decentralization

Political decentralization shifts to lower levels of government the decision-making power itself. In a fully decentralized structure, the lower levels of government formulate and implement policies in their assigned spheres of responsibility independently, without any intervention from higher levels of government. (This corresponds to the concept of devolution discussed later.)

Fiscal Decentralization

Fiscal decentralization (sometimes called "fiscal federalism") involves the transfer of expenditure and revenue responsibilities from the central government to subnational governments. Fiscal decentralization can take a number of forms, including: (1) tax sharing; (2) joint or coordinated provision of certain public services; (3) expansion of local tax and nontax revenue authority; (4) intergovernmental transfers; and (5) local borrowing. (Fiscal decentralization is discussed in detail in chapter 6, owing to its close linkage to the principles and practice of public finance in general.)

Degrees of Decentralization[7]

The degree of decentralization can be measured by the extent of autonomy of the subnational entities from the central government, which progressively increases from "deconcentration" through "delegation" to full "devolution."

Deconcentration

Deconcentration shifts the management workload from central government officials in the capital to subordinate field staff in the regions, provinces, or districts. Deconcentration is basically an efficiency measure internal to central government and therefore does not involve a downward transfer of decision-making authority and autonomy from the national level. However, since it does reduce the workload at the center and brings government activity closer to the people, deconcentration can be considered a first stage of decentralization. Furthermore, it permits greater administrative flexibility in the implementation of central directives by giving field staff some latitude, within prescribed guidelines, to make adjustments to suit local conditions. And, at least in principle, provides greater "voice" to the local community (see chapter 11).

In a deconcentrated system, the local government leadership inevitably faces stiff competition from the field offices of the central government agencies, which are typically better equipped with technology and manpower. Turf problems are also frequent. In Algeria, for example, the local managers of central ministries, torn between their technical accountability to the home ministry and their service responsibility to the *wali* (provincial governor) are often unable to do full justice to either. Thus, for deconcentration to be effective, central authorities need to draw clear lines of responsibility and control.

Delegation

More extensive than deconcentration is delegation. The subnational government organizations to which authority is delegated (1) are technically and administratively capable of performing specialized functions; (2) may be exempt from central rules on personnel; (3) may be able to charge users directly for services; and (4) have broad authority to plan and implement decisions without the direct supervision of central ministries (although they are ultimately accountable to the government). Examples are housing and transportation authorities, school districts, public corporations, special service districts, special project implementation units, and regional development corporations.

A major advantage of delegation is that it helps insulate the implementation of special high-priority projects from political interference and bureaucratic conflicts. It also prevents revenues gained from income-earning ventures from being mixed with regular government budgets. (This is generally appropriate, however, only when there is a direct link between the revenue and the beneficiaries from the service provided [see chapter 6]. As implicit in the term, delegation is revocable.)

Devolution[8]

Devolution carries the highest degree of decision-making independence and involves total relinquishment of certain functions to subnational governments. It entails creating autonomous subnational governments that (1) have corporate status; (2) recruit their own staff; (3) occupy clear and legally recognized geographic boundaries; (4) raise revenues to finance their functions; and (5) can interact reciprocally with other units in the government system of which they are a part.

In most countries, despite devolution of functions to subnational governments, the central government still retains some supervisory powers and plays a significant financial role. Also, the central government sometimes tries to keep its hold on local governments through formal and informal controls or regulatory instruments, often linked to project or program funding. This is intended to ensure that subnational governments act consistently with national policies and plans and follow prudent financial practices. Sometimes, this is true; sometimes, it reflects merely a reluctance to let go of central power and control.

Rationale, Advantages, Costs, and Risks of Decentralization

Let's start with two obvious points, because they are so often neglected in practice. First, *decentralization is a process, not an event,* and as in any other process the manner in which decisions are made is critical to their likelihood of success. Second, *decentralization is not a panacea,* and can neither remedy deep-seated governance problems nor quickly improve economic efficiency. Decentralization offers large potential benefits and equally large potential costs and there can be no a priori blanket judgment for or against it. The right question is not whether to decentralize, but what to decentralize, to whom, how, when, and with what resources.

The Political Impulse

Much of the decentralization that occurred especially during the 1980s and 1990s was associated with broader political developments. In Latin America, fiscal and administrative decentralization grew out of democratization movements by which elected governments operating under new constitutions replaced autocratic central regimes in most countries of the continent. Subsequently, strong local democracy fed back into contributing to more accountable national government. In most of Africa, regionalism, ethnicity, and the spread of multiparty systems gave rise to greater local control and participation in administrative decision making. (Regrettably, lack of resources has made such local control inoperative in many countries.) In continental Europe, the growing unresponsiveness of the central government apparatus fueled a widespread push toward greater regional and local control of service delivery.

In extreme cases, decentralization has been a desperate attempt of the state to keep the country united. For example, political and ethnic cleavages and the long civil wars in Mozambique or Uganda paved the way for the granting of greater autonomy to all localities, or for the forging of "asymmetrical federations." Ethnic conflicts have also exerted strong pressure for decentralization in Sri Lanka, Indonesia, the Philippines and Sudan. All these countries have managed to remain united thus far—other countries have not. (The jury will be out for many years in the case of Sudan where, in addition to the tragedy of Darfur, the much longer conflict with the South produced an agreement in 2005 for full autonomy to be followed by a referendum in South Sudan, after six years, to decide whether to secede or remain within a unified Sudan.) The breakup was peaceful in Czechoslovakia after its "Velvet Revolution" and mostly peaceful in the former Soviet Union—where Mikhail Gorbachev's last-ditch effort at a union treaty to prevent the USSR from splintering was nullified by the abortive August 1991 coup. But national "divorces" are more often bloody and messy, as shown by the tragic breakup of the former Yugoslavia. In some Asian countries that were previously governed by autocratic central regimes, decentralization came to be seen as the natural and only alternative to repressive central authority.

In any event, as William Dillinger (1993) has pointed out, decentralization has generally come from a series of ad hoc reactions, rather than as a sequenced set of well-conceived policies by the national government.[9]

The Economic Rationale: Oates' Theorem and the Subsidiarity Principle

Aside from political motivations, the literature sets out a clear economic rationale for decentralization. The efficiency of allocation of public resources can be raised if expenditure decisions are made at lower levels of government, which are supposedly more responsive to local demands than a remote central administration. This closer nexus between expenditure decisions and their beneficiaries also provides opportunities for more efficient use of public resources. From a pure efficiency standpoint, the rule governing the geographic articulation of government services is provided by Oates' "decentralization theorem": a public service should be provided by the government jurisdiction that has control over the smallest geographic area that would internalize both the benefits and the costs of providing the service.[10] Oates' theorem has a strong proof, given its assumptions, but it is intuitive as well: if one can clearly identify the residents of a particular area who receive all the benefits from a particular service, they are also the ones who should shoulder all the costs of providing it. For example, trash collection in a mountain town should be provided and paid for by the authorities of that town because only the town inhabitants benefit if the trash is collected and suffer if it is not. In reality, this test is pretty tough to set up and satisfy in practice, partly because technology and people's consumption habits are not static and partly because people do have a tendency to move around. Thus, while Oates' decentralization theorem remains a sound conceptual guidepost, a more practical criterion is needed.

Such practical criterion is found in the principle of "subsidiarity." According to this principle, spending, taxing, and regulatory functions should be exercised by lower levels of government unless a convincing case can be made for assigning these functions to higher levels of government. This turns the cumbersome analytical challenge of the Oates theorem into a simple burden-of-proof test—more political and thus better suited to decisions that are themselves inherently political. The principle of subsidiarity is embedded in the U.S. Constitution, albeit modified by clauses giving the federal government broad powers to regulate any state action which can be construed to materially affect interstate commerce. Subsidiarity was also introduced in the Catholic Church by Pope Leo XIII in 1891, in its internal process of renewal and partly in response to a plea for expanding the authority of local bishops and parish priests. In contemporary times, the principle of subsidiarity has been adopted by the European Union, incorporated as "fiscal decentralization" in the Single Europe Act of 1987, and formally adopted by the European Commission in 1993.[11]

The Potential Advantages of Decentralization

The potential gains of decentralization derive mainly from the presumably closer contact of local government institutions with local residents:

- Decentralization may create opportunities for more accountable government. Residents who participate in decision making can more easily monitor and evaluate the government's compliance with the decisions made, demand speedier government operations, and push local institutions to enhance their capabilities.
- Decentralization may be a step to greater transparency in government. Planning, policy making, and project implementation can be made accessible even to the remotest residents, given appropriate policies for information transfer.
- Decentralizing fiscal powers to local leaders can ease the financial strain on the central government since subnational governments can more readily mobilize funds by collecting fees and charges for the services they provide. (Unfortunately, as discussed later, this generates the temptation to download expenditure responsibilities to subnational governments but without giving them the authority or capacity to raise the required resources.)
- Greater closeness may open up public participation in government decision making, resulting in (1) more flexible administration, since the government can tailor its services to the needs of the various groups; (2) more effective administration, as local leaders can better locate services and facilities within communities; and (3) political stability and national unity, as civil society organizations are given a stake in maintaining the political system (for an illustration of the latter, see Box 5.1).

The Potential Costs of Decentralization[12]

Decentralization carries various costs and risks as well—which are almost the mirror image of its potential advantages:

- Decentralization can entail the loss of scale economies and generate unnecessary duplication and underemployment of staff and equipment.

BOX 5.1

Rural Development and Community Participation in Northeast Brazil

The chronic poverty in northeast Brazil was caused partly by the weak resource base in the region and the virtual absence of a financial system for the rural poor. Efforts to reduce rural poverty in the 1980s cost the central government large sums with little impact. In mid-1993, the Brazilian federal and state governments reformulated the poverty intervention programs and made the projects community-based, with funds going directly to community associations to finance small-scale subprojects they had identified themselves. Unlike previous rural development programs, the reformulated program also addressed institutional issues such as community organization and participation, transparency in decision making, and technical assistance to municipalities.

The results were a general improvement in the living conditions of the rural poor and an increase in productivity and employment in the region. In addition to better project design, what contributed to these positive outcomes were the increased participation by residents in subproject selection and execution, the transparency in project design and implementation, and the decentralization of fiscal and investment decision-making to state and local governments.

Source: Johan van Zyl et al. (1995).

- Decentralization can create coordination problems and conflict where none existed. Especially relevant for ethnically diverse countries, decentralized decision making may subvert the overall resource distribution and macroeconomic management objectives of the central government. More importantly, decentralization can jeopardize the civil and social rights of certain minorities, and, in time, contribute to national disintegration. For example, the argument of "states' rights" was used in the southern states of the United States to preclude federal interference with their "Jim Crow" discrimination policies against African Americans.

- Where resource endowments and capacities are uneven, as in large countries or across the various islands in an archipelago, decentralization may deepen regional inequalities. Also, in countries where different ethnic groups and secessionist movements control large areas, if wrongly approached, decentralization can contribute to severe internal societal conflicts. From Kosovo in the Balkans to Aceh in Sumatra, the serious implications of the issue cannot be overestimated.

- Decentralization can worsen rather than improve overall governance in the country. The generic test here is whether the legitimacy and quality of governance is higher at local level than at national level. If the answer is no, decentralizing into a comparatively worse governance climate will tend to worsen the quality of governance in the country as a whole. Plainly, it is possible that corruption is worse at local level than at national level, and local autocrats can be as bad as or worse than central government bureaucrats.

- The potential efficiency gains from decentralization can be undermined by institutional constraints: subnational governments, especially in developing countries, generally have weaker administrative capacity than central government, and this can cause services to be delivered less efficiently (see Box 5.2).

What Belongs Where? The Assignment of Government Functions

Table 5.1 (p. 106) classifies government activities in accordance with their attribution to different levels of government. The information it contains, while associated with actual experience in most countries, should be interpreted as indicative and not prescriptive. (See the Note to the Table for an explanation of the symbols.) As shown in the table, governmental functions such as defense, foreign affairs, external trade and finance, and monetary policy are performed almost exclusively at central government level; others, such as water supply, waste management, firefighting, almost exclusively at local level; and responsibility for all other normal state functions is shared in some fashion among the central, intermediate, and local levels of government.

INTERGOVERNMENTAL RELATIONS AND COORDINATION[13]

There are two sets of separate but interrelated relationships: the horizontal relationships between local government and civil society, and the vertical relationships between levels of governments. Complications are introduced when different levels of government look after different aspects of the same service (e.g., education or health care). The issue of service delivery then becomes much more than just a central-local option; it becomes a question of apportioning accountability among multiple providers. For example, if the national government is responsible for defining rules and financing a child vaccination program, with the provincial government in charge of procuring the vaccine and needles, and local government responsible for providing the nurses and physical facilities—each side has a potential alibi if the program is ineffective.

Intergovernmental relations are primarily defined through:

- formal constitutional provisions;
- statutory obligations, such as intergovernmental fiscal transfers;
- nonstatutory central-provincial agreements setting out obligations and commitments in specific policy areas of concurrent responsibility, such as the environment; and
- informal agreements among the respective political leaders.

The Legal Framework for Decentralization

However decentralized a country may be, the actions of subnational government must be subject to some form of central regulation and monitoring. Central control is, of course, its most obvious in deconcentrated structures, where local government bodies merely carry out functions on behalf of the central government. But a degree of regulation is also essential in devolved administration, not only to ensure uniform national standards of public services but also to prevent local government actions from interfering with or contradicting national policies and goals.

Normally, the country's constitution embodies the outline of decentralization (i.e., the territorial divisions, the broad responsibilities of different levels of government, the major institutions at central and subnational levels, and the process by which these can be amended). Consistent with

BOX 5.2

Local Government Capacity: The Personnel Dimension

One of the classic objections to decentralization is that local governments are incompetent. Citing statistics on illiterate mayors, crude accounting systems, and widespread nepotism, critics of decentralization argue that local governments are incapable of taking on expanded functions. Even when the facts are true, this argument is not as compelling as it may appear at first. As a practical matter, when a major public service is decentralized, existing field personnel are normally decentralized with it. Thus, when primary education was decentralized in Colombia and Mexico, corresponding central government teachers were decentralized at the same time. They became no less (or more) competent than they had been when employed by the central government.

However, technical competence has emerged as a problem when central government employees have refused to be decentralized. In Peru, for example, many central government highway engineers chose to retire rather than accept employment in local government. Local staff then proved incapable of taking up the job, which eventually led to the collapse of the initiative and recentralization. Governments can make it easier for central government employees to transfer to local level by requiring local governments to offer them the same wages and benefits they received as central government employees. But this also makes it difficult for local government to adapt wages and benefits to local conditions or to introduce management and personnel reforms, and may generate resentment among less well paid local personnel.

Even when employees are decentralized along with the functions, the overall management weakness of local government remains a concern. Extensive interference by local politicians in personnel decisions can make it difficult to attract and retain competent staff, particularly in very small jurisdictions.

It is important, however, not to allow these very real problems from stopping an otherwise well-conceived decentralization initiative. The reality that local governments suffer from staff and management weaknesses is a reason for helping them remedy those weaknesses, and not a reason to keep them in a state of administrative submission until—magically—they become ready to perform the delegated functions. The assignment of responsibilities should not get too far ahead of the capacity to perform them, but it should nonetheless come first; capacity cannot grow without responsibility.

Source: Adapted from Burki, Perry, and Dillinger (1999).

the constitution, other laws define intergovernmental fiscal relations, election and accountability procedures, the division of functions and resources among different levels of subnational government, and so on. Finally, administrative rules define the implementation details.

It is sensible not to build excessive detail into the laws. While decentralization mandates are

Table 5.1

A Representative Assignment of Governmental Responsibilities

Function	Policy and Standards	Provision & Administration	Production & Distribution
External trade	U	U, N, S	P
Financial transactions	U, N	P	P
Environment	U, N, S, L	U, N, S, L	N, S, L, P
Foreign direct investment	N, L	L	P
Defense	N	N	N
Foreign affairs	N	N	N
Money and banking	U, N	N	N, P
Interstate commerce	N	N	P
Immigration	U, N	N	N
Transfer payments	N	N	N
Criminal and civil law	N	N	N
Fiscal policy	N	N, S, L	N, S, L, P
Natural resources	N	N, S, L	N, S, L, P
Education, health, welfare	N, S, L	S, L	S, L, P
Highways	N, S, L	N, S, L	N, S, L
Parks and recreation	N, S, L	N, S, L	N, S, L, P
Police	S, L	S, L	S, L
Water and sewerage, waste management, fire protection, street lighting, etc.	L	L	L, P

Source: Adapted from Shah (1998); Annex Table 1.

Note: U: Supranational responsibility;
　　　N: National government;
　　　S: State/provincial government;
　　　L: Local/municipal government;
　　　P: Private nongovernmental entities.

usually formulated at the center, implementation is shaped and influenced by the local context and environment. Flexibility in implementation is very different, however, from piecemeal and ad hoc formulation of decentralization laws and rules. In cases when this has been allowed to occur in the past, the first order of business is to review and codify all such laws and regulations—not only to construct a coherent legal framework and to spot duplications and inconsistencies, but also to provide public administrators with a clear set of policy objectives and rules of authority and accountability. A good example of such codification is the local government code of the Philippines (see Box 5.3)—although its implementation has not always been effective. Also, the practice of granting "pork barrel" funds to national Congress members to dole out at their discretion has made local budgeting and planning much less meaningful and effective than the Code calls for.

National Control of Subnational Government

In deciding on the appropriate central monitoring and control on the activities of intermediate and local government, three risks must be avoided: over-control, which defeats the purpose of decentralization and reduces subnational governments to mere administrative arms of the central government; under-control, which fragments national unity and generates destructive competition;

BOX 5.3

The Philippine Local Government Code of 1992

The Local Government Code is landmark legislation, considered the most far-reaching to address the decades-old problem of an overcentralized system in the country. It was promulgated in 1991 in accordance with the 1987 Philippine constitution, after the fall of the Marcos dictatorship, and declared that "the state shall ensure the autonomy of local governments" by transferring substantial political and administrative authority and responsibilities to units of local government.

The Code defined the transfer of responsibilities in "mandatory" services—such as rural health and hospitals, environment and natural resources, agricultural extension and on-site research, local roads, waterworks, minor infrastructure, and social welfare services—as well as certain non-mandatory services, such as school building, tourism facilities, telecommunications, and housing.

The Code also provided for the transfer to local government of power and authority in the enforcement of certain regulations (e.g., on the environment, food inspection, building codes, local transport, zoning, cockfights) and in fiscal management. In the latter area, the Code broadened local governments taxing powers, provided them with a share of the proceeds from the exploitation of national resources in their area, raised their share of national tax revenues, and granted authority to generate revenues from local fees and charges.

Finally, the Code gave local government some powers to negotiate partnership arrangements with the private sector, to float bonds and borrow from private institutions. At the same time, it provided for expanded participation of civil society in local governance, including the allocation to civic organizations of specific seats in certain local bodies, such as the local development council, health board, and school board.

Source: Republic Act 7160 (Local Government Code of the Philippines), 1992.

and perverse regulation, whereby the rules on monitoring local governments inadvertently lead to dysfunctional behavior and "gaming the system."

In general, these risks can be avoided by eschewing detailed and rigid regulation and ex ante controls in favor of monitoring process and results. However, some normative controls are essential as well, especially on local borrowing, employment and safety standards, and, of course, protection of human rights and minorities. Transparency must be always and aggressively promoted by the national government, especially in local budgets and procurement. Strong local resistance to transparency measures is a clear symptom of local governance problems.

Vertical Intergovernmental Coordination

The challenge of effective intergovernmental relations is to achieve *balance:* balance between autonomy of subnational units and necessary central control; balance between promoting efficiency and protecting equity; and balance between ensuring responsiveness and assuring sustainability. In Australia, for instance, the Council of Australian Governments gathers together federal and state ministers, as well as the presidents of the Local Government Association, for increased cooperation among levels of government. Central governments in Scandinavian countries regularly consult local associations on financial matters and on legislation affecting local authorities. Post-apartheid South Africa offers an encouraging example of good vertical coordination (see Box 5.4).

BOX 5.4

Cooperative Intergovernmental Relations in South Africa

The principle of cooperative governance is articulated in Chapter 3 of the South African Constitution and has proven to be a cornerstone of intergovernmental relations. Where government functions are a shared responsibility of national and provincial government, as in the social services, the national government provides the policy framework while the provinces are responsible for delivery of services. This division of responsibilities, combined with the considerable economic disparities across provinces, requires a coherent coordination process to ensure that expenditure planning is aligned with policy goals and to promote equity in social services access.

To facilitate this coordination, each of the major government sectors has a policy forum comprising the competent national and provincial ministers. Joint meetings are also held between the finance forum and individual sector forums to review the policy issues in light of the budget constraints. These joint meetings enhance understanding of the cost of policy choices and encourage the development of alternative methods of delivering services.

The policy forums for finance, education, health, welfare, and transport are supported by technical committees comprised of officials from the national and provincial line departments and treasuries. These committees deal with policy implementation, developing coherent policy within sectors, setting norms and standards for service delivery, evaluating the affordability of policy choices, and evaluating other issues of a technical nature. A key focus of the technical committees for the near future is to develop service delivery indicators against which to measure government performance.

Source: Laura Walker, personal communication, May 2000.

Conversely, lack of constructive interaction can damage well-designed national policies, as in Indonesia where the central ministries formulated and implemented their own decentralization policies with very little discussion among themselves or with local governments, leading to conflict, inefficiency, and duplication (see Box 5.5).

ADMINISTERING LOCAL GOVERNMENT

In the two-tier system of North America and many European countries, below the province (or state, in the United States) the counties are the upper level of administration, and the municipalities and villages are the lower level. Both entities provide services directly to the citizens. Some Asian countries (e.g., Japan) have instead a single tier of local government under the intermediate level of province or region. Normally, the national and provincial governments have the authority to vary the territorial boundaries of urban districts and merge the units in different ways. But the units, too, may initiate a merger or separation, usually with the concurrence of the higher level of government. Depending on their size, the cities can report directly to the central government or

---

BOX 5.5

Poorly Coordinated Decentralization in Indonesia

Although the legal framework for decentralization was established in 1979, the Indonesian government remained highly centralized. In April and May 1999, after the fall of the Suharto regime, the Indonesian Parliament passed two laws to replace the earlier legal framework. The Regional Law (Law 22) revised the assignment of functions and roles of institutions at all levels of government, and the Fiscal Law (Law 25) defined the financing for devolution, deconcentration, and coadministration of government functions. These laws have improved the statutory framework, although there were initial implementation problems that hampered the transition from a centralized to a decentralized administration.

Five working groups were formed to draft implementing regulations and to plan and monitor the implementation process. However, the activities of the groups were not coordinated and harmonized because of lack of interaction among the ministries. Duplication of regulations and unnecessary competition among the concerned ministries resulted. The Ministry of Home Affairs claimed that thirty additional decrees were needed to support the Regional Law, and drafted several, while the Ministry of Finance separately drafted implementing regulations to support the Fiscal Law. Much progress has been made since then, but many local regulations still have to be enacted and it may take more time for Indonesia to work as a fully decentralized system.

Source: Claudia Buentjen, personal communication, June 2000.

to the province or to the county. Submunicipal bodies, such as neighborhood committees, school boards or community councils, constitute the final links in the chain between the government and the citizens.

Administering Rural Areas

Administrative systems for rural areas are strongly influenced by cultural factors and traditions in most countries. In former colonies in Africa and parts of Asia, village organizations were used as intermediaries in the "indirect rule" system of colonial control and after independence became the building blocks of local government. However, as noted earlier, the strong central control of the colonial power was typically retained by the post-independence governments, which placed their representatives in charge of administering and coordinating the activities of districts and villages. In Asia too (e.g., Sri Lanka), the traditional system of elected village chiefs was simply and arbitrarily junked in favor of direct appointment of chiefs by the central government. In China, a start has been made in this century with the election of local leaders in some villages, but local leaders remain in practice subservient to officials of the Chinese Communist party and their "private sector" partners, and are more often than not agents of local exploitation rather than representation.

The legal underpinnings of rural administration differ. In India, the system of rural administration is embedded in the constitution (the *panchayat raj* organizations); in Indonesia, the 1999 law on decentralization gives the elected district governments authority to draw up the development plan for the district. Similar autonomy was provided to groups of villages in South Africa after the fall of apartheid, as well as in other African countries; and in North America the "town meeting" evolved naturally as a form of direct democracy—closely related to the Aristotelian ideal (see chapter 2).

The establishment of local government poses special problems for ethnically plural countries. Under colonial rule, customary patterns of organization along tribal lines were reinforced as an instrument of colonial control and persist today alongside formal systems. Governments of countries in sub-Saharan Africa, in particular, labor under the arbitrary state boundaries set by colonial powers in their parceling out of territory. There are a few exceptions. Uganda has made serious attempts to decentralize authority through local councils that cross ethnic boundaries, and Senegal has managed ethnic diversity reasonably well, but only Tanzania has really succeeded in devolving authority to local level while building a genuine national consciousness beyond tribal lines.

In post-colonial Asia, too, although plural societies generally do not carry the African countries' handicap of arbitrary colonial boundaries, severe tensions continue between the aspirations for local autonomy and the need to preserve central control. The worst "solution" is found in Burma (Myanmar), where ethnic differences have been repressed by a brutal and corrupt military oligarchy. Hopeful signs have emerged in Indonesia with the settlement of the autonomy claims of the people of Aceh province (tragically, it took the devastating tsunami of 2005 to produce such a settlement), and in the Philippines with a halting process for greater autonomy in the Muslim parts of the island of Mindanao.[14] At the same time, however, new conflict has surfaced in Thailand with the Muslim population of the south of the country. It is likely that the accommodation of ethnic pluralism within a unified state will remain as the core political and administrative challenge in multiethnic societies for years to come.

In the Pacific island countries, by contrast, the dispersion of the islands and their ethnic homogeneity have made decentralization easier.[15] The problem is instead that the traditional role of customary leaders has been distorted by their concurrent formal role within the framework of local government as, in the process of induction into local government, the chiefs have lost some of their traditional accountability to the people. As Hughes (1998) perceptively put it, custom once codified ceases to be custom, as it loses its inherent capacity to adapt to the changed circumstances and aspirations of the community.

In any event, effective rural administration is important to the quality of life of hundreds of millions of people everywhere and genuine local self-government is therefore a must. The typical model of good self-government for rural areas is a village council at the base, with elected leaders, a subdistrict to represent a block of villages, and a larger district with indirectly elected leadership. This formal structure naturally should allow sufficient space for traditional chiefs and other customs, but even when traditional chiefs are the cultural norm, it is desirable to submit them to periodic popular confirmation.

Managing the Cities[16]

The Weight of Place and History

A country's attitude toward the city is largely determined by its history and geography. Thus, the stereotypical American mistrust of "city slickers" is to some extent derived from the vastness of the country and the accepted mythology of the self-reliant rural pioneer. In Europe, by contrast, where population density is high and the city was always a place of protection and security, anti-rural snobbery is frequent. In developing countries, policies and attitudes vary, depending largely on the pattern of decolonization. Thus, as noted earlier, the urban roots of the educated post-independence elites produced in most African countries an anti-rural bias in government policies—particularly by engineering unfavorable terms of trade for agricultural products—and a severe negative impact on exports and economic development. In post-colonial Asia, instead, political leaders tended to come from the rural areas, which led to channeling vast resources into rural development—whether viable or not. Fears that city services would be overwhelmed by rural migrants made the city authorities determined to discourage migration, even by denying basic services to newcomers, while at the same time the dominance of the political system by rural voters continued to bias government expenditure against investment in essential municipal infrastructure. Not surprisingly, the opposing outcomes in the two continents have been a pauperized countryside in Africa and ghastly urban slums in Asia.

Urbanization and Fragmentation

Although every country has experienced urbanization, its rate, magnitude, and character have differed significantly across countries. There is a frequent misperception that the largest cities are in developed countries. On the contrary, in terms of population, of the more than 300 cities in the world in 2007 with more than a million inhabitants, over 200 are in developing countries; of the twenty "megacities" with more than 10 million inhabitants, seventeen are in developing countries—of which twelve in Asia alone; and projections indicate that by 2025 there will be some twenty-five such megacities outside Europe and North America, with a combined population of 500 million people, or an average of 20 million inhabitants each.

Urban problems in North America and Europe, where the smaller cities still dominate the urban scene, pale in comparison. Thus, nine out of ten cities and towns in the United States have fewer than 10,000 residents, and three out of four of France's 36,000 communes have fewer than 1,000 inhabitants. Two contrasting tendencies are at work here. In many countries, such as the United States and in Eastern Europe, citizens have the right to split into new urban units recognized by the government. And in Eastern Europe (largely as a reaction to pre-1990 centralized structures), the freedom granted to settlements to govern themselves has produced thousands of municipalities, with an average population of 2,000 to 4,000.[17] In other countries, by contrast (e.g., Japan and the United Kingdom), smaller municipalities have been merged to achieve more viable administrative entities, producing a much larger average city size.

City size aside, the municipal incapacity to tackle major capital investments, combined with the failure to adjust municipal boundaries to accommodate urban growth, created peripheral settlements, slums, and unregulated development of areas abutting large cities. The solution would be to expand municipal boundaries in order to regulate development and provide services efficiently. The problem is that any boundary change runs up against entrenched political interests. Consequently, urban administration all over the world is characterized by geographical fragmentation, where an urban area and its periphery are divided among several jurisdictions (e.g., metro Los Angeles, or Metro Manila with a dozen contiguous "cities" forming a single unplanned conglomeration); and functional fragmentation, where responsibility for urban government is divided among several agencies (e.g., Calcutta with 107 different urban government bodies). This is especially problematic for those functions that need to be linked, such as water supply, sewerage, roads and traffic management, and environmental management.[18]

What All Cities Do

Notwithstanding the large differences between size of cities in different countries, urban government generally comprises the following public services:[19]

- garbage collection/waste management/street cleaning;
- water supply/sewerage;
- recreation services (street lighting, parks);
- home social welfare (e.g., homeless shelters, neighborhood clinics);
- local transport;
- zoning, city planning, and regulatory enforcement;
- local public works and housing;
- firefighting and other emergency services; and
- traffic regulation.

Types of Urban Governance

The status of municipalities in different countries varies. Urban government is explicitly recognized in the constitution in most Asian, African, Latin American, and continental European countries, but not in the United States and the United Kingdom. At the same time, there are varying traditions of local administration in countries with dispersed settlements and disparate cultures. The only possible generalization is that the legal and regulatory system of the country should allow the rise of different management modalities in municipalities of different sizes.

Within elected municipal governments, executive authority can reside in:

- an executive mayor elected directly, along with an elected council (as in parts of Europe, Japan, and most of North and South America);
- an elected council along with an administrator appointed by the government (as in South Asia);
- an elected council, which in turn selects the mayor (as in several western European countries); or

- a mayor-in-council system, whereby the mayor is elected from the members of the majority party in the council (as in some Asian cities), symmetrical to the parliamentary system of government.

Mayors elected directly or indirectly by an elected council are becoming increasingly common, partly as an answer to the fragmentation of authority within the municipal administration. In many cases, such a system is more effective when it is supported by a professional administrator as "city manager." This arrangement is analogous to good corporate governance, whereby policy is set by the board of directors headed by a chairman and day-to-day management is entrusted to a chief executive officer. In particular, the elected mayor can represent local interests before other public agencies and levels of government and make collaborative bargains for resource mobilization and program implementation, while the city manager handles the operational aspects of city administration.

Experience shows that the capacity of a mayor to exercise strong leadership depends on the manner of election, the length of tenure, whether the mayor functions in an individual or a collegial mode, and the extent of interference by the provincial or central government levels. In the United States, Japan, Eastern Europe, and a number of countries in Latin America and Asia, city mayors are directly elected, cannot be removed by the council (except for criminal behavior), and have full executive authority—subject only to council approval of budgets, staffing levels, senior appointments, and major policies. Depending mainly on the personal qualities of the individual, this system can produce either bad outcomes or opportunities for effective and responsive leadership. (For example, the mayor of Colombo, Sri Lanka, was able in the 1990s to open up the municipal administration to people-friendly partnerships with business and civil society, involving the citizens in planning and decision making. Similarly, the mayor of La Paz, Bolivia, in the early 1990s turned a corrupt and bankrupt city into a reasonably efficient and financially stable entity—although unfortunately there has been severe slippage since then.)

The model of the mayor elected by the city council—symmetrical with that of a parliamentary system where the prime minister is elected by the parliament and not directly by the people—is followed mainly in Asian and African countries in the British administrative tradition. This model has the advantage of avoiding conflicts between the mayor and the elected council, but makes the mayor more vulnerable to party maneuvers and her authority dependent on her placement in the hierarchy of the ruling political party. The system is also prone to delaying necessary decisions.

A variant of the model of an indirectly elected mayor is the "mayor-in-council" system adopted in a number of cities, such as Calcutta. The majority party elects a group of councilors at the same time as a person to head the council. Each councilor is responsible for a particular department, but functions as a member of a collective executive under the leadership of the mayor. This system yields greater attention to administrative detail, as well as guidance to the departmental heads, but is subject to the same risks of personal politicking as a cabinet government system. Thus, it can function effectively only when the discipline of the ruling political party is strong enough to prevent internal dissension from undermining collective work.

Where city mayors are not elected but appointed by the national government, their authority depends on the extent to which they are allowed to function independently and to carry influence with the city administration, but their responsiveness to local needs and demands is invariably more limited.

In any case, as noted, political authority must be supported by a strong administrator (city commissioner, city manager, town clerk, or whatever title). In British-tradition countries, the chief administrator is responsible to both the mayor and the city council. In Latin American countries that follow the U.S. administrative tradition, the strong mayor selects the chief administrator, subject to endorsement by the city council (analogously to the "advise and consent" function of the U.S. Senate for presidential appointments), but after appointment the chief administrator is responsible only to the mayor. In many Asian countries, the chief administrator of large cities is a career bureaucrat appointed by the provincial or central government. This practice creates divided loyalties and dilutes local political control. Indeed, the practice is inherited from the deep-rooted colonial mistrust of local native administrations and the resulting wish to install a colonial functionary to guard against wasteful expenditure and to give early warning of "restless natives." Not surprisingly, mayors in Asian countries see the practice as undermining local democracy and empowerment. On balance, local appointment of the city administrator, recruited on merit and by transparent procedures, is best.

Personnel Organization

General government employment policies and practices are discussed in chapter 7. In urban government, three broad personnel models are found, each with its own advantages and limitations:

- separate, whereby the city itself appoints and controls its own staff;
- unified, whereby the senior positions (but not lower-level employees) are filled from a central cadre of service for local government; and
- integrated, whereby the employees of central and local government form a common cadre and are exchanged freely between levels of government and localities according to central policies.[20]

Managing Metropolitan Areas and Megacities[21]

The growth of metropolitan areas and megacities (i.e., urban agglomerations with more than 10 million people) is the most striking feature of turn of the century urbanization. Megacities comprise a built-up area at the city core, a metropolitan ring and an extended metropolitan region. Examples are Sao Paulo in Brazil, the Jakarta region in Indonesia, the Bangkok metropolitan region in Thailand, Metro Manila in the Philippines, and—the largest of all—China's Chong Qing "municipality" with over 35 million people. The governance issues raised by such agglomeration are as massive as their population.

Megacities are economically larger than most countries, and their contribution to the country's GDP is substantial (e.g., 36 percent of Thailand's GDP is generated by Bangkok, 35 percent of Japan's GDP by Tokyo, almost 30 percent of Mexico's GDP by the Mexico City Federal District, 24 percent of Philippines' GDP by Manila, 22 percent of Brazil's GDP by Sao Paulo). Unfortunately, equally substantial are problems of urban poverty, disease, slums, exclusion, environmental pollution, crime, and violence. Thus, megacities are in special need of good governance to improve policy and service coordination, enforce the rules, make administration more responsive to neighborhood needs, and address social and geographic exclusion.

Whether it is a single "megacity" or a "metropolitan area," the key common administrative features are multiplicity of authorities and responsibilities, and vast unfilled needs. For example, the Chicago metropolitan area encompasses 1,250 different local governments and authorities; the national capital region of Delhi encompasses cities from three surrounding states in addition to the state of Delhi proper; in China, provincial status has been given to the cities of Beijing, Shanghai, and Tianjin; and a two-tier system (a metropolitan authority and city governance) applies in Manila, Tokyo, Karachi, and New Delhi.

Consequently, the responsibility for services is badly fragmented, not only among the municipalities within the megacity, but also among the functional agencies of central governments. The traffic and pollution problems in Asian megacities are legendary—Bangkok, formerly the uncontested "leader" in this field, has been surpassed by Manila in scale and severity of traffic and pollution problems. But the adverse impact of bad metropolitan coordination is now evident in urban areas elsewhere—and not only in the usual suspects such as Los Angeles and Mexico City. Thus, sections of the Washington Beltway now make visitors from Manila and Bangkok feel right at home.

As grave and complex as the problems of megacities are, solutions do exist. Unfortunately, it is far easier to apply them with foresight at the start of the problem (as in Tokyo or, to some extent, Seoul) than to remedy a disastrous situation after it has been allowed to worsen for decades (as in Mexico City or Jakarta). But solutions can be found, if the central government plays a significant role, both enabling and affirmative—enabling mainly by removing unnecessary regulatory obstacles and enacting sensible policies, and affirmative mainly by assuring adequate infrastructure. Consider the experience of Singapore, which demonstrates the huge payoff from effective traffic management policies (Box 5.6).

One feasible option for handling megacity problems is to set up metropolitan-level authorities for major services such as water supply and sewerage, housing, transport, and area planning—provided that sufficient provision is made for adequate maintenance of the system as a whole, as a breakdown in any part of it compromises the entire system. For example, Curitiba in Brazil is a model for structuring the metropolitan network around the transport system. Seoul, too, has managed its growth pains reasonably well. And the Tokyo metropolitan government exercises the authority of both city and prefecture over seventeen cities, twelve towns, and other areas in the metropolitan region. It also controls and supervises sector authorities, with established channels for public feedback and participation, and the reliability of its public transport system is rightly celebrated. By contrast, coordination is minimal in some metropolitan areas in developed countries (e.g., the Washington metropolitan area, with the three jurisdictions of the District of Columbia, Virginia, and Maryland apparently unable to cooperate in even the most obvious common problems, such as traffic congestion). In the developing world, Metro Manila is still searching for the right answer to balance metropolitan coordination with local government needs (Box 5.7).

THE SITUATION IN THE UNITED STATES

Some General Observations

The United States offers a striking example of variety and profusion of local authorities, all delivering different public services and managing their affairs in their own way. As of 2007, there were about 90,000 local government units in the fifty states of the union. These comprised about 3,000 counties, 19,000 municipalities, 20,000 townships, 15,000 school districts, and 30,000 special districts. With such variety, useful generalizations are difficult.[22] Moreover, the core principle of subsidiarity enshrined in the U.S. Constitution—that powers not explicitly assigned to the federal government are reserved to the states—means that those vast non-enumerated powers are exercised in very different manner in the different states.

The principle of subsidiarity, however, does not apply *within* states. On the contrary, states operate on the *ultra vires* principle, reserving to themselves all powers except those they explicitly delegate to counties, municipalities, and other local government. This is referred to as the Dillon Rule, from federal judge John F. Dillon who formulated it in 1872. The historical and legal logic of this differential approach is that the founding blocks of the entire U.S. political system are the individual states. Thus, just as the

BOX 5.6

Dealing with Traffic Congestion in Singapore

Dealing with traffic congestion in big cities calls for active demand management and differential pricing. Fiscal and regulatory measures to restrain private car ownership and use are important to enhance the efficient use of road space. Of course, to be politically and economically acceptable, such measures must be accompanied by provision of good alternatives to private cars, in the form of safe and affordable public transportation.

Singapore provides an interesting example of a policy to contain traffic congestion through the assignment of road-use rights to the government and the use of market mechanisms to reallocate those rights to the car owners. For starters, owners of a new car pay an import duty of 40 percent and a 3 percent goods and services tax. If they actually want to drive the car, they pay a registration fee of 140 percent of the value of the car and hefty yearly road taxes that vary with the engine capacity of the vehicle. Moreover, a "certificate of entitlement" (COE) must be acquired before the vehicle can be registered. The COE, which is valid for a ten-year period, can be bought at a monthly closed auction held by the Land Transport Authority by bids submitted electronically via ATMs. Accordingly, the price of a COE fluctuates accordingly with the supply and demand for COEs, from as "little" as $10,000 to as much as $40,000. All told, to drive a $20,000 car in Singapore for ten years can easily cost $150,000, or $15,000 per year—not counting fuel, maintenance, repairs, and parking.

Moreover, the area licensing scheme, an example of intelligent road pricing, requires private motor vehicles entering the central business district during working hours to display a color-coded area license, and pay differential monthly or daily entry charges for peak and nonpeak hours. The scheme is enforced by traffic wardens eyeballing the traffic past the entry points, and is being replaced by electronic monitoring. These measures help reduce both traffic problems and pollution levels.

It is hardly surprising that only one in four households in Singapore own a car, compared to at least one car per household in the United States. But it is also not surprising that Singaporeans can get around everywhere in their city-state by the inexpensive, squeaky clean, fast, safe, and reliable public transport system. Nor is it surprising that the levels of air pollution are among the lowest of any large city in the world. In Mexico City, Lagos, or Manila, you can belch smoke from your ancient jalopy all year long for very little money—if you don't mind moving at five miles an hour and getting emphysema by age 40.

Although elements of the Singapore experience are worth considering elsewhere, it is evident that such measures, taken in a compact city-state with an authoritarian government, cannot be easily transplanted to other countries.

(*Vide* the "taxpayers revolt" in Virginia in 2001 that led to the sharp reduction of a comparatively modest car tax—almost wrecking the state's finances and aggravating suburban sprawl and traffic congestion.) Nevertheless, the basic *quid pro quo* is the same everywhere: if a state wishes to effectively limit private motor vehicle use, it must (1) make the use of motor vehicles expensive *and* thereby (2) use the money to provide public transport facilities that are at least equivalent in convenience and reliability.

Sources: Adapted from ADB (1995); Singapore Government (www.gov.sg; keyword "Certificate of Entitlement"); Jon Quah, personal communication, 2004.

United States was formed by the individual states (the former separate colonies), which freely decided to cede specific powers *up* to the federal government, substate government levels are also creatures of each state, which consequently decides what specific powers to delegate *down* to them.

Aside from their subjection to federal constitutional provisions and applicable federal laws, the only major institutional feature that states have in common is the requirement to live within their means. Because, unlike the federal government, a state does not have the power to print money, the requirement of a balanced budget applies to all states, explicitly or implicitly. This requirement can be avoided for a time, with accounting gimmicks or "special" borrowing, but sooner or later expenditure cuts and/or tax increases become inevitable. In other federal countries (e.g., Brazil in the 1990s), the possibility of a federal bailout of a state in severe financial difficulties has weakened fiscal discipline at subnational government level. In the United States, by contrast, the federal government has typically abstained from coming to the rescue of a state or locality in financial trouble. (In 1975, when virtually bankrupt New York City applied to President Gerald Ford for federal help, the response was, in a celebrated Daily News headline: "*Ford to City: Drop Dead.*" Yet, New York City today has become in many respects an example of good megacity governance.)

The realization that a federal bailout is extremely unlikely has tended to keep U.S. states and cities on a generally responsible fiscal course. However, the other side of the fiscal discipline coin (as discussed in some detail in chapter 6) is the perennial tendency of the federal government to "solve" its own fiscal problems by downloading expenditure responsibilities onto the states and localities, but without the revenue necessary to finance them. Thus, the sound appearance of states' finances may camouflage a host of unmet needs and repressed financial problems. Plainly, the underlying challenge of vertical coordination in the United States does not revolve around issues of bailout or control, but calls for much greater cooperation among the various levels of government—not only in the fiscal and financial area, but in general. Such cooperation is particularly relevant to the contemporary concern with the risk of terrorist attacks.

Coordinating the Response to National Emergencies: A Key Contemporary Issue

Taking the lead from the disaster associated with the unprecedented hurricane season of 2005, some knowledgeable observers (e.g., David Broder, "The Right Minds for Recovery," *The Washington Post,* September 29, 2005) have argued that a structural weakness of the Constitution is the lack of a mechanism to coordinate the work of federal, state, and local government, partly because in

BOX 5.7

Metro Manila: From Centralized Corruption to Decentralized Confusion

The evolution of seventeen different local governments into what is now known as Metropolitan Manila occurred in three different time frames. The first was during the Ferdinand Marcos regime from 1975 to 1986; the second during the term of President Aquino from 1986 to 1992; and the third during the term of President Ramos from 1992 to 1998.

Metro Manila was created in 1975 during the Marcos regime as a geopolitical entity, and was governed by a national agency called the Metropolitan Manila Commission. The lawmaking powers of the seventeen local governments in the metro region were transferred to the new commission, which was a single governing board with five members and chaired by the president's wife, Imelda Marcos. The commission was responsible for all metropolitan services, the levy of taxes and charges, and comprehensive planning. However, it acted in practice as a bribe-producing mechanism for the regime. In reaction, after the fall of Marcos, the commission went into limbo. Legislative councils were elected for the local governments and the larger municipal units kept pressing to break away. Centralized thievery gave way to decentralized chaos.

In recognition of the situation, in 1995 the Philippines Congress designated Metro Manila as a special development and administrative region and set up the Metro Manila Development Authority. Policy was made by an expanded Metro Manila Council consisting of mayors, government officials, and the chief of police, and powers of the Authority included transport management, waste disposal, urban zoning and land use planning, health and sanitation, pollution control, and public safety. The problem from the start was the unclear accountability and jurisdictional conflicts generated by the overlapping authority with the legal powers of the municipal councils.

Completion in 2002 of the light rail transport around the city was a major accomplishment to reduce Manila's legendary traffic problems, and the situation as of 2007 is better than either the centralized corruption of the Marcos era or the confusion of the subsequent twenty years. However, the right institutional balance between managing activities that have a metropolitan impact and preserving municipal autonomy has not yet been found in the Philippines.

Source: Adapted from Bunye (1999).

the event of an emergency requiring the three levels to work together, there is no forum in which they can meet. However, the core issues lie elsewhere—in local initiative to identify the needs and problems and present them to federal authorities; federal intervention to lead and coordinate efforts to address those problems; and the flow of information between the two.

There is already a consensus on the supremacy of the federal level. Good cooperation, however, is contingent on the quality of leadership at all levels; effective coordination to anticipate and respond to national emergencies can only be exercised by the federal authorities; and, most obviously, timely intervention requires *interoperability,* that is, the ability of different government jurisdictions to communicate with one another. Sadly, many of the deaths on September 11, 2001, could have been avoided if only the police and firemen had been able to talk to each other on compatible radios. Astonishingly, four years later Hurricane Katrina showed that federal, state, county, and local officials were *still* unable to share information and communicate with one another and the situation in 2007 is not much better.

Indeed, Katrina was not only a monster natural storm, but triggered a perfect storm of leadership failures. These failures spanned the entire chain of authority, from municipal to county to state to federal, but fundamentally underlined the reality that whether natural, accidental, or from terrorist attack, national emergencies in a federal system demand vigorous coordination and leadership from the federal level of government, including timely action *before* the emergency.[23] The Katrina debacle also showed the importance of providing the government emergency agencies with the clear mandate, adequate resources, and competent leadership required by any organization—public or private (see Box 5.8).

GENERAL DIRECTIONS OF IMPROVEMENT

Because a core requirement for accountability is a clear assignment of responsibility, it is advisable to specify by law the powers of each level of subnational government. (While some functions entail shared responsibility between different levels of government, to avoid turf competition and confusion, the number of these functions should be carefully circumscribed.) It is highly inadvisable, however, to codify into law the local administrative customs or other informal modes of behavior, because when it is codified custom loses its natural capacity to adapt to change as noted earlier. This would be particularly damaging in developing countries, which depend to a large extent on time-tested but dynamic informal norms.

Decentralization

Experience worldwide shows that decentralization can serve to improve political stability, deliver service more efficiently and effectively, reduce the level of poverty, and promote equity. However, certain considerations apply:

- Decentralization is a means for better governance and service delivery and not an end in itself.
- Decentralization measures need consensus and support from different sectors.
- Subnational governments should be given time to learn and gradually adapt to the new system.
- Selective control and monitoring mechanisms of local government are important.
- Decentralization policies should be carefully designed and implementation closely monitored. The risks of hasty decentralization are particularly great in developing countries.
- In countries where decentralization laws were enacted piecemeal, the relevant legislation should be reviewed to eliminate duplications and inconsistencies.
- Mechanisms for effective public participation at local level should be provided.

BOX 5.8

Federal-State-Local Interaction: A Contemporary Horror Tale

When in the future a good bureaucrat wants to scare her unruly child, she may say the FEMA Monster will "get him" if he doesn't behave, and tell him the following story.

"Once upon a time, there was an effective government organization in the USA called the Federal Emergency Management Agency—FEMA. It was called that because it actually dealt with emergencies, managed the federal response efficiently, and provided real assistance to those affected by the emergency. FEMA had all the attributes of an effective organization: a clear mission, political support in the form of cabinet status, well-defined focus, operational independence, experienced staff, adequate resources, and an excellent track record of intervention, including in its earlier coordination of the activities of state and local authorities. Unfortunately, poor FEMA itself had no defenses against political rape, and the sad day came whenas a result of such rape, it mutated into a monster of patronage and inefficiency. Between 2000 and 2004, many of the experienced people were pushed out or quit in disgust; most top management jobs were given to hacks whose only qualification was their previous fundraising and campaign activities for the president of the United States (the director's previous job consisted of organizing horse shows); the agency's budget was cut year after year; and the agency lost cabinet status when a much bigger monster was created in 2002—the Department of Homeland Security—which grabbed FEMA and ate its focus.

Since FEMA wore the same clothes, nobody noticed the body snatching for quite a while. A first hint was provided by the string of hurricanes in Florida in 2004—when, instead of devoting their time to actually coping with the emergency, local first responders had to attend lengthy FEMA "brainstorming retreats to achieve a holistic response to the weather-related situation, including awareness-raising" (personal communication from a Florida sheriff whose modesty does not permit him to be credited). The true nature of the mutation of FEMA, however, came to light only with the disaster caused to New Orleans and the entire Gulf Coast by Hurricane Katrina in August 2005. Not only was the agency shockingly unable to intervene promptly, but it actually sat like a drugged elephant in the doorway, preventing others from helping. (Just one example: a hospital ship with medical staff and thousands of beds was kept off the coast for days without reply to its repeated requests to FEMA for authorization to assist the hurricane victims.)

And so, many of the victims *lived unhappily ever after . . ."*

A footnote. The respected conservative commentator David Brooks claimed in a September 12, 2005 *New York Times* column that FEMA's failure was the failure of government itself. Nonsense. The failure had nothing whatever to do with a public versus private dichotomy, but came from the violation of the most basic requirements for organizational effectiveness. A simple mind experiment may help: if a private corporation saw its competent managers replaced by pinheads, budget slashed, business model shredded by outside meddlers, technical staff decimated and demoralized, and operational freedom curtailed by having to ask for "higher" permission before acting, that private corporation would become as ineffective as FEMA had become by 2005.

The general directions of improvement in decentralization are the same for developing as for developed countries, although the emphasis will differ. The approach should:

- ensure that subnational governments possess the capability to carry out the functions and responsibilities given to them by transferring appropriate technology, skills, and financial and manpower resources;
- ensure provision of human resource and organizational capacity until such time when subnational governments can independently perform their functions;
- put in place central regulation to ensure national standards of public services and prevent local government actions from interfering with or contradicting national policies and goals, especially in devolution; and
- allow some flexibility to local government in implementing central mandates.

Effective decentralization requires sufficient administrative capacity at the relevant government level. However, a weak capacity of subnational government to exercise certain functions should be an indication of the need to strengthen such capacity and not taken as an excuse for withholding legal sanction for the responsibilities it is expected to exercise. Central and intermediate levels of government can strengthen both the powers and the capacity of local government by:

- entrusting to elected local bodies the government of urban and rural areas, with clear functions and commensurate resources;
- avoiding the central appointment of local leaders and resisting the temptation to intervene except when local governance is violated or at risk;
- fostering the creation of mechanisms for accountability and responsiveness of local government to the citizens and for appropriate public participation;
- enabling local governments to appoint qualified staff, and providing—on request—such technical and managerial assistance as local government may require to function; and
- assuring the effective audit of local government activity, as well as an appeals channel for the redress of citizens' grievances.

Large Metropolitan Areas

It is much easier to anticipate and address problems of large agglomerations and megacities than to remedy them after they have surfaced in severe form. Nevertheless, improvements in metropolitan governance are essential to keep those problems from becoming worse still and can succeed if they are well-coordinated and sustained over a period of time. Considering the large number of people residing in megacities and the severe problems of urban slums and poverty, the central and provincial governments concerned have a responsibility to:

- help devise region-wide solutions for land-use, transport, traffic and environmental problems, as well as for a minimum level of services to the poorer groups—primarily shelter, clean water, and waste disposal in developing countries and good quality education and basic health care in developed countries;
- assure that megacity governance meets the same basic requirements as good governance in general—especially participation;
- support targeted solutions for the special problems of slums and other poor urban neighborhoods;
- prevent interests of individual municipalities, or of privileged neighborhood groups, from exploiting the unplanned expansion of megacities for their own advantage; and
- help address the issues of internal migration, along with measures to assist the recovery of impoverished inner cities.

QUESTIONS FOR DISCUSSION

1. "Obviously, it is easier to administer a province that corresponds to a natural physical region—such as a large valley—than a province with artificial boundaries and a variety of different physical features." Discuss.
2. Why shouldn't all powers and responsibilities of government be allocated among subnational government units in accordance with the scientific basis provided by Oates' decentralization theorem?
3. What's the key difference between deconcentration and delegation? For which kind of public services would deconcentration be more appropriate?
4. Pick one of the following two statements, and make a credible argument for it:
   a. "Decentralization is a dangerous fad."
   b. "Decentralization is an overdue necessity."
5. "Central governments are forever praising the virtues of devolution and local rights, only to interfere with the exercise of those rights when the result is not agreeable to the party in power in the central government." Discuss.
6. With general reference to Table 5.1, discuss which government services are best delivered by central government, state government, counties, or a city mayor.
7. In a country characterized by severe ethnic fragmentation and hostility, is it better for the central government to appoint directly the leaders of provinces and cities, or to have them directly elected by the people concerned?
8. If whenever a function is delegated to a local government the central government must also give the money to implement it, why not simply have the central government perform that function directly? And if no money is given for it, why should the local government accept the responsibility?

NOTES

1. New Zealand has organized its local authorities into three categories: regional, territorial, and special-purpose authorities. The regional councils set the regulatory environment for managing natural resources, while the territorial councils provide local services within a defined regulatory framework.

2. Paradoxically known as the "Congo Free State," King Leopold's immense private domain was set on a foundation of systematic atrocities and deliberate terrorizing of the population in order to force it to collect ivory and, later, rubber for the world market. An estimated 10 million Congolese lives were lost during that period and nobody can even guess at the much greater number of amputations of children's limbs as punishment for their parents' failure to collect enough of the desired commodities. Hochschild (1999) gives a carefully researched and vivid account of what must rank at the very top of the long history of colonial brutalities. In our times, the armed conflict of the last fifteen years has caused an estimated 4 million Congolese deaths, mainly in the eastern parts of the country. Again, this has basically happened for control and exploitation of the country's natural resources, but this time with active meddling by neighboring African countries rather than by Europeans—not that the dead, raped and maimed care about the difference.

3. It was at the University of Edinburgh, partly through his encounter with Fabian theory, that Nyerere began to develop his particular vision of connecting socialism with African communal living—the later *ujamaa* (family) villages (see Nyerere, 1962).

4. This section draws partly from Smith (1985), a still-current treatment to which the reader interested in a comprehensive discussion is referred.

5. Cf. H. J. deBlij and Peter O. Muller (2005).

6. Originally published in 1949 and popular during the 1950s. Cf. *Concept of a Growth Pole*. www.applet-magic.com/poles.htm. Also see: David Darwent, 1969, "Growth poles and growth centers in regional planning—a review," *Environment and Planning*, vol. 1, pp. 5–32.

7. This section is based mainly on Rondinelli and Cheema, eds. (1983).

8. Some political scientists define "devolution" and "decentralization" as separate processes: devolution as the dispersal of power and authority, and decentralization as the geographic and territorial subdivision of the state. This is a tenable distinction, but we believe the definitions provided here are more practical.

9. Dillinger (1993).

10. Oates (1972).

11. In its broadest formulation, subsidiarity entails that government should not, at any level, undertake any activity other than those that demonstrably exceed the capacity of individuals or private groups.

12. See, among others, Rondinelli (1983); Ter-Minassian (1997); and Bahl (1998, 1999).

13. This section draws in part on OECD (1997a); Dillinger (1993); Davey (1993); Asian Development Bank (1998b); World Bank (1997b).

14. For the Philippines, see Pertierra and Ugarte, in McFerson (2002).

15. Fiji, with its endemic conflict between ethnic Fijians and Fiji Indians, is an exception—but even in nominally monoethnic Pacific countries extremely violent inter-island conflict can emerge, as in the Solomon Islands from the late 1990s until 2004. See, for example, McFerson (1996).

16. Various bodies exist below the level of cities and towns—such as the community councils in the Netherlands, the *barangays* (villages) in the Philippines, and the ward committees in India. The diversity of organization is such that no generalization is possible—except for the requirement that all such submunicipal bodies must operate with the full transparency and direct contact with citizens that their very existence implies.

17. Davey (1993).

18. Oakerson, in Perry (1989); Davey (1993).

19. Primary education and health are sometimes provided by cities, but as an adjunct to county or central government services, and responsibility for police and prisons is usually entrusted to central or provincial government, with some exceptions (e.g., in the United States).

20. Davey (1993).

21. This section draws in part on Sivaramakrishnan and Green (1986); UN (1993); ADB (1995a and 1998b); and Bunye (1999).

22. The reader interested in a fuller discussion of state and local government in the United States is referred to Andrisani, Hakim, and Savas (2006); and to Hondale, Cigler, and Costa (2004).

23. The single most effective (and simplest) measure would be to set aside a frequency for police, firemen, and other first responders, as recommended by the 9/11 Commission. See: Final Report of the National Commission on Terrorist Attacks Upon the United States, Official Government Edition. www.gpoaccess.gov/911/index.html. To the unitiated, such as the authors, it is a puzzling mystery why a no-brainer measure of this sort was still not in place six years after 9/11 and two years after Katrina.

PART II

MANAGING GOVERNMENT ACTIVITY

CHAPTER 6

Managing the Money: Preparing, Implementing, and Monitoring the Budget

> It is better to rise from a banquet neither thirsty nor drunk.
> —*Aristotle*

> Annual income, twenty pounds, annual expenditures nineteen six, result happiness. Annual income, twenty pounds, annual expenditures twenty pounds six, result misery.
> —*Mr. Micawber (in Charles Dickens'* David Copperfield)

WHAT TO EXPECT

Adam Smith, the founder of modern economics, famously said that what is wise conduct for a family cannot be folly for an entire nation. This assertion is often wrong and embodies what logicians call the "fallacy of composition"—assuming that what is true of a part is necessarily true of the whole. However, in the management and implementation of the government budget the assertion is almost always true, and the analogy between a household budget and the national budget is apt. Thus, in the heavily technical discussion that follows, when readers feel a need for concreteness and a better connection to the material, it will help them to think of the particular issue in terms of their individual finances or of household decisions.

The word "budget" comes from a Middle English word signifying "the king's purse," when a country's resources were deemed to be the personal property of the king. The meaning has of course changed since then, along with the political evolution from absolute monarchy to constitutional government. In most countries today, approval of the budget (the "power of the purse") is the main form of legislative control over the executive, with public money raised and spent only under the law. In some developing countries, however, the public perception persists that some of the country's resources are the personal property of the leader or of the ruling group. This perception should progressively be dispelled, and executive accountability established, as the system evolves toward greater legitimacy and better governance. The chapter discusses, in turn, the basic rationale and forms of taxation; the meaning and objectives of the budgeting system; the principles and process of its preparation, approval, execution and monitoring; and the financial management controls, including the key role of external audit. The budget system in the United States is described next, and the chapter concludes with suggestions for general directions of improvement in budgeting. Appendix 6.1 describes in some detail the most common dysfunctional budget preparation practices to be avoided and Appendix 6.2 discusses some technical issues in budget execution and financial control.[1]

PAYING FOR YOUR GOVERNMENT

The subject of taxation and public finance in general is much too vast for even a basic summary to be included in this book on public management. The interested reader is referred to the classic text in public finance (Musgrave and Musgrave, 1989) and to Gruber (2004) for a more recent treatment including discussion of contemporary American issues. Most of this chapter is devoted to the principles and practices of government *expenditure* management. However, we start with a telegraphic indication of the elementary rationale for taxation and a description of the main types of taxes—to provide the minimum context without which a discussion of government budgeting is like the sound of one hand clapping.

First Principles: Why Taxes?

In recent years, the case for cutting taxes in the United States has rested on the statement that the tax revenue is "the people's money, and the people should decide how to spend it." This proposition is true, appealing, and meaningless. Whether for national security, social protection, law and order, and so on, government services do not materialize out of thin air as the result of political decrees, strong willpower, or fervent wishes. Like any entity in the public or private sector, government too requires resources—labor, materials, supplies, equipment, and information. Those resources must be provided by the country's own citizens, who are collectively the presumptive beneficiaries of those activities, mainly through taxes. If you want a government, you have to pay for it. In the words of Justice Oliver Wendell Holmes, inscribed on the front of the Internal Revenue Service headquarters in Washington, taxes are the price we pay for a civilized society.

In principle, a country's citizens, through their votes and the actions of their elected representatives, first determine what they wish their government to do and then decide how to pay for it. (In practice, the two decisions are made in an iterative manner and through the same process of annual budgeting, in fairly disorderly ways and influenced by pressure from various interest groups.) If the taxes and other revenue collected are insufficient to pay for the desired government activities, the government will need to finance the resulting fiscal deficit by printing the money, issuing bonds to borrow it from foreign sources or from the citizens, or simply by not paying its bills. In all these cases, there are inevitable economic and financial repercussions (mainly, inflation) that have the equivalent effects of taxes—although in very diverse and less visible forms and affecting different groups.

In reality, the only real tax cut is a cut in government *expenditure*, for it is that expenditure that will have to be paid for in one form or another, by one group or another, now or later, by the present generation or by their children. Since you do not get what you do not pay for, in considering whether to reduce taxes society must balance the gains to some groups against the losses to other groups from the reduced government services—hopefully in view of the country's long-term interests. This is the very essence of politics. Thus, the fundamental meaning of "fiscal responsibility" does not lie in whether government expenditure is lower or higher, or taxes are raised or reduced, nor even in a balanced budget, but in confronting honestly the real worth of government activities and their short- and long-term financial implications, and in finding transparent and efficient ways to pay for them. Accordingly, a serious discussion of taxation cannot rest on the truism that taxes are "the people's money" and on fairy tales of getting something for nothing, but must revolve around the hard political, economic, and social issues of how well the tax money is spent, for whom, and which groups in society should pay more for the country's government and why.

Types of Taxes

What Is Taxed

Taxes can be levied on property, on income, or on transactions. *Property taxes* include mainly real estate taxes—the main source of revenue for local government in the United States—and other property taxes, e.g., the estate tax on inherited assets. (The estate tax is the single most equitable and least burdensome form of taxation. It is sometimes deliberately misnomed as the "death tax." But dead persons cannot be taxed. They are dead. The tax is on their heirs, who have contributed little or nothing to the accumulation of the assets being taxed.) *Income taxes* are levied on the income of corporations and of individuals. Corporations are taxed on their net income (i.e., corporate profits). In turn, individual income taxes are levied on income from work (wages and payroll taxes to finance Social Security and medical care) and income from capital and other assets (e.g., taxes on stock dividends or on rents and royalties). Capital gains taxes are levied on the difference between the sale price and the original price of an asset. *Taxes on transactions* include mainly sales taxes and customs duties. Some of these taxes are typically levied by central governments and others by provincial or local governments, based on the principles mentioned later in this section.[2]

Who Is Taxed

Progressive, Proportional, and Regressive Taxes. A progressive tax is one where the tax rate increases as the taxpayer's income increases; in proportional taxes, the rate is constant; and a regressive tax takes a greater bite out of the income of lower-income taxpayers. For example, sales taxes are regressive because they take the same percentage of the value of the transaction whether the buyer is wealthy or poor—and hence a lower percentage of wealthier buyers' income. The same is generally true of real estate taxes and customs duties. (Government-run lotteries are the single most regressive and least equitable form of tax, almost entirely hitting the poor.) Income taxes, instead, are typically progressive, with wealthier persons paying a higher rate of income in tax and people below a certain income level exempt from income taxes altogether.

Why a Progressive Income Tax? It is easily understandable that the rich should pay more taxes because they have more income. But is it fair that they should pay a greater *proportion* of income? As in much of economics, the main justification is related to basic psychology. The criterion of tax fairness is to try and equalize the subjective "pain" of taxation across all citizens. The basic consideration is that the satisfaction we derive from consuming or owning more of any particular thing generally diminishes the more we have of it. A loaf of bread means far more to a starving person than to somebody who just had a big lunch. A first TV set is much more valuable than a second set, and to add a fifth TV set to a never-used guest room will yield very little additional satisfaction. Because the utility of money, as a medium of exchange, derives from the utility of the things that money can buy, this basic consideration underpins the principle of "diminishing marginal utility" of money—an extra $1,000 in annual income will mean far more to someone making $20,000 than to someone making $200,000 a year. Therefore, the only way to try and equalize the pain of taxation is to tax a smaller fraction of the additional $1,000 for the low-income person than for the wealthier one—which leads to a progressive income tax structure. A second justification of progressive income taxation is that it offsets the regressivity of the many other forms of taxes. In reality, when *all* taxes are considered, in the United States the relative tax burden on lower- and middle-income persons is the same or higher than on the wealthiest individuals. An important caveat is in order, however. When the top tax rates on income become too high, they reduce individual incentives to work harder, innovate, and invest, and increase the incentives to find ways to avoid the tax—including relocating outside the country. A reasonable balance must be found between tax equity and tax efficiency. A rough-and-ready rule of thumb from international experience is that the highest income tax rate should be kept comfortably under 50 percent and becomes seriously dysfunctional when it exceeds 60 percent.

A Flat Income Tax? In recent years, some have proposed replacing the progressive federal income tax structure with a "flat tax" (a proportional income tax with the same rate regardless of income level), or a national consumption tax—along with the elimination of most deductions and special tax provisions. This would simplify tax administration enormously and, incidentally, put a lot of tax lawyers and accountants out of business. However, if the tax rate is high enough to generate the same revenue, it would make the *overall* tax structure sharply more regressive; otherwise, it would create a huge hole in government revenue, which would then require a drastic cut in government expenditure—most probably to the disadvantage of lower- and middle-income taxpayers and thus equally regressive in its net impact. Moreover, the strong political resistance to eliminating the various deductions and loopholes would almost certainly doom the chances of the drastic tax simplification that a flat income tax rate (or a national consumption tax) would require.

Who Does the Taxing

In every country, tax policies must be coordinated between central, intermediate, and local government jurisdictions in order to avoid distortions in the movement of economic resources (labor, capital, goods, and services) from one region to another and to prevent mobile taxable bases (such as capital) from migrating to regions with lower tax rates. Such migration would cause jurisdictions to compete with one another through lower taxes or other inducements and thus create an inefficient and opaque overall fiscal system. Rules are also needed for allocating tax revenues among jurisdictions in a way to avoid double taxation or tax gaps. What follows is a summary of the basic criteria for deciding at which level of government to assign different types of taxes.

Central Taxes. In keeping with the previously stated objectives, good central government taxes are mainly progressive and should:

- cover mobile tax bases (e.g., corporate income, capital gains, inheritance taxes) in order to avoid movements of assets and factors of production and interjurisdictional tax competition;
- be "buoyant" (i.e., sensitive to changes in income) in order to provide the central government with macroeconomic stabilization instruments and to partly shelter the budgets of subnational governments from cyclical fluctuations; and
- cover tax bases that are unevenly distributed across regions, such as taxes on natural resources. (In this case, however, since the local environment will be affected by natural resource exploitation, the proceeds of the tax should be shared with the local government.)

Local Taxes. Symmetrically, taxes appropriate for local government are mainly regressive and should:

- have a relatively immobile tax base (e.g., real estate);
- provide a stable and predictable yield (e.g., "sin" taxes on alcohol, tobacco, etc.);
- be relatively easy to administer (e.g., sales taxes); and

- prevent nonresidents from shifting their tax liabilities to other communities.

Distribution of the Overall Tax Burden

It is analytically and practically very difficult to assess the distribution of the burden of taxation on the various regions, groups, and individuals in society. Even the most thorough analysis will have gaps and ambiguities, and the data are so diverse as to allow persons of opposing political viewpoints to pick and choose from the numbers to support very different conclusions. However, some general criteria do help form a correct impression, if not of the actual distribution of the burden of taxation, at least of how such distribution is likely to change in response to a proposed major tax policy measure. (These criteria also help debunk misleading partisan claims.)

First, it is important to understand the distinction between those who carry the "first-line" official responsibility for collecting and paying the tax and those who ultimately end up bearing the burden of the tax. Two illustrations may help. A sales tax is officially paid by the buyer and collected by the seller, who turns it over to the government. However, it is the nature of the transaction that determines who actually ends up paying for the tax. If the good or service being sold has a very inelastic demand (i.e., if it is a necessity without close substitutes), the seller will not need to reduce the sale price to offset the sales tax, which is therefore indeed paid by the buyer. If instead the purchase is more discretionary, the seller may be forced to reduce the net sale price to avoid losing customers and ends up in effect paying for part or most of the sales tax even though it is formally charged to the buyer.[3] Similarly, Social Security and medical insurance taxes are shared between employer and employee. However, if the labor market has a surplus of the skills of the employees and there are few employers, the employers may in fact make the employees pay for some of the employers' own contribution, in the form of lower salaries. On the contrary, if the labor market is very tight and the industry is expanding fast, employers may have to raise worker salaries to offset part or all of the employee payroll taxes and will end up in effect paying more than their official share. The point here is that just because a tax is charged to one party it is not always ultimately paid entirely by that party. The nature of the tax, the characteristics of the market, and the interaction between the supply and demand of the good or service being taxed should be carefully considered.

Second, when trying to assess the distribution of the tax burden, it is essential to consider the totality of the tax system—all types of taxes, at central, state, and local government levels—and not just one category of tax or another. In the United States in 2006, for example, the federal revenue from the individual income tax (which affects higher-income persons to a greater extent) made up less than half of total federal receipts and was barely higher than the taxes paid for Social Security and Medicare (which are borne mostly by low- and middle-income persons). A shift from individual income taxes, which are progressive, to other taxes automatically shifts some of the overall tax burden onto lower- and middle-income individuals.

Third, one must also take into account the tax assignments between central, intermediate, and local government. Because state and local revenue depends heavily on sales and real estate taxes—both of which are regressive—shifting the tax burden from the central government to intermediate government and municipalities makes the overall tax structure less progressive.

Finally, the challenge is even more complex if one wishes to understand the impact of overall government activity on people in different income groups or regions of the country. Doing so would require taking into account the distribution of the benefits from public expenditure as well as the distribution of the burden of taxes. For example, Social Security benefits go disproportionately to lower- and middle-income people, while other subsidies (e.g., to energy and agriculture) accrue largely to wealthy corporations and individuals, and the benefits of protection of property are naturally most important for persons with valuable assets to protect.

THE ROLES AND OBJECTIVES OF PUBLIC EXPENDITURE MANAGEMENT

The Centrality of the Government Budget

The government budget is commonly viewed as a technical collage of words and numbers, profoundly boring and to be left to the bureaucrats and a few politicians. The budget documents are certainly not exciting, except to a few specialists. But in reality the government budget is at the center of public policy and the development prospects of the country.

In legitimate governance, the government is expected to fulfill the roles and respect the limitations decided by society. Those roles are articulated into policy objectives—quantitative, such as reducing the rate of a disease by a certain amount, or qualitative, such as fostering competition in a particular market. Some of these policy objectives may be met by issuing regulations or prescriptions or by other interventions that do not require direct and immediate expenditure (see chapter 3). Most policy objectives, however, require financial resources, which can only come from the public in the form of taxes and fees (complemented in developing countries by foreign aid). The fundamental principle of fiscal management in good governance countries is that the executive branch of government can take no moneys from the public, nor make any expenditure from those moneys, except by explicit approval of the legislature as the representative organ of the citizens. Consequently, when properly understood, *the budget is the financial mirror of society's economic and social choices,* and is thus at the very center of the country's governance structure. As such, the budget is far more than a boring technical document, and the budgeting process should reflect all four components of good governance. As summarized in chapter 1, these are: accountability, predictability (through the rule of law), participation, and transparency.

Accountability in budgeting entails both the obligation to render account of how the public's money has been used and the possibility of significant consequences for satisfactory or unsatisfactory performance in the preparation or implementation of the budget. *Predictability* of financial resources is needed for strategic prioritization and to permit public officials to plan for the provision of services, as well as a signpost to guide the private sector in making its own production, marketing, and investment decisions. Also, budgetary rules must be clear and uniformly applied to everyone. Appropriate *participation* can improve the quality of budgetary decisions and provide an essential reality check for their implementation. Finally, *transparency* of fiscal and financial information—normally through the filter of competent legislative staff and capable and independent public media—is a must for an informed executive, legislature, and the public at large. It is essential not only that information be provided, but that it be *relevant* and provided in understandable form. Dumping on the public vast amounts of raw budgetary material does nothing to improve fiscal transparency.

The IMF Code of Good Practices on Fiscal Transparency underlines the importance in every country of clear fiscal roles and responsibilities; public availability of information; open processes of budget preparation, execution, and reporting; and independent reviews and assurance of the integrity of fiscal forecasts, information, and accounts, as summarized in Box 6.1.

BOX 6.1

Selected Requirements for Fiscal Transparency

Clarity of Roles and Responsibilities

- A budget law or administrative framework is necessary, covering budgetary as well as extra-budgetary activities and specifying fiscal management responsibilities.
- Taxation should be subject to the law and the administration of tax laws should be subject to procedural safeguards.

Public Availability of Information

- Information on extra-budgetary activities should be included in the budget documents and accounting reports
- Original and revised budget estimates for the two years preceding the budget should be included in the budget documents
- The level and composition of central government debt should be reported annually, with a lag of no more than six months.

Open Budget Preparation, Execution, and Reporting

- A fiscal and economic outlook paper should be presented with the budget, including (among other things) a statement of fiscal policy objectives and priorities and the macroeconomic forecasts on which the budget is based.
- A statement of "fiscal risks" should be presented with the budget documents.
- All general government activities should be covered by the budget classification.
- The overall fiscal balance should be reported in budget documents, with an analytical table showing its derivation from budget estimates.

Independent Assurances of Integrity

- Final central government accounts should reflect high standards and should be audited by an independent external auditor.
- Mechanisms should be in place to ensure that external audit findings are reported to the legislature and that remedial action is taken.
- Standards of external audit should be consistent with international standards.
- Working methods and assumptions used in producing macroeconomic forecasts should be made publicly available.

Source: International Monetary Fund, *Manual on Fiscal Transparency,* 2001. Available at www.imf.org. The IMF is in the process of updating the code to reflect recent fiscal developments and practices, but the core principles remain the same.

The Objectives of Public Expenditure Management

In order to perform the roles assigned to it by the people, the government needs, among other things, to collect sufficient resources from the economy in an appropriate manner, and allocate and use those resources efficiently and effectively. Hence, one should always keep in mind the integral relationship between revenue and expenditure (i.e., between the money collected from the people) (and, in most developing countries, from aid donors), and the use of that money in a manner that reflects most closely the people's preferences.[4] Also, close cooperation between tax and budget officials is a must for many economic management areas (e.g., budget forecasting, macroeconomic framework formulation, trade-offs between outright expenditures and tax concessions, etc.).

Public expenditure management, as a central instrument of policy, must pursue all three economic policy goals of growth, stability, and equity. Financial stability calls, among other things, for fiscal discipline; economic growth and equity are pursued partly through the allocation of public money to the various sectors; and, most obviously, all three goals require efficient and effective use of resources in practice. Hence, the three goals of overall policy translate into three key objectives of good public expenditure management: fiscal discipline (expenditure control), allocation of resources consistent with policy priorities ("strategic" allocation), and good operational management.[5] In turn, good operational management calls for both efficiency (minimizing cost per unit of output) and effectiveness (achieving the outcome for which the output is intended).[6] But as stressed earlier, attention to proper norms and due process is essential as well.

There are linkages between the three key objectives of budgeting, their major function, and the government level at which they operate. Fiscal discipline requires control at the national level; strategic resource allocation requires good expenditure programming, which entails appropriate top-level and interministerial arrangements, and operational management is largely an intraministerial affair, albeit within the guidelines and standards set centrally. These linkages are articulated in different ways in federal countries such as the United States than in unitary systems such as France, and the allocation of resources is partly influenced by the organizational arrangement of central government discussed in chapter 4. Also, fiscal discipline and operational management are more amenable to "technical" improvements than is the strategic allocation of resources, which is the more obviously political dimension of budgeting. As Petrei (1998) puts it:

> Resource distribution among programs is perhaps the least technical part of the budget process. With the exception of investment projects, spending decisions are rarely based on technical principles or on detailed work to determine the population's preference. The allocation of funds results from a series of forces that converge at different points of the decision-making process, with an arbitrator who rules according to an imperfect perception of present and future political realities. The ministries, the headquarters of the principal agencies, and many other decision-making positions are occupied by politicians who, theoretically, have developed a certain intuition about what people want.[7]

The scheme in Table 6.1 summarizes these relationships.

Complicating the Issue

The scheme of Table 6.1 is a simplification intended to help fix the key concepts in one's mind. The reality is more complex. First, as noted, the three objectives may be mutually conflicting in the short run (and trade-offs and compromises must be made) but are clearly complementary in the long run.

Table 6.1

Key Objectives of Fiscal Management

Objective	Revenue Function	Expenditure Function	Organizational Level
Fiscal discipline	Reliable forecasts	Expenditure control	Aggregate
Resource allocation and mobilization	Tax equity and incidence	Expenditure programming	Interministerial
Operational efficiency a. Economy b. Efficiency c. Effectiveness d. Due process	Tax administration	Management	Intraministerial

For example, mere fiscal discipline in the presence of arbitrary resource allocation and inefficient operations is not worth much. Second, good aggregate budgetary outcomes must emerge from good outcomes at each level of government: while fiscal discipline must ultimately be manifested at the aggregate level, it should emerge as the sum total of good expenditure control (and reliable revenue forecasts) in each ministry and agency of government, rather than being imposed top-down. Similarly, in federal countries such as the United States, central government budgeting should ideally take into account the fiscal needs and possibilities of the states, and mechanisms must be in place to prevent lack of discipline at state level from compromising the overall expenditure goals of the country. (In the United States in recent years, as discussed later, the problem has been rather the reverse, with gross lack of fiscal discipline at the federal level causing costs and uncertainties for the states.)

Therefore, an overall expenditure constraint is necessary but not sufficient for good budgeting; on the contrary, imposing the constraint *only* from the top may result in misalllocation of resources and inefficient operations. Typically, such top-down aggregate limits are intended to root out waste, fraud, and corruption. But waste, fraud, and corruption are hardy weeds. If the top-down limit is imposed *in isolation* and without any attention to the internal workings of the public expenditure system, the outcome may well be to underfund the more efficient and worthwhile activities, precisely because they do not carry benefits for the individual bureaucrats and their private "partners." In Latin America, for example, "pressure to spend less has led to better spending in many cases, but in many others it has led to the opposite result."[8] Similarly, the best mechanisms for interministerial coordination are worth little if the sectoral expenditure programs are inappropriate or inconsistent with overall policy. Finally, management and operational efficiency cannot normally be improved except in an overall context of fiscal discipline and sound allocation of resources—to which good management itself makes a key contribution.

A Word About Sequencing

If you cannot control the money, you cannot allocate it, and if you cannot allocate it you cannot manage it. Fiscal discipline, in many ways, comes first; resource allocation and operational efficiency come next. This is literally true in those few developing countries that have extremely weak revenue forecasts and cash management systems. In those countries, the objective of improving expenditure control is first and foremost, and any effort at addressing the other two objectives of public expenditure management would be futile and possibly counterproductive. However, it is essential to (1) design and implement improvements in expenditure control in ways that do not jeopardize the improvements in sectoral allocation and resource management; and (2) have a clear ex-ante sense of how far to push improvements in expenditure and cash control before it becomes timely to address strategic allocation and operational management issues.

In countries where expenditure control and cash management are already minimally acceptable, none of the three objectives of expenditure control, resource allocation, and good operational management should be pursued in isolation from the others (just as the overall policy goals of growth, stability, and equity are interrelated). Improvements in one or another area can and should go forward as and when circumstances permit. But a coherent vision of the entire reform process is needed to prevent "progress" in any one objective from getting so far out of line as to compromise progress in the other two, and thus the public expenditure management reform process in its entirety. Hence, a multiyear perspective is essential for good annual budgeting.

The Policy–Budget Link

For the budget to be an efficient instrument to implement the government policy objectives, the budgeting system must provide for a strong link between resource allocation and the policies. In the first place, however, the policy choices themselves must meet certain basic criteria. Decisions on what is to be done belong to the political leadership of the country. With that authority, however, comes the responsibility to make sound decisions. To recall the discussion in chapter 4, the main criteria of good decision making are:

- discipline—policies should be consistent, without internal contradictions;
- realism—policies should be affordable and implementable;
- stability—frequent policy reversals should be avoided, as a clear vision and sense of direction for the medium term is necessary for good policy making;
- openness and clarity—while the deliberations leading to budgetary policy decisions must usually be confidential, political accountability requires that the criteria and processes of decision making be explicit and public;
- selectivity—the focus ought to be on important issues and an appropriate mechanism is needed to filter out minor matters and prevent wasting the time and concentration of the political leadership; and
- communication—a badly understood policy cannot be implemented and is unlikely to be properly reflected in the budget.

BUDGET SYSTEMS, ANNUALITY, AND COMPREHENSIVENESS

The Basis of Legislative Authorization

The budget system is defined by the nature of the authorization given by the legislature, which can be in three forms. The legislature could authorize the executive to:

- spend for certain programs up to a certain amount, without specific time limit; or
- enter into *commitments* up to a certain amount, within the fiscal year only; or
- make *payments* on the proposed expenditures, within the fiscal year only.

The first type of authorization produces an "obligation budget," which is appropriate for investment projects, which take years to complete, or special programs, but doesn't permit knowing when the budget will be implemented. To use it as the general basis of budgetary authorization would allow the executive too much discretion and make economic programming difficult. The second type of authorization produces a "commitment budget," which is most suitable for keeping track of government contractual engagements, but generates uncertainty as to the timing of actual payments. The third type of authorization produces a "cash budget." A cash budget is used in most countries, and permits reconciling the government's fiscal operations with monetary and balance-of-payments developments. However, cash budgeting must be complemented by a system to keep track of government commitments in order to have a clear picture of future claims on the state finances and to preclude the temptation for the executive to get out of a tight spot by unduly delaying payments. Such "payment arrears" have the same adverse impact on the economy as overspending but also damage the credibility of the government vis-à-vis the public and the suppliers and eventually lead to a vicious circle of overbilling and underpaying.

Annuality of the Budget

Whether for commitments or for payments, the legislative authorization to collect revenue from the public and spend it must cover a reasonable period of time—neither a week nor ten years. In almost all countries, therefore, the budget covers twelve months (the "fiscal year"), and the authority to collect revenue and make expenditures expire at the end of the fiscal year. (The fiscal year usually corresponds to the calendar year, but not always; in the United States, for example, the fiscal year begins on October 1.)

The annuality rule is justified by the desirable balance between the need for legislative control and the need of the executive to adapt to changes. A budget period shorter than a year would hamper the executive capacity to manage, and a longer budget period would, in most countries, preclude sufficient legislative control over the executive branch. It is important to keep in mind the distinction between the *budget,* which contains the legislative authorization to tax and spend and covers only one fiscal year, and the multiyear *forecasts* and projections that are needed to frame the preparation of the annual budget, as discussed later.

Budget Comprehensiveness

It is clearly impossible for the government budget to reflect the choices of society and embed the principles of good governance if it includes only a part of revenues and expenditures. In such a case, the legislature would be able to review and approve only a part of government activities. The lack of information on the other expenditures would lead to abuses of executive power and, most probably, also provide an opening for theft and mismanagement. The major issues are two. First, if the budget excludes major expenditures, there is no assurance that scarce resources are allocated to priority programs. Only if all proposed expenditures are "on the table" at the same time is it possible to review them in relation to one another and choose those with higher relative benefits for the community.[9] Second, if a category of expenditure is not included in the approved budget, the amount is itself likely to be uncertain and opaque. In turn, this makes macroeconomic programming more difficult and increases the risk of corruption and waste.

Imagine that, as the head of household, you have large sources of income in addition to your salary, but only discuss with your family the allocation of your salary. At best, even if the extra income is allocated well, the family cannot cooperate in making sure that it is *spent* well, nor will it later feel any responsibility to help resolve your mistakes in this respect. At worst, the extra income will be frittered away in frivolous expenditures, with adverse impact on the family future finances and well-being.

For all these reasons, in principle, the budget should cover all transactions financed through public financial resources. Budget comprehensiveness, however, does not mean that all expenditures should be *managed* according to the same set of procedures, nor authorized each year. As will be discussed, there are practical reasons why special arrangements for administering some programs financed through public resources may be established.

Also, each public sector unit responsible for spending decisions must prepare its own budget. (As explained in the appendix to chapter 2, the "general government" consists of the central government and subnational levels of government, and the public sector includes the general government and all entities that it controls, such as state-owned enterprises.) However, it is essential that all these budgets fit together in order to compare the expenditures of different entities, calculate how much money goes to each program, and prevent duplication or gaps. Therefore, all budgets of all levels of government must be prepared on the basis of the same classification and accounting system and, for accountability and control, financial reports should consolidate the operations of general government and (to the extent possible) the financial activities of all nongovernment public entities.

"Extra-Budgetary" Funds

Operational efficiency requires taking into account the specific characteristics of different expenditure programs, and special arrangements may be needed in some cases. *Extra-budgetary funds are expenditure programs that are not subject to the annual budgetary approval process*, but are financed by approved multiyear allocations or by dedicated revenues—either because of their characteristics or their long duration. Also, when the budget process is not fully effective, high-priority expenditures may need to be protected by setting up special funds to finance them. These "extra-budgetary" funds (or "off-budget operations") are very diverse, ranging from the "road funds" common in developing countries to assure financing of highway maintenance, to such funds in the United States as black lung disability, hazardous substances superfunds, and oil spill liability funds. While they may need separate administrative arrangements, all such activities should be submitted to the same scrutiny as other expenditures. For this, they must follow the same expenditure classification system as other expenditure programs, and their transactions must be shown in the annual budget documents.[10] Equally important, their management should be representative of the main stakeholders as well as independent of political interference. In Africa, in contrast with the "first-generation" funds established in the 1980s to finance road maintenance, some "second-generation" road funds meet many of these criteria. Box 6.2 shows illustrations of the evolution of road funds in Africa from the earlier problematic arrangements to more efficient approaches. Even so, the special autonomy of extra-budgetary funds must always be accompanied by special oversight to protect against fraud and abuse.

Revenue Earmarking and User Fees

Earmarking government revenues for specific expenditures (not to be confused with the entirely different and very bad practice of "earmarks" in the U.S. government budget discussed at the end of this chapter) comprises three options:

- earmarking a *general tax for a specific use* (e.g., a percentage of income tax collected devoted to a specific expenditure);
- earmarking a *specific tax for a general use* (e.g., using proceeds from a lottery to finance infrastructure improvements);

- earmarking a *specific tax for a specific use* (e.g., using gasoline taxes to pay for road improvements).

BOX 6.2

Evolution of Extra-Budgetary "Road Funds": Contrasting Experiences in Africa

Established in 1985 to assure financing of road maintenance, twelve years later the *Ghana* Road Fund had still not created the basis for sustainable road maintenance financing. The main reason was the fund's lack of the authority and autonomy needed to resist political interference and raids on its resources. Financing of road maintenance was therefore unpredictable, which made it difficult to plan properly and issue contracts on a timely basis, while also providing the fund with an excuse for inaction. As a result, significant portions of the road network in Ghana remain in very poor condition.

After a promising start, *Malawi's* Road Fund, created in 1997, experienced similar difficulties. While at first the governing board was selected on the basis of technical competence, from the early 2000s many of the members were chosen on the basis of political influence. In particular, the board chairman came under the control of the president, who paid him board-sitting allowances for every day of the month. Critical decisions were made by the president, board chairman, and roads minister alone, and private sector participation and consultation with civil society were perfunctory.

The experience of *Tanzania* is different. The country's "second-generation" road fund came into operation in 2000. Its board is composed of a chairman from the private sector, the top civil servants from the main concerned ministries, and representatives of the private sectors and civil society. The road fund has its own dedicated secretariat, a stable resource base originating from a fuel tax, and predictable allocations for road maintenance and development. All these allocations are governed by performance agreements between the road fund and the implementing agencies, specifying the responsibilities of each party, a budget detailing the works to be performed, performance indicators, verification procedures, and reporting requirements. Political interference is minimal, and the road network in Tanzania has improved significantly.

Still, while a "good" road fund may help maintain and improve roads in developing countries, it is not essential. For example, *Burkina Faso* has been able to finance most of its road maintenance requirements through the regular budget process and without a dedicated road fund. It appears that when the budget system works reasonably well, it can meet priority expenditures without

(continued)

Box 6.2 *(continued)*

the need for extra-budgetary funds to finance them. The overall reform priority remains improving the budget system, rather than looking for ad hoc patches to remedy its weaknesses.

Sources: On the general issue, Robin Carruthers, personal communication, August 2007; Zietlow (2004); and Gwilliam and Kumar (2002). For Ghana and Burkina Faso: Sam M. Mwale, "Africa Transport Technical Note," No. 8, World Bank, May 1997. www.worldbank.org. For Malawi and Tanzania: Adam Andreski, "Case study of road funds in Ghana, Malawi and Tanzania." Senior Executive Course, 2005. University of Birmingham.

Earmarking general revenue for specific uses should generally be avoided, as it makes it difficult to compare the relative worth of different expenditure programs. Nor does earmarking of a specific tax for a general use make much sense, except possibly to sugarcoat the introduction of a new tax. However, when there is a strong link between the revenue and the expenditure, and the service is provided to clearly identified groups, the costs and the benefits are "internalized" within the same group. Thus, earmarking a *specific tax* for a *specific use* may be justified both on equity grounds and as a way to induce agencies to improve performance and facilitate cost recovery. Also, the use of earmarked taxes could increase taxpayers' knowledge of how their money is used, possibly making it more likely that they will keep an eye on the efficiency of the services.

The same principle of internalizing costs and benefits applies to *user fees* (charging the users of a public service for all or part of the cost of providing the service, e.g., public university tuition). An additional practical consideration is at work here, however: the user fees collected by the government must be sufficiently high to justify the administrative costs of defining and collecting them. When the service is provided in small units to large numbers of people, it is usually more cost-effective to just deliver it for free. (In poor developing countries, the moral and social implications of charging people struggling to survive for essential services such as basic health care argue strongly against user fees for such essential public services—whether or not they would be administratively cost-effective.) When instead user fees are easy to collect, e.g., road tolls, they can be an important spur to efficiency.

Budgeting: A Bird's-Eye View

The entire budget cycle is discussed in the next section, in terms generally applicable to all countries, whether developed or developing. (The budget system in the United States is described in the last section.) The budget cycle comprises the preparation of the budget, its execution, financial accounting and reporting, and audit and control—discussed in turn below. Owing to the technical complexity and large scope of the subject, certain topics may be of limited interest to some readers and other topics may require additional explanations provided in fuller treatments of the subject.

BUDGET PREPARATION

In keeping with the three key objectives of public expenditure management, the budget preparation process should aim at (1) ensuring that the budget fits resource constraints, (2) allocating resources in conformity with government policies, and (3) providing conditions to enable good operational management.

Three Prerequisites

The Need for a Medium-Term Fiscal Perspective

Because most government policies cannot be implemented within a single year, the starting point in the preparation of the annual budget should be the formulation of a fiscal perspective of several future years.[11] Specifically, the annual budget must reflect three paramount multi-annual considerations:

- The funding needs of entitlement programs (for example, pensions and transfer payments) where expenditure levels may change, even though basic policy remains the same. (This is especially relevant for developed countries, such as the United States, with large Social Security and public health obligations).
- The future recurrent costs of capital expenditures (which constitute the largest single category of public expenditure in most developing countries).
- Contingencies that may result in future spending requirements (e.g., government loan guarantees).

A medium-term outlook is especially necessary because the discretionary portion of the annual budget is small and most of the expenditures are already committed. Salaries of civil servants, debt service payments, pensions, and the like cannot be changed in the short term, and other costs can be adjusted only marginally. In most countries, the available financial margin of maneuver is typically about 5 percent of total annual expenditure. This means that any real adjustment of expenditure priorities, if it is to be successful, has to take place over several years. For instance, should the government wish to substantially expand access to health insurance coverage, the expenditure implications are substantial and stretch over several years and the policy can hardly be implemented through a blinkered focus on each annual budget.

Aaron Wildavsky (1993, p. 317) has summed up the arguments against isolated annual budgeting: ". . . short-sightedness, because only the next year's expenditures are reviewed; overspending, because huge disbursements in future years are hidden; conservatism, because incremental changes do not open up large future vistas; and parochialism, because programs tend to be viewed in isolation rather than in comparison to their future costs in relation to expected revenue."

We add that multiyear spending projections are also necessary to demonstrate to the administration and the public the direction of change and allow the private sector time to adjust. Moreover, in the absence of a medium-term perspective, adjustments in expenditure to reflect changing circumstances will tend to be across the board and ad hoc, focused on inputs and activities that can be cut in the short term. But often, activities that can be cut more easily are also the more important ones, such as major public investment expenditures or socially essential programs. Finally, by illuminating the expenditure implications of current policy decisions on future budgets, a government is enabled to evaluate cost-effectiveness and to determine whether it is attempting more than can be financed. (Naturally, a medium-term perspective is not worth much unless the government does use it as a robust frame for decisions on the annual budget.)

The Need for Early Decisions

By definition, budgeting entails hard choices. These can be made early, at a cost, or avoided at far greater cost. The ostrich that hides its head in the sand gets it chopped off when the train comes by. It is important that the necessary trade-offs be made explicit when formulating the budget. Partisan political considerations and administrative weakness often lead to postponing these hard choices until budget execution. This postponement makes the choices harder, not easier, and the overall consequence is a less efficient budget. An unrealistic budget cannot be executed well.

When revenues are overestimated and/or expenditures underestimated, expenditure cuts must be made later when executing the budget. On the revenue side, overestimation can come from technical factors (e.g., a bad appraisal of the impact of a change in tax policy), but often also from the desire of politicians to keep in the budget an excessive number of programs, while downplaying the difficulties of financing them. Similarly, on the expenditure side, underestimation can come from unrealistic technical assessments of their cost, but can also be a deliberate tactic to launch new programs with the intention of requesting increased appropriations later during budget execution. This tactic plays on the natural reluctance of the public to abandon an expenditure program after it has started—forgetting that one should never throw good money after bad. When combined with the bureaucratic and political momentum and vested interests, this natural reluctance leads to continuing an expenditure program even when there is a broad consensus that it is ineffective and wasteful. No technical budgeting improvement can by itself resolve institutional and political problems of this nature. It is that essential, therefore, to have robust gate-keeping mechanisms to prevent bad projects and programs from getting started in the first place. By the time they are in the budget pipeline, it's usually too late.

The Need for a Hard Constraint on Expenditure

To set a hard expenditure limit for each line ministry from the beginning of budget preparation favors a shift away from a "wish list" mentality and forces each ministry to make the necessary tough choices early in the process, knowing that its expenditure proposals will be automatically rejected if they add up to an amount higher than the initial limit. The absence of a hard expenditure constraint at the start of the budget preparation process invariably leads to various dysfunctional practices in budgeting. Because of their more technical nature, these practices are described in Appendix 6.1.

Can Fiscal Responsibility Be Legislated?

Several countries have enacted laws and rules that restrict the fiscal policy of government ("fiscal rules") and prescribe fiscal outcomes.[12] For example, the so-called "golden rule" stipulates that public borrowing must not exceed investment (in fact prohibiting a deficit in the current budget, as in Germany). In the United States, the Gramm-Rudman-Hollings "Balanced Budget and Emergency Deficit Reduction Act" of 1985 required Congress to compensate tax cuts with other revenues and provided for automatic spending cuts if Congress and the president failed to do so—but utterly failed. In the European Union, the Maastricht Treaty stipulated specific fiscal "convergence" criteria, defining both the maximum permissible ratio of fiscal deficit to GDP and the debt/GDP ratio. (The former criterion has been by far the more important.) EU member countries whose fiscal deficit is higher than the permitted 3 percent of GDP are supposedly liable to large penalties. Unfortunately, the Maastricht rules have been selectively enforced, with no penalties imposed on the largest and most important members of the Union.

A frequent criticism of "fiscal responsibility" rules is that they favor creative accounting and encourage nontransparent fiscal practices by "burying" expenditures or listing one-time revenues as regular revenue. Conversely, when the rules are effectively enforced, the criticism is that they prevent governments from adjusting their budgets to the economic cycle, thus aggravating both recession and inflation.

The real problem with fiscal rules is they are usually a government's contract *with itself*. In a presidential system of government, it is extremely difficult for the system to enforce a fiscal discipline rule on itself when the chief executive feels the need to violate it—he or she can always claim "national security" or "emergency" needs. In a parliamentary system, where the government is a creature of the legislature, for the legislature to enforce a fiscal rule is equivalent to declaring "no confidence" in its own government. The real issue is therefore the oldest issue in contract law: a contract has no legal or practical meaning unless it is enforceable, and there cannot be an enforcement mechanism in a government's contract with itself to abide by certain fiscal rules.

This reality still allows three situations in which fiscal rules may bite. First, in countries with a vibrant civil society and active political exchange, breaking a major and public fiscal commitment may entail a political price. Second, in countries with fragile coalition governments, fragmented decision making, and legislative committees acting as a focus for bargaining, setting up legally binding targets may be effective to limit political horse trading. Third, and probably most relevant, fiscal responsibility rules may be applicable to states in a federal country, for in this case the "contract enforcement" authority does exist—it is the national government. In general, however, if a government is not serious about exercising fiscal responsibility from the top leadership on down, a "fiscal responsibility law" is the fancy equivalent of a New Year's resolution.

The Stages of Budget Preparation

Annual budget preparation should be organized in the following three stages:

- The *top-down* stage, which consists of:
  - defining aggregate resources available for public spending over the fiscal year, within a medium-term fiscal perspective;
  - establishing for each line ministry or department the spending limits that fit government priorities; and
  - notifying the line ministries of these spending limits.
- The *bottom-up* stage, during which the spending agencies formulate their proposed expenditure programs within the given spending limits.
- The *iteration/negotiations* stage, to ensure overall consistency between expenditure aims and resource availability.

It is at the top-down stage that the hard expenditure constraint, or ceiling, should be communicated by the ministry of finance to all spending agencies because it is the most effective way to induce them to confront the hard choices early in the process.

These stages are broken down in the following specific activities, in sequence:

- preparation of the medium-term fiscal framework;
- issue of a budget circular or instruction, which gives expenditure ceilings by spending agency, guidelines for preparing their budget proposals, and the timetable;
- preparation of the spending agencies' budget proposals based on these guidelines;
- budgetary negotiation between the ministries/agencies and the ministry of finance;
- finalization of the draft budget by the ministry of finance;

- approval of the draft budget by the top levels of the executive; and
- submission of the draft budget to the legislature, which debates it and approves it, with or without amendments.

The amending powers of the legislature vary widely in different systems. In general, because the budget must remain coherent with the fiscal framework and established government policy, amendments are allowed but only to the extent that they do not cause changes in the basic fiscal targets (fiscal deficit, etc.) and thus offset an expenditure increase with a revenue increase or an expenditure cut somewhere else in the budget—an approach known in the United States as the "pay-as-you-go" rule.

Investment Programming and Aid Management

In developed countries, with their complex and advanced economy and primacy of private investment, there is no need for a national public investment program as such, and public investment decisions are made on a project-by-project basis—although guided by national policy and constrained by resource availability. The need for formal and detailed programming is primarily in developing countries, where public investment is critical for the profitability of private sector activity and for development and poverty reduction.

Preparing the Investment Budget

In developing countries, the annual investment budget should be based on a medium-term public investment program (PIP) consistent with both government policy and available resources. When badly prepared and implemented, a PIP becomes a wish list of projects or a shopping list for donor money and can harm the expenditure management process. However, a well-prepared PIP can improve the budgetary process as well as foster economic development and strengthen the recipient country's control over foreign aid. PIPs cover a three- to four-year period and are on a "rolling" basis (i.e., updated each year by adding a year at the end). Ideally, a strong PIP should:

- include only economically sound investment projects that are clearly related to government policy—procedures to prevent the birth of "white elephant" projects (costly and unproductive "prestige" investments) are especially important;
- cover all central government investment as well as investments by other public entities that are financed by the central government;
- stay within the ceilings set by the fiscal framework (although public investment should never be defined as a mere residual derived from the other fiscal and macroeconomic targets);
- include in the first year only projects for which financing is certain;
- assure that the budget includes adequate local funding complementary to public investment—funding problems are likely in any event, but they are a certainty if the aggregate budgetary provision for investment is insufficient;
- include in the out-years only projects for which financing is highly probable; and
- prevent overreliance on external expertise and foster systematic improvements in local capacity. If the PIP process becomes a mechanism for replacing local responsibility with expatriate experts, it will neither improve the budget process nor contribute to local capacity.

Aid Management in Developing Countries

In aid-dependent developing countries, all three objectives of government expenditure management require that the recipient government and not the donors should "drive" the allocation and use of aid funds—while respecting, of course, the procedural and fiduciary requirements of the donors concerned. Experience worldwide shows that there are several requirements for effective aid management. Among these, the following are essential:[13]

- External resources must be integrated with overall resource use, and thus included in the budget.
- There should be one, and only one, aid management entity (preferably in the ministry of finance) covering all external aid, including technical assistance.
- Aid management should be structured along donor lines (e.g., a US aid desk, a World Bank desk, etc.) rather than sectoral lines (e.g., a health assistance desk).
- The aid management entity should function to facilitate, not obstruct, and avoid interfering in ministries' budget proposals or project selection.

BUDGET EXECUTION

Objectives of Budget Execution

Budget execution is the phase when financial resources are used to implement the policies incorporated in the budget. The basic responsibility of the executive to—in the words of the U.S. president's oath of office—"take care that the laws are faithfully executed" encompasses the responsibility to assure that the budget is implemented as in the budget approved by the legislature. Unfortunately, while it is possible to implement a well-formulated budget, it is not possible to implement well a badly formulated budget.

There is no satisfactory way to correct during budget execution the defects of an unrealistic budget. If the numbers don't add up during budget preparation, they will not add up during budget execution. Thus, simply delaying payments erodes the credibility of government and generates a vicious circle of overbilling and underpaying. Across-the-board "sequestering" (temporary cancellation) of budget appropriations leads to inefficient dispersal of insufficient resources among an excessive number of activities. Selective sequestering combined with a mechanism to control commitments partly avoids these problems, but the spending agencies will still lack predictability and time to adjust their programs and commitments. Finally, cash rationing politicizes budget execution, enables corruption, and often substitutes suppliers' priorities for program priorities.[14]

However, good budget execution does not come down simply to ensuring compliance with the initial budget. It must also adapt to intervening changes and enable efficient operational management. Even with excellent forecasts, unexpected changes in the macroeconomic environment will occur during the year and will need to be reflected in the budget. "Taking care that the laws are faithfully executed" implies the responsibility to keep a close watch on developments and get back to the legislature on a timely basis for approval of changes that may have become necessary. This section reviews the basic elements of good budget execution—excluding payroll and personnel management and procurement, which are the subject of the next two chapters. (Again, recall that only the essential points can be summarized here and the interested reader is referred to the fuller treatments of the subject in specialized treatises.)

The Expenditure Cycle

Once the budget is adopted by the legislature, the expenditure cycle consists of the following phases:

- *Allocation of appropriations/release of funds to spending units*—in many countries, including the United States, this stage includes two steps: (1) "apportionment" by the central budget office, which consists of defining what part of the approved budget appropriation the spending ministries and agencies can use in a given period of the fiscal year; and (2) "allotment" by the spending ministries and agencies to their subordinate spending units.
- *Commitment*—a commitment consists of placing an order, awarding a contract, and so on, for goods to be received or services to be performed. It creates an obligation to pay, but only if and after the other party has complied with the provisions of the contract.
- *Verification*—at this stage, when goods are delivered and/or services are rendered, their conformity with the contract or order is verified.
- *Payment*—after verification that goods have been received or service performed, payments are made through checks, cash, electronic transfers, debt instruments, tax deductions, vouchers, or other means. E-transfers are becoming more and more common, although the majority of payments are still by check.[15] In most countries, payments are recorded at the time the checks are issued or the transfer ordered, rather than the time when they are received or credited to the recipient's account. Payment arrears are defined as the difference between expenditures due at the verification stage and actual payments.

Assuring Compliance

The basic compliance and control mechanisms during budget execution are as follows:

- At the commitment stage, *financial control* is necessary to verify that the proposal to spend money has been approved by an authorized person, money has been appropriated for the purpose in the budget and sufficient funds remain available in the proper category of expenditure, and the expenditure is proposed under the correct category.
- At the verification stage, *documentary and physical control* ascertains that the goods have been received and that the service was actually performed and physical spot-checks are made.
- At the payment stage, *accounting control* is necessary to confirm that:

  - a valid obligation exists;
  - an authorized person has verified that the goods have been received or the service performed as expected;
  - the invoice and other documents requesting payment are correct and suitable for payment; and
  - the creditor is correctly identified.

- After payment is made, *audit* is necessary to examine and scrutinize expenditures and report any irregularity.

Various technical requirements that must be met for good budget execution and financial control—release of funds, carryovers and virements, cash and debt management, monitoring and financial control, and accounting and reporting—are described in Appendix 6.2.

MANAGEMENT CONTROLS, AUDIT, AND EVALUATION

Management Controls and Internal Audit

Management controls (also called "internal controls") are the policies and procedures put in place by the managers of an entity to ensure its proper and effective operation. There are many kinds of management controls. Developing an effective system of controls first requires a careful assessment of the risks facing the organization. Policies and procedures can then be selected to control those risks effectively and at reasonable cost.

Management controls are a basic responsibility of any manager. To be effective, the management control system must have the strong support of the entity's leadership. Policies and procedures must be observed consistently throughout the organization. Irregularities revealed by the control system must bring prompt and effective corrective action. To assure the continued effectiveness of the system, both the risks facing the organization and the control system itself must be reassessed frequently.

No system of controls can provide an absolute guarantee against fraud, abuse, inefficiency, and human error. However, a well-designed system of controls can give reasonable assurance that significant irregularities will be detected. At the same time, even well-designed controls can be defeated by collusion, especially if that collusion involves senior executives who have the power to disarm or bypass the control system. Thus, as stressed in chapter 10, effective accountability requires appropriate *external* feedback and "voice."

Internal audit is part of an organization's management control structure. The most important functions of internal audit are to test the management controls themselves and assist senior managers in assessing risks and developing more effective control systems. The obvious corollary is that internal auditors are responsible to the head of the agency, and not to any outside entity such as the ministry of finance. By contrast, external audit must be exercised by an independent external entity.

External Audit

"Doveriay, no proveriay. . ." "Trust, but verify" was the motto so liked by Ronald Reagan—which actually originated with Vladimir Lenin. This basic principle has been understood for centuries. Two millennia ago, Aristotle stated the essential requirement for financial integrity crisply: "Some officials handle large sums of money: it is therefore necessary to have other officials to receive and examine the accounts. These inspectors must administer no funds themselves . . . call them inspectors or auditors." In public expenditure management, *there cannot be efficiency without trust, or integrity without verification.*

External audit of government operations is typically performed by a "supreme audit institution" (SAI), normally independent of the executive branch of government and reporting its findings to the legislature, as well as to the audited agency itself. There are two basic organizational models of a SAI: the "office" model, headed by an "auditor general" (typical of British Commonwealth countries), and the "tribunal" model, in which the auditors have the status of judges (as in France and Italy). Combinations of these two basic models are also seen in some countries.

SAIs may perform several types of audits, including audits of compliance with the regulations, financial audits, and "value-for-money" (efficiency) audits. The appropriate emphasis of external audit depends on the particular circumstances of each country. Weak governance and accountability require a concentration on compliance and financial audit. In developed countries, external audit should look more and more into efficiency and effectiveness issues, but never loosen up on the essential function to verify that public money has not been stolen or misallocated to purposes other than those approved by the legislature.

Whatever the focus of activity, the effectiveness of external audit demands that the SAI, *by law*:

- be legally independent of the executive branch of government;
- report, publicly, to the legislative branch of government;
- have unrestricted access to required information;
- control its own budget;
- be fully autonomous, including in personnel management matters; and
- have sufficient capacity, skills, and professionalism.

Evaluation

Just as external audit closes the legitimacy loop, so does good evaluation close the programming loop by feeding into the preparation of the next budget relevant information concerning the execution of the previous one. Public financial resources are supposed to be spent for certain economic or social purposes and evaluation of the results of public spending is important both for accountability and to improve the quality of expenditure over time. The important subjects of monitoring, evaluation, and performance are discussed in chapter 10.

THE SITUATION IN THE UNITED STATES

Fiscal Developments

Overall Fiscal Trends

The U.S. federal government spent an average of $17 million a year from 1789 to 1849, and $290 million a year from 1850 to 1900. In the six years 2001–6, average *yearly* expenditure was $2,514,072 million—more than two-and-a-half *trillion* dollars, or 170 times the annual average during the nineteenth century. We give these figures for their shock value only, as they are not meaningfully comparable for various reasons, including the vast expansion of U.S. population, price increases, and the enormous differences in the composition of national production and consumption. The comparison does point clearly, however, the substantial expansion in the role of the federal government since the early days of the republic.

A much more relevant comparison over a more meaningful period of time is provided by federal revenues and expenditures as a percentage of gross domestic product (GDP, defined as the net value of goods and services produced in a year) over the last seventy-five years. In 1930, before the full impact of the Great Depression, the federal government was running a modest surplus, with revenues of just 4.2 percent of GDP and expenditures of 3.4 percent. By 1935, at the peak of the Great Depression, the spending necessary to get out of the economic crisis had risen to 9.2 percent of GDP, and the government was running a large deficit of 4 percent of GDP. Recall, as explained earlier, that it is appropriate for a government to run a fiscal deficit in bad economic times and a fiscal surplus in boom times. Ideally, the government budget should be in balance only as it goes from appropriate overspending to appropriate underspending, and vice versa. (If you lose your job, you will normally go through a period when you spend more than you earn;

if you get a better-paid job, it is wise to increase your spending by less than the entirety of the salary increase.)

The somewhat lower deficit of 3 percent of GDP in 1940, before the start of World War II, was quickly superseded by the need to finance military operations, and by the end of the war federal spending had risen to well over 40 percent of GDP. The fiscal deficit rose much less, however, to a peak of 23 percent in 1944, owing to the substantial increase in taxes and other revenues required to help pay for the war. Federal revenue rose from 7 percent of GDP before the war to a historical high of 21 percent, which has not been reached since. Following two decades of approximately balanced budgets in the 1950s and 1960s, significant fiscal deficits reappeared in the 1970s and 1980s, and fiscal health was not restored until the mid-1990s. The last six years have seen a reappearance of large fiscal imbalances. Table 6.2 summarizes these fiscal developments.

Trends in the Composition of Revenue and Expenditure

The composition of revenues and expenditure is shown in Tables 6.3 and 6.4.

The Revenue Side. Contrary to popular misconception, the individual income tax makes up less than half of total federal receipts and is barely higher than the taxes paid for Social Security and Medicare. Clearly, when discussing the "tax burden" and the groups on whom it falls most heavily, it is essential to look at *all* taxes and not only income taxes.

While, for example, the $1,044 billion paid in individual income taxes in 2006 naturally affected higher-income persons to a greater extent, the $837 billion in Social Security and Medicare taxes were borne mostly by low- and middle-income persons. The relative share of total revenue accounted for by the income tax and the payroll taxes has changed significantly from the start of this century, with the share of individual income tax declining from 48 percent to 43 percent, and the share of payroll taxes rising from 32 percent to 35 percent—thus shifting the overall tax burden to low- and middle-income persons. For a proper comparison, however, one would also need to take into account the distribution of taxes paid at state and local levels, including sales and real estate taxes. Finally, a full understanding of the relative impact of government activity on people in different income groups would require taking into account the distribution of the benefits from public expenditure as well, not just the distribution of the burden of taxes. For example, certain subsidies and welfare expenditures benefit poorer people disproportionately; other subsidies instead accrue largely to wealthy corporations and individuals; and the benefits of public safety are naturally most important for persons with valuable assets to protect.

The Expenditure Side. The largest share of federal government spending is on "human resources," mainly owing to the "entitlements" of Social Security and Medicare expenses, which account for half of the human resources expenditure. The next two largest categories of spending are defense and interest payments, which together account for more than a quarter of the total expenditure. By far the most significant development over the last thirty years has been the increase in Social Security and Medicare expenditures, which rose from under 20 percent of total spending in the late 1960s to around 25 percent in the 1980s and over 33 percent in 2006. More worrisome still are the projections of continued expenditure increases, driven mainly by the longer life expectancy of Americans and the lack of any meaningful government influence on the medical costs paid for by the taxpayers.

This is not the place for a discussion of these highly complex and politically difficult issues. It is worth emphasizing, however, that the financial situation of Social Security is comparatively manage-

Table 6.2

Revenues, Expenditures, and Fiscal Balance of the United States, 1940–2005
(in US$ billions at constant 1996 prices and percentage of GDP)

Fiscal year	In constant 1996 dollars			As percentage of GDP		
	Revenue	Expenditure	Balance	Revenue	Expenditure	Balance
1940	65	94	−29	6.8	9.8	−3.0
1944	362	755	−393	20.9	43.7	−22.8
1948	305	219	87	16.2	11.6	6.6
1952	473	484	−11	19.0	19.4	−0.4
1956	450	426	84	16.6	17.3	−0.8
1960	495	493	2	17.8	17.8	0.1
1964	556	585	−29	17.6	18.5	−0.9
1968	669	779	−110	17.6	20.5	−2.9
1972	711	792	−80	17.5	19.5	−2.0
1976	760	948	−188	17.2	21.4	−4.2
1980	956	1,093	−137	18.9	21.6	−2.7
1984	950	1,215	−264	17.4	22.2	−4.8
1988	1,154	1,351	−197	18.1	21.2	−3.1
1992	1,197	1,515	−318	17.5	22.2	−4.7
1996	1,453	1,561	−108	18.9	20.3	−1.4
2000	1,880	1,661	220	20.8	18.4	2.4
2004	1,656	1,920	−264	17.0	19.7	−2.7
2005	2,025	2,324	−299	17.5	20.1	−2.6

Source: Excerpted from Office of Management and Budget, Historical Tables, Budget of the U.S. Government. Available at www.gpoaccess.gov/usbudget.

Table 6.3

Composition of Revenue of the United States, 1940–2005
(in percentage of total revenue)

Fiscal year	Individual income tax	Corporate income tax	Social sec & retirement taxes	Excise taxes & fees	Customs & other receipts
1940	13	17	26	29	15
1950	40	26	11	19	4
1960	44	23	16	13	4
1970	47	17	23	8	5
1980	47	13	30	5	5
1990	45	9	37	3	6
2000	50	10	32	3	5
2005	44	10	38	3	5

Table 6.4

Composition of Expenditure of the United States, 1940–2005
(in percentage of total expenditure)

Fiscal year	Defense	Human resources	Physical resources	Net interest	Other functions*
1940	18	44	24	10	4
1950	32	33	9	11	15
1960	52	28	9	8	3
1970	42	39	8	7	5
1980	23	53	11	7	5
1990	24	49	10	15	2
2000	17	62	5	13	3
2005	18	66	5	9	2

*Includes offsetting receipts.

able, and its longer-term sustainability can be improved in a number of ways without changing the basic system—let alone destroying it. The precarious financial state of Medicare, aggravated by the unacceptable situation that 47 million Americans lack any medical insurance, is a greater and more urgent problem, which will necessarily call for measures on both the demand and the cost side. The only certainty about the current health care system is that when the government pays for the medical care without exercising any control over its costs, the costs of medical care will continue to rise.

In any event, the reader is encouraged to peruse the revenue and expenditure data in Tables 6.3 and 6.4, as they reflect—directly or indirectly—what the American people have wanted their government to do in the last sixty-five years and whom to charge for it.

The Budget Process in the United States[16]

Moving on to the instrumental aspects of the budgeting system in the United States, the obligatory starting point is the Constitution. Article 1, dealing with the powers of Congress, prescribes specifically, among other things, that "the Congress shall have power to lay and collect taxes, duties, imposts and excises, to pay the debts . . . No money shall be drawn from the treasury, but in consequence of appropriations made by law; and a regular statement and account of receipts and expenditures of all public money shall be published from time to time." Because of the extensive authority given to the president and the framers' core concern with preventing undue expansion of executive power, giving to the legislature this so-called "power of the purse" was seen—and proved to be—an essential component of the system of checks and balances envisaged in the Constitution.

The Budget Timetable

Beyond the broad grant of budget authority to Congress, the Constitution contains no provision on how to structure the budget system. Virtually all aspects of the current U.S. budgeting system have emerged through history for practical reasons and as separate laws. The main foundations of the current system were laid with the Budget and Accounting Act of 1921, which established the Bureau of the Budget in the Treasury Department, and the 1974 Budget Act. Although the current U.S. budgeting system has unique characteristics befitting its particular variant of a presidential system of government, it does meet the broad principles and general requirements for good budget preparation described earlier in this chapter. Whether actual budget preparation has been consistent with those sound principles and requirements is an entirely different matter, however, which has depended throughout history largely on the responsibility and integrity of both the executive and the congressional leadership of the time.

The budget preparation process is formally kicked off in February by the budget proposal by the president—even though the Constitution does not require the president to submit an annual budget. In reality, budget preparation starts the previous July, with the instruction from the White House Office of Management and Budget (OMB) to the various federal agencies to submit their budget requests, which are eventually assembled in the president's budget proposal. The conclusion of the budget preparation process is the approval by Congress of the report of the joint House–Senate "conference" reconciling the differences between the House and Senate versions of the budget and producing a single bill. As all other legislation, the budget bill does not become law until signed by the president or, if vetoed, until Congressional overturning of the veto by a two-thirds vote.

The budget timetable is shown in Box 6.3 and its stages are briefly described subsequently.

Although it appears that the formal U.S. budget cycle encompasses a total of eight months— consistent with the period of time normally required for budget preparation in most developed countries—most of the process is in effect collapsed within five months. However, the dates are flexible guidelines rather than deadlines and allow for accommodating the legislative scheduling priorities of the House and the Senate. Also, the substantial amount of time dedicated by OMB to prepare the president's budget proposal permits resolving a number of important technical and analytical issues before the budget proposal reaches Congress. Altogether, the time available for budget preparation, consideration, debate, and approval is an ample fourteen months. Delays are rarely due to technical reasons, but stem from political disagreements—between the president and Congress and/or between House and Senate—that may take a long time to resolve. If the budget is not approved by the start of the fiscal year on October 1, Congress takes up a "continuing resolution," which allows the government to continue functioning by spending at the same monthly rate as in the previous year until a final budget can be approved.

The Major Stages

The *president's budget* is a detailed outline of the executive branch's policy priorities and associated financing needs, as well as a presentation of its general outlook on the economy. The budget

BOX 6.3

Timetable of the Budget Process in the United States

First Monday of February	President submits his budget (usually the date for the State of the Union address to Congress)
February 15	Congressional Budget Office submits report to the House and Senate budget committees
Within six weeks	Budget committees submit their views and estimates
April 1	Budget committees report "budget resolution"
April 15	Congress acts on the "concurrent budget resolution"
May 15	Appropriations committees consider the annual appropriations bills
June 10	Appropriations committees report appropriation bills
June 15	Congress acts on "reconciliation" legislation
June 30	House and Senate complete action on annual appropriation bills
Before October 1	Following "conference committees," House and Senate approve an identical budget bill and send to the president for approval and signature.
October 1	Fiscal year begins

is compiled by the Office of Management and Budget, based on inputs from the various federal departments and agencies, and is broken down into twenty functional spending categories (which are in turn grouped into the five broad designations of national defense, human resources, physical resources, net interest, and "other").

Although Congress is not bound by the president's budget, it naturally takes it as the starting point for its own deliberations. The House and Senate budget committees hold *hearings* on the proposed budget, to obtain the views and advice of the administration, members of Congress, and experts. The *"markup"* phase follows, during which each budget committee makes amendments and changes in the starting budget.

On this basis, the Senate and House budget committees report their *budget resolution*, which, after approval by the full House and Senate, sets the overall spending limit for the coming fiscal year, as well as the projections of revenue, spending, and fiscal deficits for the subsequent four years and a statement on total federal debt. As per Article 1 of the Constitution, the debt ceiling for the government is set by Congress and its authorization is required—and routinely given—to increase that ceiling. At the start of 2007, the national debt was $8.7 trillion, or about $30,000 for each man, woman, and child in the country.[17]

The budget resolution thus corresponds to the medium-term fiscal perspective discussed earlier in the chapter and provides the framework for the detailed consideration of expenditure and revenue legislation to follow. Because it encompasses projections for future years, the budget resolution is not and cannot be legally binding, and thus does not have to be signed by the president. The budget resolution is expected, however, to provide a robust frame and set the expenditure ceilings for the annual budget decisions. (Whether in practice the ceilings are respected or not depends on the congressional leadership at the time.) If the revenue and expenditure levels in the budget resolution require changes in some laws, the resolution will also contain instructions to the various committees to recommend such changes.

In May, based on the allocation in the budget resolution, the relevant committees of the House and Senate then consider the thirteen annual *appropriations bills* for the coming fiscal year. Each of these bills proceeds through the same hearings and markup process as precede the overall budget resolution and, after committee approval, it is sent to the two budget committees of the House and Senate to be assembled into an "omnibus" (i.e., comprehensive) package, which is then submitted to the full House and Senate for approval. By end-June, both House and Senate are expected to have acted on the appropriations bills and thus to have assembled a complete draft budget for the coming fiscal year.

Inevitably, there are differences between the House and Senate versions of the draft budget. For the purpose of ironing out those differences, which are sometimes major, and to arrive at a single budget, *conference committees* are established, with joint House–Senate membership and (in principle) bipartisan participation.[18] It is at this stage, which is not open to the public, that most of the horse trading takes place—constructive compromises as well as corrupt deals, including the stealth insertion of the wasteful expenditure "earmarks" discussed at the end of this section.

The joint conference report is then submitted for House and Senate approval, following which it is submitted for the president's signature, upon which the budget bill becomes law and is strictly binding for the revenue and expenditure operations of the fiscal year beginning October 1.

Limited Congressional Debate and Amendments

Congress has a general rule to prohibit adding to any bill provisions unrelated to its subject. However, because there is no hard-and-fast criterion to decide whether a provision is or is not germane to the subject of the legislation, observance of this rule has been contingent on the political balance of power and extraneous amendments are added to pending legislation all the time. The prohibition is much stronger for the budget bill, however. To prevent the budget (and thus the functioning of the entire government) from being used as hostage to push unrelated agendas, both the House and Senate prohibit consideration of amendments that are not germane to the budget, introduce "extraneous" matters, or cause the fiscal deficit to increase (the "Byrd Rule").[19] Such a rule can only be waived in the Senate by a three-fifths vote. Moreover, by the Budget Act of 1974 the time for debate is limited and the bill cannot be subject to "filibuster"—preventing a vote by extended debate that can only be "clotured" (cut off) by a three-fifths vote.

The Budget Process at State Level

It is not possible to summarize the different budgeting practices of the fifty states. The principal difference from the federal government is that all states, directly or indirectly, are precluded from running a budget deficit for any sustained period of time. Many have a balanced budget provision in their constitution, but all states—unable to print money and conscious that the federal government will not bail them out if they get into serious fiscal trouble for reasons other than a genuine emergency—must follow a balanced-budget policy de facto.

The political structure of most states parallels the federal structure and so does the budgeting process. Budgets are proposed by the executive (the governor) and must be approved by both the state house of representatives (whatever name is given to it) and the state senate. Differences between the house and the senate are discussed and resolved in a conference committee. After legislative approval, the budget becomes law when approved by the governor.

States do confront special problems, however:[20]

- A timing dilemma—good budgeting requires a reliable forecast of revenue and sufficient preparation time, but transfers from the federal government are not known at the start of the process.
- Reduced budgeting flexibility—constraints from the center include restrictions on the use of transfers as well as "unfunded mandates" (i.e., assignment to the states of certain responsibilities or procedures without the resources needed to implement them).
- High transaction costs—states have the obligation to report in detail about numerous conditions of central transfers and, in some cases, inconsistency between federal and state investment programs or discontinuities in the execution of investment projects or in the timing of federal financing.

As a result, the timetables of budget preparation and the responsibilities of committees of the legislature show some differences from federal budget practice. Box 6.4 illustrates the process in Virginia.

Some Major Contemporary Budget Issues

Financing Wars

The policy of raising revenue to finance a war effort is reflected throughout the entire history of the country through the end of the twentieth century. Federal revenue:

- increased six-fold between the start and the end of World War I;
- increased three-fold, from 7 percent to 21 percent of GDP, between the start and the end of World War II;
- was raised from 14 percent to 19 percent of GDP between the start and the end of the war in Korea; and
- was raised from 17.5 percent before the war in Vietnam to about 19 percent of GDP in the heaviest Vietnam conflict years—still a significant though smaller increase owing to President Lyndon Johnson's fanciful claim that America could have both "guns" and "butter" (i.e., could fight both the war in Vietnam and the War on Poverty, a claim that contributed to producing inflation in the 1970s).

This history should be compared with the fiscal developments since the attacks of September 11, 2001, when the wars in Afghanistan and Iraq were accompanied by *cuts* in income, dividend, capital gains, and estate taxes[21] producing a *decline* in federal revenue from about 20 percent to an average of 17.5 percent of GDP. The inevitable arithmetical result was a jumbo deterioration of the fiscal accounts, from a surplus of $236 billion in 2000 to a deficit of $248 billion in 2006 (in current dollars). A deliberate policy of massive tax reduction during wartime is a first in America and is unknown in any country in world history.

Moreover, since the start of the Iraq war in 2003, the administration funded the war by "emer-

BOX 6.4

The Budget Process at State Level: The Example of Virginia

The legislature of the commonwealth of Virginia comprises a House of Delegates and a Senate. Similar to the federal Congress, it has the "power of the purse," with the ability to initiate tax and spending proposals and the authority to approve the state budget. In Virginia, budget proposals follow the same legislative itinerary as all other proposals for legislative action. Proposals for a bill may originate from a member of either the House of Delegates or the Senate, frequently as a result of constituent requests. The various steps are, in sequence, as follows:

- The proposal is presented in general terms to the Division of Legislative Services to draft it in the proper form of a bill, which is then signed and introduced by the sponsor.
- The bill is referred to the appropriate committee, which holds public hearings and decides whether or not to send it to the entire House (or Senate).
- If the committee's action is favorable, the bill is printed in the legislative calendar, to be considered by the House (or Senate) on "first reading." (Bills are considered in the order in which they appear on the calendar.)
- The next day, the bill appears on the calendar for "second reading." This is the stage at which it is debated and may be amended.
- If the bill is approved, with or without amendments, it is termed "engrossed" and again appears on the calendar for "third (and final) reading," at which it either passes or fails.
- If passed, the bill is "communicated" to the other body (Senate or House), where it goes through the same procedure.
- If the other body amends it and the house of origin does not agree with the amendment, a "conference committee" of three members from each body is formed to resolve the difference.
- When the agreed-upon bill is passed in identical form by both the House and the Senate, it is printed as an "enrolled" bill and sent to the governor by the presiding officers of the House and Senate.
- If the governor approves, s/he signs the bill, which becomes law effective on the subsequent July 1.

Source: Adapted from Virginia General Assembly Citizens' Guide; see the Assembly website http://legis.state.va.us

gency spending" and "supplemental requests," rather than including the cost in the annual budget. While this practice is understandable for 2003 and possibly for fiscal year 2004, by the middle of 2004 it was obvious that the war and its costs would continue. Elementary fiscal transparency demands that these costs (rising to $190 billion in fiscal year 2008) should be included in the regular budget process instead of a "shadow budget,"[22] which interferes with congressional oversight and distorts the country's true fiscal picture.

Among the adjectives to describe such fiscal policy and practices, the word "conservative" does not come to mind, regardless of one's views of the war in Iraq.

Fiscal Deficits and the Future of the United States

Advocates of the Bush tax cuts argue that the income, dividends, and estate tax cuts helped fuel the recovery from the post-2000 recession because the increase in after-tax income stimulated aggregate demand (i.e., the total spending on consumption and investment) and thus national production and employment. This is certainly true. However:

- A larger economic stimulus would have been provided by cutting payroll taxes instead of taxes on income and assets, to the benefit of those deriving most of their income from work. This is because persons deriving most of their income from work have a lower income and thus a higher propensity to spend. Moreover, a cut in payroll taxes would have spurred job creation and supported real wages, by reducing the cost of labor to the employers. To that extent, it would also have partly counteracted the downward pressure on wages exerted from globalization.
- The massive increases in government spending during the same years had an even greater effect on aggregate demand than the tax cuts. Unlike tax cuts, a portion of which go into savings, the entirety of additional government spending adds to aggregate demand.
- Finally, the sharp decrease in interest rates engineered by the Federal Reserve probably had a more important positive impact than either tax cuts or expenditure increases—especially through the wealth effect associated with the real estate boom.

The long-term issue, however, goes well beyond the transitional impact of either tax cuts or spending increases on aggregate demand and national production, or even the massive increase in income inequality—unparalleled since the "robber barons" age of the late 1800s. The long-term issue revolves around two items: (1) the efficiency of the increased government spending, in terms of adding to the economy's productive *potential*; and (2) the long-term fiscal health of the U.S. economy.

Regarding efficiency, it is highly dubious that the additional spending of the last few years has raised the economy's productive potential spending as war expenditure typically has a limited impact on civilian productivity; enormous waste, fraud, and abuse are known to have been associated with Iraq reconstruction and homeland security expenditures; and "pork-barrel" spending (discussed later) has little impact on productivity.

Regarding the fiscal impact, the country's fiscal health has been crippled for at least a generation by the massive deficits accumulated after 2000, the related burden of servicing the national debt, and the resulting disappearance of the fiscal headroom needed to address critical infrastructural and social needs in future years.

To return to the household analogy, if you choose to cut your earnings while spending a lot more on unproductive pursuits and accumulating new debt, more and more of your future income will go to repay credit cards; your kids' college fund will evaporate; your home will deteriorate for lack of necessary maintenance; your economic standing will diminish relative to your neighbors; and your economic future will be jeopardized. If, as economists say, "there is no such thing as a free lunch," there is certainly no such thing as a free war. Or two.

Still, despite the lasting damage to the American economic future, there are ways to gradually return to fiscal sanity in the years to come. Starting from the radical notion that "a deficit reduction plan should reduce the deficit," the Concord Coalition—a prestigious bipartisan group advocating fiscal responsibility—set out three basic rules for redressing the huge fiscal imbalance in the United States (see Box 6.5).

BOX 6.5

Three Basic Rules for Deficit Reduction

"Put everything on the table: If everyone insists on only cutting someone else's priorities, talk about deficit reduction will remain just that. The best way to end the standoff is to agree on the common goals of deficit reduction, put everything on the table—including entitlement cuts and tax increases—and negotiate the necessary tradeoffs." Deficit reduction must be real (i.e., avoid accounting gimmicks) and the process must be legitimate and thus sustainable (i.e., confronting honestly the tough choices and make the necessary tradeoffs). One needs to identify and confront the opportunity costs of different options.

"Share the sacrifice: The burden of deficit reduction should be distributed fairly. It is not fair, fiscally responsible, or politically viable to make cutbacks in limited areas of the budget while exempting most areas from scrutiny. Those who can more readily shoulder the burden should be asked to do so." Quite to the contrary, fiscal policy in 2001–07 has reduced the relative tax burden on the richest one percent, while at the same time altering the expenditure pattern in ways that have curtailed per capita expenditure in real terms on programs that benefit lower-income Americans. Regulatory changes have gone in the same direction as well.

"Implement pay-as-you-go rules and budget caps: These rules, which Congress and the president enacted in 1990 [under the Republican administration of George H.W. Bush] and extended in 1997 [under the Democratic administration of Bill Clinton], were a critical part of getting a handle on the deficit in the 1990s. Anyone who proposes a spending increase or tax cut, including the extension of expiring tax cuts, should answer the question: 'How do we pay for it?'" Congress chose to disregard the "pay-go" rules after 2001, but restored them in 2007.

Source: The *Concord Coalition,* full-page ad in the *New York Times Week in Review,* December 11, 2005.

Abusing the Taxpayers' Money

If, alongside the increase in expenditure, its quality had improved—or even remained the same—the debate would revolve only around issues of policy. Regrettably, fiscal management has deteriorated in recent years and the quality of public expenditure along with it. A larger proportion of government spending has been misallocated to unjustified subsidies (e.g., subsidies to large agribusinesses, giving "earthquake damage" compensation to producers who actually suffered no earthquake damage, etc.), to new open-ended entitlements of dubious comparative value (e.g., the prescription drugs benefit), or simply wasted in patronage projects approved entirely to satisfy the demands of powerful political barons and without any review of their economic or social benefits. These projects go under the appropriate name of "pork"—from the pork barrel that used to be a fixture of country fairs or picnics, open to all invitees to grab tasty snacks for themselves. The growth of pork-barrel spending is the most egregious aspect of the degradation of fiscal management in recent years.

In U.S. budgetary lingo, the official name for "pork" is "earmarks" (not to be confused with the general issue of revenue earmarking discussed earlier). These are the special expenditure provisions designed by and for individual members of Congress to benefit their district (or powerful constituents). At best, they bolster their political support by providing marginal local benefits and, at worst, provide opportunities for corrupt payoffs. Such "earmarks" are totally contrary to good budgeting practices, and—because they take place in the dark and as part of complex trade-offs of political favors—are incompatible with the fundamental principles of good governance and fiscal transparency.

For these reasons, the practice was banned by the House of Representatives a hundred years ago. However, it crept back up in the early 1980s shortly after the election of Ronald Reagan and grew dramatically since 2000, as summarized in Box 6.6.

Until 2007, the congressional leadership, despite much breast-beating and lip service paid to the inappropriateness and risks of earmarks, did nothing to limit them—quite the contrary. The 2005 budget resolution (which, as we have seen, is supposed to frame the annual budget) has an especially fustian provision in this regard: ". . . committees should *consider* not funding those [earmarks] *most egregiously inconsistent* with national policy" (Section 631; italics inserted). This obviously implies that after such "consideration," committees are entitled to give away taxpayers' money to activities most egregiously inconsistent with national policy; and, they don't even need to "consider" turning down requests that are "not so egregiously" inconsistent with national policy. It is hard to imagine a more irresponsible budget "instruction": think of a parent who suggests to his teenage son that he may consider the possibility of stopping his use of the most dangerous illegal drugs.

As the only response to the public outcry about earmarks, in September 2006 the House voted to require identification of members of Congress who slip "special projects" into the budget. Even this cosmetic change was temporary, subject to ratification after the mid-term elections of November 2006. Such contempt for the taxpayers' money and lack of basic fiscal discipline did not augur well for a return to earlier well-established standards of integrity and efficiency in the U.S. budget system. However, after the 2006 elections, the new Congress established rules to limit earmarks and foster transparency. Although the rules did not far enough, they make it politically riskier for Congress members to push new pork-barrel spending and are a major step toward fiscal transparency and restraining this scandalous practice.

GENERAL DIRECTIONS OF IMPROVEMENT

The priorities in this area differ substantially between developed and developing countries. In developed countries, the primary direction of reform is to assure that the management of public

BOX 6.6

"Pork" in the United States and the Philippines

For decades, there had been no "earmarks" in the U.S. budget, until the 1982 budget which included ten specific earmarks. The number grew to over 500 in 1991, exploded in 2005 to a phenomenal 14,000 "projects," and in the 2006 budget, while the number of earmarks declined to about 12,000, the total expenditure more than doubled, to $64 billion. This is equivalent on average to *twenty-five* projects and $150 million per each House member, with well-connected legislators reaping far greater booty (Alaska's Senator Ted Stevens is the undisputed Earmarks King). The most egregious example is the "Bridge to Nowhere," from the Alaskan town of Ketchikan to an island with fifty inhabitants—$223 million of taxpayers' money to make it more convenient for local congressman Young to get to the airport and to allow naming the bridge after him. The Bridge to Nowhere was finally deleted from the budget in 2007. But smaller earmarks can be equally bizarre, e.g., the allocation of one million dollars for a museum to the 1968 Woodstock rock festival.

It is particularly worrisome that one third of the earmarks in the transportation bill were added after the bill had been drafted in the House—showing the extent of under-the-table horse trading and lack of transparency of the process. Predictably, congressmen argue that their pork barrel projects only correct the "errors" in the national agencies' budgets, which do not know the needs of their particular constituencies. But consider that:

- neither the public nor Congress as a whole has any idea whatsoever of what projects are included in the bill before it is voted upon because they are typically slipped in at the last minute and without debate;
- the only certainty about the process is that none of these projects was subject to normal cost-benefit scrutiny; and
- "pork" in the 2005 budget totaled over $27 billion. This amount is about the same as the federal government spent on food and nutrition assistance and on housing assistance, and twice as much as it spent on financial assistance to college students. (To put it differently, if pork-barrel projects were eliminated, the savings would allow giving financial aid to three times as many college students.)

The practice of earmarks is fiscally scandalous and toxic to good governance. At least on this score, today's budgeting practice in the United States is far worse than before World War I. It is also worse than in a developing country whose formal budgeting system is modeled after the United States—the Philippines. Members of the Philippines Congress have drawn on pork-barrel funds to finance economic and social projects in their home districts. These include mainly the congressmen's Countrywide Development Fund and the Congressional Initiative Allocations (CIAs). The CIAs are congressional changes of the budget submitted by the president and are closest in nature to U.S. earmarks. Their amount is neither fixed nor centralized under one appropriations item but is spread across agencies, and the allocation per legislator depends on the budget of a particular agency. Since 1999, steps have been taken for an agreement between the legislature and the executive to limit the use of pork-barrel funds and promote greater participation and transparency in budgeting. Despite the Philippines' severe governance weaknesses, the problem has been declining to some extent, unlike the recent mushrooming of earmarks in the U.S. budget.

expenditure is strictly in conformity with the law and fully meets the basic requirements of fiscal transparency, accountability, and appropriate participation in the making of expenditure decisions and in their execution—within an overall context of fiscal responsibility and a long-term outlook. Although many countries exhibit some weakness in one or another aspect of the budgeting system, the most glaring example of a violation of these principles is the aforementioned explosion of budget earmarks in the United States—opaque, against the spirit of budget rules, unaccountable, and with no public scrutiny whatever. Accordingly, the single most important reform in the United States would be a flat prohibition by law of *all* earmarks. Like any addiction, the only measure certain to be effective is total abstention. Short of that, much can be achieved by publication of all bills in their final form several days before they are to be voted on—as proposed in 2006 by Rep. Brian Baird of (D-Washington). (Other measures for greater transparency can also be helpful, as discussed in chapter 13.) A significant first reduction in earmarks was achieved in 2007.

The following set of suggestions applies primarily to developing countries, but is also a useful checklist for the periodic reexamination of expenditure management procedures that is advisable even in highly developed countries.

Core Principles of Reform

The approach to improving central government budgeting should be pragmatic, providing a menu of options rather than single "best-practice" models. However, experience suggests for developing countries five practical rules for improving public expenditure management:

- The basics of expenditure management need to be firmly in place before highly sophisticated concepts of budget management can be considered.
- Reform must raise the country's own capacity to manage its public expenditure and not rely on improvements designed and implemented primarily by expatriate specialists.
- Similarly, budgeting improvements cannot last if they are imposed top-down by the central ministry of finance with little involvement or low implementation capacity of the sector ministries.
- The record of actual success or failure of the measure being recommended must be carefully assessed, by obtaining independent feedback from other countries that have experimented with it.
- The annual budgeting decisions must take into account their probable future impact.

Improving Budget Preparation

Priority actions in this phase of expenditure management are a reasonably comprehensive budget coverage, disclosure of policies that have an immediate or future fiscal impact (e.g., contingent liabilities), and a good expenditure classification. In addition, line-item cash budgeting must be established on a solid basis before considering a move to other budgeting systems. Hard expenditure ceilings flowing from a consistent macroeconomic framework are essential at the start of the budget preparation process to give the line ministries the predictability needed to design their expenditure programs, in conformity with government sector policy, and thus eventually hold them accountable for results.

To take into account the future impact of budget decisions, a multiyear expenditure perspective is necessary but should be developed gradually, begin with preparing broad medium-term estimates by function and broad economic category, and review the forward costs of major programs. Because in developing countries public investment is the largest category of expenditure with medium- and long-term fiscal and economic implications, a strong and realistic public investment program should be the first major building block of an eventual comprehensive medium-term expenditure framework. In addition, preparing a full sector expenditure program for one or two key sectors, including both capital and current expenditure, can yield useful experience in multiyear programming.

Improving Budget Execution

Improvements in execution generally entail enhanced expenditure control, improved efficiency, and better cash management. In turn, expenditure control results mainly from timely and predictable release of funds, effective controls and monitoring at each stage of the expenditure cycle, clear procedures for registering commitments, and sound and enforced procedures for procurement. Improvements in efficiency call for flexible rules for transfers between budget items, some carryover of authorized spending to the next year; and progressive decentralization of controls (but in parallel with a reinforcement of audit and financial reporting). Finally, priority actions for better cash management include realistic cash planning consistent with the budgeted expenditure, centralization of cash balances (not necessarily of actual payments), and timely tracking of government borrowings and repayments.

Accounting and Audit

The priority in accounting is to establish solid cash accounting and consolidate the operations of extra-budgetary funds. Important complementary actions are a commitment register, accrual accounting for debt, and the recording of contingent liabilities. At a later stage, improvements could include the recognition of all financial assets and liabilities and, possibly, the compilation of asset registers—but limited to the assets that are both very valuable and "at risk." A move to full accrual accounting should not be considered until the previous steps are firmly in place (except for public enterprises, where accrual accounting is essential). Indeed, for developing countries, the expected benefits from introduction of accrual accounting are far lower than the costs of doing so. Similarly, in audit, all resources should be concentrated on the basic priority of strong financial and compliance audit. Only after that may efficiency (value-for-money) audits be considered, and even then on a pilot basis to gain the requisite experience.

QUESTIONS FOR DISCUSSION

1. The text makes reference to the fallacy of composition—assuming that what is true of a part is necessarily true of the whole (e.g., if you stand up at the stadium you see the game better, but if everybody stands up they will not all see the game better). Can you think of other examples of this fallacy in public administration, economy, finance, or society in general?

2. The U.S. Constitution prohibits any spending except as appropriated by Congress in the public budget. During the Cold War, Congress made an exception of spending on "national security"—allowing the budget of the Central Intelligence Agency and other such programs to remain secret. On the one hand, secrecy is antithetical to good governance. On the other, making such budgets public could give useful information to countries or individuals hostile to the United States. *Keeping the discussion focused on the budget process,* how would you navigate between the two competing objectives of good governance and national security?

3. One man's "community project" is another man's "budget pork." In a federal system such as the United States, how would a reasonable person allow for local responsiveness without providing powerful individuals a blank check for waste and abuse?

4. Is there a connection between "pork" (budget earmarks) and corruption? If so, how could such a connection work? Try to imagine several possible links, not just one, as well as some practical examples.

5. All things considered (you decide which things are to be considered) and within the parameters set by the Constitution, would you prefer more or less influence by Congress on the formulation of the U.S. federal budget? Why?

6. Would you prefer more or less public participation and open congressional hearings during preparation of the budget? Should they be routinely televised by major channels? Would you watch them if they were?

7. During the execution of the budget, would you prefer stronger congressional oversight or greater executive flexibility? Why? If you are not sure, what pros and cons do you see in each option?

8. Why is it that the government can run a huge budget deficit for years on end, whereas your credit card is canceled if you miss a couple of payments?

9. How can the federal government run a deficit when state governments are generally obliged to balance their books?

10. Is taxation the egg and spending the chicken, or vice versa? Is the analogy appropriate? (This question can take you way out to sea; try to limit the discussion in terms of the budget process and the sustainability of the public finances.)

11. If a tax cut is always good for the economy, why not cut taxes to zero?

12. Since public spending stimulates production and carries benefits for some groups, why not increase government spending to the level necessary to satisfy everyone's reasonable claims for government help?

13. In light of available facts and recent experience, do you believe the strongest stimulus to the American economy comes from cutting income taxes; cutting dividend and capital gains and estate taxes; cutting payroll taxes; increasing government spending; or from low interest rates, including on mortgages?

14. "A fiscal deficit is just an accounting problem, and doesn't affect anything that really matters." Discuss.

APPENDIX 6.1. BAD PRACTICES IN BUDGET PREPARATION

As flagged in the text, the absence of a hard expenditure constraint at the start of the budget preparation process invariably leads to one or more dysfunctional practices in budgeting, all too common in history and still prevalent in some developed countries and many developing countries.

Incremental Budgeting

Life itself is incremental. And so, in large part, is the budget process, since it has to take into account the current context, continuing policies, and ongoing programs. Except when a major "shock" is required, most structural measures can be implemented only progressively. (Thus, carrying out every year a "zero-based" budgeting exercise covering all programs would be an expensive illusion.) However, incremental budgeting, understood as a *mechanical* set of changes on the previous year's detailed line-item budget, leads to very poor results. The dialogue between the ministry of finance and line ministries is confined to reviewing the different items and to bargaining cuts or increases, item by item. Discussions focus solely on inputs, without any reference to results, between a ministry of finance typically uninformed about sectoral realities and a sector ministry in a negotiating mode. Worse, the negotiation is seen as a zero-sum game and is usually not approached by either party in good faith. Moreover, incremental budgeting of this sort is not even a good tool for expenditure control, although this was the initial aim of this approach. Line-item incremental budgeting focuses generally on goods and services expenditures, whereas the "budget busters" are normally entitlements, subsidies, hiring or wage policy or, in many developing countries, expenditure financed with counterpart funds from foreign aid.

Budget Unpredictability

Recalling that credibility is a critical feature of a good budget, even the most mechanical and inefficient forms of incremental budgeting are not as bad as large and capricious swings in budget allocations in response to purely political whims or power shifts. There is no reason for spending agencies to prepare careful spending proposals when they can be wiped out at any moment and contracts cannot be entered into without certainty that the money will be available to honor them when the goods are delivered or services performed. Knowing this, suppliers will protect themselves by building in a hefty "unpredictability premium," thus raising substantially the cost of government activities.

"Open-ended" Processes

An open-ended budget preparation process starts by requesting proposals from the spending agencies without giving any clear indication of financial constraints. Since these requests express only "needs," in the aggregate they invariably exceed the available resources. Spending agencies have no incentive to propose savings, since they have no guarantee that any such savings will give them additional financial room to undertake new activities. New programs are included pell-mell in sector budget requests as bargaining chips. Lacking information on the relative merits of proposed expenditures, the ministry of finance is led to making arbitrary cuts across the board among sector budget proposals, usually at the last minute when finalizing the budget. At best, a few days before the deadline for presenting the draft budget to the top political leadership, the ministry of finance gives firm directives to line ministries, which then redraft their requests hastily, making cuts across the board in the programs of their subordinate agencies. Of course, these cuts are also arbitrary, since the ministries have not had enough time to reconsider their previous budget requests. Further bargaining then takes place during the review of the budget at the cabinet level, or even during budget execution.

"Open-ended" processes are sometimes justified as "decentralized" approaches to budgeting. Actually, they are the very opposite. Since the total demand by the line ministries is inevitably in excess of available resources, the ministry of finance in fact has the last word in deciding where increments should be allocated and whether reallocations should be made. Paradoxically but accurately, the less constrained the process is to begin with, the stronger is the role of the central ministry of finance in deciding the composition of sectoral programs and the more illusory is the "ownership" of the budget by line ministries.

Excessive Bargaining and Conflict Avoidance

There is always an element of bargaining in any budget preparation, as choices must be made among conflicting interests. An "apolitical" budget process is an oxymoron. However, when bargaining *drives* the process, the only predictable result is inefficiency of resource allocation. Choices are based more on the political weight of the different actors than on facts, integrity, or results. Instead of transparent budget appropriations, false compromises are reached, such as increased tax expenditures, creation of earmarked funds, loans, or increased contingent liabilities. A budget preparation process dominated by bargaining can also favor the emergence of escape mechanisms and a shift of key programs outside the budget.[23]

A variety of undesirable compromises are used to avoid internal bureaucratic conflicts—spreading scarce funds among an excessive number of programs in an effort to satisfy everybody, deliberately overestimating revenues, underestimating continuing commitments, postponing hard choices until budget execution, inflating expenditures in the second year of a multiyear expenditure program, and so on. These conflict-avoidance mechanisms are frequent in countries with weak cohesion within the government. Consequently, improved processes of policy formulation can have benefits for budget preparation as well, through the greater cohesion generated in the government.[24]

Conflict avoidance may characterize not only the relationships between the ministry of finance and line ministries, but also those between line ministries and their subordinate agencies. Indeed, poor cohesion within line ministries is often used by the ministry of finance as a justification for its leading role in determining the composition of sectoral programs. Perversely, therefore, the all-around bad habits generated by "open-ended" budget preparation processes may reduce the incentive of the ministry of finance itself to push for real improvements in the system.

"Dual Budgeting"

There is frequent confusion between the separate presentation of current and investment budgets and the issue of the process by which those two budgets are prepared. The term "dual budgeting" is often used to refer to either the first or the second issue. However, as discussed earlier, a separate presentation is needed. "Dual budgeting" therefore refers only to a *dual process* of budget preparation, whereby the responsibility for preparing the investment or development budget is assigned to an entity different from the entity that prepares the current budget.

Dual budgeting was aimed initially at establishing appropriate mechanisms for giving higher priority to development activity. Alternatively, it was seen as the application of a "golden rule" that would require balancing the recurrent budget and borrowing only for investment. In many developing countries, the organizational arrangements that existed before the advent of the public investment programming (PIP) approach in the 1980s typically included a separation of budget responsibilities between the key core ministries. The ministry of finance was responsible for preparing the recurrent budget; the ministry of planning was responsible for the annual development budget and for medium-term planning. The two entities carried out their responsibilities separately on the basis of different criteria, different staff, different bureaucratic dynamics, and, usually, different ideologies. In some cases, at the end of the budget preparation cycle, the ministry of finance would simply staple the two budgets into a single document that made up the "budget." Clearly, such a practice impedes the integrated review of current and investment expenditures that is necessary in any good budget process. (For example, the ministry of education will program separately its school construction program and its running costs and try to get the maximum resources for both, without ever considering variants that might consist of building fewer schools and buying more books.)

In many cases, coordination between the preparation of the recurrent budget and the development budget is poor not only between core ministries but within the line ministries as well. While the ministry of finance deals with the financial department of line ministries, the ministry of planning deals with their investment department. This duality may even be reproduced at subnational levels of government, in provinces and municipalities. Adequate coordination is particularly difficult because the spending units responsible for implementing the recurrent budget are administrative divisions, while the development budget is implemented through projects, which may or may not report systematically to their relevant administrative division. (In a few countries, while current expenditures are paid from the treasury, development expenditures are paid through a separate development fund.) The introduction of rolling public investment programs was motivated partly by a desire to correct these problems.[25]

Thus, the crux of the "dual budgeting" issue is the lack of integration of different expenditures contributing to the same policy objectives. This real issue has been clouded, however, by a super-ficial attribution of other deep-seated problems to the "technical" practice of dual budgeting. For example, dual budgeting is sometimes held responsible for an expansionary bias in government expenditure. Certainly, as emphasized earlier, the initial dual budgeting paradigm was related to a growth model based on a mechanistic relation between the level of investment and GDP growth. In hindsight, the implicit disregard for issues of implementation capacity, efficiency of invest-ment, or mismanagement, corruption, and theft is difficult to understand. This paradigm itself has unquestionably been a cause of public finance overruns and the debt crises inherited in Africa or Latin America from bad-quality investment "programs" of the 1970s and early 1980s. However, imputing to dual budgeting all problems of bad management or weak governance and corruption is equally simplistic and misleading. Given the same structural, capacity, and political conditions of those years (including the Cold War), the same outcome of wasteful and often corrupt expansion of government spending would have resulted in developing countries—dual budgeting or not. If only the massive economic mismanagement in so many countries in the 1970s and early 1980s could be explained by a single and comforting "technical" problem of budgetary procedure! In point of fact, the fiscal overruns of the 1970s and early 1980s had little to do with the visible dual budget-ing. They originated instead from a *third* invisible budget: "black boxes," uncontrolled external borrowing, military expenditures, casual guarantees to public enterprises, and so on.[26]

Public investment budgeting is submitted to strong pressures because of particular or regional interest (the so-called pork barrel projects) and because it gives fatter opportunities for corruption than current expenditures.[27] Thus, in countries with weak governance, there are vested interests in keeping separate the process of preparing the investment budget and a tendency to increase public investment spending. However, under the same circumstances of weak governance, to concentrate power and bribe opportunities in the hands of a powerful "unified-budget" baron would hardly improve expenditure management or reduce corruption. On the contrary, it is precisely in these countries that focusing first on improving the integrity of the separate investment programming process may be the only way to assure that some resources are allocated to economically sound projects and to improve over time the budget process as a whole.[28]

By contrast, in countries without major governance weaknesses, dual budgeting often results in practice in insulating current expenditures (and especially salaries) from structural adjustment. Given the macroeconomic and fiscal forecasts and objectives, the resources allocated to public investment have typically been a residual, estimated by deducting recurrent expenditure needs from the expected amount of revenues (given the overall deficit target). The residual character of the domestic funding of development expenditures may even be aggravated during the process of budget execution, when urgent current spending preempts investment spending that can be postponed more easily. In such a situation, dual budgeting yields the opposite problem: unmet domestic investment needs and insufficient counterpart funds for good projects financed on favorable external terms. Insufficient aggregate provision of counterpart funds (which is itself a symptom of a bad investment budgeting process) is a major source of waste of resources.

Recall that the real issue is lack of integration between investment and current expenditure programming and not the separate processes in themselves. Forgetting the real issue has often led to considering the problem solved by a simple merger of two ministries—even while coordination remains just as weak. A former minister becomes a deputy minister, organizational "boxes" are reshuffled, and a few people are promoted and others demoted. But dual budgeting remains alive and well within the bosom of the umbrella ministry. By contrast, when coordination between two initially separate processes is close and iteration effective, the two budgets end up consistent with each other and with government policies and "dual budgeting" is no great problem.

Thus, when the current and investment budget processes are separate, whether or not they should be unified depends on the institutional characteristics of the country. In countries where the agency responsible for the investment budget is weak and the ministry of finance is not deeply involved in ex-ante line-item control and day-to-day management, transferring responsibilities for the investment budget to the ministry of finance would tend to improve budget preparation as a whole. (Whether this option is preferable to the alternative of strengthening the agency responsible for the investment budget can be decided only on a country-specific basis.) In other countries, one should first study carefully the existing processes and administrative capacities. For example, when the budgetary system is strongly oriented toward ex-ante controls, the capacity of the ministry of finance to prepare and manage a development budget may be inadequate. A unified budget process would in this case risk dismantling the existing network of civil servants who prepare the investment budget, without adequate replacement. Also, as noted, coordination problems may be as severe between separate departments of a single ministry as between separate ministries. Indeed, the lack of coordination *within line ministries* between the formulation of the current budget and the formulation of the capital budget is in many ways the more important dual budgeting issue. Without integration or coordination of current and capital expenditure at the line ministries' level, integration or coordination at the core ministry level is a misleading illusion.

On balance, however, the general presumption is in favor of a single ministry responsible for both the investment and the annual budget (although that entity must possess the different skills and data required for the two tasks).

APPENDIX 6.2. TECHNICAL REQUIREMENTS FOR BUDGET EXECUTION AND FINANCIAL CONTROL

Budget execution must conform as closely as possible to the budget approved by the legislature, although flexibility is also needed to enable operational efficiency and responsiveness to changed circumstances. We previously listed capricious swings in budget allocations among the undesirable practices in budget preparation. Similarly, predictability is equally important when the budget is to be implemented and the critical requirement in this respect is timely release of funds to the spending departments and agencies.

Release of Funds

To ensure effective budget implementation, the authority to spend must be given to agencies in useful time. Of course, funds must be released in conformity with budget authorizations, but the actual release must be regulated through the fiscal year in keeping with the estimated timing of expenditures. Because revenues do not come all at once at the start of the fiscal year, it would be impossible for the government to release to the spending ministries and agencies the entirety of the cash corresponding to their budgetary appropriation for the year. At the other extreme, funds are released to spending agencies through day-to-day or week-to-week cash rationing (rare but not unknown, including Ukraine in 1976 and China in the early 1980s) because of extreme liquidity problems or a badly overestimated budget. The resulting "cash budget" de facto replaces the approved budget, funds are often released on political and patronage grounds, and corruption opportunities proliferate. Moreover, such cash *rationing* cannot even achieve its control objective, as the spending agencies can continue to make commitments in accordance with the approved budget—accumulating payments arrears but formally complying with budget procedures.

In normal situations, cash must be released periodically but on a predictable basis. In different countries, the budget may be sliced into four quarterly parts; or one twelfth of the budget appropriation may be released every month; or, ideally, a detailed budget implementation plan is prepared at the start of the fiscal year and cash released in accordance with the plan. Generally, monthly releases are inefficient, as for many commitments, even for simple purchases of goods, one month is insufficient. In any case, whatever the periodicity of cash releases, the system for releasing funds should ensure efficient implementation of the budget and avoid generating payment arrears and thus be grounded on the following considerations:

- Spending agencies must know in advance what funds will be allocated and when.
- Funds must be released in time. In case of unforeseen liquidity problems, the cash release plan should be revised, but in consultation with and timely communication to the spending agencies instead of just delaying the release of funds.[29]
- Particular attention must be paid to agencies located in remote areas. This calls for good coordination between the central ministry and regional offices.[30]
- Regulating cash flows without regulating commitments generates payment arrears. In many cases, it is unclear whether spending units are allowed to make commitments up to the ceiling given in the budget or up to the cash limit.
- The financial requirements of ongoing commitments must be taken into account.

Carryovers

The budget annuality rule, explained earlier, can create a spending spree at the close of the fiscal year, partly because "the money is there" and partly as a defensive tactic to ensure that underspending in one year does not lead to reduced appropriations the following year. (This practice was standard in the Soviet system and was called *shturmovschina*—"the storming.") Occasionally, the bulge may simply reflect commendable prudence on the part of a ministry concerned with keeping its expenditures down as much as possible throughout the year as protection against unexpected mid-course cuts in appropriations. More often, the bulge of spending at year end is likely to be for low-priority or even wasteful purchases, and rushed expenditures almost invariably require some avoidance or bending of the procurement rules (see chapter 9). In both situations, a small "carryover" provision can serve to remove the temptation to get rid of leftover funds before the spending authority comes to an end.

In some developed countries (e.g., Australia), the annuality of budget appropriations has been altered slightly to authorize the "carryover" to the beginning of the following fiscal year of up to 10 percent of current expenditures. In most countries, carryover of capital expenditures to the following year is authorized or routinely approved by the ministry of finance. On balance, in developed countries a limited carryover provision can eliminate the wasteful spending rush at the end of the fiscal year and provide spending agencies with additional flexibility at a negligible cost in terms of the integrity of budget execution. Note, however, that a wasteful spending bulge at the end of the year would not occur if: (1) the budget was well-prepared to begin with; (2) a realistic cash plan had been formulated and implemented; and (3) intervening changes had been reflected in appropriate modifications to the budget and the cash plan. Thus, a carryover provision should not divert attention from focusing on improving these three characteristics of good budgeting.

Virements

Virements is the technical term for transfers of money between budget items—e.g., reallocating budgeted expenditure from vehicle purchases to office equipment. For efficient operations, spending agencies should have some flexibility to reallocate resources internally, without going beyond the total expenditure authorized for the agency. For example, an investment project may be delayed for technical reasons, while another should be speeded up; or, it may transpire that subcontracting some data processing may be more cost-effective than the purchase of computers that was originally envisaged. Clear rules for virements are therefore necessary for good budget execution, and must distinguish between virements that may be made entirely at the discretion of the spending agency concerned; those that require approval of the ministry of finance; and those that are prohibited.

To give spending agencies maximum flexibility, several developed countries have recently gone to block appropriations, leaving spending ministries and agencies free to determine the best composition of inputs to implement their programs and achieve results within each "block." However, flexibility should not be so great as to allow changing during budget execution the spending priorities defined in the budget approved by the legislature. Also, when financial controls in the spending ministries are weak or there are internal governance weaknesses, flexibility can too easily become an opening for misallocation and theft. Thus, because conditions in all these respects vary between countries, the proper boundary between permissible and impermissible virements will also differ depending on country circumstances. In general, the case for budget execution flexibility is strongest in countries where the administrative capacity of the spending agencies is high and their internal governance and controls are robust.

Cash and Debt Management

As noted earlier, it is not practical for the whole sum corresponding to the budget appropriation to be allocated to each spending agency at the start of the year. Centralized cash and debt management are necessary to: control total spending, implement the budget efficiently, minimize the cost of government borrowing, and maximize return on government deposits and financial investments. In this light, the first requirement for good cash management is careful cash planning as previously discussed. Secondly, government cash must be centralized.

Centralization of cash balances (not to be confused with centralized payments) is best made through a "treasury single account"—although advances in information technology now make several treasury accounts feasible. A treasury single account is an account (or a set of linked accounts) through which all government payment transactions are made. It should have the following features: (1) daily centralization of the cash balance; (2) accounts open under the responsibility of the treasury; and (3) all transactions recorded along the same classification.

The challenges of debt management are primarily to assure that new external borrowing increases debt-servicing capacity by more than the cost of borrowing and finance government borrowing needs in a way that minimizes its cost by careful management of placement and maturities. In developing countries, there is also a need to build up the capacity to negotiate with external creditors. In all countries, naturally, a complete and up-to-date debt database is essential to keep track of forthcoming payments and thus budget them properly. For all this, a borrowing policy should be set in advance and a borrowing plan should be made public consistent with the budget and the multiyear fiscal perspective. Finally, borrowing by subnational governments must be regulated and should be consistent with overall fiscal targets.

Monitoring and Amending the Budget

An integral part of good budget execution is to keep a close eye on developments to ensure that programs are implemented effectively, identify any financial or policy slip-ups, and, when necessary, propose timely amendments to the legislature. Monitoring should cover both financial and physical progress, as measured by a variety of performance indicators (as discussed in chapter 10). Financial implementation of the budget should be reviewed monthly, and a comprehensive midterm review is needed.

It is difficult to make accurate forecasts for the implementation of certain programs or for changes in economic parameters such as inflation, interest rate or exchange rates, and certain urgent needs may emerge that are not foreseen during budget preparation. In addition to flexible rules for virements, a mechanism to accommodate such changes is the inclusion in the budget of a "*contingency reserve*." The amount of such reserve, however, should normally not exceed 3 percent of the total budget, lest budget execution degrade into bargaining on the use of the contingency reserve. Also, there must be clear and well-understood criteria for the allocation of the reserve.

For changes that would alter the composition of the budget or increase expenditure by more than the small contingency reserve, the budget should be formally amended. The government must be allowed to address urgent major problems promptly, and it is appropriate to permit exceptional expenditures without prior legislative approval. However, this authority should be regulated and limited and the executive branch should request ex post legislative sanction as soon as possible.

In general, amending the budget should be done only through prior approval of the legislature. The process for budget amendments (sometimes called "supplementaries") is symmetrical with the process of budget preparation and approval—albeit much more limited in scope and time. Such budget amendments should be considered only at fixed times and the number of in-year revisions should be strictly limited (preferably to only one budget revision). In some countries, supplementary budget requests are presented to the legislature on a case-to-case basis, each time the executive approves a request from a spending ministry or agency. As a result, an excessive number of supplementary requests are made every year (e.g., up to forty in Sri Lanka). Aside from frittering away legislative attention and time on small individual requests, such an approach makes it impossible to compare the economic and social worth of one additional expenditure request with others, and budget execution is difficult to control when the budget is continually being revised. Thus, various requests from spending ministries and agencies should be "bundled" and reviewed together.

Accounting and Financial Reporting

Accounting is a subject that causes many eyes to glaze over. Yet, without reliable numbers, it is impossible to follow the execution of the budget and to hold anyone accountable for misbehaving or underperforming. The critical importance for the private sector of honest and competent accounting has been brought home with a vengeance by the failure of the profession in the well-known collapses of Enron and so many other large corporations in the early 2000s. Good accounting is no less important for the public sector, although its bases and methods need to be different because of the various objectives of public sector activity.

Accounting systems are classified as follows:

- *Cash accounting*, which focuses on cash flows and cash balances. Cash accounting is appropriate for the objective of expenditure control, provided that it is complemented by an adequate system for monitoring commitments and reporting on expenditure arrears.[31]
- *Accrual accounting*, which covers all liabilities and all assets. Accrual accounting, which is used in commercial enterprises, gives the framework for assessing full costs and performance and is appropriate to private enterprises and to autonomous public sector entities. However, its requirements in terms of data and technical and administrative implementation capacity are heavy, making it very unreliable if inappropriately or prematurely introduced.
- *Modified accrual accounting*, which covers, in addition to cash, all liabilities and *financial* assets. Modified accrual accounting gives a framework for registering liabilities and all expenditures and is an improvement over cash accounting, when circumstances permit.

The essential requirement is to have an accounting system that is reliable and suitable to the administrative capacity of the country in question. A strong cash accounting system is far better than a bad accrual accounting system and is appropriate in virtually all developing countries and several developed countries. In any event, whatever the basis of accounting, the accounting system should have the following features:

- adequate procedures for bookkeeping, systematic recording of transactions, adequate security system, and systematic comparison with banking statements;
- uniform methodology for recording all expenditures and revenues (including expenditures from extra-budgetary funds and autonomous agencies, and aid-financed expenditures);
- common classification of expenditure along functional and economic categories;
- clear and well-documented procedures; and
- robust arrangements for the retention, access, and security of records.

Consistent with the accounting system, financial reporting must be designed to fit the needs of the different users (the legislature, the public, budget managers, policy makers, etc.). In addition to regular statements of accounts, minimum requirements for financial reporting are:

- budget management reports, showing all movements in appropriations and line items (allotments, supplementary estimates, virements, etc.);

- accountability reports to the legislature;
- financial reports (consolidated accounts of the general government, statement on arrears, report on debt and contingent liabilities, and report on lending); and
- budget policy assessment reports and line agencies' reports.

NOTES

The material in this chapter is in part summarized and adapted from Schiavo-Campo and Tommasi (1999) by permission of the Asian Development Bank. The reader interested in a comprehensive treatment of the subject is referred to that book.

1. Because budgeting practices vary significantly according to local circumstances, readers interested in different regions may wish to consult ESCAP (1993), for Asia; Petrei (1998) for Latin America; and Shah (2007), mainly for Africa.

2. Of particular concern for governance, because of their lack of visibility, are *tax expenditures,* that is, the loss of revenue from special subsidies, exemptions, and the like.

3. This phenomenon, called "tax incidence," is more complex than described here, as the extent to which payment of the sales tax is effectively shared between buyer and seller depends on the interaction between the supply and demand for the good or service, and not simply on the characteristics of demand.

4. In this book, we do not address the complex question of how the people's preference can be ascertained. We underline, however, the inherently political nature of the process of allocating public monies to various users and beneficiaries. Indeed, Kenneth Arrow proved mathematically almost forty years ago the "impossibility" of aggregating individual preferences into a single social preference function that is stable, consistent with economic efficiency, and not dependent on coercion (in Arrow and Scitovsky, 1969). Other contributions, known collectively as "public choice theory," look at the government budget as being determined by a mechanism similar to the market mechanism where a variety of rational actors interact to maximize their own individual satisfaction.

5. The distinction originates from Campos and Pradhan (1998). The latter two objectives of strategic resource allocation and good operational management are easily recognizable in the distinction traditionally made in economics between allocative efficiency and efficiency of use.

6. As chapter 10 will explain in detail, efficiency relates to the concrete results of government activity (e.g., number of schools built), while effectiveness relates to the achievement of the intended purposes of those activities (e.g., higher literacy).

7. Petrei (1988).

8. Petrei (1988, p. 338).

9. Similarly, when cutting the budget deficit, *all* taxes and expenditures must be on the table. Excluding a priori certain types of revenues or expenditures makes cost-benefit comparisons impossible and thus produces inferior policy packages. In reality, of course, certain entitlement programs (e.g., Social Security in the United States) are extremely difficult to modify and thus end up de facto excluded from the debate. However, the principle of looking at revenues and expenditures in their entirety must still be kept in mind as the optimal guideline.

10. For efficiency and anti-corruption reasons, the transactions should be shown in gross terms without "netting out" receipts and expenditures, as it is necessary to know the magnitude of the receipts and the expenditures made from them.

11. The future is obviously more uncertain the longer the period considered: the general trade-off is therefore between policy relevance and certainty. (The reader familiar with statistical inference will recognize here the familiar trade-off, for a given sample size, between the precision of a statistical estimate and its probability of containing the true value, with narrow-band estimates being more precise but less likely to include the true value for the population and wide-band estimates more likely to be correct but more vague as well.) Such an expenditure perspective has been referred to as "indicative multiyear programming," "medium-term public expenditure programs," "multiyear estimates," and "medium-term expenditure framework." In practice, the fiscal perspective should cover two to five years beyond the budget year—with the shorter period appropriate in developing countries given their more fluid situation, and the longer period appropriate in developed countries. In the United States, a five-year perspective is contained in the "budget resolution," as discussed later in this chapter.

12. For an early definition of the fiscal responsibility issue, see Kopits and Symansky (1998).

13. See Schiavo-Campo (1994).

14. Such an approach has recently come to be known as "cash budgeting." This term is highly misleading. First, it has nothing to do with the basis of budgetary appropriations, which are on a cash basis almost everywhere. Second, it is merely a tactic during budget execution to deal with the inevitable consequences of an unrealistic budget. "Cash budgeting" is, simply, cash *rationing* and not a budgeting *system*. The problem lies upstream, in a budget that is unrealistic in the first place.

15. Payments through deduction from taxes, frequent in some countries of the former Soviet Union, have negative consequences for both tax collection and competition among suppliers and reduce transparency, and vouchers are simply a way to delay payments when the government has a liquidity problem.

16. This section is based in part on official U.S. government sources. See mainly www.rules.house.gov/archives and www.gpoaccess.gov/usbudget. We do not include here all the nuts and bolts of the system, but only its main features. Also, for a fuller definition of some of the technical terms used in this section—as well as a more complete list of those terms—the reader is referred to www.senate.gov/reference/glossary.

17. The interested reader can follow the increase in the national debt at www.brillig.com/debt_clock.

18. Such bipartisanship can be genuine or bogus. Both parties, when controlling Congress, have engaged in the practice of excluding members of the other party from debate on the crucial decisions, which are then presented to the full conference committee and inevitably approved by its majority without meaningful input from the minority.

19. The rule was successfuliy invoked in December 2005 to remove from the defense spending bill a provision to permit drilling for oil in the Alaska National Wildlife Refuge.

20. For a full analysis of the commonalities and differences between national-level budgeting and budgeting at subnational government level, see Premchand and Schiavo-Campo (2004).

21. As noted earlier in the text, the estate tax is often deliberately misnamed "death tax." But dead persons cannot be taxed. The tax is on the *estate* (i.e., on the assets which they leave behind, and thus on their heirs). Estate taxes are among the most efficient and equitable ways to raise revenue, with an incidence almost entirely limited to the richest one percent of American households. They are also intended to prevent the emergence of an inherited aristocracy and the perpetuation of rigid economic and social class stratification. Moreover, the spirit of the capitalist system is to assign financial rewards to those who earn them by their efforts or ingenuity and not as an unearned accident of birth.

22. The expression was used by the outgoing and incoming chairmen of the Senate budget committee in their December 2006 request to the administration to include the war costs in the regular budget.

23. "In Japan, where bargaining takes place in respect of the main budget account, greater controls are exercised by the Finance Ministry on the Fiscal Investment Loan Program, involving substantial borrowed funds and outside the traditional budget" (Premchand, 1983).

24. Budgeting by norms and formulae also reduces conflict and has the advantage of simplicity. Whether it results in good allocation and efficiency depends largely on whether the formulae are appropriate and used to facilitate estimates and budget preparation, rather than mechanical straight jackets.

25. "Aside from the legacy of the planning practices of the past, other factors contributed to dual budgeting, such as pressure or recommendations from donors or international financial institutions (IFIs). The desire of donors to 'enclave' their projects to minimize risks of mismanagement and maximize provision of counterpart funding has also increased the fragmentation of the budget system. For example, at the recommendation of IFIs, Romania attempted in 1993–1997 to implement an investment coordination unit outside the Ministry of Finance, to prepare the capital budget and screen projects through its own investment department. A frequently debated issue in the World Bank is the tendency [of enclaves] . . . inherent in any project-centered approach to lending [to] reduce the pressure on government to reform, and . . . weaken domestic systems by replacing them with donor-mandated procedures" (World Bank, 1997b).

26. Sometimes, in countries with poor governance, the spending-developmental approach of the ministry of planning is opposed to the thrifty-financial approach of the ministry of finance. Again, reality is inconvenient: it is the financial authority that approves extra-budgetary loans, releases cash beyond spending limits, grants the guarantees, and so on.

27. See Tanzi (1997).

28. What evidence does exist is in conflict with the hypothesis that separate investment budgeting has been fiscally expansionary. From 1990 to1994, countries participating in structural adjustment programs had slightly *lower* capital expenditure relative to total expenditure, and higher current expenditure than countries not undergoing adjustment. (Participating countries also had a much lower military spending and civilian wage bill.) This took place at a time when these countries were in effect required by the donors to have a separate public investment programming process.

29. These mechanisms for fund release in the various Asian countries do not always ensure that funds are released in due time for use by the spending authorities. Delays in authorization may be intentional, with the finance ministry withholding release orders if they are uneasy about the cash position of the government. The finance ministry may indeed make some informal reprioritization of expenditure of its own (ESCAP, 1993).

30. "In the pre-computer age, which still prevails in some Asian countries [e.g., Nepal until 1997], there were frequent logistic problems over fund release when spending agencies had to make repeated visits to the Controller's office, particularly in the districts which claimed that authorization had not reached them from the Finance Ministry, the line ministry or the head office of the Controller" (ESCAP, 1993).

31. Modified cash accounting, which adds to cash accounting a "complementary period" for recognizing year-end payments, is also possible, but should be avoided as it is cumbersome and risky and opens up possibilities for corruption.

CHAPTER 7

Managing the People I:
Employment and Wage Policy

Sire: A vast majority of civil servants are ill paid . . . the result is that skilled and talented men shun public service. . . . Intelligent, hardworking, competent and motivated individuals should direct the Empire civil service. If treated as they well deserve, the employment of such persons may well reduce the number of civil servants to one fourth of its current size.
—*Ali Pasha, 1871*[1]

In giving pay or rewards to men, [it is a bad thing] to do it in a stingy way
—*Confucius, Analects, 1.20*

WHAT TO EXPECT

Institutions do not implement policies—people do. Without competent employees at all levels, the best government policies cannot be implemented well. The strategy and practice of recruiting, compensating, managing, and training human resources is therefore as central to administrative effectiveness as the efficient management of public financial resources. Because of the large scope of the topic, it is addressed in two chapters. This chapter describes the main principles and criteria of policy on government employment and compensation, leaving to chapter 8 the discussion of the practice of government personnel administration and development.

After reviewing the fundamental reasons why a good civil service is important, this chapter proceeds to outline the criteria for government policy concerning employment and compensation. Concerning government employment, its right size depends on the functions assigned to government. As it is the case, however, that many countries have some excess government employment, the discussion turns to how to reduce the workforce in ways that are socially and economically sound. Concerning compensation of government employees, the chapter sets out the objectives of compensation policy and design of a compensation plan and highlights certain major issues, such as ethnic and gender discrimination. The customary section on general directions of improvement concludes the chapter. Owing to the inter-relation between the topics, the section on the situation in the United States is included at the end of the next chapter—covering the personnel administration aspects as well as the employment and wage policy.

INTRODUCTION: THE IMPORTANCE OF A GOOD CIVIL SERVICE

Civil service issues are not a new concern. Ancient China and Rome built their empires on competent and efficient civil servants, and the quoted advice given to Ottoman Sultan Abdul Aziz by Ali Pasha, his Chief Minister, is as fresh and current today as it was 140 years ago. (The Sultan's disregard of this advice was a key ingredient of the continued decline of Turkey's public administration apparatus, and a few years later the Ottoman Empire was overturned by the Young Turks movement.) A good civil service is important in five major areas.

Civil Service and Good Governance

There is strong evidence in the history of the United States and other countries that an efficient government workforce is a necessary condition for genuine accountability, transparency, participation, and the rule of law. It is not a sufficient condition for good governance—without the right political accountability mechanisms the best government workforce can accomplish little. However, a very bad civil service is sufficient in itself to eventually produce bad governance.

Civil Service and Production of Public Goods

The quantity and quality of public goods and services, as any branch of production, are a function of capital, social and economic infrastructure, materials, the technology of production, and, of course, the labor employed in it. It would be as nonsensical for the analysis of government activity to exclude consideration of the number and skills of civil servants as it would be for the analysis of production in a private company to neglect the quantity and skills of its employees.

Civil Service and Economic Policy

As discussed in chapter 15, economic policy reforms can be "enabling" reforms (e.g., removing an unnecessary regulation) or "affirmative" reforms (i.e., improving the budget preparation system). The former may be politically difficult, but do not call for much administrative effort. The latter, however, depend crucially on competent and motivated personnel for their implementation. Affirmative change does not occur by decree, and a policy paper is just a paper until the policy is actually implemented. Nor is it enough to have obedient civil servants following instructions, for reforms are always complex and require voluntary commitment by those charged with putting them in place.

Civil Service and Fiscal Management

It is impossible to imagine that revenue collection or the budgeting processes discussed in the previous chapter can be managed effectively without employees with the competence and integrity to do so. This requires a permanent nucleus of civil servants, with enough continuity and institutional memory to give sound advice to the political leadership and remind it of the good budgeting practices and mistakes of the past. This necessity is well understood and well established in developed countries. In many developing countries, instead, the weakness of the regular government workforce is often addressed by band-aid solutions, such as setting up enclave arrangements for managing expenditure programs or hiring expatriate consultants to do much of the fiscal and budgeting work.

In the long term, these band-aid solutions lead to an even weaker public administration and less reliable revenue collection and expenditure management.

Moreover, the "wage bill" (i.e., the cost of government employment) is considerable in countries with a comparatively large public sector. Thus, on the one hand, a judicious combination of measures affecting both the number and the pay of public employees can reduce the wage bill and free up fiscal resources for other uses. On the other hand, a blinkered focus on short-term fiscal savings may jeopardize the effectiveness of government action and be more costly in the long term. Either way, attention to the fiscal implications of government employment and pay policies is a necessary ingredient of sensible fiscal policy.

Civil Service and Institutional Development

As defined in chapter 1, institutional development is a move from a less efficient to a more efficient set of basic rules and procedures, measured by the reduction in "transaction costs" (i.e., all costs other than out-of-pocket expenditure that are associated with the time and opportunities lost in concluding the transaction in question). The effectiveness of organizations and their interaction with the regulatory framework is an obvious ingredient of the process and depends to a large extent on the people in the organizations. More efficient rules, including on personnel incentives, can lead to improved performance of employees; conversely, skilled and motivated public employees are instrumental for the formulation and implementation of more efficient rules. Thus, a good government workforce is both effect and cause of institutional development.

GOVERNMENT EMPLOYMENT POLICY

The overall objective of government employment and pay policies is to achieve a government workforce of the "right size" and with the skills, motivation, and integrity needed for responsive and efficient administration. But let's first look at the international facts.

How Big Is Government, and Why?

Why Does Government Tend to Grow?

Let's start by pointing out that the several possible measures of the size of government—employment, expenditure, revenue—are closely correlated. A large government shows large employment relative to population as well as large revenue/GDP and public expenditure/GDP ratios. Thus, a discussion of government size can adequately be framed in terms of government employment.

Adolph Wagner (1835–1917), a German economist, presciently argued 125 years ago that the public sector tends to expand faster than the economy. According to "Wagner's Law," economic growth is positively correlated with the share of public expenditure in GDP (and with the share of fiscal revenue and size of government employment along with it). The explanation is not that a larger public sector helps accelerate economic growth. On the contrary, it is the expansion of the economy which tends to bring about a more than proportionate expansion of government activity. The standard explanations are three: the need for larger government in order to countervail the power of large industries, the higher costs of regulating an increasingly more complex economy, and the assumption that many public goods are socially superior goods. Moreover, organizational theory argues that there is an inherent *tendency* of all large organizations to expand. In the case of government activities, much less open to competition, this tendency of *all* large organizations is more likely to translate into *actual* expansion of government organizations.

There is strong empirical support for this proposition.[2] It is surely not accidental that relative government employment has been almost twice as high in developed countries, at over 7 percent of population, as in the rest of the world. However, Wagner's Law is only a tendency—and can be counteracted by deliberate policy to contain the size of government, as shown by the containment in government employment in developed countries over the last decade. Also, the size of the public sector is a function of several other factors in addition to the size of the economy and level of development of the country.

A Global Snapshot[3]

In the 1990s, government employment worldwide averaged just under 5 percent of population, with education and health accounting for half of government employment and central government and local government for roughly one fourth each. Substantial interregional differences are evident, with the rich countries that are members of the OECD showing the largest government employment relative to population and Africa and Asia relatively the smallest. In the United States, total government employment, at about 7 percent of population, is in line with the developed countries' average. Federal government employment, under one percent of population, is somewhat lower than the developed countries' average and local government employment somewhat higher—which is consistent with the federal structure of the country. The major change worldwide in the past twenty years has been the growth of local government employment to almost the same level as central government—especially visible in Latin America.

Determinants of the Size of Government Employment

High Level of Country Development. The global evidence shows a close positive association between per capita income and government employment. Countries at higher levels of development tend to have larger governments. When added to the results of earlier studies[4] this finding removes all reasonable doubt about the general validity of Wagner's "law." However, the employment–income association ceases to operate beyond certain income levels and is no longer found *within* the OECD group of countries. This means either that the Wagner tendency was counteracted by deliberate policies in the 1980s and 1990s, or that Wagner's law itself becomes inoperative beyond a certain level of development—or most probably both.

Low Wages. There is a close negative association between central government employment and relative wages. This confirms the standard expectation that higher numbers of employees are associated with lower compensation, other things being equal. However, again, this association does not appear within the OECD group. Among the possible explanations is that, in these countries, greater psychological satisfaction is derived from public service. The implication would be very important: when public servants are respected and trusted, they are willing to accept comparatively lower pay. The opposite is also true—mistrusting and devaluing the contribution of government employees leads in time to the necessity of paying them higher salaries.

The Fiscal Situation. There is no significant association between the size of the fiscal deficit and the size of government employment—except in Africa. In general, whatever influence government employment would have on the fiscal deficit seems to be largely offset by the associated lower wages. Because excessive employment is not translated into higher deficits but into lower wages, the issue is generally not the fiscal impact but the adverse effect on the motivation and productivity of the government workforce.

Population Size. Finally, there is a negative association between size of population and of relative government employment in the OECD countries and in Latin America, but not in other regions. This suggests the existence of economies of large-scale production in public services, but only in the more developed countries. It is probable that information technology, with its expensive equipment and vast efficiency gains, is at the root of the phenomenon of lower relative labor requirements in the governments of rich countries. If so, with the expansion of IT, these economies of scale should become more and more accessible to smaller countries as well.

The Regional Picture. Among developing countries, the results are most striking in Africa, where there is conclusive evidence that the proportion of the population employed by central governments is higher in countries where per capita income is higher, the fiscal deficit is higher, and government wages are lower. In Latin America, the correlation between high government employment and low wages is almost as close as in Africa, but there is no association with population size or the fiscal deficit. In this region, local government employment is strongly correlated with the country's income level; thus, within Latin America, the richer countries appear in general to have progressed further on the road to decentralization. No other significant relationships emerge from the evidence for other regions of the developing world. In any event, inter-country differences swamp whatever regional patterns exist, and decisions on the right size of government employment must be country specific, as emphasized next.

The "Right Size" of Government Employment

What is clear from the above is that there is no universal rule to determine how many employees a government *should* have. Understaffing and overstaffing are relative notions. That government employment is comparatively large or small in a particularly country is a useful flag for analysis but proves nothing in and of itself. The role of the government may be different in that country—in which case the issue is the appropriate role of government. Or, the degree of government centralization may differ—in which case the issue is the geographic articulation of state responsibilities. (For example, while the French central civil service is among the largest and the British among the smallest, *total* government employment accounts for about the same percentage of population in both France and the United Kingdom.) Thus, a very small government organization can still be "overstaffed" if the same level and quality of public service could be provided with fewer employees; conversely, a large government agency can nevertheless be "understaffed" if its size and skills are not adequate for the responsibilities assigned to government by the population. Clearly, the issue must be addressed sector by sector, and public service by public service—rather than by reference to international "norms."

The civil service regulatory framework and country geography are also relevant. In particular, greater mobility within the civil service permits a smaller workforce without affecting service delivery, or may improve services, or both. Thus, other things being equal, one would expect that a small and homogeneous country with good internal communications will need a smaller government workforce. Again, the opposite is also true: restrictions on mobility may lead to the necessity to enlarge the workforce or to reduce service delivery. Aside from personnel regulations and geographic characteristics, the use of information and communication technology can have a vast impact on lower labor requirements (see chapter 13).

Consequently, an assessment of the "right size" of government employment must be country and time specific, and must consider the functions assigned to the state, the degree of administrative centralization, the skill profile of the civil service, the availability of resources and of information technology, and the personnel regulations and constraints on staff mobility—not a fit subject for facile prescriptions.

Getting to the "Right Size"—Approaches to Retrenchment

When the civil service is understaffed, getting to the right size of employment calls for a combination of more active recruitment and more attractive compensation. This is by far the easier and more agreeable problem, politically and humanly. The tough choices emerge when the government is overstaffed and a reduction in force is required.

Retrenchment is often socially and politically costly, particularly when general unemployment is high and alternative job opportunities are scarce. However, the social costs can be cushioned by appropriate provisions and the political costs are not inevitable. There are circumstances when the support of the public for reductions in government employment offsets the loss of support from those directly involved—as in many Eastern European and former Soviet Union countries. This is certainly the case when civil servants have earned the hostility of the public through inefficient service delivery or corruption, as in much of Africa, South Asia, and Latin America, and some European countries. Also, political opposition can be defused if the change is enacted for good reason and is well managed, transparently and with appropriate explanations and equity of action. However, a mechanistic approach to reduce the workforce by some arbitrary number, without analytical and empirical justification, gives civil service reform a bad name and heightens resistance to change. All that being said, as any other reform, government employee retrenchment carries benefits as well as costs, and the balance between the two is heavily influenced by the quality of design and implementation of the reform.

The Benefits of Retrenchment

If done right, workforce retrenchment can provide the financial wherewithal to improve incentives for the remaining employees, produce net fiscal savings, or both. In addition, retrenchment can sometimes actually raise morale (by revaluing public service) and stimulate the performance of the remaining employees. Nothing demoralizes a good performer more than to work next to a less-qualified, underperforming, and uncaring individual with the same salary and nominal responsibilities. And, if retrenchment is accompanied by a review of the effectiveness of the organization, as it should be, it holds the potential to raise public sector productivity and the quality of public service for the benefit of the population as a whole.

The Costs of Retrenchment

When it's not done right, retrenchment can be very counterproductive:

- The *immediate risk* is skill reduction—if the program inadvertently encourages the best people to leave. (This risk is referred to as "adverse selection.") Voluntary severance and early retirement are especially problematic in this respect. The people more likely to leave are those with more options, hence the better qualified. The difficulty is that it is precisely voluntary severance and early retirement that are more humane and administratively easier to introduce. The government ought therefore to retain the right to refuse applications to take advantage of severance and early retirement when the applicant's skills should be retained in government. Since it is difficult to force people to stay in their jobs when they wish to leave, appropriate moral incentives and recognition are needed.

- The *medium-term risk* is the recurrence of overstaffing—if personnel management practices and control systems are not strengthened before or at the same time as retrenchment occurs. If wages have been raised in the meantime to improve incentives, the new hiring ratchets up the fiscal cost of government employment, and the eventual outcome is worse than the initial situation. It is thus essential to introduce tighter provisions to prevent new recruitment and the re-employment of the same retrenched individuals as contractual consultants.

- The *broader risks* from a retrenchment program that is perceived as arbitrary and opaque are demoralization of employees, lower service quality, and possibly social conflict in countries with religious, ethnic tribal, or clan differences.

The Devil in the Details

The upshot of this discussion is not that retrenchment measures should be avoided. In many circumstances, downsizing is virtually mandated by fiscal needs; in others, it is an important component of necessary structural reform. But *retrenchment must be approached as part of an overall improvement in the efficiency and quality of government action and not as an isolated cost-cutting exercise.* Rightsizing of government employment is not an end in itself but a means toward the end of better provision of public services. Thus, the right size of the government workforce must be derived from an appropriate vision of the role of the state and functional reviews of the efficient organizational structure of government.

In any event, whatever the need and the rationale, experience shows that retrenchment programs must be designed carefully—including the recognition that retrenchment is almost always financially costly in the short term because severance payments must be added to the normal pension obligations. It is also important to preserve progress made in bringing into the government workforce women and members of minority groups. Thus, a "last-in-first-out" approach to retrenchment is by definition discriminatory against groups recently included, and modifications of a strict seniority rule would be needed.

In any event, retrenchment must meet clear and specific criteria determined in advance, implemented with ferocious attachment to the established rules and criteria, and without any personal or group favoritism. Transparency, candid internal communications and active cooperation with the media are therefore critical. It is difficult to overstate the importance of this element. In a time of difficult change with potentially significant implications for many individuals, suspicion becomes the rule and destructive rumors spread very fast. Moreover, lack of honesty in the process unnecessarily adds insult to injury. Causing some employees to lose their job may be inevitable; causing them to lose their dignity is unforgivable.

A special approach to the "right size" of government employment is the Japanese way of handling government employment, called the "bonsai" approach by Anne-Marie Leroy (Box 7.1). Although vast differences naturally separate Japan from other countries, there is much in the "bonsai" approach that is worth considering.

BOX 7.1

Japan: The "Bonsai Approach" to a Small and Efficient Civil Service

The Japanese approach to the civil service can be likened to a bonsai tree—the careful grooming and nurturing of a well-proportioned and very small system.

There is substantial evidence linking the quality of Japan's civil service with the country's economic performance. Japanese civil servants comprise the best and brightest, working long and hard. The bureaucracy is very small and has been deliberately kept that way. Petty corruption is minimal. Retirement comes early and smoothly, leaving top positions open to be filled by individuals in their late forties and early fifties (unlike politicians, typically much older). Competition among agencies is also extensive, building an emulative spirit within the civil service that is often lacking in government agencies in other countries. Moreover, the legal structure of public administration protects the civil service from partisan politics and assists in maintaining a corps of professional employees. Civil service recruitment and promotion decisions are largely on merit and strictly insulated from political patronage.

The Japanese civil service has played a crucial and proactive role in promoting Japan's earlier catch-up economic and technological strategy. The good performance of the Japanese civil service was facilitated by cooperation between the civil service and the private sector, instead of jostling for supremacy. On retirement, many top civil servants relocate to new positions in the private sector, a phenomenon known as *amakudari,* or "descent from heaven." (Although the practice raises certain governance risks, it also brings valuable skills to the private sector. Stiglitz (1996) identified the cooperation between the public and private sectors as a key ingredient of the Asian "economic miracle.") The Japanese civil service model has shown signs of strain and incipient arteriosclerosis in the last decade, but its effectiveness in sustaining Japan's economic recovery in the 1950s and its remarkable economic development of the 1960s, 1970s, and 1980s cannot be overestimated.

WAGE AND INCENTIVE POLICY

Background

Don't Destroy Administrative Effectiveness to Fix a Fiscal Problem

Not surprisingly, much civil service reform has taken place under conditions of fiscal crisis. Government responses to fiscal crisis have understandably tended to avoid the harsh requirement of retrenchment and have instead eroded real government pay, compressed salary structures, and reduced expenditure on complementary inputs. Certainly, in cases where public wages are too high relative to private wages, cutting them improves resource allocation and equity as well. However, when compensation is just adequate or less than adequate, short-term fiscal savings must not be allowed to drive government wage policy.

Reductions in real wages below their level of adequacy set in motion a vicious circle of demotivation and underperformance that provide justification for further wage reductions. The long-term impact on administrative effectiveness can be devastating. The bottom of this spiral is a de-skilled labor force, too poorly paid to resist temptation, cowed when faced with pressures from politicians and influential private interests, and unable to perform in minimally adequate ways. Furthermore, because everyone is aware of the problem of inadequate compensation, and petty corruption is widely tolerated, society loses its legitimate claim to honest and efficient performance by its public servants. Beyond the direct deterioration in the provision of public goods and services, the result is a worsening economic climate for the private sector, corruption, and an increase in transaction costs.

The lesson of international experience is to resist the temptation to fix fiscal problems by distorting incentives. In the old Soviet Union, employees quipped: "We pretend to work and the government pretends to pay us." In Uganda in the 1980s, "the civil servant had either to survive by lowering his standard of ethics, performance and dutifulness or remain upright and perish. He chose to survive."[5] Complicating the matter are the lack of evidence on comparable pay in the private sector and the misperception of wage adequacy. Civil servants typically believe they are more underpaid than is in fact the case, while the public at large has the opposite misconception that government employees are overpaid.

Comparability: The Basic Criterion of Public Compensation

The nexus between pay and performance is complex. In the private sector, wages are market-determined and, at least in theory and under optimal conditions, correspond to the value of the employees' contribution to the company's production. Instead, it is difficult to value the labor of civil servants, given that their output is generally not marketable. The general solution is to make compensation comparable (not equal) to that for equivalent marketable skills (i.e., private-sector pay). This is no easy matter. As with everything else in the public sector, determining civil service compensation is not a purely technical issue but is influenced by the political climate, applicable legislation, and executive rules, tempered and interpreted by judicial decisions. In addition, a number of public policies have an impact on civil service compensation—limitations on political activity of public employees, equal pay and anti-discrimination statutes, and so on.

The Objectives of Compensation Policy

Although in practice there are severe problems in formulating a compensation policy that meets all of its different objectives, the four main objectives themselves are intuitive and reasonable—beginning with the objective of comparability itself.

Government Pay Comparable to Private Pay

Comparability must be both internal (i.e., between salaries for different government jobs and in different locations) and external (i.e., between government and private sector salaries). Comparability has both an efficiency dimension and an equity dimension. If government compensation is less than comparable private compensation, either the best-qualified government employees will leave or they will have to accept inequitable treatment.

But note that "comparable" does not mean equal. In the unlikely cases where public service demands especially high qualifications and additional prior investment in education, government wages higher than their private equivalent may be justified (e.g., in Singapore). In the much more typical cases, the greater job security and (sometimes) greater prestige of public service justifies a somewhat lower compensation package. In international practice, the "discount" on government work averages between 10 and 30 percent. (As explained at the end of chapter 8, in the U.S. federal government wages are comparable to private wages for similar occupations, allowing for the advantage of greater job security.)

Equal Pay for Equal Work, Performed Under the Same Conditions

As morally and economically obvious as this objective is, the evidence shows that this is not always the case. The major deviations are underpayment of female employees and the distortions caused by personal and political patronage.

Periodic Review of Compensation

Circumstances change, and a compensation structure that may be sound and adequate may acquire distortions over time. Periodically, it is necessary to give a fresh look at government pay. In the United States and other rich countries, this principle is usually observed. In developing countries, it is not always the case. In Jamaica, for instance, while the consumer price index rose by 470 percent from 1972 to 1982, the salaries of the three highest grades of civil servants rose by only 40 to 90 percent, while salaries of casual laborers rose by 360 percent. In Guyana, between 1986 and 1991, real wages in the central government fell by almost 20 percent, with even greater deterioration in the managerial, professional, and technical grades. Similarly, real salaries in Uganda declined 20 to 33 percent *per year* between 1975 and 1983. Real per capita salaries generally declined throughout Africa during this period, the decline being particularly marked in Ghana, Nigeria, and Zambia. Naturally, periodic adjustments of compensation are appropriate only when the compensation structure and level were adequate to begin with. In the infrequent cases when compensation is higher than warranted, gradual wage erosion through inflation may be the best way to bring compensation levels back into line. But internal comparability of incentives must be preserved during this process, and care must be taken to determine when the adjustment in real wages must stop.

The Design of a Compensation Plan

There are two main approaches to determining civil service compensation in actual practice. One is demand-driven *trial and error*—ascertaining what salaries will attract and retain employees with the appropriate skills. By its very nature, this is an ex-post method and therefore can be effective only at the margin. The second approach, more widely used, is *comparison with the private sector.* These approaches are not mutually exclusive; on the contrary, each can improve the other.

Job Classification

What is job classification? The starting point for designing a compensation plan is usually a job classification exercise, in which the positions are described in detail and systematically arranged in a coherent structure. As noted, a sound compensation system should provide equal pay for equal work and equal pay for comparable jobs. This in turn involves acquiring and analyzing the skill and responsibility attached to each job; the specific duties; the degree of supervision needed; and the difficulty, hazards, or other characteristics of the job. On the basis of such information, similar jobs are grouped into *classes* (e.g., cabinet-maker); classes involving similar work at different levels of difficulty are grouped into *occupations* (e.g., carpenter); and occupations are grouped into major *occupational categories* (e.g., construction worker).

Job classification schemes are complex and costly, and require the following:

- A formal procedure for measuring the level of difficulty, effort, knowledge, and responsibility requirements of each class of jobs. Techniques used to do so include factor ranking, point rating, factor comparison, and hybrid comparisons.
- Identification of grades, each constituting a specified level of difficulty and responsibility.
- A single pay range for all positions in classes assigned to each grade, without duplication (although the maximum salary for one grade is normally higher than the minimum salary for the next higher grade).

If done badly, in a rush, or with a hidden agenda, job classification exercises can produce phony or self-serving classifications (especially when supply-driven by donors or international consultants). In these cases, the high cost is not even justified by a better outcome. Moreover, where governance and accountability are weak, complexity is the enemy of integrity. Developing countries should thus consider operating on the simplest practicable job classification instead of attempting to implement the finely tuned classifications used in rich countries. (Even simple paired comparisons can give good results for mid-level and senior positions.)

Content of a Compensation Plan

A compensation plan for public employees should cover, in the following order:

- Identification of the kinds of positions and employees to which it is applicable
- Statement of the basic pay policy—for example, the relationship to private compensation or the kinds of compensation encompassed (base salary, allowances, and benefits)
- The pay schedule, showing the classes of jobs and the pay range assigned to each
- The schedules of premium pay rates and rules on overtime pay and holiday and weekend pay, among others; and

  - rules for determining pay on promotion, transfer, demotion, etc.;
  - rules of pay under special conditions (e.g., dual jobs in the same jurisdiction, military and jury duty, weather emergencies, etc.);
  - rules regarding special pay rates (e.g., to alleviate recruitment difficulties for a specific class of positions);
  - rules on pay for overtime or different kinds of leave (e.g., maternity leave); and
  - rules for resolving anomalies and discrepancies and redressing employee grievances regarding pay decisions.

Non-Wage Benefits

Identifying and quantifying non-salary benefits is a major problem in comparing private and public compensation and the impact of inflation on real compensation. Non-salary benefits take such various forms as spouse and dependency allowances, pensions, health and liability insurance, free or subsidized housing and social services, free or subsidized meals, transportation allowances, paid leave, and others too numerous and varied to mention. In the public sector in most countries, pensions, health insurance, and family dependency allowances are standard. But other benefits are also provided. In rural France, for example, municipalities are responsible for housing public school teachers. (This is partly to compensate for the fact that the salaries of teachers in rural areas are considerably lower than that of teachers in large cities.) In India, too, civil servants are given subsidized housing and some jobs, such as superintendent of prisons, carry free housing. Free education and health care are widespread means of compensating public employees, both in Eastern Europe and Central Asia (where state-owned enterprises used to provide such services) and elsewhere in the world. Food subsidies ranging from subsidized food shops and employee canteens to direct food distribution are also common. In Afghanistan, for example, civil servants were given rations of vegetable oil and wheat flour, along with a free meal per day, instead of a minimally adequate salary. In former colonies, such benefits are a colonial legacy, having been designed for the colonial administrators but kept after independence.

While some non-wage benefits can have a positive incentive role in a well-designed compensation package and may be necessary to assure comparability with private sector compensation, others are inefficient and can weaken work motivation and distort incentives. (A particularly inefficient benefit is the meeting allowance used in some countries, such as Tanzania until the 1990s. Not surprisingly, aside from its cost, such allowance results in maximizing the number of administrative meetings and minimizing their substance, which is a perfect way to interfere with administrative efficiency.)

The argument for scrutiny of non-wage benefits is stronger the more precipitous the decline in real wages has been. In-kind benefits tend to proliferate as the real salary declines because they provide a way to cushion the salary decline, and the short-term cost is usually very small (although the fiscal impact balloons later). Diligence in probing fringe benefits is, however, no guarantee of success in uncovering them, since they are often specific to the country, region, organization, or service, and lodged in the nooks and crannies of the budget documents. Some, like free housing or transportation, may be off-budget altogether. Indeed, a proliferation of extra-budgetary funds, discussed in chapter 6, in addition to weakening the integrity of public expenditure management process, also distorts the civil service compensation system. The fact that such giveaways are rarely subject to outside knowledge or review is convenient for both the granters and the beneficiaries.

Countries such as Botswana and Indonesia have replaced some in-kind benefits with a compensatory adjustment in pay. Guinea eliminated rice rations, Cameroon reduced housing allowances, Tanzania stopped the meeting allowances, and Bolivia abolished special "performance" premiums in the effort to rationalize remuneration and reduce undue discretion. However, effective measures must be taken to prevent the reemergence of the same in-kind benefits that had been monetized and added to basic pay. Frequently, a rationalized compensation system has reverted in time to the earlier complex and opaque system, of allowances, but with higher base wages to boot.

Finally, it's healthy to recall that, in most developed countries, fringe benefits to government employees pale into insignificance when compared with those enjoyed by private sector executives—company cars, private jets, club memberships, and so on.

The Gender Gap

Although most countries now explicitly prohibit discrimination on the basis of gender, there remains a difference between women's and men's wages. Salary inequalities between men and women government employees are persistent. Although these reflect inequities in the larger society, government has typically failed to provide the model and the leadership for putting into practice the elementary fairness and efficiency principle of "equal pay for equal work." It should be a continuing priority for governments to push for increasing convergence in pay for men and woman in government service—albeit in a manner that is mindful of the social structure and norms of the country. Gender discrimination has also been implicit in "nepotism" rules, with spouses (almost invariably women) prohibited from employment. For example, until 1947 a female civil servant in the United Kingdom was required to resign when marrying another civil servant.

The gender gap is widest in developing countries, but the problem has persisted for a long time even in highly industrialized economies. The following reminders are worth mentioning:

- In Denver, Colorado, government nurses were paid less than tree trimmers.
- In Australia, the principle of equal pay for equal work was not adopted until 1972. Indeed, a landmark judicial decision in a 1912 case justified lower wages for women because, unlike men, they did not generally have to support a family. That judge began the practice of fixing the female pay rate as a percentage of the basic male wage rate. The rate was officially fixed at 54 percent until 1949, when it was increased to 75 percent. By the end of the 1970s, the base pay for women had risen from 74 percent to 94 percent of that for men, and in government service the gap has now disappeared.
- New Zealand officially sanctioned different wage rates for men and women in 1903, and legislatively authorized them in 1934 and 1945. As in neighboring Australia, only in 1972 was the Equal Pay Act passed. As a result, hourly earnings of females rose from 71 percent of male earnings in 1973 to 79 percent in 1977 and are today close to parity.
- Britain explicitly countenanced gender-based pay discrimination until 1975, when the Equal Pay Act of 1970 came into effect.

Salary Compression

The Issue

The *compression ratio* is the ratio of the midpoint of the highest salary grade to the midpoint of the lowest salary grade. Internationally, the ratio varies widely, from highs of 30:1 or more to lows of 2:1—with a mode of around 7:1. (Note that a lower ratio means a more compressed salary structure.) In the U.S. federal structure, the compression ratio is about 8:1.

In addition to erosion in general pay, salary compression (i.e., the shrinking of the difference between the highest- and lowest-paid employees) has been a typical result of fiscal crisis in many countries. When an otherwise sound salary structure is unduly compressed, the impact is negative for the individuals affected and the public administration, and is both inequitable and inefficient. It is inequitable because the investment made by the individual in acquiring skills and experience is no longer adequately rewarded, nor is compensation commensurate with the individual's contribution to the organization. It is inefficient because the higher-level employees will either leave for better-paying private sector jobs, or remain and do as little work as possible. On the other hand, especially in poor countries, there is very little room for cutting the salaries of the lower-paid employees. The response to fiscal pressure is neither to make the poor poorer, nor to destroy the incentive structure for the public service, but to reduce the government workforce and/or find savings elsewhere in the government budget. In any budget, there is scope for raising some revenues or reducing certain expenditures at a much lower opportunity cost to the country than the cost of making overall wages inadequate or fiddling with their internal structure.

In developing countries, in the absence of well-designed civil service reform programs, fiscal difficulties in the 1980s tended to cause government wages to become more compressed and incentives to suffer as a result. The lesson was slowly and finally learned, and reform programs from the mid-1990s began to include an explicit objective of decompressing the public salary structure. These reforms were generally successful in countries such as Ghana, Laos, Mozambique, Uganda, and others. In this century, reviews of the wage structure have become a fairly common component of reform programs in countries experiencing severe civil service problems.[6]

Although not within this book's concern with the public sector, it is worth noting that, during the same years, top executive compensation in private corporations has increased vertiginously—especially in the United States—as a result of the ratchet mechanism of company boards of directors setting the compensation of their top executives by reference to the average for top executives in other companies. Decompressing salaries to provide adequate incentives to the highest skilled is one thing; raising compensation of top executives to 500 or 600 times the salaries of average workers is another. This action does not demonstrate a search for appropriate incentives but an embarrassing disconnect between ownership and control, giving free rein to stupendous greed.

Promotions, Raises, and Nonmonetary Incentives

Linking Incentives with "Performance"

In recent years, largely from an understanding of the disadvantages of compressing the wage structure, the question of targeting wage increases to scarce skills or essential functions has moved to the forefront of policy attention.[7] Similarly, training is now seen more as a focused way to fill selected skill gaps rather than an across-the-board program to lift the general educational level of the workforce (see chapter 12). This is a valid approach. So, in theory, is the attempt to create a closer link between employees' performance and their monetary rewards or penalties. In practice, however, such an attempt is fraught with difficulties.

The issue of performance in the public sector is discussed in detail in chapter 10. A word is in order here because of its direct connection to public wage policy. In some sense, of course, all pay should be for performance. It is therefore intuitively appealing to link monetary incentives to yearly employee achievements in terms of specific quantified measures. Unfortunately, the actual empirical evidence shows that performance bonus schemes have been only marginally effective in improving performance (see, for example, Milkovich and Wigdor, 1991),[8] especially in the public sector where outputs remain difficult to quantify or are of limited relevance to the purpose of the activity. Monetary bonuses and similar schemes can also introduce an additional element of political control over the civil service. In developed countries this may or may not be a serious problem; in developing countries it is a central concern. Moreover, in multiethnic, multireligious, or clan-based societies, performance bonus schemes can upset a delicate social balance. Even when such schemes are administered fairly and well (which is not likely in such societies) the perception of favoritism is next to impossible to prevent. For example, African-American members of the U.S. Secret Service have alleged that the performance bonus scheme of the Service is implemented in discriminatory fashion. The intent here is not to dismiss the option of performance bonuses outright, but to interject a strong note of caution.

While performance bonus schemes are generally inappropriate in the public sector, meaningful performance *incentives* are a must. First and foremost, the overall recruitment and advancement system must reward good performance and penalize (and improve) underperformance. Nothing demoralizes good public servants and destroys effectiveness more than favoritism and patronage in recruitment and promotion. In addition, nonmonetary incentives, such as peer recognition, can be very important, especially among the professional ranks. In any case, informed, frank, and contestable performance assessment by the supervising managers is the cornerstone of any incentive system. Extensive paperwork and detailed performance evaluation forms are far less important than fair and informed judgment.

Promotion

A critical element in the motivation and morale of employees is the opportunity for promotion to higher levels. Career management involves, among others, assigning the right people to the right jobs and making full use of employee skills. But promotion, with its higher salary and—equally important—enhanced status and responsibility, remains the key to motivation and rewards. Personnel specialists see as the norm two to four promotions in a career. In many countries, promotions are limited to existing vacancies in the higher grade, and such limits are normally stricter at the higher grades in order to prevent "grade creep" as a response to inadequate salaries or as a result of weak management.

Criteria. Promotions should be based on a number of factors including performance, potential, skill, knowledge, and seniority (as a proxy for experience and good judgment).

There are differing approaches to the use of seniority and merit as criteria for promotion. Most developed countries and many developing countries use a combination of the two. Some developed countries (e.g., Singapore) consistently promote people entirely according to merit, while most developing countries (e.g., India) give much greater weight to seniority. A seniority-based promotion system tends to produce inefficiency over time and weakens incentives for effort and self-improvement. However, one should remember that the seniority principle was originally introduced around the end of the nineteenth century in many developed countries as a necessary *reform* to professionalize the civil service and insulate it from both the vagaries of politics and the personal connections of individual employees. These risks may have largely disappeared in developed countries but remain a reality in most developing countries, especially in multiethnic plural societies or countries with weak governance. On balance, it is important to give a progressively much greater role to merit considerations in civil service promotions than is typically the case, but to do so carefully and without discarding the seniority principle. Unlike "performance" or "merit," the number of years of service is the only objective criterion that is not subject to interpretation and manipulation by vested interests, personal agendas, or discrimination. It is also important to note that using seniority as the main criterion for promotion is less problematic to the extent that the initial recruitment was based on merit. Good personnel policy starts with good recruitment.

Procedures. Most countries follow the practice of constituting a committee for promotion within the ministry or agency concerned. This committee prepares the list of persons to be promoted as available vacancies emerge. To be eligible for promotion a candidate often must have served a minimum number of years in the current grade, earned a prescribed performance rating for a number of years, and acquired the qualifications relevant to the higher post. Promotions to higher-level positions and to senior executive services (see chapter 8) are decided on the basis of in-depth assessments and interviews, which may be undertaken by a public service commission or central personnel office in consultation with the ministry concerned. In some countries, employees are placed under probation in the higher position for some time before being confirmed in the job. Japan used to assess the eligibility of senior officials for higher posts through a system of peer rating.

Indeed, evaluation by peers and subordinates—unthinkable until recently—has been increasingly used (see chapter 10 for a discussion of performance appraisals).

Salary Increments

Promotion is only one form of reward, albeit certainly the most important one. Other monetary incentives include salary increases within a grade and "performance" bonuses. Unlike promotion, in-grade salary increases in many countries have traditionally been automatic and have been withheld only as a form of punishment. In other systems, salary increments are expected and standard, but not fully automatic and are withheld from inadequate performers.

Although most countries tend to award increments automatically within the maximum of the salary range, the size of such increments is in part based on an assessment of the employees' diligence and efficiency. When the pay structure is such that employees reach the maximum of their pay scale and stagnate there, any incentive value of salary increments obviously disappears and morale is adversely affected. (As noted earlier, the temptation to "solve" the problem by promoting the person to the higher grade should be resisted.) Some countries have therefore moved to a more nuanced system of salary increases, as illustrated by the case of South Africa (Box 7.2).

Annual Performance Bonuses

To the extent that one wishes to reward good performance during a particular year, it makes little sense to do so by giving a *permanent* increment in the base salary. Thus, in principle, a bonus is more appropriate, as it rewards performance over the relevant period of time without changing the base salary for all future years. One-time bonuses for special achievements are awarded in various countries, including the United States. Singapore introduced an interesting system in 1989, giving large performance bonuses of up to three months' salary for the top-level employees, but linked to the overall performance of the economy and not paid in times of poor economic performance. (Singapore also gives quality-service awards to staff dealing with the citizens.) In Korea, incentive bonuses are awarded every three months on the basis of points earned by employees on several parameters. Often, cash rewards are given to employees in revenue and enforcement functions (e.g., to customs inspectors and investigators for the seizure of smuggled goods or illicit drugs, usually as a percentage of the value of the goods). There may be a place for such a practice, but mainly as a transitional measure and only in conjunction with stronger oversight. In itself, it is a risky practice, as it is likely to be abused and is vulnerable to collusion.

The few bonus schemes that have had some success in the public sector have provided for performance bonuses for the entire organizational unit, as well as additional bonuses for successful teams. Awards based on *team effort* are naturally applicable mainly in activities that depend on the collective efforts of many persons in a unit (e.g., immunization or literacy programs in rural areas, or the efficiency of municipal transport). Also, team-based schemes are less likely to engender resentment and suspicions of favoritism. However, it is important to develop clearly the criteria for group effort, the procedures for obtaining feedback from the user groups, and—in order to avoid the free rider problem—the rules for distributing the cash reward among the members.

Unfortunately, whether individual- or team-based, bonuses tend over time to become viewed as de facto entitlements and an element of wage negotiation and thus lose any positive influence they may have had on incentives.

BOX 7.2

Performance-Based Compensation Systems in South Africa

The following performance-based compensation systems are used in the South African public service to grant special recognition to personnel who distinguish themselves from their peers through sustained above-average performance:

- *merit awards* for which all public servants are eligible—depending on evaluation of performance—entailing a cash award equivalent to 18 or 19 percent of basic annual salary;
- *special recognition,* through cash payments or commendations for useful suggestions, inventions, improvements, and so on;
- *department-specific awards* whereby each department may give awards, bonuses, or allowances to employees of exceptional ability, those with special qualifications important for the departmental functions, and employees who have rendered sustained meritorious service over a long period.

Source: Commonwealth Secretariat (1996).

Nonmonetary Incentives

These rewards are particularly important in times of fiscal restraint and of insufficient funds for monetary incentive schemes. In any case, men and women do not live by bread alone. Nonmonetary recognition and rewards are useful to foster performance—so long as they are used judiciously and avoid gimmickry—building on the natural desire of public servants for recognition of their efforts (or for avoiding embarrassment). Nonmonetary incentives are commonly assumed to have a particularly important role in countries where social sanction and "face" matter greatly (e.g., most East Asian countries). However, the importance attached by French civil servants to obtaining the *Legion d'Honneur* or by British government officials to receiving a title from the Queen show that public recognition can be a powerful motivator almost everywhere.

Nonmonetary incentives may include:

- National honors (e.g., inclusion in the annual Honours List in the United Kingdom, the *Legion d'Honneur* in France, and similar forms of official recognition in other countries).
- Agency-based recognition and awards schemes (e.g., certificates, plaques, or commendations). Scholarships can be instituted, or lectures arranged, in honor of an outstanding official. In addition to national awards, ministries and agencies should normally be allowed to operate recognition schemes specific to their organizational culture, including awards for field staff in regional programs. It is important to celebrate such recognition in open gatherings and to publicize it in the media.
- Career development opportunities (e.g., rewarding good performance with high-profile training opportunities such as foreign fellowships, attendance at international conferences, etc.).

- Postretirement options (e.g., appointment as board members, advisors, etc.). A signal example is the Japanese *amakudari* ("descent from Heaven") practice of postretirement assignments in the private sector to foster individual competition for excellence in the bureaucracy. Similar incentives are available after retirement to senior civil servants in many countries. (Where governance systems are weak and accountability is loose, however, postretirement incentives are a very dangerous practice—especially in industries that are heavily dependent on government, such as defense production.)

Job Transfers: An Opportunity and a Problem

Job rotation and transfers are an important influence on incentives and efficiency, but carry risks when they are abused. On the one hand, fostering the mobility of government personnel within large ministries and between ministries offers a regular opportunity to develop different skills and experiences. From the government's standpoint, such mobility helps avoid the stagnation and decline resulting from rigid systems and can alleviate as well the adjustment and personal costs of needed retrenchment. To the employee, mobility can be a welcome source of new challenges and improved prospects for higher positions.

On the other hand, frequent job rotation and arbitrary transfers can lead to poor performance in constantly changing jobs, reduced morale, and disrupted career development and family life. The ability of political superiors to transfer personnel to other locations at short notice is a powerful form of pressure and makes a mockery of the legal protections against arbitrary demotion or dismissal that were designed precisely to insulate civil servants from political pressure or personalistic interventions. Imagine being protected by law from being fired or demoted, but exposed at any time to be transferred to some place in the boonies—where you don't know anyone, and there's no adequate housing, schooling for your children, or employment for your spouse. Your temptation to "play ball" with your political boss would be very strong. For a variety of historical reasons, the problem of arbitrary transfers of senior civil servants is especially severe in South Asia (see Box 7.3). Thus, like all other public administration practices, job rotation and transfers must also be based on clear and transparent criteria, developed in consultation with the employees and other relevant stakeholders, and contain a mechanism for appeal of arbitrary decisions to an independent entity.

Grade Inflation and "Band-Aid" Remedies: The Worst Response to Inadequate Incentives

A public sector manager, confronted with deserving but poorly paid staff, is tempted to promote them to levels for which they are not qualified or to provide special ad hoc payments or perks as a way to prevent further deterioration in their real salary and keep them from leaving the government. This is entirely understandable, and most managers would yield to that temptation. However, in a very short period, such grade inflation and ad hoc remedies produce all the disadvantages of inadequate incentives and *in addition* diminish the capacity of the government to manage its human resources, as these ad hoc remedies are not transparent and tend to be "sticky" once given.

Examples abound, especially in the developing world. Thus, in Trinidad and Tobago and in Guyana, disguised pay increases were given by not filling upper and middle professional vacancies with permanent appointees but instead with underqualified staff in an "acting" capacity, causing severe imbalances in employment. The payment of special salaries and allowances to staff in some ministries but not others caused resentment and loss of morale among civil servants, and unapproved recruitment and temporary hiring at higher rates produced distortions in the compensation structure.

BOX 7.3

Arbitrary Rotation of Civil Servants in Bangladesh and India

A major weakness of the Bangladesh civil service is the too-frequent rotation of civil servants. The practice erodes accountability, forfeits the benefit of accumulated experience, and weakens commitment to the immediate task. Glaring cases of inappropriate rotation in key ministries include the transfer of secretaries (the highest-level career civil servant in a ministry) soon after major credit agreements with donor agencies are signed; the transfer of secretaries in key ministries after less than six months; the frequent shifting of chief engineers of major spending departments; and the short tenure of members of the Planning Commission. Departmental secretaries with a reputation for good management of crises are periodically shifted between departments and secretaries who fall out of favor with the political leadership are transferred elsewhere. The "spoils system" associated with Bangladeshi electoral politics is the root cause of these problems.

In India, a conference of chief ministers noted similar problems of political interference in the transfer of senior officials and the effect of such instability on the morale and efficiency of field and secretariat officials. In some provinces, massive transfers were ordered with every change of government. In times of short-lived governments, offices could be shuffled every six months or less. With political middlemen entering the fray, transfers have become a productive industry. (As noted, this is not an argument against transfers, but an argument against the threat of the use of transfers as an instrument of political pressure to force inappropriate behavior of senior civil servants.)

In Yemen, the practice of bringing in unqualified outsiders to fill high-level positions for which they were totally unsuited was widespread, especially after the unification in 1990 of North Yemen and South Yemen (formerly Aden), and was a major factor in the degradation of the civil service that has occurred since that time, until major reforms from 2002 onward. Ad hoc partial responses to the basic problem of inadequate compensation ruin the very system onto which more adequate incentives could be built in the future. Because it is reasonable and realistic to expect that managers will behave as normal human beings and try to give favorable treatment to their employees, the adverse outcomes of grade inflation and ad hoc remedies can be averted only by penalizing managers who resort to these devices. Naturally, the long-term solution is to build a government workforce that is competent and small, and thus can be adequately compensated in affordable ways.

GENERAL DIRECTIONS OF IMPROVEMENT

In developed and developing countries alike, the objective of reform is to take measures to achieve a government workforce of the appropriate size, skill mix, motivation, professional ethos, and accountability.

Most of the major issues of government personnel employment and compensation have already been tackled in developed countries—with the exception of gender equality and the ethnic diversity of the workforce, in both of which there remains substantial scope for further improvement. The government workforce has reached a size that is roughly consistent with the functions of government in each country, and employee compensation is also more or less appropriate as a result of the operation of an open and efficient labor market that precludes large deviations from private sector compensation. In developing countries, by contrast, the problems are more basic and, in general, harder to resolve.

Civil service reform in developing countries is often identified with personnel retrenchment and real-wage reduction for fiscal reasons. Although, as noted, the goal of civil service reform is much broader, the necessity of cost containment places a priority on getting the government workforce to a size that is both appropriate and affordable.

Government Employment: Getting to the "Right Size"

The reality in most developing countries is a bloated workforce resulting from weak recruitment controls, years of patronage hiring, and an earlier view of government as "employer of last resort." In practice, therefore, the reform direction is to reduce the size of government employment. Doing so gradually and mainly by attrition—reducing recruitment below the rate of normal retirements, resignations, and deaths—can help, and is preferable. However, in countries where the workforce is in substantial excess, sharper measures may be required.

A retrenchment program should be designed and implemented in phases. Because in developing countries institutions are fragile and ethnic pluralism is a dominant reality, it is critical that the process be clear to all concerned and administered with ferocious attachment to the established rules and criteria and excluding any personal or group favoritism. On the other hand, it is also important to preserve progress made in bringing into government women and members of minority groups. Thus, a "last-in-first-out" approach to retrenchment is by definition discriminatory against the groups recently included and modifications of a strict seniority rule would be needed. Subject to these considerations, a possible sequence of measures is suggested below.

Immediate measures could include:

- a freeze on recruitment, with swift penalties for violation and a carefully circumscribed procedure for exceptions in order to avoid the rigidities and inefficiencies of a prolonged recruitment freeze;
- the sequestering of job vacancies arising out of retirement, termination, death, or resignation, as they occur;
- the strict application of regulations on regular retirement and separation of employees beyond the retirement age, with normal pension and other separation benefits;
- a temporary moratorium in promotions except in individual cases expressly approved by high authority; and
- a halt to the practice of absorbing contractual and temporary employees into permanent positions.

Short-term measures would involve:

- a complete census of all types of employees;
- the removal of "ghost workers" from the payroll and correction of other irregularities revealed through the census;

- an improved personnel management information system;
- an improved and secure payroll system; and
- studies on job classification, personnel procedures, and salary structure.

Medium-term measures would include:

- implementation of the findings and actions emerging from the previous phase;
- streamlining of personnel regulations;
- a review of the functions, organization, operational effectiveness, and staffing of government, starting with the key ministries;
- definition (not implementation) of a new salary scale befitting the country's level of income and consistent with good practice in this regard;
- a mechanism for recertifying government employees in order to screen out those without adequate qualifications;
- implementation of a program for redeploying other employees to more useful jobs; and
- where necessary, a program of involuntary early retirement of employees found redundant through the organizational review process, with an appropriate safety net.

As part of a *long-term program,* each ministry and agency could be required to submit a concrete restructuring plan consisting of a clear statement of objectives; strategies for achieving these objectives; a staffing program; a timetable of reform measures; simple indices of administrative performance; training needs, based on a sound assessment; and financial requirements. Once the plan is approved at the highest level and irreversible initial reforms have been implemented, the ministry in question may be allowed to freely recruit from other ministries, resume normal wage increases and promotions, have its reasonable budget requests met, and implement for its employees the new salary scale established in the meantime. Such a process would create incentives for all government entities to improve their organization and operations in order to be allowed to "move up" to the new flexible structure and for individual employees to move to the more dynamic government entities. In time, all government entities would operate in accordance with the new system and the coherent vision formulated to begin the process would be fulfilled. (This process, naturally, is an ideal, and carries heavy requirements in terms of consistency, persistence, and political determination and continuity.)

Compensating Government Employees

Compensation of state employees in many developing countries is notoriously inadequate. The main problem with a bloated government workforce lies not only in itself, but in its consequence of inadequate wages across the board. Given fiscal constraints, achieving more adequate compensation is only possible if the overall workforce is reduced. Because such reduction takes time, the main conundrum in a poor country is how to provide in the interim sufficient incentives to government employees charged with essential functions without either balkanizing the public service or busting the budget. A few practical transitional measures can be suggested:

- It is possible to create a temporary two-tier system (as in Poland) whereby new staff are recruited at the new salary scale and are expected to meet higher standards of qualification and performance. Over time, the new system will expand as the old one contracts, eventually leading to a unified system with better-qualified, better-paid staff. Like dual exchange-rate systems, this approach will work only if it is transitory and compressed in a relatively short period of time.

- Even at inadequate salaries, young and better-trained people can be induced to join government service for limited periods if given challenging responsibilities and solid training (as in Estonia). When they leave, others can be recruited. The training requirements within the government sector are semi-permanent, but the capacity of the economy as a whole is enhanced; the understanding of the work of government is improved.
- The average performance of government employees rises and positive models are offered to permanent employees for their own betterment.
- Special transitional arrangements for fixed-term contract employees (higher-skilled, paid above the existing scale) can be workable (as in Lebanon), provided that the allocation to the different government bodies of such contractual posts is decided at high levels; each appointment is cleared individually and personally by high authority; and these arrangements are part of a genuine transition to an overall salary reform.

In any case, individual negotiations between new staff being recruited and ministries should never be permitted in developing countries, as they result in glaring distortions and inequities, maximize suspicions and resentment, and compromise prospects for sustainable improvement.

QUESTIONS FOR DISCUSSION

1. Why is the relative size of government employment larger in rich than in poor countries? Will it necessarily grow in the poor countries as they develop?
2. All things considered, do you expect the overall size of government employment in the United States to grow or decline? Do you also expect a shift from federal to state and local government employment, or vice versa? Why?
3. "As a general rule, the workforce of general government should be between 2 and 4 percent of the country's population, and that of central government between 1 and 2 percent." Comment.
4. If government employment is excessive and a fiscal crisis occurs, is there any practical alternative to retrenching (terminating) very quickly as many employees as necessary to restore the fiscal balance?
5. "Last hired, first fired." Discuss the possible implications of this general principle for ethnic and gender equality in government employment.
6. "Because full comparability and equity are a chimera, supply and demand in the market for labor should be allowed to set the salary of individual government employees—just as they do in the private sector." Discuss.
7. Pick one of the following statements and make a credible argument for it:
   a. "Promoting people by seniority rewards employees for longevity—not merit—and damages government efficiency."
   b. "Promoting people by merit without regard to seniority damages morale of older workers and government integrity."
8. Aside from the arguments made in the previous question, are there situations where hiring and promoting exclusively on the basis of individual qualifications and merit could reduce the *efficiency* of the public administration as a whole?
9. Since a salary structure must be sufficiently decompressed to provide adequate incentives to top managers and professionals, shouldn't the government adopt a system similar to that used in very large corporations to set compensation for their top executives?

10. Discuss the pros and cons of annual "performance-based" bonuses for government employees. Try to frame the discussion with a concrete scenario with specific hypothetical illustrations.

NOTES

1. Quoted in Andic and Andic (1996).
2. Among others, Bird (1971); Diamond (1977); (Martin 1982).
3. This and the following sections are based largely on Schiavo-Campo et al. (1997a, 1997b).
4. Among others, Lindauer (1981); Heller and Tait (1983); Kraay and Van Rijckeghem (1995).
5. Report of the Public Commission of Uganda (1982), cited in Lindauer and Numberg (1994, p. 27).
6. Measuring compression raises a number of methodological issues. First, changes in the compression ratio of highest to lower salary midpoints may not indicate changes in the structure as a whole. For example, placing a cap on the highest salary may weaken incentives at the highest level (as in the case of the United States—see chapter 8), but has no effect on the remainder of the salary structure. Second, international comparisons based on compression ratios are difficult because the ratio is necessarily higher where there are a greater number of salary grades, other things being equal. Thus, a government could easily demonstrate an "improvement" in incentives without changing the compensation structure at all by simply splitting each salary grade in two, which would automatically increase the difference between the highest and lowest midpoints. The best measure of salary "compression" would be the coefficient of variation—the deviation of the salary grade midpoints divided by the overall mean salary—divided in turn by the number of salary grades. This calculation is much too demanding to be practical for large-scale international comparisons, but it should be a requirement of any serious effort at reforming the salary structure in a given country. However, if the specific issue is one of monetary incentives for one particular grade or occupation, the appropriate measure is the ratio of the salary midpoint for *that* grade to the mean salary for the ministry or sector or civil service as a whole—depending on the purposes of the analysis. In any case, the imperfections of the usual compression ratio should be kept in mind when interpreting the data.
7. See, on these issues, Commonwealth Secretariat (1996); Armstrong (2006); Milkovitch (1997); Klingner and Nalbandian (1998); Riley (1993); Corrigan, Hayes and Joyce (1999); Pearce and Rich, in Perry, ed. (1989).
8. Milkovich (1997).

CHAPTER 8

Managing the People II: Personnel Administration and Development

Every man is good at some thing; it is the task of the Chief to find it.
—Malay proverb

WHAT TO EXPECT

Different social values have led to different personnel systems in different countries. A system where personal rule is prevalent tends to be characterized by political appointments. Where social equity is important, affirmative action and minority protection are introduced. Where the focus is on efficiency, the personnel system stresses disciplinary action against nonperforming employees and rewards for strong performance. In general, the evolution of government personnel systems has shown a transition from political patronage and personalism to a system based on merit, political neutrality, continuity, integrity, and professionalism, as in the United States. However, many developing countries and countries of the former Soviet Union still show an uneasy coexistence of informal rules and personal considerations with formal merit-based personnel management.

In any country, good management of government personnel begins with clear personnel planning, a discussion of which starts this chapter. The types of job classification and evaluation are discussed next, highlighting the trade-off between cost and complexity on the one hand and accuracy and equity on the other. A discussion follows of the procedures for hiring, promotion, and discipline that are consistent with the basic principles of personnel management, among which merit and nondiscrimination rank highest, tempered by other social and equity considerations. The various possible organizational arrangements are discussed next, generally requiring uniform national rules, terms of employment, oversight, and appeal, with actual personnel decisions delegated to each agency. The chapter outlines the rights and responsibilities of public servants and has an extensive discussion of training. A section on the United States covers both personnel management and the policy issues addressed in the previous chapter, and the chapter concludes with the customary section on general directions of improvement. An appendix outlines the rationale for establishing elite executive personnel corps.

GOVERNMENT PERSONNEL MANAGEMENT

The public's view of government employees has typically mirrored public views about government in general. High status attaches to government employees in countries where the role of government is viewed positively, and civil servants enjoy little public trust in countries where government

198

is viewed as part of the problem. The latter has been the case since the 1980s in North America, the United Kingdom, and other countries in the "Anglo-Saxon" administration tradition, such as Australia and New Zealand. But the picture is not uniform. In France, for example, surveys by the Ecole Nationale d'Administration (ENA) have shown that over 80 percent of ENA graduates are still in the civil service and that the citizenry is keen to retain them by offering adequate salaries. In many countries, especially in Asia (e.g., China, Japan, Korea, Sri Lanka), there is respect for civil servants and government employees have high social status.

Personnel Planning[1]

The *objectives* of government personnel planning are to:

- monitor and control the growth of government employment consistent with the fiscal targets;
- ensure that staff are utilized effectively in response to government policy and development priorities; and
- enable the government to achieve its strategies for staff acquisition, retention, development, and separation.

A planning and information system for government provides the mechanism for reconciling the demand for government employees, the likely supply, and financial constraints. Thus, a fully developed system typically contains the following elements: (1) workforce inventory, (2) framework for position control, (3) demand forecasting, and (4) supply forecasting.

Adequate *personnel records* are a prerequisite for government personnel planning, and the information required can be grouped into three categories:

- *The people*—numbers and characteristics of employees (age, gender, qualifications, skills, experience), their location (ministries, departments, agencies, and field offices), and data on their entry, promotion, transfer, resignation, retirement, and dismissal;
- *The jobs*—number, location, types, and grades of authorized positions, positions filled, and vacancies; and job types, grade, pay, and other employment conditions; and
- *The finances*—current pay and allowances structure, personnel expenditure trends, termination benefits, pension forecasts, etc.

Job Classification[2]

Grading Government Jobs

Positions are grouped in a hierarchical grade system. Each grade contains all jobs with features that are judged to be similar and has a salary scale associated with it. The appropriate number of grades is a matter of judgment and depends on the conditions in a particular country. (For example, the Philippines and India have about thirty salary grades and the United States half that number.) With too many grades, the distinction between work levels becomes too fine, jobs more difficult to classify, and disputes more frequent. Too few grades, on the other hand, dilute the strong motivation provided by the chance of promotion and a higher-sounding title.

There are two basic approaches to the grading of government jobs: rank-in-person and rank-in-job. Under the *rank-in-person* approach, the employee rank is independent of specific duties or organizational location. For example, a military general remains a general, whether in the field or at headquarters. The rank-in-person system encourages mobility but tends to become top-heavy, give undue weight to seniority, and suffer from inbreeding.

Under the *rank-in-job* approach, it is the job—not the person—that is ranked. The rank-in-job system permits recruitment through lateral entry and enables more efficient younger employees to leapfrog over more senior employees. However, necessary updating of the classification will be resisted by the incumbents. Also, agencies are tempted to create too many higher-level positions or to shift professional specialists to administrative positions to improve their chances of retaining or recruiting them. Third, the system hampers the mobility of personnel and keeps them from gaining new experience.

Country experiences show, however, that the contrast between rank-in-person and rank-in-job systems is not as stark as it may appear. The systems are not mutually exclusive, and elements of rank-in-person systems are found in predominantly rank-in-job systems and vice versa. Thus, developing countries in the British administrative tradition inherited the British administrative elite system, along with functional services for different specializations like health, engineering, accounts, and audit. In parallel, both France and Japan also established elite civil service systems after World War II. The rank-in-person system blended well with the traditional stratification of these former British colonies and has continued substantially in the same form until now in many countries (e.g., India). Similarly, the creation of a "senior executive service" in developed countries that practice the rank-in-job system has served to bring into the higher civil service the advantages of the rank-in-person system.

Job Evaluation

Job Analysis and Evaluation. Job analysis involves describing the responsibilities of the job, its relationship to the organizational hierarchy, supervisory content (if any), and the qualifications and skills it requires. Evaluation is the next step. The evaluator looks at all the jobs in the government or in a particular agency and assesses their relative difficulty and contribution to the organization. The jobs are then grouped into categories and features, and points are assigned accordingly.[3]

Job Classification. Job classification requires that the duties of every position be described by the incumbents, their supervisor, and finally by a classification specialist in the central personnel office. Positions are then grouped into classes according to occupation (e.g., clerk-typist, civil engineer) and level of qualifications and responsibility. This allows the determination of "grades" (also called "skill levels"), each corresponding to a specified level of difficulty, skill, and responsibility, and a single pay range for all positions in all classes assigned to a particular grade.

The System in Practice

Developed countries show a diverse picture. The French system is unique in following a highly structured internal organization based on the civil service "corps" concept, with each corps corresponding to an occupational specialization. The number of corps (over 1,700) is larger in France than in most other developed countries. Each corps falls into one of three major hierarchical classes—A, B, or C. In the systems structured along the British tradition (except in Canada and Australia), the entire civil service is organized into the same set of categories—usually executive, administrative, clerical, and messenger.

In developing countries, far more important than the choice of classification system is the transparency of the grading system. Limited availability and poor quality of information on jobs lead to arbitrary assignment of personnel, opaque decision making, and a grade structure complicated by an excessive number of wage brackets. Moreover, the staff responsible for grading jobs is often not adequately trained in job evaluation and lack technical skills, and the systems are too easily influenced by political considerations. Experience calls for caution in transplanting to developing countries the job classification systems of developed countries. (Transplants of institutional arrangements to countries in different circumstances are always risky—see McFerson, 2007.) As a broad generalization, simple classifications with a limited number of grades are most appropriate in developing countries.

In any case, all job evaluations and classifications are time consuming, expensive, and potentially subject to manipulation. Their strong subjective component is camouflaged in numerical complexity and can be used to rationalize political or top management decisions already taken informally. Caution is especially necessary when the classification exercise is carried out by consultants paid by senior management, who are naturally responsive to its wishes. Integrity, common sense, and contestability of results are critical because, if job evaluation and classification produce phony or self-serving results, their substantial cost is unlikely to be justified by a better outcome. For example, Fesler and Kettl (1991)[4] point out that organizational distortions and wrong assignment of staff members accounted for about 30 percent of the upward grade creep in the U.S. federal government, from an average grade of GS 5.4 to GS 8.3 between 1950 and 1983.

Recruitment, Advancement, and Sanctions[5]

Guiding Principles

Recruitment, advancement, rewards, and sanctions in the public service should be based on the principles of merit and nondiscrimination. As noted earlier, in government employment there has been a steady move in the twentieth century away from political patronage and favoritism toward recruitment based on merit and open competition—even if for higher-level appointments "merit" may well include an element of personal commitment to the political leadership and its agenda. Although this move is comparatively recent, consideration of individual merit in government personnel decisions has a long pedigree, as Box 8.1 illustrates.

However, efficiency is hardly the sole criterion for personnel selection. In many countries (e.g., India or South Africa), social peace or group equity and the objective of promoting a more inclusive society justify provisions for "affirmative action," sometimes extending to specific job quotas. (For excellent analyses of the complex subject of affirmative action, see Broadnax, 2000; Miller, 2005; and Weisskopf, 2004.) Equal opportunity laws have been passed in most countries, including virtually all developed countries, to ban employment discrimination against women, minorities, and the disabled. However, the passage of formal laws cannot by itself change deep-rooted attitudes. For example, the proportion of women hired for civil service in Bangladesh actually fell in the last twenty years, despite the existence of anti-discrimination legislation. Aggressive enforcement is needed, as well as addressing the structural roots of discrimination.

Recruitment Procedures

The recruitment process entails, in sequence:

- identify the post to be filled;
- draft the job description and specifications;

BOX 8.1

The Merit System in Historical Perspective

From ancient times, in the objective of establishing well-ordered societies, governments have attempted to recruit, promote, and penalize personnel at least partly on the basis of individual merit and qualifications-assessed in various ways.

In China, a system of competitive examinations for recruiting imperial government officials ("mandarins") based on a Confucian curriculum (see chapter 2) dates back to the Han dynasty (202 B.C.E. to 220 C.E.). Candidates for government employment faced fierce competition in a series of exams, dealing primarily with classical texts and conducted on the municipal, provincial, and national levels. The exams continued to be administered for almost two thousand years, albeit of course with various changes, and were only abolished in 1905. The system created an administrative elite grounded in a common body of teachings; provided continuity to state administration through revolts, revolutions, and dynastic upheavals; and lent credibility and enormous prestige to the state meritocracy.

In pragmatic ancient Rome, merit was assessed more on the basis of subjective judgments of the individual's abilities than by objective criteria. However, the performance of government officials was then evaluated mainly by results—especially in public works construction—with typically Roman severe penalties for bad performance and substantial rewards for good results.

In the pre-Arab Middle East, there are indications that individual merit played a role in the appointment and advancement of government servants in both the Babylonian kingdom and in the Persian Empire from the days of Darius the Great. In the early period of Arab states after the Arab conquest, government administration required from its employees not only religious piety but also a measure of effectiveness, especially in southern Spain.

In the Ottoman Empire, good performance of state employees was a major ingredient of public administration. Indeed, some observers consider that the slow decline of the Ottoman Empire after the 18th century was partly caused by the increased reliance on patronage and loyalty networks and by the progressive disregard of the qualifications and performance of government employees.

In Europe, civil services based partly on personal qualifications and ability date back to 18th-century Prussia, with Frederick the Great and his successors—whereas in France and southern Europe the role of merit in government employment was introduced later, largely through the influence of Napoleonic concepts at the start of the 19th century.

- publicize the vacancies, allowing for a reasonable period of time to apply, and provide prospective applicants with all necessary information;
- assess the candidates; and
- select the most suitable candidate.

The standards and criteria of personnel selection are normally prescribed by law, with detailed procedures defined in the subsequent general civil service regulations. However, the line ministries and agencies are usually also allowed to establish additional specific recruitment criteria for their own positions, in consultation with the central personnel agency and in conformity with the national norms.

In countries that use examinations, practices vary widely. Examinations are usually coupled with other selection mechanisms, such as interviews and sometimes psychometric tests. For recruitment for middle or higher ranks, examinations are unusual and candidates are selected on the basis of experience, qualifications, references, and interviews.

Open competition based on clear criteria and transparent procedure is the best way to assure merit-based recruitment and good outcomes. Often, however, the preferred candidate has already been informally selected and the public competitive procedure is only a formalistic smokescreen. This is not only a waste of time and resources, but also produces unnecessary frustration for unsuccessful candidates and damages the credibility of the whole system. Where this practice is widespread, it is preferable to give openly more space for direct selection of preferred candidates under clear rules and for specified situations, while at the same time enforcing strictly the competitive selection process in the regular cases. (Also, at the very least, vacancy announcements should give potential candidates a candid and honest signal by including the standard expression that "a suitable candidate has already been identified.")

Types of Appointment

The terms and conditions of appointment of the candidate selected are usually set out in a formal letter. The vast majority of government service employees are appointed on a permanent and full-time basis, referred to as *indefinite-duration* contracts. Normally, a probationary period of service needs to be satisfactorily completed. Increasingly important, however, are fixed-term and part-time contracts, which enable ministries to use their budget effectively, respond more readily to changes in needs and in supply of labor, and meet demands from employees for flexible arrangements suited to their family and other circumstances. Usually, limits are set on the percentage of posts that can be filled by fixed-term contract, but there are rarely limits on part-time working arrangements.

In many developed countries, there has been a move in the last decade away from the traditional "tenured" permanent employment and toward *fixed-term contracts,* especially for senior and professional staff. In New Zealand, fixed-term contracts are the uniform practice for all senior staff. The objectives are to provide greater flexibility to the government and to establish a stronger link between employees' performance and employment (see chapter 10 for a full discussion of performance issues). An imaginative innovation is that of "rolling" contracts, which are also fixed-term but are rolled annually for two or three years, thus offering somewhat greater long-term security for the employee and no sharp discontinuities in employment.

Note that whether the contract is permanent or fixed-term or part-time, the individual in question is a government employee, with the responsibilities and rights attached to this status. Instead, when a service or activities are outsourced to an outside private entity, the persons performing such services do not become government employees and do not have the rights attaching to government employment. Sidestepping the standards and constraints of direct employment has been a serious problem in the outsourcing of government activities. In many developed countries, however, the courts have ruled that the government is obliged to make sure that contractors give their employees some of the same basic protections enjoyed by government employees. (See chapter 11 for a discussion of outsourcing.)

The extent of *part-time work* in government service has also grown in many developed countries. Part-time employment is any employment that entails less than the standard working hours for full-time jobs (varying in developed countries from 35 hours per week, in France, to the more frequent 40 hours per week). Part-time work may be permanent or temporary. A variant of part-time employment is job sharing (e.g., the sharing of the responsibilities of a full-time job between two or more people). Some observers foresee a considerable expansion in job sharing in the years to come, to allow for better balance between work and personal life.

Finally, *casual appointments* are temporary appointment to meet short-term needs, such as an unexpected increase in workload, and combine elements of fixed-term and part-time work. They are a necessary adjunct to the government workforce, but can easily be abused as well. Most commonly, central government "freezes" on the filling of permanent position are circumvented by casual or contractual appointments and the employees concerned are later converted to permanent job under political pressure. Like price controls, across-the-board recruitment freezes may have an important role in situations of severe fiscal pressure or unforeseen developments, but are rarely effective and cause distortions that become worse and worse the longer the duration of the "freeze."

Advancement

Advancement includes progression to the next salary step within a grade and promotion to the next higher grade. The former is almost automatic in every system except for demonstrated underperformance; the latter instead requires a major review of employee performance and, usually, also some well-founded expectation that further advancement is possible in the future.

The mix of salary step raises and promotions depends of course on the degree of detail of the grade structure. When the structure has a large number of grades, it becomes impossible to raise the salary of employees who have reached the top of the salary scale in their grade unless they are promoted—an action for which they may not otherwise qualify. Thus, a number of governments and large organizations have moved toward "flatter" organizational structures and "broad-banding" (i.e., the reduction in number of grades and widening of salary ranges to allow monetary rewards for good performance without promotion or transfers). When pushed too far, however, broad-banding has proved to weaken individual incentives, which, in every culture, are much stronger for promotion and a higher-sounding title than for salary increases in and of themselves. It is likely that the pendulum will swing the other way in the future and return to greater grade differentiation.

In any event, advancement must be grounded on the same principles of merit, qualifications, nondiscrimination, and due process that underpin recruitment, and so does, of course, the imposition of penalties and sanctions for disciplinary reasons or underperformance.

Penalties and Sanctions

Performance management, outsourcing, changing contract modalities, reorientation to results—these and other major changes that have occurred in public administration since the 1980s have led to some confusion over what is acceptable behavior for a civil servant. There is a persuasive argument that in several developed countries, including the United States, these changes have carried some costs in terms of a deterioration of probity and integrity among both government employees and elected politicians. Codes of conduct for civil servants have therefore come into increasing use in recent years. While these are discussed in chapter 13, it is important to advance here the essential point that codes of conduct are useless if they are not grounded on internalized ethics, clear values, and a strong accountability regime—and are worse than useless if they are enacted to whitewash unpleasant corruption realities, or as an alibi for not undertaking necessary reforms.

Disciplinary Measures. Measures against a government employee range from minor (e.g., a warning or small fine) to severe depending on the gravity of the violation. For poor performance or misconduct that stretches over an extended period of service, disciplinary action proceeds in stages, from oral to written reprimand to more serious action—progressively, denial of salary raise, suspension, demotion, and finally, dismissal. Because there can be no greater administrative penalty than dismissal, persons who have already left government service are beyond reach. They might, however, lose their pensions if they violate post-retirement provisions and, of course, if the misconduct is criminal, the former employee is liable to prosecution like anybody else. Naturally, different disciplinary regulations apply to civilian and military employees.

Disciplinary Regulations. These should be covered in appropriate detail in a manual drafted to ensure clarity and due process, including:

* types of misconduct;
* types of punishments;
* proceedings for minor and major punishments, respectively;
* supervisor's report detailing the circumstances and substance of the misconduct, the steps taken, if any, the documentary evidence and witnesses, and the penalty proposed;
* action taken on the report by the competent authority;
* for major punishments, inquiry and recommendations by an investigating officer;
* action taken on the recommendations by the competent authority;
* issue of a notice informing the employee of the punishment decided;
* consultation with the central body responsible for disciplinary matters, if required;
* decision on the punishment; and
* appeal procedures.

Disciplinary Proceedings. A qualified panel of current or retired staff should be appointed to review the case and complete the inquiry within a reasonable period (usually not more than six months). The competent authority, in turn, should process the report quickly and decide the case on the basis of the facts and the law. There should be a single-stage appeal to a competent authority (normally the central or state personnel agency, or a public service commission), which should itself decide within a stipulated time. The rules should allow no scope for outside interference at any stage of the disciplinary proceedings. When disciplinary proceedings are dilatory and badly conducted, the innocent employee suffers the trauma of inquiry, uncertainty, and the injustice of being denied promotion and other rewards, while the guilty person is able to prolong the ultimate decision and carry on as before. As always, justice delayed is justice denied.

In most countries, it is widely felt that laws protecting job security in government employment and the lengthy procedures for dismissal make it nearly impossible to remove incompetents or malfeasants. The answer is not to dilute government job security but to put in place and enforce measures for better management and greater accountability. Managers are the first line of response to underperformance and misconduct. They should be held responsible for weak disciplinary action or inattention to bad performance and penalized when they pretend to "resolve" the problem by transferring the nonperformer to another post. All this is much easier written than done: the reality in most countries is that it is unduly difficult to fire regular government employees, even when their performance is consistently sub-par.

It is generally advisable to introduce rapid summary proceedings for imposing minor punishments quickly in order to create a deterrent effect. To this end, the central personnel agency should make an effort to build a cadre of experienced inquiry staff. The central personnel office should intervene to stop instances of outside influence in the conduct of the case or deliberate victimization. Throughout, it is important to again note that swiftness and certainty of punishment are a more effective deterrent than the severity of the penalty, particularly where its probability is low and its timing far off into the future.

Organizational Arrangements for Personnel Management

Centralized personnel management systems are more common than decentralized systems whereby each government ministry or agency handles its own personnel recruitment, advancement, and terms of employment without central controls. Successful centralized systems exercise effective control over personnel functions and professional standards; unsuccessful centralized systems turn control into micromanagement, and protection of professional standards into paralysis.

Authority over personnel at the national level is generally shared among a number of entities: a policy agency, an oversight agency to ensure due process, and a financial control and monitoring unit. However, in most countries the line ministries and agencies have in recent years assumed increasing responsibility for many personnel functions.

Delegation and Decentralization

Delegation involves reallocating personnel responsibilities *within* the central government, from the central public service commission to function-based commissions and from the central personnel office to the line ministries and agencies. Delegation of personnel management to line ministries should, of course, be part of a more general devolution of functions. Many developed countries have retained the centralized system for the higher levels of civil servants, but use a delegated system for other personnel. In general, over the last two decades, most developed countries have moved in the direction of keeping central standards and norms but leaving all recruitment and other personnel decisions to each department and agency. So far, no significant problems appear to have emerged.

In developing countries, by contrast, there is no hard evidence of the benefits of agency-based recruitment, but plenty of evidence of the risks in terms of inequity and corruption. Decentralized recruitment requires a healthy accountability regime, a strong tradition of public service, and a robust personnel system. The priority in developing countries is clearly to develop well-functioning, merit-based, and accountable central recruitment systems before even considering giving their line ministries and agencies discretion in recruitment. This is especially important when the political arrangements in ethnically plural countries assign different ministries to different ethnic groups. In the absence of strong central control and employee protection, such assignments are bound to produce enclaves founded entirely on kinship and ethnic ties and unwilling to cooperate with one another—thus turning an arrangement for social peace into a recipe for longer-term conflict. (The same realities strongly militate against the introduction in plural societies of "performance-pay" practices, as discussed later.)

Delegation in International Experience

The varieties of delegation in recruitment in different countries are shown in Box 8.2.

Public Service Commissions

Central public service commissions (PSCs) can play a major role in ensuring merit-based recruitment and advancement policies and practices. In many countries, such commissions enjoy constitutional status. Their members are expected to be men and women of integrity, appointed on merit and without regard to partisan political considerations. Legal provisions for security of tenure and conditions of service safeguard the status and independence of the members of the commission.

The mandate of a public service commission generally includes administering competitive examinations and selecting the successful candidates according to transparent and objective criteria. The central PSC typically also enforces the merit principle in promotions, senior appointments, and lateral entry; assists the government in recruiting and managing a senior executive service; regulates disciplinary procedure; hears appeals from employees; and is consulted before major penalties for misconduct are assessed.[6]

Despite sound formal structures, public service commissions have often not functioned effectively. In some countries, they have been mere rubberstamps for politicized personnel decisions. Conversely, in other countries they have functioned in micromanagement mode, causing long delays and precluding any hiring flexibility by public managers—forcing them to take illicit shortcuts to fill their vacancies. In several developing countries, moreover, there have been instances of malpractice in commission-supervised examinations, political interference in selection of candidates, and the induction of unqualified political appointees into the public service commission itself. These difficulties are real, and have led many to push for the elimination of central personnel bodies. However, the solution lies in improving their functioning, not in eliminating them.

Below the national level in some countries, the provinces have set up their own public service commissions to recruit personnel for provincial administration and, in a few cases, for local governments as well. Similarly, the elected local governments and various different types of local authorities are often authorized to recruit all or most of their employees, in accordance with national or provincial guidelines (especially regarding merit and non-discrimination). A group of local authorities may engage in collective recruitment for certain common jobs, to save transaction costs and attract better candidates, or they may rely on specialized recruitment agencies for help in selecting candidates for senior positions like those of city manager and heads of departments.

Performance Management and Appraisal

This subject could be equally well addressed in this chapter as in the chapter on performance and managing for results. It is briefly previewed here but discussed in greater detail in chapter 10. The interested reader is advised to now turn to the appropriate section in that chapter.

The objective of personnel performance management and appraisal is to guide individual employees toward making an effective contribution to the work of the organization while at the same time meeting their own personal goals. Because of the impact of performance appraisal on salary and career pros-

BOX 8.2

Different Organizational Arrangements for Personnel Management

In *India,* major departments, such as railways, are allowed to set up their own recruitment boards for lower-level personnel. Department heads have limited powers to appoint staff to lower-level jobs and contractual positions. Service commissions also operate at the individual states level to recruit staff for state and local government agencies.

In *Malaysia,* core personnel management functions are concentrated in the Public Service Department and, instead of a single Public Service Commission, four separate commissions recruit people for police, education, railways, and judicial and legal services—in consultation with the departments concerned.

In *New Zealand,* department heads are responsible for hiring all staff, on fixed contracts, and agencies are allowed to devise their own procedures in conformity with national guidelines.

In the *Philippines,* both key central agencies, the Department of Budget and Management and the Civil Service Commission, have legal responsibility for setting pay scales and salary grades. The overlapping legal mandates of the two agencies create problems for the line agencies in getting permission to create a new position and to recruit externally, and lead to delays in filling positions. There is also a conflict between the definition of qualifications done by the Commission and the grading of positions done by the Department of Budget and Management.

In *Singapore,* the Ministry of Finance has two divisions for personnel matters: the Budget Division handles manpower control, while the Public Service Division develops policy, coordinates implementation, and is responsible for pay and grading, training, and productivity improvement. Most personnel actions were delegated in 1995 to personnel boards in each department, composed of senior managers of the department and acting on the basis of merit and rigorous selection. However, the central Public Service Commission continues to be in charge of recruitment for the elite administrative service, promotion to the highest ranks, disciplinary cases, and all appeals.

In the *United Kingdom,* the line ministries are allowed to recruit persons for most positions, except for the fast-stream administrative trainee program.

In the *United States,* subject to the oversight of the Office of Personnel Management, departments and agencies are authorized to conduct their own recruitment.

Source: Commonwealth Secretariat (1995); Various news reports, 2000–2, and official websites.

pects, its framework and methodology have important consequences for the motivation of employees, and thus for improved performance. Performance appraisal can also serve as a strategic tool for raising overall standards in government service and for increasing accountability to citizens.

In principle, performance appraisal and feedback should be a continuous process, but periodic formal appraisal is dictated by the practical need to review performance over a defined period of time and on a uniform basis for all individuals in a work unit. The starting premise of personnel appraisal must be recognition of the reality that *any* appraisal of individual performance is inherently subjective and entails an element of qualitative judgment. The goal of a sound appraisal system should therefore be to minimize arbitrariness and undue discretion, while leaving room for nuanced supervisors' judgment. The worst outcome is obtained when performance appraisal is reduced to mechanistic bean counting or, worse, used as a smokescreen for arbitrary personnel decisions unrelated to job performance.

Thus, the question is not whether employee performance should be systematically evaluated—obviously it must—but rather how to do so fairly, reliably, economically, and without generating dysfunctional behavior or unnecessary conflict. If the country circumstances or characteristics of the organization raise serious doubts as to the capacity to rate employee performance fairly, it may not be desirable to have a formal performance appraisal system in the first place. A bad performance appraisal system is worse than none at all. That said, in most countries a good performance appraisal system improves the productivity of employees and thus the quality of government action.

Employee Rights and Obligations

The obligation of public employees is to perform the duties detailed in the employment contract, with efficiency and respect for the public interest and without favoritism or attempts to derive personal gain from their official position.

Basic Public Employee Rights

A government employee, as any citizen, should have six basic rights in any country:

- protection from arbitrary penalties without due process;
- equal treatment without regard to race, ethnicity, religion, or gender (and, depending on the country's cultural norms, sexual orientation);
- freedom of speech and of religion;
- individual privacy;
- political participation; and
- right of association.

Although some of these rights are routinely violated in a number of countries, owing to weak governance or ingrained cultural traditions, they provide the beacon for efforts to reform and improve personnel management.

Legitimate Restrictions of Employee Rights

The right to due process is as strong for government employees as for any other citizen. Owing to the special nature of public service, however, the other basic rights can be subject to reasonable restrictions.

Free Speech. The right to free speech is generally weaker for government employees than for other citizens, owing to the reputational risk to the government agency or the government as a whole. In some countries, a private company may, if it wishes, tolerate racist remarks by its employees; a government organization can never do so. (In the United States, however, private companies are liable for such behavior by their employees, as part of the general prohibition against creating or allowing a harassing work enviroment.) Conversely, public employees are entitled to be shielded—at government cost if necessary—against slander and unsubstantiated allegations.

Privacy. Similarly, the individual right to privacy may be restricted for government employees by prohibiting excessive consumption of alcohol and drugs or other pursuits that, without being illegal or improper, might nevertheless embarrass the government or bring disrepute to the civil service.

Political Participation. Political activity of government employees is restricted in most countries (e.g., in the United States through the 1939 Hatch Act). While retaining full rights of political association and voting, public employees are generally not allowed to campaign actively for political parties, run for elective office, or publish articles of a partisan political nature or critical of government policies. (One exception is France, where civil servants may hold union positions or local political office and have broader rights to involvement in national political activity than in most other developed countries.) These restrictions are required by the principle of political neutrality for career civil servants, but are also intended to insulate them from partisan political pressure.

Right of Association. Freedom of association is of two kinds: the right to join various associations, including political parties, and the right to join a union to defend common economic interests. The first right is rarely restricted; indeed, governments encourage employee membership in professional associations and permit membership in cultural clubs and associations—provided that such membership does not create a conflict of interest or lead to public perception of bias. It is a different matter regarding employees' rights to unionize and engage in collective bargaining. In general, public employee unions exert a positive influence on good governance, as shown for some Latin American countries and elsewhere (Tendler, 1997).[7] However, some restrictions are necessary and common. Most countries that allow public employees trade unions have restrictions on the right to strike and take other job actions that paralyze critical government functions. In particular, employees in essential public services (e.g., police, firefighting, prisons, some types of urban transport) do not have the right to strike. A signal application of this principle in the United States was President Reagan's decision in 1981 to dismiss striking air traffic controllers.

Beyond these basic rights, the specific rights of employees are defined by the job and spelled out in the employment contract, and thus are legally enforceable. Court decisions in many countries have extended to temporary and casual employees the legal protection of some of the rights of permanent employees—partly to preclude government temptation to recur to temporary or casual employment as a way of avoiding respect for basic employee rights. (A similar temptation is at the basis of some outsourcing of government activities.) Although formal rights are no guarantee against arbitrary actions, in countries with an effective judicial system they go a long way in making such actions very unlikely.

Protecting Employee Rights

Most countries have internal grievance redress procedures to hear employees' claims of violations of their rights, as well as complaints of employment and working conditions. While enforcement of these procedures is effective in all developed countries and some developing countries, in many developing countries and transition economies they have no effect in practice. The grievance redress system is normally institutionalized through a unit in the central personnel agency, linked to complaint officers designated by each ministry or agency, but standing ministerial committees with employee representation also exist in some countries.

The central personnel unit can also conduct employee surveys, obtain feedback on the effectiveness of the grievance redress system, and analyze recurring complaints in order to initiate action at the central and ministerial level to address their systemic causes. The central personnel unit also keeps track of court decisions in order to update its regulations. In some countries, the ombudsman (see chapter 11) can mediate in staff complaints and prevent the matter from becoming a formal legal dispute.

Gender Discrimination

Most countries have on the books policies to increase the number of women in government employment and redress disparities of access to different occupations. In many countries, enforcement of these policies is lax, for a variety of cultural factors and vested interests. In some countries, by contrast, gender equality is pursued forcefully beyond employment, and applies also to elective positions through legal reservation for women of a certain proportion of parliamentary or city council seats (fully one half in Scandinavian municipalities).

In addition to improving the gender composition of the government workforce, most developed countries have devised procedures and a machinery to deal with complaints of *sexual harassment* and discrimination. Sexual harassment is not only a source of individual pain and discomfort for its victims, but also a severe hindrance to the efficiency and productivity of the organization because it creates a hostile work environment.

In the United States, the earlier narrow construction defined sexual harassment as unwelcome sexual advances and other conduct of a sexual nature to which an individual is required to submit as a condition of employment (Saltzstein, 1989).[8] From the mid-1990s, the definition was expanded to include the existence of a sexually offensive environment—both in itself and also because the evidence shows that it is conducive to individualized sexual harassment. As in all personnel procedures, it is not enough to draft a policy on sexual harassment; effective and credible enforcement must also be ensured. Real progress against sexual harassment has been confined almost entirely to the developed countries, however. Elsewhere, attitudes on this subject remain highly peculiar, as Box 8.3 illustrates.

Racial and Ethnic Discrimination

Equal employment opportunity and prohibition of racial discrimination are part of the personnel system in all developed countries and in most developing countries. Despite this, discrimination in government employment persists almost everywhere in varying degrees, manifesting itself in job segregation, disparity in earnings, and disproportionate representation of one group in supervisory and senior executive jobs. Although discrimination in government employment is part of a larger societal problem, and equality is a long-range goal, the government itself should give the good example, with strong provisions to combat discriminatory practices against individuals as well as to remove the barriers to career opportunities.

In societies with a heritage of discrimination, affirmative actions (including, in some countries, quotas in recruitment and promotion) are viewed as necessary to remedy the effects of past

BOX 8.3

An Original View on How to Reduce Sexual Harassment in
the Workplace

"There are far too many pretty women in the government offices at the moment, distracting male workers and lowering business efficiency with their
pert and yielding tightness. We must be ever watchful for possible immoral
activities, and it is well known that pretty women cause unhealthy activities
that lead to insanity, blindness, sickness and bends. That is why from now on
thorough ugliness must be considered a deciding factor at all job interviews.
Since the prettier candidate has already been blessed by God, it is only right
that we should hire the uglier one. After all if we do not choose the ugly
candidates, who will?"

This is an *actual quote* from a leading politician in a major Asian country during a recent lecture to employees of his government—conceivably
a botched joke. Extra credit for the reader who can imagine the workplace
climate for women employees in that government. (Neither the politician nor
the country are named as this viewpoint does not fairly represent the social
climate of the country.)

exclusion, equalize the playing field, and build a broad social consensus on the equity of the civil
service system. The balance between the necessary redress of past discrimination and the risk of
new unfair practices vis-à-vis individual employees is a delicate one, which must be achieved in
different ways in different societies.

In several former colonies the ethnic majority was historically discriminated against, in favor
of a smaller ethnic group serving as "intermediary minority" between the colonial power and the
majority of the population (e.g., the Chinese in Malaysia and Indonesia, the Tamils in Sri Lanka,
the Indians in Uganda, the Tutsis in Burundi and Rwanda). In these cases, affirmative action in
favor of the ethnic majority was justified after independence, and in some cases may have helped
defuse the majority's deep-seated resentments. In all cases, however, the compensatory provisions
should not be allowed to persist past the point where the initial historical disadvantage has been
eliminated.

Even more importantly, both the problem and the specific solutions must be conceived in a
positive way. The objective must be to uplift the conditions and capacity of the previously disadvantaged group and never to put down or exclude individuals of any other group. For example,
there is a vast difference between affirmative action policies in Bolivia in favor of the indigenous
Aymara or in Malaysia for the Malay majority, and the objectionable treatment of the Tamils by
the Singhalese majority in Sri Lanka—let alone the odious anti-Indian policy of the Idi Amin
regime in 1970s Uganda, the large-scale massacre of Chinese in Suharto's Indonesia, and the
genocidal horrors of Rwanda.

Unionization in Government[9]

As noted, the right to form and join employee unions is inherent in the right of association that public employees have, as any other citizen. However, unionization in government raises specific issues.

Labor-Management Relations in the Public Sector

By their very nature, labor-management relations are conflictual, in government as in the private sector, and therefore need to be regulated in order to manage and resolve conflicts within the framework of labor laws common to all employment relations. Thus, in most developed countries and many developing countries, government employees do have the right to unionize and engage in collective bargaining just as in private industry. However, labor relations in the public sector have an inevitable political dimension that is absent from private sector labor relations. Three major differences exist:

- Government employment has an inherent public interest, particularly vital public services such as fire protection or law enforcement.
- Government differs from the private sector in how it is organized for decisionmaking on employment issues. A government official designated to negotiate with public employee unions, no matter how senior, lacks the authority to commit the legitimate political executive to accept specific changes in employment conditions.
- Changes in government wages or other conditions may affect the overall fiscal situation and prospects in ways that may not necessarily be consistent with fundamental objectives of stabilization, economic growth, or equity.

These differences are real, and can justify certain restrictions on public employee unions and their rights. However, there is an ever-present risk that a particular government in power may use them as excuses to dilute employee rights for less valid reasons.

Nature of Public Sector Unions

The nature of unionization varies in centralized and decentralized personnel systems. Unions in centralized systems generally support the system of initial appointment by merit and the government personnel agencies in opposing political patronage of any kind, which undermines the job security which unions value highly. However, committed to protecting the interest of their members, unions typically resist executive attempts to introduce performance considerations in personnel management, and particularly to discipline or dismiss employees for poor performance. By contrast, in decentralized systems the relations between employer and employees in the ministries and agencies are much closer to those in the private sector and are regulated mainly by the same contractual legislation that applies to employment in the private sector. (This is also true of the senior executive service.)

Unions in centralized systems may include various types of professional associations, such as those comprising teachers, engineers, public health workers, construction workers, or railway employees. These professional unions may either federate at the central or provincial level or form a loose coalition of occupational groups to deal with common problems. It is often left to individual ministries, on the basis of centrally prescribed criteria, to grant recognition to employee unions in the ministry while the central personnel office decides on recognition of national unions. In some countries, such as France, unions are represented on government civil service boards.

Collective Bargaining

There are three basic arrangements for collective bargaining in the public sector:

- Direct negotiation between government and union representatives negotiating on behalf of all employees. (The agreements negotiated are normally submitted to a referendum by the entire union membership and to approval by the political leadership.)
- Independent determination of salary and allowances by an expert body. Despite its apparent attractiveness, such a system may produce unacceptable results, as the expert body lacks the necessary perspective on the overall fiscal situation and on other social objectives. In some cases, as in India's Pay Commission, the system has turned into a mechanism to ratchet public wages upward, to the point where they are significantly higher for most grades—despite the complete job security—than in comparable private sector jobs, and has contributed to severe fiscal difficulties of the central government and of many state governments.
- Joint decisions on *both* private and public wages by independent councils, with representation from the government, private employers, employees, and technical experts, as in Singapore. This system has worked well, but generally only in small countries with authoritarian government.

Bargaining should be broad in scope, or inconsistencies with other human resource policies may arise (Delaney and Horton, in Perry, 1989). Also, a broad scope may allow negotiators from both sides the flexibility to trade changes in wages for changes in work conditions, or to offer other concessions in exchange for higher productivity. However, labor issues specific to individual ministries are best negotiated at the ministry level (consistent with national norms). The collective bargaining process ends with a written agreement, whose terms should be made known to all the employees and line managers and which, like any other contract, must be drafted in clear language to prevent future disputes.

The responsibility for collective bargaining rests on the political executive, even though the actual negotiations may be conducted by professional negotiators. In view of the complex government structure in most countries, it is useful to have a "pre-bargaining" stage within government, whereby the government negotiators, the budget and personnel officials, line managers, and ministers agree on goals and threshold responses to employee union demands. Resolving beforehand any conflicts among the government stakeholders themselves and reaching political agreement on the negotiating approach strengthens the hand of the executive and reduces the scope for the union to exploit internal government differences. At the same time, this assures the unions that the agreements negotiated will be respected by all government stakeholders and supported by the political leaders.

Strikes and Arbitration

If collective bargaining does not lead to an agreement, there are three alternatives: mediation, arbitration, and strike, usually in that order. Mediation is usually compulsory but not binding, whereas arbitration may be both compulsory and binding on the union as well as the government. If after mediation and arbitration there is still no agreement, a strike becomes the last resort.

There are restrictions on strikes by government employees in most countries. In the states of the United States and in many large municipalities, strikes by public employees are either prohibited altogether or allowed only when they do not affect essential public services. Canadian law authorizes the government to prohibit strikes during the period of general elections. Even in France, where the right to strike is enshrined in the civil service code, the law prohibits strikes by the police, armed forces, judiciary, and prison personnel and sets a minimum period of notice for strikes in other safety-related areas such as air traffic control. However, with or without a legal right to strike, government employees in many countries have resorted to a variety of tactics to press their claims after failing to do so through collective bargaining—such as public demonstrations, walkouts, "sick outs," "hiccup strikes," or "work to rule."[10] These tactics are more common in developed than developing countries and, among developed countries, far more frequent in continental Europe than in North America or East Asia. They have been losing steam in recent years, however, in the face of mounting resentment by the public.

INVESTING IN GOVERNMENT PERSONNEL DEVELOPMENT

> "If I am told, I forget. If I am shown, I remember. If I do, I understand."
> —*Confucius*

Training: Ingredient of Success or Alibi for Failure?

Governments rely on the knowledge, skills, and abilities of employees to produce goods and services efficiently, effectively, and responsively. As governments modify their responsibilities in a globalized world and face increasing competition from other service providers, they must renew and upgrade their human resources. Training can also have a key role in motivating and retaining government employees. However, training is still too frequently used by managers as a way to avoid unpleasant but necessary personnel decisions, and by nonperforming employees as a temporary refuge. Moreover, even when well run, government training programs are often unrelated to the employees' actual or prospective tasks, thus giving them new skills that quickly atrophy from lack of use. Finally, in the absence of efficient procedures and adequate incentives, upgrading of skills only generates frustration among employees. Indeed, while solid training for skills required by the job is critical for good administrative performance, ill-conceived training programs have been one of the single largest sources of waste in government.

Rarely can training alone make an organization more effective. Except for short and targeted training for keeping employees up to date in their jobs, training of employees normally helps only when there are accompanying changes in rules and incentives, improvements in the organization, or advances in technology (especially information and communication technology). *Training will never fix a dysfunctional system.* If employees perform poorly because the compensation structure is inadequate or conditions of employment inefficient, the answer is pay and employment reform. If they perform poorly because they are unaware of expected performance standards, these standards should be clarified and enforced. If weak performance is linked to the failure to reward good work and to penalize bad work, the solution is a good performance appraisal and appropriate personnel action. None of these situations call for training per se. Investing in training is warranted only if employees have inadequate skills for the jobs where they are already best placed, and the new skills will actually be used right after the training; if specific skills are needed for the employee career advancement; or if the training is required for the educational upgrading of an entire workgroup.

Otherwise, training is simply a bureaucratic alibi for avoiding the real issues of weak performance, distorted incentives, or inefficient organization.

With these qualifications in mind, well-designed and well-imparted training can achieve some or all of the following objectives:

- improve efficiency (reduce unit cost);
- help make government personnel more flexible and adaptable;
- motivate employees and assist their career advancement;
- keep up the expertise of government agencies; and
- achieve specific personnel objectives, such as diversity or equity.

Types of Training

Activity-Related and Career-Related Training

Activity-related training includes skill formation, task-specific training, and executive development. Most of the training for government personnel is focused on general skill formation. Career-related training consists of four categories: pre-entry training, in-service training, project-related training, and training for personal effectiveness. A number of countries (e.g., France) require civil servants to undergo pre-entry training (usually including internships) as a condition for appointment, and in-service training as a condition for promotion. In some countries (e.g., Italy and Spain), these conditions are specified in collective bargaining agreements. Countries in the British administrative tradition, instead, generally regulate pre-entry and in-service training through executive instructions.

Formal and Informal

Formal training includes structured courses, classes, and formal development programs. Informal training takes place in everyday work. Because most learning takes place informally and on the job rather than through formal education, much can be achieved by creating a favorable climate for informal coaching and learning. While this costs little money, it has a potentially large payoff in improved performance and employee satisfaction. The expanded use of the internet and e-mail has offered new opportunities in this direction. On the other hand, "face time" remains an invaluable source of professional interaction and renewal. Indeed, it can be argued that the takeover of interoffice communications by e-mail and texting has greatly diminished the kind of personal interaction—including through body language—that can convey positive and negative signals that are extremely valuable to transmitting work norms and performance expectations. A similar drawback can be attributed to the disappearance of the office watercooler, which in older times served as the micro-equivalent of a village square in which important information was exchanged.

On-the-Job and Off-the-Job

On-the-job training is done informally at all levels in the organization, but more often for new employees, including various forms of apprenticeships and internships. Since the feedback from informal coaching and training is immediate and the new skills are put to active use right away, on-the-job informal training can be highly motivating and successful. (The typical example is when learning to use new computer software).

The utility of on-the-job training is often overlooked. In addition, on-the-job training is rarely seen as a responsibility of supervisors, who get little or no credit for coaching and mentoring. To the contrary, training of subordinates or of counterparts should be considered an integral part of a manager's responsibility and rewarded as such (or penalized when it is not provided)—especially in the case of expatriate technical assistance in developing countries. Job rotation, too, can give employees a broader perspective on the inner workings of their organization or of several ministries, generate new skills through exposure to different tasks and revitalize their interest. For this reason, a number of large public organizations make promotion to higher levels contingent on the employee having worked in different units of the organization.

Traditional vs. "New" Training

Traditional training—classroom lectures, discussions, and case studies—is usually delivered by external institutions—whether on site or through distance learning—and is indispensable when seeking to acquire a coherent set of new skills or to reach higher educational levels. Practical problems are frequent. There is rarely an effort to identify the skill and level of preparation of participants or to consult with the client agencies beforehand. Unlike college and university students, who can be assumed to meet certain common standards, government employees are generally a heterogeneous audience. It is therefore more difficult to define program content and to pitch lectures at the right level. Also, when training is provided by international experts, there is often a problem of language. "New training" methods (e.g., interactive video, role playing, etc.) have their place, especially when specific new innovations are to be introduced, but cannot replace traditional training, notwithstanding its problems. *No matter what training method is used, competence in the subject matter is always far more important than mastery of teaching techniques.*

In-House vs. External Delivery

The question of who will do the training and how will depend on the target group of participants, the content of the training, and the relative capacities of in-house and outside training organizations in the public or private sector. Different countries follow different mixes of delivery, although in recent years there has been an increasing tendency to contract training of government employees to outside entities and to move away from permanent government training institutions. Generally, in-house units have the advantage of knowing the policies, programs, and culture of the government agency concerned, and the agency has greater control of the training program. The outside provider, on the other hand, can be more flexible and able to cater to a variety of training needs. In-house and outside training alternatives are not mutually exclusive, and some national training organizations (e.g., those in Malaysia) are able to capture the advantages of both.

Policy, Needs Assessment, and Evaluation

The Need for a Training Policy

As stressed earlier, training delivered with no attention to the preconditions for its effectiveness leads only to inefficient use of resources and duplicated efforts. A sound training policy is therefore essential. In turn, the skills provided through training will actually be used only if they are germane to the institutional and organizational environment of the individual employees.

While training is often misunderstood as coterminous with "capacity-building" it is in fact only one of four components of administrative capacity. The first three components are institutional capacity (i.e., the efficiency of the basic rules and incentive frameworks); organizational capacity (i.e., the soundness of the structure designed to administer those rules); and information/communication capacity (i.e., the physical ICT infrastructure as well as the provisions for easy flow of information across the organization). Human skills are reinforced by use and atrophy very quickly if not used after the training. This leads to the key requirement to *design training programs as a corollary of the institutional, organizational, and information changes,* and to initiate the training only after these changes have been put in place, or at least implemented concurrently.

At the national level, a training policy should formulate training objectives for different sectors; set the guidelines for planning, delivering, and monitoring training of government personnel; specify the complementary measures; and estimate the financial resources available. A draft of the training policy should be widely circulated for comments among the ministries, their employees, and the legislature. Moreover, because upgrading of the government workforce has a major impact on the overall national labor market, the views of trade unions, business organizations, and other selected outside groups should be sought. The final national training policy should be approved by the highest political authority, endorsed by the legislature, and widely disseminated to provide public managers at different levels with a concrete framework for planning and implementing training programs for their own employees.

A training policy should be as much as possible demand-driven and it is essential to make sure that the training is appropriate and valued *by those for whom it is meant.* Too often in government the training specialists formulate programs without reference to the needs and wishes of the prospective beneficiaries and their managers. Indeed, training programs are often developed primarily in order to provide continuous employment for those who design and deliver the training. Thus, as with all other costly government programs, it is important that the training itself be subjected to clear performance criteria. The first of these criteria must be the relevance of the training to the needs of employees and their managers, as defined and evaluated *by them* as clients, not by the training providers or by experts hired by them.

Assessing Training Needs

The first step in articulating the training policy is a fact-based assessment of training needs. Training needs must be identified at three interrelated levels: national, organizational, and individual. A broad assessment of skill availability, new skill requirements, and the resulting identification of skill gaps and training needs should be undertaken at regular intervals, so that a menu of relevant training options may be developed and the training institutions have the information essential to plan their curriculum and staffing.

Training needs of the organization should be defined by each ministry or agency, integrated within the overall training policy, and related to the availability of training from educational institutions. Training needs can also be assessed by the training institutions themselves, but if so, they should be carefully reviewed—mindful of the temptation to define needs as a function of the institution's preferences and capabilities rather than the government's requirements.

Training needs of the employees must be assessed in relation to their work context, as well as to the future skills required by technological advances or other changes. Evidently, the more rapid the pace of technical change and the deeper the reorientation of the role of government, the more important it becomes to have a forward-oriented training needs assessment. Most training, however, is remedial in nature (i.e., intended to fill specific skill gaps and/or to address employee performance problems). Here again, there is a common tendency to throw training at performance problems instead of taking the stronger actions that may be required.

To assure the relevance and good quality of the training, managers should agree with the employee on a training program, reviewed every year. In practice, this does not often happen. At a minimum, however, training requests and requirements should be discussed during the periodic personnel evaluation. (Quite frequent is the practice of perfunctory attendance at an "executive development" or "leadership" course, the real purpose of which is not to impart higher skills, but to serve as a marker of the intention to promote the individual.)

Finally, as noted, a good training-needs assessment must reflect the views of all major stakeholders in the exercise, including the public managers, the employees, and concerned outside groups. A good assessment would normally include:

- inventory of current employees' skills;
- determination of skills required for the functions of the organization;
- the resulting skill gaps;
- ways to fill the skills gaps—types of training and target participants;
- institutions that can provide the training; and
- estimated training costs, constraints on release of employees for training, and other practical issues.

Training Evaluation

As noted, training that is badly designed or supply-driven or not accompanied by requisite institutional changes is a waste of resources. The cost-effectiveness of the training investment must therefore be assessed rigorously, comparing the *results* with the *objectives*.

In addition to the evaluation of the immediate results of training, governments should also develop outcome indicators to evaluate the overall effectiveness of the training program, using information from trainees, peer groups, supervisors, the personnel unit, the client agencies, and, where relevant, the citizens. Performance measurement is a complex and tricky area, however, and must be approached with care and common sense, as discussed in detail in chapter 10.

Organizational Arrangements for Training

Most countries have entrusted training policy and monitoring to the central ministry in charge of public administration or personnel, or to a public service commission that can relate training to career advancement and promotion.

When training funds are centralized, a training unit in the central personnel agency pays the designated training institutions, meets all the cost of ministry and agency training programs, and provides grants and loans to employees for educational leave and self-development programs. When training funds are decentralized, they are allocated to each ministry or agency, which then manages the funds, pays the training institutions, and meets the educational needs of employees. There is no *a priori* preference for centralized or decentralized administration, and both arrangements have disadvantages. In centralized administration, where the central unit meets all the costs of training and the training is free, the government agencies obviously tend to ask for more training than needed, and the resulting bargaining does not necessarily ensure the optimal utilization of training funds. When training funds are fully decentralized, it is difficult to assure that the overall educational needs of the government workforce are met.

In countries where training is mainly centralized, the central unit assesses the training needs of individual ministries and of government as a whole based on consultation with the ministries, training institutions, and stakeholders outside government. The training unit is responsible for all aspects of the design and funding of government training, including the cost estimates, identification of training providers in the public and private sectors, interaction with the client ministries and agencies, and the training plan. Often, advisory councils composed of representatives of training institutions and user groups are set up to assist the central training unit.

The United States provides an example of how the training function can be integrated into the central personnel agency. The Office of Personnel and Management (OPM) has a training and development division grouped around clusters of states to assist federal agencies in designing training courses and devising training solutions.

In countries with decentralized training, the overall training policy remain the responsibility of a central unit, but the actual management of training is entrusted to the line ministry and agency concerned, subject to central monitoring of outcomes. Effective incentives are to allow budgetary savings by individual ministries to be used for their own training, and to encourage interagency competition for excellence in training (e.g., the Investing in People program in the United Kingdom).

Most countries follow a mixed arrangement. The central unit is provided with funds for the centralized training of senior personnel and for training to address important skill gaps that cut across ministries and agencies. Other training funds are allocated to the ministries and agencies to meet their specific training needs. In such an arrangement, the ministries and agencies have flexibility and discretion in the use of their portion of the training funds, consistent with the plans submitted, and may of course also finance specialized training themselves. (However, the creation of separate training and research institutes attached to specific ministries, which was the norm in the former Soviet Union and Eastern Europe, is inefficient and should not be encouraged.)

In any organizational arrangement, the central unit is generally responsible for training senior executives and elite cadres. For reasons of economies of scale and convenience, the central training unit normally also serves as a clearinghouse of information on all matters related to training institutions and experts, training practices, needs assessment, and evaluation.

Training Institutes

Training institutions for government personnel include:

- autonomous civil service academies;
- university-affiliated institutes, which offer public management degree or nondegree programs to both public employees and private individuals;
- business schools, originally set up to provide training in business management but which have diversified into also training government personnel; and
- sector-specific training institutes.

Civil Service Academies. A civil service academy is engaged primarily in orientation courses; training of new recruits into government; and in-service training, mostly for mid-level and senior personnel. The civil service colleges in India (mainly, the Indian Administrative Service institute), Singapore (the Civil Service College, under the Public Service Division), and the United Kingdom typify this model. A civil service academy offers training in general administration as well as functional subjects (e.g., public procurement). Often, there are separate academies for different technical specializations and some countries also have dedicated academies for secretarial and other support staff. Civil service academies can be autonomous entities or attached to the cabinet office, as is the British civil service college, incorporated in the Cabinet

Office as the Centre for Management and Policy Studies and renamed in 2005 as National School of Government.

The principal advantage of a dedicated civil service academy is the formation and dissemination of common norms and a public service ethos. Critics argue, however, that the courses in public administration and related disciplines already offered in existing public and private universities are more than ample to meet the various demands of government service and, to the extent that specific knowledge gaps exist, they can be filled better with specific training related to the job.

In the United States, creation of a public service academy has been debated for a long time. The proposal acquired fresh momentum in 2006 when it was endorsed by a sizable group of senators and representatives. It would be modeled after the Army academy at West Point—albeit with a different curriculum and without the military structure and disciplinary regulations—and would enroll up to 5,000 students, who would commit themselves to working in federal, state, or local government after graduation for a specified period of time. The costs are estimated to be comparable to those of mid-range private universities, but every student would attend on a full scholarship basis. As of 2007, it was not clear whether the idea of a publicly funded civil service university in the United States would get off the ground this time around.

University-Affiliated Institutes. The primary task of university departments of public administration is to prepare young graduates for a career in government through pre-entry education and training. Some of these departments (as in the Philippines and Singapore) also provide in-service training on behalf of ministries and government agencies, offer courses for personnel sponsored by the government, and support sabbatical studies by individual government employees. There are doubts, however, whether the curriculum and teaching orientation of university departments is suitable to the needs of government employees. In part, this is because the currency of an academic career is scholarly research, which is necessary, but does not meet the practical and operational requirements of government work.

Business Schools. These were originally set up to meet the training needs of private managers. As the role of government has shifted in many countries, these institutes now also cater to the training needs of government personnel. Smaller countries, for which it would not be practical to set up specialized management schools, depend on excellent regional facilities such as the Asian Institute of Technology in Thailand, the Korean Development Institute, or the Asian Institute of Management in Manila.

Sector-Specific Training Institutes. Some countries have created sector-level management institutes and training centers and specialized training organizations for local government employees. Generally, these initiatives have been wasteful. Training specific to a sector can be ensured at a lower cost and, usually, better quality through participation in the design and conduct of training programs by a single central training institution. Also, fragmentation of training among sectors leads to the creation of specific vested interests, which tend to perpetuate themselves and feed the supply-driven nature of many training programs. (As noted earlier, particularly wasteful has been the practice of creating specialized training institutes as part of individual ministries.)

Combining Cost-Effectiveness with Public Purpose

Clearly, training of government personnel need not be conducted by the government or by state institutions. Indeed, for higher-level training, it may be more cost-effective for the government to use the existing network of universities and private institutions. In turn, the universities have to adapt and be responsive to the specific training needs of government while obtaining adequate financing. While training of government personnel is increasingly run on a commercial or quasi-commercial basis, it remains a public function that must be exercised with an eye to the public interest. There are of course a number of ways to combine cost recovery with public purpose. The School of Public Policy at the University of Birmingham in the United Kingdom provides a good model of an educational organization that is entirely self-financed but still fulfills a public sector function (Box 8.4).

Issues in Transition Economies and Developing Countries

The Special Case of Transition Economies

The vast changes in government training in transitional economies deserve a separate word. Before 1990, in the Soviet Union and Eastern Europe, each ministry typically had its own research and training institute, consistent with the logic of central planning. Changes in training arrangements in the former Soviet Union and Eastern Europe in the 1990s have been more in the nature of experiments than of systematic efforts. The ministry-based training institutes atrophied from lack of resources and clientele and had almost all disappeared by 2005, but a variety of problems prevented their replacement with a comprehensive new policy and organization.

The enormous legal, organizational, and procedural changes accompanying the post-Soviet transformation gave rise to a need for suitably qualified public servants. Although most government employees were highly qualified technically, they needed very different skills suited to the new role of the state. Also, deep-seated attitudes had to be changed—from the habits of passive execution of orders to the exercise of initiative, the use of personal judgment, and the taking of certain risks for the sake of innovation. The efforts to provide coherence in public sector training and impart these new attitudes led to the creation of a focal point in a coordinating ministry (usually the ministry of interior), or of a state office specifically created for the purpose of retraining and reorienting government employees. In most transition economies, however, these efforts had meager results. The skill and attitude gaps were filled more by replacing older civil servants with young new recruits than by retraining the older employees.

Problems in Developing Countries

Training of government personnel in developing countries is beset by problems related to the supply-driven orientation of most training, the low priority given to training, and deficiencies in the staffing and organization of training centers. The training infrastructure is fragmented and poorly utilized; the content of training is often irrelevant to the current needs of government and the employees; and the teachers are inhibited by civil service regulations and practices, lack material incentives or career prospects, and often have weak competence in the subject. In some countries, public training institutions have been used as a dumping ground for supernumerary senior officials. Not surprisingly, the quality of public service training in most developing countries is very low.

The situation in Bangladesh (Asian Development Bank, 1997b) exemplifies many of these problems, but is unfortunately typical of the public sector training in developing countries. In Bangladesh, the curriculum is not responsive to the needs of the trainees. Training is based on choices made by the training institutions mainly for their own internal reasons and is not based on any systematic needs assessment, nor is consideration given to planning the employees' training in relation to their career development path. Training of civil servants is provided by more than

BOX 8.4

A Public Educational Organization in the Marketplace

The School of Public Policy at the University of Birmingham in England is a self-financed organization that receives no public subsidy and sells its services, but is nonprofit and works for and with the public sector. It includes an International Development Department (IDD) for postgraduate training and advisory services to various countries. Created in 1964 to train public officials, the School could not use normal university finance, oriented mainly to undergraduates, and alternative funding had to be found. Yet, the School still had to meet the academic standards of the university as a whole. Hence, it has had to conform to two imperatives—one market based and the other professional.

Each department operates as a budget center, balancing its expenditure against its income, and has to pay the university for its full costs—where "full" really means full, including rental of its building, utilities and supplies, and use of the university facilities and services. As a result, members of the School staff are expected to demonstrate that they earn from external clients over twice their salary. But in addition, they have to demonstrate that they are worthy members of the academic community, based on high independent ratings of both their research and their teaching.

Clients benefit from quality advice from a responsive provider with a public service mission, unlike its private consulting firm competitors, and which carries the intellectual guarantee of being part of a major university. Staff pay a high price in terms of workload—heavier than their colleagues in other parts of the university—but also benefit from working in a collegial environment in which they have considerable influence over the activities of the organization and managing their own future and enjoy a much more varied professional experience than the typical academic or consultant.

The difficulty is to manage such an organization within the constraints of a university and of academic individualism. The School cannot use the incentives and sanctions of the business manager because pay levels and hiring and termination procedures are governed by university requirements. Organizational effectiveness thus depends on the intangibles of the goodwill, energy and mutual support of the staff, and on the shared pride in winning business and influence.

This model may or may not work in other sectors or other countries, but shows that it is possible to harness market pressures to public service training, while maintaining standards of academic and educational professionalism.

Source: www.publicpolicy.bham.ac.uk and Richard Batley, director of the IDD. Personal communication, 2000.

300 institutions, most of low quality and whose programs are poorly coordinated, if at all. There is a huge backlog of pre-entry training for new civil servants. Many new government employees take up their positions without any orientation and receive induction training after several years, by which time the "pre-entry" training is obviously irrelevant. Finally, promotion requires specified in-service training, but the relevance and quality of the programs are highly questionable. All in all, the productivity of the government workforce would not be much affected if most of the training for public servants were eliminated. The resources provided are, in effect, mainly a subsidy for the employment of the trainers and administrative staff. Clearly, they could be far better utilized by subsidizing the specific educational needs of employees as defined by them and their direct supervisors.

In civil service systems in large and diverse developing countries, the national civil service must be representative of the population while remaining merit-based. Thus, special measures are needed to identify strong candidates from disadvantaged or previously excluded groups and provide them with appropriate pre-entry training. For example, India has special coaching programs to help candidates from the lowest castes or outside the caste system to gear up for the entry exam into the Indian Administrative Service institute. (There are also quotas reserved for such candidates, so that the intent of the coaching is as much to assist them to handle the demands of the Institute as to help them compete for entry.)

Recouping training costs is problematic. Training is obviously undesirable if is it not cost effective. Paradoxically, however, when training is effective, it also makes the employee's skills more marketable and thus raises the chance of losing the employee to more remunerative employment in the private sector. From a national viewpoint, so long as the individual remains in the country, the training cost is a loss to the government, but not to the economy. However, when trained individuals leave government for employment abroad, the cost of their training is a dead loss to the country. The issues of "brain drain" and emigration are beyond the scope of this book, but the risks must be explicitly recognized in the design of a training program for civil servants and, to the extent possible, measures could be taken to address it. For example, some countries (e.g., Burkina Faso) require public service for a certain period of time from persons trained at government expense and offer additional allowances as a motivating factor. Such quasi-contractual agreements can be helpful to limit the brain drain without infringing on individual freedoms.

The International Dimension of Government Personnel Training

Opportunities Through International Organizations

For all countries, the United Nations organizes seminars and conferences in public administration and produces and distributes relevant publications through its public administration network (see www.un.org, search for "UNPAN").

For developed countries, government personnel training is facilitated and supplemented by the activities of the Organization for Economic Cooperation and Development (OECD). While the OECD rarely organizes training events, it produces a wealth of material on the entire gamut of public administration issues through its Public Management division (see www.OECD.org, search for "PUMA").

For developing countries, the capacity gap in national training has been partly filled by a variety of intergovernmental institutes mostly established under the auspices of the international financial organizations. The World Bank, through the World Bank Institute, offers training programs in Washington, in the countries themselves, and through long-distance methods (see worldbank.org, search for "WBI"). The International Monetary Fund provides training in financial and macroeconomic programming for government officials of member countries through the IMF Institute and has set up regional technical assistance centers (TACs) in the Caribbean, Africa, Asia, the Pacific and the Middle East (see imf.org, search for CARTAC, AFRITAC, etc.). In 1998, the Asian Development Bank established the ADB Institute (see ADBI.org) and other regional development banks have done the same. All of these institutes have substantial resources and staff with extensive country experience and expertise in different subjects, including public management.

In addition, there are the Asian and Pacific Development Administration Center in Kuala Lumpur, the Arab Administrative Development Organization (ARADO) in Cairo, the African Training and Research Center in Administration and Development in Tangiers, and the Latin American Center for Development Administration in Caracas. There are also a variety of regional training centers, such as the Macroeconomic and Financial Management Institute headquartered in Zimbabwe, the East and South African Management Institute in Tanzania; the Central American Institute for Public Administration in Costa Rica; and the Caribbean Center of Development Administration in Barbados. Other regional institutions, although autonomous, are supported by multilateral agencies—an example is the Asian Institute of Technology[11] in Bangkok, which is supported by the ADB. Finally, technical information is exchanged under various forms of regional cooperation, such as the regional associations in Southeast Asia and Latin America, including information in public administration.

Other Transnational Training Opportunities

Universities and institutes in developed countries offer degree programs and short-term courses for government officials from developing countries. As noted earlier, for example, ENA in France runs a regular international course for officials from developing countries, similar to its course for domestic candidates, as well as short-term specialized courses. In the United States, major universities offer advanced training in public administration to developing country officials—for example, the master in public administration programs by the John F. Kennedy School of Government at Harvard University. Similar programs for international participants are organized by the British Civil Service College, the National Institute of Public Administration (INTAN) of Malaysia, and the Lee Kuan Yew School of Public Policy at the National University of Singapore.

Finally, a major example of intercountry cooperation is the public management network among countries in the British Commonwealth, sponsored by the Commonwealth Secretariat. The network is supported by the independent Commonwealth Association for Public Administration and Management (CAPAM), which arranges annual conferences on diverse topics for officials, experts, and practitioners; disseminates experiences and country profiles; and supports innovations in individual countries. CAPAM and the Commonwealth Secretariat also arrange training courses for developing countries and offer consulting services to governments in different areas (see www.capam.org).

Evidently, scarcity of good training opportunities is not a constraint on the effectiveness of training for government personnel of developing countries—at least for the senior levels. Training effectiveness is constrained instead by the institutional and incentive weaknesses mentioned earlier.

"Twinning"

Twinning between training institutions in developed and developing countries can be an especially constructive form of capacity-building, as it provides continuity of advice and the building of trust and mutual commitment. Such agreements cover exchange of faculty and curriculum development. Examples include the agreement entered into between the ENA of France and the national training institutes in China, India, and other countries. While twinning, too, cannot remedy deep-seated institutional, skill, and incentive problems, it can be the vehicle for suggesting useful organizational improvements in the host institute. Twinning can also be very helpful to transfer knowledge in specific areas of public management and to provide regular contacts between colleagues in the same field and confronted with similar problems, but operating in a very different context and with varying expertise. For example, the International Organization of Supreme Audit Institutions (INTOSAI.org) facilitates the twinning of external audit offices in developed countries with their counterparts in developing countries—as between the Swedish National Audit Office and the Tanzania Auditor General.

A variant of the twinning concept is sector-specific training, such as that provided for the housing authorities by the Dutch-supported Habitat coalition, which is organized around the Dutch Institute of Housing Studies and comprises Ghana, India, Indonesia, and Peru. Another variant is the regional network of sector institutions that is sponsored and partly financed by UN agencies. For example, the UN Economic and Social Commission for Asia and the Pacific (UNESCAP.org) has successfully sponsored a network of training institutions in urban development and housing, as well as a network of city mayors and managers called CITYNET (Citynet-AP.org).

THE SITUATION IN THE UNITED STATES

Overview

The Number of Government Employees

As of 2005, there were approximately 20.2 million full-time government employees in the United States, of whom about 1.7 million were in the federal government and 18.5 million in state and local government. Among state and local employees, almost two thirds were employed in county, municipal, and other local government. (Recall that local government in the United States employs teachers and health workers, who account for the largest part of government employment in most countries and an even larger proportion in federal systems.)

As a proportion of the population, at 6.9 percent, general government employment (federal, state, and local combined) in the United States is fairly limited, compared to the 7.7 percent average for the developed countries as a group. Although, as we have seen in chapter 6, government has expanded substantially in the United States since the early days of the republic, overall government employment remains somewhat smaller than in other rich countries—a reflection of U.S. structural characteristics, historical roots, and cultural and political preferences. Consistent with the country's federal structure, federal government employment, at 0.6 percent of population, is less than half the OECD average, whereas state and local government employment, at 6.3 percent of population, is slightly higher than the 5.9 percent average in the other rich countries.

Among the states, the largest government in terms of numbers employed is found, not surprisingly, in the largest states: California, with over two million state employees, followed by New York and Texas with about 1.3 million each. In terms of population, the largest relative government employment is found in the smaller states, with Wyoming and Alaska at around 8 percent of population. Again, this is not surprising, because economies of scale in public administration mean that the need for employees rises less than in proportion with the population. Overall, government employment in the fifty states clusters around 5 to 6 percent of population.

At the federal level, government employment has been reduced significantly from its Gulf War

Table 8.1

Distribution of Civilian Federal Employment, 2005

Total Civilian Federal Government	**1,744,758**
Legislative branch	9,288
Executive branch	1,735,470
Executive office of the president	1,114
Departments	1,561,258
Agriculture	91,525
Commerce	31,316
Defense (civilian employees)	628,897
Air force	149,013
Army	217,454
Navy	177,608
Other civilian employees	84,822
Education	4,284
Energy	14,794
Health and human services	57,821
Homeland security	135,971
Housing and urban development	10,195
Interior	66,047
Justice	100,234
Labor	15,389
State	19,908
Transportation	56,914
Treasury	118,682
Veterans affairs	209,280
Independent agencies	173,808

Source: Office of Personnel Management, available at www.opm.gov/feddata.

peak of 3.1 million in 1991. As of 2006, the largest civilian employer in the federal government was the Defense Department, with 36 percent of the federal workforce—not counting military personnel. When adding the 210,000 civilian employees of the Department of Veteran Affairs, almost half of total federal civilian employment is accounted for by defense-related programs. Taken together, Treasury, Justice, and Homeland Security account for another 20 percent, leaving less than a third of federal employment, or around half a million, distributed among all the other federal departments and agencies. (Table 8.1 shows the distribution of federal government employees among the various government departments and agencies in 2005.)

The Pay

With an average annual salary of $47,000,[12] federal employees earn slightly more than the U.S. GDP per capita of about $42,000. State and local employees earn much less than federal employees, on average a little over $30,000.

Table 8.2

Base Annual Salary, General Schedule (GS) federal employees, 2006 ($ thousands)

Grade	Step 1	Step 5	Step 10
1	16.3	18.5	20.5
2	18.4	20.2	23.1
3	20.1	22.7	26.1
4	22.5	25.5	29.3
5	25.2	28.6	32.8
6	28.1	31.8	37.5
7	31.2	35.4	40.6
8	34.6	39.2	44.9
9	38.2	43.3	49.6
10	42.0	47.6	54.6
11	46.2	52.3	60.0
12	55.4	62.7	72.0
13	65.8	74.6	85.6
14	77.8	88.2	101.1
15	91.5	103.7	119.0
Average (*unweighted*)	40.8	46.3	53.1

Source: Office of Personnel Management, available at www.opm.gov/oca/06tables.

Table 8.2 shows the base salary scale for "General Schedule" (GS) federal employees (i.e., career employees) in 2006. The base annual salary ranges from $16,352 for the lowest step in GS, grade 1, to a maximum of $119,000 for the highest step, grade 15.

To the base salaries shown in Table 8.2, since 1994 the government has added "locality payments" to allow for the cost of living in different regions, ranging from a low of 12 percent to a high of 26 percent in Houston and 29 percent in the San Francisco area. This salary differentiation is a sound practice, to prevent distortion of incentives—both horizontal, with the *real* compensation of employees different only because of where they happen to work, and vertically, with government employees earning either much more or much less than private sector employees in the same region. When taking into account the locality payments, the lowest entry salary rises to between $18,000 and $20,000 per year and the top salary to between $133,000 and $153,000 (depending on the region).

In addition to the GS salary scale, there are special salary scales for administrative law judges, senior scientists and professionals, and members of the Senior Executive Service (SES—the federal government corps of senior public managers). These salary scales are higher, but not by much, than the top GS-15 compensation. The SES salary schedule goes, in principle, from $136,000 to $187,000 per year. However, the salary is capped at about $167,000 for "comparability" with the salary of members of Congress. Such comparability is fictional, however, as the duties, time commitment, and required qualifications of congressmen and of senior public managers are entirely different. (Moreover, in agencies without a "certified appraisal system," the salary cap is $152,000, or about the same as the top GS-15 salary including the locality payment.)

Are Government Employees Under- or Overpaid?

At first glance, average government salaries compare favorably with private sector salaries. However, the proportion of professional and technical personnel is much higher in federal government employment than in the private sector, which has a very large proportion of low-paid service employees. Also, federal government employees are by definition concentrated in higher-cost localities. Accurately correcting for these differences is anything but simple: an appropriate analysis would require a comparison of public and private pay for *each* specific skill in *each* different locality, then weighted by the number of public and private employees in each skill and locality. Short of such a careful detailed analysis, it is easy—but wrong—to pick and choose from the data to find examples to support the contention that government employees are overpaid or underpaid—depending on one's ideological predilection.

There are two other rough but valid approaches. The first relates government employee compensation to the country's standard of living by taking the ratio of average compensation to the per capita income in the country and then comparing it with the same ratio in other countries at similar levels of income. As we have seen, the compensation of U.S. federal government employees is slightly higher than the U.S. per capita GDP, compared to the average of 1.5 times per capita GDP in the other developed countries that are members of the OECD. A second approach looks at the salary trend in the public and private sectors: since the 1970s, average compensation of U.S. government employees has not increased in real terms (after inflation), whereas private salaries have shown a slight improvement. By both approaches, U.S. federal employees would appear to be somewhat "underpaid." On the other side of the ledger, however, is the much greater job security of government employment, especially compared to the sharp increase in private job volatility over the past decade. Job security contributes greatly to individual well-being, not only in itself, but also because it permits better planning of personal finances—and security of government employment becomes all the more attractive as insecurity of private employment increases.

As a broad generalization, therefore, when taking into account the greater job security and, in many cases, the "psychological income" from public service, compensation for government employees in the United States appears to be more or less in line with both the requisite incentives and private compensation for comparable skills and locations. (The major exception is the small group of top scientific personnel and most senior public managers, who would generally do much better financially in the private sector but, in exchange, enjoy substantial influence over public policy). Whether this broadly acceptable state of affairs will change in the future depends largely on whether the recent erosion of the influence of public sector unions continues. In any event, the problem with inadequate employee compensation in America is not found in the public sector, but in the declining real salaries and increasing insecurity of middle- and lower-income workers in the private sector.

The Development of the U.S. Personnel Management System

The Main Stages

Public administration theorists are fond of defining their own sequence of stages in the evolution of the personnel management system in the United States. Any such exercise has severe analytical limits. Time is a continuum and, as explained in chapter 1, "path dependence" means that the vast stock of accumulated institutions and norms does not permit institutional changes to occur suddenly. Established practices disappear only gradually and the evolution of institutions does not occur in discontinuous ways. "Nature does not make jumps," as the Romans said, and neither does institutional development. Still, there is some utility in broad generalizations of this sort, and we can suggest here our own classification of five major "stages" in U.S. administrative history—at the federal level but also percolating in time to state and local levels:

- "citizen-servant" stage, from the establishment of the country until the 1830s;
- "patronage/populism" stage, from the election of Andrew Jackson in 1828 through the mid-1880s;
- "transition to professionalism," until the 1940s;
- "mature merit" stage, from the late 1970s through the mid-1990s; and
- "moving toward results"—the current stage, still in its infancy, with personnel management evolving toward a combination of ex ante individual qualifications and ex post results.

Citizen Servant

During the first forty years of the republic, government service was seen as a civic duty of men of means and intellect, who would return to their private pursuits after a stint of helping run the country. The citizen-servant model could not survive the increasing demands for full-time employees. Even if the model had managed to hang on for a few years longer that it did, it would certainly have broken down when the huge territories of then-northern Mexico (comprising today's Texas, California, New Mexico, and Arizona) were added to the United States in 1848 following the Mexican-American War.

Patronage/Populism

In any event, the citizen-servant model of state employment was dealt a sudden final blow with the inauguration of President Andrew Jackson in 1829, and the general reaction against elite government. The weakness of formal institutions and lack of public demand for competency in those still raw years of American political life meant that service-by-elite could not yet give way to a professional civil service and was instead replaced by a jobs-for-loyalty system. Power over hiring and promotion was unapologetically seen as an adjunct of political victory, with supporters of an outgoing administration fired and supporters of the winner hired in their place. (In the words of Senator William Marcy in 1832, "To the victor belong the spoils of the enemy.")[13] By 1840, the patronage system was dominant in federal, state, and local government employee recruitment.

In addition to the right-to-spoils assertion, the argument in favor of the patronage system was that it stimulated political activism and participation. However, the reliance on personal loyalty and political support inevitably entailed an ill-trained government workforce, always looking up for approval instead of down to the needs of the public. Moreover, what employees did manage to learn on the job was wiped out by the next political turnover, when they were replaced by a brand new and inexperienced cohort of supporters of the new administration.

Transition to Professionalism

The patronage system thus came under increasing strain as the economy expanded and the role of government along with it, creating the demand for trained and dedicated personnel. After the Civil War, public and policy attention turned to the issue of the efficiency of civilian government, and the patronage system in its crassest form eventually ended in the 1880s. However, unlike the earlier sharp and rapid break from the citizen-servant to the patronage model, elements of patronage and politicization of government employees remained in the system for a long time after meritocratic criteria were first introduced into government personnel management.

The introduction of merit into government employment practices occurred mainly through the 1883 Pendleton Civil Service Act, which built on the earlier work and pressure of a number of reformers[14] and was triggered by the public revulsion at the assassination of President Garfield, a strong opponent of the patronage system. In a convincing demonstration that civil service reform can be a dangerous thing, Garfield was shot by Charles Guiteau, who was furious at being turned down as U.S. consul in Paris, a job for which he had no qualification whatsoever other than his credentials as Republican party hack.[15] The Pendleton Act introduced the merit system by subjecting the selection of some categories of government employees to competitive exams administered by a new and nonpartisan Civil Service Commission.

Only 10 percent of government jobs were originally covered by competitive recruitment, however. It was to take almost a century before a professional civil service system in America was fully consolidated but substantial progress was made in various ways during the intervening period:

- The coverage of competitive selection was gradually expanded until it eventually included more than 90 percent of federal employees.
- The next most important single advance was in 1939, when the Hatch Act[16] prohibition of partisan political activity by federal employees completed their insulation from political pressures that was presaged by the Pendleton Act.[17]
- Finally, the 1974 Civil Rights Act made racial discrimination illegal, including in all aspects of government personnel management, and created the Equal Employment Opportunity Commission to enforce the law.

Mature Merit

The merit system reached full fruition with the 1978 Civil Service Reform Act. The Carter presidency launched two major initiatives to modernize public administration—in budgeting and in personnel management. The former, "zero-based budgeting" (ZBB), was a failure. The premise was valid—bureaucratic inertia and vested interests do allow expenditure programs to persist long past the end of their usefulness. But the requirement to rejustify all major programs each year and rank them in order of importance generated a huge amount of paperwork. The ZBB approach was dead on arrival at Congress and was quickly abandoned. By contrast, the second initiative, on personnel management, was a major success. The 1978 law consolidated the merit system, through both appropriate expansion and functional differentiation. Most importantly, it also redefined the objective of personnel policy and management as producing "a competent, honest, and productive Federal work force *reflective of the Nation's diversity*" (italics added).

The Current System

Principles

The main principles of the merit system as enumerated in the 1978 law are:

- recruitment of qualified individuals from all segments of society, determined solely by ability, knowledge, and skills, after fair and open competition;
- fair and equitable treatment of all employees and applicants without regard to political affiliation, race, color, religion, national origin, sex, marital status, age, or handicap;
- equal pay for work of equal value and incentives for excellent performance;
- high standards of employee integrity, conduct, and concern for the public interest;

- efficient and effective use of employees;
- protection of employees against "prohibited personnel practices," such as arbitrary action, personal favoritism, coercion for partisan political goals, or reprisal for their disclosure of violation of the law, mismanagement, or risks to public health and safety; and
- prohibition of employees from using their position to influence elections.

Organizational Arrangements

The head of each department and agency is accountable in the first instance for the implementation of these principles and for preventing prohibited practices. For personnel policy formulation, oversight, and appeal, the law replaced the century-old Civil Service Commission and distributed its functions primarily among three agencies:

- Office of Personnel Management (OPM);
- Merit Systems Protection Board (MSPB); and
- A strengthened Equal Employment Opportunity Commission (EEOC).

These three agencies encompass the mandate of the "public service commissions" existing in many countries and discussed earlier in this chapter. Responsibility for personnel policy (including criteria, standards and appeals) is reserved to these central personnel agencies. However, for efficiency, actual appointments and other personnel actions are normally delegated to the departments and agencies, under the control and oversight of the central agencies to protect against prohibited personnel practices. This division of labor between policy and transactions is in keeping with good international practice (and symmetrical with the arrangements for government procurement—see chapter 9).

Office of Personnel Management. OPM is the focal point for all personnel management in the federal government and its mandate is to execute, administer, and enforce all civil service rules (except for the appeal functions assigned to the Merit Systems Protection Board or the Special Counsel), as well as to formulate policy proposals on all aspects of federal employment, in pursuit of "the systematic application of the merit principles." It is led by a director and a deputy director, both presidential appointees for four years, subject to Senate confirmation.

Merit Systems Protection Board and Special Counsel. The Board is composed of three specially qualified members, not more than two from the same political party, and appointed by the president for seven years, subject to Senate confirmation. The chairperson, selected from among the members, is the chief executive and administrative officer. The Board mandate is broad and includes both protecting the rights of employees and imposing sanctions on employees for violation of the rules. To this end, the Board has quasi-judicial functions, hearing and adjudicating appeals of adverse personnel actions, and has authority to give orders to any federal agency or employee and to enforce these orders. Closely associated with these functions is the Special Counsel, who receives and investigates any allegation of a prohibited personnel practice.

Equal Employment Opportunity Commission. The EEOC was originally created under the 1964 Civil Rights Act. It has five commissioners, appointed by the president and confirmed by the Senate, for five-year staggered terms. As for the Merit System Protection Board, the chairperson is selected from among the commissioners and becomes the chief executive officer of the Commission. The General Counsel is responsible for conducting EEOC enforcement litigation under the Civil Rights Act of 1964 (Title VII), the Equal Pay Act (EPA), the Age Discrimination in Employment Act (ADEA), and the Americans with Disabilities Act (ADA). The mandate of the EEOC was expanded from the original fight against racial discrimination to enforcing provisions against discrimination on the basis of age and disabilities and to an active search for diversity in the government workforce. The Commission was also given added responsibility to coordinate all federal equal employment opportunity programs.

Other Features

The 1978 law also:

- reaffirmed the federal employees' *right to organize,* bargain collectively, and participate through labor organizations in decisions which affect them (the Federal Labor Relations Authority—FLRA—was created to oversee the process of collective bargaining in the federal service);
- established a *Senior Executive Service* (SES) to give agencies flexibility to recruit and retain highly competent and qualified executives at a higher salary scale and with stronger obligations for performance (the SES broadly follows the model of "elite civil services" described earlier in this chapter);
- gave federal agencies *authority to experiment,* subject to congressional oversight, with new and different personnel management concepts; and
- introduced the new idea that, in appropriate instances, pay increases should be based on quality of *performance* rather than length of service.

To that end, each government agency was expected to develop systems for periodic appraisals of job performance of employees and to use them as a basis for rewarding or penalizing employees—under regulations to be prescribed by OPM and respecting due process.

Moving Toward Results

Personnel management in the United States is currently in the midst of a fifth stage—an effort to mesh the emphasis on ex ante employee qualifications with the new attention to the ex post results of employee activities. The 1978 law injected into the system a new orientation to individual performance as a basis for personnel actions. Actual progress has been slow, however. First, the natural reluctance of public managers to record substandard performance and their unwillingness to go through the complex process required has meant that penalties for nonperformance are very rarely assessed. (This is typically the case in most countries, as discussed earlier.) Also, "performance" is still too often defined in terms of diligence, timeliness, economical use of inputs and compliance with the rules, rather than in terms of actual accomplishments and results.

As explained earlier, personnel performance evaluation is a tricky exercise in every country, especially in the public sector. Moreover, as chapter 10 will elaborate, an attempt to focus only on results would be as misleading and ineffectual as exclusive attention to inputs and rule compliance. Thus, it is not a surprise, and is probably a good thing, that it is taking a long time to define and put into practice the right balance between ex ante merit and ex post results, between effort and outcomes, and between experience and one-time achievement.

A critical ingredient of a robust and fair system of government personnel management is still missing: the systematic involvement of public service users and civil society in evaluating the quality of employee efforts and their results on the ground. In this area, more (and more fruitful) initiatives have been taken at state and local level than at federal level. Future improvements in personnel management may well depend on the federal government adopting some of the innovations of state and local government.

Major Current Issues

The Functioning of the Senior Executive Service

Currently, SES personnel number about 7,000, of whom about 90 percent are career employees. Non-career SES appointments have been stable at around 10 percent of the total number since the introduction of the system. The logic of the introduction in 1978 of a Senior Executive Service was sound. A higher salary scale was created to raise SES compensation to levels adequate to attract or retain managerial and professional talent. The converse was that SES employees would be subject to commensurately greater demands for performance. In practice, neither side of the bargain was fully respected.

While somewhat better than the highest GS pay levels, SES salaries have been capped to a maximum that does not exceed congressional salaries and, although it is somewhat easier to penalize underperforming SES employees, their performance has not been assessed as rigorously as might have been expected. The system of annual merit awards has helped make up for both the discrepancy between theoretical and capped salary and for the weaker assessment of underperformance, with merit awards averaging several thousand dollars per eligible employee.

A significant and undesirable change has occurred, however, between the merit award practices of the 1990s and those in the first years of this century. The average merit award jumped from an average of slightly over $7,000 a year during 1994 to 1998 to an average of over $12,000 during 1999 to 2005. This increase is, in principle, consistent with the logic of the system, by which merit awards must be substantial enough to serve as reward for unusually good performance, and thus incentive for the future. Not consistent with the logic of the system, however, was the increase in the number of SES employees receiving merit awards—from an average of just over one third of employees during 1994 to 1998 (already much too high) to over 50 percent during 1999 to 2005. Almost three out of five SES employees received merit awards in 2004 and 2005. It appears that, just as in Garrison Keillor's Lake Woebegone[18] "all the children are above average," a large majority of SES employees show much higher performance than the standard that is expected of them.

On balance, the SES system has served to attract, and help retain, thousands of highly skilled personnel, and the efficiency of the federal workforce has certainly improved as a result. However, the incentive framework would be stronger and the system would work better still if the artificial and irrelevant comparison with congressional salaries were removed, thus allowing implementation of the full SES salary scale, and if the merit awards were larger but limited to the small minority who show truly outstanding performance—at most one employee in five. (Doing so may also help reduce some of the dysfunctional aspects and corruption temptations of the "revolving door" between government and private companies doing business with the government.)

Politicizing Scientific and Medical Decisions

As noted, the 1939 Hatch Act protects and prohibits government employees from partisan political involvement and the 1978 Civil Service Reform Act refers to their responsibility for technical integrity. Recent years, however, have seen the exercise of a different form of political pressure to countermand technical decisions for political reasons or to censure scientific advice prior to its publication. When employees are insulated from the pressure to become engaged in partisan political activities but the results of their work are subject to subtle or not-so-subtle pressure to conform to a partisan political agenda, the spirit of the U.S. civil service laws is violated and the integrity of public policy is compromised. Two major instances, among many others, have been the censoring of parts of scientific reports on global warming and the intrusion into medical decisions of the values and preferences of particular religious groups, as illustrated in Box 8.5.

National Security and the Right to Organize

As noted, the 1978 civil service legislation, among other things, reaffirmed the federal employees' rights to organize, bargain collectively, and participate through labor organizations in decisions that affect them. (The Federal Labor Relations Authority—FLRA—was created to oversee the process of collective bargaining in the federal service.)[19] After September 11, 2001, the administration argued that, in areas related to national security, the need to deal with pending threats, disrupt potential terrorist plots, and respond quickly and effectively to national emergencies called for constraining or eliminating some of these rights—in particular, the right to bargain collectively.

The political debate in summer and fall of 2002 revolved around the question of whether the employees of the new Department of Homeland Security (DHS) that was to be created should be allowed to unionize. The Democratic Party support for their right to unionize, and resistance to approve the new department until that right was reconfirmed was interpreted by some as an inappropriate delay in creating an essential new government agency. Even though the creation of the DHS had been pushed by Democrats and was originally resisted by the administration, the Democratic position was portrayed as "softness" on national security. In the political climate of the day, the opposition caved in, and the law creating the new department gave the executive power to unilaterally set new pay scales and performance evaluation and discipline systems with only pro forma "consultation" with representatives of the affected workers. In effect, this took away from the 170,000 employees in the department the right to union representation and collective bargaining, even when they were continuing in the very same job that had enjoyed union protection for more than fifty years.

In August 2005, however, Federal District Judge Rosemary Collyer blocked the entry into force of the new personnel rules by the Department of Homeland Security, finding that they violate the congressional requirement to ensure collective bargaining rights for federal employees. Essentially, the decision states that the department claims the right to modify contractual provisions practically at will, while the unions will be bound by the contract. As reported by the *Washington Post* (August 15, 2005), the judge concluded that "a contract that is not mutually binding is not a contract." (Moreover, the Department proposed to virtually eliminate the capacity of employees to appeal to the Merit Systems Protection board.)

As of 2007, Judge Collyer's decision was under appeal. The issue is a test case, because there are other administration plans to revise drastically the conditions of employment of federal employees, as set in the existing legislation. On deck is the Defense Department plan to modify the rules for its 650,000 civilian employees, and next would be the additional federal employees affected by legislation proposed by the Office of Management and Budget—thus effectively eliminating collective bargaining rights of almost all federal employees. However, with the Democrats regaining control of both House and Senate as a result of the November 2006 elections, the future of all such plans is seriously in doubt, regardless of the outcome of the appeal of Judge Collyer's decision. Stay tuned.

BOX 8.5

"Plan B": Protecting Women's Health or Dictating Their Morality?

The so-called "morning after pill" or "Plan B" is medication to prevent pregnancy if taken within seventy-two hours from sexual intercourse. It has been available with prescription in the United States and is available over the counter in most developed countries. Plan B works primarily by preventing ovulation and only occasionally by preventing implantation of the ovum after fertilization. After implantation, Plan B does not work. Thus, the U.S. Food and Drug Administration (FDA) itself considers emergency contraception to be just that—prevention of pregnancy, rather than somehow equivalent to abortion. (Indeed, like all other forms of effective contraception, it unquestionably reduces the number of abortions.) Nevertheless, the morning after pill was strongly opposed by certain influential political groups associated with the administration.

Here is Plan B's three-year obstacle course through the FDA bureaucracy:

• In June 2003, the FDA agreed to review Barr Laboratories' application for over-the-counter sale of their emergency contraceptive.
• In May 2004, after a six-month review, the FDA's own Nonprescription Drugs Advisory Committee and Advisory Committee for Reproductive Health jointly concluded that the product was safe and recommended that it should be sold without a prescription.
• The FDA rejected the recommendation, allegedly because of insufficient data on the safety of Plan B for teenagers.
• Barr Laboratories revised its application to exclude over-the-counter sales to girls younger than 16.
• The FDA rejected the revised application because it was "incomplete and inadequate."
• The application was again revised by the manufacturer, to exclude girls younger than 17.
• The application was again turned down in January 2005, but the FDA promised to make a final decision by September.
• In August 2005, the FDA indefinitely postponed consideration of the application for over-the-counter distribution of Plan B.
• In August 2006, the FAD authorized over-the-counter sale of the morning after pill to women 18 years and older.

Considering the favorable recommendation of the competent technical committees; the support of more than seventy medical organizations, including the American Medical Association, the American Academy of Pediatrics, and the American Association of Family Physicians; and the fact that the pill has been safely used by 2.5 million American women and by tens of millions in other countries, it is hard to see the FDA stalling and objections as anything other than the result of pressures from politico-religious pressure groups. Indeed, it was only in order to gain Senate confirmation that the acting FDA administrator finally authorized in August 2006 over-the-counter distribution. Actual distribution began in December. He was subsequently confirmed by the Senate.

There can be no debate on the absolute right of individuals and groups to their moral and religious values or on their freedom to exert all legal efforts to have those values prevail in public policy. There is, however, a clear and dangerous disconnect between the mandate of the FDA for "protecting and advancing the public health" and its disregard for the integrity of the work of its employees and technical advisors in order to impose on American citizens a particular set of moral and religious values.

Source: Food and Drug Administration, www.fda.gov, and various media accounts.

GENERAL DIRECTIONS OF IMPROVEMENT

The Major Issues in Different Countries

In developed countries in general, personnel management has achieved a reasonably stable and efficient state. The general direction of future improvement is the judicious introduction of performance orientation in the management of government employees and the achievement of the requisite balance between personal qualifications and effort compared to results.

In some countries of continental Europe, lackadaisical work habits of yesteryear and lack of responsiveness to and respect for the public still persist in some sectors (especially at subnational government level), despite very substantial progress during the last two decades. In those countries, the priorities are to strengthen transparency and the mechanisms of external accountability, particularly the methods to identify individual employees responsible for specific services, penalize those who receive persistently negative feedback from the service users, and reward the better performers.

In other countries, both in Europe (France) and Asia (Japan), "mandarin" attitudes of superiority and condescension by the elite civil service are now increasingly resented, and major corrections are urgent lest the entire concept of senior executive services be discarded in the future.

In the United States, grave and dangerous tendencies to revert to earlier cronyism and politicization of government personnel have been resurrected in the twenty-first century. These include the politicization of scientific and technical decisions; inappropriate pressures on civil servants to accommodate the values and wishes of particular religious groups; appointments of unqualified partisan cronies to important and sensitive government posts; and, under the cover of the "war on terror," a systematic attack on the right of public servants to associate and on the role of the public sector unions.

In many developing countries, government personnel management systems are in a state of disrepair—riddled with patronage, lacking relevant information, and neither rewarding good performance nor disciplining underperformance or misbehavior. Often, weak personnel administration is associated with inefficient policies for government employment and compensation. In these cases, it is difficult to change personnel management substantially without policy reforms (e.g., motivating employees is very hard when they don't get a living wage). In other countries, with the opposite situation of adequate personnel policies but unsound personnel administration, major improvements in administration are both possible and likely to be greatly beneficial to the effectiveness of the public management apparatus. In all developing countries, the role of merit, nondiscrimination, and openness in government personnel recruitment and promotion should be strengthened at every opportunity.

Classification Systems

Both the need for simplicity and the limitations of capacity suggest the desirability of unified classification and pay systems, as in Japan, France, and the Netherlands, rather than differentiated classifications for different entities of government. Lack of reliable data also affects the grading of different government jobs and allows the system to be manipulated, especially when complicated by an excessive number of wage brackets. Efforts at improvement in this area should concentrate on reducing the number of wage brackets and conducting a basic survey of who works where and on what rather than attempting complex job classification exercises.

Mobility is a related issue. In particular, the fragmentation of the civil service into a variety of separate professional "cadres" fosters rigidity and lack of communications within the civil service, and opportunities for streamlining and consolidation of cadres should be explored. In general, mobility within government should be encouraged, and, to the extent possible, obstacles and artificial constraints removed. Consideration should also be given to introducing the requirement of prior mobility to other departments and regions as a condition for promotion to top civil service posts. In some countries, however, transfer provisions have been abused by politicians to put pressure on senior civil servants to behave in inappropriate ways. Transfer rules and provisions should therefore be reviewed to enable individual mobility while precluding abuse, and revised as needed after appropriate consultation with the main stakeholders.

Central or Decentralized Personnel Management

Although a handful of developed countries have adopted a system where terms of employment and most other personnel matters are decided by each government agency, the desirability of a common public service ethos and the imperatives of equity call for qualification requirements and terms of employment to be uniform throughout the central government. In developed countries, actual recruitment is best left to the individual government agency—but subject to the national rules and requirements and with central oversight and appeal mechanism. In developing countries, it is generally better to put in place a strong and accountable centralized recruitment system to preclude the inequity and corruption risks of agency-by-agency recruitment. A robust and agile public service commission of integrity and independence is a must for improving government personnel management in developing countries. However, it must operate efficiently and not be allowed to become a bottleneck in recruitment, promotion, and discipline—as has too often been the case.

Performance Management

In "western" developed countries, the challenge is to encourage individual achievement, innovation, and intelligent risk-taking. In other countries, the challenge is much more complex, as the understanding of "performance" is influenced by different cultural factors and social norms. Many Asian countries stress rule compliance and group cohesion; in some Latin American countries family ties are important; and African countries put a premium on ethnic loyalty. Propitiating superiors with gifts and bringing personal considerations into hiring and promotion decisions are often not seen as ethical violations. On the contrary, a failure to help one's own people can be judged by society as selfish and immoral behavior. The practical challenge of improvement is how to adapt good management principles to the reality of informal practices and local cultural influences. Here, the comparative merits of group versus individual performance appraisal deserve consideration, as—depending on the cultural milieu—the individual's performance may be stimulated more by sanctions or rewards for his workgroup than by the probability of short-term personal gain or loss.

Training

In most developed countries, improvements call for selective skill upgrading in order for government employees to stay abreast of technological improvements, particularly but not exclusively in informatics and communications technology. Because government-run training institutions are of good quality— where they exist—and educational and training facilities outside government are plentiful, the issues are primarily the identification of the specific skills gaps and the provision of the requisite funding.

In developing countries, the skill gaps are much more extensive and basic, and in most countries the educational and training facilities are in very bad shape, especially in Africa. An important priority is to restore formerly great institutions of higher education, such as Makerere University in Uganda or Ibadan in Nigeria, that have gradually fallen into grave disrepair during the last forty years. Government-run civil service training institutions, instead, are mostly beyond repair, with very few exceptions. Generally, in most developing countries, the underpinning for reform is a comprehensive and tough-minded review of both the demand and the supply of training of government personnel.

On the demand side, the foundation for such a review must be a revision of the roles of the state and a factual assessment of the resulting training needs. In addition, there should be a clear link between training and staff careers, because new skills atrophy quickly when not used. On the supply side, many countries have an unnecessarily large number of institutions for training government workers and those that exist are typically weak. Major improvements can be expected from a rationalization of the system, eliminating overlapping, duplication, and waste of resources and phasing out the weak institutions. The guiding criterion should be the actual needs of agencies and civil servants, to combat the supply-driven mentality of most training programs.

Foreign aid can provide a useful role in this process of improvements, especially through the permanent commitment entailed by "twinning" arrangements between local training institutions and public administration institutes in developed countries. But foreign aid has often been a major part of the problem, too, supporting vast training programs with neither clear aims nor the essential institutional and organizational prerequisites, and in some cases inadvertently weakening further the capacity of local training institutions. It is therefore important for developing countries' governments to reassert "ownership" of external aid programs for public administration training. In turn, this requires a simple but clear national policy for the training of civil servants.

QUESTIONS FOR DISCUSSION

1. What are the pros and cons of government executives keeping their rank and grade when they transfer to other departments or jobs?
2. Pick one of the following statements and make a credible argument for it:
   a. "Without a strong central unit to make all personnel decisions, there cannot be a homogeneous public service or equity in government employment."
   b. "Without the autonomy of each government agency to hire and promote people as it judges

best, there cannot be good standards of public service nor efficiency in government employment."

3. "A recruitment freeze may be inevitable on occasion, but should be lifted as soon as possible lest it cause distortions in the structure of the government workforce." Discuss.

4. Getting rid of incompetent government employees is notoriously difficult. Are there practical ways in which consistently bad performance can be penalized without affecting the job security expected from government employment?

5. Hypothetically, what percentage of your salary would you be willing to give up in exchange for an assurance of reasonable job security? How much less pay would you be prepared to accept in exchange for an assured six weeks paid vacation a year at a time of your choosing?

6. Pick one of the two following statements and make a credible argument for it:
   a. "Unless government has the flexibility to hire and terminate employees, it cannot manage the public's business efficiently, nor adapt to changes in fiscal circumstances."
   b. "It is inhuman and, in the long run, inefficient to fire an employee with two weeks' notice after thirty years of faithful service."

7. Pick one of the two following statements and make a credible argument for it:
   a. "An elite civil service corps is antithetical to all notions of equity in public employment and eventually generates an attitude of arrogance vis-à-vis the public and the ensuing backlash."
   b. "Without an elite civil service corps, it is not possible to recruit and retain in government top executives and high-level professionals, which eventually results in mediocrity across the board and the ensuing deterioration of public services."

8. Pick one of the two following statements and make a credible argument for it:
   a. "When a person accepts a public service job, he or she must also accept strict restrictions on political activity and the right to unionize."
   b. "When a person accepts a public service job, he or she does not surrender constitutional rights of freedom of speech and freedom of association."

9. "Most training by government of government employees has been a waste of time and resources and has only served to create employment of teachers and trainers. When government employees need new specific skills, they can be sent to a specialized facility of their choice, or simply pick up the training in their spare time." Do you agree?

10. Are U.S. federal employees paid too much? Too little? Just right? What about state and local government employees? How would you decide?

11. In recent years, it has been argued that the current national security environment requires greater flexibility in government employment practices and thus greater restrictions on public employee unions. Do you agree? If yes, in what way does the current national security environment justify greater restrictions compared to years past? If not, how would you change government employment practices, if at all, to address presumed security concerns?

12. How would you draw the line between legitimate instructions to government employees by their duly elected or appointed political superior, and illegitimate political interference with their job duties and professional responsibilities?

APPENDIX 8.1. ELITE CIVIL SERVICE CORPS

Background and Rationale

An elite corps of senior civil servants (called in the United States "Senior Executive Service"—SES—see the last section) is defined as a small group of the most senior staff members, who provide policy advice, have higher managerial and professional responsibilities, and may be deployed wherever they are needed to promote the efficiency of the government. They have special conditions of employment, with higher salaries and correspondingly less job security and greater demands for performance.

In *developed countries*, when elite services have been introduced it was mainly in response to three problems:[20]

- increasingly inadequate compensation for the highest-skilled staff in comparison with the private sector, and ensuing difficulties in attracting or retaining highly qualified professionals;
- absence of a public-spirited, interagency, service-wide elite cadre; and, in some countries,
- perception that the senior permanent employees were insufficiently responsive to the priorities of the political leadership.

In many *developing countries,* the senior cadres (such as the Singapore Civil Service, the Indian Administrative Service, or the Sri Lanka Civil Service) inherited the mantle of the elite civil services set up during colonial times and generally kept the same roles while replacing the expatriate elite with a national one. The pluralistic nature of society in many of these countries, and the centrifugal tendencies in the larger countries, justified after independence the continuation of the tradition of a cross-cutting professional elite corps. The challenge was to convert this instrument, which had been so effective (and so disliked) as an agent of colonialism, into an agent of development and national public service—sensitive to the needs of the population and the demands of independence.

Variants

A Senior Executive System is a rank-in-person system, where one is hired as a fungible individual suited to a variety of senior jobs. However, there are many variants of elite civil service in both developed and developing countries.

Recruitment in "Mandarin Systems" (e.g., Japan) is usually through a central agency such as a public service commission. Applicants are normally screened by means of both general and specialized examinations followed by intensive interviews of the short-listed candidates and other forms of individual and group assessment. The successful applicants enter directly a particular class of service, usually on a fast track to senior positions.

In many British Commonwealth countries, the candidates are recruited into a national generalist elite service or in a number of central functional services, such as accounting, taxation, and communications and are liable to be rotated from one job to another both within the service and between ministries.

In India, candidates for the elite Indian Administrative Service (IAS), after graduating from the IAS Institute are recruited directly into individual ministries, where they tend to remain throughout their careers. Job rotation is within the ministry, but they may also rotate back and forth between service in central government and in state governments. (Many states have their own administrative service, closely modeled along the lines of the all-India IAS.)

In contrast to the centralized mandarin systems, a few countries favor an open model of senior recruitment, stressing flexibility, delegation, and market orientation. In the United States, the Senior Executive Service permits horizontal entry without age restrictions and allows considerable mobility between jobs (although interagency mobility is rare). Each government agency sets qualification standards for its SES positions and may choose both career and noncareer employees recruited directly from outside.

Keeping elite senior staff within the same ministry builds knowledge, provides continuity, and inspires loyalty to the objectives of the ministry. The downside is factionalism among the ministries and the lack of a common public service ethos throughout the government—paradoxically, this is precisely what elite senior services are supposed to provide.

In recent years, the advantages of interagency mobility have been increasingly recognized, and promotion to the highest posts often requires prior service in several ministries. (This was already a well-established practice in Britain and its colonies.) Canada, for example, has tried to develop a new interdepartmental identity for senior managers by increasing their mobility throughout the government, and introduced an executive development program (*La Relève*) particularly to strengthen policy analysis ability across sectors. (A similar mobility requirement is applied by the major international organizations for advancement to the managerial ranks.)

Issues for Developing Countries

The risks of an elite civil service system in a developing country are vulnerability to political and sectarian alignments and lack of sensitivity to the citizens' needs. In Asian SES systems, problems have arisen from politicization, weak incentive and penalty systems, and lack of recognition and rewards for initiative and integrity. Rivalry among the different service corps and the uneven opportunities for job enrichment and career mobility hamper the strengthening of a common service ethos. Faulty assignments of senior personnel often result in lopsided distribution of scarce expertise in government, leading to strong skill enclaves in high-profile ministries such as finance and planning and relatively weaker capacity in ministries such as education and health. In some countries where civil servants are supposedly insulated from political pressure (e.g., in India), a variety of practices (especially transfers at short notice to undesirable locations) keep civil servants vulnerable to politicians' whims and particularistic interests.

The problems in Africa are starker, with many senior civil service positions still occupied by expatriates. Changing the ethnic composition of senior government employment is probably the most sensitive challenge of personnel management in postcolonial plural societies. A delicate balance must be achieved between short-term efficiency, which calls for some continued—albeit diminishing—reliance on skilled expatriates, and long-term efficiency, which requires building strong local capacity and grooming national talent. (In certain cases, however, appointing a foreigner permits avoiding the risky choice between equally qualified members of contending ethnic groups.) The imperative to foster equity and social peace while assuring reasonably good public service provision is one of the challenges of plural societies and is particularly true in the new South Africa, where during apartheid the 10 percent white minority held 60 percent of government jobs and all the senior positions.

Training of Executive Government Personnel

In countries that have an elite-type civil service, successful applicants usually enter a prestigious national training institution, such as the Indian Administrative Service Institute, or the Ecole Nationale d'Administration (ENA) in France, which combines formal instruction with structured internships (Box 8.6). Throughout the training and subsequently, the candidates undergo intense socialization to internalize core public service values. Thereafter, they follow different streams of service. Again, the issues of training of government executive personnel are different in developed and developing countries, particularly concerning the cost-effectiveness of permanent training facilities in-country as compared with specialized and targeted training in foreign institutions.

BOX 8.6

Combining Instruction with Internships: The ENA Program

Perhaps the best known among elite civil service academies is the Ecole Nationale d'Administration (ENA) in France, which for generations has served as incubator for both the bureaucratic and political leadership of the country. The ENA continues to produce the supply of new elites for government service, although the "Enarchs" have been criticized for being out of touch with the average citizen and have run into increasing popular resentment since the late 1990s. Indeed, in 2007 France elected as President Nicolas Sarkozy, whose street savy background and personal traits make him in many ways the "anti-enarch."

The typical program at the ENA combines formal course instruction with internships. The school admits only about 100 French students and 40 foreign students a year, on the basis of tough competitive examinations. The formal courses comprise mainly international issues, economics, budgeting and finance, public law, and administration. The training includes two six-month internships—one with a prefect in a French province and the other with a French ambassador or with a company abroad. ENA graduates are ranked according to their performance and, on that basis, assigned to one or another of the elite services, among which the highest status is that of "inspector of public finance."

The ENA also offers short-term specialized programs, and its curriculum is complemented by the courses of similar schools that exist for the senior cadres in health, taxation, and the judiciary.

Source: Ecole Nationale d'Administration (www.ena.fr/en); Robert Chelle (former ENA director of administration), personal communication, 2000.

Developed Countries

The grooming of senior staff for higher management and advisory responsibilities calls for analysis of the required competencies and existing skill gaps. Eligibility to attend "executive development" programs requires not only job-related skills of a high order, but also communication skills, "people skills," and leadership potential. The development of executive personnel must be the responsibility of the central personnel unit in both centralized and decentralized training systems.

For this purpose, the United States has set up the Federal Executive Institute, which certifies candidates for entry into the Senior Executive Service discussed earlier in the text. (The government also conducts executive seminars for personnel below SES level.) The French ENA and the National School of Government of the United Kingdom (formerly the Civil Service College) have been performing this role for their senior cadres. Generally, executive development programs for senior staff of central governments are well-established and reasonably effective—the executive training programs of Singapore and Canada are among the best organized (see Box 8.7). By

---

BOX 8.7

Executive Personnel Training in Canada and Singapore

In *Canada,* senior government executives are trained through the Canadian Center for Management Development. Understanding that executive training should be complemented by appropriate career incentives, such as the opportunity to leapfrog over more senior colleagues, the program "La Releve" identifies executives for leading positions through a prequalification process and then facilities their advancement through the Accelerated Executive Development Program.

In *Singapore,* after merging several schemes of service into a single senior staff scheme in 1996, the government provides the senior staff with training in line operations, human resource management, finance and corporate services, public affairs, research, and information support. Training beyond orientation is provided at five career levels. The staff thus attends different courses at different stages in their career, totaling a minimum of 100 hours of training a year. (The training centers are well equipped to handle these demands.) Each ministry is expected to organize its own specialized functional training, while the Civil Service College handles training in four general areas: managing service excellence, managing change, managing people, and managing self. The latter, which is unusual in government employee training, is known as the "life skills" area and includes such topics as balancing work and home responsibilities, managing one's health, and planning for retirement.

Source: Commonwealth Secretariat (1998a).

---

contrast, training of executive personnel of subnational government is still insufficient in most countries, although some successful examples of executive training at provincial and local government levels do exist (Box 8.8).

Developing Countries

Government executive development programs have been provided in a few developing countries. However, the evidence shows that the benefits are not commensurate with the large investment required because of the poor link to career development and the lack of performance incentives. Executive personnel do not attend the course regularly, or attend only because they are required to do so. This may indicate either lack of incentives, as noted, or more likely, lack of relevance of the material or poor quality of the training itself. In any case, reliable and systematic feedback surveys are essential to either improve the training or halt the waste of resources. In general, considering the comparatively small number of senior employees concerned, it is highly likely that to use the international and transnational training opportunities described here would be much more

BOX 8.8

Executive Training at Subnational Levels in New York and Ontario

The *New York* public service training program includes two practical, skill-based curricula—one on supervision and individual performance, and the other on administration and organizational performance (cf. Flanders, in Perry, 1989). The funding modality for this program is highly unusual in that the funding is included in the agreement between the state and the collective bargaining unit for professional and scientific employees. The New York program is implemented along the lines of the national certified public manager consortium, which accredits executive personnel for state government positions, based on six job-related, competence-tested management courses. These courses parallel the executive continuum, from supervisory to senior levels, and are delivered in association with state university systems or with a government institute.

In *Ontario, Canada,* the provincial government has developed a human resource plan for senior management incorporating core competencies and combining just-in-time learning with long-term education. Within twenty-four months of appointment, all senior appointees are expected to take at least the leadership program as well as one foundation program related to transforming government, mastering business issues, and managing relationships. Later, the senior staff can also take advantage of a menu of supplementary programs, depending on their interests and needs, and may pursue university-accredited courses in information technology, in a unique partnership between the government institute and three universities.

Source: Fesler and Kettl (1991); Borins (1999).

cost-effective than to build an entire executive development program in the country. Exceptions are the largest developing countries, where the number of candidates is sufficiently high to justify the investment—see Box 8.9 on the next page.

BOX 8.9

Mixed Record of Executive Training in Some Large Countries

In *India,* the National Academy of Administration organizes, on behalf of the government Department of Personnel and Training, two types of training for officials in the elite Indian Administrative Service—orientation courses on various topics, where staff of different seniority are grouped together; and a series of short courses throughout the year, tailored to staff of different ranges of seniority. Some of these courses involve the collaboration of overseas institutes such as the French ENA and the National Institute of Public Administration (INTAN) in Malaysia. Staff members are also given opportunities to spend short periods in the National Academy doing case studies or research and teaching. Although training is mandatory for all senior staff, except those in the top two grades, there is a weak link between training and career development and no conscious effort to prepare staff for higher positions.

Argentina has created a permanent training system, whereby executive personnel must obtain a certain number of credits in training, either to remain in their posts or to be promoted. What evidence exists suggests that the training is often perfunctory, the link between the courses and the jobs weak, attendance is unmotivated and mechanical, and thus few lasting skills are imparted.

Similarly, *China* organizes training for senior executives through its own National School of Administration, and has made it mandatory for all persons in "leading positions" to attend a minimum period of training. There is no evidence on the effectiveness of this program. However, the dramatic rise of China's economy and the attendant vast new problems and challenges call for a thorough evaluation of the system and, in all probability, a large-scale overhaul and modernization.

NOTES

1. This section relies in part on Armstrong (2006); Commonwealth Secretariat (1996); Riley (1993); Grindle and Marshall (1977); and Patten (1971).

2. This section has drawn on Chew and Teo (1991); Fesler and Kettl (1991); Klingner and Nalbandian (1998); Riley (1993); Schiavo-Campo (1998); and Starling (1998).

3. The techniques of job evaluation include market-based evaluation, whole-job ranking, point rating and factor comparison, and position classification. Point rating and factor comparison identify specific job factors, which are assigned point values. The jobs are then grouped on the basis of point totals, and the various job categories are accordingly ordered by rank.

4. Fesler and Kettl (1991).

5. This and subsequent subsections have drawn on Commonwealth Secretariat (1996); Klingner and Nalbandian (1998); Nunberg (1995); Starling (1998); Local Government Center (1996); and Salzstein in Perry, ed. (1989).

6. Depending on the size of the country and its personnel management system, there could be a number of other commissions, working under the guidance of the principal PSC, for specific categories of civil service, such as police and teachers, or at the regional level.

7. Tendler (1997).

8. Saltzstein (1989).

9. This section draws on Commonwealth country profiles; Coleman (1990); Delaney and Horton, in Perry, ed., (1989); Riccuci (1997); and Riley (1993).

10. "Work to rule" is the deliberate slowdown of activity through strict and literal adherence to every single provision in the regulations. While such slowdowns are theoretically possible only when the rules are cumbersome or inefficient, even the best-designed regulations can be abused when they are followed to the very letter in a systematic attempt to disrupt the activity. "Hiccup strikes" are short-duration strikes of a few hours or even an hour at a time, designed to cause maximum inconvenience through their unpredictability.

11. The websites of each of these institutes and organizations can be easily obtained by googling their name.

12. On a weighted basis, obtained by dividing civilian federal payroll by number of civilian federal employees.

13. *Encyclopedia Britannica,* Premium Service, November 3, 2005. www.britannica.com/eb/article-9050821. See also William Safire, *Safire's New Political Dictionary,* 1993.

14. Civil service reform began in earnest under the Hayes presidency, including the creation of a Civil Service Reform Association in 1880.

15. To add posthumous insult to lethal injury, the first entry in *Wikipedia* under "Garfield" is for the cartoon cat, not the president. (Note to the reader: despite its wonderful utility as free first-line on-line resource, information in Wikipedia remains suspect, as it can be "improved" by anyone without verification or immediate correction. Important facts and conclusions must be confirmed with other sources, even if originally found through *Wikipedia.*)

16. Titled "An Act to Prevent Pernicious Political Activities," the legislation was named after Senator Carl Hatch of New Mexico (1889–1963), and is also known as the Hatch Act of 1939.

17. George Pendleton (1825–1889), a United States senator from Cincinnati, Ohio, authored the Pendleton Act, on January 16, 1883. The Pendleton Act still serves as the basis for civil service positions today.

18. Keillor (1986).

19. The FLRA is an independent administrative federal agency that was created by Title VII of the Civil Service Reform Act of 1978 (also known as the Federal Service Labor-Management Relations Statute).

20. See, for example, O'Toole (2006).

CHAPTER 9

Managing the Purchases and the Contracts: Public Procurement

> Where there is honey, there are bees.
> —*Nepali proverb*

WHAT TO EXPECT

In addition to financial resources and personnel, which were discussed in the previous chapters, government needs a variety of supplies, equipment, and materials, as well as consultants and other services. Government contracting and acquisition of goods and services is referred to as public procurement. The chapter first reviews the nature and objectives of public procurement and the differences from private sector purchasing. While "economy" (i.e., the timely purchasing at least cost and given quality) is the procurement criterion in both private and public sectors, public procurement must also meet certain broad policy objectives. In this light, the chapter discusses the legal and procedural framework for public procurement, advances key management considerations, and presents the major issues of procurement risk, corruption in procurement, and neglect of procurement by top public managers. The procurement process is then described in some detail, beginning with international competitive bidding—the most appropriate method for large purchases—and including the scope, limits, and risks of sole-source (no-bid) procurement. Good public procurement does not stop with the selection of the winning bidder and contract negotiation. Close and careful contract management and monitoring by the government are critical, including provisions to assure that technical and quality specifications are met. The chapter then examines the special problems raised by military procurement, which accounts for the bulk of government procurement spending in a number of countries. The costs and risks of military procurement are described and various measures are suggested to minimize the costs while meeting legitimate military needs and genuine emergencies. The procurement policies and practices in the United States are described next. The customary section on general directions of improvement rounds out the chapter. Appendix 9.1 describes in some detail the stages of competitive procurement and Appendix 9.2 the various other forms of procurement.

GENESIS, OBJECTIVES, AND SCOPE OF PUBLIC PROCUREMENT[1]

Background

Historically, the main role of public procurement was to obtain goods and services for the military (see Box 9.1). Procurement activities gradually expanded along with the roles of

---

BOX 9.1

Procurement in Seventeenth-Century England

Samuel Pepys was appointed by the British monarch to look into the reasons why the quality of ships and supplies for the British Navy was so unreliable and their prices so high.

His diary gives a striking description of the procurement function in seventeenth-century England and the uncontrolled scope for self-enrichment by government officials in those times. Pepys did manage to clean up the defense procurement process by delving into administration as a professional, learning what was required by the navy and why, negotiating fiercely on quality and price, and following up to see that contracts were properly fulfilled. He was troubled by the ease with which he (like many others before him in his position) could receive "tokens" of appreciation from successful contractors. On occasion, Pepys himself yielded to the temptation. The diary also speaks about the required reporting on procurement to an increasingly assertive Parliament in its watchdog role and the type of detailed documentation that is needed to justify the conduct of the executive.

His progress notwithstanding, Pepys' conclusion was a resigned acknowledgement in 1662 that "it is impossible for the King to have things done as cheap as other men."

Source: Adapted from Latham (1978).

---

government, and became a core function of public administration. A substantial proportion of public expenditure at every level of government goes for acquisition of goods and services and for construction activity—about one fifth of expenditure in developed countries and up to one half in developing countries. The range of government contracting and purchasing is vast, from weapons systems and large industrial plants to road surfacing, raw materials, paper, milk, custodial services, and so on.

Contracting for public works and construction (roads, bridges, ports, buildings, etc.) is usually treated separately from purchase of goods and services, for a number of reasons.[2] Unlike goods and services that are consumed in short order or serve as intermediate inputs, public works represent long-lasting final outputs. The standards and specifications for bids and contracts are different. Also, the contracting process for works lends itself to unbundling into separate contracts for each component (e.g., design, technical services, and actual construction). The process of contracting therefore stretches over a much longer period than the acquisition of goods and services and calls for closer and continuous supervision.

As a part of the broad procurement process, contracting-out (outsourcing) has become more prominent in some countries. Outsourcing the delivery of services, such as transport and garbage collection, has been common for years, but has increased in use since the late 1980s at both national and subnational levels of government, and accelerated in this century especially in the United States. (Outsourcing is discussed in chapter 11.)

As discussed later, procurement can be centralized or decentralized in different degrees. As a general proposition, government departments and subnational governments should have autonomy to contract and to buy goods and services, but uniform policies and standards should be set at the central government level and supervision and appeals should be the responsibility of a central procurement entity.

Some Basic Terms

The following terms can help clarify the discussion in this chapter:

- the term "procurement" includes all stages of the process of acquiring property or services, beginning with the process for determining a need for property or services and ending with contract completion and closeout;
- "procurement system" refers to the integration of the procurement process, the professional development of procurement personnel, and the management structure for carrying out the procurement function;
- "procurement standards" are the criteria for determining the effectiveness of the procurement system by measuring the performance of its various elements;
- "competitive procedures" means procedures under which an agency enters into a contract pursuant to full and open competition;
- "full and open competition," when used with respect to procurement, means that all qualified sources are permitted to submit sealed bids or competitive proposals on the procurement.

The Differences Between Private and Public Procurement

There are essential differences between the procurement process in government and in private companies. A private company places less emphasis on formal competitive bidding, documented procedures, and conflicts of interest than governments do. This is because private managers have built-in incentives to purchase goods that provide high value for money and to hire contractors who will do high-quality jobs at competitive prices. Their accountability is related to results, not process, and private procurement inefficiencies will show up in their impact on overall company profit.

In contrast, the public manager must follow prescribed procedures that give a major weight to fairness and equity, and public procurement is subject to oversight by the legislature and public audit (in addition to internal administrative accountability mechanisms). Also, public procurement is often used as a tool for public policy goals (e.g., fostering the growth of local industry, benefiting groups of poor women or disadvantaged groups, etc.). Moreover, mistakes or malfeasance in public procurement can have vast political repercussions owing to the attention that the media and the citizens place on the subject. Finally, private companies and nongovernment organizations prefer stable relationships with suppliers and long-term contracts for certainty and easier business planning, but public agencies are prevented from developing such long-term relationships by several factors (including the fear of collusion with contractors and financial integrity rules).

Objectives of Public Procurement

Economy

The general objective of government procurement is to acquire goods and services, and to work in a manner providing the best value to the government and the people. The performance criterion for evaluating procurement activities is thus "economy" (i.e., acquisition at the lowest price and on a timely basis, without sacrificing quality). From an economist's point of view, economy is subsumed under the broader criterion of *efficiency* (i.e., lowest *unit* cost of production). Obviously, the lowest unit cost of the product can only be achieved if, among other things, the inputs needed to produce it are themselves obtained at lowest cost. However, economy remains a very useful separate criterion for public administration purposes, as it is the main criterion on which to assess the performance of the public procurement function. Also, poor procurement management has an impact beyond direct cost: it reduces the benefits of government programs, hampers private sector performance, and enables major corruption.

Wasteful procurement can arise from duplication and overlap in government operations, from lack of funding predictability (which leads public agencies to use funds available when they happen to be available, entailing higher cost of storage), and from lack of incentives for employees to make the best use of supplies. Sound procurement, therefore, depends also on a variety of organizational and incentive factors within government, well beyond the control of the individuals in charge of the procurement function itself.

The basic criterion of economy is pretty much the only one applicable in private procurement. In public procurement, instead, the criterion of economy is complemented by, and often balanced with, the following other objectives.

Fostering the Growth of Competition

Competition in procurement is defined as equality of opportunity for qualified suppliers to compete for public contracts. Competition and impartiality are needed not only to ensure a beneficial outcome in price and quality, but also to promote public accountability for the process. Fostering the growth of competition in public procurement is a goal of most governments and is supported by international organizations as well. In the United States, for example, the Competition in Contracting Act of 1984 aims to increase competitive efforts within departments and to narrow the justification for "sole-source" contracting (also called "no-bid" contracts or "direct selection"). Several European countries require their local governments to resort to compulsory competitive bidding for all purchases and services (partly to conform to European Union directives). Many countries require their national and subnational governments to take measures to attract more firms to compete for government business. Because the degree of competition is partly a function of the number of qualified suppliers, many developing countries and most aid agencies support the provision of information and technical assistance to potential bidders to better understand the rules of procurement and thus become qualified to compete.

Import Substitution and Domestic Preference

By giving preferences to local suppliers, or restricting purchases from foreign firms (which is equivalent), the procurement strategy may deliberately try to encourage the growth of local industry. These preferences are very different in motivation and impact from regulations to offset market imperfections preventing domestic suppliers from competing on a fair and equal basis with international suppliers. Unlike those regulations, domestic preference practices are generally suspect from both an efficiency and a development viewpoint.

In *developing countries,* giving some preference in public procurement to domestic firms has traditionally been accepted by donor agencies—the World Bank, the African and Asian Development Banks and others—and a means to stimulate the growth of domestic competitors to large multinational suppliers. Similarly, although the World Trade Organization (WTO) prescribes uniform treatment of domestic and foreign suppliers in procurement, it provides for special treatment of developing countries in order to safeguard their balance-of-payments position, promote the development and establishment of domestic industries, and support industrial units that are substantially dependent on government procurement. The European Union allows central and eastern European countries applying for membership to keep domestic preference provisions, but only for a limited time.

While political interference and corruption are certainly a reality in public procurement, competition is often restricted by market imperfections as well, such as barriers to entry and information gaps for small and less-experienced suppliers. These barriers are sometimes put up by the administration itself, such as the tendency to float large bids in order to save time with a single decision, or the formalistic overspecification of requirements that small and less-experienced firms find very costly to fulfill. In some areas (e.g., emerging technology, specialized services, or complex equipment, as in military procurement), developing countries may be obliged to deal with only one or two suppliers because the aid is "tied" to purchases from the donor country's firms. In these cases, the long-term strategy consists of:

- encouraging the development of the domestic contracting industry;
- lowering the barriers to entry for small business and voluntary agencies; and
- pushing to untie aid as much as possible through better cooperation among donors and stronger leadership by the multilateral financial institutions.

In *developed countries,* competition is usually restricted by political interference, corruption, or emergency—or a combination of all three, as inprocurement of goods and works for the Iraq war. The solution in such cases is essentially political, via pressure from the public or from opposition parties to clean up the operation of the system and enable more vigorous competition.

Protecting Public Service Provision

Whether or not public service delivery is outsourced to private entities, government retains the basic responsibility—reaffirmed in judicial decisions in many countries—to ensure that the services paid for by the taxpayers reach the citizens. In procurement, this responsibility implies setting up recourse mechanisms in case of contractor failure, carefully monitoring contract execution by private suppliers, giving credible information to citizens about the actual providers of service, and opening avenues of complaint.

Protecting the Environment

The preservation of environmental quality and the reduction of waste is a recognized factor in public procurement.[3] Government purchasing policies, including those related to packaging and recycling, should be reviewed to reduce where possible their adverse environmental impact or foster positive impact (e.g., encouraging the use of recycled materials).

BOX 9.2

Procurement in the New South Africa

Procurement reform in South Africa is part of the extremely difficult challenge of balancing short-term efficiency with the imperative of dismantling the discriminatory structure of the old apartheid regime. The old procurement system was not only racially discriminatory, but also fragmented, hard to use, and biased toward large, established businesses. The onerous procedures often caused delays in delivery and prevented the government from taking advantage of its size in negotiating procurement contracts. All contracts had to be approved by ten Tender Boards (one national and nine provincial), and there were separate boards or committees for parastatal and local authorities. Each of these boards was autonomous, with its own procedures, requirements, and policy interpretations.

Owing to this background, South Africa is among the minority of countries whose constitution contains a special provision on government procurement. Section 187 of the new 1994 constitution provides that:

- the procurement of goods and services for any level of government is to be regulated by an act of Parliament and by provincial laws, providing for the appointment of independent and impartial tender boards;
- the tendering system must be "fair, equitable, transparent, competitive and cost-effective" and the tender boards shall have to justify their decisions at the request of interested parties;

Fostering Equity and Remedying the Effects of Past Discrimination

Last but certainly not least, and especially important in ethnically plural countries, the procurement system can be designed to include certain preferences for ethnic or regional minorities previously excluded or discriminated against. There is a risk that such preferences may persist long after the underlying impact of past discrimination has been corrected. Conversely, they can be circumvented or abused by putting up "front companies" devised exclusively to take advantage of the procurement preference regime. These risks exist and must be addressed in the regulations, but do not at all mean that minority group preferences are impractical or inadvisable. South Africa offers a good illustration of how to move from a discriminatory system to one with an explicit equity component—Box 9.2.

THE LEGAL AND REGULATORY FRAMEWORK FOR PROCUREMENT

The Governance Dimension

Predictability, a key principle of good governance, presupposes clear principles and regulations for bidding, qualification of contractors, award of bids, and contract management. Information and documentation on these rules should be widely available, and the rules should be enforced fairly and consistently. Predictability in procurement also requires a well-functioning system for dispute settlement, and checks on arbitrary behavior of procurement managers and the inconsistent exercise of discretionary power.

Accountability and transparency are vital to procurement management as well. Lack of oversight mechanisms to ensure accountability undermines the capacity of governments to secure the confidence of contractors in the public procurement process and the trust of citizens that public funds are being properly used to acquire goods and services. Trust and confidence can be eroded by secrecy in procurement transactions (although a degree of confidentiality is essential to protect business privacy and the legitimate interests of individual bidders). Transparency reduces uncertainty and inhibits corruption in procurement by assuring equality of access to information for all bidders before, during, and after the bidding process.

The Legal Framework[4]

A country's legal framework for public procurement includes obligations arising from international agreements; specific domestic legislation on procurement; contract and commercial law in general; and other pertinent laws, mainly on patents and copyright and on labor relations. Some countries (e.g., South Africa, as described earlier) even have constitutional provisions governing procurement.

The emphasis in developed countries in recent years has been on adopting a uniform procurement framework, supplemented by more detailed rules promulgated by each ministry in accordance with its specific needs. For example, in Australia, the procurement framework is contained in the *Commonwealth Procurement Guidelines* issued in 1997. At the subnational level, the *Model Procurement Code for State and Local Governments* in the United States has been the most comprehensive attempt to adapt the elements of good procurement practice to particular state and local circumstances. The EU requires from prospective member countries certain uniform procurement reforms as a condition for EU membership (Box 9.3).

The most widely used model public procurement law is the one adopted by the United Nations Commission on International Trade Law (UNCITRAL), updated in 1995 consolidating previous laws. The law was intended to be a model for developing and transition countries in modernizing their procurement, but is also expected to remedy the inefficiencies and the potential for abuse in the procurement laws of many other countries, and make these laws more compatible with international trade practices. The UNCITRAL model law has formed the basis for national procurement legislation in many developing countries, with support from international donor agencies. Although as a "framework" law the UNCITRAL model law does not itself set forth all the necessary regulations, it recommends open bidding as the method of procurement that is generally most effective in promoting competition, economy, and efficiency in procurement.

Regulations and Procedures

The Scope of the Rules

As compatible with general contract law, most countries regulate public procurement by internal rules that prescribe the formal process of bidding, the evaluation of bids, the awarding and conclusion of contracts, and contract management (see the United Kingdom example in Box 9.4). The rules also mandate procedures for dealing with court challenges from unsuccessful bidders and for contract interpretation, breach of contract, and dispute resolution and arbitration.

BOX 9.3

Procurement Requirements for European Union Accession

Countries seeking European Union (EU) membership are required to establish and maintain procurement systems that meet standards of transparency
and of open and fair competition. Central and eastern European countries
have been working to establish modern public procurement systems from
the start of their transition to a market economy in the early 1990s. Creating
such systems is part of the process of forging an efficient and competitive
market economy and is necessary for full integration into the international
trading community.

To build and implement the procurement system, significant changes have
had to be made from the days of the command economy, when procurement
was part of the central planning system and goods and services were supplied
by direct government instructions. In particular, central and eastern European
countries are designing a legal and administrative framework that facilitates
the integration of the myriad procurement entities throughout the public sector
into a functional and coherent network with high professional standards and
that is consistent with international obligations. Such a framework defines
the financial and legal responsibilities of all participants in the procurement
process, including suppliers and procurement entities in central and local
government.

New members of the EU have passed national procurement laws consistent
with international standards and some have set up a central organization to draft
and disseminate procurement regulations and rules for decentralized operation.
The Organization for Economic Cooperation and Development and the International Labor Organization have collaborated on the preparation of a public
procurement manual for central and eastern Europe.

Source: Updated from OECD (1997a).

The procurement regulations place great reliance on competition and objective decision making
(except in specified emergencies such as natural disasters). This approach often results in extensive
regulatory control and oversight by external agencies and heavy bureaucratic review and approval
processes. Many government agencies feel that the procurement process has become an end in
itself, stressing compliance with rules to the neglect of economy or efficiency. In 1993, the United
States had 889 laws on defense procurement alone, causing a product to be on average 50 percent
more expensive simply because it was purchased by the Defense Department. Federal regulations
filled 1,600 pages, supplemented by 2,900 pages of agency-specific regulations, supplemented in
turn by instructions and case law.

Many countries are consequently moving to streamline and consolidate existing laws and
regulations, or writing simpler laws and regulations to govern procurement transactions. In the

BOX 9.4

Procurement Guidelines in the United Kingdom

In the United Kingdom, the Procurement Practice and Development team is the central unit in the Treasury that promotes best practices and the development of procurement strategies by government departments. The government has stipulated the following key criteria:

- value for money;
- compliance with national and international legal obligations;
- cost-effective fulfillment of users' needs;
- appropriate level of competition; and
- honest and impartial relationships with suppliers.

The procurement process is also intended to ensure:

- fairness, efficiency, courtesy, and firm dealings;
- high professional standards;
- wide and easy access to information on the procurement process and documentation;
- prompt notification of the outcome of the bidding;
- efficiency and integrity in contract management; and
- prompt response to suggestions and complaints.

In the selection of bidders, undue emphasis should not be placed on size, and the standards of financial and technical capacity should be proportionate to the nature and value of the contract in question. The criteria for the award should not consist of price alone, but should also consider other factors such as lifetime cost (including operations and maintenance cost), quality, and delivery. Lifetime cost is relevant in complex procurements, including large supply and service contracts and construction projects, to offset the higher cost of better quality against the lower maintenance costs over the asset life.

New Zealand has published *Government Purchasing: A Guide for Suppliers* to help suppliers understand and operate in the government purchasing environment. It is intended to improve communication between public-sector buyers and industry to their mutual benefit. *Canada* provides an integrated electronic public tendering service, which supports open, cost-effective procurement for all levels of government and all sizes of suppliers in the private sector.

Sources: United Kingdom government (www.directgov.uk) and World Trade Organization websites (www.wto.org).

United States, as recommended by the National Performance Review, the Federal Acquisition Streamlining Act of 1994 repealed or modified 225 provisions and raised the value thresholds for full compliance with the regulations, thus exempting 95 percent of the transactions.

Manuals and Procedures

Public procurement manuals typically comprise: (1) a policy manual, which includes the purchasing criteria and main rules; (2) an operations manual of internal practices and procedures; and (3) a vendor manual, which often takes the form of a booklet entitled something like *Doing Business with the Government*. Matters of policy (e.g., giving preference to domestic suppliers in international competitive bidding) are generally issued as binding instructions for all ministries and departments, but different countries allow different degrees of departmental discretion in devising procurement regulations. In Singapore, for example, all government entities must strictly follow the administrative procurement procedure laid down by the ministry of finance. By contrast, the United Kingdom, New Zealand, and other developed countries issue central guidelines but allow individual departments to issue regulations specific to their own needs within those guidelines. There are advantages to issuing a single set of procurement guidelines for common guidance while allowing individual agencies to supplement and vary these according to their needs and those of their clients.

THE MANAGEMENT OF PUBLIC PROCUREMENT

Defining and Assessing Performance in Procurement

As noted earlier, the performance criterion for procurement function is easily defined as *economy* (i.e., least cost and timely acquisition). It is less easy in practice to organize and manage the procurement function to meet this criterion. The United States General Accountability Office has developed a framework for the organization of procurement and the assessment of its performance. Table 9.1 shows an adapted and simplified version of the framework.

Organizational Arrangements[6]

The central organizational question is whether procurement transactions should be carried out by one central purchasing agency or decentralized to the spending ministries and agencies concerned. The main advantages of a central agency are that the staff become very familiar with the law, policies, and procedures and have the institutional memory to gain the best value for the government. The main advantage of decentralized procurement is that it speeds up the process and places greater emphasis on the quality and appropriateness of the goods and services. The conflict between central procurement offices and the spending agencies is typical, and is part and parcel of the general issue of central versus decentralized authority.

Instead of inquiring whether procurement should be central or decentralized, it is more constructive to ask *which* of the several procurement functions are best performed by a central agency. The general answer is that a central entity is essential to set uniform procurement rules and standards, exercise oversight, and handle appeals, while the actual purchasing and contracting should be left to the spending ministry and agency directly concerned. As far as local governments are concerned, subnational units should have the autonomy and flexibility to procure their own goods and services within the overall rules and standards. (This

Table 9.1

Framework for Organizing and Assessing the Procurement Function

Critical area	Elements	Success factors
Organizational alignment and leadership	Aligning procurement with agency goals/needs	Appropriate location of procurement function
		Organize the function to meet strategic goals
		Define clearly roles and responsibilities
	Leadership	Competent and strong leadership
		Providing role model for integrity
		Good communications
Policies and processes	Planning strategically	Assessing internal needs and the impact of external events
	Effective management	Partnering with other organizations
		Managing suppliers
		Robust monitoring and oversight of contracts
		Enabling financial accountability
Personnel management	Investing in human capital	Tailor recruitment to organizational needs
	Fostering ethical behavior	Targeted training
		Enabling a culture of integrity and providing robust oversight.
Information	Data and technology to support procurement decisions	Tracking procurement data
		Putting financial data into "friendly" formats
		Analyzing spending
	Safeguarding operational and data integrity and confidentiality	Ensuring effective controls
		Good records protection and management

Source: U.S. General Accountability Office, GAO-05–218G, available at www.gao.gov/new.items.

approach is symmetrical with the approach to government personnel management discussed in chapter 8.)[7]

While the objectives of public procurement are generally the same everywhere (albeit assigned different relative weights in different countries), the organizational arrangements vary. In Slovakia, procurement is the sole responsibility of the Ministry of Construction and Public Works. In Singapore, with some exceptions (e.g., pharmaceuticals) the government has decentralized the bulk of purchasing to the ministries, departments, and statutory boards, under uniform binding rules. In the United Kingdom, a procurement policy team, joint between the Treasury and the Department of Trade and Industry, advises the ministers on procurement policy. Australia's structure is a good example of strategic coherence in procurement, combining central agencies and decentralized departments. Australia and other countries (e.g., Canada, and a number of Asian and European countries) have also set up a specialized purchasing agency to provide certain common services and materials for several departments (Box 9.5).

BOX 9.5

Organizational Arrangements for Federal Procurement in Australia

In the federal government, procurement management is substantially decentralized, with each department and agency responsible for its own procurement within a centrally prescribed framework of procurement policy and advisory guidance on best practices and techniques. (The framework also covers government business enterprises.) The Department of Administrative Services coordinates purchasing policy.

A special office to handle purchasing of goods and services needed throughout government is "Purchasing Australia," which also supports the supplier community through:

• a Supplier Development Program, which assists small to medium enterprises in gaining access to the Commonwealth marketplace by linking suppliers with buyers, providing information, and facilitating skills development; and

• the Government Electronic Marketplace Service (GEMS), which provides information through the Internet about the purchasing policies of the Australian government and special purchasing opportunities in the government.

The Office of Government Information and Advertising provides advice and assistance in advertising, market research, public relations, and related matters. It manages the centralized arrangements for federal government advertising, disposal of surplus assets, contracting assistance, facilitation of electronic purchasing, buyer training, and publications and other advisory material on procurement matters.

The Public Works Policy Group (PWPG) assists agencies in applying public works policies. The PWPG promotes the implementation by agencies of best practices in the procurement of construction and related services and facilitates the ongoing development of best-practice strategies.

Finally, the National Procurement Board monitors, reviews, and reports on the efficiency and effectiveness of the government's buying framework and plays a key role in ensuring that all agencies carry out the government's policies.

Source: World Trade Organization (www.wto.gov).

It is useful to build a consultation mechanism into the procurement process not only to give the spending agencies the benefit of expert advice but also to check imprudent procurement. As an outgrowth of such consultation, spending agencies may be exempt from the bidding requirement if the purchases are made from an approved contractor preselected by the central procurement agency. Alternatively, agencies may be required to consult specialized entities or experts when acquiring computer systems and scientific services. Interagency committees may be set up for the procurement of supplies involving several sectors or agencies. Various other coordination and flexibility mechanisms may be established for effective consultation between the procurement entity and the spending agencies.

MAJOR ISSUES IN PUBLIC PROCUREMENT

Systematic Neglect by Senior Management

A fundamental problem in public procurement is disinterest and neglect by senior managers, who tend to leave procurement to the "specialists." There are several reasons for this neglect. Top managers are typically more interested in policy and find the purchasing tasks dull by comparison. Also, they rarely have enough time to understand the intricacies of product quality, pricing structures, and technical specifications. Moreover, in a climate where the integrity of government operations is coming under increasing scrutiny, keeping some distance from purchasing operations insulates a manager to some degree from potential charges of corruption. Finally, management distance from procurement decisions is often encouraged by the procurement staff themselves—usually because they view management involvement as interference with little value added, and occasionally for less honorable reasons. (A time-honored defensive response to a sudden interest by managers in procurement is to provide them with a large volume of indigestible technical material.)

The general disinterest of public managers in procurement matters finds its expression in, among other things, the cursory treatment of the subject in public administration schools. By contrast, business and management schools normally offer one or more courses in purchasing and in contract monitoring.

This is not a healthy state of affairs. In the first place, as noted earlier, the entire field of public administration has its historical origin in the ruler's concern with a malfunctioning procurement system. Second, as stressed throughout this book, the effectiveness of public management depends largely on achieving a good balance between control and flexibility; between protection of systemic equity and the provision of individual incentives for performance; and between short-term results and long-term sustainability. These are all vital considerations in procurement—particularly for large civil works and informatics contracts. Unfortunately, rank-and-file civil servants, including procurement staff, have an understandable aversion to risk, because of the lack of corresponding rewards and of the special external scrutiny to which public service is exposed. Only a climate of trust and strong higher-level support can prevent such risk aversion from turning into operational paralysis. In the area of procurement, this calls for more involvement by managers and consequently greater support for (and control of) the actions of the procurement specialists.

Accordingly, top public managers have a central responsibility to become much more involved in the procurement function, especially for large contracts, than is currently the case in most governments. A failure to do so can have heavy financial and political repercussions, as illustrated in the United States by the Air Force tanker aircraft scandal described later in Box 9.8. When questioned, former Defense Secretary Donald Rumsfeld disclaimed any responsibility for overseeing the department procurement of almost $100 billion a year: "I have got 50 million things on my desk and this isn't one of them."[8]

The political leadership can persuade senior managers to accept their responsibility to keep an eye on procurement by making its exercise part of their explicit performance expectations. Of course, senior managers cannot and should not become procurement specialists, and never interfere in particular procurement transactions, but they must be fully aware of the process and its risks. There are many ways by which senior public managers can obtain competent and independent advice. (Greater attention to procurement by senior public managers finds a parallel in the earlier evolution in the private sector from product orientation to client orientation. As a result of this evolution, beginning in the 1970s the separate purchasing activities of companies were merged and brought more and more under top levels of management.)

Centralize or Decentralize?

As emphasized in chapter 5, the issues of delegation and decentralization pivot around the right balance between efficiency and risk. Typically, line ministries and spending agencies always push for the delegation of the procurement function, on the grounds that they are the best judge of their own requirements and can meet them faster and at less cost than going through a central procurement agency. This would be almost always true, except for the problem of the senior managers' disinterest and neglect of the procurement process discussed earlier. The disinterest of senior managers implies that once procurement is delegated to the spending agency, it then falls under general administration and is no longer given the prudential attention it deserves and, presumably, it received when it was handled centrally. Thus, the general questions to be considered when deciding to decentralize procurement are:

- whether it is more effective to develop strict purchasing procedures and contractual safeguards at the center, or to give public managers more discretion to develop procedures and safeguards tailored to the particular goods and services they need;
- how to delegate procurement to the line agencies while installing appropriate safeguards to prevent abuses;
- the role of the central procurement agency in a context of delegated procurement responsibilities;
- the comparative degree of corruption and inefficiency at different levels of government; and, most importantly,
- the degree of risk at different stages of procurement and in different sectors.

Managing Risk and Combating Corruption in Procurement

That there are risks associated with delegating procurement does not at all imply that procurement needs to be centralized. On the contrary, the previous section has pointed to the advantages of decentralized purchasing and contract decisions, subject to central rules, criteria, and oversight. The risks of delegating procurement, however, must be carefully identified and addressed.

The Determinants of Procurement Risk

The degree of risk differs in different sectors, countries, agencies, and transactions. Therefore, to achieve a good balance between efficiency and risk, one should unbundle the procurement issue. Generally, three variables determine the degree of risk: specificity, market structure, and size and complexity of the transaction.

Specificity is inversely related to risk: the more specific the product or contract, the fewer the opportunities for manipulating the procurement process. However, artificial specifications may be included in the standards in order to favor a particular supplier. Also, all things being equal, greater specificity also entails a smaller market and thus less competition. The market structure in the sector is itself important, with a more restricted and less competitive market associated with greater risk. Finally, large transactions are normally also more complex technically, thus offering greater openings for manipulation and making oversight more difficult. (Note also that in the area of procurement the riskiest level of management is middle management, either in terms of inefficiency through a narrow insistence on the literal application of every extant rule, or in terms of corruption.)

To illustrate, information and communication technology is an especially sensitive area in terms of procurement risk, as it normally entails the bulk purchase of expensive equipment and requires a level of buyer expertise that is not normally found in government. There is little competition among the few suppliers and information technology is frequently supply- or donor-driven or both—irrespective of the real needs of the users in the company or the government. In this and similar sectors, it is essential to set up a mechanism to obtain independent technical advice, as well as to assure much greater participation by the final users of the equipment or the software from the very beginning of the process.

The time-phasing of delegating procurement functions is important. Government may delegate certain phases in the procurement cycle first, keeping close tabs on their functioning and maintaining strong central control on the other phases—progressively delegating more and more procurement phases as experience permits and performance warrants. Delegation may begin first in the less "risky" sectors or agencies and gradually be expanded to other sectors.

Quantifying Procurement Risk

The main four phases of procurement are the setting of standards and criteria, bid evaluation, contract negotiations, and contract monitoring. Risk differs in each phase. A simple scheme may help categorize the degree of risk, and hence help decide which procurement phase to delegate and in which sector. In the hypothetical illustration in Table 9.2, the risk of delegating a specific stage of procurement is measured on a scale of 1 to 10 (10 being highest risk) and the risk in sectors V through Z is assessed on the three risk determinants discussed earlier (specificity, market structure, and size of transactions). In this illustration, in sector V the entirety of procurement can be fully delegated; in sector Z no aspect of procurement should be delegated at all; and strong central control should be kept in the monitoring phase for sector W, in the standard-setting phase for sector X, and in both the bid evaluation and negotiations phases for sector Y. (The difficult analytical work consists of assigning realistic ratings of risk to the various phases of procurement and in the different sectors of the economy—but the scheme in Table 9.2 is useful to frame the results and facilitate decision making.)

Corruption in Procurement

Although the subject of public corruption is discussed in chapter 14, corruption in public procurement is best addressed in this chapter, as it is intimately related to the other issues and procedures in procurement. Lack of integrity in the procurement process is a major problem in all countries—developed and developing—and at all levels of government and administration. It can occur mainly when regulation is excessive, unclear, or not accessible to the public; the bid documents are poorly drafted or ambiguous; the specifications and standards are not

Table 9.2

Risk Matrix for Delegating Procurement Functions

Sector	Phase of procurement			
	Criteria & standards	Bidding & bid evaluation	Contract negotiations	Contract monitoring
V	1	1	2	2
W	3	3	3	9
X	9	2	2	2
Y	2	8	7	1
Z	8	8	8	9

Note: The sectors are hypothetical and the degree of risk is on a 1–10 scale, where 1 denotes lowest risk and 10 highest risk.

clear; contract monitoring is loose; or, of course, when the regulations are violated without any consequence or sanction. Accordingly, either the procurement personnel or the suppliers can corrupt the procurement process.

To extract private gains out of the bidding process, the public procurement staff can:

- tailor the specifications to benefit particular suppliers or contractors;
- restrict information about bidding opportunities only to some potential bidders;
- claim urgency as an excuse to award the contract on a sole-source basis;
- give "preferred" bidders confidential information on offers from other bidders;
- disqualify potential suppliers through improper prequalification or excessive bidding costs; and
- act directly in collusion with the bidders or outside influences to distort the entire process.

The private suppliers, too, can take a number of actions to distort the bidding process to their advantage, such as:

- collude to fix bid prices;
- collude to establish a "rotation" or other system by which bidders take turns in participating to bids, or in deliberately submitting unacceptable or technically unsuitable offers—thus favoring the supplier whose turn it is to "win" the contract. Even the most careful scrutiny of *individual* transactions will not reveal this tactic, because every rule will appear to have been strictly followed. It is therefore necessary from time to time to review all the procurement *results* for a given period and see if suspicious patterns emerge;
- promote discriminatory technical standards; or
- use their influence or bribes to push political leaders or senior public officials to interfere improperly in bid evaluation.

However, the most direct approach to bribery is to avoid competitive bidding altogether and manage to have the contract awarded to the desired party through direct contact and without any competition.

After the bids are submitted, other opportunities for misbehavior arise. Transparency is critical for the fairness of the bid evaluation. Where the rules do not require that all bidders be present when the bids are opened, it is easy for the procurement officer to reveal the lowest bid to the desired bidder and enable the latter to submit an even lower bid, which is then included in the bid evaluation process.

Serious corruption problems arise also after the award of contract and during the contract execution phase, through practices such as:

- failing to enforce quality standards, quantities, or other performance specifications of the contract (it is often "understood" in advance that enforcement will be superficial or nonexistent);
- agreeing to pay for shoddy construction or for the delivery of unacceptable goods and services, or acceding to fictitious claims of losses in transit or false deductions for material losses in construction;
- permitting "lowballing" (accepting artificially low bids, which are then jacked up by mutual consent);
- delaying payments to extort a bribe; or
- giving individual legislators influence over the award of contracts in their constituencies.

By far the easiest and most profitable form of corruption in public procurement or works is simply to not deliver the goods or build the works.[9] In countries with weak accountability systems, very low administrative capacity, or widespread systemic corruption, it is not difficult to falsify delivery documents or certificates of work completion. It is in this area that citizens' feedback can be a particularly powerful weapon against corruption. The peasant who still gets his feet wet crossing the stream is best placed to know that the government bridge was not completed—regardless of what the paperwork says.

Local Government Procurement and Intergovernmental Aspects

Local government procurement is becoming more important with increasing decentralization and the greater range of functions performed by local governments in most countries. However, legal restrictions on procurement apply much more at the local level because of conditions attaching to grants from the central government or because of national mandates in areas such as environmental protection.

Some developed countries have been enforcing compulsory competitive bidding at the local level for years, in the interest of service efficiency and quality. Model procurement codes for state and local governments developed in countries such as the United States envisage a procurement policy unit reporting to the city manager or the district or county commissioner. The unit has no operational responsibility for procurement, but provides research support, maintains a contractor database, and monitors complaints.

As noted earlier, there is substantial agreement on the advantages of combining centralized procurement policy with decentralized measurement operations. In developing countries, with their scarce skills at local levels and the greater scope for questionable discretionary expenditure, such delegation has to proceed carefully. The higher levels of government must be cognizant of the risk of corruption and waste in local government procurement and take steps to build local capacities, along with nonintrusive oversight mechanisms. Of course, in countries where the central government is especially corrupt, to decentralize procurement is likely to improve matters by itself, even without special safeguards or capacity-building technical assistance.

Once the authority is delegated, the higher government level should have the power to monitor and conduct audits, but should not intervene in the award or administration of any specific contract. To address the problem of limited capacities in local units, the state or provincial government could encourage joint procurement by a number of jurisdictions, as is done in France. Also, the provincial government could have the important functions of removing barriers to entry for small contractors in local jurisdictions, organizing training programs for contractors and construction firms, and providing support services. Some countries have set up public-sector consultant organizations staffed by experts to assist local governments in planning and managing large construction and irrigation works and in procuring supplies and services from domestic and foreign sources. Finally, the subnational units could take advantage of central rate contracts with reputable suppliers (as in India).

Although not subject to the same rules and constraints, a good deal of procurement takes place *between* levels of government. This partly takes care of the problems of auditing and overseeing contracts with private parties. In addition, contracting with another government agency may ensure a more stable level of assured services for smaller local units. It is important, however, to avoid making local government a captive consumer of higher government entities. Thus, the choice of whether to purchase from higher-level government or from private suppliers should be left to the local government concerned, except in specified instances.

THE PROCUREMENT PROCESS[10]

The forms of procurement practiced in different countries depend mainly on the nature of the goods and services, the size and complexity of the contract, the administrative level, and the market structure. International organization guidelines and bid documents recognize various forms of procurement (although special procurement procedures may also apply in certain cases). These are listed here in descending order of complexity of the required procedures:[11]

- competitive bidding (international or national);
- "shopping" (international or national);
- sole-source contracting (also known as direct selection or no-bid contracting);
- "force account"; or
- procurement through agents.

Normally, the different forms of procurement are applied to contracts of different value, with the simplest procurement modality used for low-value purchases and the pricey items requiring full international competitive bidding. For example, the World Bank requires international competitive bidding for purchases worth more than $200,000; permits national competitive bidding for purchases between $30,000 and $200,000; and allows shopping and direct selection for purchases of less than $30,000, consulting contracts of less than $50,000, or vehicles costing less than $100,000.

Competitive Bidding

Also known as open tendering, competitive bidding is by far the most common and preferred form of procurement and is discussed here at greater length than the other forms. Competitive bidding aims at providing all eligible bidders with timely and adequate notification of the requirements of the procuring agency and with an equal opportunity to bid for the required goods, services, or works. *International* competitive bidding is required for very large purchases. *National* competitive bidding is normally used when foreign bidders are unlikely to be interested, either because of the nature of the goods and services or when the purchase is not large enough. In turn, *limited competitive bidding* without public advertisement is indicated when the purchase is small or there are only a few qualified suppliers. In this method, bids are sought from a number of potential suppliers that is limited and yet broad enough to assure competitive pricing. Many local governments float such limited competitive bids on an annual basis for repetitive purchases (e.g., engineering items and construction materials) and place repeat orders with one or more contractors.

The complexity and specific modalities of the competitive bidding process depend on the country and on the value and nature of the goods or services being procured, but the main requirements of competitive bidding are similar in all cases: (1) a clear and fair description of what is to be purchased, (2) a publicized opportunity to bid, and (3) fair criteria for selection and decision making. In accordance with these three requirements, the five stages of competitive bidding are:

- pre-bid;
- public notice and invitation of bids;
- bid evaluation;
- contract award; and
- resolution of complaints.

Each of these stages is discussed at some length in Appendix 9.1.

Shopping

As noted, virtually all countries and international organizations have established a value threshold below which formal competitive bidding would not be cost effective, procurement is delegated to lower levels of authority, and small repetitive purchases may be permitted on the basis of limited price quotations. "Shopping" involves comparing price quotations obtained from at least three suppliers for readily available off-the-shelf goods of small value, such as standard office equipment and supplies, furniture, medicines, books and educational materials, and information and communication materials.[12] The contract may be awarded on the basis of an evaluation of at least three quotations obtained from a number of known suppliers, and the agreement is simple and often consists of a mere exchange of letters. Some countries permit the registration of authorized vendors and the placing of orders with these vendors by rotation during the year. Many countries have made provisions for contracts to be awarded, at a negotiated price, to labor and community associations, after ascertaining their competence and experience. All of these procedures present no problem provided that they are administered in efficient and honest fashion. (If not, for example, a registered-vendor list can become a tool for extorting money from vendors who wish to be placed on the list.)

Also mentioned earlier is the practice of avoiding procurement rules by splitting purchase requirements into several small packages below the value threshold that requires competitive bidding. However, the practice may also be forced on an agency by fluctuations in the availability of funds during the year (see chapter 6). Also, splitting up a large purchase may be the only way for an agency to get around the roadblock of a badly inefficient central purchasing office. When contract-splitting is forced on public managers by inefficient central procurement, insufficient budgetary transfers, or overly complex rules, the solution is not to prevent the practice but to reform the central procurement entity or streamline the procurement rules. Still, since small purchases can add up to a significant part of the budget, the overall scope for corruption and waste is substantial. The main safeguards are vigilant public managers and robust ex-post audits of such small purchases on a sample basis.

Sole-Source Procurement

Variously also known as "direct selection," "no-bid" contracting, or "single-tender" procurement, sole-source selection is cost-effective for small contracts and in the procurement of specialized consultant services, when a track record of technical expertise is essential and timing is important. It is also appropriate for the purchase of highly complex systems and equipment; in emergencies; or when the standardization of equipment or spare parts justifies additional purchases from the same supplier. Thus, combining all three elements, war provides the strongest rationale for sole-source procurement, as well as the best excuse for corrupt procurement and large-scale profiteering.

All countries limit sole-source procurement to specific types of purchases and circumstances, normally when:

- the value of the purchase is low (thresholds vary greatly between countries);
- there is only one qualified supplier of, and no close substitutes for, the good or service;
- it is required by international agreement or specifically by national law;
- it is justified by national security considerations; or
- there are emergencies or other unusual urgency.

Because several of these exceptions entail a judgment call, frequently "sole-source selection" is also "sole source of abuse." Fake "emergencies" are used to justify sweetheart contracts to a favored supplier; contracts are artificially split to stay below the no-bid threshold and then all the contract pieces are awarded to the same bidder; or the regulations are simply disregarded—trusting that the sheer mass of government transactions will hide the violation. Special care must be exercised in evaluating the bids in spot purchases of commodities like crude petroleum and armaments, as these typically involve very large sums and have been the subject of scandals (e.g., the Food for Oil program in pre-invasion Iraq).

Frequently, unwarranted sole sourcing does not start as deliberate abuse, but as the result of plain laziness on the part of the procurement staff. The easiest way for a procurement employee to avoid the "homework" and careful processes required for competitive bidding is to award repeat contracts to the same individuals or firms. Some excess cost is bound to be the result. Moreover, such laziness then tends to lead to corruption, when the relationship between government buyer and private seller loses its arm's length distance and becomes a cozy affair between "friends." (As discussed in the concluding section, in recent years no-bid contracts have mushroomed in the United States to a historical record, with predictable consequences in terms of increasing fraud, waste, and abuse.)

Force Accounts

A "force account" is the provision to government of goods, services or works by the government's own personnel and with its own equipment. (The practice should more properly be called "command procurement," as it consists of an administrative instruction to a government agency to deliver certain goods or perform certain functions for another government agency.) It is justified where the works are both small and scattered, the amount of work cannot be specified in advance, or in emergencies. In all other cases, procurement by force accounts has tended to be less economical owing to the lack of any competition for the services. Force accounts were the standard method of procurement in the former Soviet Union and other centrally planned economies, and their use has dropped drastically with the end of the USSR and the transition to a market-oriented economic system.

Other Forms of Procurement

Other forms of procurement include procurement by agents, requests for proposals (RFPs), indefinite-quantity contracts (IQCs), procurement from other government agencies, and procurement of consulting services. These are discussed in Appendix 9.2.

CONTRACT MANAGEMENT AND MONITORING[13]

Importance of Contract Management

Choosing the winning bid and awarding the contract is not the end of the procurement process. The goods and services still must be delivered as ordered and the works begun and completed as per the contractual agreement. As in budgeting, while it is possible to execute badly a good and clear contract, it is difficult to execute well a badly formulated contract. In the first place, therefore, the effectiveness of contract management is strongly influenced by decisions made prior to contract signature. Ambiguous, unrealistic, or conflicting agreements make it very difficult for the public manager to oversee their execution. Also, many contracts do not have clear performance standards, which would permit the contractor's work to be assessed and also protect the contractor from arbitrary interference. Procurement managers should be encouraged to draft contracts that, insofar as appropriate, emphasize results, make monitoring feasible, and are easily understandable to field officers and contractor representatives alike.

However, even when the contract is clear, realistic, and comprehensive to begin with, it is unlikely to be executed well without appropriate supervision. Contract administration and monitoring is a critical but often-neglected area in many developing countries and some developed countries—reflecting either weak supervision capacity and inattention by senior management, or both. Experience in all countries is rife with examples not only of long delays and excessive costs of implementation, but also of abuse, waste, and fraud in contract execution. Indeed, unscrupulous suppliers count on administrative disinterest in the nuts and bolts of contract execution to take shortcuts in quality or justify supplemental payments for "unforeseen" changes.

It is important to note that while government activities cover the entire country, the government's procurement for very large contracts is concentrated at the center. Consequently, the field administrative units responsible for supervising contract execution often have no idea of the basis for the award of the contract and are in a difficult position to supervise it effectively. Coordination between the central ministry and its field offices is therefore critical for effective contract administration and monitoring.

Nature of Contract Monitoring

Contract Monitoring

Monitoring should continue through the life of the contract. No amount of careful preparation of the contract or detailed specifications will ensure adequate performance if the actual performance is not monitored. Monitoring contract execution includes reviewing contractor reports, making inspections, commissioning audits, and obtaining citizen feedback. The relationship between the public official and the contractor should not be adversarial and antagonistic. Nevertheless, direct inspection and observation of the progress of the work remains the most important element. Financial audits, while necessary and usually required, come too late to remedy problems of execution—though they can provide evidence of wrongdoing, which can be used to sue the contractor or disqualify the contractor from future work. On the positive side, establishing good and professional relations with the contractor can do much to assure good contract execution.

Quality Assurance

Quality is a component of "economy," and quality assurance is a critical aspect of contract monitoring. It is influenced critically by the clear drafting of the technical and other specifications of the product, work, or service to be provided under the contract. The nature of the quality assurance task will depend on the nature of the output. Inspectors of construction work, for example, must demand compliance with building codes and similar legal mandates, in addition to compliance with the contract specifications. (Most countries have established quality control units in their public works ministries.)

Some developed countries have a policy of making the contractor responsible for verifying and certifying product quality prior to delivery. This policy requires a high degree of contractor responsibility, contract management skills, and swift dispute resolution. All three factors may be deficient, especially in developing countries. Accordingly, governments should be especially careful about excessive reliance on physical output performance indicators, as this could lead to undetected lower-quality output (see chapter 10 for a full discussion).

The four principal requirements for robust contract monitoring are:

- the central procurement office should disseminate guidelines for the inspection and testing of goods and services under different types of contracts, including information on testing facilities and other quality assurance (e.g., a requirement to obtain certificates of compliance or certified test results to accompany deliveries);
- there should be a formal system for reporting complaints against vendors by user agencies and the public, for taking action on deficiencies noted during inspection, and for dealing with product warranties and latent defects in goods;
- the payment schedule should be tied to satisfactory inspections, so that payments can be withheld when problems occur and until they are resolved satisfactorily;
- citizen associations should be systematically consulted, not only because of their involvement as stakeholders, but also because feedback from informed citizens is a highly reliable and cost-effective way of monitoring contracts and ensuring the integrity of public officials.

Procurement Practices of International Development Organizations

These practices are very important for aid-dependent developing countries. Consistent with the good practices in procurement discussed earlier, four considerations generally guide the requirements of aid organizations):

- economy and efficiency in the implementation of the aid-supported project;
- opportunity for all eligible bidders from developed and developing countries to compete to provide goods and works financed by the organization;
- promotion of domestic contracting and manufacturing industries in the aid-receiving country; and
- transparency in the procurement process.

Cognizant that in developing countries a faulty procurement process is often caused by weak administrative capacity, the international development organizations, and particularly the World Bank and Asian Development Bank, have assisted member countries to incorporate sound principles of procurement in new or amended regulations and to devise procurement procedures and tender documents that meet international requirements of international conventions. A similar objective has guided the efforts of the OECD and the European Union to assist the countries of central and eastern Europe in reforming their procurement regulations and practices. And, as noted, the United Nations has developed the UNCITRAL model procurement code. However, even when good new procurement laws and regulations are introduced, as with all formal legislation the real problem is enforcement. Because enforcement depends on various governance and capacity factors, the challenge of improving public procurement in developing countries is long term and the enactment of good formal rules is only the beginning.

THE SPECIAL ISSUES OF MILITARY PROCUREMENT[14]

Scope and Size of Military Purchases

Military procurement differs from civilian procurement, as it is affected by considerations of national security and is thus politically sensitive and conducted in a less transparent manner than other forms of procurement. Equally important is the bilateral monopoly structure of the market for military equipment and weapons in the United States and major European countries. On the supply side, the number of suppliers is limited to one or very few due to the high barriers to entry generated by the high research and development (R&D) investment and the enormous fixed costs and scale economies in the production of costly defense equipment. On the demand side, the government exercises monopsony ("sole buyer") control as single buyer of the equipment and spare parts produced by the defense industry.

As noted in chapter 1, after its reduction in the 1990s following the end of the Cold War, military expenditure has bounced back, amounting in 2005 to almost one trillion dollars worldwide ($150 per year per person), of which almost half, $480 billion, was spent by the United States. To comprehend the magnitude of military procurement, military expenditure must be considered together with the turnover of arms-producing companies. The top 100 arms-producing companies combined sell over US$200 billion a year, with the United States, France, and Russia as the major producers.

Moreover, official military expenditure figures understate the actual amounts. Military expenditure is rarely disaggregated and is often shown as a single line item in the budget. The additional income from arms exports and the earnings from the business activities of the military frequently are not shown on the revenue side. Off-budget items, such as expenditure on paramilitary or intelligence forces, food or housing subsidies to army personnel, military research and development, and subsidies for arms production and imports are often not shown in the budget at all. Secrecy in security matters leads to omitting expenditures made for major equipment purchases. However justified, all this makes it difficult for oversight agencies to exercise audit and vigilance and thus raises the inherent potential for waste and abuse.

Military spending goes for salaries and pensions for military personnel and civilian employees, various forms of civilian supplies and amenities (e.g., housing), and military equipment and supplies. In the United States, about three fifths of the amount spent on weapons systems and maintenance supplies is acquired under contract. Regional agreements, such as those of the European Union, seek to regionalize procurement by eliminating preferences for locally produced civilian goods, but exempt military equipment.

Constraints to Economical Military Procurement

It is usually very difficult for the public finance authorities in any country to regulate expenditure on defense procurement, because of overriding political perceptions of threats to national security, internal solidarity within the military, and the sensitivity and secrecy surrounding the purchase of major weapons systems. In developing countries, moreover, the superior bargaining advantage of foreign suppliers limits the ability of government to negotiate favorable deals.

A distinction should be drawn between sophisticated equipment with a specific defense use and commercial off-the-shelf defense supplies—including items for both civilian and defense use. The purchase of special military equipment cannot easily be subject to the normal procurement principles. However, for purchases of foodstuff, transport, and civilian supplies, there is no justification for the defense establishment not to apply the principles of good public procurement. But even here there are stories of grotesque overpricing—$5,000 coffeepots, $200 pliers, and similar absurdities (Gregory, 1989). Aside from possible fraud, such extreme overpricing usually arises from excessive specifications in military contracts even for everyday items and from grossly inadequate oversight by the responsible authorities. The argument is also made that the contractor must recover the entire overhead cost of production from the few items supplied to the army (as opposed to spreading the cost across millions of items in a production run for civilian sales). This is quite unconvincing in large countries, where the scale of the military purchases of ordinary supplies is more than ample to absorb production at lowest unit cost.

In the case of military equipment and supplies, many countries prefer to buy from home producers, even at additional cost. The label "military-industrial complex" sums up popular perceptions of the nexus between domestic industry and the defense establishment. Military hardware (aerospace equipment, telecommunications and electronics, explosives, shipbuilding equipment, etc.) accounts for the single largest share of total equipment expenditure. Contracts for defense equipment and R&D can give suppliers a competitive advantage in technological, commercial, and financial terms. Some form of arms production is undertaken by some forty-five countries, and many of them, including (in addition to the large producers) Israel, Korea, Brazil, South Africa, and Singapore, undertake military exports.

Reliance on arms and supplies produced a country's own government factories is alleged to reduce dependence on private suppliers and vulnerability to arms embargoes. Direct production of arms by the public sector *may* help avoid the overpricing, abuse, and long-term dependence associated with procurement from private domestic and foreign arms suppliers. However, such production usually covers small arms and ammunition rather than high-technology equipment. Also, when properly costed, it may in the end prove more expensive than outright purchases. For this reason, some countries in Europe and Asia have sought to achieve a compromise between dependence on imports and self-sufficiency in defense, by setting up production units licensed by foreign companies.

Costs, Risks, and Special Procedures

The risks and costs of military procurement are markedly different between countries with and countries without an advanced defense industry.

Developed Countries

Typically, the process of military procurement is complex, normally including a protracted approval itinerary through various levels, from contracting officers to their superiors, then the treasury, and finally a ministerial committee. The process is further complicated by unnecessarily detailed requirements and specifications, compelling the industry to prepare costly and voluminous proposals, which then have to be analyzed in great detail by a large team of evaluators. Not surprisingly, all this red tape is then used by suppliers to justify their overpricing. Much of the military waste and delay that has been publicized in the United States has been attributed to overregulation and overspecification; excessive paperwork and compliance requirements; too many layers of authority and supervision within the executive; and micromanagement by the Defense Department and the Congress (Gregory, 1989). Paradoxically, while these requirements were partly introduced to combat corruption, they have not even succeeded in doing so (see Anechiarico and Jacobs [1996] on the need to avoid the "pursuit of absolute integrity.").

This experience should be contrasted with that of Canada, which devised a "Smart Procurement Initiative" in consultation with the defense industry to improve the procurement process. This included innovative measures such as incremental acquisition, greater flexibility and delegation for small-value and off-the-shelf items, streamlined decision making, and partnerships with business.

Developing Countries

The situation is very different for most developing countries, which have no defense industry and depend entirely on imports, where the balance of bargaining power is with the suppliers. In countries with inadequate purchase evaluation capacity, the potential for bribery is aggravated by the danger of purchasing inefficient equipment such as weapons that do not fire or planes that do not fly. At the same time, building a domestic defense production capability is neither possible nor desirable. Apart from problems of patents and secrecy, the research and development costs of defense equipment and supplies are unaffordable in developing countries. And when they can be afforded, as in large countries such as Brazil and India, the large investment required would add far more to the country's well-being and long-term security if it were spent on improving basic health care and education and lifting millions of citizens out of poverty. (The extreme case is North Korea, where vast expenditures are made on weapons production, in the midst of deprivation of virtually the entire population and starvation of a large segment of it.) Moreover, as argued in chapter 1, a country's national security is not necessarily guaranteed by higher military spending and in some cases may be enhanced by not having an army in the first place—as the example of Costa Rica demonstrates.

Unlike in arms-producing developed countries, the administrative challenge is not to make life easier for the contractors by reducing overregulation and complexity, but to move toward transparent and consistent practices for military procurement, adequate legislative and audit oversight, and the reduction of individual discretion by institutionalizing decisions relating to the acquisition of costly equipment from foreign suppliers.

Where military aid loans are tied to purchases from the lending country, the recipient country has little control over the cost and quality of the equipment and spares, and merely watches as its foreign debt rises along with its "defense" spending. When locked into the use of particular equipment and transport, the country also becomes vulnerable to a cutoff in supply of spare parts and replacements. Military procurement thus becomes the handmaiden of the vagaries of foreign policy. Conversely, developed countries seeking to buy locally the supplies needed in connection with their military assistance are often confronted with collusion and corruption (as in Korea in the 1960s—see Klitgaard, 1998).

The military procurement process is permeated by the interplay of international and domestic companies, liaison agents, arms bazaars, bribes and contributions to political parties, and is punctuated by the outbreak of scandals and media exposés. The best single cover for corruption in international defense procurement is the commission paid to a local agent by the foreign arms supplier. The agent is given sufficient funds to land the contract by any means necessary and without the company having to know the details, thus creating a comfortable distance between the supplier and the bribery, and enabling all the parties in the recipient government and the company to disclaim any association with the unsavory details of the deal, should these be exposed.

Are Improvements in Military Procurement Possible?

It is certainly possible, at least in principle, to apply sound procurement principles to military purchases while fully protecting confidentiality and secrecy for national security reasons. For example, while protecting the confidentiality of transactions, Singapore has declared and implemented a transparent policy for defense procurement based on open bidding. The principle is to go for the best source that meets Singapore's military requirements, plugs up the openings for corruption, and gives best value for money—mainly by dealing directly with overseas and domestic suppliers and avoiding intermediary agents in contract negotiations. Other countries (e.g., Canada) have established specialized divisions for military procurement, based on similar principles. At a minimum, even military procurement must be subject to oversight by the supreme audit institution, as in the United States with the publication of General Accountability Office audit reports for the benefit of the legislature and the public.

However, these practices are unlikely to be adopted in most developing countries, where accountability and public management are not strong, as well as in large developed countries where the domestic arms industry holds great sway over the defense department. If, as Samuel Johnson said in 1775, "patriotism is the last refuge of scoundrels," national security is a natural cover for crooked deals. Moreover, in countries and situations where the survival of civilian government depends on the support or goodwill of the military, touching military procurement is akin to touching the electrified third rail of the subway.

THE SITUATION IN THE UNITED STATES

Purchasing and contracting by the U.S. federal government dates back to the earliest days of the Republic and, as in Britain and many other countries, began as a way to assure reliable supplies for the armed forces. As observed in 1781 by Robert Morris, then-superintendent of finance and major financier of the American Revolution: *"In all countries engaged in war, experience has sooner or later pointed out that contracts with private men of substance and understanding are necessary for the subsistence, covering, clothing, and manning of an army."*

In general, beyond military procurement, the federal government acquires most of its goods, services and works from private entities. Federal agencies bought more than $235 billion in goods and services during fiscal year 2001, reflecting an 11 percent increase over the amount spent five years earlier (GAO-03–443).[15] Additional growth since then has resulted from increased spending on defense and homeland security. The Defense Department is the largest agency in terms of contracting dollars spent, accounting for about two thirds of the government's total spending on goods and services—more than twice the amount spent by the next nine largest federal agencies combined. (The Air Force, Army, and Navy each spend more than the largest civilian agency, the Department of Energy.)

In 2006, the total value of federal government contracts was about $416 billion. Apparently, the money was spread around 176,172 companies, for an average yearly contracts value of $2.4 million. Of this, however, about $100 billion went to six companies—the big five defense contractors plus Halliburton's KBR—for an average total yearly contract value of $15 billion each. The remaining $315 billion went to the other 176,166 companies, for an average yearly total contracts value of $1.8 million. (Oh, and of the $100 billion going to the Big Six, more than half was contracted without full competitive bidding.)

Policies, Regulations, and Organization

Federal Procurement Policy

In the United States, the main procurement-related laws are the Office of Federal Procurement Policy Act of 1974, the Competition for Contracting Act of 1984, and the Federal Acquisition Streamlining Act of 1994. The 1974 act (related to the budget reform act of the same year—see chapter 6) created the Office of Federal Procurement Policy (OFPP) and placed it in the Office of Management and Budget (OMB). The OFPP was created mainly to formulate government-wide procurement policies to be followed by executive agencies in all procurement activities and to establish a standard for procurement systems.

The 1974 act also includes the training of professional procurement staff. Subsequently, in 1990 an interagency group developed a plan for procurement professionalism.[16] Partly on this basis, OMB promulgated in 1992 a policy for government-wide training in contracting and purchasing, and in 1997 established career management, education, and training requirements for acquisition personnel in civilian executive agencies.[17]

The Federal Acquisition Regulations System (FAR)

The Federal Acquisition Regulations System is established for the codification and publication of uniform policies and procedures for acquisition by all executive agencies. The system consists of the Federal Acquisition Regulation (FAR), which is the primary document, and agency-specific regulations that implement or supplement the FAR. The FAR is issued jointly by the General Service Administration (GSA), and the Department of Defense (DOD) and National Aeronautics and Space Administration (NASA) under their separate statutory authorities. The development of the system is in accordance with the requirements of the Office of Federal Procurement Policy Act of 1974. Its bedrock principle is that government business shall be conducted in a manner above reproach and, except as expressly authorized by statute or regulation, with complete impartiality and no preferential treatment.

Organizational Arrangements

As noted earlier, a central question in procurement is whether responsibility should rest with the agency that requires the goods and services or with a central purchasing agency. In most countries, standards and rules are set by a central agency, but actual purchasing is done by the individual agencies in conformity with these standards and rules. This is the case in the United States as well, albeit with certain differences.

In addition to the standard-setting responsibility of the OMB Office of Federal Procurement Policy, the General Services Administration is the central office for administering the procurement regulations. (The Department of Defense and NASA have their own procurement approaches, to fit their special missions.)[18] The general mandate of GSA is to "help federal agencies better serve the public by offering, at best value, superior workplaces, expert solutions, acquisition services and management policies." GSA includes the Federal Technology Service (FTS), the Federal Supply Service (FSS), the Public Buildings Service, and various staff offices, including the Office of Governmentwide Policy. Eleven regional offices extend GSA's outreach to federal customers nationwide.[19] An anticipated GSA reorganization will consolidate the FTS and FSS into a single new organization, the Federal Acquisition Service (FAS), which will include six zones within GSA's eleven geographic regions.

Conforming to good international practice, actual procurement is done by each federal department and agency on its own account. For this, many U.S. agencies have been relying increasingly on outside intermediaries to do their purchasing and contracting, a practice with advantages and risks discussed in chapter 11. The past decade has seen the emergence of several changes in the way in which the government buys goods and services, as Congress and the administration have sought to simplify the acquisition process and contract negotiation, to shorten procurement delays, reduce administrative costs, and improve results.

Recent Changes

The Services Acquisition Reform Act of 2003 covered the definition of acquisition requirements, the measurement of contract performance, and technical and management direction.

In April 2005, the federal government established a government-wide framework for creating a federal acquisition workforce with the skills necessary to deliver best value supplies and services, find the best business solutions, and provide strategic business advice to accomplish agency procurement/acquisition missions.[20] This is intended to recognize the need for a professional workforce through the passage of the Defense Acquisition Workforce Improvement Act, and the Clinger-Cohen Act, which amended a section of the 1974 OFPP Act. These acts established education, training, and experience requirements for entry and advancement in the acquisition career. Policy Letter 05–01 defines the implementation of the new legislation, building on the previous efforts of 1992 and 1997 to improve the skills of procurement personnel.

Procurement in State and Local Government

The Model Procurement Code for Subnational Government

Although the underlying principles and basic procedures of procurement are the same as in the Federal Acquisition Regulations system, each state and locality has its own particular features in public procurement. These cannot be summarized here. However, as noted earlier, a model procurement code for state and local governments has been developed. The code envisages a procurement policy unit reporting to the city manager or the district or county commissioner, as the case may be. The unit would have no purchasing responsibility, but would provide research support, maintain a contractor database, and monitor complaints. This could be a suitable system for smaller cities and towns, with limited staff and skills.[21]

The Case of New York City[22]

The dynamics of change in public procurement in large American cities have followed a similar pattern, which is well illustrated by developments in New York City. Beginning in the late 1800s, with the attack on the political spoils system and patronage jobs, through the "progressive era" of the 1930s, efforts have focused on how to improve the efficiency of city government. In more recent years, a basic mistrust of direct government provision of public services was generated in part by the city's failure to have streets cleared in a timely manner after a major 1969 snowstorm, followed by the fiscal crisis in the 1970s and the explosion of street crime in the 1980s and early 1990s.

However, the obstacle to improving government services was voter opposition to raising taxes—as in many other large cities. To square that circle, New York City officials began to contract out the delivery of work or services previously provided directly by city government, while maintaining city responsibility. Subsequently, three major scandals put the public spotlight on the city's contracting system: Mayor Koch's Talent Bank that mutated from a job referral service for women and minorities to a patronage mill; the push by Bronx Democratic party boss Stanley Friedman of a multimillion dollar contract for the issue of parking tickets to a company largely owned by him; and the case of a Bronx congressman using his political influence to obtain federal contracts for the WedTech company that benefited his friends. As a defensive reaction to the negative publicity generated by the scandals, the city began to saddle the contracting and acquisition process with an ever-increasing plethora of rules, procedures, and reviews by different oversight bodies.

In 1987, Governor Mario Cuomo created the New York State Commission on Government Integrity, known as the Feerick Commission, to investigate New York City's procurement practices and make recommendations. The Commission's blunt report (*A Ship Without a Captain: The Contracting Process in New York*), concluded that: " . . . the city's labyrinthine contracting system wastes millions of dollars, . . . is mired in red tape, scares away vendors, and remains vulnerable to corruption,"[23] and made five major recommendations:

- the city should try to expand the contractor base rather than just identify bad contractors;
- a temporary deputy mayor should be appointed, with the sole responsibility of overseeing and reforming city contracting procedures;
- each city agency should appoint a chief contracting officer with a professional procurement background;
- contracting personnel must be trained with the skills and tools necessary; and
- selective ex-post audits of contracts should be carried out to make sure that procurement rules were followed.

The simplicity and basic nature of these recommendations underlines how dysfunctional city procurement had become. Although the city did not act until after heavy pressure, when it finally acted it did so vigorously, taking a fresh look at the entirety of its procurement practices and drawing on the expertise of the private sector and of organizations such as the National Institute of Government Purchasing and the National Association of State Procurement Officers. As a result, the New York City charter was completely revised in 1989. Major changes—all constructive—included:

- bringing procurement as an executive function under the mayor;
- removing from the Board of Estimate its authority to approve contracts;
- restricting the award of contract without competitive bidding to contracts urgently required by a threat to life, safety, or property;
- establishing the Procurement Policy Board, including members from the private sector, to set citywide rules that promote competition, fix accountability with each agency, provide

each agency with the authority to make timely and efficient procurements, and define ethical guidelines; and

- establishing a vendor database (the Vendor Information Exchange System—VENDEX), which contains relevant information on contractors' qualifications and background (i.e., debarments, indictments, convictions, or other violations).

Since then, other changes have been introduced, including the creation of the post of chief procurement officer and of the Procurement Training Institute (PTI). Also, from 2001, to combat corruption, all procurement staff are required to divulge their personal finances and the Department of Investigation (DOI) was given broad powers to investigate city employees' finances and contractors eligible for a city contract. Also, in keeping with the old Feerick Commission recommendations, the New York City comptroller has been given authority to review all contracts on a post-audit basis. Unfortunately, the comptroller has overinterpreted this role to include preauditing of contracts and investigations of a contractor's background, and to reject a contract based on suspicion of possible fraud or corruption. While such investigations are a necessary precaution and are facilitated by the existence of the VENDEX system, accountability is diluted unless the procurement staff under the procurement rules exercises responsibility for all phases of procurement up to contract award.

Currently, over $7 billion worth of goods, services, and construction are contracted out annually in New York City using the Procurement Policy Board rules (less than 200 pages, compared to the thousands of pages of federal regulations). Although public procurement problems have certainly not disappeared from New York City, the state of public procurement is a far cry from its disrepair of twenty years ago. (It is now time to address the inefficiencies and delays in the services still provided directly by city government—particularly, but not exclusively, in the morass of housing and construction regulations.)

Some Major Current Issues

First Plan, Then Buy

It is important to realize that procurement is part of the overall process of managing government expenditure and, as such, the procurement function cannot be exercised efficiently without good advance planning. You cannot decide what to buy, and when, unless you have previously decided what you want to accomplish, and how. Box 9.6 provides an illustration of what happens to the efficiency of procurement when prior planning is deficient or nonexistent.

The Risk of Cozy Relationships

In virtually every country, after leaving government service government officials are prohibited from working for a corporation that they oversaw or did business with while in government, at least for a significant period of time. Among the most indefensible peculiarities of the American administrative system is the extraordinarily permissive attitude toward the revolving door from public service to private employment and back again. In the United States, a public official responsible for purchasing and contracting with a private entity, or overseeing regulations affecting it, can go to work for *the same* private entity immediately after leaving government employment—albeit with minor restrictions that do nothing to alleviate the incestuous nature of the relationship.

BOX 9.6

Good Procurement Requires Good Planning

According to the General Accountability Office, a "gross error" was committed in late 2004 by the Air Force in its $45 million award of contracts to Operational Support Services (OSS), a private translation company, on a sole-source (no-bid) basis. The contracts were for identifying and paying bilingual English-Arabic speakers to act as translators in the preparation of Iraq's constitution and the holding of elections.

There are reports that political pressure was exerted by the Defense Department to use the contracts to pay "friendly" Iraqi exiles. Be that as it may, competing firms that had not been allowed to bid for the contracts protested the sole-source award to OSS. The Air Force argued that the no-bid procedure was required by the urgency of the situation, with only a short time remaining before the Iraqi elections in January 2005. The GAO didn't buy it. Not only did the Air Force issue a second sole-source contract several months after the elections, but the first contract could easily have been put up to competitive bid if the Air Force had done its planning in time. With the invasion of Iraq occurring more than 18 months earlier, the need for Arabic translators should have been obvious long before.

Aside from partisan political pressure and favoritism, the lesson from this episode is that good procurement requires good advance planning—which specifies in useful time the nature of the services, their quality, the qualifications required of the service provider, and all other matters needed to proceed to normal competitive bidding. If the government entity is able to do its planning in good time but does not, it cannot then use the "urgency" of the situation as an excuse to short-circuit the procedures that protect against abuse and misuse of the taxpayers' money.

Source: General Accountability Office, Report B-296984, November 14, 2005.

Such looseness is extreme even by the standards of Japan, where the symbiosis of government and business is legendary (the so-called "Japan, Inc."). The pervasive practice of *amakudari* ("descent from heaven") allows former high-ranking civil servants to systematically cash in upon retirement by going to work for private corporations, but *not* in the same industry which they used to regulate. In America, the easy revolving door game has been played under Democratic as well as Republican administrations, and both by legislators (Box 9.7) and members of the executive branch (Box 9.8). The fact that practices such as those described in Box 9.7 are technically legal only demonstrates the extraordinary weakness of the federal conflict-of-interest laws.

For years, the needed reforms have been as obvious as their chances of approval were nonexistent. After leaving government employment, all elected members of the legislature and staff of the legislative and the executive branch should be prohibited for a minimum of two years from private employment in the area of their direct responsibility and should *never* be permitted to work for private entities on which they had direct oversight or allocative authority. A timid but still meaningful first step was implemented in 2007 prohibiting former members of Congress from lobbying activity for at least two years after leaving office. This will prevent future occurrences of extreme cases such as the one described in Box 9.7.

Flexibility Without Accountability: The Root of Procurement Waste and Fraud

The Druyun-Boeing case summarized in Box 9.8 is merely a fairly extreme illustration of a deep-seated problem: the assignment of greater managerial discretion and autonomy without the more robust supervision and oversight that such autonomy demands. (This is the obverse of the problem of administrative paralysis through the pursuit of absolute integrity signaled by Anechiarico and Jacobs [1996].) It is possible to achieve greater efficiency through more autonomy, but only if accountability is strengthened along with it. When public spending is stable or grows at a slow and steady rate, greater flexibility is less risky, as abuses are more visible and thus less frequent. When spending increases rapidly, it becomes more and more difficult for supervision to keep pace and, unless special protective measures are taken, procurement waste and fraud have a tendency to grow. Moreover, when this tendency is compounded by a "national security" rationale and various other emergencies—real or manufactured—the proportion of public funds that are stolen, misallocated, or wasted is bound to rise rapidly.[24]

Between 2000 and 2005, annual discretionary federal spending increased by $354 billion. Nearly half of this increase—$174 billion—was spent on private contractors. As a result of the rapid increase in contracting, the size of the shadow government represented by federal contractors is now at record levels. In 2005, nearly 40 percent of every discretionary federal dollar was paid to private contractors, compared to 33 percent in 2000. Contract mismanagement has kept pace with the surge in spending. Federal procurement without full and open competition has increased from about $70 billion in 2000 to $207 billion in 2007, partly as a result of practices such as the assignment of contracts by federal officials to their former colleagues in the private sector.[25] The primary areas of mismanagement have been:

- award of noncompetitive contracts;
- reliance on types of contracts known to be prone to abuse;
- abuse of contracting flexibility;
- poor procurement planning;
- inadequate contract oversight;
- unjustified fees; and
- straight bribery.

The increase in contract disbursement to $745 billion to 118 private contractors has resulted in increased waste and cost to the taxpayers. The worst instances have occurred in contracting for "homeland security," the war in Iraq, and Hurricane Katrina recovery. Thankfully, the new procurement flexibility has resulted in easing procurement for such vital national security priorities as a petting zoo in the Midwest.

In the Department of Homeland Security (DHS) alone, a weak control environment has enabled wasting over $19 billion on ill-conceived purchases and misuse of credit cards.[26] The GAO and the Department of Homeland Security's own Office of Inspector General estimated that almost

BOX 9.7

Hiring the Overseer

Congressman Billy Tauzin (R-Louisiana) was until 2005 the chairman of the House committee that oversees the pharmaceutical industry. In that capacity, he had substantial authority to push for new regulations or for waivers of existing regulations, as well as the lead in initiating and clearing new legislation affecting the industry:

• In 2003, he sponsored the prescription drug legislation that, among other things, prohibited the government from negotiating with drug companies to keep down the price of the drugs the taxpayer would ultimately have to subsidize, and kept the ban on importing from Canada the identical drugs at a much lower price.

• In 2004, he resigned his chairmanship and did not run for re-election.

• In January 2005, right after the expiration of his term in Congress, Tauzin started working for the pharmaceutical industry lobby for a reported $2 million a year plus perks. Incredibly, he had been having private discussions about this new job for the drug industry while he was still in Congress chairing the committee with oversight authority over the selfsame industry. (Even more incredibly, none of this was technically illegal.)

Mrs. Letitia White was a senior staff member of the House Appropriations Committee, which is responsible for funding all federal programs. Unlike congressmen, congressional staffers must wait twelve months before lobbying the committee on which they served. This prohibition, itself extraordinarily mild, is made laughable by its application only to staff with a salary above a certain amount—currently about $120,000 a year. A year before resigning from the staff of her House committee in January 2003, Mrs. White took a pay cut that brought her $80 (eighty dollars) under the annual salary cap. *One day* after resigning she joined a lobbying firm (reported by Paul Kane in *Roll Call,* July 27, 2006; www.rollcall.com). With enough imagination, the more perceptive readers might perhaps be able to connect the following dots:

• at the House Appropriations Committee, she oversaw the award of "earmarks" (see Box 6.6), of which $22 million worth went to sixteen defense companies;

• the lobbying firm she joined is partly owned by a former congressman, a very close friend of Congressman Jerry Lewis, the chairman of the committee;

• in her first year at the lobbying firm, Mrs. White was paid $670,000;

• she did so by attracting to the firm sixteen new clients;

• the new clients were the same defense contractors who had received the "earmarks"; and, of course,

• she was and is free to lobby the committee she used to work for, on behalf of the firm owned by the friend of the committee chairman. (All this, too, perfectly legal . . .)

BOX 9.8

Buying the Buyer: Boeing and Air Force Procurement

As the number 2 procurement executive for the Air Force, Darleen Druyun was in charge of negotiating a bizarre deal by which the Air Force would spend billions to lease from Boeing tanker planes that the department's own experts said were not needed—at a cost higher, when properly calculated, than the cost of buying the planes outright. Not only did she agree to a $100 million lease price per aircraft, much higher than appropriate, but also gave Boeing confidential information about a competitor.

This was no isolated billion-dollar peccadillo, however. Among Mrs. Druyun's many other "favors" to Boeing, in chronological order:

• in 2000, she agreed to pay $412 million to Boeing as settlement over a clause in an aircraft contract...
• then Boeing hired her son-in-law;
• in 2001, she was the lead procurement official in awarding Boeing, over four competing firms, a $4 billion contract to modernize the C-130 plane...
• then Boeing hired her daughter;
• in 2002 she awarded $100 million to Boeing as part of the "restructuring" of a NATO AWACS contract...
• then came the tanker plane deal, and, right after Druyun retired from the Air Force...
• Boeing hired *her.*

Under the authority provided by the Competition in Contracting Act of 1984, the General Accountability Office received protests alleging Druyun's exercise of improper influence on contracts awarded to Boeing by the Air Force. The GAO sustained the protests and recommended, among other things, that the C-130 contract be resubmitted to competition. The tanker deal was stopped altogether. Darleen Druyun was sentenced to less than a year in jail and fined a mere $5,000. No manager or employee of Boeing was prosecuted (although the CEO was eased out, with all his perks and golden parachute intact).

Aside from all other considerations, what is really curious in this affair is how cheap it is in America to buy your government buyer. For the price of three jobs, adding up to perhaps a measly half million dollars a year, Boeing got preferential treatment in the award of contracts worth several billion dollars—a "return on investment" of over 10,000 to one.

Source: GAO, *Air Force Procurement: Protests Challenging Role of Biased Official Sustained,* Report GAO-05–436T, April 14, 2005, and various news accounts.

half of DHS purchase-card transactions were not properly authorized; more than half did not give priority to designated sources, and for an astonishing two thirds there is no evidence that the goods or services were ever received. The review also found frequent failures to dispute incorrect transactions; improper use of the purchase card (e.g., $460,000 for prepackaged meals); abusive transactions (e.g., purchase of a beer-brewing kit and a 63-inch plasma TV costing $8,000 and found unused in its box six months after purchase); and tens of thousands of dollars for golf and tennis lessons at resorts.[27]

But the main driver of waste, fraud, and abuse has been the award of contracts without full competition. While it is understandable that no-bid contracts may be needed in the early days of a new agency, the value of noncompetitive contracts at DHS *increased* from under $800 million (25 percent of total contracts) in 2003, when DHS was created, to $5.5 billion in 2005, seven times the initial amount and more than half of the total value of DHS contracts. The charitable explanation of this phenomenon would be a remarkable lack of procurement planning and of elementary oversight and monitoring responsibility.

Although there are no precise estimates of waste and fraud in war contracting and for Iraq reconstruction, the amount is certainly much higher than that of no-bid contracts for homeland security. It must be reiterated that the issue here is not the wisdom of the activities or the underlying policy decisions, but the risks and costs associated with authorizing "special" flexible procurement procedures to deal with emergencies. If the emergency could have been anticipated, proper planning would have avoided the need for special procurement procedures. And, if the emergency is genuine and of a nature sufficient to justify deviations from established practices, it then also demands much tighter supervision and scrutiny by top managers and the political leadership in order to minimize the stupendous waste and grand theft of taxpayers' money that has occurred in the last five years.

GENERAL DIRECTIONS OF IMPROVEMENT

Improving the procurement system to meet standards of economy, competition, accountability, and integrity generally requires moving to:

- simplified legal and regulatory framework and transparent process of procurement;
- clear organizational arrangements, combining centralized procurement policy/oversight/appeal with decentralized operations;
- improved public access to information and documentation;
- measures to ensure that only civil servants of competence and integrity are in charge of government procurement and to provide for commensurate rewards, as well as frequent rotation of staff;
- effective mechanisms to curb fraud, abuse, and corruption; and
- more attention to contract execution and monitoring.

In many countries, efforts to close openings for corruption or to achieve social goals through procurement have led to increasingly detailed regulations and centralized control. This is especially important for the acquisition of technology, but poses a problem for purchasing items that change rapidly and have a short product cycle. Also, because low-value items make up the bulk of procurement transactions, especially in local government and field offices, applying to small transactions the complicated regulations intended to prevent large misappropriation generates transaction costs far greater than the savings that can be achieved. A major improvement would therefore be to raise the generally low value thresholds above which the complex bidding rules apply and index the thresholds to inflation. The main direction of improvement is to achieve a better balance between controls and managerial flexibility.

In some countries, including the United States, conflict-of-interest rules are much too weak and loosely enforced. In particular, the "revolving door" between public service in procurement and employment by the private suppliers is the major enabling mechanism of inefficiency and corruption. The general direction of improvement in most countries is thus to clearer and more robust rules, together with swift and predictable enforcement. In general, every government could benefit from a quick review of good practices followed by other countries to close the major avenues of conflict of interest and potential corruption. In particular, in the United States, legislators should be precluded for life from employment in the industries over which they had oversight responsibility when in Congress, prohibited from lobbying for at least two years, and deprived of their privilege of access to the floor of the House and Senate; former congressional staffs ought to be prohibited from lobbying their former committee for a minimum period of two years; and, similarly, civil servants and military officers ought to be legally precluded from employment in companies vis-à-vis which they had purchasing or oversight or service responsibilities. These measures, apparently so radical in the U.S. context, are standard in almost every well-run country in the world.

In developing countries, the uneven documentation and bidding procedures of the different government entities are a major part of the procurement problems. Major improvements in both economy and integrity would result from extending to all government procurement the standard bidding documents required by international development organizations for projects they finance, which would reduce opportunities for arbitrary decisions, collusion, and extortion.

Other improvements in procurement in developing countries could be realized by addressing the slowness of the dispute resolution mechanisms, which is due partly to weaknesses in the judicial system and partly to the complexity of appeal procedures. The process of recovering money from government suppliers in case of bad performance or default is cumbersome and often fruitless because of antiquated foreclosure laws and the manipulation of bankruptcy laws by defaulters. Contractors, too, face protracted legal battles in recovering disputed sums from government. With the government and the contractors thus forced to take steps to protect themselves from these eventualities, transaction costs increase on both sides, making the purchase of goods and services and contracting much more costly in government than in the private sector. Introducing formal but nonjudicial dispute resolution would help, as well as setting up a fast-track procedure for appealing administrative court decisions on procurement disputes.

Finally, although the process of procuring works, goods, and services is critical for the economical and effective use of public funds, procurement issues do not receive much attention from senior public managers and political leaders. Senior managers are not interested in the mechanics of procurement and are also concerned with keeping their distance (and deniability) from potential waste or corruption scandals. Yet, they must be made to realize the great importance of procurement for efficient, effective, and honest government, and place it at the center of their responsibility rather than shunting it off to lower-level staff. This suggests factoring their involvement in procurement into the appraisal of their work performance. In turn, political leaders must give senior public managers full support in the exercise of this delicate responsibility.

QUESTIONS FOR DISCUSSION

1. What are the main differences between contracting to buy goods and services and contracting for works?

2. "There is no good reason why government procurement should work any differently than procurement in the private sector. In both cases the procurement system is supposed to obtain the goods or the contracts at least cost, at a given quality, and at the right time." Agree?

3. Pick one of the two following statements and make a credible argument for it:
   a. "Government procurement is best carried out by one central office to assure uniformity of criteria and respect for the rules."
   b. "Government procurement is best carried out by each separate agency to assure speedy purchasing and a good fit with the agency's own needs."

4. Is giving preference to national firms in government procurement mainly a form of protectionism? Is it less or more justifiable in developing countries?

5. How would you achieve a proper balance between speed and efficiency in government procurement, on the one hand, and protecting competition and precluding corruption, on the other?

6. The U.S. Pentagon, the largest office building in the world, was built in under two years. The construction of most ordinary government buildings today takes several years from initial decision to occupancy. Why?

7. Give a concrete illustration of the various ways in which formal procurement processes can be circumvented to produce undue private advantage.

8. Discuss the various reasons, with reference to a concrete example, why sole-source (no-bid) procurement is usually a recipe for waste and corruption.

9. "Whether for goods, services, or works, good procurement must always assure the lowest price at the time designated for delivery." Discuss.

10. "The defense and national security implications of procurement for the armed forces make it dangerous and impractical to apply to military procurement the same procedures as standard civilian procurement." Comment.

11. Pick one of the two following statements and make a credible argument for it:
    a. "The federal procurement system in the United States is an awful mess, which calls for a thorough overhaul."
    b. "The federal procurement system in the United States is in excellent shape and only needs a few minor adjustments."

APPENDIX 9.1. THE STAGES OF COMPETITIVE BIDDING

As noted in the text, competitive bidding involves, in sequence, five stages: pre-bid; public notice and invitation of bids; bid opening and evaluation; contract award; and resolution of complaints. These are discussed in turn.

The Pre-Bid Stage

The pre-bid stage includes the preparation and distribution of standardized bid documents; rules for the registration of contractors and suppliers; rules for prequalification; and procedures to eventually decide on winning bids.

The documents must contain specifications, instructions, and definition of contracting terms. Contractors and suppliers need clear and substantive specifications in order to respond competitively to the requirements of the purchaser. Often, the bidding process is marred by deliberately unclear specifications for the purpose of leaving room for "discretion." Conversely, the specifications and required qualifications are sometimes made so detailed as to apply to only one or two potential bidders. This is almost invariably done to circumvent the requirements of competitive bidding and award the contract on a sole-source basis, for good or bad reasons.

Enough time must be allowed for potential suppliers to bid; for the contracting agency to evaluate the bids and make the award decision; for the final contract to be negotiated; and for the goods and services to be received or the works to begin. The purchasing agency thus needs to begin the process early enough to ensure that the goods and services will be ready when needed and avoid short-circuiting the process or making rush decisions. (Both unnecessary delays and rush decisions, whatever their cause, are unlikely to lead to high-quality procurement. Recall that timeliness of purchase is one dimension of the basic procurement criterion of "economy.")

Dividing the service area into a number of smaller regions, or dividing the contract into a number of similar packages of equipment and works and then encouraging competitive bidding for each area or package, can facilitate the participation of small contractors. This advantage should be weighed against the higher transactions cost of handling a number of smaller contracts (which is the major reason for the typical bias of central governments in favor of large tenders).

Public Notice and Invitation to Bid

A prerequisite of competitive bidding is the easy and timely availability of bidding documents, in comprehensible language, to all interested bidders. An increasing number of governments and international organizations make the information and documents available in electronic form, through the internet or other convenient outlets, or through associations of contractors.[28] The bidding documents should be both in the local language and in an international language (normally English).[29]

Notification of bidding opportunities should be published in local and national newspapers, official gazettes, or electronic bulletins, depending on the nature of the purchase. Information should also be available at the purchasing agency website and offices. Bid notices should be publicized in the local language, in cases where small contractors and community organizations are likely to be interested in bidding. International bidding opportunities should be published in widely circulated trade journals and newspapers, through the internet and normally in English.

Two-stage bidding may be used for complex works, "turnkey" contracts, or large consultancies, where the quality of the goods or services is critical. Unpriced technical proposals are solicited first, on the sole basis of technical and performance specifications. Bidders whose proposals are judged to meet the technical criteria are then invited to submit price bids.

Prequalification of bidders is also usually necessary for complex works and large technical contracts, as well as in cases when the high cost of preparing bids may discourage competition (e.g., for custom-designed equipment). Prequalification ensures that invitations to bid are extended only to those with adequate capability and resources.[30] Prequalification entails assessing the capacity, experience, and resources of the contractors to perform the particular contract satisfactorily, taking into account their past performance in similar contracts. Prequalification also serves as a check on the integrity of the contractor by precluding bids by firms that have been declared ineligible for previous corrupt and fraudulent practice. Such declarations of ineligibility are increasingly frequent, in parallel with the emphasis on fighting corruption (see chapter 14). Of course, as in all stages of procurement, prequalification must be based on transparent and well-publicized guidelines.

The *bidding documents* should furnish all the information necessary for a prospective bidder to bid for the goods, services, or works to be provided. While the detail and complexity may vary with the size and nature of the proposed procurement package, the bidding documents generally include the following:

- invitation to bid;
- instructions to bidders, including the criteria for bid evaluation;
- form of bid;
- form of contract;
- general and special conditions of contract;
- specifications (and drawings where relevant);
- list of goods or quantities;
- delivery time or schedule of completion; and
- necessary appendixes for such items as the types of deposits required.

To assist developing countries, international aid organizations have prepared standard bidding documents for different types of procurement. In many cases, the aid-receiving government is required to use the standard bidding documents of the donor organization. This practice may appear to be intrusive, but it saves resources and provides needed protection for both the donor and the recipient. Equally important, potential bidders who may be unfamiliar or uncomfortable with the country's own procurement system are encouraged to participate when they know that the procedures are those established by a major international organization.

Bid Evaluation

The objective of bid evaluation is to determine the winning bid—the bid that is substantially responsive to the bidding documents and offers the lowest cost (properly calculated).

The key to transparency and fairness is to open the bids at a designated time and place in the presence of all bidders or their representatives who wish to attend. Such public bid openings reduce the risk that bids will be leaked to competitors, "lost," or otherwise manipulated. However, after the bids are opened, no information whatsoever should be disclosed until after the successful bidder is notified of the award.

Notwithstanding such safeguards, bid evaluation is one of the most difficult procurement steps to carry out correctly and fairly and one of the easiest to manipulate. To reduce this risk, most countries have bid evaluation committees for acquisitions above a threshold value and experts are called in to assist in evaluating complex bids. Conversely, decisions on bids on small purchases may instead be delegated to the appropriate lower level.

A report on the evaluation of bids should be prepared giving the specific reasons for the award recommendation. This process also calls for the exercise of judgment in spotting unrealistically low bids, which during project execution would lead to requests for changes in specifications, supplementary payments during project execution, or lower quality or other unsatisfactory performance. Especially in developing countries, public managers have to be on guard against rigging of the process by a group of suppliers or contractors making private arrangements to share the market or rotate purchases. Such practices are not revealed by case-by-case audits, as each case will show that the procurement requirements were strictly adhered to. It is important for the results of the bidding process *as a whole* to be evaluated periodically in order to identify suspicious trends.

As in vote counting after elections, unusual delays in bid evaluation are often a sign of trouble—an indication that someone in the system is attempting to discourage the best bidders or to give extra time to favored bidders to modify their bids on the basis of leaked information. Such delays should be strongly discouraged by triggering a special scrutiny of the contract award.

Contract Award

The contract should be awarded to the winning bidder within the period of validity of the bid. The bidder should not be required to undertake responsibilities not stipulated in the bidding documents or to otherwise modify the bid. However, if the winning bid exceeds the pre-bid cost estimate, the agency may then negotiate with the successful bidder to reduce the scope of work or reallocate responsibility. This process, as always, should be transparent and according to explicit criteria. In this phase, too, delays are often a symptom of unfair or corrupt practices.

The European Union requires purchasing agencies to make the results known by means of a contract award notice published in the official journal and the data bank of the European Commission (EC), specifying the criteria applied and the price. Agencies are also required to give unsuccessful bidders the reasons why the successful bidder was selected, and the bidders are entitled to ask for review on the basis of a claim that proper evaluation procedures were not followed. In most countries and agencies, however, there are no uniform requirements for explaining the selection to the unsuccessful bidders.

Rejection of all bids is justified either where there is lack of effective competition or none of the bids are substantially responsive. If all bids are rejected, the purchasing agency should examine the reasons for the lack of responsive bids or the low number of bidders and repeat the process, with wider advertising and suitable revisions in the bid specifications if necessary. Note, however, that rejection of all bids is sometimes a danger signal that improper negotiations are being conducted "on the side." As with undue delays in evaluating bids, rejection of all bids may be a device to elicit bribes from bidders, or to provide privileged information to "friendly" contractors who can then place an artificially low bid to be discreetly augmented after the contract is awarded.

Resolution of Complaints

There must be channels for entertaining legitimate grievances and complaints from bidders and providing explanations. This is not only necessary for the integrity of the contract in question, but also serves to educate the unsuccessful bidders and thus improve the foundation for competitive bidding in the future. Attitude is also important. Unresponsive or uncaring behavior of procurement staff to complaints and suggestions can make it less attractive for companies to do business with the government and can thus reduce effective competition in the future. (This may sometimes be precisely the goal of the unresponsive behavior in the first place.)

In some countries (including Scandinavia), when the purchasing agency is unresponsive complaints can be addressed to the *ombudsman*.[31] Other countries provide for a review of the contract award decision only if complaints are received from other bidders within a prescribed period, but in most countries all procurement decisions are open to judicial challenge in any event.

Most countries provide for the investigation of complaints from contractors and their redress or disposition by the procurement entity itself, but practices vary. In Japan, a special unit in the Cabinet office considers complaints relating to international competitive bidding. The EU requires the establishment of formal complaint procedures, which allow the bidding firms to challenge procurement decisions either in general courts or in courts with standing jurisdiction over public procurement, or by administrative commissions. The model UNCITRAL law recommends creating specialized institutions to deal with public procurement complaints. (Hungary and Poland, among others, have adopted this recommendation.)

APPENDIX 9.2. OTHER FORMS OF PROCUREMENT

Procurement by Agents

Where the buying agency lacks the necessary organization or skills, it may employ as its agent a specialized procurement firm, or—for construction of works—a project management firm. Consultants are also often used to draw up contracts and project documents or to inspect supplies and works. The earliest and best example of procurement by intermediaries is the firm of Crown Agents, which had its start as the sole agent for all purchases of goods, services, and equipment for the British crown. (Now a private international consulting firm, Crown Agents still retains some of its original public purpose ethos and orientation.)

In various forms of build-operate-transfer contracts or under turnkey construction projects, the private company is allowed to procure the goods and services for the project, in accordance with the designs and specifications agreed in the contract. Conversely, government agencies in developing countries sometimes handle international bidding and related services for small local firms.

Requests for Proposals

Requests for proposals (RFPs) are negotiated bids wherein the parties enter into a contract after discussing its terms, provisions, costs, and other elements. RFPs are most common in consulting or other personal professional services, such as those of architects. RFPs can be subject to competition or used for sole-source suppliers of specialized products such as computer software or special patents (as for experimental programs). Thus, unlike the invitation to bid in competitive bidding, which focuses on minimum qualification, RFPs focus mainly on the quality of the service.

The RFP process starts with the definition of the scope of services and proceeds to the identification of the possible bidders, who are then encouraged to make an umbrella offer to provide the service or product. The price and other terms are then negotiated with the bidder chosen. These RFPs are a useful addition to the panoply of procurement instruments, but are inherently judgmental, often not transparent, and may lead to higher costs. The combination of technical judgment and negotiating ability calls for skills that are in short supply in many governments. The RFP procedure needs clear and transparent guidelines and regulations, personnel skills adequate to manage the process, and tight management scrutiny.

Indefinite Quantity Contracts

Indefinite quantity contracts (IQC) are used when the need for certain goods or services is clear, but there is uncertainty as to how much will be needed and when. IQCs define the goods to be supplied or tasks to be performed, establish general criteria for satisfactory performance, and set the time frame and overall expenditure limit. Although formal and negotiated between the government and the supplier or service provider, IQCs are not contracts in the binding sense, as the specific amounts of goods or services and the time of delivery cannot be defined in advance. IQCs can be awarded on any of the procurement methods—competitive, shopping, or sole source.[32]

Procurement from Other Government Entities

Much purchasing by government agencies is from other agencies of government. Such intergovernmental purchasing is different from force accounts insofar as the interagency agreement is entirely voluntary and negotiated. A simple example is where a county agrees to collect trash for a city. The city would bill the customers directly and the county may be paid by the city or use property tax levies to cover its costs.

Joint service agreements, as in countries following the French tradition, are formal agreements between local government units (and sometimes state agencies) for joint planning, financing, and delivery of services (e.g., water supply or sewage, road maintenance, or data processing) to the inhabitants in the participating jurisdictions. These agreements generally entail formal service contracts approved by the legislature or the government and are legally enforceable. A newly incorporated city would compare the cost of providing these services through its own employees with the cost of having them provided by another city and make a rational choice between self-provision and joint services.

In developing countries, intergovernmental contracting is also a useful means of governmental integration. It can ensure uniformity of services and economies of scale, avoid many of the hassles of contract management, and, more importantly, create a habit of cooperation among local government units, or what we may call "governmental social capital." Among other things, this may help alleviate the coordination problems of metropolitan areas and megacities discussed in chapter 5.

Procurement of Consulting Services

Nature of Consulting Services and Special Procurement Risks

The term "consultant" includes a wide variety of private and public entities, including individuals, management firms, engineering firms, investment and merchant banks, and universities. These consultants may help in a wide range of activities, from policy advice to engineering services and project supervision.

Because the wrong advice can be costlier than the wrong purchase of goods, selecting the right advisory expertise is a very important procurement decision. However, selection of proper consultant is not an easy process:

- Advice is intangible, thus its value is difficult to assess in advance.
- Unlike a commodity or a piece of equipment, a consultancy cannot be realistically tested prior to contracting.
- The buyer cannot have the same degree of specialized competency as the consultants and thus finds it difficult to choose among different candidates.

While the specific rules and procedures to be followed for employing consultants depend on the circumstances of the particular case, five main considerations should guide the consultants' selection process (World Bank, 2004):

- high-quality services;
- economy and efficiency;
- an opportunity to all qualified consultants to compete in providing the services;
- transparency in the selection process; and
- in developing countries, encouraging the development and use of national consultants.

Methods of Selection

The overriding consideration in consultants' procurement is the quality of the advice, rather than the price per se, as in most cases the consulting fees are a small fraction of the total project cost while good advice is key to its success. Accordingly, the following methods are used in consultants' selection:

- Both quality and cost-based selection is appropriate when the assignment and the staff time and associated costs can be defined with reasonable precision (e.g., for feasibility studies when technical solutions are already known).
- Quality-based selection is appropriate for specialized assignments for which it is difficult to define precise terms of reference.
- Cost selection is appropriate for selecting consultants for assignments of a standard or routine nature.
- Sole-source selection, which is generally to be avoided, is appropriate for small contracts with highly specialized individual consultants. However, repeat contracts to the same consultant for larger assignments flowing from the initial contract should generally not be awarded on a sole-source basis. Indeed, it is best to make the consultant ineligible to compete for major follow-up work in order to avoid giving any temptation to slant the advice in order to obtain such work.

For all the above reasons, selection of consultants must rely heavily on their demonstrated qualifications, prior experience and actual track record in similar assignments. Because even the weakest experience can be manipulated and embellished into a nice-looking resume, confidential references and direct feedback by the consultant's former clients are a must.

NOTES

1. The introductory section of this chapter has drawn in part on Pope (1996); Hauck and Leighland (1989); WTO statistics; Commonwealth Secretariat (1996); and Cooper and Newland (1997). Reflecting the growing importance of the procurement function and the risks of mismanagement and corruption, a new journal emerged in 2005, the *Journal of Public Procurement.* Readers wishing to follow current developments in this area are encouraged to keep track of articles published in the new *JoPP.* Two respected older journals are the *Public Contract Law Journal* and *Public Procurement Law Review.* The interested reader should also peruse Arrowsmith and Hartley's *Public Procurement* (2002). This is a two-volume set including fifty-two reprints from edited books and major academic journals. Each volume is divided into parts covering a different theme, issue, or problem in public procurement. Volume 1 covers outsourcing versus internal provision; competition and transparency in public procurement; and procurement as an instrument of industrial, social, and environmental objectives. Volume 2 covers more specialized issues such as the relation between procurement and external trade; enforcement, contracting, and military procurement.

2. The World Bank, for example, has stipulated the use of a separate set of documents for construction contracts.

3. Following the adoption of Agenda 21 in the International Conference on Environment and Development in 1992.

4. This section relies partly on WTO statistics; OECD (1997e, 1999a); Sherman (1987); and Cooper and Newland (1997).

5. The UNCITRAL is a UN commission set up to promote the harmonization of international laws relating to trade. It has formulated other model laws, on international commercial arbitration and conciliation, international sale of goods and related transactions, cross-border insolvency, international payments, international transport of goods, electronic commerce, and international construction contracts. See www.uncitral.org/uncitral/en/uncitral_texts/procurement_infrastructure.html

6. This section has drawn partly on Dehoog in Cooper and Newland, eds. (1997); Perry (1989); WTO statistics; and Corrigan et al. (1999).

7. In countries where autonomous "executive agencies" are set up for operational functions (see chapter 6), the framework agreement provides for financial autonomy in procurement, subject to certain binding features of national procurement policy.

8. As reported by the *Washington Post,* June 20, 2006.

9. Even this pales in comparison to the single most efficient and least verifiable form of corruption, i.e., privileged access to undervalued foreign currency, which is then resold at a premium on the informal market, for a riskless, costless, and almost instantaneous profit. In developing countries with an overvalued currency, poor governance and weak accountability, the black market for foreign exchange is conveniently located very near the Central Bank.

10. This section has drawn from Walsh and Leigland in Perry, ed. (1989); Dehoog in Cooper and Newland, eds. (1997); OECD (1999); the official procurement guidelines issued by the World Bank and the Asian Development Bank; and the details of national practices available in the statistical data published by the World Trade Organization.

11. These may include procurement from UN agencies, procurement under build-operate-transfer (BOT) and similar private-sector arrangements, and community procurement.

12. As an example of the value threshold, World Bank projects in India permit "shopping" procedures for items estimated to cost less than the equivalent of US$30,000 per contract, up to a specified overall maximum.

13. This section relies mainly on Sherman (1987); Dehoog, in Cooper and Newland, eds. (1997); and John Rehfuss (1989).

14. This section relies in part on Stockholm International Peace Research Institute (SIPRI) (2006); Gregory (1989); Brzoska (1999); and Jones (1999).

15. "Federal Procurement: Spending and Workforce Trends," April 30, 2003. As of 2007, 2003 was the last year for which the data was collected.

16. In July 1990, an interagency group was established to develop a detailed Procurement Professionalism Plan for agencies to identify a comprehensive program of workforce improvement to include an enhanced Federal Acquisition Institute (FAI), which develops instructional materials to support training in classroom settings, work sites, and on the job. Examples of FAI courses offered by the General Services Administration Interagency Training Center are "Introduction to Contracting," "Procurement Planning," "Price Analysis," "Basic Contract Administration," and "Construction Contracting."

17. See Policy Letter 92–03, "Procurement Professionalism Program Policy-Training for Contracting Personnel," June 24, 1992, and Policy Letter 97–01.

18. To disseminate regulations appropriate to its special mission, the DOD has established the Defense Acquisition University, partly to integrate operations and contracting for support of operations. The Civilian Faculty Plan establishes opportunities for a preeminent faculty in support of acquisition education. There are approximately 235 civilian faculty and 70 military positions in DAU. The NASA Procurement Management System is part of the NASA Acquisition Information System and includes the Simplified Acquisition Process for the Goddard Space Flight Center; the Industry Assistance/Small Business Office, for contracts of $25,000 or more; and the Offices for Earth Sciences, for Mission Enabling, and for Space Sciences Support.

19. The GSA Regional Offices are in Boston, New York, Philadelphia, Atlanta, Chicago, Kansas City, Fort Worth, Denver, San Francisco, Auburn (Washington), and Washington, DC.

20. Policy Letter 05–01, April 15, 2005, of the Office of Federal Procurement Policy (OFPP) Act, and sections 307(b)(3) and (g) of the OFPP Act, as amended.

21. See Del Duca (1996).

22. This section is based in part on Anechiarico and Jacobs (1996).

23. Quoted in ibid., p. 134.

24. The new flexibility in procurement, which was partly responsible for these problems, was proclaimed by an anonymous official source in "Emergency Procurement Flexibilities: A Framework for Responsive Contracting & Guidelines for Using Simplified Acquisition Procedures," *Journal of Public Procurement,* 2004, vol. 4, no. 1.

25. For example, a no-bid contract was awarded by the DHS to the former colleagues of a senior DHS official who used to work for the same firm before joining the Department—as reported by Robert O'Harrow, Jr., in the *Washington Post* of September 8, 2007. The reader should not be too surprised if the DHS official returns to the employ of the same company after leaving government service.

26. U.S. House of Representatives Committee on Government Reform—Minority Staff Special Investigations Division. *Dollars, not Sense: Government Contracting Under the Bush Administration,* June 2006.

27. *Purchase Cards: Control Weaknesses Leave DHS Highly Vulnerable to Fraudulent, Improper, and Abusive Activity,* GAO-06–957T, July 19, 2006.

28. Pre-bid action in the case of construction and works also requires the prior assembly of land and the

site where the work will be performed. Potential bidders cannot possibly be expected to guess how to obtain the land and how much it would cost to do so.

29. The fee charged for the documents should be reasonable and should reflect only the cost of printing and delivery and not be so high as to discourage small bidders. Bid deposit should also not be set so high as to discourage bidders. The deposit could be in any acceptable form, such as a certified check, bank draft, letter of credit, or cash.

30. Sometimes contractors may be prequalified for a group or type of contracts over a period of time.

31. An *ombudsman* is a person or an office enjoying broad respect and confidence, appointed by the executive or the legislature to represent impartially the interests of the public by receiving and handling complaints about the administration by individual citizens. The term, and the institution, originates from Norway but has been introduced in many other countries. See chapter 11 for a fuller discussion.

32. Along with "requirements contracts" and "definite quantity contracts," indefinite quantity contracts are one of the three types of "indefinite-delivery" contracts. The interested reader is referred to any of the various specialized treatments of procurement (e.g., the Federal Acquisitions Regulation system—www.acquisition.gov/far).

CHAPTER 10

Managing for Results: Performance, Monitoring, and Evaluation

> Success can be a great liar.
> —*Friedrich Nietzsche*

> Man does not live by bread alone
> —*Deuteronomy 8:2–3*

WHAT TO EXPECT

"Performance," a very attractive term, is an inherently relative concept. Performance can be defined in terms of the use of resources, or of the immediate results, or of the ultimate results, or of the process followed—and good performance in one respect does not necessarily imply good performance in the other respects. Performance is also country-, sector-, and culture-specific. Thus, depending on the circumstances of the country and the characteristics of the sector, introducing performance measures carries a great potential to spur administrative effectiveness but also severe risks of misleading findings. Analyzing the concept of performance suggests an "accountability trade-off," by which accountability can be either tight or broad but not both; the resulting need is to use a combination of a few relevant indicators. Next, ten caveats are listed for successful reorientation to results, based on international experience. The major ones warn against proceeding as if performance indicators were easy to measure, implement, and monitor; focusing only on benefits and neglecting costs (including transaction costs) and disregarding due process in the name of results—which is liable to eventually lead to bad process and bad results as well. The practice of "outsourcing," discussed more fully in chapter 11, is then very briefly introduced, followed by a discussion of monitoring and evaluation, which are necessary to close the feedback loop and to stimulate continuous improvement of efficiency and effectiveness in public service provision. The chapter concludes with suggested general directions of improvement.

THE CONTEXT

The Increasing Emphasis on Performance

"Performance" is one of those seductive terms whose meaning appears self-evident but is not. Who would not praise an actor's great performance, wish for a high-performance engine, or expect good performance of contractual obligations? When such terms themselves become a basis for actual policies and practices, however, it is prudent to look past their allure and inquire into their substantive meaning.

The introduction of performance semantics and measurements into public administration has gathered steam since the early 1990s and carries a potential to stimulate greater effectiveness but also substantial risk. It is thus necessary to unbundle the concept and identify the country circumstances and sector conditions that make for successful or disastrous insertion of "performance" systems into the management of the public sector.

In recent years, several developed countries and some developing countries have made increasing use of performance concepts and results indicators, both in their administrative practices and in the formulation and execution of public programs, assisted—and often pushed—by external aid agencies. In some countries, the results have eventually justified the substantial investment in time, effort, and stress; in other countries, they have not. The key determinant of success or failure is whether the changes were realistic, introduced gradually, and consistent with both the methodological complexity of the topic and the specific country realities (especially administrative capacity and the governance regime).

Several factors have led to the focus on performance. The main ones were the pervasive dissatisfaction with government employees' unresponsiveness to the public; the dynamics of Wagner's Law, by which the size of government tends to grow more than in proportion to the size of the economy (see chapter 7), and hence puts pressure on the public finances;[1] and the New Public Management (NPM) paradigm. As previewed in chapter 1 and discussed in chapter 16, the genesis of the NPM can be dated to the early 1980s (essentially starting from Prime Minister Margaret Thatcher's reforms in the United Kingdom) and its heyday was marked by the completion in the early 1990s of the public sector revolution implemented in New Zealand.[2]

The caricature of the bureaucrat investing a lot of time and diligence to save one dollar or to comply to the letter with the smallest technicality in the rules, thereby causing far worse delays and additional expense, is surely not a model to be followed. To forget the real purpose of spending monies obtained from the people eventually generates a culture of means rather than ends, disregard for the public, and the legendary "green eyeshade" mentality that considers it a success to formulate tight and internally consistent controls and implement them strictly—regardless of whether they are necessary or even helpful in executing the functions assigned to the government. Thus, a focus on policy and performance is highly appropriate—provided that it does not lead to forgetting the importance of integrity and of due process. (This real risk, which has already materialized in some countries, carries serious costs in terms of corruption and government credibility (as discussed in chapter 14).

The reforms that have introduced performance-based management practices have only rarely taken into account the country context and circumstances (including administrative capacity). In most cases, they have been introduced mechanically, without regard for the need to adapt to local circumstances or even to correctly identify the real problems. Not surprisingly, the result has been to waste time and resources and create unnecessary new problems without solving the existing ones.

The first basic requirement is to be clear about the complexity of the performance issue. To recognize such complexity helps lead to adopting those performance-oriented reforms that have a good chance to last and to be effective. Experience shows that introducing performance-based systems as if they were easy and simple has led to serious mistakes and damaged the credibility of the concept itself. But what *is* performance?

The Meaning of "Performance"

Performance: In Terms of What?

Dictionary definitions of "performance" include such alternative terms as "accomplishment," "achievement," "realization," and "fulfillment." Most of these terms have to do with the objective effect of public actions, but some relate to the subjective sense of satisfaction and accomplishment experienced as a result of one's actions. Naturally, the economic and public management literature emphasizes the former meaning, not only because of its direct implications for the population, but because subjective satisfaction is extremely difficult to measure and impossible to aggregate.

Accordingly, performance may be defined in terms of effort or in terms of results. To pay attention to individual effort is often looked at as a "soft and gentle" approach to salve human feelings. It is that. But it is also an eminently practical proposition. Consider what happens if you completely neglect the subjective dimension of "performance" and focus *only* on objective results. The brighter though lazier persons will be rewarded for their better results and the less capable but harder workers will be penalized. The former will therefore receive the clear message that underachieving carries no negative consequences; the latter will get the equally clear message that working hard carries no rewards. Both groups being composed of rational individuals, the level of effort will decline across the board and, in time, the entire organization will be populated by underachievers.

Recognizing (even if not rewarding) genuine individual effort can do much for morale and also serve as a demonstrator for others, thus fostering the effectiveness of the organizational unit. More fundamentally, most human beings consider a sense of accomplishment (what the early twentieth century economist Thorstein Veblen called the "instinct of workmanship"—Veblen, 1914) as a strong motivator of their action independent of salaries, penalties, or other material incentives. Thus, if public sector reforms inadvertently remove that motivation, the efficiency of personnel is likely to decline—and the effectiveness of public action along with it.[3] The normal human drive to do things right should be harnessed, not disregarded or depreciated. This is certainly recognized in the more efficient private corporations. Nonetheless, while we should keep these factors in mind, to introduce stronger performance orientation it is advisable to rely mainly on results because, among many reasons, "effort" is less easily measurable and is an excellent alibi for lack of results.

Understanding the Administrative Culture

In any event, it is critical to realize that *"performance" is a relative and culture-specific concept.* Government employees are considered "well-performing" if they stick to the letter of the rules, in a system where rule-compliance is the dominant goal; if they account for every cent of public funds, in a system where fastidiousness is the ultimate virtue; if they obey without question their superiors' instructions, in a strictly hierarchical system; if they compete vigorously for individual influence and resources, in a system where such competition is viewed positively; if they cooperate harmoniously for group influence and cohesion, in a system where conflict is discouraged; and so on.

Must we then infer that all the diverse administrative cultures are equally efficient? Certainly not. Indeed, the objective of institutional reform in public administration is to move from a less efficient to a more efficient set of behavioral rules. But we must also remember that administrative cultures do not come from Mars, but evolved through time in response to man-made incentive structures and concrete problems. Even when an administrative culture has become obsolete or dysfunctional, it is *still* necessary to understand its institutional roots in order to improve it in a durable way.

For example, the practice of advancement by seniority has rightly come under fire as preventing the recognition of individual merit and achievement. This is generally true. However, as noted in chapter 7, it must be remembered that the seniority principle was originally introduced in public administration largely *as a reform* to insulate the system from the vagaries of patronage and political pressures on government employees. Thus, depending largely on the quality of governance and the ethnic makeup of the country, a change to a "merit-based" system may carry the risk of reopening the door to such pressures. The change may still turn out to be highly desirable, but the reformer should become familiar with the historical roots of the administrative culture and the accountability regime, recognize the risks of change and address them explicitly.

It is an unfortunate reality that many public administration reform programs never took the trouble to assess how and from where the problems to be resolved arose in the first place; it is an unfortunate corollary of that reality that those programs produced no lasting improvement and, in several cases, real damage.

MEASURING AND USING PERFORMANCE INDICATORS

The Types of Performance Indicators

The measurement of "objective" performance can focus on inputs, results, process, or a combination of these. In turn, results can be outputs or outcomes.[4] Using law enforcement as the example, the taxonomy of performance is recapitulated in the sections that follow. The typology of performance indicators is summarized in tabular form in Table 10.1, and Table 10.2 gives examples of input, output, outcome, and process indicators in various sectors. Some of the indicators shown in Table 10.2 are good, but others are bad and their use would be likely to reduce or distort performance rather than improve it. The reader should decide which is which, and imagine the likely consequences of using one or another indicator.

Inputs

Inputs are the resources used to produce the goods or services—in the example of law enforcement, the policemen, prisons, police cars, handcuffs, and other necessary equipment and supplies. The social value of inputs is measured by their acquisition cost—the salaries to measure the human input, the purchase price of the equipment, the cost of supplies. The performance criterion corresponding to inputs is *economy*—the timely acquisition of high-quality inputs at lowest cost. (As we have seen in chapter 9, this is the guiding criterion for assessing the performance of the public procurement function.)

Outputs

The output is the good or service itself—in this example, the number of arrests, or the conviction rate, or the number of inmates. The social value of outputs is approximated by the market price for the good or service, or for its closest equivalent service. (In the absence of a market for the service, as in this case, the value can be approximated by the price of a close substitute, such as the price

Table 10.1

Typology of Performance Indicators

Type of Indicator	Definition	Measure of Social Value	Performance Criterion
Input	Resource needed to produce the good or service	Acquisition cost	Economy
Output	The good or service itself	Market price of the service or of close substitute	Efficiency
Outcome	Purpose for which the good or service is produced	As revealed by public preferences	Effectiveness
Process	Manner in which inputs are acquired/outputs produced/ outcomes achieved	Indeterminate	Consistency with societal norms; stakeholders' satisfaction

Table 10.2

Illustrations of (Good or Bad) Performance Indicators in Different Sectors

Sector	Type of Indicator			
	Input	Output	Outcome	Process
General administration	Number of employees	Number of policy papers	Better decisions	Openness of debate
Education	Student/teacher ratio	Retention rates	Higher literacy	Encouragement of student expression
Judicial system	Budget	Cases heard	Low appeal rate	Assistance for indigent defendants
Police	Number of police cars	Number of arrests	Decline in crime rate	Respect for rights
Corrections	Cost/prisoner	Number of prisoners	Recidivism rate	Prevention of abuse
Health	Nurse/population ratio	Number of vaccinations	Lower morbidity	"Bedside manner"
Social welfare	Number of social workers	Number of persons assisted	Exits from the system	Dignified treatment

of private security.) The performance criterion corresponding to outputs is *efficiency*—minimizing total input cost per unit of output (or maximizing the quantity of output in relation to a given total cost of inputs).

Outcomes

The outcome is the purpose that is achieved by producing the service—in this case, reduction in the crime rate. The social value of outcomes is difficult to assess, as there is no market for outcomes—you cannot buy and sell reductions in the crime rate—but may be gleaned from the public reaction through opinion surveys or, finally, in the political arena. The performance criterion corresponding to outcomes is *effectiveness*—maximizing outcomes in relation to the outputs produced.[5]

Process

Process is the manner in which inputs are procured, outputs produced, or outcomes achieved. The value of good process is high but inherently undetermined, partly because it becomes evident only when it is violated. In some areas of public activity, as in our example of law enforcement, "due process" has its own independent validity and is a key element of good governance. Thus, extracting confessions by torture is no longer considered "good performance." For inputs, good process consists of integrity and of intelligent compliance with acquisition and utilization rules. In other areas, process indicators are a useful proxy for performance when outputs or (more often) outcomes cannot be defined with clarity (e.g., "bedside manner" in health services, "rules for free debate" in policy formulation). Process indicators can be quantitative (e.g., percentage of class time dedicated to student questions) but are usually qualitative. Even then, they can frequently be transformed into quantitative indicators by feedback from users: for example, hospital patient satisfaction can be numerically assessed through a patient survey.[6]

The Link to Accountability

The whole point of measuring results is to improve performance through the intermediate process of making individuals more accountable for the results of their actions. The hierarchy of results given here suggests a sort of complex production function of public services whereby the out-*come* of one stage is an out*put* of the next stage. (For example, trash collection is an output whose outcome is a reduction in the rodent population, while the outcome of that reduction is a lower incidence of disease.) In "downstream" activities—i.e., activities close to the ultimate user (e.g., urban transport)—the output-outcome link is clear and immediate enough to permit using output indicators (e.g., passenger-mile) as a good proxy for outcomes. In "upstream" activities this is not the case (e.g., in government regulation, "maximizing" the number of rules is hardly a desirable measure of public performance).

These statements imply an "accountability chain"—with accountability clearest and most immediate by the narrowest performance criterion (i.e., compliance with input allocations) and most ambiguous and diffuse by the broadest performance criterion (i.e., net impact).[7] There is an *accountability trade-off*, by which accountability for performance can be either tight but with narrow relevance, or broadly relevant but diffuse—never *both* tight and broadly relevant. For example, it is fairly easy to hold a village nurse strictly accountable for the output of number of vaccinations and to reward or penalize him accordingly; it is difficult to hold him responsible for the outcome of improving the health of village children, which is affected by a variety of other factors. Conversely, his active involvement in household sanitary conditions or nutrition or other contextual health factors may have more influence on the outcome of improving children's health than a greater number of vaccinations, but he cannot be held strictly accountable for the quality of that involvement. The relevant point here is that such involvement will not be motivated by an incentive system that focuses only on the narrow outputs.

Moreover, in the absence of close supervision, it is difficult to prevent immunizations from being performed with less than the recommended quantity of vaccine (with the remaining vaccine "leaking" out of the health delivery system). Therefore, it is risky to let go of controls on inputs, when moving toward rewarding results. To protect against these risks some controls on both the input and the quality of the service should be retained alongside the result indicators for as long as may be needed to shake the bugs out of the results-oriented system.

These considerations are not meant to suggest that outcome indicators are "better" than output indicators, or vice versa. Other things being equal, output indicators are closer to the desired outcomes, and hence are more realistic, the closer the activity is to the final user. However, the greater specificity associated with output indicators comes with a loss of relevance. Conversely, outcomes are of greater policy relevance, but public servants cannot be held strictly accountable for them.

Putting It Together

The process of deciding which of the indicators in Table 10.2 are good and which bad, and the thought experiment of imagining the consequences of using the wrong types of indicators, should have brought the reader to a fundamental conclusion: It is unwise to rely on any single indicator to measure performance. An adequate understanding of performance in a sector can be gained only by using a *combination* of indicators. The implication of this conclusion is very important. Since in most cases there is no defensible way to attach relative weights to the various indicators, they cannot be aggregated into a single number and should therefore be used only as the necessary starting point of a robust *dialogue* on performance. Mechanistic rankings of performance and bean counting of individual achievement measures are to be avoided for both conceptual and practical reasons. However, once a baseline is established, it becomes more and more feasible over time to track the progress of the organization or of the individual and thus strengthen the dialogue on performance.

On the other hand, it is obviously impractical to try and use all the indicators that have even a slight connection to the topic. Thus, a pragmatic choice must be made to select those few indicators most relevant to the function at hand and which, taken together, provide a reasonably good picture of how the function has been performed. (We'll give later a suggestion in this direction.)

As noted, the measurement problem becomes more complex as one proceeds up the scale from narrow input measures through outputs, outcomes, and finally process indicators. Although the quality issue is ever present, there is no great difficulty in defining and measuring outputs (and, even less so, inputs)—the issue with output indicators is their relevance. Similarly, the interpretation of outcomes is rarely in doubt—the issue with outcome indicators is their feasibility as a motivator of better performance. Outcome indicators are almost always more meaningful and output indicators almost always more feasible. Combining these two considerations, we arrive at an important principle: *performance measurement is most appropriate for those government activities where there is a direct and immediate relationship between the government agency's outputs and the desired public outcomes.*

The selection of output or outcome indicators (in cases where they are appropriate to begin with) is also heavily influenced by data availability and information technology. First, good data and good monitoring permit better definition of outputs and thus justify greater reliance on them as a measure of performance. Conversely, when data are lacking or unreliable or monitoring is weak, measuring performance by outputs generates only gamesmanship and self-delusion. In such cases, the priority must be to strengthen rule compliance and responsibility for input use and to improve the relevant data and monitoring capability before even considering the introduction of results-based performance indicators.

Moreover, data collection costs and, more generally, the transaction costs of introducing performance indicators in a systematic manner can be enormous. These costs must be assessed realistically and weighed against the benefits expected. It is simply wrong to consider only the benefits expected from introducing performance indicators. Yet performance-based systems have

---

BOX 10.1

How Not to Define "Performance" in Contracting

The U.S. government decided in 2006 to drop Bechtel, a giant construction firm, from a project to build Basra Children's Hospital in southern Iraq. The project was a year behind schedule and was expected to cost two and a half times as much as had been contracted. The company claimed that the delays and cost overruns were due to security problems, while the Iraqis argued the project had been badly mismanaged. The cause of the mismanagement was reportedly the roundabout way in which Bechtel went through a complex chain of companies and subcontracted a Jordanian company to supervise the work, even though the work was done by local construction firms in southern Iraq.

The interesting point is that Bechtel was not dropped for failure to fulfill the contract, as the contract did not actually require the company to complete the hospital. As a spokesman for the U.S. Agency for International Development stated, despite not finishing the hospital, the company did technically complete the contract, which "was a 'term contract,' which means *their job is over when the money ends . . .*" [Italics inserted]

Source: James Glanz, "Series of Woes Mark Iraq Project Hailed as Model." *New York Times*, July 28, 2006.

---

been introduced only on the basis of a reasonable expectation that they would improve performance—*with no consideration of costs.*

What is clear, regardless of the choice of results indicators, is that "performance" should never be defined as simply the ability to spend the public's money. Regrettably, public contracts are sometimes written precisely in these terms, and a project is considered "successful" when the financing has been fully disbursed. (In the United States, the bureaucratic term is the "burn rate" of the funds, which speaks volumes about the underlying attitude.) See, for example, the story of the Bechtel corporation contract for a children's hospital in southern Iraq—Box 10.1.

Assembling all these considerations together, the only universally valid rule is the following: If and when results measurement is appropriate and cost effective, performance should be assessed according to that particular combination of a few output, outcome, and process indicators that is realistic and suitable for the specific activity, sector, country, and time.

PERSONNEL PERFORMANCE APPRAISAL[8]

The previously stated principles and considerations are pertinent also to the assessment of the performance of individual government employees. (Although the subject is addressed here, it is equally relevant to chapter 8 on government personnel management, where it was first flagged.)

The General Outlook

To repeat the brief introduction of the subject in chapter 8, the objective of performance management and appraisal is to guide individual employees toward making an effective contribution to the work of the organization while at the same time meeting their own goals. Because of the impact of performance appraisal on salary and career prospects, the framework and methodology have important consequences for the motivation of employees and thus for efficient and improved performance. Performance appraisal can also serve as a strategic tool for raising overall standards in government service and for increasing accountability to citizens.

Ideally, performance appraisal should be specific to the job and measure only observable behavior. It should be participatory and tied to long-range employee objectives as well as to the mission of the organization. A good performance appraisal system should also promote a climate in which performance, achievements, and difficulties can be discussed openly and supportively. However, the critical importance of the cultural context, emphasized in chapter 1, must not be disregarded. For example, an open discussion of individual strengths and weaknesses may be unacceptably embarrassing in most East Asian countries.

In principle, performance appraisal and feedback should be a continuous process, but periodic formal appraisal is dictated by the practical need to review performance over a defined period of time and on a uniform basis for all individuals in a work unit. The starting premise must be recognition of the reality that *any* appraisal of individual performance is inherently subjective and entails an element of qualitative judgment. The goal of a sound appraisal system should therefore be to minimize arbitrariness and undue discretion, but without reducing the exercise to mechanistic bean counting or, worse, providing a smokescreen for arbitrary personnel decisions unrelated to job performance. Here, too, the cost-benefit issue comes to the fore.

Thus, the question is not whether employee performance should be systematically evaluated—of course it should—but rather how to do so fairly, reliably, economically, and without generating dysfunctional behavior or unnecessary conflict. If the country circumstances or organizational characteristics raise serious doubts as to the capacity to rate "well," it may be undesirable to have a formal performance appraisal system. A bad performance appraisal system is worse than none at all.

That said, performance management in any organization is an integral part of effective people management. Effective performance management must not be confused with a mechanical evaluation exercise or with purely monetary rewards. On the contrary, a well-designed system must rest on a realistic assessment of the complex motivations of human beings, as well as the need to generate and preserve cohesion within the organization while avoiding unproductive conflicts. The special characteristics of public service should also be recognized.

Appraisal Procedures and Techniques

Performance appraisal has traditionally been associated with communication from a supervisor to an employee. This tradition is consistent with the view of organizations as hierarchies of command and control. Formal appraisal, undertaken annually, is nested in routine administrative procedures and documented in forms and reports. The demand for procedural and substantive fairness requires formal appraisal systems as well as specific criteria and procedures for rewards or penalties. Because equity considerations are weighted more heavily in government than in the private sector, appraisal procedures are typically more complex and time consuming in public organizations.

Person-related or Goal-related Appraisal

Person-related appraisal compares the employee against other employees, while goal-related appraisal assesses employee performance against previously established behaviors and standards. Person-related systems are easy to design and interpret, but have low reliability and are of dubious value for improving performance or assuring equity. Furthermore, an ineffective or underachieving employee in a group of even less effective individuals will be rated higher than a good employee in an outstanding work unit. And, as argued earlier, higher-skilled persons who are systematically rated higher than their colleagues lose all incentive to do better.

For these reasons, most specialists advocate the use of goal-related appraisal, which clearly communicates managerial objectives relevant to the job. The participation of the employees themselves in the formulation of the evaluation criteria validates the criteria. In principle, goal-related appraisals enable supervisors and employees alike to determine if the objective standards have been met; personnel decisions can be better explained to employees, and changes in salary, promotions, or dismissals can be better justified and accepted. This approach permits the identification of areas where performance can be improved as a basis for counseling, job assignment, and training.

Although theoretically superior to person-related appraisal, goal-related methods also have weaknesses. First, despite all rhetoric about the employee agreeing in advance with the supervisor on aims and achievements, in reality the goals are pretty much set by supervisors and employee "ownership" is at least in part a sham. Second, since there will always be a number of goals listed, at appraisal time the problem will surface of how to weigh each of these goals and how to aggregate different achievements into a single rating of performance. Here, too, the supervisor's preferences will tend to prevail, as she can choose to emphasize as "area of weakness" an especially damaging trait (e.g., inability to cooperate with others) or a relatively harmless one (e.g., maintaining an orderly desk). Thus, an intelligent combination of person-related and goal-related appraisal is usually preferable to either approach taken in isolation.

Appraisal Methods[9]

There are seven possible kinds of appraisal methods (Klingner and Nalbandian, 1998):

- graphic rating and ranking;
- forced choice;
- essay;
- objective;
- critical incident;
- behaviorally anchored rating scales; and
- psychometric analysis.

Graphic rating scales are the most easily developed, administered, and scored. Desirable and undesirable traits (quality of work, work output, work habits, safety, personal relations, supervisory ability, etc.) are listed, with a box or "scale" next to each for the ratings (usually some version of "outstanding, above average, satisfactory, below average, unsatisfactory").

In *forced choice,* statements of traits for a given position are couched in multiple-choice form and the rater must choose the statement that corresponds most closely with the employee's performance. This method helps somewhat to reduce supervisory bias and simplifies comparisons. (However, the specific drafting of the multiple choice items can itself introduce a source of bias.)

The *essay,* with the supervisor making narrative comments about the employee, is the oldest form of appraisal and the one that can best capture the complexity of a human being's performance. (The essay need not be long, as in the legendary put-down of a mid-career officer by his superior: "This officer is admirably placed in his present position.") However, this method is usually time consuming and depends largely on the supervisor's writing ability. Moreover, comparisons of performance between employees doing different work are unfair and cannot be used as sole basis for decisions affecting their careers. Finally, different supervisors have different ideas of what a "good job" is: To one, it may mean excellent work; to another, it may mean work that is merely acceptable. Therefore, the essay is often used in conjunction with the rating method.

The *objective method* measures work performance against previously established standards using workload indicators. It is most relevant to physical or technical jobs, where the workload reflects the substance of the job, but can be artificial and misleading otherwise.

The *critical incident* technique records representative examples of good or bad performance, in relation to agreed work objectives.

The *behaviorally anchored rating scale (BARS)* employs objective performance criteria in a standard appraisal format. It is time consuming to develop and administer, deceptively precise, and ultimately unsatisfactory.

Psychometric analysis based on psychological tests has attempted over the years to fine-tune the performance appraisal process. Although valuable for first recruitment into special occupations where personal temperament is critical to good performance (e.g., police, submarine crews, astronauts), in general these methods risk giving a false sense of pseudoscientific accuracy, and demoralize employees by implicitly treating them as experimental subjects. In any event, psychometric tools are too expensive and sophisticated for most government organizations (especially in poor countries) and are not worth the effort and resources invested—except, as noted, in specific cases before recruitment.

Table 10.3 summarizes the relationships between the purpose, criteria, and these methods of appraisal. Clearly, no single method applies to all occupations or situations, but all methods have some degree of validity in most cases. Therefore, evaluative narrative and "objective" rating methods may often have to be combined.

Feedback

It is said that who does the rating matters more than how the rating is supposed to be done. It is important, therefore, not to leave the appraisal of employee performance exclusively to the immediate supervisor without input from others knowledgeable about the employee's performance. Normally, various persons are involved in rating the performance of an individual. Of course, the immediate supervisors do assess the performance of their subordinates because they presumably possess more relevant information than other sources and carry the responsibility for managing their personnel. However, complementary inputs can and should be sought.

Self-rating has been employed with some success to promote an honest discussion between superior and subordinate and is in some cases a formal annex to the superior's report. Though less frequently used, *peer ratings* or group ratings provide additional valuable information, including observations on the employee's teamwork and collegiality. The late 1990s have witnessed an introduction in several large public organizations of *upward feedback* (i.e., confidential comments by subordinates on the performance of managers or supervisors). Upward feedback was, naturally, strongly resisted at first, but has had remarkable results in terms of fostering the accountability of managers and their effectiveness in leading the work team, and good managers have become the

Table 10.3

Personnel Performance Appraisal: Purposes, Criteria, and Methods

Purpose	Criteria	Methods
Communicate objectives	Goal-oriented	Critical incident, objective measures, BARS
Allocate rewards	Person- or goal-related	Graphic rating, ranking, forced choice, BARS
Improve performance	Goal-related	Critical incident, objective measures, BARS
Research on personnel	Goal-related	Essay, critical incident, objective measures, BARS

Source: Adapted from Klingner and Nalbandian (1998).

strongest supporters of the method. In some cases, upward feedback has been expanded to *360-degree feedback,* by which superiors, subordinates, peers, and clients are all asked for their views of the individual's performance. All-around feedback is the most comprehensive, but obviously also the most time-consuming method. The argument can be made that such expansion provides for the fullest description of an individual's performance. However, although logical in principle, 360-degree feedback has often been used in practice to dilute the heavy impact of negative upward feedback on the performance of managers.

In ministries and agencies that provide direct services to the public, citizens' feedback can be an invaluable adjunct of performance appraisal for civil servants (see chapter 11).

Managing Poor Performers

Factors of Weak Performance

Assessing good performance and rewarding it is much more agreeable as well as easier than dealing with unsatisfactory employees. The handling of weak performance is the single most difficult aspect of personnel management, especially in public organizations. Incompetence or unwillingness to meet job standards are the main reasons for weak performance, but other factors outside the control of the employee may contribute heavily. The supervisor must first try to separate the factors within the employees' control from those external to them:

- poor job design;
- poor work environment;
- inadequate planning and unrealistic deadlines;
- ineffective recruitment and mismatching of people and jobs;
- unclearly defined responsibilities and expectations;
- insufficient skills or experience for the expected role;
- lack of required equipment and supporting staff;
- disruptive personality clashes;
- gender and racial bias;
- personal or family problems; and
- communication difficulties.

Whatever the reasons, unsatisfactory performance becomes ingrained and self-reinforcing in an organization that is reluctant to impose demonstrative sanctions against incompetent or erring employees, or that inhibits robust action by supervisors through informal rules and constraints, or that resists making the changes in environmental factors that contribute to poor performance. A reluctance to apply the rules not only permits poor performance to continue but also demoralizes good performers and, in time, erodes the entire organization. Most governments require the termination of an employee with two successive unsatisfactory reports, but weak supervisory accountability and supervisory reluctance to give candid ratings often disable this rule. Among other things, therefore, supervisors should themselves be assessed for the consistency, fairness, and candor of their evaluation of subordinates.

Dealing with Unsatisfactory Performance

There are four sequential ways of managing unsatisfactory performance:[10]

- early intervention and informal counseling;
- formal counseling with the help of a performance improvement plan;
- follow up on the improvement plan; and
- sanctions.

Early intervention and informal counseling address the problem as part of daily supervision. When unsatisfactory performance persists, formal counseling is called for: On the occasion of the annual performance appraisal, the supervisor would agree with the employee on a performance improvement plan then follow up on its implementation. The performance improvement plan may include the acquisition of required skills and/or a "test" assignment, as well as the removal of constraints outside the control of the employee, if any. If the employee has not improved at the end of the stipulated period, appropriate sanctions—from minor penalties up to dismissal—should be imposed, subject to appeal procedures.[11] The Philippines follows the interesting practice of publishing a "Hall of Fame" to recognize outstanding employees and a "Hall of Shame" that lists the very poor performers.

Rewarding Good Performance

Material and Nonmaterial Motivations

According to Riley (1993, p. 213), the main sources of motivation are as follows:

- general social motivators, and the prevalent ethic in the society;
- the mission of the organization;
- the content of the job;
- working conditions; and
- money.

There are obvious differences in respect to all of these factors between the private and public sectors. The weights of those factors also differ between private and public employment, with the work environment generally more important for private sector employees and the mission of the organization generally more important for government employees. In any event, it is clear that nonmaterial factors such as peer recognition and colleagues' esteem have an important role as motivators of good performance. Ethical values and the desire for achievement—what Thorstein Veblen called "the instinct of workmanship" (Veblen, 1914)—often drive individuals as much or more than material rewards or the threat of performance assessment based on output indicators. This is as true of private-sector workers as it is of government employees. By and large, however, government employees tend to have a stronger public service ethos, by definition, either at entry or as an adaptation to their public mission.

"Performance Pay": Linking Compensation to Employee Performance

As previewed in chapter 8, the concept of performance pay, or merit pay, was first introduced into the U.S. public sector by the 1978 Civil Service Reform Act in imitation of similar schemes in the private sector. In general, private business practices are not necessarily—nor even frequently— applicable to the public sector, for a number of reasons ranging from the absence of the profit motive to the lack of genuine competition, the need for equity and uniformity of treatment of employees, and many other reasons. With particular reference to performance pay, its record as a motivator of better results is very mixed even in the private sector—as shown, among other things, by the granting of multimillion-dollar bonuses to top executives whether their company did well or badly, and the strong evidence that higher executive compensation is generally not correlated with better company performance. (The disconnect between company performance and executive compensation is most evident in the United States, but the distortion is spreading. Consider, for example, the ailing British telecom firm Cable and Wireless' plan to pay its top managers over $400 million equivalent, two months after its financial difficulties led to the firing of 3,000 employees.)[12] When applied in government, pay for performance is even more questionable—as should have been made clear by the earlier discussion of the complexities and difficulties of measuring performance in the public sector.

Let's go back to basics. In a sense, *all* pay in government should be for performance—whether the performance consists of protecting government resources, applying regulations, behaving in accordance with probity and due process, or producing different sorts of results. Moreover, there has always been performance pay in almost every government, in the form of promoting the better performers to higher positions, which of course carry higher salaries. There is no possible argument, therefore, that public sector salaries should be given on any basis other than "performance" in some sense, or that promotions should be an entirely mechanical consequence of surviving to an older age.

The issue of performance pay revolves instead around the specific question of whether giving annual bonuses to the "best-performing" employees—fairly common in private corporations in North America and several other developed countries—succeeds in motivating improved efficiency and productivity of employees. In this narrower sense, the record of performance pay in the public sector is uniformly disappointing—as shown by, among many others, Milkovich and Wigdor (1991); Kellough and Lu (1993); and Ingraham (1993).[13] Nevertheless, these problems, identified more than a decade ago, have not entirely tarnished the continuing appeal of "merit pay" for politicians as well as some public managers.

Managing for Performance Around the World

While the advantage of performance bonuses in "western" developed countries' governments can at least be debated, it is all risk and no advantage in other cultures and can be positively lethal to good government in developing countries—particularly where ethnic or religious differences are important. A country's cultural factors and social values have a great deal of influence on the nature of performance appraisal, the manner of imposing sanctions and granting rewards, and the relative emphasis on group versus individual achievement. For example, in an environment of guaranteed job security such as the Japanese civil service, with the great importance given to personal dignity, it is a severe penalty to give the employee minor assignments and little work. In extreme cases, underperforming employees are given nothing to do and assigned to a "desk by the window"—thus making them immediately recognizable to all passersby as substandard employees. In such an environment, obtaining challenging assignments is a far stronger motivator of good performance than an extra few hundred thousand yen.

Also, many nonwestern countries stress rule-based compliance and group cohesion, whereas western countries tend to emphasize values of individual achievement and risk-taking. Accordingly, other things being equal, a consensus person will generally be evaluated more favorably in, say, Korea, than in the United States, and giving a performance bonus to an individual member of the group will generate dissatisfaction among all other members of the group, and undercut the effectiveness of the individual concerned to boot. In many developing countries, particularly in Africa and parts of Asia and Latin America, propitiating a superior with gifts and incorporating personal considerations in personnel decisions are not seen as violating public ethics. On the contrary, not doing so may be viewed as rudeness and disloyalty. Also, a failure to discriminate in favor of relatives may be considered a violation of basic family duty. In these circumstances, everyone is likely to assume that the annual bonuses have been distributed by the manager for personal or family reasons and not for performance on the job—whether or not this is the case. Again, the consequences for morale and productivity are bound to be negative.

The difficult practical question, then, is how to reward good performers in an environment of group primacy and informal norms. Good answers can be found, provided that they are tailored to the relevant economic and social context. (A promising approach is to consider rewarding the good performance of work groups rather than individuals.) But, whatever the best answer might be in a given country, the worst answer is to transplant mindlessly personnel management practices evolved in other countries, without careful examination of their suitability to the different context.

Manipulation of personnel appraisal systems, however, may occur in any cultural context, and is a far greater issue than the pros and cons of performance pay. In every country there is a risk that formal appraisal systems are used only to ratify and rationalize wholly subjective and arbitrary judgments. Without strong safeguards and external monitoring, therefore, personnel appraisal may become administrative lipstick rather than a tool for performance management and motivation.

INTRODUCING PERFORMANCE REFORMS

The previous discussion underlined the care, common sense, and sector knowledge needed to introduce performance indicators successfully. Indeed, the careless introduction of performance indicators has often generated unintended consequences so serious as to provoke a general backlash against all performance measurement. (This explains the apparent paradox of why some public officials who would stand to lose from a new and robust focus on performance generally support the introduction of simplistic performance indicators.)

The Ten Commandments of Performance

This section offers a variety of analogies, metaphors, and anecdotes to illustrate the main issues. The intent is not to add analytical content, but to provide "memory aids" to anchor these issues, and, not so incidentally, to take some of the dryness out of the topic of public sector performance.

The Patton Premise ("Know Where You're Going Before You Get Moving")

In the 1970 movie *Patton,* the actor playing General George Patton stumbles on a sleeping soldier while inspecting the sorry state of the U.S. Army after the disastrous defeat in their first battle against the Germans at Kasserine Pass in Tunisia in 1942. The soldier says: "Hey! I am trying to sleep!" then, realizing it's the new commanding general, mumbles some apology. Patton replies: "Don't worry, son, you're the only s.o.b. in this army who knows what he's trying to do."

The first, and most obvious, requirement for strengthening performance is to be crystal clear about the objective of the activity being performed. Yet, often because of the force of fashion and to imitate "cutting edge" practices, in many countries performance indicators were introduced without defined goals, and in some countries resulted in weakening control and accountability systems that had been working reasonably well.

The Stepsisters' Predicament ("If the Shoe Doesn't Fit, Get Another")

In the original uncensored version of the Cinderella story, one of her stepsisters cut off her toe to fit in the glass shoe; the other cut off part of her heel. Both ended up with mutilated feet and got neither the shoe nor the Prince.

We have stressed throughout the book that all institutional innovations must be viewed in the light of the local cultural, social, and historical context and—above all—administrative capacity. In some countries, instead of carefully designing the reform to fit local conditions, the approach to improving performance has ignored administrative capacity limitations and other institutional constraints. The result has been failure of the reform and loss of credibility of the approach itself.

The Accountability Trade-off ("There's No Free Lunch Here Either")

In statistical inference, there is an inverse correlation between precision and probability (given the size of the sample). A point estimate is highly precise but carries near-zero probability of being right (i.e., corresponding to the true value of the variable). Conversely, a very wide band estimate is highly likely to comprise the true value but is too broad to be useful. Similarly, as noted earlier, in the domain of performance there is an "accountability trade-off": *accountability can be broad or tight, but not both.* Tight and immediate accountability is by definition narrow accountability; conversely, the link between action and results becomes more ambiguous the broader and the more meaningful the results.

We can either measure very accurately the performance of specific things (and then we are able to hold those in charge strictly accountable for those specific things), or resign ourselves to getting a rough idea of the important results (and then tolerate the resulting vagueness in attributing responsibility). In practice, it is advisable to do both, in order to get a more rounded sense of the overall results. It follows from the accountability trade-off that performance monitoring through outputs is least appropriate for complex tasks (e.g., mental health services) but can be very effective for simple processes (e.g., street lighting).

The Titanic Warning ("It's What You Can't See That Can Sink You")

The great ship *Titanic,* which was considered unsinkable, sank in its maiden voyage in 1912 after its below-water compartments struck an iceberg in the North Atlantic. There are two lessons here. The first is that it is not sensible ever to believe that any particular institutional reform is "unsinkable" and bound to succeed. The second lesson is that the *Titanic* was sunk by the unexposed portion of the iceberg.

The total stock of institutional rules in any society is always much greater than the portion visible as formal rules. Indeed, sometimes the visible formal rules are simply not operative. For example, the Soviet Constitution of 1936 was considered as a model document, protecting individual rights at the same time as it facilitated the achievement of social objectives. In reality, anyone who was foolish enough to act as if this were really so found himself in serious trouble. In reforms intended to encourage stronger performance orientation in government, a design failure to recognize and take into account the key informal rules (which are generally below the surface) is likely to lead to a failure of the reform itself. This does not mean that reformers or external advisers are supposed to acquire their own expertise in the inner workings of society, which would be presumptuous and unrealistic. It does mean that they have a responsibility to identify those who do know and understand the local informal rules, and to get them to participate in the design of the institutional reform—or at least to "kick the tires" before the reform is introduced.

The Heisenberg Dilemma ("Beware the Law of Unintended Consequences")

In physics, the Heisenberg "uncertainty principle" states that one cannot measure with precision the values of pairs of observable characteristics of the same phenomenon. Loosely interpreted, this means that the action of observing a phenomenon itself alters it. In the context of performance measurement, it is never advisable to be too sure that the actions undertaken will have the effects intended and *only* the effects intended. Introducing new ways of evaluating the results of human action always leads to changes in behavior (*provided* that the evaluation is attached to concrete changes in incentives). Of course, it is precisely a change in public servants' behavior—toward results—that the use of performance indicators is intended to generate. However, attempts to influence people often produce unintended behavior that may be at odds with the desired objective or even defeat it altogether and worsen the initial situation.

Some examples of the law of unintended consequences, all from real life, follow:

- When police performance is measured by the number of police officers "on the beat," important statistical and analytical functions are neglected, with adverse long-term consequences for law and order policy. If the measure is the overall crime rate, the implicit incentive is for policemen to underreport all crimes. If performance is assessed on the basis of specific crimes, underreporting of those crimes and neglect of crime prevention in general are likely.
- When agricultural subsidies are given with the intention to preserve small family farms, the increase in the price of land—now more profitable because of the agricultural subsidies—puts small farmers at a competitive disadvantage vis-à-vis large agribusiness.
- If hospital subsidies are based on the number of patients waiting for treatment, hospital managers have a perverse incentive to keep as high as possible the number who are waiting, by neglecting noncritical cases and focusing entirely on other cases; if the subsidies are based on the number of patients treated, an incentive is provided to process patients as fast as possible, letting them out of the hospital much too early after surgery, etc.
- When the 2002 "No Child Left Behind" legislation in the United States provided education grants to stimulate states to spend more on poor children, the richest states, which spent more anyway, ended up with the lion's share of the grants.
- When an aboriginal tribe in Australia was informed that its sanitation and other subsidies from the government would depend on their performance in keeping the sanitary facilities

clean, they did so most effectively by thoroughly cleaning the toilets, and then closing them to the public.[14]

The Turkish Evasion ("If It Ain't Worth Doing, It Ain't Worth Doing Well")

A traditional Turkish folk story tells of a man who searched diligently for his purse on the main street because, he said, it was too dark in the back alley where he had lost it. To be sure, it is very difficult to measure performance in meaningful ways, but this can never justify measuring performance in easy but meaningless ways. The "tyranny of the measurable" is in evidence here. Let's elaborate.

According to a well-known management consulting rule, "what gets measured, gets done." This may be valid in private sector activity, where the bottom line of profit (or sales, or return on investment, or stock price, etc.) is both measurable and meaningful. It is much more doubtful in the public sector. There are three obvious conditions for this rule to make sense: (1) the right thing must be measured; (2) the thing must be measured right; and (3) there must be consequences if it does not get done. As we have seen earlier, none of these conditions is easy to meet.

Even more of a complication is the obvious corollary of the rule: what does *not* get measured, does *not* get done. The Turkish Evasion warns us that, in the public sector, the least measurable activities may be the most important ones (e.g., equity or social peace). Finally, as noted, it is never enough to assess the short-term consequences of changes in organization or in incentives, which are usually positive (nor, as stressed earlier, to limit attention to the benefits expected without considering the costs). Both the expected costs and benefits of performance measurement must be considered, and in a long-term rather than immediate perspective.

The Dreedle Illusion ("Better About Right than Exactly Wrong")

In Joseph Heller's classic antiwar satirical novel, *Catch-22,* the commanding air force general Dreedle, enamored of "tight bombing patterns," praises a pilot whose raid produced an orderly set of bomb craters in an empty field and scolds another who destroyed the assigned target with bomb hits scattered all over it.

Clean spreadsheets with neat indicators of clear results and timely monitoring do nothing to stimulate performance if the indicators are not relevant to the outcome sought (or, worse, if the data themselves are phony). In fact, this false accuracy can result in channeling civil servants' energies toward presenting the data better, or even manipulating the data to make them appear to fit an orderly pattern. Either way, their energies are channeled away from the real objective of their work—to improve public service.

The Mechanic's Principle ("If It Ain't Broke, Don't Fix It")

If the public management function under consideration is performing tolerably well, reformers should be particularly mindful of the risk that changes may worsen the situation. Even if this doesn't happen, resources and attention should be devoted to the more serious problems. This principle does not imply the need for passive acceptance of mediocre performance, but simply the need to assess downside risks and address them properly. (Symmetrically, however, if the process is dysfunctional or thoroughly corrupt, radical changes may be the only way to improve it.)

The Gym Prescription ("Stretch Before You Exercise")

In basic economics, the "production possibilities" concept makes a distinction between getting actual production closer to the ceiling set by resource and technological constraints, and raising the ceiling itself. By analogy, it is advisable to first stimulate all improvements possible under the existing regulatory and incentive framework before introducing new results-based performance indicators and incentives. Second, when the time is right and the right indicators of performance have been chosen, the specific levels to be achieved need to be set. The general principle is that *the performance target must be challenging but achievable.* Both overambitious and easy targets lead to underachievement. Overambitious targets discourage effort; easy ones do not stimulate better performance. In turn, targets may be set by reference to norms and standards prevailing elsewhere or, better still, by reference to earlier performance in the same country and sector. ("Benchmarking," discussed in the next section, is often used for this purpose; the method has its uses and limitations—see, for example, Powers, 1998.)

The Missouri Test ("He Who Lives by the Sword Must Be Willing to Duel")

The motto of the state of Missouri is: "Show me." It is inherent in the logic of any performance-based system that *the system,* too, must be subject to a reality test.

Operationally, therefore, it is essential to build into performance reforms specific provisions for the systematic assessment of the performance of the performance system itself. But even before the reforms are introduced, government officials, or the public and the media, should demand that the proponent of the reform take the plain but powerful Missouri Test. The test calls for a *demonstration* that the concrete benefits are likely to outweigh the costs and that there is a good answer to the simple question: How and when will one know whether this practice has performed well or badly in this particular country? If the advice is good and the experts are right, they will be able to pass the Missouri Test and the performance-based reform should be vigorously pursued. If not—inverting the slogan of a well-known athletic shoe company—the only sensible course of action is: Just Don't Do It.

The "Cream" of Good Performance

Keeping these warnings in mind, a good performance indicator must meet the "CREAM" criteria. It must be:

- *C*lear—precise and unambiguous (not necessarily quantitative);
- *R*elevant—appropriate to the objective at hand (not used simply because it is readily available);
- *E*conomic—the data required should be available at reasonable cost;
- *A*dequate—by itself or in combination with others, the measure must provide a *sufficient* basis for the assessment of performance; and
- *M*onitorable—in addition to clarity and availability of information, the indicator must be amenable to independent scrutiny.[15]

If *any one* of these five criteria is not met, formal performance measurement should not be introduced and other ways of assessing and stimulating good performance would be needed—including the old-fashioned method of open give-and-take with competent and honest managers. At the same time, however, statistical and analytical capacity-building efforts should be made toward meeting the CREAM criteria in order to permit the introduction of good performance measures in the future. And, even where data limitations and other circumstances are inimical to the successful introduction of results-based performance indicators, it is still possible to assess performance in service delivery through opinion surveys and other means of obtaining feedback from those who know the situation best (i.e., the users of the services).

Setting the Targets: Benchmarking[16]

Benchmarking and performance measurement are closely linked. Performance measurement can be the first step toward improving the performance of a public-sector organization and, if backed by an appropriate incentive system, it can help shift organizational focus from inputs to outputs and outcomes and thus improve efficiency and effectiveness. However, the real benefits come from using the performance measures as the basis for internal or external comparisons, with the objective of improving the performance of the organization as a whole. This is called "benchmarking," the technique of comparing business practices and performance levels between organizations to identify opportunities for making improvements in the economy, efficiency, or effectiveness of an organization's activities. The two main approaches to benchmarking are metrics and process benchmarking.

Metrics Benchmarking

Metrics benchmarking focuses on the calculation of numerical performance indicators, such as unit costs, response time, and number of customer complaints, which can then be compared with similar data from other organizations in the same field. Metrics benchmarking is a useful diagnostic tool, as it can help an organization to identify the areas where it is less efficient areas and provide targets. Metrics benchmarking can be used to produce the so-called "league tables" (by analogy to the ranking of teams in sport leagues). However, it compares apples with oranges and can be misleading, as different organizations are subject to different constraints on which they have little control.

It is more useful to benchmark the performance of an organization against the performance of the same organization in the past. Because one is then comparing apples with apples, benchmarking gives a measure of progress achieved. Even this, however, does not indicate what future improvements can be made and how. For that purpose one has to turn to process benchmarking, which focuses on the comparison of the processes and activities underlying performance. In sum, metrics benchmarking identifies the problem areas and process benchmarking helps to find ways to deal with the problems.

Process Benchmarking

The first steps in process benchmarking involve preparing "process maps" for the activities in the selected area of focus, collecting information on resources consumed by those activities, and analyzing the practices, working methods, and policies that determine the performance of those activities. This stage usually reveals many obvious inefficiencies in processes, which if eliminated can yield significant performance improvements. The next steps are to obtain comparator data, compare the processes, develop recommendations, and implement changes. After the changes have been introduced, the new values of the performance indicators provide a measure of the improvements achieved and the basis for starting the next round of benchmarking. Therefore, this technique is often referred to in the literature as "continuous improvement."

For the purposes of benchmarking, comparators can be either internal or external. The former refers to a situation where comparisons are made between separate divisions of the same organization where similar processes are performed (e.g., multi-site organizations such as the tax, health, or education department can compare the performance of their offices, hospitals, or schools in different cities). External comparators can be direct competitors (i.e., organizations providing the same product or service). For example, the public sector could benchmark schools or hospitals it runs against those run by the private sector or nongovernmental organizations (NGOs) in the same area; by other public-sector bodies performing similar processes, such as land registration and vehicle registration agencies; or by the best organization around, public or private, in the case of similar business processes, such as in the areas of accounting, information systems, procurement, payroll, or customer service. However, it is often helpful to start with internal benchmarking (i.e., comparing performance measures between different offices or sites), understanding the processes and methods that explain the differences in the measures, and deciding what the best internal practice is before going to outside comparators.

In the public sector, benchmarking can yield additional benefits by introducing a form of competition. If the results are publicized and general recognition, promotions, and career opportunities of public-sector managers are linked to the relative performance of their offices, divisions, or ministries, it can be a powerful force for improvement in the public sector. However, the league table approach can be demotivating for those at the bottom of the league. Motivation is better fostered by focusing on the gap between the individual unit and the best unit and, as noted, the changes over time. Benchmarking also enables meaningful and realistic performance targets to be set and can help to increase the client orientation of the organization.

Some of the problems encountered in the application of the benchmarking techniques are necessarily the same as those for performance measurement (i.e., capturing the important attributes of the product in question, agreeing on what is to be measured and how to measure it, and ensuring the comparability of performance between organizations). In addition, because benchmarking is a resource-intensive technique, the scope of any single benchmarking exercise must be restricted to the key areas—those that account for the largest component of costs or where the performance gaps are widest, or both. It is also important to avoid excessive detail in collecting data or mapping processes as it could divert effort from the primary purpose of benchmarking, which is identifying better practices and implementing the lessons learned. Finally, a critical success factor in benchmarking is the commitment of the senior management to improving the performance of the organization. (Box 10.2 summarizes Hong Kong's good experience with benchmarking of railway performance.)

Whether the performance improvements produced by process benchmarking are worth the complexity, time, and resources associated with the approach depends largely on the characteristics of the country and the sector concerned. In many cases, it may be best to first establish a solid baseline of good performance indicators and monitor changes in performance over time. Provided that adequate publicity is given to the results, this may allow leaving to the organization itself the task of determining how to sustain excellent performance or improve deficient areas. Thus, as emphasized throughout this discussion, the choice of good performance indicators (and the *process* of choosing them) remains the basic prerequisite.

Outsourcing (Contracting Out)

Outsourcing is discussed thoroughly under the heading of "exit" in chapter 11, but is also germane to the subject of performance in this chapter. Suffice it to say here that outsourcing a public service could under certain circumstances improve performance in terms of cost, quality, or access. Under other circumstances, instead, outsourcing has led to less desirable outcomes than direct service provision by the government. Either way, contracting out the delivery of a public service

BOX 10.2

Benchmarking Mass Transit in Hong Kong

The Mass Transit Railway Corporation (MTRC) carries 2.4 million customers daily and has been consistently rated as one of the best in the world. MTRC conducts performance benchmarking annually. Considerable time was spent at the outset to define the key performance indicators. To improve areas classified as weak, the company set up special task forces that met regularly and made site visits to the best-performing companies to learn from their practices. On the basis of the benchmarking, MTRC revised its supplier selection criteria and created a fully computerized purchasing system, achieving substantial savings, reducing its error rate, and improving the pricing structure because of quantity discounts and better shipping arrangements.

Social and cultural differences make it difficult to adopt in other countries the lessons learned by the MTRC experience. However, the eighteen KPI provide useful guidance, and are listed here. A rank of 1 denotes best comparative performance.

Categories	Key Performance Indicators	MTRC Rank
Financial Performance	1. Total cost per passenger	2
	2. Operating cost per passenger	2
	3. Maintenance cost per revenue car operating km.	5
	4. Fare revenue per passenger	4
	5. Total commercial revenue/Operating cost (including maintenance)	1
	6. Operating cost/Revenue car operating km	3
	7. Total cost/Revenue car operating km	2
Efficiency	8. Passenger journey/Total staff + contractor hours	2
	9. Revenue capacity km/total staff + contractor hours	2
	10. Revenue car km/total staff hours	7
Asset Utilization	11. Passenger km/Capacity km	3
	12. Capacity km/Track km	1
Reliability	13. Revenue car operating hours between incidents	1
	14. Car operating hours/Total hours' delay	1
	15. Trains on time/Total trains	1
	16. Revenue car operating km/Total incidents	1
Service Quality	17. Total passenger-hours' delay per 1,000 passenger journeys	1
	18. Passenger journeys on time/Total passenger journeys	1

Source: Powers (1998).

to a private entity never resolves weaknesses of the administration itself. Also, outsourcing does not relieve the government of its responsibility for the manner in which the service is provided or the work constructed, and for the quality of both.

MONITORING AND EVALUATION (M&E)

Monitoring is the regular tracking of inputs, outputs, outcomes, and processes in a given area of activity. Based on the results of monitoring, evaluation is the systematic assessment of the positive and negative factors affecting the results. The best organizations and the most conscientious workforces will eventually perform less and less well if they are never called to account for the utilization of the resources entrusted to them and for the results they have achieved with those resources. Nor will good performance last and bad performance improve unless the activities are evaluated by external entities with the requisite competence and experience. Monitoring and evaluation are not only instruments of static accountability—the constructive dialogue that good evaluation engenders often generates new ideas for improving performance. Thus, monitoring is necessary for evaluation, and evaluation is necessary to close the feedback loop and improve future performance based on the lessons of past experience.

Monitoring

Effective monitoring must take into account the reality that outputs and outcomes are not equally observable in different government organizations. The literature makes the following distinctions to determine the scope of administrative accountability and hence the mechanisms to put in place to monitor the performance of different government entities:

- in "production organizations"—such as the tax agency or the postal service—both outputs and outcomes can be observed;
- in "procedural organizations"—such as hospital administration, armed forces during peace time, or employment agencies—the outputs can be observed but not the outcomes;
- in "craft organizations"—such as law enforcement or the judiciary—outputs may not be meaningful, but outcomes can be evaluated; and
- in "coping organizations"—such as the diplomatic service—neither the outputs nor the outcomes can be observed and process indicators are paramount.

Monitoring and evaluation are most applicable at both ends of the public service continuum. It is at the "bottom end"—the interface with the citizens—that the connection between physical outputs and accountability is clearest and most immediate (e.g., trash collection, pest control, water purification). But it is at the "top end" of policy review and program formulation that process indicators are most relevant, and performance can in those cases be assessed by judicious feedback from the main participants in the process.

Evaluation

By Objectives or by Results?

The classic approach to evaluation consists of assessing the degree of achievement of the objectives stated at inception of the task. The pragmatic approach consists of assessing the results actually achieved, whether or not they match the initial objectives. The two approaches do not necessarily produce the same verdict.

The classic approach has been criticized for lending itself to excessive formalism and enabling a mutation of simple and useful ideas into monsters of red tape. A case in point is the transformation of the concept of "logical framework" (usually abbreviated as "logframe") from a simple and useful instrument to spell out the key links between objectives and activities into long and indigestible matrices assembled to meet bureaucratic requirements. The pragmatic approach has been criticized because it can become an alibi for perennial postponement of reckoning and accountability by evading the simple requirement to be explicit in advance about the objectives to be pursued. On balance, most organizations, including public organizations, have found it best to complement the classic approach of evaluation by objectives with some form of mid-course assessment of actual results and the ensuing revision of the initial objectives. Thus, evaluation shades into supervision.

Program Evaluation

Program evaluation is a systematic effort to identify and measure the effects of government policies and programs. The more sophisticated forms of evaluation—experimental design and time-series analysis—involve the collection and statistical analysis of large volumes of data to isolate reliably the effects of the program from other factors that might have caused these effects (impact evaluation). Case studies provide less reliable information about causes and effects but have proven useful in identifying ways of improving efficiency. For an impact evaluation to be useful there must be clear agreement on the matter being examined and the data required to provide a reliable answer. Those performing the evaluation must have the professional skills and resources needed to collect and analyze the data. The evaluator often must depend heavily on the cooperation of operating units to gain needed access and to collect data. Program evaluation itself, like value-for-money audit (see chapter 6), must show that it is cost-effective relative to the improvements identified or the progress expected.

The Link to the Budget Process

There isn't much point to monitoring and evaluating performance unless the results of the evaluation are systematically used to strengthen accountability and improve future performance. As noted earlier, one should beware of mechanistic links between the evaluation findings and actions to be taken—especially in the process of preparation of the government budget. The evaluation findings can and should be taken into explicit consideration. However, a robust dialogue on performance between knowledgeable civil servants familiar with the hiding places of bureaucratic skeletons is far more effective than the uncritical use of formulas.

This leads to a strong word of caution about the use of formal, detailed contracting *within* the public administration. While some highly developed countries have gone in that direction—with mixed success—diminishing returns set in quickly. In brief, while an explicit (and therefore written) *understanding* of the key results expected is useful for the later dialogue on performance, it must not be allowed to expand into detailed fine-print "contracts," which can dilute accountability and lead only to a time-consuming paper chase. The exercise of judgment and good sense is essential, and the guiding rule for monitoring and evaluation remains the KISS principle: "Keep It Simple, Sir."

Introducing M&E in Developing Countries[17]

The standard assumption is that M&E capacity should be created within the government itself. Whether this is correct or not, it is surely fallacious to assume from the start that because evaluation *of* government activities is important, it must be conducted *by* government. In-house evaluation has the obvious advantage of inside expertise, savvy, and intimate operational knowledge of the programs being evaluated (as in Australia). The other side of the coin is a natural tendency to overstate results and, where accountability systems are weak or nonexistent, even to provide a coat of whitewash to failed programs.[18] The advantages of external evaluation are, first, presumptively stronger independence, and second, the greater probability that the evaluators are familiar with similar programs in other sectors or other countries.[19] The disadvantage may be a lack of understanding for the operational realities of the organization.

These advantages are not exclusive, however. In-house evaluation organs can be guaranteed a degree of independence close to that enjoyed by external entities. Conversely, if external evaluators contribute on a regular basis, they will develop the intimate understanding of operations that is needed for an informed assessment. The disadvantages, too, are not exclusive: in particular, if the governance climate is not conducive to candid evaluations, it is most likely that even the best external evaluations will be suppressed, or distorted to produce the desired results. Therefore, the choice is entirely pragmatic.

Thorough evaluations require substantial input by economists, engineers, scientists, researchers, auditors, and other specialists—skills that are in limited supply in most developing countries and are best used in designing and running sound programs, not in evaluating them. Thus, it is inevitable that evaluation in developing countries should be conducted largely on the basis of expertise external to the government and, in many cases, external to the country. At the same time, an organic link to the regular administrative apparatus must be created. The approach to creating M&E capacity in African developing countries should therefore rest on two complementary efforts: (1) relying on external evaluations, especially for major expenditure programs; but (2) working to create a small but strong in-house capacity to design, guide, contract, *and monitor* the external evaluators. Such in-house capacity should not be pigeonholed into a small "evaluation ghetto," but should instead enjoy systematic connections to the public finance function and to the line ministries, in whatever manner is effective in the specific country.

One more observation: the capacity to monitor and evaluate government action is too important to be left entirely to government either directly or through contracting. One should also consider possibilities for using the users of services themselves to provide feedback and contestability. Appropriate participation by civil society can augment limited governmental capacity for M&E. The role of NGOs is especially relevant here. The Uganda experience, among others, has shown the potential contribution of NGOs to effective M&E as well as the NGOs concern with the risk of being co-opted. The issue is delicate, but a balance between cooperation and independence can be struck.

Other lessons of experience in introducing M&E capacity in developing countries are summarized in Box 10.3. Of these, perhaps the most important is that excessive monitoring, through a large number of indicators, produces little effective monitoring and insufficient evaluation.

THE SITUATION IN THE UNITED STATES

Given the abundance and rich diversity of monitoring and evaluation activities in the United States by governments as well as nongovernment entities, watchdog organizations and, increasingly, the

BOX 10.3

Some Lessons from the Experience of Introducing M&E in
Developing Countries

• Simply placing M&E on the government agenda is itself a significant accomplishment (as in Sri Lanka and Malawi).
• It is also significant to help build a common monitoring and evaluation
language and conceptual understanding (as in Egypt).
• Cross-fertilization of ideas and country comparisons can be helpful, as in
the effective use of the Chile experience for other countries.
• An excessive focus on "macro-level" public management efficiency issues
detracts from robust M&E of services to the public—thus, better links of evaluation activities with line ministry staff and service providers are important.
• Similarly, focusing M&E on the provision of services of specific sectors can be
a highly promising entry point for M&E development, which is often neglected.
• The mere availability of funding is insufficient to advance the M&E agenda
if it does not include efforts at capacity building for the long term.
• Too much monitoring, through an excessive number of indicators, produces
little real monitoring.
• Inattention to bureaucratic realities produces delays or weak ownership.
• It is not advisable to rely overmuch on one-time workshops or similar
events. While these events can be important to explain the role of monitoring
and evaluation, sustained capacity-building efforts are required to improve the
performance of the public sector on a lasting basis.

Source: Adapted from *Evaluation Capacity-Building Self-Evaluation*, Operations
Evaluation Department, World Bank, 2004. See particularly the Uganda and Egypt
case.

blogs, this short section is limited to providing a mini case study of faulty government monitoring of
public services and describing the main program evaluation instrument of the federal government.

Public Health in the United States: Who Monitors the Monitors?

Medicare is the nation's largest health insurance program, covering nearly 40 million Americans
(65 and older, and persons with disabilities) at a cost of over $200 billion per year. (An additional
36 million people are eligible for the state-level health care program, Medicaid.) Since almost
all these medical services are performed by private providers, adequate monitoring of the quality
of care is paramount. The federal government has contracted out such monitoring to fifty-three
private "Quality Improvement Organizations" (QIOs—one per each state, plus Puerto Rico, the
Virgin Islands, and the District of Columbia). Under a contract worth over $400 million a year,
the QIOs are supposed to measure health care quality, work with doctors and hospitals to improve
care, investigate patient complaints, and recommend appropriate sanctions. In the initial phase after

establishment of the system in 1982, the emphasis was on peer review to identify cases of violation of professional standards. In the second phase, the emphasis shifted to quality measurement. The rub is that QIOs consist mainly of doctors and health-care company executives.

Critics allege that the domination of QIOs by these doctors and executives has resulted in secrecy, lack of oversight, and little accountability to consumers and taxpayers and that the organizations have mutated from impartial inspectors to interested partners of hospitals, nursing homes, and doctors—becoming highly profitable and paying generous salaries and perks to executives. A *Washington Post* inquiry in July 2005 found that:

- QIOs have been collecting nearly as much from their outside work as from Medicare, with total revenue of more than $500 million;
- eleven QIO executives received over $300,000 in salary and benefits and thirty others more than $200,000;
- in New Jersey alone, PRONJ, the Healthcare Quality Improvement Organization of New Jersey, Inc., in 2003 paid more than $500,000 to its directors, including thirteen physician board members who received between $34,000 and $45,000 each;
- patients have just a 1-in-4 chance of having their complaints investigated, and the number of QIO sanctions against doctors and hospitals on quality matters has dropped dramatically, from hundreds each year to a few;
- even more offensive, the results of QIO investigations are kept secret, including from the patient's family, who have to sue in order to find out how their loved one was mistreated.

In response, the government initiated certain measures to improve the functioning of the system, described in a 2006 report to Congress.[20] Although the majority of these measures are empty rhetoric, certain actions are likely to bite, mainly by increasing the competition for QIO contracts and directing QIOs to focus on the local achievement of national quality goals. However, given the continuing basic problem of domination of the QIOs by medical industry interests, it is not clear than these measures will have a lasting impact on the monitoring of medical services.

Whether the QIOs will improve or not, this experience illustrates how risky it is to contract out the regulatory function unless government exercises robust monitoring of the monitors themselves. It also shows that the phenomenon of "capture"—de facto private control of administrative action (see chapter 3)—is equally applicable to private exploitation of administrative *inaction*. What is important is not whether the regulations are administered by public or private operators, but the strength of the accountability mechanisms. Indeed, outsourcing can reduce transparency, on the excuse of company confidentiality, and dilute accountability even more, as in this case. Despite the publicity given to these problems, given the confluence of interests between the monitors and the monitored there isn't much of a chance that health care monitoring will improve.

The "PART" Approach to Program Evaluation in the United States

In contrast with mechanistic and overly complex attempts in the 1960s and 1970s at linking resources and results, a simpler and much more effective evaluation approach was introduced in the United States in 2002. This is the "Program Assessment Rating Tool" (PART), by which the White House Office of Management and Budget (OMB) uses a 30-item survey to evaluate four dimensions of any program—objectives, planning, management, and results. The expenditure program is then ranked along a four-point scale, from "ineffective" to "adequate," "moderately effective," and "effective" (www.whitehouse.gov/omb, keyword "PART").

In so doing, the OMB approach eschews the technocratic delusion of the earlier initiatives and combines to some extent the classic evaluative emphasis on the match between results achieved and results expected, with the pragmatic consideration of good results whether or not they are tightly linked to the original objectives. As of mid-2005, OMB had evaluated more than 600 federal expenditure programs (accounting for about 60 percent of the Federal budget), of which fewer than 30 percent had been found "ineffective"—thus belying the myth of systematic inefficiency in the federal government. Equally important, the results are placed on the White House Web site, which creates a potential for public comment and reaction, and thus improved accountability.

There are four interrelated reason why the PART approach is more sensible and useful than the earlier methods:

- its relative simplicity;
- the comparatively low cost;
- the lack of a mechanistic link to budget allocations; and, most importantly,
- the space allowed for informed individual *judgment.*

Precisely because of these advantages, the approach stands or falls on the credibility of those doing the evaluations. This credibility can only flow from technical integrity and absence of politicization of the process. So far, OMB implementation of the PART method appears to have been highly professional and relatively bias-free. (The independent Government Accountability Office also conducts in-depth evaluations of government programs—see chapter 11.) As the public learns to use more and more the valuable information placed on the OMB Web site and add its "voice" to the results, the quality of government expenditure can be expected to gradually increase.

GENERAL DIRECTIONS OF IMPROVEMENT

Injecting formal result-related elements into public management requires great care, both because better performance orientation is critical for improving public administration and because there are many wrong ways and only a few ways of doing it right. In particular, special care is needed not to yield to the "tyranny of the measurable"; very often in the public sector the nonmeasurable results are the most important ones.

The suitability of performance measurement and the specific indicators themselves depend on the sector in question, among other things. Thus, the subject must be addressed in country-specific and time- and sector-specific ways. However, there are general lessons of international experience concerning the overall approach to fostering better administrative performance in all countries:

- The goal of stronger performance orientation should not be confused with the specific means for achieving it. There are many ways to foster performance, including quantitative results indicators, qualitative indicators, dialogue, moral suasion, and peer pressure.
- When performance indicators are appropriate, they should be piloted at first without making wholesale changes in administrative or budgetary systems.
- The process of choosing the right performance indicators is critical and should assure upfront involvement of both "front-line" employees and the users of the public service in question.
- The probable impact of introducing certain performance indicators on individual behavior should be considered—especially in multiethnic societies.
- The use of the different input, output, outcome, and process indicators of performance should be tailored to the specific sector and program in question.

- A combination of a *few key* indicators should be used to assess performance rather than either a single one or a large number of indicators.
- The indicators should meet the "CREAM" test—they should be Clear, Relevant, Economical, Adequate, and Monitorable.
- Swift and predictable consequences for both good and inadequate performance are critical; however, while indicators can underpin a robust dialogue on the performance of administrative units, they should not be mechanically linked to procedures, staffing decisions, or budgetary allocations.
- Periodic assessment of the performance of the performance management system itself is necessary to continually assure that the concrete benefits outweigh the costs of administering the system.

In developed countries, the process of introducing performance indicators into the public administration is already advanced and, in certain sectors, well-established, and no general recommendation can be advanced other than performing periodic reality checks, by seeking direct user feedback when possible.

In developing countries, the process can consist of the following stages:

- Select one or two government departments that provide services directly to the public;
- Define, in consultation with front-line employees and service users, a few key and simple performance measures that entail an acceptable cost of collection, reporting, and monitoring (including transaction cost);
- Monitor closely the functioning and impact of the measures;
- Debug the measures and adjust and revise as needed, again with input from employees and the users;
- Gradually expand the application of performance measures to other governmental areas;
- Stop when reaching the point of diminishing returns.

QUESTIONS FOR DISCUSSION

1. "Good performance has always been the key objective of public administration." Discuss.
2. "Performance should be defined and assessed in terms of actual results." Discuss.
3. Pick one of the following two statements and make a credible argument for it:
   a. "The challenge of measuring performance in the public sector consists of identifying that indicator of results that best sums up the objective of the activity."
   b. "The challenge of measuring performance in the public sector consists of identifying all indicators that are relevant to the objective of the activity."
4. "Because you can only hold managers strictly accountable for specific outputs, managerial performance should be assessed in terms of a combination of output indicators." Comment.
5. "Ultimately, appraising personnel performance is a subjective judgment of the manager concerned, and the various assessment methods serve mainly to rationalize that subjective judgment (as well as provide jobs for personnel administrators)." Agree?
6. "Man does not live by bread alone." What are the implications of this statement for motivating government employees?
7. Give an illustration of the difference between metrics and process benchmarking, and on that basis identify the relative advantages of the two approaches.
8. "In Monitoring and Evaluation, there is usually way too much monitoring and too little evaluation." Discuss.
9. What's the point of a good program evaluation methodology such as the PART system devel-

oped by the U.S. Office of Management and Budget, if most program selection and funding decisions are made for political reasons?

NOTES

1. See Bird (1971). There is evidence that Wagner's Law may have ceased to be operative in developed countries in the early 1990s, but it is still very much in evidence in developing countries, where the size of government is closely correlated with the country's per capita income (Schiavo-Campo, 1998).

2. See Hood (1991) for an exposition of the NPM, and Borins (1995) and Savoie (1995) for a summary of the arguments for and against the NPM approach, respectively.

3. In the ancient adage, man does not live by bread alone. A reductionist view of human nature may eventually sharply reduce public sector effectiveness and increase the risk of corruption.

4. These measures are discussed in a variety of sources, including Fédération des Experts Comptables Européens (1991).

5. *Impact,* often used as a synonym for outcome, is more properly defined as the value added from the activity—the "gross" outcome minus the contribution from other entities or activities. The notion is important in that it takes some account of favorable or unfavorable circumstances beyond the control of those responsible. However, impact (in this sense of value added) is nearly impossible to measure and is not discussed further in this chapter.

6. Note that not all useful data concerning a public service are necessarily performance indicators. For example, the percentage of arrests stemming from citizens' direct complaints is a useful statistic for law enforcement, but says little about the performance of the law enforcement apparatus.

7. For process indicators, accountability can be stronger or weaker depending on the nature of the public activity. Thus, it is easy to assess a doctor's "bedside manner" by asking her patients, but difficult to hold a politician's advisor responsible for the politician rambling on beyond the time allowed for his speech.

8. This section has drawn on Commonwealth Secretariat (1996); Armstrong (2006); Milkovich (1997); Lovrich in Perry, ed. (1989); Klingner and Nalbandian (1998); Riley (1993); Corrigan et al. (1999); Pearce in Perry, ed. (1989); and Rich in Perry, ed. (1989).

9. Klingner and Nalbandian, 1998.

10. Lovrich, 1989.

11. However, unsatisfactory performance during the probationary period, which is normally required for government employment, should result in termination of the employee rather than counseling.

12. As reported in the *Economist,* May 20, 2006.

13. Kellough and Lu review the rationale and expected advantages of merit pay and identify the four most critical problems associated with merit pay practices in the public service. Ingraham questions the basis for the common assumption that pay-for-performance has been successful in the private sector to begin with, explores the additional difficulties of implementing the practice in the public sector, and demonstrates the gap between expectations and realities by examining the experience of the United States and other developed countries.

14. We owe this illustration to Michael Heppell.

15. Shand (1998) lists many more requirements for performance indicators. However, several are desirable but not mandatory and others are in fact different dimensions of the five requirements listed earlier.

16. We are indebted to Naved Hamid and Gie Villareal for the main points made in this section.

17. This section is based in part on Schiavo-Campo (2005).

18. As described in the last section, the United States has created a framework to address this problem. Line agencies are required to rate the performance of all their programs. These self-ratings are reviewed and often overridden by the OMB, which manages the budget process in the federal government. The OMB's reviews of the departments' self-ratings include an assessment of the reliability of the departments' M&E findings, and constitute, de facto, a critique of departments' M&E methods. However, these approaches are much too demanding in terms of data and resources to be of value in most developing countries.

19. Chile is one of a small number of countries that rely largely on commissioning independent evaluations, although the process is managed by a government ministry. In contrast with the U.S. approach, the cost-effectiveness of the Chile approach may be a useful example for developing countries.

20. DHS, "Improving the Medicare quality improvement organization program," July 2006.

PART III

GOVERNANCE AND PUBLIC MANAGEMENT

CHAPTER 11

Accountability: "Exit," "Voice," and Institutions

> Power tends to corrupt, and absolute power corrupts absolutely.
> —*John Dalberg-Acton, 1887*

WHAT TO EXPECT

Lord Acton's dictum on the corrupting effect of power has been degraded by overuse to the unfortunate status of cliché. Nonetheless, it remains as relevant today as it was in 1887 or, for that matter, in 1887 BCE. Conceptually, the dictum is at the basis of Montesquieu's doctrine of separation of powers later enshrined in the U.S. Constitution (see chapter 4), because all concentration of government power is dangerous. Practically, without the requirement to give account of one's use of power and to accept consequences for misuse and abuse, management cannot be either efficient or equitable either in the public or the private sector. At various times in different countries, people living under oppressive and corrupt regimes have yearned for a "Man on Horseback"—a strong leader who could sweep out the thievery and extortion and give them a clean and well-functioning system. Unfortunately, this wish carries the seed of its own demise: history is full of examples of unaccountable leaders who started with good intentions and ended as corrupt as their predecessors because there were no mechanisms to *keep* them honest. Good public management does not need a Man on Horseback; it needs systems to make Men on Horseback unnecessary. Among those systems, none are more important than those that provide for accountability of public officials, both internal accountability within the administration and external accountability vis-à-vis the citizens. The chapter reviews the role of "exit"—the extent to which citizens have access to alternative sources of service—and "voice"—the extent to which they are able to complain to seek better government performance. The discussion includes the advantages and risks of outsourcing, and the chapter concludes with a review of the institutions that enforce public accountability. Suggested general directions of improvement in accountability round out the chapter. (Neither this chapter nor subsequent ones includes a special section on the situation in the United States, owing to the breadth and diversity of the issues discussed.)

THE ROLE OF "EXIT" AND "VOICE" IN PUBLIC ACCOUNTABILITY

In his pioneering work of 1970, Albert O. Hirschman, the brightest economist never to get the Nobel Prize, identified two determinants of external accountability. One is the opportunity for

325

the citizens to *exit* the government system, i.e., the extent to which they have access to alternative suppliers of a given public service (or access to good substitutes for the service). The other is *voice*, the opportunity for the citizens to complain and seek better performance from public service providers, while remaining within the government system of supply. We will give plenty of examples and illustrations later. For now, a brief description of the two concepts.

. "Exit" is an economic mechanism operating through competition and the market, while "voice" is more of a political response operating through organizations such as political parties, voluntary agencies, and citizen groups. "Voice" is the degree to which the public can influence the quality and access of the public service by some participation or expression of protest or views (irrespective of whether exit options exist).

The two forms of external accountability are not mutually exclusive, and exit and voice options can both substitute for and complement each other. Certain activities are difficult to specify or are not "contestable," i.e., the entry and exit of competitors is difficult. In these cases, there are no realistic exit options. Improved delivery can result only through voice mechanisms, and through incentives and penalties for better performance by the civil servants responsible. For other services, it is instead possible to offer formal exit options to citizens through the use of markets, the voluntary sector, and community-managed service delivery.

People's decision to use either exit or voice, or a combination, will depend partly on the cost of acquiring information about alternative suppliers, in the case of exit, and on the cost of various forms of collective action, in the case of voice. The relative effectiveness of exit and choice is determined by the characteristics of the service, such as the degree of market failure, economies of scale, barriers to information, education, legal and other factors. Poor and marginal population groups are particularly limited in their use of either voice or exit, owing to their inability to move or to access more expensive alternative providers. This makes governmental or nongovernmental initiatives to expand exit and voice options especially beneficial for the poor and most vulnerable.

EXIT: PROVIDING CHOICES AND OUTSOURCING[1]

Providing Choices

As noted, exit is the extent to which the public has access to alternative suppliers, public or private, of a given public service. Government should behave toward consumers *as if* they had an exit choice, even when it has a full monopoly. *Contestability* is the key concept here. Contestability is *potential* competition: under certain circumstances, the very possibility that new competitors can enter the market is sufficient to make a monopolist behave almost as if he were operating in a competitive market and keep monopoly profit down, in order not to induce potential rivals to enter the industry. The government, by appropriate policies, can create contestability for the public providers of services and thus spur them to greater efficiency and responsiveness.

In the absence of contestability mechanisms, the population may in time be led to exercising more drastic forms of exit, such as refusing to pay taxes and service charges or organizing locally to have private suppliers deliver the service (e.g., private trash collection or water supply). When exit takes the literal form of out-migration of skilled professionals and private firms, it has a lasting impact on the economic and revenue base of the local or national government concerned. With globalization (see chapter 1), most governments have had to recognize this risk and accordingly pay more attention to creating "moderate exit" options through providing contestability for public service delivery.

Exit possibilities depend on the scope for unbundling the service. An apparent government monopoly of a service does not preclude the operation of small and informal private suppliers in slums and peripheral areas not covered by the government. In many cities with an official monopoly of public transport, the share of private transport can be as high as 90 percent. Health care, too, is typically provided by a variety of private practitioners, and neighborhood organizations often make up for the inadequacy or absence of other public services. Even for services that can only be provided by the government, extreme inefficiency will generate exit pressures. For the poor, however, exit possibilities are more theoretical than real, if they cannot afford to take advantage of them.

An increasing cause for concern in developing countries is the exclusion of large numbers of the poor from services provided by public monopolies. In the long run, there is no contradiction between public-sector efficiency and the encouragement of exit alternatives. On the contrary, the active search for alternatives to direct governmental service delivery is an essential means of stimulating public efficiency and—more importantly—assuring that the basic needs of the poor and the vulnerable are met.

Outsourcing Public Services[2]

The General Setting

Direct service provision by government bodies continues to be the predominant form of public service delivery. In most countries, the proportion of local and national expenditure on public services delivered through private business and voluntary organizations is not significant. However, interest in private delivery of public services has grown in both developed and developing countries in the last decade. "Contracting out" (or "outsourcing"—we will use the two terms interchangeably, despite minor technical distinctions between them) public services is an important way in which government can provide citizens with an exit option at the same time as it spurs efficiency within the public administration itself.

The prospect of losing customers is a well-known and powerful stimulus for performance in a private enterprise, but—despite the absence of the profit motive—can also prod a public sector organization to perform better. In addition, contracting the delivery of social services to the private sector can, if done right and under certain circumstances, lead to savings in and of itself. Therefore, the possibility of contracting out certain public services or functions should rank among the questions to be asked periodically in government organizations.

Outsourcing is the delivery of public services by an external organization or person under contract with the government organization that is (and remains) responsible for the service. Outsourcing is thus different from "privatization," which is the transfer of the function itself out of the government into the private sector. (Outsourcing certain aspects of production is even more widespread in private companies than in government, enabled by the rapid improvement in information and communication technology, and is increasingly related to the globalization trend discussed in chapter 1.)

Although the practice has experienced a recent resurgence, it is common in history although mainly on the revenue side. "Tax farming" (i.e., contracting with private entities for the collection of taxes due the government), was prevalent in ancient China, Greece, Rome, parts of medieval Europe, the Ottoman Empire and, more recently, Thailand, which as late as 1875 did not have a governmental organization for tax collection.

In the United States, the delivery of certain public services has been occasionally outsourced since the late 1970s, but in a limited way—for example, the operation of cleaning services and cafeterias in government buildings. The practice of outsourcing did not really take off until the

1990s, with the "National Performance Review." Currently, federal functions are distinguished between those that are "inherently governmental," which may not be outsourced, and the remainder. (See chapter 2 for a discussion of the basic roles of government and of "public goods.") All functions that are not considered "inherently governmental" (which employ almost half of the federal workforce) are potentially eligible to be contracted out, under detailed guidelines promulgated by the Office of Management and Budget.

Reasons for Outsourcing

Whatever the reason for contracting out, the contracting agency always remains responsible to the government and to the population for the quality of service and for the contract outcome. The reasons for contracting out include one or more of the following (Rehfuss, 1993):

- reducing service delivery costs,
- lack of in-house expertise;
- providing a higher-quality product;
- obtaining a yardstick for cost comparisons between government delivery and private delivery ("market testing");
- gaining access to specialized skills and equipment;
- avoiding high start-up costs;
- initiating new functions;
- encouraging the private sector to develop a particular line of business.
- limiting the size of the permanent government workforce;
- weakening the influence of employees;
- avoiding labor rules or restrictions; and
- keeping flexibility to adjust the size of the program.

Private companies are often contracted to perform certain tasks internal to government agencies, such as courier services, cleaning and security, and travel, normally based on straight cost advantages. Of greater relevance to the citizens' exit options is the manner of external service provision. Other than direct provision by the government department, three modes of service provision exist: regulated, grant, and contract. In the regulated mode, the government is involved in planning, but not in financing or producing the service (for example, enforcement of land zoning regulations). Under the grant mode, the government provides financing for studies or technical and legal assistance, but doesn't plan or produce the service. Under the contract mode, the state both plans and finances the service, but contracts out its delivery (for example, the maintenance of parks and community centers).

Because different services require different modes of provision, the nature and mix of the services provided by a government agency will determine whether and how reliance on outsourcing is appropriate. Services never recommended for contracting out are mainly those involving the use of the state coercive power (e.g., police) and essential services whose disruption would create a major crisis (e.g., air traffic control). Even in those cases, however, partial aspects of those services, but not all, may be potentially suitable for outsourcing—such as security for diplomats abroad.

When Is Outsourcing Appropriate?

Contracting out must not be considered as a cure-all for inefficient service provision by government agencies—nor should it be allowed to lead to a reduction of voice and exit for users, or to open new opportunities for corruption and waste of resources. Consistent with a central theme of this book, Rosenbloom and Piotrowski (2003) argue that "scholars and practitioners, anxious to improve administrative practice, often jump from accurate diagnosis of complex problems to the prescription of untested, flawed, or ill-conceived reforms—many of which fail largely because they emphasize managerial values over political and constitutional values." This explanation of an "anxiety to improve" is more benevolent than the alternative hypothesis that, since the late 1990s, outsourcing has been increasingly used in doctrinaire fashion without regard to its probable cost-effectiveness, and occasionally designed to benefit the private supplier rather than the taxpayer. This hypothesis is easily tested. If in the specific instance outsourcing fails to produce a net cost saving and/or an improvement of service quality, it is reasonable to conclude that it was either ideological or corrupt or both--and hence inefficient and a waste of taxpayers' money. For example, contractors from Blackwater Security Consulting—mostly former soldiers—have been hired by the State Department to protect diplomats in Iraq at an average cost of $1,100 per day, more than ten times the cost of using a current soldier to perform the same duty.[3]

Accordingly, contracting out of public services should be considered only if six basic conditions are met:

- there are demonstrable cost savings or improved benefits to the users;
- outputs relevant to the desired outcomes can be clearly specified;
- performance can be effectively monitored;
- the contracts can be enforced;
- robust accounting and audit mechanisms are in place; and
- the established procedures for competitive contract award are strictly followed.

Accordingly, contracting out is of particular relevance for local government services—sometimes as the consequence of limits on local government staff, more often because of the efficiency advantages of private delivery of certain local public services. Major areas of local government contracting include airport operations; building maintenance; security; vehicle maintenance and repair; parks, landscaping, and recreation facilities; waste collection and disposal; streetlights and road maintenance; and similar services meeting the six conditions listed. In some developed countries, local government is required to submit most internal and external services to competitive bidding. (For example, the Australian state of Victoria requires 50 percent of budget-financed activities to be submitted to competitive bidding.) The corresponding government departments are thus put under pressure to bring their cost and quality of services to the level of the most-responsive private bidder if they wish to continue to provide the service and thus retain their staff and resources. Actual experiences vary widely in different countries and within the same country, as illustrated in Box 11.1.

Outsourcing also requires making distinctions between different facets of a public function. For example, while the notion of outsourcing law enforcement in general is absurd, contracting out specific aspects of law enforcement may be efficient. In addition to the use of private security services, which are common, this point is exemplified by the growing pressures for outsourcing the management of prisons in the United States—see Box 11.2.

The Special Case of Build-Operate-Transfer Schemes

Build-operate-transfer (BOT) or build-lease-transfer (BLT) schemes relate to private financing of public investment. In BOT schemes, the private sector finances the initial investment; recoups

BOX 11.1

Outsourcing: The Good, the Bad, and the Ugly

In *Argentina,* the city of Buenos Aires delegated in the late 1990s to a private consortium the management and investment responsibility for its water and sanitation systems. Under the 30-year concession, the consortium was to invest $4 billion in upgrading, rehabilitating, and extending the systems. In the first three years, the consortium brought dramatic operational and financial improvements through reduced waste and higher bill collection rates. The success can be traced to the significant steps the Argentine government took to ensure the financial viability of the concession: raising tariffs in advance, assuming the state water companies' liabilities, financing a voluntary retirement program, providing a guarantee that the concession company would be permitted to cut off service to consumers for nonpayment, and creating an independent regulatory authority to prevent politicization of the concession.

In *Malaysia,* the government signed in 1993 a similar 28-year concession with a private consortium to upgrade, rehabilitate, and extend the entire country's sewerage system. Progress under the $2.8 billion contract was slow, primarily because of significant public and commercial backlash from tariff collection and large tariff increases. Malaysia's experience points to the unique risk allocation issues raised by private provision of retail sanitation services in instances where these services have never been centrally provided before, there is no legal right to cut off service for nonpayment, and sewerage and water services are billed separately.

In the *United States,* the Equal Employment Opportunity Commission (EEOC) performs the essential function of enforcing federal nondiscrimination laws. In 2005, several EEOC district offices were downsized as part of a reorganization. Staff members were transferred and inquiries rerouted to an outsourced private call center staffed by contract workers. The $5 million, 5-year contract was expected to cut EEOC costs by eliminating twenty-one regular staff positions without affecting the volume or quality of responses to inquiries. The staff reduction turned out to be only six positions, for a total savings of $420,000 a year (at an assumed yearly salary of $70,000), or $2.1 million over the life of the contract. The scorecard for this particular instance of outsourcing government work is thus an outlay of $2.50 for each dollar of salary savings. Worse, the private contractors didn't understand the work of the EEOC or their own role in the process, and the volume of calls decreased to one fifth—thus raising the effective cost of the outsourcing to twelve times the savings. Even without taking into account the reduction in the quality of responses, due to the contractors' lack of familiarity with the process, this is a pretty ugly deal for both U.S. taxpayers and the effective enforcement of civil rights laws. Much more expensive, much less effective, much lower quality service: The negative impact of outsourcing is so large in this case that it is impossible to avoid the conclusion that the EEOC call centers were contracted out for purely doctrinaire reasons—or worse.

Source: Finance and Development, March 1997 for Argentina and Malaysia; for the United States, Christopher Lee, "EEOC is Hobbled, Groups Contend," *Washington Post,* June 14, 2006.

BOX 11.2

Privatize Prisons?

The management of prisons is a major and growing issue in the United States, in light of the 2.2 million inmates—proportionately five times as many as in Britain and ten times as many as in Japan. A number of private prison management companies have emerged, accounting in 2005 for over 5 percent of total prison population. While outsourcing all prisons would be both undesirable and impractical, contracting out the confinement of certain categories of prisoners *may* improve their treatment as well as lower the cost.

Private prisons do carry special moral and safety risks. The appropriate comparison, however, is not with an ideal situation of state-run prisons but with their reality, which is notorious for overcrowding, gross abuse of prisoners by prisoners, pervasive influence of prison gangs, and the mixing of violent criminals with persons guilty of comparatively minor infractions—mainly drug-related. In addition to lowering the cost (which in fact has been the case), the option of privately managed prisons may add flexibility to the system by its capacity to respond more quickly to needed expansion of facilities and a greater ability to expand or contract the prison workforce.

The risk is that this lower cost and greater flexibility may lead to lower security and greater mistreatment of inmates. Thus, the case for private prisons is stronger for confining inmates not guilty of violent crimes and for quickly filling temporary capacity problems in the prison system. Even so, there are real issues of visibility and monitoring. Outsourcing prisons may make a positive contribution—albeit limited and partial—but only if the contract includes ironclad transparency and due-process requirements and if security and inmate conditions are monitored as least as effectively as in the state-run prisons.

---

it through the profits from a government concession to operate the project over a determined period; and, at the end of the concession, transfers the assets to the government. In developing countries, BOTs are seen as a means of attracting private and foreign capital. BOT schemes have been used for years in some developed countries[4] (the most publicized being the Anglo-French Channel Tunnel).

Recently, these schemes have been introduced in developing countries. Asia has a variety of BOT projects, including the new airport in Hong Kong, power and railways in China, highways and airports in Malaysia, telecommunications in Thailand, and mass transit in the Philippines. The $1.8-billion Hub River thermal energy project in Pakistan involves BOT arrangements second in size and complexity only to the Channel Tunnel.[5]

Some BOT contracts guarantee the contractor against losses in operating the project (in the example of a toll road, if traffic is less than projected, the government could ensure the servicing of debt contracted for the project).

Managing the Contracting-Out Process

As noted, in certain cases and under specific conditions, contracting out can be an effective tool for promoting efficiency and improving the delivery of certain public services. When reviewing line ministries' budget requests, it is always advisable to ask whether a more cost-effective private solution could exist to implement the various programs and, if the answer is yes, to explore the possibility of contracting out the service. However, the process must be carefully managed, including the following seven stages:

- identify specifically the activities to be contracted out, and specify clearly the objective of the outsourcing (e.g., cost saving, quality improvement, or expansion of access);
- review issues of coordination between the activities to be contracted out and the other relevant governmental activities;
- assess costs realistically, when possible based on the experience with similar outsourcing;
- evaluate the experience and quality of the contractor;
- consider the contractual options—lump-sum contracts, price-per-unit contracts, shared profits, etc.;
- stipulate clear performance standards and specify provisions regarding contractor nonperformance and dispute resolution; and
- define monitoring procedures—and make sure the government has employees with sufficient technical knowledge to monitor the private delivery of the service.

Even when the case for outsourcing appears solid in principle, practical issues may intervene to cause severe unexpected problems, as in the instance of power distribution in New Zealand, summarized in Box 11.3.

Risks of Outsourcing

Most importantly, as noted, contracting out delivery of a public service does not relieve the government agency from its responsibility for the service, and the various risks of contracting out must be identified and addressed. The three major risk categories are the dilution of constitutional rights, the impact of lack of competition, and fiscal and corruption risks.

Compromising Due Process and Constitutional Rights. As discussed by Rosenbloom and Piotrowski (2003), the constitutional constraints and legal requirements imposed on government agencies in the United States are often not applicable to private entities performing outsourced public administrative activities, and some democratic norms may be lost. This issue has generally been neglected in a debate dominated by cost-effectiveness or ideological considerations. Indeed, the detailed OMB contracting guidelines contain no mention of contractors' responsibility for observing due process norms, or even a reference to the existence of such norms. Except for the prohibition of slavery in the 13th amendment, the U.S. Constitution does not typically apply to purely private relationships, as between a private contractor and its employees. However, a private entity is subject to constitutional constraints by becoming a "state actor," i.e., when it is:

- engaged in a public function;
- effectively controlled by the government;
- a party in a joint public-private venture;

BOX 11.3

Why Did the Lights Go Out in New Zealand?

Following the deregulation of the New Zealand energy industry under the 1992 Energy Companies Act, Mercury Energy Limited was incorporated in October 1993 as the successor to the Auckland Electric Power Board (AEPB). The 1992 Energy Companies Act set the deregulation process in motion by requiring all power boards to come up with a plan to turn themselves into successful businesses. Mercury Energy's plan, which was accepted by the government, included creating shares and placing them in the hands of newly formed Auckland Energy Consumer Trust (AECT). That made the AECT principal shareholder of Mercury Energy. Each year, Mercury Energy was to pay the AECT a dividend of at least 50 percent of its after-tax profit. The AECT, after meeting its operating costs, would then distribute the surplus to customers of Mercury Energy.

On February 20, 1998, a power crisis hit Auckland when four major cables feeding the central business district crashed. International experts engaged by Mercury Energy found various possible causes for the cable failures, including the exceptionally hot and dry weather, problems in the backfill and ground in which the cables were installed, steep slopes down which some sections of the cables were laid, vibrations from road and rail traffic, and the cutting of control cables by contractors.

Whether the causes of the power failure were under the control of Mercury Energy or not, the company's competence, standards, and practices as Auckland's major provider of power have been put into question. The ministerial inquiry distributed blame between Mercury Energy and its predecessor, the AEPB, because both neglected the evidence of increasing unreliability of the cables. Mercury Energy, however, gets a bigger share of the blame, as it seems likely that it did not properly evaluate the risk of supply interruptions from the rising load on unreliable high-voltage cables.

Moreover, the inquiry report concluded that the indirect nature of the trust ownership of Mercury Energy may have had an effect through "absence of clear Board accountability through effective shareholder and/or market disciplines," a vital objective in a network industry with monopoly characteristics. Likewise, Mercury's contracts with its customers did not clearly define what supply risks are involved and unless exclusions and limitations were freely and equitably negotiated between supplier and customer, the supplier should bear the residual liability.

Sources: The Age, Melbourne Online, various issues, 1998; and Rob Laking, Director, Master of Public Management, Victoria University of Wellington, 1998.

- "entwined" with government to the extent of functioning as a single organization; and
- empowered to use government's coercive power (e.g., the power to seize assets).[6]

Hence, one needs to raise the critical question of why the relevant constitutional and administrative norms should not themselves be "outsourced" along with the activity being contracted out—that is, whether contractors should not routinely be made to abide by the same requirements imposed on public agencies (e.g., whistle-blowing and privacy protection, freedom of information, etc.). In certain cases, the answer is obvious: if management of a prison is outsourced, the contractor must assume obligations on how to treat inmates; if a public school is subcontracted, the private management must not be allowed to practice racial discrimination; and so on. In many other cases, the process norms included in a contract differ according to the nature of the service. It is important to underline that the decision rests with the executive branch of government. In the United States, for example, nothing would prevent the Office of Management and Budget to require contractors to abide by certain legal norms that would apply if the activity were not outsourced. Transparency of information would be at the top of the list of such requirements, especially to assess responsibility in cases of emerging problems or disasters.

Lack of Competition. A competitive environment is generally necessary to benefit from contracting out. After reviewing several surveys of outsourcing experiences in the United States that showed uneven results, John Donahue (1989) concluded that: "Public versus private matters, but competitive versus noncompetitive usually matters more. . . . Half of a market system—profit drive without meaningful specifications or competitive discipline—can be worse than none."

Fiscal and Corruption Risk. Contracting out is sometimes a way of evading budgetary constraints rather than a deliberate choice on efficiency grounds. In theory, the financial risk should be transferred to the contractor, but government contracts often include explicit or implicit guarantees. When the service is important to the public, if the contractor fails to provide the service correctly or goes bankrupt, the government has no practical alternative but to intervene and give financial support to the activity previously contracted out. Contracting out may also diminish transparency, since it substitutes "commercial confidentiality" for accountability and thus escapes legislative controls.[7]

The fiscal cost may be especially high when the government is obliged to support an ailing project implemented under a Build-Operate-Transfer (BOT) contract, as shown by the Mexican experience described in Box 11.4. Beyond the usual cost-benefit analysis, for projects undertaken under BOT schemes careful analysis is required of the legal aspects and fiscal risks. The bottom line is that a BOT arrangement should never be an excuse to launch an unviable project. In such cases, a wholly private solution must be considered and, when the government cannot find a genuine private solution, the reason is often that the project is not viable in the first place.

The corruption risk of unmonitored outsourcing is of special concern. For example, in a country such as France, where corruption within the civil service is nearly nonexistent, several judicial proceedings at the turn of the century revealed corruption of local authorities through BOT contracts. And in the United States, where contracting out has about doubled since 2000 to almost $400 billion in 2007, an investigation revealed that 118 contracts worth a *cumulative* total of $745 billion had been awarded in a questionable manner and were plagued by mismanagement and overcharging. The reasons are easily found in the violation of the basic conditions for outsourcing, listed earlier: a recent audit of forty-nine privatized contracts revealed that three out of five contracts were awarded uncompetitively, lacked oversight, and raised legal issues.[8]

BOX 11.4

Avoiding Fiscal Discipline by Outsourcing: Two Examples

In the 1980s, local authorities in the United Kingdom, faced with financial problems, resorted to dubious private funding vehicles to evade public expenditure control. These unconventional means of finance involving private parties become known as avoidance instruments. For example, many local authorities "improved" their financial situation by selling assets and then leasing them right back—including the entirety of the sale profit in the current fiscal year but spreading the lease payments over a number of years. In some cases, the practice reached the extreme of realizing cash through sale and leaseback of street furniture, such as lamp posts or parking meters.

In 1987, Mexico launched an ambitious program for contracting out the building and operation of roads under Build-Operate-Transfer arrangements. Initially, the arrangements appeared to be successful, and more than 5,100 km of new toll roads were built. However, construction times turned out to be more than 50 percent longer than had been agreed with the contractors, vehicle traffic was less than two thirds the volume projected, and investment was almost one third higher than agreed. Obviously, on all three accounts the profitability of the roads was a fraction of what had been anticipated. The Mexico economic crisis of 1995 aggravated the financial situation of the toll roads under concession to private companies, forcing the government to implement a plan of emergency support of US$2.2 billion. As a consequence, the participation of the public sector rose to 40 percent of the capital stock of the companies holding the concessions, and the concession terms were extended to allow private investors a greater opportunity to recover their investment. Instead of being spread out between public and private sector, the fiscal risk bounced right back on the Mexican government and was magnified to boot.

Sources: Adapted from David Heald, "Privately Financed Capital in Public Services," The Manchester School (1997); and Robert Barrera, "Contracting-Out Highway Development and Operations in Mexico," in *Contracting Out Government Services,* OECD (1997d).

Baby Steps

In light of the significant potential risks of outsourcing, it is always preferable to begin with small steps toward outsourcing than with impressive-sounding government-wide initiatives. Small improvements permit those involved to gain experience, make timely mid-course corrections, experiment at low cost and, perhaps most important, build consensus within the administration rather than fostering resistance and obstruction. Moreover, it is easier to expand outsourcing practices than to curtail them after they have been undertaken, as strong vested interests are created in the meantime.

Involving the Community

Possibly the single best antidote to the risks of outsourcing is to involve the communities concerned, either in cooperating with the delivery of the service itself or in looking over the shoulder of private contractors. Cooperating with nonprofit agencies and local community groups may also carry special benefits in terms of community development and social capital formation, as discussed to a greater extent in the next chapter.

The Global Dimension of Outsourcing

The advantages of outsourcing have been compounded by the new opportunities offered by globalization—and so have its costs and risks. However, global outsourcing is almost entirely a private sector phenomenon and comparatively few government activities have been contracted out to firms in other countries. The literature on international outsourcing is now extensive. For a good start, the interested reader is referred to a survey done in late 2004 by the *Economist* magazine. Unlike most of the current debate, that survey adopts an explicitly global perspective and thus looks beyond the impact on consumers and workers in the outsourcing country to consider also the impact on the countries on the receiving end of the process.[9]

VOICE: COMMUNICATING AND LISTENING TO THE CITIZEN[10]

To meet collective needs efficiently, governments must be able to ascertain the needs of all segments of the population, including the poor and marginalized groups. This requires opening avenues for individuals, user groups, private organizations, and civil society to express their views. Periodic elections, while indispensable, cannot serve the purpose of providing timely feedback on government performance in specific areas. In almost all countries, therefore, citizens seek to project their views and interests between and beyond elections, in their diverse capacities as taxpayers, consumers of public services, recipients of public assistance, and members of civil society organizations.

Through pressure on policymakers, publicity, protests, and participation in key decisions, the voice of the public can cut through hierarchical control in public administration and help strengthen accountability and motivation. The influence of voice is strengthened when the organizational structure and incentives in the public administration motivate civil servants to be responsive to the public. Internal and external accountability are thus complementary.

Beyond accountability for services, "voice" also requires that governments *consult* the citizens in the formulation of expenditure programs and in major project decisions, in order to secure broad consensus and lay the basis for effective implementation. In developing countries, voice must involve education, social mobilization, and even social marketing, in order to increase the utilization of socially desirable programs such as immunization, family planning, literacy, and nutrition. In developed countries, candid evaluations and open communication channels may instead be sufficient, given the wide use of the internet and an active print, radio, and TV media.

The downside of the exercise of public voice is the risk of delays and administrative overload, and the problems and costs of sorting through a large number of views from the public—some of which may represent only campaigns organized by vested interests. Through the internet, millions of form letters or other communications can be generated to put pressure on politicians or government agencies. It is difficult to ascertain the extent to which such campaigns reflect the concerns and interests of the public, or simply the financial and organizational muscle of the specific interest group. In the United States, the National Rifle Association, the American Association of Retired Persons (AARP), and the American-Israel Public Affairs Committee (AIPAC) have been especially effective in influencing government policy. Riskiest in terms of good governance is the ability of the leadership of these vocal and well-equipped pressure groups to drown out the views of their broader constituency—whether hunters or seniors.

In such cases, the broader constituency has a civic and moral responsibility to voice its disagreement with the position of the group purportedly representing it. This occurred in 2004, with the outcry of a large number of AARP members against the AARP support of the prescription-drug legislation. Unfortunately, it was an exception. It is also important to keep in mind that poor and disenfranchised groups usually do not have the ability to have their voice heard in the first place. *Government does not only have a responsibility to listen, but also to ascertain to whom it is listening and to make an affirmative effort to elicit the views of the broader constituencies and of the less vocal groups as well.*

Establishing a Client Orientation

Citizen or Client?

Government deals with the citizen in various capacities, only some of which resemble the private-sector supplier-customer relationship. It is important to distinguish between citizens and customers. Citizens have rights and responsibilities vis-à-vis their government that go well beyond their role as clients of public services.

The use of the term "customer" or "client" is appropriate when the government delivers specific services (e.g., electricity or medical care). The "client" perspective is central to the rationale for setting up executive agencies for service provision and for hiving off commercial activities from public entities and is valid to the extent that private management principles can improve public service.[11] However, a citizen is more than just a client. The interests of specific client groups may differ from the interests of the taxpayers and the citizens at large. Citizen orientation, then, becomes part of the movement for responsive public administration, which incorporates the interests of the public *both* as customers of specific public services and as members of the polity.

That being said, a client orientation can be a very important component of an overall effort to improve the effectiveness of government. Clear and credible statements of public service standards, action in accordance with these standards, attentiveness to customers, and quick response to complaints are needed to improve the level and quality of public service. The importance of client orientation is especially in evidence where it is lacking—nothing engenders resentment and a cynical attitude toward government as much as a dismissive and contemptuous attitude of government employees toward the citizens they are supposed to serve. Client orientation can also improve the overall quality of the government-citizen interaction by challenging the attitude that citizens are passive recipients of services delivered by a public monopoly, empowering the ordinary citizen to confront government agencies, and replacing the patronage culture with a service orientation that has an element of external accountability.

The potential for client voice is stronger in some services than in others. Services with stronger potential for voice are those which:

- are more visible (e.g., garbage collection as opposed to garbage disposal);
- are locally provided;

- can be commercialized and supplied through the market; and
- can rally user groups into pressuring public agencies.

Citizens' Charters

What Is a Citizens' Charter? A citizens' charter is a proactive initiative by government to organize the actions of government agencies around an explicit and public statement of service standards and obligations. The premise is that, since citizens contribute to all public services as taxpayers and have basic rights as members of society, they are entitled to certain standards of quality, responsiveness, and efficiency. Citizens' charters are statements of principles and standards most appropriate to each different public service, and their content can vary from a general list of performance expectations to a listing of legal rights of the service users.

The principles of the Citizens' Charter movement as originally framed by the Conservative government of Britain's Prime Minister John Major in 1991 were:

- Improving the quality of services;
- Provide choice wherever possible;
- Specify standards and what to expect and how to act if standards are not met
- Give value for the taxpayers' money;
- Assure accountability of Individuals and Organizations; and
- Provide for transparency of rules/procedures/schemes/grievances.

In 1998, these principles were rechristened "Services First" by the Labor government of Prime Minister Tony Blair and elaborated into nine requirements for service delivery, as described in Box 11.5.

The U.K. Citizens' Charter initiative aroused considerable interest around the world and several countries implemented similar programs during the 1990s, e.g., Australia, Belgium, Canada, France, India, Jamaica, Malaysia, Portugal, Spain.

Among the most comprehensive, *on paper*, was India's initiative of May 1997, embedded in an "Action Plan for Effective and Responsive Government." Central and state governments were to formulate citizens' charters, starting with sectors that have a large public interface (e.g., railways, postal service, etc.), and including standards of service and time limits to which the public was entitled, avenues of grievance redress, and a provision for independent scrutiny with the involvement of citizen and consumer groups. As of 2006, 111 Citizens' Charters had been formulated by central government ministries and 668 by various state governments. Most of the national charters are posted on the government's website (www.goicharters.nic.in) launched by the Department of Administrative Reforms in 2002.

How to, and Not to, Implement Citizens' Charters. Whatever the format and scope of the charter, it should be accompanied by information detailing the complaint and compensation procedures, and the names and addresses of offices and officials to be contacted. A mere list of promises without specific information and guidance for the users has little use or credibility.

Next, the actual implementation of citizens' charters must be effectively monitored, which requires political support from the highest level. Typically, monitoring is done by a central unit attached to the office of the competent minister or the cabinet secretary (as in the United Kingdom and Malaysia). Potential implementation problems include inadvertent differences in service quality and cost for customers in different locations, and a discrepancy between the interests of taxpay-

---

BOX 11.5

"Service First" Charter in the United Kingdom

Service First, the new charter program in the United Kingdom, takes the Citizens' Charter of 1991 into the 21st century. It is part of the wider Better Government program to transform and modernize public services. Its nine principles, aimed at improving service responsiveness, quality, effectiveness, and cross-sectoral cooperation, are:

- set standards of service;
- be open and provide full information;
- consult and involve;
- encourage access and the promotion of choice;
- treat all fairly;
- put things right when they go wrong;
- use resources effectively;
- innovate and improve; and
- work with other providers

Service First charters have been adopted and are being implemented by a large number of government agencies and local governments. A "charter mark" scheme organized by the central unit recognizes and encourages excellence in public service by motivating all the charter organizations to apply for and earn a charter mark. A people's panel has been established to give people more say in how services are delivered and how they can be improved. The panel consists of 5,000 persons, representing a cross-section of the country by age, location, background, and other characteristics.

Source: UK Cabinet Office. 1995. *Report of the Committee on Standards in Public Life.* London: HMSO.

---

ers as a whole versus the interests of particular client groups. Realistic evaluation is important as well, to ensure that the benefits of the citizens' charter, in terms of improved service quality and access, justify the costs of introducing and monitoring the initiative. This leads to the most important consideration.

Citizens' charters should not be a mere symbolic gesture with no provision for systematic implementation. This has unfortunately been the case in a number of developing countries, often with the active encouragement of international organizations. Thus, the apparently impressive initiative of India mentioned earlier fell short of the capacity to deliver on the service standards promised—partly because it had been dictated from the top down, without a sense of ownership on the part of employees and consumer groups, who were not consulted.

Citizens' charters can be an impressive adjunct of administrative reform, but only when well designed in participatory ways and efficiently and forcefully implemented. Their effective implementation involves, among other things, a major revision of administrative procedures; appropriate delegation of powers; adequate resources; changes in the attitudes and skills of public employees; and systematic feedback by the service users. Substantial administrative capacity is required in all these respects. The specific obligations under the charter, such as maximum waiting times for patients, passengers on public transport, or the timely redress of complaints, should also correspond to what the agency can *actually* deliver under its resources, staff, and other constraints.

These problems should not discourage practical initiatives towards stronger client orientation in developing and transition countries, where citizens are commonly viewed as passive recipients of public services "granted" by the government. Such initiatives for stronger client orientation should, however, be focused on the most critical areas of public dissatisfaction. Selectivity is therefore a must, starting with services that are more visible and around which citizens can organize themselves, such as primary health care and sanitation, as well as services delivered by local government. Such efforts should be accompanied by consultation with both users and employees and by a quick review of administrative procedures to identify potential stumbling blocks.

In any event, when citizens' charters are seen as mere public relations gimmicks and are not effectively implemented, they can do lasting damage to the credibility of government. If a government is not sure of *both* its commitment and its ability to deliver on certain service standards, it should not promise to do so in the first place—or the "citizens' charter" will be only an expensive joke.

Public Consultation and Feedback

Note at the outset that, in a democracy, the question is not whether the public will voice its feelings, because it will do so in one way or another. Protests, riots, and street violence usually indicate that people are not given reasonable opportunities to express their views, or have their complaints redressed swiftly, or be involved in some way in public programs. These so-called "disorderly voice" movements have affected policies of countries in different areas and even the destiny of governments. The challenge is therefore to build channels for citizen voice to be expressed in orderly ways and before major problems arise. Consultation and feedback overlap and shade into one another, but it is useful to discuss them separately, both because the methodologies differ and because, in general, consultation occurs before decisions are taken, whereas feedback is mainly ex post on the results of these decisions.

Consulting the Public. Organized public consultation can take a range of forms:

- simple transmission of information;
- eliciting substantive input from the public through a dialogue;
- delegating to community representatives the task of developing policy implementation options; and
- granting to citizens control over final decisions (e.g., through the referendum mechanism in Switzerland, or "initiative petitions" in many states of the United States).[12]

Administrative responsiveness to citizens, too, can be enhanced in a variety of ways, as shown in Box 11.6. As noted earlier, the relative infrequency of elections underscores the need for continuous feedback and consultation mechanisms to supplement the electoral mechanism.

Feedback. Feedback mechanisms may seek to obtain information from the clients of a particular public service about the service itself, such as its price, quality, timeliness, access, suitability, or

BOX 11.6

Increasing Administrative Responsiveness to Citizens

From the mid-1990s, most developed countries have given priority to improving the relationship between the administration and the citizens and have introduced measures of different sorts to increase responsiveness to the public.

Procedural measures: Redesigned forms, less red tape, streamlined procedures, staff training, easier access, and the like. Examples include a special office in France and Norway joining civil servants and private sector people to recommend improvements in communication with citizens and in procedures; Austria's review of almost the entire body of laws to eliminate obsolete and unnecessary regulations; Britain's publication of "management guidelines" including standards to minimize the number of forms and simplify communications.

Information measures: Establish communications offices, adopt promotional devices, make information more freely available, and publish government documents. Examples include, in Australia, Holland and Norway, the passage of freedom-of-information laws making all public documents available to citizens unless specifically barred by law; France's establishment of interministerial centers to provide citizens by telephone with information regarding laws, rules, and administrative procedures; New Zealand's directory providing information about manuals, rules and procedures, and the addresses and phone numbers of officials to contact; and, of course, the current Web sites for public agencies, which have simplified enormously transactions with the administration and also spurred internal efficiency improvements. (Such Web sites, now commonplace, were almost unknown ten years ago and a rarity even in the first years of this century.)

Consultative measures: Obtain citizens' feedback on administrative matters affecting them (e.g., the Swedish "red tape commission" to survey the public on the difficulties faced in contacting the administration and possible improvements, a national "suggestion box," and a special directorate in France to analyze media content and to conduct opinion polls).

Institutional measures: Setting up special appeals courts, commissions, and advisory agencies to ensure support and protection for citizens. Examples include an "ombudsman" office to receive appeals against administrative decisions in countries such as Austria, Finland, and Norway; Australia's requirement that public officials must give citizens the reasons for an administrative decision within a month; the surveillance agency within Spain's government to check the activities of service providers, and enforce rules regarding the economic rights of citizens and conflicts of interest.

Source: Adapted from OECD (1997g).

safety; about the helpfulness of staff; or about the effectiveness of the complaint redress mechanism. But clients may be involved beyond giving feedback on consumer satisfaction. There is a continuum of client involvement and discretion, proceeding from information to consultation, partnership, delegation, and control.[13]

The general mechanisms for consultation and feedback may include:

- employee feedback;
- service user surveys;
- publicity and information campaigns;
- public hearings and local meetings;
- user advisory groups and user representation on agency boards;
- channels for consumer complaints;
- comments through the internet; and
- media interventions and feedback from nongovernmental organizations (discussed in chapters 12 and 13).

In addition, ad hoc methods of eliciting consumer feedback include user boards, electronic bulletins, suggestion boxes, focus groups, brainstorming groups, and increasingly, the blogs. User boards and e-comment allow more direct communication about service issues, but are not representative, particularly of the less internet-literate users. Similarly, suggestion boxes may provide useful feedback from individual clients, but again tend to provide a fragmented view of general customer preferences. By contrast, systematic service user surveys follow standard statistical techniques and structured questionnaires. Even though they carry significant resource and time costs, there is no adequate substitute for them. Box 11.7 gives illustrations of user surveys in various countries, and Table 11.1 shows the questionnaire used in Korea.

Citizen Report Cards

An especially promising variant of user surveys is the *citizen report card* pioneered by Samuel Paul's Public Affairs Center in Bangalore, India. The system allow citizens and businesses to give grades to public agencies (1 to 10, A through F, etc.) in terms of such criteria as information availability, transaction costs, staff courtesy and helpfulness, delays, and corruption (Box 11.8). Report cards were used first in a number of Indian states and cities and later imitated with varying degrees of success in several other countries. As of 2006, at least thirty countries have some form of citizen report card for some public service. The report cards have been very effective to stimulate performance and merit very serious consideration in all countries. Their main benefits have been the sparking of a constructive dialogue between government agency and the users and the inducement of healthy competition among government agencies to provide better services. However, they are much more meaningful for tracking changes in agency performance over time than for comparing the performance of agencies to one another—as the circumstances and clients can be very different from one agency to another. (See the discussion of benchmarking in chapter 10.)

As mentioned earlier, improvement in public services is unlikely until there is an effective public demand for such improvement. The responses report cards can engender have a positive effect on both the supply and the demand for good services, giving the public an appreciation of the value of their role in improving governance. Client/user surveys gain in value when people realize that their views influence the performance of agencies or the choice between alternatives: constructive public pressure on service providers tends to generate more such pressure, at the

---

BOX 11.7

Illustrations of User Surveys in Different Countries

Sweden uses an opinion survey instrument called the Swedish National Satisfaction Barometer to contact citizens who are customers of the largest public enterprises and to measure their satisfaction with the services provided. This longitudinal survey provides information on the success of enterprise reforms and spurs efforts to improve services.

A number of cities in the United States, such as Portland, Oregon, survey their citizens in an effort to appraise—and potentially improve—police, fire, sanitation, parks, and a range of other municipal programs. The results of the survey give leaders an indication of how programs are or are not working. Portland is also developing benchmarks in areas like law enforcement and education, and uses an interactive computer-based system to allow people to express their views on these benchmarks in electronic town meetings.

In Canada, the media regularly publishes report cards on issues that are considered important by the public, to complement the information released by government agencies. These media report cards have a discernible effect on policy formulation.

Source: Commonwealth Secretariat (1998b); Barrett and Greene (1994).

---

same time as it expands the public's understanding of the real constraints and problems faced by the public agencies—a "win-win" outcome.

Conversely, if the government agencies take no meaningful action in response to the survey results, the credibility of the exercise disappears quickly and participation rates fall, thus calling into question the representativeness of subsequent surveys. User surveys or report cards can be conducted by nongovernmental bodies as well as by government agencies, but public awareness and subsequent citizen action depend on wide dissemination of results and on mobilization, both of which normally require the active involvement of the government.

Next only to consumers, government employees are an important source of valuable feedback on service quality and problems. If you wish to know the reliability and safety of power supply in a household, you need to ask both the residents of the home and a professional electrician. Thus, Canada among several other countries regularly surveys government employees. The views of employees can be elicited in ways other than formal surveys, of course. For example, in Singapore, where feedback mechanisms for service improvement have existed since 1991, "work improvement teams" elicit feedback from junior employees by offering rewards for the best suggestions. Singapore also appoints a "service quality manager" in each department to receive feedback phoned in by the public using toll-free numbers or online. Finally, to minimize bias in reporting and to ensure the usefulness of this type of feedback, the information obtained in these ways should be supplemented by user surveys, data on complaints, and systematic observation. Incentives and rewards for employees could be linked to consumer satisfaction, as they are in some East Asian countries.

Table 11.1

Customer Satisfaction Survey Questionnaire in Korea

Quality Dimensions	Some Questions Asked
Accessibility and availability of service	Is the service guidebook adequate?
	Is the application procedure easy to understand?
	Was the public servant kind to you when you asked for service?
Convenience	Were application forms and procedures simple and convenient?
	How many branches and counters did you have to visit to receive public service?
	How many documents were needed in public service applications?
	How many times have you been to the government office to receive service?
Speed and correctness	Did the public servant do the job quickly and correctly?
	Are you satisfied with the time required to receive public service?
Pleasantness	Are you satisfied with the parking space at the government office?
	Are the restrooms in the government office sufficient?
	Was the government office clean and orderly?
Responsiveness	Did the public servant let you know beforehand how long it would take to finish the service, and really finished it at the appointed time?
	Did the public servant correct and explain errors when he/she made them?
	Was it easy to receive information that you think can be made public?
Equality	Did the public servant do the job impartially based on relevant regulations?
	Did the public servant offer service impartially without considering the social position of the customer?
	Did the public servant ask for pecuniary or nonpecuniary remuneration when you asked for consultation?
Feedback	Could you anticipate the result of the public service?
	Are you satisfied with the result of the public service?

Source: Asian Productivity Organization (1998).

Voice and Decentralization

As mentioned earlier, the potential for voice is stronger in services that are more visible and are locally provided, thus making it easier to mobilize user groups. Decentralization therefore offers great possibilities for increasing user voice. There are qualifiers. First, and most important, there must exist responsive and representative local structures. Second, there is a risk that improvements will focus on the visible services and inadvertently entail a worsening of the provision of the "invisible" services. The classic example is the attention paid to timely trash collection, compared to the disinterest in the appropriate location of waste disposal sites, the neglect of which can severely damage environmental quality over the long term.

The introduction of user fees, too, can make users more vigilant and encourage them to demand accountability from the service provider, in addition to their impact on revenue and improved resource

BOX 11.8

Citizens' Report Cards in Bangalore

A "report card" on urban public services systematically gathers citizens' opinions on the performance of government service agencies. The first use dates to 1993, when local civic groups in Bangalore, the capital city of the Indian state of Karnataka, used a report card prepared by the Public Affairs Center, a local nonprofit think tank.

The report card was sent to the heads of all agencies and the findings were widely disseminated through the media. The survey was repeated several times to assess changes in responsiveness, information barriers, and corruption in urban public services, from the citizens' point of view.

The first agencies to take action in response to the report card "grades" were the Bangalore Development Authority, the Bangalore Municipal Corporation, and, later, the state Electricity Board. Internal service delivery was reviewed and improved; lower-level staff received appropriate training; and imaginative experiments were initiated in waste disposal and other areas. The results in terms of better quality and timeliness of services were significant and visible in a very short period of time. A virtuous interagency competition for improvement ensued.

Particularly important has been the impulse given by the report cards to the creation of new voice channels. The Municipal Corporation created a joint forum of NGOs and public agencies to address the key concerns and an expert panel of private citizens was formed to monitor the quality of road construction; the State Electricity Board has formalized periodic dialogues with residents' associations; and, by and by, several other agencies have improved their response to customer complaints.

The Public Affairs Center then prepared report cards on services in several other large cities of India, mostly in partnership with NGOs and local civic groups, making it possible to compare citizens' satisfaction with public services in different cities, and was consulted more and more frequently by organizations in other countries wishing to learn from its experience. The practice of report cards has been widely imitated in the subsequent years in a number of other countries. It was successful when the results of the report cards were publicized and followed-up by the government agencies involved. As can be expected, report cards produced nothing but red tape and cynicism when they were introduced for purely cosmetic or public relations reasons.

Source: Adapted from Samuel Paul, Director, Public Affairs Center, Bangalore; personal communications, 2002, and updated.

allocation. (See chapter 6 for a discussion of user fees.) Having to pay something for a public service is a natural way to foster user groups and create new effective voice channels, as shown, for example, by the "water user councils" set up in a number of Latin American and Asian countries. The major risk here is the familiar one of "capture" of the user association by a few powerful individuals or groups. In a semi-feudal society such as central Pakistan, for example, or an upper caste–dominated village in India, the central government has a duty and responsibility to assure that the user group includes representation of all users and minority groups and thus speaks for the "common good" and not only for the interests of the dominant individuals. Of course, if the user group is representative and active, the public service organization must then stand ready to consider and implement changes recommended by the group, as without meaningful follow-up the users' interest will not last long.

Other Channels for Voice

Broad *citizen surveys* provide both detailed and aggregate data on attitudes and expectations and tend to avoid the bias of overly restrictive estimates of needs and wishes that often characterize specific user surveys. Surveys where all the relevant social groups are statistically well represented can be a source of valuable information on a diffuse public. The sample size can vary: it can cover only those persons directly affected by a decision, or a particular sector of the population, or an entire region. (A well-known type of citizen survey is the *opinion poll*.)

Circulating for comment proposed policies or draft legislation to organizations with a direct interest in the outcome or calling for open public comments is sometimes used to elicit broad opinions. *Public meetings* to discuss issues take this type of consultation still further. *Public inquiries* are designed to investigate and report on a specific issue and are conducted formally by a person or group with judicial powers sufficient to receive evidence and compel the attendance of witnesses. These inquiries can help in specific instances, but are expensive and time consuming and should not be overused.

Public hearings, often mandated by law for proposed land use or major proposals, give experts and the general public a structured opportunity to question public officials. In many provinces in India, local officials are required to inform the citizens of development projects at public hearings held by the government at the village and district level. The local people can also take advantage of those hearings to bring out instances of corruption or misallocation of funds, and the government is obliged to report back to them on the action taken. Public hearings do tend to strengthen the legitimacy of proposals. However, once again, it is important to ensure that all the relevant interests are represented and that the hearing does not merely paper over or worsen conflicts over the issue.

Finally, *joint public-private councils* can give open consideration to issues of general concern and have been institutionalized in different ways in a number of countries (Box 11.9). Labor unions, industry, service users, and the government are normally represented in these councils, which relay the viewpoints of these groups to the government agency concerned. These councils can be helpful, too, in creating a consensus for improvements in the interface between the government and the public. However, they can also be easily misused—to whitewash administrative actions already informally decided, to give a mere semblance of consultation, or to silence opposition by co-opting outside interests.

ACCOUNTABILITY INSTITUTIONS

Redress of Public Complaints[14]

In the absence of exit options, individuals need to find ways of settling their grievances against government organizations and service agencies quickly and fairly. Systematic redress mechanisms bring wider

---

BOX 11.9

Deliberation Councils as a Consultation and Feedback Mechanism

Deliberation councils are forums through which stakeholders and the government can regularly exchange information and discuss policies to resolve specific problems. They reduce uncertainty and present opportunities for key stakeholders to provide inputs. Governments may use such councils to test the effectiveness of their policies and programs and to draw up stable long-term policies based on understandings with the key interests. Examples are the Joint Public Sector–Private Sector Consultative Committee in Thailand in the mid-1980s; the industry-based councils in Japan; the "Malaysia Incorporated" concept; the business-labor councils in Canada; and the Singapore National Crime Prevention Council, which is chaired by a private sector chief executive and composed of representatives from civil society, professional bodies, and universities. The council commissions studies on various issues on different criminal activities and recommends specific prevention and control measures.

The key to the success of these councils is their capacity to act as a credible mechanism for the government to show commitment, as well as their focus on clear and relatively narrow sets of issues. The councils can act like a rolling meeting of all the different interests and work toward the consensus options. The conditions for the success of the councils are broad representation of the stakeholders, public education to garner widespread support, technical assistance and support for the council, and emphasis on mutual monitoring.

Source: Adapted from World Bank, *World Development Report* (1997); and OECD (1997d).

---

benefits. They act as checks on the actions of service providers, bring out causes of recurring grievances, and correct underlying problems in policies and procedures. The institution of the ombudsman, which formally originated in Sweden in 1809, can play an important positive role as well.

The right of redress assures citizens that an administrative wrong or malpractice will be put right, through personal or written explanation, apology, compensation, restitution, disciplinary action against the concerned official, or other remedy. The right of redress should begin with establishing a complaint mechanism in every public agency, at all levels of public contact.

Characteristics of a Complaint Mechanism

Ideally, the complaint mechanism should be:

- readily accessible to users of services;
- simple to operate, with clearly defined procedures and responsibilities;

- transparent and widely disseminated to the public;
- speedy, with time limits for dealing with complaints and communicating the decision;
- objective, with complaints investigated independently;
- linked, to the extent possible, to performance appraisal and reward of employees;
- confidential, with protection for the privacy of the individual; and
- integrated with the management information system of the agency, to keep track of the nature and frequency of complaints and of actions taken.

Setting Up a Complaint Mechanism

In keeping with these requirements, the main steps involved in setting up a complaint and redress mechanism include:

- establishing convenient and inexpensive channels for the public to lodge their complaints;
- specifying and publicizing the procedures for investigating complaints, defining the roles and responsibilities of the staff, and allowing complainants to present their case, setting time limits for each stage beginning from receipt of the complaint;
- requiring senior officials to make themselves available at preannounced hours to consider public complaints;
- having formal and understandable communications with complainants, specifying the reasons for rejecting complaints and indicating further avenues of redress; and
- establishing procedures for appeal or review.

Numerous other actions may be taken, such as:

- computerizing the tracking of complaints to facilitate monitoring by the agency and issue periodic reports to the public;
- devising mechanisms for dealing with collective or class-action complaints, as well as complaints from disadvantaged persons;
- consulting with members of the legislature and other elected officials;
- setting up telephone help lines and Web site complaint boxes to provide information and assistance and improve employees' phone courtesy;
- reviewing the training and orientation program for front-line employees and managers;
- requiring service agencies to treat consumer complaints as a valuable source of information, which should be systematically analyzed and considered in evaluating policies and programs; and
- publicizing the performance of the grievance redress function and taking steps to replicate good practices.

Naturally, not all of these actions are possible or necessary in every country and for every public service. As we keep repeating, the expected benefits of new initiatives must always be weighed against the probable costs, and several of those actions may not meet the cost-effectiveness test. However, some means of redress of public complaints must exist in any country, in clearly understandable form, and must be effective and credible. Whatever its specific content, the process must be related to measures to make service delivery and regulatory administration more responsive. A central complaint monitoring unit could be set up at the center of government, such as the prime minister's or president's office, with adequate staff support and under an official with appropriate status and authority. An example is the Public Complaints Bureau under the prime minister's office in Malaysia (Box 11.10).

BOX 11.10

Dealing with Public Complaints in Malaysia

As far back as 1971, Malaysia set up a Public Complaints Bureau as an independent organization to look into complaints against public agencies. The bureau was reorganized in 1992 to strengthen its administrative machinery for monitoring the promptness and effectiveness with which public agencies act on public complaints and for taking action to correct causes of recurring complaints. The bureau is the main channel through which the public can put forward complaints or grievances regarding: (1) public officials who provide poor-quality services or are discourteous or dilatory; and (2) administrative actions and decisions that are alleged to be unfair, contrary to laws and regulations, or entail misconduct, misappropriation, abuse of power, or other forms of faulty administration.

The bureau is backed by the full authority of the prime minister's office and has a staff of professionals, enabling it to perform its job effectively and credibly and to enforce compliance by all the departments. In addition to monitoring the response of agencies to complaints it forwards to them, the bureau also investigates important complaints on its own. It reports regularly to a committee headed by the chief secretary (the top civil servant in the government) and consisting of executive heads of major departments and the police chief. This committee reviews actions taken by the different departments and issues directives to lagging departments. The Bureau has operated with success for thirty-five years and the public is reportedly well satisfied with the system.

Source: Commonwealth Secretariat (1996).

Ombudsmen

Several governments in both developed and developing countries (about forty countries as of 2007) have established the institution of the "ombudsman." The ombudsman—meaning "people's representative" in old Norse language—is a person or a group of persons of unimpeachable integrity and competence who intermediate between a people and their government. This independent institution, with its origin in Scandinavia, is a means of requiring government bureaucracies to respond to citizen complaints of bad or inefficient administration or of failure to follow due process.

Ombudsmen should be appointed through an apolitical process either by the legislature or by the executive in consultation with the political opposition. The authority of ombudsmen varies widely between countries. They may act only as good-faith intermediaries and advisers or may be authorized by law to investigate administrative actions that are alleged to be unfair, contrary to laws and regulations, or entail misconduct, misappropriation, abuse of power, or other forms of bad administration, and to impose sanctions. Sometimes, an anti-corruption agency may also handle complaints against the administration, as in Hong Kong. Ombudsmen normally function at the national level, but there is no reason not to consider a similar office at the provincial or local government level or in large public agencies. Indeed, a number of large cities, including New York, have established ombudsman offices.

Regarding the effectiveness of the institution of the ombudsman, the evidence is mixed. Effectiveness is largely determined by the personality of the ombudsman, the willingness of the political system to support the ombudsman, and the effective independence of the office. Thus, in the Philippines, the ombudsman is a powerful person who can prosecute and punish offenders, but Filipinos generally consider the institution ineffective, mainly because of the last two occupants of that position. Conversely, when the ombudsman has the requisite integrity, energy, and commitment, political leaders are inclined to chafe at the independence of the position and seek either to control it or to neutralize it. In the South Pacific country of Vanuatu, for example, the ombudsman had broad jurisdiction over administrative matters, including public enterprises. However, following the tenure of an unusually assertive and active ombudsman, the institution itself was effectively neutered by the political leadership in 1998. Not too different was the fate of the "Ehtesab" (accountability) Commission in Pakistan in the late 1990s. The Commission was highly successful for its first few years; however, its good record led not to stronger political support but to President Nawaz Sharif demoting it to a "bureau" attached to his office and draining it of independent investigating authority.

As in all cases of institutional transfer, countries should exercise caution in importing successful institutions from other countries. The ombudsman institution succeeded in Scandinavia because of specific local circumstances, its fit with local traditions and the political culture, and the strong governance climate. Indeed, if an ombudsman is established as a symbolic or cosmetic gesture, with no serious political or administrative will to ensure its efficient functioning for the public good, the institution would be a mere whitewash and damage further the credibility of government.

However, even assuming an independent and honest ombudsman with political support, the institution cannot be a substitute for the proper functioning of the regular organs of government. In fact, at one extreme there is no major need for an ombudsman if the government feedback and grievance mechanisms are functioning very well and the administration itself is responsive, accountable, and effective. At the other extreme, an unresponsive and unaccountable government would render an ombudsman completely ineffective. Hence, the institution can be an important adjunct to public accountability but cannot substitute for the good functioning of the regular accountability mechanisms. The exception is in periods of major transition and change, when an ombudsman of courage and integrity can be instrumental in supporting the forces for better government or in preventing a temporary weakness in governance from becoming entrenched and permanent.

External Audit Institutions: The Heart of Public Accountability

The role of external audit was briefly described in chapter 6 in the context of the public expenditure management cycle. External audit, however, is not limited to verifying that public moneys were not misappropriated ("financial audit") or financial rules violated ("compliance" or "regularity" audit). External audit, as the lynchpin of public accountability, must also look into the efficiency and effectiveness of government operations to the extent permitted by the capacity of the organization and the priorities of the country.

The Lima Declaration of Guidelines on Auditing Precepts, which was agreed upon almost thirty years ago and proved to be a watershed in the development of public accountability worldwide, opens with the following statement: "Audit is not an end in itself but an indispensable part of a regulatory system whose aim is to reveal deviations from accepted standards and violations of the principles of legality, efficiency, effectiveness and economy . . . early enough to make it possible to take corrective action in individual cases, to make those accountable accept responsibility, to obtain compensation, or to take steps to prevent—or at least render more difficult—such breaches."[15]

It is not enough for the public to be sure that its tax dollars were used in accordance with the rules; it is also necessary to have independent assessments of the degree of waste and of the achievement of the purposes for which these tax dollars were mobilized from the public. This latter "value-for-money" audit examines an entire government agency, program, or activity to suggest ways of improving its efficiency and effectiveness. The auditor searches for areas of waste and mismanagement which, if eliminated, would permit the same purposes to be achieved at less expense, or where the same resources would produce greater value if used better. This type of auditing can make a major contribution to increasing the efficiency of government.

Such independent assessments can only be carried out by an institution that is genuinely independent as well as technically competent. Thus, in every country there is a need for a "supreme audit institution" (SAI) charged with carrying out all external audits of public sector operations—financial, compliance, and value-for-money audits. The SAI may have different juridical forms in different countries, but must be independent of the executive branch of government and should normally report its findings to the legislature and the public (as well as to the audited entity itself for comments and possible corrections).

The appropriate emphasis of external audit depends on the particular circumstances of the country. Weak governance systems require a concentration on compliance and financial audit. In developed countries, external audit should look more and more into efficiency and effectiveness issues. But in no country or situation should the SAI ever loosen up on its core function to verify that public monies have not been misappropriated or misallocated to purposes other than those approved by the legislature.

Whatever the focus of activity, the effectiveness of external audit demands that the SAI:

- be legally independent of the executive branch of government;
- report, publicly, to the legislative branch of government;
- have unrestricted access to required information;
- control its own budget;
- be fully autonomous, including in personnel management matters; and
- have sufficient capacity, skills, and professionalism.

The General Accountability Office in the United States

The General Accountability Office (GAO) is the supreme audit institution in the United States, responsible for external audit of all operations of the government and public sector agencies. It was created as the General Accounting Office in 1921 by the Budget and Accounting Act to take over the tasks of auditing and accounting previously carried out by the Department of the Treasury. Public spending during World War I had increased substantially and legislators felt they needed better and more independent information on government expenditures than could be provided by an arm of the executive branch itself. The Act made the GAO independent of the executive branch and gave it the mandate to investigate how federal funds are spent. Its mission was later clarified and expanded through the enactment of subsequent legislation and, in July 2004, the name was changed to the Government Accountability Office in keeping with its broader mandate.

The GAO, an independent and nonpartisan agency, serves Congress and the public interest by keeping an eye on virtually every federal program and activity. It is headed by the Comptroller General, who is appointed by the President, with the consent of the Senate, to a non-renewable fifteen-year term and cannot be removed except for special cause, in order to insure independence and continuity. The Office has full autonomy of budget and operations and functions through a team of highly trained evaluators, who examine federal programs ranging from missiles to medicine, from aviation safety to food safety, from national security to social security.

The GAO audits federal expenditures, evaluates the effectiveness of federal programs, issues legal opinions, publishes its findings and reports, and recommends actions to Congress and the heads of executive agencies to make the program in question more effective and responsive. The evolution of the GAO mandate and activities since 1921 has occurred in the following stages.

The Early Years

The years between 1921 and 1945 became known as the "Voucher Checking Era" because the GAO focused on examining the regularity of individual government expenditures. The volume of GAO activities expanded substantially in the 1930s during President Franklin D. Roosevelt's New Deal, owing to increased federal spending to fight the Great Depression.

The GAO volume of work increased further during World War II, alongside the expansion of defense production, and encompassed the review of defense contracts and the audit of the accounts of the Army and Navy departments. The agency also became responsible for reviewing government vouchers for transportation of soldiers and material, examining all paid transport bills, determining any overcharges, and requesting refunds from carriers.

Moving to Economy and Efficiency

After 1945, the GAO moved away from simple and time-consuming voucher checking—which it transferred back to the executive branch—and shifted to broader audits of the economy and effi-ciency of government operations. Instead of mechanical scrutiny of every government transaction, the GAO began to review the systems of financial control and management in federal agencies and the cost-effectiveness of operations. Starting in the late 1940s, the GAO also worked with the Department of the Treasury and the Bureau of the Budget (now the Office of Management and Budget) to help executive branch agencies improve their accounting systems and controls over spending. With this move to more substantive auditing, the GAO reduced drastically the number of clerks and began to hire accounting professionals. By 1951, the GAO's staff had been cut to 7,000—less than half the number on the payroll at the end of the war.

The 1950s saw a further rise in government spending because of the Cold War and the buildup of U.S. military forces in Europe and Asia, and the GAO's audit work increasingly focused on "big-ticket" defense spending and contract reviews. Although the agency first began doing field-work in the 1930s, it formally established a network of regional offices in 1952 and also opened branches in Europe and the Far East. During the Vietnam War, for example, the GAO opened an office in Saigon to monitor military expenditures and foreign aid. At the request of Congress, the GAO evaluated the Johnson administration's War on Poverty efforts in 1967 and did other impor-tant work in areas such as energy, consumer protection, and the environment. In 1972, some of the GAO's reviews touched on aspects of the Watergate scandals.

Transition to a Full-Service Supreme Audit Institution

In 1974, Congress broadened the GAO's evaluation role and gave it greater responsibility in the budget process. The agency's staff, mostly accountants, began to change to fit the evolving nature of the work, and scientists, actuaries, and experts were recruited in various fields such as health care, public policy, and informatics. During the last thirty years, the GAO has sought more and more to strengthen accountability by alerting policy makers and the public to emerging problems throughout government. In the 1980s, for example, the agency reported on the problems in the savings and loan industry and repeatedly warned about the consequences of the government's failure to control deficit spending. The GAO also worked with the executive branch to strengthen financial management, modernize outmoded systems, and improve the reliability and timeliness of financial statements. As the twenty-first century began, the GAO was doing important evaluation work on a wide range of issues, including computer security and conditions at nursing homes. As of 2007, the agency that once checked millions of individual government vouchers had become a multidisciplinary organization equipped to handle the most complex value-for-money audits and toughest evaluation challenges.

The U.S. GAO meets all the requirements for an effective supreme audit institution—independence, reporting to the legislature and the public, integrity, and technical capacity. Indeed, the GAO is known as one of the most effective external audit institutions in the world. With its in-depth and robust but balanced assessments it has performed the invaluable function of informing Congress and the American people about the efficiency and effectiveness of government operations and programs. While several observers have lamented the decline in fiscal responsibility and efficiency in U.S. public administration in recent years, the GAO has stood out as an island of excellence and integrity.

GENERAL DIRECTIONS OF IMPROVEMENT

Strengthening internal administrative accountability of civil servants to their superiors for their job performance is important but rarely sufficient in itself to produce improvements in government efficiency. External accountability (also called "social accountability") is also essential. One component of external accountability is the opportunity for the citizens to "exit" the state system (i.e., the extent to which they have access to alternative suppliers of a public service [or access to good substitutes]). The other component is "voice," the opportunity for the citizens to seek better performance from public service providers while remaining within the government system of supply. The heart of public accountability is a strong external audit institution—independent and reporting to the legislature—to protect public integrity and oversee the use of public resources.

Exit

Outsourcing (contracting out) is the main governmental mechanism to provide choices to the users of public services. The effectiveness of government delivery of public services, relative to alternative delivery by private business and NGOs, should be kept under periodic review—especially in local government, which is normally responsible for providing those services that are generally more suitable for nongovernmental delivery. Close monitoring is needed, however, to prevent service quality and access from declining as a result of "capture" by powerful local private interests or insufficient contract monitoring capacity in government. Thus, contracting out of public services should be considered only under five basic conditions:

- There are demonstrable and lasting cost savings and/or improved benefits for the users;
- The outputs relevant to the desired outcomes can be clearly specified;
- Performance can be monitored (and there is sufficient administrative capacity to do so);

- Contracts can be enforced (and there is administrative capacity to do so); and
- There are robust accounting and audit mechanisms.

When these conditions are met, the outsourcing process must be carefully managed, including the following stages:

- define clearly the service goal (e.g., cost saving, quality improvement, or expansion of access) and identify specifically the activities to be contracted out;
- review issues of coordination between the activities to be contracted out and the other relevant governmental activities;
- assess contract costs based on the experience with similar outsourcing;
- evaluate the quality and experience of the contractor;
- consider carefully the contractual options—lump-sum contracts, price-per-unit contracts, shared profits, and so on;
- stipulate clear and monitorable performance standards and include provisions regarding contractor nonperformance and dispute resolution; and
- define monitoring procedures for which the government needs employees with technical knowledge of the service.

The risks of outsourcing, too, need assessment. These risks are mainly contractor violations of due process and constitutional rights of its employees, encouragement of monopoly owing to lack of competition in the private market, and fiscal and corruption risk. The two major protections against these risks are careful piloting of outsourcing and provisions for contract cancellation and obtaining frequent and direct feedback from service users on access to and quality of the service as it is delivered by the nongovernment entity.

Voice

Among the myriad possible ways of fostering public consultation and feedback, the following merit particular attention:

- Whistle-blower laws to protect state employees who go public on inefficiency or dishonesty in their agency.
- Citizens' charters listing the users' rights to certain service standards. These require substantial resources as well as administrative and monitoring capacity and are thus not effective in developing countries, where impressive charters have often been promulgated without any capacity to deliver on the service standards being set.
- Public "report cards" on the performance and integrity of different government agencies have been effective in every country. The desire to preserve a good public image or improve a low standing has proven to be a powerful motivator for government agencies.
- Public opinion polling and client surveys are the most common way to elicit views on government efficiency and service quality. In developing countries where sophisticated surveys may not be affordable, quick and simple surveys can still provide reliable information at low cost.
- The same is true of grievance redress mechanisms, which can be expensive and highly burdensome for developing countries with their limited administrative capacity. Simpler variants can be implemented, however.
- The media can perform a crucial role in facilitating communications to and from the public.

Exit, Voice, and Poverty

Exit and voice possibilities are very limited for poor and vulnerable groups and for minorities. Outsourcing may limit further their access to the service, and merely improving communications will typically give greater voice to the better-off and to more vocal groups. Thus, affirmative actions are necessary to assure that the poor and vulnerable do not become even more excluded and less visible as a result of attempts to improve government responsiveness in general. Similarly, because the potential for voice is stronger in the services that are more visible, the focus on those services may lead to neglect of less-visible services. For example, an increase in users' voice might lead to better (visible) garbage collection and worse (less-visible) garbage disposal—causing environmental damage and adverse effects on the poor communities that become the unwilling host of garbage disposal sites. Thus, greater client orientation must be sought in the context of stronger *citizen* orientation.

QUESTIONS FOR DISCUSSION

1. When actual competition is lacking, as in most government services, is contestability essential for integrity and efficiency?
2. The concept of "exit" means that citizens should have choices. Why is it not justified for individuals who are dissatisfied with public garbage collection to pay for private trash hauling and subtract the cost from their local taxes?
3. Has globalization increased or reduced accountability of governments to their citizens?
4. Pick one of the two following statements and make a credible argument for it:
   a. "Outsourcing (contracting out) of public services is essentially a way to increase profits of private firms at the expense of the citizens."
   b. "Outsourcing (contracting out) of public services is necessary to spur efficiency in government and reduce the costs of the services to the citizens."
5. Under what conditions is outsourcing of public services appropriate? Does violation of one or more of those conditions necessarily mean that the service should not be contracted out?
6. Pick one of the two following statements and make a credible argument for it:
   a. "Outsourcing is a necessity when the public administration is weak."
   b. "Outsourcing is a danger when the public administration is weak."
7. "Because 'the customer is always right,' government functions best when it treats the citizen as a customer." Discuss.
8. "The institution of *ombudsman* is typically Scandinavian and thus not suitable to other cultures and countries." Discuss.
9. Why is external audit described in the text as the heart of public accountability? Is this the only way in which the legislative branch of government can be both strong and active?
10. Try to connect the evolution of the General Accountability Office to the main political and social events in the history of the United States in the twentieth century.

NOTES

1. This section should be read in conjunction with the discussion in chapter 2 on the continuum of service delivery option. It draws partly on OECD (1996c); Peters (1996); Paul (1995); Girishankar (1999); and World Bank (1997b).

2. This section has drawn partly on World Bank (1997b); Caiden (1996), Donahue (1989); Gidman (1994); Commonwealth Secretariat (1996); Rehfuss (1989).

3. Walter Pincus, "U.S. Pays Steep Price for Private Security in Iraq," *Washington Post,* 10 October 2007.

4. For about forty years in France for toll roads and water supply under the name of "public service concessions" (see Heald, 1995).

5. Leigland (1996), in Naomi Caiden (1996).

6. Similar principles apply in the individual states of the United States.

7. For example, at a congressional hearing in October 2007 on the actions of employees of Blackwater, a private security firm operating in Iraq under contract with the State Department, the company CEO refused to answer certain pertinent questions on the grounds that Blackwater is a private company—notwithstanding the grave nature of the allegations against the company and their damaging implications for U.S. policy and image in Iraq.

8. "Tracking Outsourced Bonanzas," Editorial, *New York Times*, January 11, 2007. (The audit mentioned therein was reported by the *Washington Post.*)

9. "A World of Work: A Survey of Outsourcing," *The Economist,* November 13, 2004.

10. The discussion in this section is drawn partly from Paul (1995); Berry, Pourtney, and Thomson, in Perry, ed. (1989); OECD (1996c); Feinberg (1997); OECD (1997d); World Bank (1997b); and Hirschman (1970).

11. See, for example, the term "customer-driven government" in the U.S. National Performance Review (1999).

12. Arnberg, in OECD (1996c).

13. Lunde, in OECD (1996c).

14. This section draws on Commonwealth Secretariat (1995a, 1996); and Government of India (1997).

15. See the Web site of the International Organization of Supreme Audit Institutions, www.intosai.org.

CHAPTER 12

Participation and Social Capital

Pick an onion you know.
—*Starting advice for a Gullah recipe*[1]

Citizen participation is a device whereby public officials
induce nonpublic individuals to act in a way the officials desire.
—*Daniel P. Moynihan*

WHAT TO EXPECT

As these quotes suggest, participation, as one of the four pillars of governance, is fundamental to good public management, but can also be manipulated to give top-down decisions the appearance of legitimacy. Participation should therefore be encouraged not as a way to elicit people's views and pick and choose among them, but as the bottom-up outgrowth of a strong civil society and a manifestation of the social capital of mutual trust that is built among citizens through their free interaction. The chapter thus begins with a summary of the concept of social capital and its implications for public management and society—both the advantages and the risks, for there can be nasty forms of social capital along with the positive ones. The meaning of participation is then examined, along with its advantages and possible misuse. Participation is viewed by some as a narrow instrument to obtain feedback on the results of government action. Its scope is broader, however, and includes a systematic contribution to the decisions and design of public policies to improve their quality and sustainability. Various ways to encourage appropriate public participation are presented, with reference to the experience of a number of countries. The chapter discusses the important roles of different types of civil society organizations, particularly "nongovernmental organizations"—pointing out, as well, how NGOs can be misused when they do not meet the same standards of accountability and transparency as are required for public administration—and concludes with the customary suggestions for improvement.

"SOCIAL CAPITAL"[2]

Evolution of the Concept

Mr. Smith, a contractor, receives a request for house renovation from a stranger. Because he has no information on the buyer, he requests payment in advance. The potential buyer, unsure of whether the work will be performed after he pays, refuses. The contractor doesn't get the job and the house doesn't get renovated. Mr. Jones, another contractor, receives a request for services from an established customer, from whom he expects further business in the future. They agree on specs, schedule, and

357

price through a couple of e-mails, an advance payment is made, the services are performed well and on time, and Mr. Jones is paid. Possibly, the two of them then have a couple of beers together, swap a few jokes, and develop a friendly acquaintance which also strengthens their commercial relationship and reduces further the "transaction costs" of doing business in the future. The difference between the two situations is "social capital"—present in the second case but not the first. Fundamentally, *social capital is the stock of trust created through networks of reciprocal support based on common interests.*

The concept can be traced to the seminal views of Lynda J. Hanifan, superintendent of schools in West Virginia in 1916, who stressed the importance of the things that " . . . count for most in the daily lives of people: namely good will, fellowship, sympathy, and social intercourse among the individuals and families who make up a social unit." French sociologist Pierre Bourdieu wrote that "the volume of social capital possessed by a given agent . . . depends on the size of network connections which can be effectively mobilized" (Bourdieu, 1986). Thus, Woolcock and Narayan (2000) summarize the essence of social capital as "it's not what you know, it's who you know."

Robert Putnam's authoritative treatment of social capital (1993, 1995, 2000) emphasized the contribution of community networks to the creation of trust and reciprocity which, in turn, lead to social collaboration and more effective institutions. The "networks" aspect is especially important in multiethnic and multicultural societies—whether in developed or developing countries. "Bonding" networks connect people who are similar (e.g., immigrants from the same country), create a sense of particularized (in-group) reciprocity, and may form the basis of joint economic activities. "Bridging" networks help generate mutually beneficial relations *between* different groups of people, fostering cooperation and the exchange of information. This distinction implies, among other things, that vertical hierarchies of control are less efficient in the long run than horizontal relationships among equals based on common interests.

Historical traditions of civic engagement help create social capital (e.g., in the city-states of northern Italy, contrasted with the patronage relationships historically prevailing in the south of the country). However, the absence of such historical tradition and rules of behavior is not an irremediable condition. The rules and habits of reciprocity can be generated by enabling socialization and participation. As the experience of so many immigrants groups demonstrated, the shared experience of one good generation may suffice to create a stock of social capital where none existed. A sound public education system can make a crucial contribution in this respect.[3]

Social and Physical Capital

Physical capital and social capital are complementary and both are necessary for good government and economic progress with equity. However, there are major differences between the two:

- First and most obviously, physical capital is tangible, consisting of equipment and other material assets; social capital is not. This does not mean, however, that social capital cannot be measured. Acceptable proxy indicators have been developed, particularly to quantify the level of trust in a community and the density of community networks.
- Physical capital is accumulated through financial savings and used for direct production; social capital is accumulated through the exchange of mutually relevant information and used for constructive interaction.
- Physical capital is marketable; social capital is a collective asset that cannot be bought, sold, or (under most conditions) transferred.
- Physical capital is depleted as it is used; social capital tends to grow as it is used—reliance on trust leads to more trust, and networks become stronger the more they are relied upon.

The differences between physical and social capital are summarized in the table below.

PHYSICAL CAPITAL	SOCIAL CAPITAL
Tangible	Intangible (but measurable)
Accumulated through savings	Accumulated through information
Used for direct production	Used to facilitate interaction
Marketable, transferable	Not marketable, rarely transferable
Depleted by use	Increased by use

Implications for Society and Public Administration

Advantages

Some view social capital as simply an ingredient of a friendlier social climate and of a more humane society. It is that, certainly, but it also has very practical implications. These are best understood by imagining how inefficient economic exchange and government would be without sufficient trust among individuals and between groups. Individuals would need to expend substantial resources to protect themselves against breaches of understandings and violations of contracts by those with whom they have economic transactions. Much closer supervision, and thus much greater expense, would be needed by government to ensure that public services are not misappropriated by persons who are not entitled to them. The "free rider" problem would be pervasive: Individuals may not contribute their share if they can get a free ride from others paying for a service from which everyone benefits and, with each individual having an incentive not to contribute, the service is less likely to be provided.

Finally, compliance with common rules would be enormously weakened by lack of social capital. Recall from chapter 3 that, in a legitimate state, most citizens accept the rules set by the proper authorities, rule violation is the exception and compliance is the norm and largely voluntary. Indeed, the rules can *only* be enforced effectively if most people obey them voluntarily. However—and here's the link to social capital—people are unlikely to obey the rules voluntarily if they cannot be reasonably sure that others will also abide by them. (If you assume that most other drivers will run red lights, you are not likely to stop at one.)

To sum up, social capital is economically beneficial because constructive social interaction generates three important practical effects:

- Trust facilitates the transmission of knowledge about the expected behavior of others. This reduces the risk of opportunistic behavior by others, and thus the need to expend resources to protect yourself. (Consider the cost and time advantages of a "handshake" contract as opposed to the need for a lengthy legal document replete with details to cover every possible infraction.)
- Trust facilitates the transmission of knowledge about technology, markets, and other relevant economic information and thus improves the competitiveness and efficiency of the market mechanism. (See, for example, the enormous impulse given to the growth of informatics by the "open source" movement for software development.)[4]
- Trust reduces the "free rider" problem. The knowledge that others in a group will do their part is an incentive for everyone to pitch in, thus making the group better off as well as every individual in it.

Note, however, that the social capital built by bonding networks among poor and vulnerable people cannot be sustained for long in the absence of linkages to supporting organizations and of assistance by government at all levels. While it is true that social capital tends to grow as it is used, the incentive of network members to "cheat" on agreements made with one another may be too strong for poor individuals living on the margins of survival. Physical resources and other protections must be provided by the state or others in order for bonding networks to survive and prosper when their members are extremely poor and vulnerable.

Risks

Like everything else, social capital has a potential negative side as well. A first category of disadvantages is the potential of social capital for discouraging individual inventiveness, for draining individual resources in order to preserve the cohesion of the group, or for weakening broader social norms. Thus, in cultures where a special premium is placed on tradition, individual behavior viewed by the group as "uppity" or simply different is strongly discouraged—small towns and villages everywhere are known for both a high level of mutual trust and a heavy pressure to conform. (See the delightful film *Pleasantville* for a visual illustration of this reality.) Similarly, in a perverse manifestation of the free rider problem, individual incentives to get ahead are weakened when the economic gains are expected to be shared with the other members of the group—making it that much harder for the group as a whole to improve its economic position. Finally, the bonds of extended family and social group may impose on individual members certain behaviors that are not conducive to integrity and efficiency (e.g., promotion to a responsible government position may lead to enormous group pressures to give jobs to relatives and friends, and a failure to do so is punished by painful exclusion from the group).

A second category of risks can be described in terms of the earlier distinction between bonding and bridging networks. When bonding networks are neither complemented nor kept in check by bridges to other networks, the greater cohesion and trust built within one particular group can be used to exclude or even destroy persons outside the group, and generates pressures to divert resources from the broader society for the benefit of the bonding network.

The most obvious example is organized crime. While the old saying that there is "no honor among thieves" is true, there can indeed be "*trust* among thieves." Members of organized crime groups have a powerful incentive to cooperate and keep their word to one another—not from a mythical and nonexistent loyalty among criminals, or even from fear of penalties, but because it is in the long-term interest of the network and thus of its members. The "social capital" generated within a criminal bonding network is genuine but creates huge negative externalities for society in the form of lost lives, wasted resources, and pervasive uncertainty.

Moreover, a contagion effect is at work. Changes in legal environment and economic incentives can turn positive social capital into negative social capital. Thus, in Colombia, the mounting profits from illegal drugs, combined with a weakened legal system, turned existing positive networks (e.g., among small farmers) away from productive endeavors towards illegal activities. The same trust that underlies legitimate economic activities can be exploited to support infant relationships between partners in new crime.

Equally obvious is the negative impact of "bonding" within military dictatorships. The strong interpersonal attachments created by military training, uniformity of incentives, and mutual support among "brothers in arms" that are essential to defend one's country against external enemies can be equally useful in enforcing rapacious oppression of the citizenry, systematic plunder of society, and preservation and enrichment of the regime. From Burma to Nigeria, all too often the soldier is the worst enemy of the citizen.

Less obvious but equally real is the risk that, in the absence of bridges to other groups or other checks and balances, economic bonding networks may appropriate power and resources. Again, because this incentive operates in all bonding networks, a situation is created whereby stronger cooperation within each group may be accompanied by a loosening of bonds in society as a whole. For example, in the 1960s some business interests in East Asia set up networks that generated internal social capital and thus increased group profit, but largely by excluding other groups (e.g., the *chaebol* conglomerates in Korea). When cooperation becomes exclusion and a bonding network becomes a closed circle of privilege and influence, the eventual impact on society can be negative—as was demonstrated by the Asian financial crisis in 1997–1999.

Finally, there is the dark side of social capital in multiethnic countries. The challenge of how to overcome entrenched hostilities and pervasive mistrust between groups with a history of conflict or even genocide is a daunting one. Indeed, severe civil conflict invariably creates very strong social capital within each contending group and in the extreme cases of genocide the bonds among members of the genocidal units are further reinforced by the psychological need to suppress one's guilt at the acts perpetrated collectively—whether by SS guards at Auschwitz, Serb chetniks in Bosnia, Interahamwe killing squads in Rwanda, or Janjaweed militiamen in Darfur.

These risks can be addressed, and the great positive potential of social capital utilized, if the state and organized civil society enable *both* the formation of social capital within affinity groups and the building of bridges and linkages among the different groups. A stable and prosperous society needs not only strong building blocks but also the cement to hold them together. Participation is the operational watchword.

PARTICIPATION

The Meaning of Participation[5]

Like the other three pillars of good government, the concept of participation is universal but inherently relative. Except in ancient Greek city-states, small towns in New England, or rural villages everywhere, it is impossible to provide for participation by everybody in everything, and one must therefore specify participation *by whom, to what,* and *how.* Moreover, like social capital, participation is not necessarily a good thing: a violent riot, for example, is a highly participatory event. With these caveats, effective and responsive public administration in every country provides for appropriate participation—participation by concerned government officials, public employees, and other stakeholders in the sound formulation of public policies and programs; participation by interested external entities in the monitoring of integrity and operational efficiency; and participation and feedback by users of public services in the assessment of the access to and the quality of the services.

The promotion of participation in public administration by citizens and civil society has been fostered in contemporary times by a number of key factors: the vastly expanded role of the public sector called for a commensurate improvement of the mechanisms for popular and user involvement; the growth of international exchange amplified the global scope of government involvement while increasing the distance between the center and the field agencies; and the success of many public programs was seen to be contingent on consultation of the intended beneficiaries.

The Benefits of Participation

The evidence shows that public programs that take an appropriate participatory approach are far more successful than those based solely on hierarchical structures. In the Philippines poverty alleviation projects, for example, the biggest improvement in living conditions was registered in the case of *barangays* (villages), which took an active part in planning and service delivery. In the process, social acceptability increased and the local minorities were included in the planning process.

Beyond the managerial benefits, participation can:

- enhance the design of public programs by taking advantage of knowledge of local technology and other conditions, and adapting the program to the social organization;
- improve program sustainability and cost recovery;
- make resource mobilization easier and facilitate community contributions of labor and materials;
- foster a more equitable distribution of benefits (although there is always the danger of capture of the program by strong local interests);
- lower information barriers between the government and the people, leading to useful feedback from users of public services;
- encourage the use of public goods such as immunization, prevention of AIDS and communicable diseases, and family planning;
- nurture the creation of community institutions, which will continue to produce social capital even after the program has run its course; and
- avoid the negative consequences of not consulting the intended beneficiaries, such as local rejection of sanitation or housing designs.

Fostering Participation

The Emerging Approach

Traditionally, participation has been narrowly viewed as obtaining user feedback on the implementation of government programs or on their results. The contemporary approach to participation is much broader than just improving the implementation of activities already decided. It stresses participation as integral also to good decisions and quality of program design, thus emphasizing also ex ante, rather than only ex post, involvement in public service provision. The approach has been in part validated by evidence showing that government programs that involve citizens early in the decision process—rather than merely after program structure and guidelines have been decided—have generally been more successful. Indeed, such involvement can have radical consequences, as shown most dramatically by the clause "with maximum feasible participation by the poor" inserted by an unknown and unsung bureaucrat into President Lyndon Johnson's "War on Poverty" legislation.

At local level, citizen participation has been mandated in a number of countries, including the United States, as Box 12.1 illustrates.

Limits and Risks

As a broad generalization, the results of participation for public service effectiveness and expansion of access have been mixed. First, as often mentioned, the risk of capture of the community group by a small elite is ever present, to the neglect of the interests of others, and particularly of the poor and the minorities. A second major challenge for genuine participation comes from excessive and prescriptive involvement by government agencies. The natural bureaucratic instinct to

BOX 12.1

Examples of Local Participation in Various Countries

In 1994, *Bolivia* promulgated the Law of Popular Participation. Among other things, the law required the involvement of grass-roots organizations in local decision making. Twenty percent of national revenue was to be transferred to municipalities for the implementation of public services, according to the needs identified by community organizations in a municipal plan. These community organizations also were to propose and supervise local investment projects in social sectors and urban and rural development. (It became clear much later that this initiative, while praiseworthy, was insufficient to address the problem of poverty and ethnic exclusion, which eventually led to the 2006 election of Evo Morales, the first indigenous president in Bolivian history.)

In *India,* there is a legal framework for community participation in local government, in the form of ward committees with citizen representatives. The ward (corresponding to an electoral constituency) committees can be given responsibility for many local functions, along with the necessary resources.

In the *Philippines,* neighborhood (*barangay*) committees may be given the responsibility for managing the delivery and maintenance of local services and for running community facilities. In practice, the assistance depends substantially on the "connections" of the barangay to the local political elite

In *Indonesia,* community participation was incorporated in the environmental improvement of slums through the KIP (Kampung Improvement Program) and other programs to improve basic infrastructure and low income-housing. As in Bolivia, despite their contributions these programs could not make up for the much broader social problems and governance weaknesses.

Sometimes, a project involving the local community management in one area can expand into other areas. For example, in *Pakistan,* starting with a low-cost sewer program, the Orangi Pilot Project in Karachi expanded to encompass low-cost housing, basic health and family planning, a women's work centers program, supervised credit for small family enterprises, and the upgrading of private schools with poor physical and academic conditions. (www.opprti@cyber.net.pk).

In the *United States,* the Parent-Teacher Association (PTA) has been the traditional conduit of public participation in education, with substantial success throughout the years. Community councils have also been set up in various cities, such as St. Paul, Minnesota, with an independent budget, the opportunity to suggest priorities for the larger city budget, and the ability to raise additional resources for local schemes.

Many other countries have legally constituted user groups for different services in rural and urban areas such as irrigation, education, waste collection, and sector projects, and often draw on the support of civil society associations for the prevention and treatment of disease, low-cost sanitation, safe water supply, solid waste management, school health surveillance, care of street children, and local maintenance of community facilities.

regulate and the push for quick results are at odds with the long gestation period needed to develop effective participation, and may suffocate worthwhile initiatives. Nurturing local participation is very different from smothering it in excessive "help." Third, the opposite problem has also been common, with participatory modalities introduced in public programs as mere window dressing to justify decisions already taken or to sidestep the responsibility for faulty policies, as alluded to in Moynihan's mordant quotation at the start of the chapter. These three constraints to effective participation can be successfully addressed, but only if they are recognized at the outset. The risk of capture, in particular, can be addressed by a judicious assessment of the power structure within the group and the ensuing prescription of genuine and broad participatory modalities.

Citizen participation at the community level in different countries shows a type of plateau effect at work. In communities where participation was designed to meet only the minimum requirements of the government program, participation fell dramatically when the program ended. By contrast, in communities that had developed a strong internal justification and standards for effective action (including links to local government and nongovernmental organizations), participation continued to grow even after the end of the government program.

There is a major concern relating to the tension between representative democracy—entailing the notion that governments are elected to take decisions on behalf of citizens—and the pressure for more direct public participation in the policy process. It may be argued that giving people a direct say in individual decisions makes decision making by elected government obsolete. But public participation should be a complement to, rather than a substitute for, public policy processes and the decisions of elected representatives and should not be allowed to blur the lines of accountability between ministers, members of the legislature, and government employees.

There is also a concern regarding the representativeness and accountability of the participatory groups themselves. It is unacceptable for pressure groups not accountable to anyone to paralyze elected government bodies that are directly accountable to the legislature and indirectly accountable to the citizenry. There is a difference between legitimate expressions of people's voice and pressures by "voluntary" organizations serving mainly as vehicles for individual egos and vested particularistic agenda. However, to the extent that public confidence in elected government bodies is eroded by incompetence, lack of responsiveness, and corruption, pressure by outside groups is increasingly justified.

Effective citizen participation does not come easy to communities that lack management skills and suffer from discrimination and poor access to information. Training and other capacity-building for community groups, voluntary associations, and local government personnel are needed to develop both skills and attitudes. (See chapter 8 for a discussion of training of government personnel.) A number of countries thus provide special subsidies to assist in developing citizens associations, and most developed countries assist disadvantaged groups in getting relevant information on public issues and opportunities (e.g., the Rotterdam social housing program in the Netherlands—see Lambla, 1998).

There are also costs to participation, at least in the short term: delays in finalizing and starting public programs; costs associated with negotiations with the affected groups; higher staff requirements; other costs arising from the inability of communities to organize themselves; and the risk of inadvertently reinforcing existing racial, gender, and caste discrimination if participation is dominated by elite groups. The raiding by richer local persons of new public housing for low-income people is a typical example of the effect of planning public programs for the poor without broad community involvement beginning at the design stage. These costs and risks are less likely to the extent that government officials are recognized and rewarded for successful efforts at encouraging participation.

Success Factors

Four criteria are essential for a serious participation effort at the project and program levels (Berry et al., 1989):

- *effective outreach*—the participation effort needs to be tailored to a specific target population and to the problem at hand;
- *equal access*—there must be a realistic opportunity for large numbers of the target population to participate on an equal basis;
- *significant policy impact*—to be more than symbolic, participation should have at least a potential influence on final policy decisions; and
- *enactable policy*—the participatory effort must be capable of being expressed through an actionable government program.

These criteria lead to two important conclusions:

- *Build on the existing forms of community participation,* by designing the public program flexibly to accommodate the input of existing local organizations, as opposed to rigid program blueprints;
- *Identify and promote community leadership,* especially from the traditionally excluded groups, with the help of the elected local structures. In urban areas, for example, successful urban renewal efforts can be built on the support of the affected neighborhoods and on the informal power of the community to influence the decision-making hierarchy.

The Link to Outsourcing

As noted in the previous chapter, the single best antidote to the risks of outsourcing is to involve the beneficiary communities—either in delivering the service itself, or in looking over the shoulder of private contractors. Outsourcing to nonprofit voluntary agencies and local community groups may also carry special benefits in terms of community development and social capital formation. In some countries (e.g., the Philippines), voluntary agencies have agreed to perform important social services in exchange only for support in kind such as laboratory, equipment, or transport. Government contracts may also be awarded to community organizations in pursuit of social and economic objectives that are broader than narrow efficiency and cost considerations. (These objectives, however, must themselves be defined clearly and communicated publicly.)

Many developing countries (e.g., Uganda, Bolivia, India) have entered into noncompetitive contracts with voluntary agencies and civil service associations for the local and national management of certain social services—typically, nutrition centers, health care and immunization, women's development, day care centers, slum improvement, and sanitation. Because the outputs are difficult to specify, these services are unsuitable for contracting out to private businesses, but may be entrusted to nonprofit, nongovernment agencies whose objective and rationale is to serve the public. Also, in many cases, such agencies are better placed to deliver the services because of their proximity to and affinity with the local community, and more efficient as well. As an illustration, public health spending in Cambodia was barely $2 per person per year, compared to $30 per capita spending in private health facilities. In the two pilot projects that entrusted the operation of the public health care system to NGOs, the cost was substantially reduced and responsiveness to the community needs increased. (As emphasized later, however, there must be careful scrutiny of the integrity and effectiveness of the NGO concerned through appropriate accountability and audit mechanisms.)

Governments could also consider introducing healthy competition between government and nongovernment providers in areas like education and health care, such as the workers' training fund on the basis of vouchers in Kenya and the Philippines, and the management of preschools in India.

In a number of countries, it is deliberate government policy to involve cooperatives in aspects of service provision, such as the distribution of essential commodities and inputs, the management of public housing, extension services to farmers, and the like. Compensation is either a specific sum or a percentage of income.

A special form of participation of NGOs in public service delivery is co-production. In a co-production arrangement, service delivery becomes a joint venture between the government agency and a citizens' group. This collaboration is not always easy to administer, but can be most fruitful with community groups for a variety of local services such as fire protection, public safety, refuse collection, area beautification, emergency medical services, care of the elderly, and cultural activities.

Enabling Partnerships[6]

Benefits of Partnerships

Partnership broadens the range and deepens the base of participation. Within a partnership, each actor contributes "hard" resources (financial, human, technological), and "soft" inputs (information and organizational support), and participates in the decision-making and implementation process on the basis of mutual agreements.

Public-Private Partnerships

Partnerships between government agencies and nongovernment entities may be mandated or voluntary. An example of mandated partnerships is the citywide partnership of government and nongovernment agencies in urban basic services program in India and the Philippines. Voluntary partnerships normally begin with the formation of an informal network of community organizations or user groups, which then expand to other groups in the area. Partnerships can also be permanent, to pursue a continuing goal, or temporary, disbanding when the specific objective is achieved.

Partnerships help build social capital in two ways. They can strengthen the capacity of individual stakeholders, their organizational structures and skills, the capacity for working together, and the confidence to build enduring relationships based on the recognition of successful outcomes. Also, the learning process during the partnership helps to break down barriers and creates trust. Again, the prerequisite is a process of monitoring to prevent the capture of the partnership by particularistic interests. The key to successful partnerships is not just to establish links to another group, but also to put in place agreed processes for joint decision making.

A good partnership must first deliver the services for which it was set up, and do so with a modicum of efficiency. However, it should also be based on effective mechanisms of accountability to ensure that those for whom the activity is intended are able to help shape it. Legitimacy is as important as short-term efficiency. In addition, government-community partnerships must partly be judged by the extent to which they give voice to marginalized and minority groups. For example, a project for rural water supply may be fully accountable in terms of access to information, review processes, and key decisions by the village council and may even ensure timely service at low cost. But if it doesn't address issues of distribution and a fair share of benefits to the weaker groups it cannot be considered a success.

BOX 12.2

Examples of Public-Private Partnerships in Brazil and India

In Brazil, the combined action of NGOs and community groups was responsible for the passage of the Prezeis law for the legalization of *favelas*—the squatter slums in Rio de Janeiro typically without any city services or public infrastructure. This was one of the few occasions when a law drafted by nongovernmental grassroots organizations was approved by the government. The law established two levels of community debate and oversight. The commission at the squatter settlement level is composed of representatives from the settlement, NGOs, and the city, and controls and monitors the funds and coordinates services in the area. The forum at city level develops citywide policies, including the administration of the Prezeis Fund, which is funded by the municipality. The fund and the participatory budget process give fiscal teeth to community control over the process. The law has turned the erstwhile slum dwellers without legal tenure into masters of the development process in their settlement (www.e-local.gob. mx/wb2/ELOCAL).

In India, a national newspaper launched an innovative idea in the large city of Pune for the citizens and the municipality to conduct a continuous dialogue on the provision of services and neighborhood issues. The newspaper organized an Express Group of Citizens for every municipal ward, with representation from all sections, including slums. The monthly meetings of the groups, also attended by local municipal officials, discuss local problems and find locally suitable solutions. These joint meetings have helped the political and administrative leadership of the Pune municipality to get reliable feedback on the quality of public services and have generated greater trust among the people about the city's responsiveness. The initiative has led to public consultations even on such technical matters as taxation and city planning. The Pune experience contrasts sharply with that of some other Indian cities, where similar local groups were set up as partisan political endeavors to mobilize votes and were disbanded when a new municipal government was elected.

Source: Asian Development Bank (1999a).

Often, inefficiently run national programs could improve substantially with support by the community, raising local acceptance and thus program effectiveness. In the Philippines, for example, health services were expanded to previously underserved areas through the dispatching of the government's mobile health units to remote villages under the endorsement and support of local community groups. Such partnerships not only lead to fuller utilization of the existing facilities for public services, but also improve their quality and outreach in countries with dispersed settlements. Partnerships can also produce tangible benefits in dense urban areas, as shown in Box 12.2.

Private-Private Partnerships

The initiative for the creation of partnerships need not always involve government agencies. Community organizations, such as women's organizations, or communal savings groups, or even slum dweller committees (see Shack/Slum Dwellers International, www.sdinet.org) can federate at the city level for the advocacy of common causes and for providing support services. Private groups can also network with parallel community organizations concerned with the same service and with community organizations in other cities and districts. Local NGOs can often facilitate the formation of these groupings by demystification of government functions, provision of information and training, and fostering of linkages to financial institutions, business, media, trade unions, and even to international NGOs. A dramatic example is the network of cooperatives of local milk producers in Indian villages, which helped decentralize milk collection and larger scale processing, permitted vastly expanded sales outlets, and eventually raised the capacity of the cooperatives to expand into many other areas of rural development and improve community literacy and health.

Consumers, too, link themselves in associations at the local and national level. Active in most developed countries, these associations are the prime mover behind the enactment and enforcement of laws to protect consumers, such as proper labeling and health and safety regulations. (In the United States, the main such association is Consumer Union, the sponsor of the print and web magazine *Consumer Reports,* which tests a variety of consumer products and publishes the results. *Consumer Reports* guarantees its independence by relying entirely on member subscriptions, refusing to accept advertisements, and never giving permission to cite its findings for commercial purposes.

The Role of Volunteers

Volunteers devote their time to assist in providing public services from which they do not benefit, for minimal or no compensation. They figure prominently in the delivery of government services in many countries. For example, at the turn of the century, unpaid volunteers were used by three-fourths of American cities. In the United States, as in many other countries, the growing elderly population provides a large pool from which to recruit volunteers. Volunteerism takes many forms, ranging from firefighters to senior citizen assistance, library aides, and so on.

The services of volunteers are utilized mainly by non-profit organizations, but volunteers are also used directly in many government programs. In the United States, retired professionals and civil servants donate time to adult literacy programs, or to help small businesses. The use of volunteers brings many of the gains possible with co-production, especially an increased service level, at little additional cost to the government. Also, the dedication of volunteers tends to have a beneficial demonstration effect on the regular employees in the government organization.

To achieve these gains, however, managers must carefully structure and plan volunteer programs to ensure that the positions filled by volunteers complement rather than compete with regular positions, that the volunteers have the necessary skills, and that employee resistance to volunteer involvement is defused in time by proper communication. It is also necessary to build the capacity of volunteers to perform their roles adequately. The most common problem in many countries is getting enough people to volunteer for government programs, because there are so many opportunities for volunteers in the nonprofit sector. However, other government efforts for community participation can bring potential volunteers into contact with government programs that need their contribution.

Volunteers can play a highly constructive role in the provision of public services and in strengthening the fabric of local communities. This has been especially true in the United States, with its Peace Corps created in 1961 for volunteer work in developing countries and, later, the AmeriCorps-VISTA program (Volunteers In Service To America—Americorps is a network of local, state and national service programs involving some 70,000 Americans a year in serving needs in education, safety, health, and the environment—see www.americorps.gov). There are tens of thousands of full-time members working in NGOs and other community organizations, as well as in public agencies, to create and expand programs primarily for the benefit of low-income individuals and communities. With the right vision and sustained government support, such programs have an immense potential for further expansion.

Indeed, a strong argument can be made in favor of a universal draft, by lottery but without exceptions, whereby young men and women would dedicate a year of their life to serving their country in any number of civilian public services. A compulsory draft would not be volunteerism, of course, except insofar as the choice of service would be left to the individuals. With the increasing segmentation of American society, including in higher education, and the elimination of the military draft, few if any opportunities remain for young Americans of different income classes and ethnic groups to interact with one another. A civilian draft could provide such an opportunity, in addition to making a major contribution to the community and expanding the provision of services to needy persons and groups.

The Role of Business

Business can contribute to effective partnerships by training managers of micro-enterprises, NGOs, and local authorities; running employee volunteer programs; supporting community projects; and cooperating with both government and nongovernmental agencies in social development and environmental management.

There are good examples of private companies joining forces with government to mobilize local skills and resources or support specific activities related to education, health, the environment, or central-city improvement. Among these examples is the Brazilian Abrinq Foundation to support needs of children, the Jamaican coalition for access to information technology, and company encouragement of employee volunteer work in Colombia and Mexico. These initiatives should be scrutinized with some care, of course, but they can make a useful social contribution even when motivated primarily by public relations concerns.

Studies show that the towns that provide more efficient services are those where private business played a direct positive role in administrative life (as in the cities of Anand, Manipal, and Bangalore in India). In developed countries, private associations such as the Paris Chamber of Commerce have also performed a constructive role in encouraging partnerships for better service delivery (Box 12.3).

The creation of collaborative networks among business, government, and the community has generated a new type of leader—the civic entrepreneur. These individuals combine business initiative with civic virtue and link community competencies with economic interests.[7] They are neither opportunists nor pure philanthropists, but contribute time, talent, and network membership to strengthen their community in the interest of everyone.

This edifying and hopeful picture of business must, unfortunately, be tempered by the much more frequent instances of collusion and corrupt transactions between private business and local government. Particularly in small countries and in small communities, public authority is often in effect largely exercised by powerful private entities using local government as their instrument of control and personal enrichment.

BOX 12.3

The Chamber of Commerce and Industry in Paris

The Paris Chamber of Commerce and Industry is a public corporation currently governed by a 1898 law. It was originally founded by Napoleon Bonaparte in 1803 to replace the old merchant corporations in Paris. The missions of the Chamber are to:

- represent and defend the interests of all companies, trade, industry, and services vis-à-vis public authorities;
- train future technical personnel, managers, and executives and all working men and women;
- inform and advise companies on legal, social, fiscal, commercial, and international issues and to back them at all stages of their development; and
- help in urban planning and infrastructure development in the Paris region.

Funding for the Chamber comes from a tax levied on companies and professionals in the district, revenues on operations, and a tax for training levied on all companies. The Chamber has about 4,000 employees, 62 percent of whom work in the field of education.

Source: Alain Billon, Associate Dean, Ecole Nationale d'Administration, personal communication, 2002.

CIVIL SOCIETY AND NONGOVERNMENTAL ORGANIZATIONS

Civil Society and Governance[8]

"Civil society" fills the space between the individual and the government. Civil society thus comprises all groups interacting socially, politically, and economically for the common interest of their members. Civil society has historically grown around traditional welfare and craft associations and religious groups and has been fostered by political, social and religious protest movements in different countries. In developed countries today, civil society includes organizations as diverse as trade unions, professional associations for architects and engineers, political parties, civic improvement groups, and social clubs. A strong and active civil society is the foundation on which rest the four pillars of good governance—accountability, transparency, participation, and predictability through the rule of law.

The idea of civil society as both counterweight and complement to government can be traced back to the writings of John Locke in the late seventeenth century, and was further developed in the nineteenth century, including its potential as a corrective force of imperfect markets. In contemporary times, the impetus for democratic change has generally come from grassroots movements. Examples include student protests in the 1960s and 1970s in Europe and the United States, the "velvet revolution" of the late 1980s in the former Czechoslovakia, and the "people's power" movements in Georgia, Korea, Philippines, Ukraine. Often, the root of these movements is alienation and lack of consultation in the major decisions affecting the people. These movements have generally, but not always, been a catalyst for positive change; occasionally they have been anomic and merely destructive, as in the more extreme "anti-globalization" demonstrations early in this century.

In countries where the transition from authoritarian or colonial regimes has produced fragile new forms of government superimposed on older habits of collusion and control, civil society organizations have represented, and will continue to represent, the only potential countervailing force to arbitrary administrative action. Quite aware of this potential, government in some countries (e.g., Russia under Vladimir Putin) has acted to systematically weaken civil society organizations in a variety of legal and extralegal ways.

When the regime in power is not hostile, civil society organizations can help address problems of social exclusion and a "democratic deficit." Social exclusion refers to the marginalization of minorities, women, and weaker groups from the processes of policy making, local administration, and delivery of services. A democratic deficit arises from lack of sufficient "voice" mechanisms for people (beyond their voting in the periodic elections). Encouraging civil society organizations can, in time, help both problems by fostering the involvement of people in specific activities of concern to them and helping to create a new assertiveness and habit of constructive participation. On the global scene, civil society organizations have made important contributions to major initiatives, such as the UN Conference on Environment and Development (1992), the World Conference on Human Rights (1993), and the World Conferences on Women.

As emphasized earlier in this chapter, social capital also has a potential downside. Similarly, civil society should not be viewed as a benevolent homogeneous category. It includes associations motivated by vice, greed, sectarian interests, and social repression, as well as business lobbies— some of which (such as the tobacco lobby) have interests sharply diverging from those of society as a whole. With this reminder, the rest of this discussion will focus on the positive roles of civil society organizations.

Types of Civil Society Organizations

Formal and Informal Organizations

Formal organizations, such as trade unions, have a specified mandate and adhere to codified rules governing the behavior of the organization. Informal organizations consist of groups of individuals who cooperate in different ways for collective action, financing, or the provision of goods and services. Cooperation in formal organization is permanent and defined. Cooperation in informal organizations may be short-term and episodic, or long-term. Community or grassroots organizations in different forms straddle the formal/informal division.

Informal organizations include well-known forms such as neighborhood committees and public service user groups, but also slums and squatter associations, local security committees, informal transport, and so on. In developing countries, these informal groups can account for a large proportion of service provision in housing, transport, sanitation, electricity supply, health, waste collection, and urban services (as much as 90 percent in Lima, Peru, for example). They fill the void left by the inability of the public administrative apparatus to meet the needs of the broader population and particularly the poor and marginal groups (McCarney, 1999).

Civil society organizations can also be distinguished between "primary" and "apex" organizations. Primary organizations form the base, but can associate with like-minded groups in regional or national apex organizations to gain leverage, share experiences, provide mutual support, and secure visibility vis-à-vis the national government. Example of apex organizations in the United States are Common Cause, founded in 1970 to work with other advocacy organizations to make government more accountable (www.commoncause.org), and the Friends Committee on National Legislation, founded in 1943 and working with a nationwide network of individuals and organizations to advocate social justice, peace and good government. (For a recent review of philanthropy and civil society in selected developed countries, see Adam, 2004.)

Public Employee Trade Unions

It is appropriate to consider government employee unions as civil society associations with a positive role in policy and program implementation—instead of the conventional view of these unions as adversarial actors with a capacity for disrupting public services (Tendler, 1997). This positive role has been demonstrated in a number of social programs in Asia and Latin America. Also, economic reforms in the transitional economies of Eastern Europe have included the participation of trade unions, professional associations, and employers. In any event, experience shows that a failure to consult government employee unions or associations invariably slows effective implementation of government policies and programs and occasionally disrupts it altogether.

Grassroots and Traditional Organizations

Most intermediary civil society organizations are one step removed from ordinary citizens. By contrast, grassroots organizations deal with the people directly. Such organizations include farmers' groups, parent-teacher associations, and faith-based associations other than the major organized churches. Some countries (e.g., India and Philippines) have taken steps to incorporate community-based organizations into formal administrative decentralization structures, usually under the guise of mandatory consultation. In the United States in recent years, religious groups have been encouraged to participate in public service provision, in ways that do not conflict with the constitutional prohibition of the separation between church and state.

Possibilities for linkage to formal administration are limited by the grassroots organizations' problems of narrow membership, low management capacity, and risk of capture by traditional elites. However, grassroots organizations can build trust, reduce the alienation of minorities and socially disadvantaged groups, and counter the corporate orientation of many government agencies. The role of customary institutions must not be overlooked either, especially in small countries with a strong tradition, although their role is more often one of resistance to change rather than facilitator of improvements (Box 12.4).

Public Interest Lobbies

Civil society includes also citizen groups for lobbying the administration, often in adversarial relation with business interests. The need to counterbalance the vast power and influence of organized industry lobbies (e.g., in the United States, the tobacco lobby, the pharmaceutical industry, and others) has led to increased citizen participation. In most developed countries, public interest lobbies have played a major role in the enactment of regulatory legislation, environmental protection, and consumer safety. Freedom of information campaigns have pushed hard for the disclosure of public records. Citizen advocacy has led to the closure or correction of polluting factories.

BOX 12.4

Traditional Community Institutions in the South Pacific

In the small island countries of the South Pacific—in both Melanesia and Polynesia—traditional village chiefs and the Christian churches are the keepers of the ethical standards of society. By mobilizing their followers, they are able to give or withhold the political support and access to resources that government and businesses require.

Traditional chiefs, in particular, can exercise powerful growth-supporting and redistributive functions, if they are determined to do so. Their role has not always been positive, however. Some traditional chiefs have been bought off by politicians or business dealmakers, and others have opposed even the mildest forms of change. The churches, too, have often been at the center of resistance to change in many island countries.

In the South Pacific, the lines between government, business, and civil society are blurred. Institutions and individuals have multiple roles, in what is called the *wantok* ("one talk")—pidgin for communal system. Churches are involved in business and also provide public services; trade unions run investment funds; individuals can function simultaneously as elected politicians and priests, civil servants and entrepreneurs, army officers and traditional chiefs, or any other combination of roles.

This multiplicity of roles explains why the norms applying to one role can be infringed without community sanction or sense of wrongdoing. It also makes it difficult to enforce accountability, foster efficiency, and prevent diversion of public funds into private pockets. The challenge of "modernization" in the South Pacific islands is to sharpen individuals' accountability for the functions assigned to them by society at large, without destroying the customary patterns of behavior and reciprocal support that make for a strong community with its own clear identity.

Source: Knapman and Saldanha (1999).

Such advocacy tends to focus on visible issues, which can bring together large numbers of citizens. However, it also tends to be ad hoc and reactive, rarely sustainable over long periods and unable to cover a broad spectrum of issues due to inadequate resources and managerial skills.

Cooperatives

Cooperatives are an important part of civil society in most countries, and fall in between grassroots organizations and larger organized groups. The concept of cooperative is comparatively recent and is associated with the northern England town of Rochdale. The Rochdale Society of Equitable Pioneers was a group of 28 artisans who got together in 1844 to protect themselves from the displacement caused by the Industrial Revolution by opening their own store selling food and other basic items they could not otherwise afford based on eight principles:

- Open membership;
- Democratic control;
- Distributing profits to members in proportion to their purchases (not capital);
- Paying moderate interest on capital subscribed;
- Political and religious neutrality;
- Cash trading only (no credit);
- Promotion of education; and
- Quality goods and services.

Some of the original principles have been relaxed or abandoned (e.g., most obviously, the prohibition of selling on credit, originally intended to prevent members from getting into debt), and the term "cooperative" now covers a variety of entities and activities beyond food sales. The principal meaning, however, remains that of a legal entity owned and controlled by its members on a one-person/one-vote basis, and not in proportion to the capital subscribed. Anyone who meets certain specified criteria may be a member, and only members may participate in the running of the cooperative. Cooperatives have legally defined structures and memberships and are often federated into regional or national organizations.

In developed countries, cooperatives have been primarily associated with urban activities and with banking. (The "credit unions" in the United States are in effect cooperatives, run by members with only one vote each whether their account balance is ten dollars or a million.) In developing countries, by contrast, the model first took hold in the rural areas—with cooperatives created for agricultural inputs, seasonal credit, crop processing, storage, and marketing—and only later expanded to urban areas.

The cooperative model has been useful to alleviate social problems: in many cities, cooperatives have reached down to include as members the poor and the slum dwellers, and have used the support of formal financial institutions to build cooperatively-managed shelters and other facilities. The growth of cooperatives has been especially remarkable in India, with tens of thousands of housing associations, industrial cooperatives, cooperative finance groups, and various forms of production cooperatives. Cooperatives of milk producers, in particular, have been responsible for a veritable revolution in the dairy industry and for new rural prosperity in a number of provinces.

In some countries, cooperatives are subject to government control and tied to government funding, and have sometimes also been manipulated by powerful political interests for vote-buying or other partisan activities. Paradoxically, when cooperatives have been successful, their very success has generated a temptation for government to co-opt them as an extension of the public administration apparatus, instead of protecting their independence. The predictable result has been to damage their credibility. Cooperatives can be an important complement of government provision of public services, especially to the poor and marginalized groups, but only if government support is limited and carefully circumscribed.

Nongovernmental Organizations

The Nature of NGOs

All "nongovernmental organizations" are by definition part of civil society. However, the term has generally been used in a narrower sense to include only organizations oriented to a public service role (as opposed, for example, to a trade union or a cooperative, which provides services limited to its members). Because NGOs in this sense have become a major interlocutor, antagonist, or partner for government, their roles and capabilities merit separate discussion.

NGOs are also called private voluntary organizations, nonprofit organizations, charities, or humanitarian foundations. By any name, NGOs possess four defining characteristics. They are voluntary, independent, not for profit, and aimed at a public function of some sort.

The Evolution of NGOs

The historical roots of NGOs are found in the charity and welfare activities of religious institutions and other voluntary groups. Christian churches have always had a social assistance tradition; in Islam, *zakat* (charity for the poor) is one of the five fundamental obligations of the religion; and in Buddhism one gains "merit" by giving alms to temples and supporting the monks. Beyond their traditional role in these respects, over the past fifty years NGOs have also emerged as a major rallying point and lobby for social, environmental, and development concerns, at both domestic and global levels. A significant role for NGOs has been incorporated in global summits on population, habitat, and the environment, women's development, HIV/AIDS, and other major issues.

NGO work now spans the entire spectrum of basic human needs and key issues, including health, education, rural and urban development, environment, family planning, social welfare, job creation, training, gender, the informal sector, indigenous people's issues, peace, and human rights. Their activities range from care and welfare provision to service delivery, resource mobilization, research and innovation, human resource development, public information, education, and advocacy.

Apart from other factors leading to the growth of civil society in general, the growth of the private voluntary sector has also coincided with mounting concerns about government inefficiency and the resulting incentive to explore alternative modes of responsive service delivery. Also, the continuing exclusion of weaker groups from economic development and political participation gave a new focus and mission to NGOs, particularly in developing countries. Along with the growth in NGOs came criticism and misgivings. Some misgivings were legitimate, others less so, but the issue of NGO accountability has come to the fore everywhere. In developed countries, the partisan political activism of some organizations (e.g., the support of conservative candidates and causes by certain religious groups in the United States) has smothered their original mission. In developing countries, rightly or wrongly, there are suspicions about the hidden agenda of international NGOs and the role of foreign governments supporting them.

The private voluntary sector has dramatically expanded not merely in numbers but also in diversity and types of activities. In central and eastern Europe, the number of NGOs has increased at least four times after the fall of the Soviet Union, albeit from the very low base of 1990. In developing countries, India alone has over a million registered NGOs. Large NGOs in Bangladesh employ over 50,000 people. In developed countries, the private voluntary sector accounts for up to 4 percent of GDP. In the United States, the number of charities and other NGOs is estimated in the tens of thousands. Over one fifth of official aid to developing countries is channeled through NGOs, and NGO coalitions have observer status in conferences of United Nations bodies (Hailey, 1999). However, the NGO sector remains small and localized relative to the much greater reach of government or big business—with some major exceptions in the United States.

Types of NGOs

A distinction can be made between "developmental," "advocacy," "service," and "whistle-blowing" NGOs:

- Developmental NGOs are formed to help meet needs for infrastructure and social services; to secure economic and social benefits through group action; or to participate directly in community production activities. An example is CARE, one of the largest international organizations active in assisting the poor in developing countries.
- Advocacy NGOs are concerned primarily with influencing public policy decisions and bringing major concerns to the forefront of national debate. They devote themselves to mobilization, dissemination, and, at local level, usually some aspect of community organizing as well. An example is Human Rights Watch, dedicated to publicizing violations and pushing governments and international organizations to protect human rights throughout the world.
- Service-oriented NGOs emphasize the provision or improvement of specific services. The best-known are Doctors Without Borders (possibly the most effective and courageous such organization in the world, *not* to be confused with "Doctors of the World"), for medical services to the poor everywhere, and the Grameen Bank in Bangladesh (to provide micro-credit to poor people who have no access to formal credit facilities).
- Whistle-blower NGOs investigate the efficiency of government activities and publicize instances of waste, fraud, and abuse. As example is Public Employees for Environmental Responsibility, to assist government employees work as "anonymous activists."

The distinction is not clear-cut, however, with large NGOs taking on at the same time developmental, advocacy, service, and whistle-blowing roles, e.g., Common Cause in the area of government accountability. Moreover, over time, an NGO may change its original orientation and take on a different function.

Many international NGOs, such as Doctors Without Borders, the Red Cross, Red Crescent, Save the Children, Amnesty International, Human Rights Watch, Oxfam, CARE, and others enjoy high standing. In addition to their own programs, most international NGOs also support networks of local NGOs engaged in the same nature of activity through funding, operational links, partnerships on specific issues, and assistance for networking. There are also regional NGOs, which operate across a number of countries.

Membership and Legal Forms

Depending on the organization's mission, the membership of NGOs can be drawn from a specific group like farmers or construction workers, or can be broad-based within a locality or region. The procedures for membership can be formal, involving eligibility criteria and limiting the size of the membership, or informal. In most cases, membership carries a fee to cover organizational expenses.

The diversity of NGO missions and activities accounts for the diversity of legal forms. For example, NGOs that are sponsored by a government (quasi-NGOs, or "QUANGOs") have a structure and membership set from above, and their board of directors may include government appointees. But even the most localized and spontaneous NGO must conform to a clear legal structure for accountability and audit purposes. In the absence of this accountability, it may be difficult to tell the difference between a genuine public-service organization and a front for personal gain of the founders or money-laundering.

Potential Contributions of NGOs

The growth of NGOs rests on the widespread perception that voluntary private organizations are a force toward democratic and pluralist society, have special strengths in poverty alleviation, and offer the prospect of more efficient public service delivery. Indeed, the potential advantages of NGOs are many. NGOs can:

- help make government services more effective by better identifying target groups, facilitating their access to services, and coordinating the delivery of inputs from various agencies;
- help mobilize resources from the local population, especially when substantial mobilization of people is required (as in the mass literacy movement in Kerala, India) and assist in training and project implementation (as in Kandy, Sri Lanka);
- provide technical inputs for community mobilization and planning (as in the Kampung improvement project in Indonesia);
- help coordinate the implementation of government social programs at the regional and local level;
- exercise valuable checks and balances on abuse of official power; and
- provide opportunities for citizens' complaints and public hearings.

Risks and Concerns

There are, however, genuine concerns as well, particularly about the extent of NGO accountability, transparency, and representative character. The key question is: To whom is the NGO accountable? There have been many instances of unscrupulous opportunism and of misuse of funds, even by established NGOs.[9] Existing arrangements for registration and reporting to government agencies are often inadequate or poorly enforced. Without adequate external oversight, a private voluntary organization is accountable to nobody but itself, which becomes an especially serious problem when the organization is controlled by one or a few individuals. (See Edwards, 2000.)

In the United States, for example, the valuable social activities of the United Way were almost totally discredited by the gross abuse of voluntary contributions by the top leadership, and even the Red Cross came under heavy criticism for its role in the post-Katrina assistance effort. Demands on advocacy NGOs to become more accountable have also intensified following the June 2000 riots in Seattle against the World Trade Organization and the April 2002 violence in Washington associated with protests against the World Bank and the International Monetary Fund. It was indeed peculiar that small private organizations not accountable to the public felt they had the right, beyond legitimate vocal dissent, to obstruct decision making by governments elected democratically by hundreds of millions of people.

Other common problems of private voluntary organizations, especially the large ones, are bureaucratic tendencies, duplication of activities from weak coordination with other NGOs, narrow issue advocacy, centralization, closed processes for decision making without participation by the broader membership, and inadequate long-range planning.

As noted, NGOs can serve as excellent cover for personal gain or even criminal activities. Indeed, during the early years of the transition in Russia and Eastern Europe after the fall of the Soviet Union in 1991, it was noted jokingly how unusual it was that mangos were now growing in such cold climates—"MANGOs" referring to Mafia NGOs. Particularly problematic are "GONGOs"—Government-organized non-government organizations. These oxymoronic entities, which have increased in both number and influence over the last decade, are more of a camouflaged government tool than a genuine part of civil society. However, with their respectable cover and superficially attractive formal mandate, GONGOs can easily delude the public and the casual observer. Elaborating on a proposal made earlier by the U.K. Foreign Policy Centre (see below), Moises Naim has proposed therefore the creation of an international rating system for NGOs "that does for civil society what independent credit rating agencies do for the global financial system" (Naim, 2007).

Stronger accountability for performance and robust external oversight are in the interest of effective and honest NGOs, because abuse by a few organizations leads to wholesale disillusionment in all. Accordingly, in recent years a number of NGOs have themselves instituted various measures to improve their governance and operations, such as clearer mission statements; better management processes; scrutiny of top management salaries; stricter budgeting; accounting and audit; better monitoring and evaluation of the organization's programs; greater public access to information about their activities; and, in developing countries, a more humble and cooperative attitude vis-à-vis both the host government and the local private voluntary organizations.

A useful suggestion was made in 2001 years ago by the U.K. Foreign Policy Centre to combine NGO self-regulation with external verification. The proposal entails the formulation of a "code of conduct" for NGOs, incorporating standards of accountability, transparency, and internal democracy. In exchange for committing to and abiding by these principles, NGOs would be certified by a regulatory body, giving them greater access to policy decision making and validating their eligibility to receive assistance. Unfortunately, nothing has come out of this proposal so far.[10]

Functioning in a Political Environment

To be effective while staying true to their mission, NGOs have to navigate their political environment, sometimes a very difficult one. Some need to work in an environment of political repression, as in the Philippines during Ferdinand Marcos' martial law of the 1970s and 1980s, Suharto's Indonesia in the 1980s and 1990s, Brazil in the 1960s and 1970s, the Pinochet despotism in Chile in the 1970s and 1980s, or Nigeria in the 1980s and most of the 1990s until the death of the dictator Sani Abacha. An NGO forced to make unsavory deals with thugs in power, in order to be allowed to help the poor and vulnerable, faces moral and practical challenges that are as difficult as they are unavoidable.

Other NGOs have to deal with non-antagonistic but heavily bureaucratic government agencies, as in many Latin American countries and most of the Middle East and South Asia. Still other NGOs have to contend with government attempts to manipulate and control their activities. It is only a minority of private voluntary organizations that are able to work in an environment of integrity, stability and openness—as for example in India, Brazil, today's Chile and Argentina, the United States, Canada, a handful of African countries, parts of East Asia, most European countries and, increasingly, Indonesia.

NGO–Government Cooperation

Where the political environment permits, there are various possibilities for cooperation between NGOs and the government; however, they must be approached with care and realism. Advocacy NGOs are often reluctant to cooperate with government, act as agents of public agencies, or to accept grants from government. They see such involvement as compromising their ability to exert pressure on government from the outside and perform their legitimate role on behalf of civil society. Even service-oriented NGOs are wary of the long-term effects of government support on the viability and service commitment of the organization. There is indeed a risk that, in becoming "too supportive" of NGO programs, a government agency may destroy the innovative and responsive element of those activities. There is also a risk that substantial government support may create a dependency syndrome and turn the NGO into a crypto-governmental entity. Regular communication between the government and NGOs in common forums, and vigilance by the NGO membership, would help to address these risks.

More effective than simple communication and conditional government support, however, is the model of government funding of NGOs used in the Netherlands and Denmark, wherein NGOs gain access to unconditional grants given by transparent criteria and without having to bid for contracts. This permits the organizations to maintain their independence while benefiting from government support and, in turn, to assist government in areas where private voluntary organizations have a comparative advantage. Nor does government support necessarily have to be large and financial: many NGOs are willing to assist in mobilizing communities and supporting services in exchange for help in-kind, such as transportation or simple equipment.

Beyond their traditional service delivery role, some NGOs have emerged as social entrepreneurs. Successful examples are the Grameen Bank of Bangladesh, for provision of microcredit to small farmers;[11] the Sulabh International of India, for low-cost sanitation and community latrines; and various housing foundations in Latin American countries. Also in Latin America, private voluntary organizations have often been entrusted with the implementation of public works programs on behalf of many cities and rural areas. NGOs can also be contracted by national and local governments to deliver social services, channel loans to target groups, and provide training. These roles of private voluntary organizations and their ability to attract government funding without having to bid for contracts often draws complaints from businesspeople who are apprehensive about the prospect of business competitors masquerading as nonprofit voluntary organizations.

In developing countries, external funding agencies and major international foundations have played a significant role in supporting NGO initiatives for many years. This assistance has often helped to demonstrate innovative approaches such as the "basic services" strategy of the United Nations Children's Fund (UNICEF). However, the activities of local NGOs have sometimes been determined by external donor preferences rather than by community needs. Also, donors have often exerted pressure on host governments to channel funds to NGOs without first ensuring that a credible system for accountability and transparency was in place. This has tended to encourage some fraudulent NGOs while leaving the smaller organizations at a serious disadvantage. And, in countries with weak governance, external aid has even ended up in the pockets of high government officials through their setting up a "private" voluntary organization as a front. As a Nepali proverb says: "Where there is honey, there are bees."

A CONCLUDING WORD

NGOs have undoubted value. However, one must be as realistic about the proper limits and potential for abuse in private organizations as in public agencies. Moreover, it is inadvisable to place responsibility for basic government functions in the hands of organizations that are not elected, and hence—unlike government—are not accountable to the public for their actions. Clarity of the scope, value, limits, and accountability of NGOs has become doubly important with the expansion of charitable giving through huge new private contributions to resolve critical problems in developing countries. The prime example is the Bill and Melinda Gates Foundation, already extremely wealthy before being augmented in 2006 by a selfless contribution by investor Warren Buffett of the largest amount ever given for charitable purposes (giving birth to the new word "billanthropy" for billionaire philanthropy). Without close scrutiny of the effectiveness and accountability of the beneficiary organizations and continued robust external monitoring with swift and strong penalties for misbehavior, the risk of waste and abuse will rise along with the size of the new charitable contributions. Both Gates and Buffett understand this risk and have put in place a set of rules to which every recipient of their grants must abide—including financial accountability and the requirement to meet defined deliverables relevant to the purpose of the grant. Indeed, a crucial potential externality from this expansion of charitable giving would be its impact on strengthening the integrity and efficiency of the private voluntary sector around the world.

GENERAL DIRECTIONS OF IMPROVEMENT

Social Capital

Social capital is the stock of trust created through networks of reciprocal support based on common interests. These networks include "bonding" networks connecting people in similar circumstances and fostering in-group reciprocity, and "bridging" networks between different groups, fostering cooperation and the exchange of information. Social capital differs from physical capital in that it is intangible and nonmarketable, accumulated through information rather than financial savings, and depleted when it is *not* used.

Social capital is more than an ingredient of a friendlier social climate and has very important beneficial implications. Social capital:

- facilitates economic exchange and government effectiveness by increasing trust among individuals, within groups, and between groups;
- alleviates the "free rider" problem (i.e., individuals not contributing their share if they can get for free a service from which everyone benefits); and
- strengthens rule compliance, as people are more likely to obey the rules voluntarily if they can be reasonably sure that others will also abide by them.

Social capital also carries risks, however:

- Individual inventiveness can be discouraged—in cultures where a special premium is placed on tradition, individuals behaving in a manner that is viewed as different may be ostracized;.
- The cohesion built within one particular group can be used to oppress outsiders, e.g., organized crime networks and the "bonding" within military dictatorships.
- Economic bonding networks may siphon power and resources from the rest of society (e.g., business interests in East Asia set up networks that generated internal social capital and increased group profit, but largely by keeping out other groups).
- In multiethnic countries, social capital formation within groups may have particularly severe negative implications, particularly if civil conflict erupts—when strong social capital within a group is used for destruction of the others.

These risks can be alleviated, and the great positive potential of social capital utilized, if the state and organized civil society enable *both* the formation of social capital within groups and the building of bridges and linkages between different groups. This need not require vast resources. Sometimes, a public signal of encouragement from the government may be enough. Or, government may make simple infrastructural or information facilities available to local communities and the community groups will do the rest. (Among the poor, however, voluntary cooperation requires active government support to become sustainable.) Also, the government should crack down on all social exclusion and restriction of competition grounded on solidarity within the elite group.

Participation

Participation is the main mechanism through which social capital is created. The first requirement for successful improvements is to identify the major stakeholder groups and assess the legitimacy of persons claiming to represent them. Country circumstances will determine which of many possible approaches to participation is realistic, but a general prerequisite for effective participation is a representative and responsive local government prodded by an active local community

At a minimum, participation must include direct feedback by the beneficiaries of public services or investments. Such reality checks are an invaluable and cost-effective means of stimulating public service efficiency. Participation should extend beyond feedback, however, to the selection and design of government activities. For example, the open hearings on the budget that are an established practice in developed countries should be fostered in developing countries as well.

Initiatives to foster participation must be genuine. When participation is elicited for purely cosmetic reasons or in mechanical ways, or the feedback is not seriously considered, the natural result is reluctance to participate and loss of government credibility. So-called "participation fatigue" is a rational response to and a visible symptom of an insincere or ineffective approach to fostering participation.

Mainstreaming participation in government operations rests on four criteria:

- effective outreach—tailoring the approach to the target population;
- equal access—assuring participation of large numbers of the target population;
- impact—linking participation to significant policy decisions; and
- actionability—promoting the incorporation of the outcome of participation into actual government programs.

Civil Society and NGOs

Civil society organizations strengthen the interface between the citizens and their government and are thus important both for the quality of governance and for improvements in public services. General directions of improvement include:

- strengthening the roles of formal organizations (e.g., by involving educational institutions in contributing to various aspects of administrative change);
- relating to employee unions as constructive agents of change rather than adversaries;
- supporting grassroots organizations (e.g., farmers' associations and neighborhood groups) by building management capacity and protecting them from capture by local interests;
- encouraging the growth of informal voluntary groups, which are particularly important for assistance to the poor and disadvantaged;
- recognizing the roles of traditional customary institutions (mainly in developing countries); and
- facilitating the emergence of public interest citizens' groups to counterbalance organized business lobbies (mainly in developed countries).

Nongovernmental organizations are a major component of civil society, and include advocacy NGOs to advance a particular goal and service NGOs to deliver a variety of services, particularly to poorer and marginal groups. Both can be excellent partners for government by checking on execution of government programs, running alternative service delivery systems, and other ways.

However, the NGOs themselves must meet certain requirements of accountability, efficiency, and willingness to cooperate with other NGOs. Improvements can focus on creating an enabling environment for NGO–government cooperation but with provisions to assure that NGOs have transparent governance, sound financial management, and a good record of service.

Even the best and most active participation by citizens and civil society organizations, however, must not cause governments to forget that they carry the primary responsibility to provide public services, nor induce society to loosen up on holding its government accountable for doing so.

QUESTIONS FOR DISCUSSION

1. "Civil conflict destroys all forms of social capital." Discuss.
2. "Unlike physical capital, social capital is a measure of comity and friendliness in society." Comment.
3. Since "there is no honor among thieves," how can there be social capital within a criminal gang?
4. Should governments pay as much attention to enabling bonding networks as to fostering bridging networks? How do country circumstances affect this issue?
5. Since it is impossible for everyone potentially affected by a proposed government action to participate in shaping it, is "participation" mainly a cosmetic device for those in power to pretend they are following the people's wishes?
6. "The benefits of participation consist largely of providing direct feedback to the government on the efficiency and quality of execution of government programs." Discuss.
7. Since active participation must come from the people themselves, aren't top-down government efforts to foster participation useless or even counterproductive?
8. "In developing countries with weak governance and accountability mechanisms, there is no such thing as 'public-private' partnerships, but in reality only 'private-private' partnerships." Discuss.
9. Pick one of the two following statements and make a credible argument for it:
   a. "Most NGOs are controlled by a few unaccountable individuals for their own agenda, and no government that is representative of and accountable to the people should allow itself to be pushed around by them."
   b. "Most NGOs are organized expressions of genuine popular concerns, and the public interest demands that government respond to their concerns and enlist their active cooperation."

NOTES

1. From Gannt and Gerald (2002).

2. This section draws in part on Robert Putnam (1993, 1995, 2000); Fiszbein and Lowden (1999); United Nations Development Program (1997); and various international organization websites on social capital. Valuable comments were received from Mara Schiavocampo.

3. An important area for further study concerns gender differences in the formation of social capital—an area so far generally neglected. (For an exception, see Maxine, 2002.) There are indications that men tend to belong to formal networks reflecting their work status and yielding material advantages, while women rely on more informal networks centered around family and kin. One possible implication is that approaches that strengthen the existing formal networks may inadvertently heighten gender inequality.

4. The open source approach entails, among other things, that the software is released with the source code permitting anyone to use and improve it, and must allow distribution in source code as well as compiled form—see www.opensource.org

5. This section has drawn in part on OECD (2001, 2005); Bamberger (1986); Berry et al. in Perry, ed. (1989); Cernea (1992); Thomas (1995); and a variety of Internet information on different countries.

6. This section has drawn partly on Fiszbein and Lowden (1999); Tendler (1997); McCarney (1999); Berry, Portney, and Thomas in Perry, ed. (1989); and Hino (1999).

7. Henton et al. (1997).

8. This section is drawn partly from UNDP (1997); the World Bank website on civil society; the British Council; Public Affairs Center (1999); Mehta (1997); World Bank (1997); Transparency International (www.transparencyinternational.org); Robinson and White (1997).

9. In 1992, for example, William Aramony, President of The United Way, resigned amid investigation for fraud and mismanagement of the organization's funds. He was later found guilty of multiple counts of fraud, tax evasion, and money laundering. The United Way barely survived the scandal. (See Glaser, 1994.)

10. As reported by the *Financial Times,* June 19, 2000.

11. The founder of Grameen, Muhammad Yunus, received the 2006 Nobel Peace Prize for this seminal contribution.

CHAPTER 13

Transparency: Information, the Media, and E-Governance

> My whole life I've been an advocate for open records—transparency
> in government—because I think it brings with it greater accountability.
> —*Roy Barnes, former governor of Georgia*

> Even a democratically elected and benign government can easily be
> corrupted, when its power is not held in check by an independent press.
> —*Henry Grunwald, former editor of* Time *magazine*

WHAT TO EXPECT

Information is the lifeblood of the relationship between a people and their government. Neither "voice" nor "exit" can operate if the people lack the relevant information. If the public does not know who makes administrative decisions and how, its only voice will be through anomic public protests that do not contribute to improving the quality of public services. Nor is accountability possible without adequate information about the actions of public agencies and their results. Inefficiency and corruption thrive best in the dark, and the capacity to press for change requires a public with adequate information on government activities and the standards by which to judge the performance of public services. This chapter reviews the issues of transparency in public management, including the importance of good records management and the uses and limits of Freedom of Information legislation. The critical role of the media is examined next, placing the accent on both media freedom and responsibility and making a distinction between the impact of "old" and "new" media—particularly the internet. The chapter then discusses e-governance and the key guiding principles for the effective use of information and communications technology in public management and for improved legislative transparency, and concludes with the customary section on general directions of improvement.

TRANSPARENCY IN PUBLIC MANAGEMENT

Transparency and Governance

Transparency is one of the pillars of good governance. As the other three pillars, the concept of transparency is universal in application but relative in nature. The operational question revolves around what information is to be provided and to whom. Full openness can be problematic when it infringes on privacy, and there are reasons for government secrecy concerning information which, if disclosed, would jeopardize ongoing investigations, national security, or other public interests. There is also a legitimate role for confidentiality in government. For example, free and frank discussions in policy-making settings and independent advice on sensitive matters must be confidential. Disclosure would only drive such discussions underground and the formal record would then contain no information of any substance or value to the public, with serious risks for healthy governance. However, *the burden of proof must be on those who would keep the information confidential*, not on those who would want to share it with the public. Disclosure should be the rule rather than the exception, and all government information should be open to the public except when specifically provided otherwise—for good and public reasons and on the basis of clear criteria. Hence, even when the information itself is confidential, the *criteria* for keeping it confidential must be public and transparent.

Transparency of administrative information is a must for an informed executive, legislature, and the citizens at large—normally through the filter of competent legislative staff and capable and independent public media. It is essential not only that information be provided, but that it be relevant and in understandable form. Dumping on the public vast amounts of raw documents is not transparency, but a time-honored bureaucratic device for drowning the important information in an ocean of irrelevancies. Thus, genuine transparency requires *both* openness and outreach.

Transparency in public administration requires mainly that the relevant information is made available to the general public in usable form and the regulations and decision-making processes are clear and public. Both requirements run against an ingrained tendency of any large organization toward secrecy. In large organizations, both private and public, for decision makers to be open about facts and practices is rarely an advantage but always exposes them to the risk of damaging criticism. The first natural impulse is therefore to withhold information. Moreover, information that is withheld becomes an instrument of influence and is thus treated as a quasi-private asset of the individual or small group that produces or possesses it. Often, lines of communication are closed even between and within government agencies. (For example, the insufficient exchange of information between the intelligence agencies in the United States has been a major obstacle to effective national security and anti-terrorism efforts.)

Whatever its origin or justification, the habit of withholding information—without adequate and agreed justification—eventually becomes a cover for arbitrary or wrong exercise of authority, dishonest transactions, and bad decisions. Power over information and the manner of its disclosure can be as corrupting as power over resources or over people. These tendencies and implicit incentives for secrecy mean that transparency in public administration cannot materialize by itself, but requires specific mechanisms and provisions to be put in place, through determined efforts within government and sustained pressure by the public.

Transparency in public administration has two main aspects: public communication and citizens' right of access to information held by government.

Public Communication[1]

Priorities

The data the government collects and produces and the rules and regulations that it enacts are too vast and varied for the individual citizen to know. Government agencies hold masses of information on both individuals and business—vital statistics, taxes, health and education, and so on. Government also has the monopoly of certain categories of data such as the census, law enforcement, and legal information. As noted, transparency entails more than simply making this vast mass of information available. It requires a genuine willingness on the part of government to reach out and communicate, and efforts to do so effectively.

Public communication is the practical and proactive expression of open government. It lends visibility to the performance of all agencies and addresses the problem of unequal access to information by different sections of the population. Realistic public expectations and confidence in government are sustained by trust in the accuracy of the information used and provided by government. Generally, the types of information that should be made available to the public are mandated by law, including decisions affecting individuals and groups, rules and regulations, and department activities.

The different categories of information to be provided to the public include:

- information about government as a holder of data—what records are maintained and how their accuracy is ensured;
- information about government as a business—how much the government spends, on what, why, and with what results;
- information about government as a service provider—what services are available, at what price and quality, and how they are to be provided; and
- information about government as policy maker—how are major decisions made, on what evidence they are based, and what results and impact are expected.

Issues

Public communication has to contend with the longstanding bureaucratic practices and tendency for secrecy earlier and, in many countries, legal constraints. Typically, unauthorized disclosure of information to outsiders makes both the communicator and the holder of such information liable to penalties, through "official secrets" laws or similar regulations. Administrative discretion and arbitrariness hold sway in classifying public records as confidential, and differences between countries are large: some countries treat even the directory of government officials as confidential, whereas other countries make the names and telephone numbers of senior officials easily available on the internet.

A critical issue is the opaqueness of the budget and the budgetary process. The complicated and often arcane presentation of the budget inhibits informed debate and effective scrutiny by the legislature or the media. The best answer to budgetary opaqueness, however, is not to assist citizens and groups to decipher inscrutable budgets, but to compel the executive branch of government to present financial information in ways that are clear and accessible to ordinary citizens—even if through the filter of a competent media. Fiscal transparency is perhaps the most important single administrative reform introduced in developed countries since the early 1990s. (See chapter 6 for a full discussion of this and related issues.)

Public communication through the internet, the exception a mere ten years ago, has become commonplace in the United States and other developed countries, and the public has enormous information of value at its fingertips. Developing countries, however, are constrained by low ownership of computers and limited capacity to sift through vast amounts of information. Information technology has thus increased the intercountry and intergroup inequality of access to information—the so-called "digital gap." The digital gap, however, is being partly filled by offering to the public online services through post offices, district agencies, public libraries and the ubiquitous internet cafes.

The availability of more information does not itself guarantee its use, especially if educational levels are low, or the citizens cannot use the information effectively to access basic services and engage in economic activities, or there is widespread alienation from the political process. When people come to believe that their input makes no difference, it is perfectly rational for them not to waste time collecting information relevant to that input. The opposite is also true, however. When citizens are unwilling to exert a minimum of effort to inform themselves or do not press for government information to be widely available, they make government secrecy or dissemination of official lies that much more likely. There is indeed a sense in which, in a democracy, the people get the government they deserve.

Records Management

Governments cannot disseminate information in the first place if the information is not appropriately managed and recorded. The subject of good management of government records has come to the fore in the last decade as a neglected but very important aspect of administrative effectiveness. In many developed countries and in most transition economies and developing countries, government records management needs considerable improvement. The major priorities are:

- an effective system for collecting and retrieving records and information;
- regulations to oblige government agencies to define, classify, and publish the information and records they hold;
- provisions specifying the time limit beyond which government records will be publicly disclosed on request;
- procedures for preparing the documents for public dissemination in intelligible language; and
- formulating performance reports in ways that allow comparisons with performance measures and expected results.

All these activities are costly, time consuming, and require constant follow-up. Therefore, selectivity is mandatory. Improvement in the management and disclosure of public records should focus on areas where the benefit is demonstrably greater than the cost. These will differ in different countries, but budget and procurement are two areas where better records and disclosure would be beneficial virtually everywhere.

Professionalism in Communications

Effective dissemination of government information is not a task to be left to amateurs or low-level staff. There is a need in every major government agency for professional public information officers, with four major functions:

- disseminate reliable information to the public;
- develop a climate of trust between the government and the public through openness and honesty in all communications and courteous treatment of all citizens;
- provide guidance and training in communication skills to concerned government officials; and
- continuously monitor public opinion and disseminate the findings within the agency or the government as a whole.

These functions require a two-way exchange of information with citizens and civil society and the active involvement of public information officers in mobilizing citizens to participate in dialogues on key issues. A continuation of the traditional censor-and-regulate system only undermines the credibility of official communications. Improved relations with the media may include closer contacts with journalists and better-packaged information; unambiguous and honest messages, especially during crises; stronger coordination between policy advice and press functions; and alternative mechanisms for disseminating information to the public. As governments become less monolithic at central, state, and local levels, the risk of ambiguity or incoherence becomes greater and the coordinating role of the central government information office (in consultation with line agencies) correspondingly acquires greater weight. What is definitely not needed is "spin," i.e., the manipulation of information and events to convey a misleading or self-serving message.

Access to Information and Freedom-of-Information (FOI) Laws[2]

The right of citizens to have access to information from governmental bodies on request includes personal information about themselves; nonpersonal information held by the government that does not endanger national security, law enforcement, privacy of others, or other specified public interest; and information disseminated by the government on its own initiative.

There are important complementarities between the access rights of citizens and the public communication role of government. Individuals who request access to information must choose which documents they need. Given the mass of information potentially available, this presents a challenge for most citizens. Hence, public communication is also necessary to convey the relevant information to citizens. This is particularly true in developing countries, with their larger numbers of poor and less literate persons. Access rights and public reporting are therefore complementary—the government is required to assume only a passive role in the former, but must be proactive in the latter.

Most developed countries (including the United States, Canada, Australia, New Zealand, and many European countries) give citizens and organizations the right of access to all government records (other than in exempted categories) through national "freedom of information" (FOI) legislation enacted during the last twenty to thirty years. Such laws have been introduced at the subnational level as well in a few countries, such as the United States and India.

Openness has, among other things, contributed to reduced corruption in the public sector. For example, according to the Swedish Freedom of the Press Act, public documents are available to all Swedish citizens, and Korea enacted a Law on Administrative Procedures to provide citizens with information on administrative decision making. In countries where democracy was introduced a few years ago, such as central and eastern European countries, transparency was identified as the principal means to achieve democratization.

Codes of practice for access to information exist even in countries that have legal restrictions on the provision of government data, such as the Official Secrets Act in the United Kingdom (see Box 13.1). It should be noted, however, that the Committee on Standards in Public Life mentioned in Box 13.1 is only an advisory body and some critics hold that its advice is followed only when it suits the interests of the government in power.

Court decisions have fully supported the citizens' right to information and set important precedents for eventual legislative action to formalize this right. However, the process is anything but quick and simple and, in developing countries, it is of doubtful utility, as explained later. In developed countries, instead, when the process is successful, freedom of information laws can contribute greatly to expanding citizens' access, improving transparency in government, and

BOX 13.1

Openness in Executive Bodies in the United Kingdom

Despite the highly restrictive Official Secrets Act, measures were recommended in Britain more than ten years ago to open up government information to the public.

On *access to information,* a code should be in place, with procedures for implementation, to include:

- defined criteria for withholding information;
- standards for speed of response to inquiries;
- a mechanism for appeals within the organization, and then to another independent body; and
- a policy for charging appropriate fees for providing the information requested.

On *official meetings,* regulations should provide that:

- meetings should be open to the public, or their minutes should be available for public inspection, or their key arguments and decisions should be publicized;
- an open annual general meeting should be held allowing the public and the media to question managers and board members on performance and activities of the agency; and
- forums should be established for consumer groups or users, or public meetings organized on major issues, to inform the interested public.

On *government publication*, it is recommended that:

- annual accounts and reports should be produced describing the mandate of the agency, its long-term plans, performance, and targets for the forthcoming year;
- important information should routinely be published (e.g., key statistics, results of consultation, major procedures [including criteria for allocating public funds], and reports of regular investigations); and
- all publications should be made as widely available as possible through public libraries and similar facilities; and
- annual reports and accounts should be deposited in the library of Parliament.

Source: U.K. Government, *First Report of the Committee on Standards in Public Life*, 1995.

BOX 13.2

The U.S. Freedom of Information Act

> "The greatest dangers to liberty lurk in insidious encroachment
> by men of zeal, well meaning but without understanding."
> —*Justice Louis Brandeis, 1928*

Beginning in the 1960s, Congress enacted a series of landmark laws promoting "government in the sunshine," to allow the public to view the internal workings of the executive branch of government. The main law has been the 1966 Freedom of Information Act (FOIA), providing public access to information held by the executive agencies and corporations. Congress and the federal judiciary are exempted, as also is "classified" information, internal personnel actions, confidential business information, interagency or intra-agency communications, confidential business information, and records of ongoing investigations, financial institutions, and geological data.

In the 1990s, public access to government information was increased by restricting the ability of officials to classify information. A 1993 Justice Department Policy Memorandum promoted disclosure of government information under the FOIA unless it was "reasonably foreseeable that disclosure would be harmful." In the wake of September 11, 2001, public access to information has been restricted anew, in the name of national security and anti-terrorism. The Ashcroft Memorandum issued on October 12, 2001, supersedes the 1993 Memorandum.

The FOIA has been severely limited in the last seven years through procedural tactics, delays, and extensive "redaction" (blacking out portions of documents). In addition, the administration has issued guidelines permitting the withholding of a broad and undefined category of "sensitive" information, and supported statutory and regulatory changes that preclude disclosure of a wide range of other information on the country's infrastructure. The number of agencies that can classify information has been expanded to include the Secretary of Health and Human Services, the Secretary of Agriculture, and the Administrator of the Environmental Protection Agency.

A related development was the October 2001 "Patriot Act" (*Uniting and Strengthening America by Providing Appropriate Tools Required to Intercept and Obstruct Terrorism*) which expanded federal surveillance, such as wiretaps, and indirectly limited access to other information. Among other things, the Act:

• expands the surveillance measures of the 1990s *Foreign Intelligence Surveillance Act* (FISA) relating to spying in the United States by foreign intelligence agencies;

• increases the type and amount of information the government can obtain about people from their Internet Service Providers (ISPs) and permits ISPs to voluntarily give law enforcement agencies all "non-content" information without court order;

• expands the records the government may obtain (without court review), including means and source of payments of ISPs, through credit card or bank account numbers; and

• allows the FBI to require businesses to turn over all records on their clients, including financial records, medical histories, Internet usage, travel patterns, and other records.

curbing the ever-present tendency to official secrecy. The U.S. Freedom of Information Act is a good example—see Box 13.2.

Scope and Advantages

The laws on freedom of information reverse the traditional presumption in favor of official secrecy. Such laws enable any person (sometimes not only citizens) to request information from government, its agencies, or other public bodies. The laws normally apply to all entities substantially funded or controlled by government (local authorities, the judiciary, the legislature, state-funded educational institutions, and private organizations that carry out statutory functions), and cover current or past records maintained in any format, including electronic.

FOI laws set time limits within which the information request should be granted or refused by the official to whom it is made and require written communication of refusals, along with the reasons. The government agency is expected to release or withhold information on the basis of its nature and content, and not the identity of the requester or the use to which the information may be put. A reasonable system of charging the requesters for the cost of assembling and transmitting the information is provided, as the taxpayers at large should not have to pay for the information interests of an individual or group, on the same principle as user charges for public services.

Administrative and judicial remedies are available to those whose requests for information have been denied. In case of final administrative denial, the law typically grants the requester the right of appeal to either a court of law or an independent authority, such as an ombudsman, if one exists. (See chapter 11 for a discussion of ombudsmen.) The court or independent authority reviews the proceedings and either denies the appeal or issues binding orders to the agency to release the record. In keeping with the basic premise of transparency in government, the burden of proving why the information should be withheld falls on the government agency.

As noted earlier, the legal framework in all countries exempts from disclosure certain categories of information, usually those relating to national defense or foreign policy; cabinet documents; personnel and medical files; privileged or confidential financial or commercial information; law enforcement; information that will prejudice the management of public services; information that may result in the breach of a court order or parliamentary privilege; and personal privacy information.

In the United States, the protection of confidential deliberations within the executive branch has been formalized in the doctrine of "executive privilege." Although not mentioned in the Constitution, the doctrine is thought to flow from the principle of "separation of powers." (See chapter 4.) It exempts the President and some members of the executive branch from the obligation to comply with search warrants and subpoenas for information, or to testify in Congress. The doctrine of executive privilege has been in constant state of flux since the days of George Washington, and its application is in practice heavily contingent on the nature of the issue at hand and the political interaction between the President, Congress and the judiciary.

Costs and Risks

Systematic evaluations of the costs and benefits of FOI laws are rare. However, the experience so far shows that the enforcement of FOI laws entails significant costs, which may or may not be matched by commensurate benefits to ordinary citizens or society. Requests under FOI legislation have typically come from organized business seeking data for competitive purposes and from interest groups in pursuit of their own agenda, rather than from individual citizens. Large variability in implementation exists even within the same country. At one extreme, the law has occasionally been used to expose to public scrutiny even the personal correspondence of government ministers. At the other extreme, government officials have been known to hide behind FOI exemption provisions to deny even innocuous information to citizens. Between countries, the access of citizens to government-held information also shows considerable variation.

The costs and variability of implementation have led to a rethinking even within countries that were at the forefront of the movement for legal citizen rights to government information, and amendments of FOI legislation for greater clarity and to reduce both the opening for intrusiveness and the alibis for secrecy. All that being said, it was, is, and will remain true that excessive official secrecy is a major reason for the declining trust of people in their government and inefficiency in public administration. As a broad generalization, therefore, in developed countries the benefits have substantially outweighed the costs—partly because the media has aggressively used FOI legislation to get and publicize relevant information on government decisions and activities, thus making the government more accountable.

The Situation in Developing Countries

The scorecard is different in developing countries. The considerable effort needed to implement FOI legislation effectively and to process requests promptly may stretch the already limited administrative capacity, record-keeping abilities, and budgets of poor developing countries—as anyone readily understands who is familiar with government offices in poor countries, full of jumbled files in cardboard boxes stacked from floor to ceiling. Inadequate preparation for the FOI law and the failure to install the complementary regulatory and organizational framework undermine the credible enforcement of the disclosure requirements. As we keep emphasizing, unenforced law is no law at all, and by giving the illusion of action may even distract attention from the underlying problem. Foreign aid can help cover the costs of administering FOI laws and improve local capacity to do so, but the question of opportunity cost remains, i.e., whether the same resources and efforts could help access to government information more if they were invested in transparency reforms other than formal FOI legislation

Perhaps most important, beyond the question of opportunity costs there remains the issue of the distribution of benefits from FOI legislation and its impact on the relative power of different groups in society. Because making a request under FOI legislation and following it up is neither simple nor cheap, the richer and better-connected individuals and groups can easily take advantage of the opportunity to access useful government information, while the poor and vulnerable cannot. Because information is indeed power, the unintended long-term effect of FOI legislation in poor countries may be to tilt the playing field even more in favor of the richer and more powerful groups. Therefore, at a minimum, efforts at introducing FOI legislation and any foreign aid should be systematically accompanied by adequate programs to assist poorer groups and minorities to have the same access to information in actual practice.

Moreover, there are other routes to improve information flows. For example, codes of practice could be enacted on public reporting and access to information, and independent citizens' bodies could monitor the process. Specific laws and regulations that prohibit disclosure of information could be amended to make disclosure the norm rather than the exception. Service providers could be required to specify their standards of service and make this information easily accessible to the public. (See chapter 11 for a discussion of "citizens' charters.") Any of these measures can improve the transparency of public administration, short of adopting a full-fledged FOI law.

Finally, most of the useful information in the hands of government is not classified or confidential. Therefore, rather than searching for disclosure of confidential information, it may be more effective to focus on improving effective access to and retrieval of available information. With improved records management and wider use of information technology, valuable information already in the public domain can be made available in practice at a lower cost than enacting and implementing FOI laws. Also, the traditional role of government public information officers should evolve, from merely publicizing government achievements and creating photo opportunities for high government officials to providing positive support for an open information policy.

The Bottom Line

None of these considerations is intended to diminish the contribution of freedom of information laws, which have proven their worth in several developed countries in a number of very important ways. Moreover, the shift in the burden of proof, from the presumption of secrecy to the presumption that the information should be made public, is a fundamental reform which is valid everywhere. The intention of this discussion is instead to underline that formal FOI laws are far more suitable to developed than to developing countries; that there is a need for realistic complementary measures in every country; and that there are alternative ways to improve access to information in practice. What is certain is that a purely symbolic enactment of a formal FOI law without enforcement mechanisms or capacity accomplishes nothing for greater transparency in government, and may even be counterproductive if it gives the impression of reform without real substantive change. In any event, however well-intentioned the government may be and however large the legal openings for the public to access government information, there is no substitute for an aggressive, professional, ethical, and independent media to limit the scope of official secrecy and to advance the public's right to know.

THE MEDIA[3]

Role of the Media

By definition, the media (from the Latin for both "middle" and "instrument") provide an informational bridge between the government and the citizens. The media is often referred to as the "fourth estate," additional to the three estates in which pre-revolutionary French society was divided (the nobility, the clergy, and everyone else). Most citizens receive their information on what is going on in the government, and how it affects them, through the filter of the media—as the deluge of primary information makes it impossible for even the most diligent citizens to keep track of all the events or take advantage of their theoretical access to information in public agencies. The media role is a two-way bridge, as government also relies on the media to a great extent to convey its intentions and receive feedback and public opinion on policies and programs.

As all filters, the media can let through the most important information in the most factual way possible or, if it malfunctions, filter critical information out of the public domain. At its worst, the media can allow itself to be used as an echo chamber for the claims, arguments and propaganda of the government in power. An alert, professional, and gutsy media is essential to communicate information about the activities of government, the results of its actions, and how they might affect the citizens and the country—in accurate, responsible, candid, and understandable form. A failure to do so is not excused by the existence of official or corporate pressure to conform with the government line. On the contrary, it is precisely at a time of unusual pressure that independent and critical reporting is essential.

The media also plays a watchdog role in investigating misbehavior by politicians, government officials, and business leaders—a role traditionally summarized in the expression "comforting the afflicted and afflicting the comfortable." It is thus an important instrument of democratic accountability, in addition to an instrument of communication. A free media, whether print, broadcast, or online, ranks along with an independent judiciary as one of the two powerful counterforces to abuses by government and to corruption in public life. Its deepest duty is to "speak truth to power,"[4] and let the public know the facts. In particular, courageous and independent journalists have played a major role in many movements for freedom and struggle against oppression—sometimes at the cost of their own lives.

Old and New Media

The traditional "old" media are print, radio and basic TV, and remain dominant in many developing countries. Radio, in particular, continues to play an important role of information and education, reaching people in countries where television has not spread to the rural areas and remote regions. It is a mistake to confuse traditional media with traditional uses, however. Instances of innovative use of radio include local channels for public communication, distance learning, and communication of basic economic information (e.g., the world market prices of rural commodities), knowledge of which protects the small producer from being cheated by intermediaries or government officials. Note, too, that radio can cross national borders and defeat government censors more easily than television, as it doesn't require conspicuous aerials. For example, in the 1990s, BBC shortwave broadcasts managed to inform Afghans under the Taliban regime, much as they informed citizens of Nazi-occupied Europe in the 1940s.[5]

The term "new media" was coined (Davis and Owen, 1998) to describe new mass communication forms, such as talk radio and television, television news magazines, print and electronic tabloids, the internet, and computer networks. The new media can be categorized on the basis of whether they employ old or new communication technologies. New media that employ old technologies include talk radio, TV talk shows, and news magazines. New media that employ new technologies include electronic town meetings, electronic tabloids, blogs, and online news These technologies have infused communication with new immediacy so that the public can receive and send out messages with ease and speed unimaginable only a few years ago. In our view, despite the spread of the internet, the surface has barely been scratched and digital journalism, the wave of the future, is still in its infancy. This is true in developed countries but much more so in developing countries, where the reach of new media is largely confined to the richer and more literate segments of the urban population. (The harbinger of change is the imaginative use of the ubiquitous cell phone, which will evolve further as direct phone by satellite becomes more common.)

The new media, including the internet, offers greater opportunities for interaction with the public and a significant potential to educate, facilitate public discourse, and enhance public participation, beyond the time and space constraints of traditional media. In addition, new media technologies easily bypass national and international boundaries, thus bringing citizens of each country into contact with diverse cultures and distant events to an extent that was not imaginable earlier—a key dimension of "globalization."

At the same time, the role of the new media in education is incomplete and sporadic, and its very speed encourages a slide toward the superficial. Even back in the days when newspapers were the only means of mass communication, Mark Twain was said to have remarked "A lie can travel halfway around the world while the truth is putting on its shoes." The quest for ratings and profits in a highly competitive industry means that speed is becoming more important than accuracy. The sheer mass of information (and the mix of the useful and irrelevant) calls for new skills and new approaches to sift through the material to make it useful for at least public agencies, let alone for ordinary citizens. Although commercial considerations also drive mainstream print and broadcasting, the old media had a historical ethic of public service, grounded on strict professional norms of journalism. Considering the ease of unverifiable manipulation of the new media, it is not clear whether the ethics of the traditional printed media will transfer to the new media, or if the looser standards of the latter will compromise journalistic ethics across the board.

Media Freedom and Responsibilities

Freedom of the Media

Only an independent media can perform an effective scrutiny function on the conduct of public officials and release uncensored information to the public. In developed countries, this is generally the case. In developing countries, genuine media independence tends to be weak. Radio and television were government monopolies in most countries when first set up, and continue to be under state control in most countries. It is only in recent years that the private sector has been allowed entry into radio and television in most countries, but the government or government-controlled media still dominates in geographical coverage.

The print media in most countries has generally been private. The problem, however, is a long tradition of censorship, overt or self-imposed for defensive reasons. For example, it is the rare and brave journalist in Russia who dares to inquire into certain murky areas of government activity—with several having been assassinated by "persons unknown."[6]

The media and advocates of transparent government have been advancing a set of basic principles to protect media freedom and independence of the media. The global anti-corruption organization Transparency International lists the following eight rules:

- Keep to a minimum laws and practices limiting the right of the news media to gather and distribute information.
- Government authorities, national and local, should not interfere with the content of print, online, or broadcast news, or access to any news source.
- Independent news media should be allowed to emerge and operate freely in all countries.
- Government should not discriminate in its treatment, economic or otherwise, of the news media, public and private.

- Private media should have the same unrestricted access as the official media to material and facilities necessary to their publishing or broadcasting operations, including newsprint, printing facilities and distribution systems, and availability of broadcast frequencies and satellite facilities.
- Fiscal and financial practices should not inhibit the free flow of information.
- No restrictions should be placed on free entry in the field of journalism, or on its practice, except through professional certification.
- Security and full legal protection must be afforded to journalists.

Like all freedoms in organized society, media freedom is not unlimited, especially where ethnic tensions or centrifugal forces are at work. In Justice Oliver Wendell Holmes well-known phrase, *"the most stringent protection of free speech would not protect a man falsely shouting fire in a theater and causing a panic."*[7] Legitimate restrictions on the freedom of the media stem mainly from protection of the rights or reputation of individuals and groups, prevention of actions leading to inflammation of communal and religious feelings, and matters of national security. For example, media freedom certainly does not include the role played in Rwanda by the newspapers and the radio in inciting the genocide of 1994. Thus, legitimate restrictions on freedom of the media exist in almost all countries.

As implied in one of the principles listed earlier, independence of the media can be threatened without overt censorship by the exercise of the power of government over the availability of inputs like newsprint, access to loans, or infrastructure and land. Sometimes, the influence extends to overt inducements given to news organizations and journalists in the form of allotment of land and houses, or withholding of commercial advertisement by business allies of the government in power. (In the Philippines in the late 1990s, the latter was a favorite tactic of former Philippine President Joseph Estrada against opposition newspapers, most of which moderated their criticism, with the notable exception of the *Daily Inquirer*.) Often, the media is selectively used by members of government to 'leak' information, either to support official government arguments or to generate opposition to government policies.

Aside from government influence, the domination of print and electronic media by a few large companies or persons is a genuine threat to the free flow of information, as well as a barrier to the entry of small operators. Entry barriers for independent media outlets should therefore be removed and antimonopoly and antitrust principles made fully applicable to the media industry.

Responsibilities of the Media

Media accountability is a critical issue in all countries. Checks and balances on the media should not come from government, however, and should take two main forms: self-regulation and cultivation of a critical public. Although private media are guided by commercial considerations, it must still also respect the public interest and professional and ethical principles. When the news media starts competing with the entertainment media for market share and advertising revenue, the resulting "infotainment" leads to erosion of credibility in the media. Obsessing on minor scandals and fabricated crises, the media can also aggravate a decline of confidence in public leaders and institutions without real justification. For the cable news channels in particular, the need to fill 24 hours a day, every day, is a powerful force for repetition, for digging into minor details devoid of any newsworthiness, and presenting every triviality as a major "newsbreak" with dramatic graphics and flourishes of trumpets to match. Even worse, informative dialogue between commentators holding different views but abiding by the simple principle of listening when the other talks, and vice versa, has been replaced by *ad hominem* attacks and unintelligible simultaneous yelling. Possibly, but not hopefully, the viewing and listening public will eventually tire of a format which conveys conflict and hostility in place of news or opinion. Conversely, when pulling punches on controversial government policies for the sake of not offending a segment of the audience, the media abdicates its fundamental reporting responsibility. When serious issues are crowded out by prurient events, the urgent supersedes the important, blocking the information bridge between an informed citizenry and their government.

The independence of the media also implies a responsibility of media owners to guarantee independence of reporting *within* their organization. In the practice of their profession, journalists and editors must be free from any form of interference, not only from the government, but also from their employer. Civil society media watchdog organizations can play a helpful role in this direction. By the same token, however, journalists and editors found to have deliberately slanted their reporting for personal gain or outright bribes need to be swiftly drummed out of the profession.

In recent years, major American newspapers have hired, for nonrenewable fixed terms, experienced and respected journalists as ombudsmen to comment on and criticize the newspaper's coverage of the news and its observance of professional and ethical standards. This practice has had some positive impact. The television networks, however, have yet to follow suit—they should.

The most effective way of policing media accuracy and professionalism is more recent still. The phenomenal growth of the internet has spawned, among myriad blogs and web-based organizations, a vast cottage industry of individual media watchdogs, to attempt to correct urban legends and deliberate lies. (Concerning political information, a signal service in this direction is rendered by FactCheck.org.) For the first time in history, the internet has the potential to provide a broad-based mechanism for media regulation in real time by the public itself without in any way compromising media independence, for the first time in history—provided that effective ways can be developed to weed out the conveyors of myth and the purveyors of slander.

In the meantime, an efficient means of inducing the media to be responsible are the autonomous press or media councils set up in a number of countries. These councils, consisting of independent persons of integrity, provide an open forum for complaints against the media by the public and chastise the media when they are irresponsible, invade personal privacy, allow themselves to be corrupted, or parrot government claims without examining them critically. These media councils should have all the prestige and credibility needed to give moral force to their public reports on the media and to nurture the improvement of media standards.

In summary, the old motto of the *New York Times* still provides a healthy guideline: "All the news that's fit to print." A more elaborate set of principles around that guideline has been developed by the British Press Complaints Commission—see Box 13.3. (But note that the Commission is funded by the press and is partly composed of important press personalities. Such self-policing is only as effective as the integrity and vigor of the individuals concerned.)

Civic Journalism

In the context of the issue of media responsibility, a new movement known as "civic journalism" has been developing in response to the concern that mainstream print and broadcast media are too influenced by the interests of the richer groups, fail to inform and report on the issues relevant to the poor and the middle class, and are too timid in testing the claims made by governments. Small newspapers, community radio channels, and local newsletters have emerged to draw attention to

BOX 13.3

Code of Practice of the British Press Complaints Commission

The British Press Complaints Commission is charged with the application of the Code of Practice, which was drafted by the newspaper and magazine industry itself. The main provisions of the Code, formulated in 1994 but still in force, are:

- accuracy—newspapers and periodicals should take care not to publish misleading or distorted material, and to promptly follow up any incorrect reporting with a correction, and an apology to concerned parties where appropriate;
- opportunity to reply—a fair opportunity to reply to inaccuracies should be given to individuals or organizations;
- separate comment, conjecture, and fact—newspapers, while free to be partisan, should distinguish clearly among the three;
- privacy—inquiries into individuals' private life without their consent are not generally acceptable, and publication can only be justified in the public interest, such as exposing crime or serious antisocial conduct, protecting public health and safety, and preventing the public from being misled by an action or statement of the individual (this restriction covers the interviewing or photographing of children, identifying children under 16 involved in cases of sexual offenses, victims of sexual assault, and intrusion into personal grief);
- misrepresentation—journalists should not obtain information or pictures through subterfuge or misrepresentation;
- harassment—journalists should obtain neither information nor pictures through intimidation or harassment;
- nondiscrimination—the press should avoid prejudicial or pejorative reference to a person's race, color, religion, sex or sexual orientation, or to any physical or mental illness or handicap;
- financial journalism—journalists should not use for their own profit financial information they receive in advance of publication;
- confidentiality—journalists have a moral obligation to protect confidential sources of information.

Source: Her Majesty's Stationery Office. 1994. *Report of the British Press Complaints Commission.* United Kingdom.

these events and issues. Civic journalism allows greater citizen input into the reporting process and fosters collaboration between community groups and reporters.

Civic journalism is involved, among other things, in developing report cards on issues of concern to poorer citizens; obtaining information on government decisions and programs, using mechanisms of legal disclosure of information, and disseminating it to generate citizen action;

and promoting media literacy from school age onwards to provide citizens with the skills to make informed evaluations of media reports.

In some instances, civic newspapers have joined forces with citizen groups to agitate for more responsive social services, and have played an important advocacy role around issues such as slum upgrading, exploitation of marginal groups and children, rehabilitation of displaced people, right to information, and misuse of public resources.

INFORMATION TECHNOLOGY, E-GOVERNANCE, AND PUBLIC ADMINISTRATION [8]

Despite the enormous changes already introduced during the past decade, there is a good argument that the impact of the revolution in information and communication technology (ICT) on governance and public sector management is still only in its first phase in developed countries and has barely begun in most developing countries. There are also broad implications for national power from the interaction of globalization and information. (See Nye, 2004.) In any case, the subject of information and communication technology is too vast to be adequately discussed in this book. Moreover, the only certainty is that, by the time this book is published, much of its discussion of the interaction of ICT and public administration will be obsolete. A few general considerations and illustrations may be raised here, however.

General Principles

ICT has a wonderful potential to increase government accountability, transparency, participation, and the rule of law; improve the efficiency and effectiveness of public sector operations; widen access to public services; disseminate information to the public and get feedback from relevant stakeholders and service users; and help solve the centralization/decentralization dilemma by making relevant data easily available at all government levels. To realize this potential, certain principles are of universal application to ICT, in general but especially in public administration.

ICT Is a Tool

Computers are immensely powerful yet essentially no different from a photocopier or a car, in the sense that user needs and requirements must come first and dictate whether and how the tool should be used. For certain functions, pencil and paper, a telephone call, a face-to-face meeting, or a visit to the library is far more effective than computers or the internet. This obvious point must be stressed because governments, consultants, or ambitious managers often encourage computerizing everything in sight. Indeed, some argue that ICT innovation is now largely supply and marketing-driven rather than dictated by the needs and requirements of the users. Thus, as for any tool, it is essential to assess realistically and compare the costs of a given ICT change with the actual benefits expected from it. Moreover, because the built-in correction of changes in profit is not operative in the public sector, special care is needed to insure that the instrument of ICT in government does not get ahead of the uses for it.

Cooperation Between the Provider and the User

The ICT "techie" and the public manager should never work in isolation from one another. On the one hand, the lack of relevant ICT expertise among many managers (or worse, the illusion of expertise) leads to a risk for costly mistakes or missed opportunities for improving services by computerization. On the other hand, improvements in public sector effectiveness stem largely from better rules and procedures. To apply advanced ICT to obsolete rules and inefficient processes means in effect to computerize inefficiency. *Progress does not mean doing stupid things faster.*

Watch Out for Data Integrity and Compatibility

Greater risks for the integrity of the data may accompany the early phase of the introduction of ICT, especially in developing countries, and can even jeopardize the entire information database if developed carelessly and without sufficient checks, controls, security, and virus protection. Governments moving from a manual accounting and recording system to a computerized one, or from paper personnel files to e-files, should keep the manual accounts going alongside the new system until the new system is working well and is secure and free of risk. Moreover, the risk of developing inconsistent systems agency by agency should be recognized and prevented. Both of these risks are among the many reasons why a coherent strategy for the introduction of ICT in public administration is essential.

ICT Cannot Substitute for Good Management

A mismanaged government agency will not become better managed by being computerized and lax controls over expenditure or personnel will not be fixed by automating them. On the contrary, the expansion of computer use can give a false illusion of better management by producing impressive spreadsheets and just-in-time reports based on phony information—and a misleading impression of tighter control in cases where a large part of the expenditure cycle occurs in parallel and in "black boxes" outside the computerized system. Throwing computers at institutional problems has been a proven way to waste large amounts of resources without any improvement in efficiency or effectiveness.

ICT Does Not Eliminate Corruption

Some have argued that corruption is reduced by computerization. Unfortunately, this is not necessarily true. Computer technology does indeed eliminate many opportunities for corruption for those who do not understand fully the new technology—particularly by flagging internal inconsistencies and data irregularities—but opens up new corruption vistas for those who understand the new systems well enough to manipulate them. Therefore, in a sense, ICT permits an intergenerational shift in corruption opportunities.

ICT in the Private Sector

During the 1950s and 1960s, it was the government that led in the use of computers in support of business functions, including management information, payroll, and accounting applications. (The original impulse for digital computers came from military applications, with first-generation computers such as ENIAC in the early 1940s—see McCartney, 1997.) Since the 1970s, however, governments have tended to fall behind private industry in electronic systems that give direct access to information and services, and as of the early twenty-first century most innovation was generated by private companies and institutions.

The still-expanding use of the internet is helping to fully integrate producers with their suppliers and customers, to cut costs, improve quality, expand markets, and share the benefits—changing the old idea of a freestanding business. Companies are bringing suppliers and customers much deeper into their business practices and systems and thus need to develop common understandings with their partners. This in turn forces greater openness and transparency than in the past (with the exception of executive compensation). Increasingly, customized services, products, and pricing are becoming the rule rather than the exception, non-core business processes are contracted out to other providers, and just-in-time inventory systems have become common. Taken together, these developments have provided a powerful push for productivity increases and, to that extent, have also been largely responsible for the taming of inflation. Until the mid-1980s in the United States and other developed countries, expansions in employment and national production typically tended to go hand in hand with inflationary pressures. In the 1990s and the first years of the twenty-first century, there has been generally robust economic growth in a climate of price stability, mainly as a result of ICT innovation.

Uses of ICT in the Public Sector

In Developed Countries

The Broad Picture. Over the last ten years or so, government operations have been substantially transformed by the introduction of ICT, especially activities at the interface with the public. While initiatives differ considerably in scope and emphasis in different countries, they all reflect the influence of ICT. New ways of handling and communicating information can allow governments to escape the dilemma between cutting costs and increasing quality, creating an administration that works better and costs less. More importantly, ICT can enhance transparency, increase accountability, and allow greater participation. Thus, government agencies, largely in developed countries, have applied ICT to a growing range of public services. These applications focus on two objectives: to achieve major improvements in speed of response, efficiency, and accessibility of public services; and to bring government closer to the citizens.

The Main Benefits. The benefits of new information and communications capabilities for the services produced by public agencies are now well known in developed countries. The main ones have been:[9]

- *Lower administrative costs*—ICT allows a significant reduction of information handling costs and compliance costs. In particular, ICT enables more data to be shared between different information systems, thereby reducing the number of times the data have to be collected (e.g., changes of address).
- *Faster and more accurate response*—ICT allows direct access to transaction or customer accounts held in different parts of government, especially for street-level public services, and faster replies to requests and queries.
- *Location-independent access to government*—ICT supports the development of more flexible and convenient ways for citizens to access public services. For example, most governments have developed online facilities for transacting in real time welfare claims, tax assessments, visa applications, license renewals, and the like. While "smart cards" to purchase services were pioneered in public transit as far back as the late 1970s (by the Washington, DC metro system), their use to travel toll roads was virtually unknown as late as 2000 and is now commonplace in major thoroughfares. Beyond public transit, smart cards are being developed to

allow access to an entire range of government services—an electronic one-stop shop—preventing fraud or misuse of public services and resulting in increased public confidence.

* *Facilitation of government-to-business interface*—ICT can result in improved services to remote rural areas and enhanced emergency support services.
* *Better management support*—ICT enables governments to harvest and process more data from operational systems, thus increasing the quality of feedback to managers and policymakers. Governments are also able to make more information available to citizens and support new kinds of online communication between policy makers, elected representatives, individual citizens, or organized lobbies.

E-Dialogue and Daily Administrative Workflow. In addition to the use of ICT in public service delivery, now commonplace in most developed countries, some governments have encouraged the use of the internet as a public space for citizens. Examples are the U.K. Communities Online (www.communities.org.uk), the North Brabant land use consultation of the Dutch government, and the online public consultation by the U.K. cabinet on its Freedom of Information proposals.[10] The main advantages are:

* barriers of language and localism can be overcome. For example, farmers are no longer limited to learning from local people or only from those who speak their language;
* multimedia technology can help people get closer and assemble databases of innovations and innovators; and
* discussion groups may be set up to discuss specific innovations or grievances, for collective improvements in design and scope and to provide organized feedback on the quality of government services and investment projects.

Some Illustrations. The improvements brought by ICT to the speed, simplicity, and efficiency of government transactions are an everyday reality for most readers. Examples of the use of ICT in public administration in developed countries are shown in Box 13.4, but only as illustrations because, by the time this book is published, the innovations will certainly seem old hat.

In Developing Countries

The situation is very different in the developing world. While segments of the population and certain areas of particular countries are as advanced in ICT as anywhere in the world, for the vast majority of government operations in most developing countries, paper is still king. A paper trail is required for approval processing; paper forms have to filed in person; access to public information is an obstacle course; citizens have great difficulties in giving feedback to public officials and getting timely responses; document archiving is manual and cumbersome (and retrieval a major challenge); several copies of a single document are usually required, even within a single department; the inbox/outbox system remains dominant; the phone call is the preferred means of informal communication; and so on. Cell phones are the one aspect of contemporary ICT that is widespread in poor countries—but less as a result of their convenience than of the spectacular inefficiency of public telephone companies in much of the developing world and the costs and delays of obtaining a landline. (The highest ratio in the world of cell phones to landlines is in Manila, Philippines.)

Large developing countries, however, have been moving faster since the late 1990s, partly under the stimulus of globalization. India is, of course, the best-known example (see Box 13.5)

BOX 13.4

Illustrations of Information Initiatives in Developed Country Governments

In *Finland,* progress of the Information Society is among the most important goals of the government, and the public sector has opened its services massively on the Internet. As elsewhere, the intention is to distribute all government documents and information, such as tax reports, in electronic form. One important element is an easy-to-use service interface that resembles television, with the aim of providing interactive front-office services from one window. A goal of the Finnish Information Society policy is to achieve computer literacy for all citizens. To this end, the government has been investing in training programs and schools. To address the risk that a "digital divide" develops between the IT-literate and the rest of the population, network services are to be widely available in libraries and other public facilities.

In *Italy,* building on the work of the Authority for Informatics in Public Administration, legislation has been enacted to establish principles and procedures for authenticating electronic documents, and rules for private transactions, notarial deeds, and electronic signatures with asymmetric keys. These rules are not only having an initial positive impact on the efficiency and transparency of the Italian public administration, but have yielded useful experience for other European countries in the construction of the Trans-European Public Administration Network.

In *Denmark,* the informatics strategy aims to provide free access to information; support democracy and individual access to resources; contribute to personal development; make government more transparent and facilitate the delivery of better service; support the weaker segments of society; and strengthen the international competitiveness of Danish companies.

In the *United States*, among a large number of other innovations and partly as a result of the National Information Infrastructure project launched in 1996, over the last decade the federal government has again become a leading force in the use of ICT. For example, Social Security Administration (SSA) forms are on the Internet and can be transmitted directly to the SSA. In addition, passport applications can be downloaded, government jobs applied for, and publications of the federal governments easily obtained online at no charge. Also, the electronic benefits transfer (EBT) system aims at delivering government benefits electronically, at ATMs and point-of-sale terminals. In addition to the greater convenience for the beneficiaries, EBT has contributed to reducing fraud and abuse in the delivery of benefits because there are fewer steps in the process and patterns of abuse can be detected electronically. Most state governments, too, have adopted similar innovations.

BOX 13.5

Information and Communication Technology in India's Government

Chances are that readers have spoken on the telephone with a tech support person in Bangalore, the capital of the state of Karnataka in the south of India, concerning their credit card account or some online purchase. Rapid advances have been made in ICT in India, particularly in the southern states of Karnataka and Andhra Pradesh. Bangalore has become India's "Silicon Valley" and Hyderabad, the capital of Andhra Pradesh, is affectionately known by its fans as "Cyberabad."

In 1998, a high-level National Task Force on IT and Software Development was set up as a first step toward the goal of turning India into an information technology superpower and one of the largest producers and exporters of software in the world. The national IT policy aims to create a government-wide information infrastructure to simplify transactions, reduce duplication, and improve the level and speed of service to the public. This will provide business and individuals with the opportunity to send and receive, over electronic terminals, the information that currently passes between them and the government on paper. Internet service providers will be encouraged to provide access to even the most remote locations in the country, and the government will collaborate with the private sector to put in place secure electronic fund transfer systems, since this is critical to the successful implementation of e-commerce, as well as for direct service delivery to citizens. Computers are to be made available to every school and university and all public hospitals in the country.

These are very ambitious goals in a still-developing country, but efforts in the last seven years have already produced good results. In Andhra Pradesh, for example, connectivity is fully operational between Hyderabad and all the district headquarters, as well as several other major towns, and is being expanded to the other towns and will eventually expand to village level. A video-conferencing facility between Hyderabad and the twenty-five other cities in the state has been operational since January 1999 and has been extended in recent years to most major government departments.

A major success story of e-governance in India is the Computer-aided Administration of Registration Department (CARD). Under the program, property registration offices have been completely computerized; deeds are registered in one hour and other services such as liens and appraisal certificates performed in fifteen minutes. These results are truly astonishing for anyone who is familiar with the extraordinary red tape of India's public administration.

If the national IT policy achieves even a part of its goals to introduce technology into government, a heavy burden on India's economy and development will be lifted and the already remarkable economic progress of the country can accelerate much further—and with even greater equity than in the last decade.

Source: Adapted from http://it-taskforce.nic.in.

but important ICT initiatives have been taken in other large countries, e.g., budget transparency in the Philippines (Box 13.6). ICT-based improvements in administration can be made even in very small developing countries, such as the South Pacific islands although, of course, they require a realistic approach suited to their size and very limited administrative capacity (Box 13.7).

Promoting Successful ICT Innovations in Government

How to Manage Government-Held Information

Before speeding up the collection and dissemination of government information, it is necessary to have the right approach to *managing* the information. Governments are the largest single collectors and producer of information in any country, and the way in which they manage the information they hold has wide-ranging consequences for both administrative effectiveness and the private sector. There are three ways in which to view government-held information, and hence three different approaches to its management and tradeability (Heeks, 1999):

- *information as a general public asset*—In this view, government-held information is owned by the general public, since the information has been gathered about everyone and from everyone, often compulsorily. It follows from this view that government information should generally be made available either for free or at a charge that reflects only the cost of making it available.
- *information as a government asset*—In this view, information is owned by the government agency that owns the network and computers in which that information resides. It follows from this view that, since the government has invested resources to collect and store the data and the information often has considerable commercial value, the government should be allowed to sell information at whatever price the market will bear.
- *information as neither a public nor a government asset*—In this view, government information is virtually a personal asset of the particular government officials who control it. It follows from this view that government-held information does not have to be made available at all, and other individuals have no right of access to it—except through "informal payments" to the officials who hold the information.

The third approach is nowadays only seen in authoritarian and patrimonial regimes and is no longer generally acceptable. The first approach, viewing government information as a general public asset, remains the prevailing one in most countries. However, developed countries are increasingly moving toward the second approach—commercializing government information and allowing the private sector to participate in marketing it. Whether this approach is acceptable or not depends largely on whether clear and generally acceptable guidelines can be elaborated, under four headings:

- who owns the information once it is sold and whether the government retains residual rights to make it available to others;
- what regulations are appropriate to preclude private misuse of government information;
- the extent to which government compete with private data companies and the manner in which information should be traded; and, most critically,
- the potential misuse by governments of information they collect on citizens—whether under the cloak of a "war on terror," or in the guise of improving the service interface with the public, or for any other reason.

BOX 13.6

Website for the Philippine Budget

In the Philippines, the Department of Budget and Management (DBM) posts the government budget for the coming year on the Internet, after its passage by Congress and approval by the president. This practice, common in developed countries, is comparatively new in developing countries.

The DBM also posts on its website its major budgetary releases to government agencies in a bid to make transactions more transparent to the public. The website includes information on government accounts payable and on the amounts released by the DBM as payment for these accounts. The details of all accounts payable and releases for each government agency are posted on the web each month, along with the names of the contractors and the amount of payment they are supposed to receive monthly.

Private contractors and suppliers are therefore able for the first time to check online the truthfulness of the statements of departmental officials against the DBM actual budgetary releases.

Source: Department of Budget Management, Republic of the Philippines.

BOX 13.7

Information Technology and Government in the Pacific Islands

In the Pacific Islands, a number of simple ICT initiatives have helped to:

• simplify government bureaucracy—a United Nations virtual meeting linked governments and NGOs in ten countries with a listserv, saving substantial travel costs and travel time;

• break down barriers between functional domains—the Fiji Public Service Commission introduced a personnel management system to facilitate, among many things, more effective training and monitoring of the performance of participants in the newly established senior executive service;

• reorient public services to solving problems for clients—the Federated States of Micronesia uses a web-based system linked with Hawaii for medical advice on difficult cases. A listserv links over 100 doctors in the Pacific Islands, serving as an early-warning system on outbreaks of disease;

• make government accountable—the Solomon lands used the web to help assess the prior experience of international contractors bidding on a government contract for preshipment inspection of logging exports (previously, the government approved contracts with unqualified firms);

• strengthen oversight—in Vanuatu, the Ombudsman's Office set up a listserv in 1997 to get legal advice on how to defend itself before the High Court against a suit by the Council of Ministers—many of whom were themselves accused of misconduct—seeking to abolish the Office (the Ombudsman's Office won the legal battle, but lost the war when the Ombudsman Act was subsequently repealed by Parliament);

• develop new forms of citizen participation—web-based chat sites such as the Kava Bowl (southpacific.arts.unsw.edu.au/links/links_chat.htm) and Papua New Guinea's www.niugini.com/wwwboard/wwoboard/html facilitate freewheeling political discussion that could not be conducted in the strictly regulated print media. The chat sites also allow the Pacific islanders' diaspora in the United States, Australia, and New Zealand to participate in the political debates in their countries.

Source: www.undp.org.fj/governance/Index3.htm; Yvan Soures, "PACNET: The Pacific islands tuned into the XXIst Century." *Pacific Health Dialog,* 1998.

Barriers to ICT Innovation

The U.S. Office of Technology Assessment identified the following general obstacles to introduction of ICT innovation:

- inadequate attention to the human element in systems development;
- insufficient priority given to the need for affordable, accessible, user-friendly applications;
- a widening gap between the educated, technically proficient citizens and the less IT-literate; and
- failure to forge effective partnerships between government agencies and the private sector.

In addition to these general obstacles, there are specific reasons for the comparatively slower utilization of ICT in public sector institutions:

- higher costs of ICT introduction due to the large size of public organizations;
- inertia of existing habits, not corrected by the need to stay abreast of the competition;
- data security concerns;
- privacy and confidentiality;
- obsolete regulations and laws; and
- lack of ICT understanding and of computer skills.

With particular reference to public service provision, Dutton (1996) has identified a number of barriers to the introduction of ICT, of which the main ones are:

- defense of functional and organizational boundaries by agency "barons";
- fragmentation caused when government agencies develop systems exclusively for their own clients;
- overcentralization of government, leading to fewer opportunities for local innovation;
- employee anxieties caused by fears of loss of jobs and involuntary transfers, combined with the perception that cost-cutting is the overriding objective of ICT initiatives (and that claims about improving services are primarily rhetorical);
- difficulties in scaling up to larger operational systems from small pilot projects;
- incompatibilities between communication systems in different departments, local authorities, levels of government, and private companies (The severe communications problems experienced by first responders on September 11, 2001, and during Hurricane Katrina in 2005 are the most dramatic examples of such lack of interoperability—and are still uncorrected as of 2007.);
- failure to enact the requisite complementary changes in organization and procedures; and
- past ICT failures, making the agency or the users reluctant to endorse new ventures.

This long list of structural, behavioral, and attitudinal obstacles appears daunting, but the reality of the advantages of e-governance and the extraordinary progress of recent years have put many of these fears to rest. Moreover, the transfer of responsibility from the older cohort of IT-illiterate government officials to younger staff—familiar and comfortable with the new technologies—has almost wiped out the psychological resistance to ICT. This, by the way, is the same kind of generational shift that has been at work throughout history to produce gradual acceptance of new technologies.

Supporting Factors

Although several of the earlier obstacles to e-governance may no longer be operative, innovation never occurs by itself, and affirmative efforts are needed on a coordinated and well-planned basis. Several factors can spur and facilitate such efforts.

A Management Climate that Supports Risk Taking. For any innovation to be successful, there must be a willingness to take risks. However, individuals in very large organizations, including public agencies, tend to be risk-averse—mainly because the individual is unlikely to receive credit for successful innovation, but is pretty sure to be blamed for an unsuccessful attempt. While various fruitful ICT innovations in the 1990s demonstrate that there are many risk takers and innovators in public agencies, further change is likely to be fitful unless the top leadership creates an agency climate that promotes and rewards intelligent risk taking.

Encouragement of Local Initiatives. Local government entities can more easily nourish innovations relevant to their communities because they are closer to the public, community groups, and businesses. Similarly, the large number and diversity of local government entities can greatly facilitate the emergence of innovative ideas and an emulative spirit, provided that a political climate and organizational arrangements are established to nurture them. Moreover, reorganizations of local government structures can offer a "window of opportunity" for authorities to rethink and change the way they do things, including how to deploy ICT. In the United States, individual cities and states have been at the forefront of the use of ICT to make citizens' lives easier and reduce administrative costs, and have provided a cauldron of technological experiments from which other states, cities, and the federal government have benefited. This internal quasi-marketplace of administrative innovations can help spread worthwhile initiatives to other locales while weeding out the less successful ones.

An Orientation to the Goals of Public Service. Although financial constraints must be respected, the focus of ICT innovation should shift from improving "back office" administration to direct improvements in the quality of front-line services offered to the public. For example, electronic one-stop services in welfare benefits administration should be appraised not only for their capacity to produce cost savings, but also in terms of intangibles related to quality improvements in customer service.

Partnerships. A key element in effective ICT innovations is the establishment of working partnerships between government and community groups, business enterprises, ICT vendors, and local government. Partnerships have been especially important in the United States, where, as noted, local agencies have taken a strong leading role in ICT innovation.

A Strategic Framework. Finally, to ensure that the diverse ICT capabilities are effectively harnessed and the overall system expands in an efficient and consistent way, a coherent strategy is needed. This strategic framework serves, among other things, to coordinate government ICT policies with related areas such as employment and data protection, and develop a policy for user charges and provision for subsidized services. A coherent strategic vision is especially important in our times of very rapid ICT change. In the 1970s, matters were simpler and comfortably sliced: first, the initial design was decided and set in stone; next, the software was installed and tested; and then the new system was installed and ran in parallel with the old system for some time before the old system was abandoned for good. With today's rapid intervening changes in technology or requirements (e.g., for new security), cost estimates are quickly superceded, internal design coherence is at risk, and contractors are given large openings to make greater profit through change orders.[11] It is only a crystal-clear strategic vision and a nimble management that can deal with the uncertainty and preempt the cost escalation and rent-seeking potential of the rapidly changing situation.

Legislative Transparency

The previous discussion has dealt almost entirely with the role of the executive branch in either impeding or facilitating public access to important government information. In the United States in recent years, transparency in the executive branch has been drastically diminished—not only in national security–related issues, but across the board and as part of a determined push to strengthen the powers of the presidency vis-à-vis Congress, the judiciary, and civil society. The executive branch, however, is not the only culprit.

Congress has not only cheerfully acquiesced in the expansion of executive secrecy, but has compensated for its diminished constitutional role by adding some more secrecy of its own, through procedural changes that have substantially reduced the transparency of legislative processes and of impending decisions. Information technology is beginning to come to the rescue in this respect as well and, as of 2007, a healthy pushback is underway to shed light into the dark corners of congressional decisions. If sustained, this reaction should make it easier for the public to find out what laws are being proposed and what their effect is likely to be, and to restrain to some extent the explosion of unproductive patronage spending and the sly insertion in proposed legislation of provisions designed to benefit some special interest or other (see Box 13.8).

BOX 13.8

Online Transparency for U.S. Legislation

There has always been a wealth of print media and library resources on existing legislation. In the last decade, the Internet has improved enormously the accessibility of that information and thus *effective* transparency in government. For example, the Web site govtrack.us/ tracks existing legislation and regulations, voting records of members of Congress, and other governmental matters. Unfortunately, accurate and timely information on legislation that is about to be voted on remains much more difficult to come by.

On the healthy premise that unexamined proposed laws are more likely to contain questionable items, since 1996 the Library of Congress has been publishing proposed bills at thomas.loc.gov (where "Thomas" stands for Thomas Jefferson). However, it is unable to do so for those items that are slipped into the proposed legislation at the last minute and in secret by the "conference committees" that iron out differences in the version of the bill approved by the Senate and the version approved by the House. These items are typically inserted into the final bill at the behest of individual powerful congresspersons, often responding to requests by lobbyists for various organizations—sometimes quite literally in the dead of night. Consequently, and given the bulk and complexity of the legislation as a whole, neither the public at large nor most members of Congress know anything about these items before they are voted on.

The most troublesome are the budgetary "earmarks" discussed in chapter 6, whereby expenditure provisions not reviewed for their economic viability, nor debated by Congress, are pushed into the U.S. budget by influential members of Congress without any prior knowledge by the vast majority of the other members. It is only after the budget is approved that Congress and the public get to find out these penumbral activities and how much money is to be spent on them—$24 billion in 2005 for the transport sector alone.

Of the many factors allowing this indefensible practice to persist, lack of transparency ranks at the top. To begin addressing the problem, in early 2006 Rep. Brian Baird (D-Washington) introduced a bill to require the prior publication of any proposed legislation in its *final* form at least three days before it is to be voted upon. (In other countries, the issue is addressed through providing a "second reading" and a confirmation vote before the legislation becomes final.) A nonprofit organization called readthebill.org (which also uses Jefferson as its spiritual patron) has been launched to support the Baird proposal and post the proposed bills online. The intent is to use individual citizens and interested organizations as a resource to search through the proposed bills and publicize objectionable items, in order to bring pressure on members of Congress to at least pay attention to them before they become law.

Also helpful may be the Federal Funding Accountability and Transparency Act, approved in September 2006 only after the public reaction to the skyrocketing budget earmarks. Although no serious action has been taken to curtail pork barrel spending, at least the Act requires creating a Web list of all federal contracts and grants larger than $25,000. Hopefully, civil society and the healthier elements of the political system can then use the information to track the uses of the money and, more importantly, the beneficiaries.

GENERAL DIRECTIONS OF IMPROVEMENT

Because there cannot be accountability without relevant information, transparency in government is a basic component of good governance, and is a particularly good way to curb corruption. Sunshine kills germs. There are legitimate reasons for keeping confidential certain types of government information. However, openness should be the rule, and the burden of proof should rest on those who would keep government information confidential.

The categories of government information that should be provided to the public include:

- information about government as a holder of data—what records are maintained and how their accuracy is ensured;
- information about government as a business—how much the government spends, on what, why, and with what results;
- information about government as a service provider—what services are available, at what price and quality, and how they are provided; and
- information about government as policy maker—how are major decisions made, on what evidence they were based, and what impact is expected.

Records Management

Good management of government records has come to the fore as a very important aspect of administrative effectiveness. If the information cannot be found, it cannot be communicated; if it is not organized, it cannot be found; and if too much information is kept, it cannot be organized. Accordingly, the priorities are:

- regulations to require government agencies to define the relevant information they hold, and organize and publish it;
- an effective system for collecting and retrieving information;
- provisions specifying the time limit beyond which government records will be publicly disclosed on request; and
- procedures to prepare the documents for public dissemination in clear language.

All these activities are costly and time consuming. Therefore, selectivity is mandatory. Keeping too much information is as inefficient as keeping too little. The reflexive bureaucratic habit of holding onto unnecessary records must be broken, by eliminating red-tape rules and then penalizing unnecessary record holding and rewarding civil servants who free up communications.

Transparency, however, is more than just openness. An affirmative effort at outreach is also necessary. In developed countries, each major government agency should have a professional public information officer with direct access to the agency leadership. In most developing countries, the priority is in the opposite direction: ministries of information need to move away from their traditional roles of propaganda and of protecting the government from embarrassing disclosures, to the role of communicating government policies and intentions and of building trust between the government and the citizens.

Access to Information

Citizens have the right to obtain from the government, on request, personal information about themselves, as well as nonpersonal information held by the government that does not endanger national security, law enforcement, the privacy of others, or another specified public interest. This right is often enshrined in laws on freedom of information (FOI), which reverse the traditional presumption in favor of official secrecy and enable any person to request information from government and its agencies.

Despite the intuitive appeal of FOI laws, experience thus far shows that their enforcement entails significant costs, which may or may not be matched by commensurate benefits to ordinary citizens or society. FOI requests have typically come from organized business seeking data for competitive purposes and by interest groups in pursuit of their own agenda. Paradoxically, government officials have been known to hide behind FOI exemptions to deny even innocuous information to citizens. A rethinking is currently underway in many developed countries to amend FOI laws for greater clarity and to reduce both the openings for intrusiveness and the alibis for unnecessary secrecy.

On balance, in developed countries the benefits of FOI laws have substantially outweighed the costs—partly because the media has aggressively used the laws. In developing countries, by contrast, the significant costs of enforcing FOI laws are rarely warranted by the benefits, partly because inadequate record-keeping raises the costs of information retrieval and partly because of the high demands of FOI mechanisms on very limited administrative capacity. Moreover, in some countries FOI laws have inadvertently weakened the poorer segments of the population and strengthened the more powerful private groups, owing to their greater capacity to use the law to obtain information useful to consolidate their position. In these countries therefore, it is all the more important to put in place a variety of other mechanisms to channel relevant government information to the public—primarily through the media. In all countries, however, the core principle is the same: the presumption is that government information should be made public unless there are specific and demonstrable reasons to keep confidential.

The Media

To protect news media freedom and independence, Transparency International lists the following eight rules:

* Keep to a minimum the limits on the media's right to gather and distribute information.
* No government interference with the content of news or access to sources.
* Free creation and operation of independent news media.
* No government discrimination in its treatment of the news media.

- Equal access of private and official media to needed materials and facilities.
- No fiscal and financial practices inhibiting the free flow of information.
- No official restrictions on free entry in the field of journalism, or on its practice.
- Security and full legal protection for journalists.

The other side of the coin of media freedom is the need for media professionalism, integrity, and accountability—an especially critical issue in developing countries. Checks and balances on the media should not come from government, however, and should take two main forms: self-regulation and cultivation of a critical public. Because both require a long time, external aid to build media capacity in developing countries can help, including through internships for journalists and "twinning" of local media with established media organizations in developed countries.

The priority for the future, however, will be to exploit the potential of the "new media." "Old" media such as print and radio will remain dominant in many developing countries—together with basic TV news in the main cities. Radio, in particular, will continue to play a vital role of information and education in developing countries. But if internet-based new media develop in these countries as rapidly as the ubiquitous cell phones have, the positive implications for governance and administrative efficiency will be enormous.

Information and Communication Technology

ICT offers a wondrous potential for increasing government accountability, transparency, and participation and, with deliberate policies, for contributing to poverty reduction and individual empowerment. It has already transformed the provision of many public services in developed countries and will continue to do so in ways that would be hazardous to predict. A few general criteria will remain applicable in all countries as a guide for further improvements:

- ICT is a tool, and user needs must dictate whether and how it should be used.
- ICT cannot substitute for good management and internal controls.
- It is important to have a coherent ICT strategy and avoid a piecemeal approach to innovation.
- ICT eliminates corruption opportunities for those who do not understand the new technology, but opens up new ones for those who know how to manipulate it.
- It is essential to prevent income gaps from widening further in favor of those with the capacity and the resources to take advantage of the new ICT possibilities. This implies a major effort by national governments and international organizations to bridge the "digital divide" and assure that the new technology contributes to poverty reduction and to opportunities for the less-advantaged groups.

QUESTIONS FOR DISCUSSION

1. "Sunshine kills germs." Discuss, using concrete examples.
2. Pick one of the two following statements and make a credible argument for it:
   a. "Without opening up to public scrutiny all available government records and information with very few exceptions, transparency in government is severely hampered."
   b. "Without a presumption of confidentiality of government decision making and information, effective government is impossible."
3. Is good management of government records really necessary for genuine transparency, or should one rely on the citizens to demand and obtain what they consider relevant information?

4. "A law on freedom of information may not suffice for overall transparency of government action, but it always helps." Agree?

5. Pick one of the two following statements and make a credible argument for it:
   a. "The media has several roles. However, as an intermediary between the government and the citizens, the principal role of the media is to transmit the views of the government on the major issues of the day."
   b. "The media has several roles. However, as an instrument of transparency, the principal role of the media is to query and contest the rationale and credibility of government actions."

6. Pick one of the two following statements and make a credible argument for it:
   a. With the extensive and just-in-time information available on the internet, there is no longer any point in reading newspapers or listening to TV news."
   b. "The internet is full of unverified junk and cannot be trusted as a source of information."

7. "The attention span of viewers has become so short that TV news has been forced to become flashy, telegraphic, and misleading." Comment.

8. "There should be no restriction on the freedom of the media—period, end of story. Any restriction, even if initially justified in itself, eventually snowballs into one form of censorship or another. Let the public decide which sources are credible and which opinions worth paying attention to." Discuss.

9. Pick one of the two following statements and make a credible argument for it:
   a. "The new information and communication technology is a boon for efficient public administration."
   b. "The new information and communication technology is a menace for responsible public administration."

10. Does the internet have the potential to strengthen public discourse and generate a new competitive stimulus for the traditional media? In the long run, are new media and old media complementary or substitutes?

NOTES

1. This section draws partly on OECD (1997d); Commonwealth Secretariat (1997d); Cooper and Newland, eds. (1997); Government of United Kingdom (1997); Guhan and Paul (1997); Transparency International (1996); Schachter (1997); and Government of India (1997a).

2. This section draws on Schachter (1997); OECD (1997d); Government of India (1997a); Commonwealth Secretariat (1997c); U.K. Government (1997b); U.S. Government internet reports; Transparency International (1996); and Schartum (1998).

3. This section has drawn in part on the OECD Occasional paper No. 17 (1997); Davis and Owen (1998); Transparency International (1996); Bjornlund and Bjomlund (1996); and various web sources. Valuable comments were provided by Mara Schiavocampo.

4. The term was a charge given to Quakers in the eighteenth century.

5. We owe this point to Trevor Robinson.

6. See, for example, "Journalists in Russia face death, violence, censorship because of their work," www.marasonline.net.

7. In his opinion in *Schenck v. United States*, 1919.

8. Review of this section by Tommie Porter is gratefully acknowledged.

9. Dutton (1996).

10. Coleman (1998).

11. We owe this point to Trevor Robinson.

CHAPTER 14

The Rule of Law: Assuring Public Integrity and Preventing Corruption

> That which is lawful is clear and that which is unlawful likewise, but there are certain doubtful things between the two from which it is well to abstain.
> —*Hadith of the Prophet Muhammad*

> Physicians say of consumption that in the early stages . . . it is easy to cure but difficult to diagnose; whereas later on . . . it becomes easy to diagnose and difficult to cure. The same thing happens in affairs of state.
> —*Nicolò Machiavelli*[1]

WHAT TO EXPECT

No country and no age have a monopoly on corruption. Official corruption is one of the oldest and most stubborn problems confronting governments and is found in different forms and degrees in virtually every political system throughout history. Also found throughout history are rationalizations that corruption is culturally determined, or that it is not harmful, or even that it is a useful lubricant for transactions with government. These arguments fail the test of common sense and actual experience. While cultural norms may facilitate official corruption, gradual improvements are possible. The evidence also shows that corruption carries substantial costs for society, both direct and indirect, and is especially bad for vulnerable groups and the poor. Moreover, official corruption rarely stands still—like a cancer, it tends to grow and permeate all public activity, eventually eroding the institutional infrastructure of the country and leading to permanent economic decline.

An inadvertent side effect of the public management reforms of the past decade has been to create uncertainty about the behavior expected of civil servants and to dilute administrative integrity. It is therefore critical to put in place new accountability mechanisms to accompany those reforms. A major international consensus has been reached during the past decade on agreements to combat official corruption, and elements of effective strategies have been elaborated. These strategies are articulated in very different ways in developed and developing countries and must be adapted to the specific country context, but rest everywhere on three complementary efforts: creating an ethics infrastructure to foster voluntary honest behavior; reducing the opportunities for corruption, thus lowering the expected gains from corruption; and raising the expected costs of corrupt actions by robust enforcement. Official corruption has never and will never be eliminated, but the outlook for reducing and containing it is more promising than it has been for decades.

WHAT IS CORRUPTION?

Problems of corruption in government are hardly new. Indeed, official bribery has been known as the second oldest profession and—in different forms and degree—can be found at all times in virtually every political system. Over 2,000 years ago, the Indian philosopher and public administrator Kautilya wrote in *Arthasastra: "Just as it is impossible not to taste honey or poison that one may find at the tip of one's tongue, so is it impossible for one dealing with government funds not to taste, at least a little bit, of the King's wealth."* Corruption can also be found within the private sector, of course. Indeed, with the Enron and other major corporate scandals, the linkage between public and private sector corruption has reemerged since the late 1990s as an area of special concern, particularly in the United States, Europe, and East Asia.

Definitions

Although there is no universal comprehensive definition as to what constitutes corrupt behavior, the most prominent definitions share a common emphasis on the abuse of public position for personal advantage. The succinct definition utilized by the World Bank (1997a, p. 8) is *"the abuse of public office for private gain."* The OECD defines it similarly as *"the misuse of public office, roles or resources for private benefit"* (OECD, 1999, p. 13). These simple statements are elaborated in the definition employed by Transparency International, the leading nongovernmental organization active in the global anti-corruption effort: *"Corruption involves behavior on the part of officials in the public sector, whether politicians or civil servants, in which they improperly and unlawfully enrich themselves, or those close to them, by the misuse of the public power entrusted to them."*[2] These definitions do not cover the problem of corruption within the private sector and cover only limited aspects of the role of private individuals in fostering corruption in government. A major improvement, therefore, is the definition of the Asian Development Bank (1998a), by which *"corruption is the abuse of public or private office for personal gain."*

Longer and more detailed definitions of corruption are necessary to address particular types of illicit behavior and underpin criminal prosecution or other legal action. In the area of procurement, for example, the World Bank (1997a) defines corrupt practice as *"the offering, giving, receiving, or soliciting of anything of value to influence the action of a public official in the procurement process or in contract execution."* A fraudulent practice is defined as *"a misrepresentation of facts in or to influence inappropriately a procurement process or the execution of a contract . . . and includes collusive practices among bidders . . . designed to establish bid prices at artificial, noncompetitive levels and to deprive . . . of the benefits of free and open competition."*

Types of Corruption

The Athabascan and Inuit people have several different words for "snow" depending on its specific characteristics. Corruption, too, takes different forms, not all of which are equally important or costly. A variety of analytic tools have been developed over the last decade to identify and quantify the precise nature of the corruption problem at hand. The policy and operational responses will vary in accordance with the type of corruption being addressed.

First, bribes given to induce public officials to deviate from their duties must be distinguished from "speed money" (or "grease money," i.e., bribes given to get them to do what they are supposed to do in any case, or to do it faster). The corrupting effect is the same, but in the former case the allocation of resources and services is distorted as well. Second, it is useful to distinguish between syndicated corruption in which elaborate systems are devised for receiving and disseminating bribes, and nonsyndicated corruption, in which individual officials may seek or compete for bribes in an ad hoc and uncoordinated fashion.

The most important distinction, however, has been made by Transparency International between "grand corruption" and "petty corruption." Grand corruption typically involves senior officials, major decisions or contracts, and the exchange of large sums of money. Petty corruption involves low-level officials, the provision of routine services and goods, and small sums of money. A related distinction is between systemic corruption, which permeates an entire government or ministry, and individual corruption, which is more isolated and sporadic. Systemic corruption is a basic governance and public management issue; isolated corruption is a run-of-the-mill law enforcement problem.

Although large-scale corruption either starts from or is tolerated by the top political levels, petty corruption itself can in time destroy the integrity of public administration—in addition to causing significant transaction costs on business and citizens. Moreover, corruption rarely stands still and has a tendency to increase over time. It is in this sense that the analogy with cancer is apt—since the disease of corruption only gets worse through time, by a competitive dynamic that leads otherwise honest employees and officials to conform to a culture of bribery. When corruption becomes accepted as normal ("everybody does it"), the noncorrupt minority of government officials are viewed as fools rather than honest, bribery comes to be considered necessary "lubricant for the machine," efficiency and effectiveness in government become impossible, the poor and powerless suffer the most, and the economy is gravely hampered.

A last major distinction is between economic corruption, as previously described, and *political corruption*. Political corruption includes such practices as the financing of political parties in exchange for contracts or official posts, or co-opting of legislators by giving them influence over the awarding of contracts in their constituencies. Political corruption is frequent in many developed and developing countries, but goes beyond the scope of this book. While illicit political financing and pork-barrel politics are blights on the integrity, efficiency, and effectiveness of public management, the problem is essentially political and so are the remedies—which are thus not amenable to technical or administrative solutions. (This is a major reason why illicit political financing is not included in the international anti-corruption agreements, such as the OECD Anti-Bribery Treaty and the UN Convention Against Corruption.)

Some Illustrations

The term "corruption" is shorthand for a wide variety of illegal and illicit behaviors, ranging from the outright theft or pilfering of state assets, to collusion in procurement, exchange of favors for recruitment and promotions, and bribes to obtain basic services. An illustrative list (not exhaustive) of illicit behavior typically referred to as "corruption" is presented in Box 14.1.

The list in Box 14.1 shows that some types of corruption are internal—interfering with the ability of a government agency to recruit or manage its staff, make efficient use of its resources, or conduct impartial in-house investigations. Other forms of corruption are external—involving efforts to manipulate or extort money from clients or suppliers, or to benefit from inside information. Still others entail unwarranted interference in market operations (e.g., the use of official power to artificially restrict competition and generate monopoly rents). In parallel with the different forms of corruption, an extensive terminology has emerged throughout the world, as described in Box 14.2.

BOX 14.1

An Illustrative List of Corrupt Behaviors

Corruption includes, among others, any of the following actions:

- Theft or embezzlement of public property and monies;
- Design or selection of uneconomical projects because of opportunities for financial kickbacks and political patronage;
- Procurement fraud, including collusion, overcharging, or the selection of contractors, suppliers, and consultants on criteria other than the legal procurement criteria;
- Illicit payments of "speed money" to public officials to facilitate delivery of goods, services, and information to which the public is legally entitled (e.g., permits);
- Illicit payments to public officials to facilitate access to goods, services, or information to which the public is not entitled, or to deny others access to goods, services, or information to which they are entitled;
- Illicit payments to public officials to prevent the application of regulations in a fair and consistent manner, particularly in public safety, law enforcement, or revenue collection;
- Payments to public officials to foster or sustain monopolistic access to markets in the absence of a compelling economic rationale for restricting public access;
- Misappropriation of confidential information for personal gain (e.g., using knowledge about intended public transportation routes to buy real estate that is likely to appreciate);
- Deliberate disclosure of false or misleading information on the financial status of corporations that would prevent potential investors from accurately valuing their worth (e.g., nondisclosure of large liabilities or the overvaluing of assets);
- Sale of official posts or promotions, nepotism, or other actions contrary to the civil service regulations;
- Abuse of public office (e.g., using the threat of a tax audit to extract personal gain); and
- Obstruction of justice and interference in the duties of agencies tasked with detecting, investigating, and prosecuting illicit behavior.

CORRUPTION—ARGUMENTS AND COSTS

The Cancer of Corruption

As mentioned, corruption has not always been seen as having a negative impact on the economy or society. In earlier decades, arguments were advanced that it could have beneficial effects. It was alleged that corruption could advance economic efficiency by helping to restore government-

BOX 14.2

The International Semantics of Bribery

Different countries have come up with different terms—some very elegant—for bribery, either as a euphemism or for deniability. Most of these terms have to do with petty corruption. Grand corruption usually goes under the more pedestrian all-purpose names of "commissions" or "agency fees," which of course can also cover legal payments for real services and not bribery. Aside from the very common "instant fine" payable on the spot and in cash to police or other minor officials, and "reimbursement of (nonexistent) expenses," an international sampling of the semantics of bribery includes:

- *bustarella:* Italian for "little envelope"—sometimes quite large!—either to perform a service to which the citizen is entitled or to avoid a legal obligation, or to gain a head start over a less generous or less dishonest competitor. (The term "envelope" is also used in most other European countries to refer to bribes.)
- *expediting fee:* used pretty much everywhere as a euphemism to refer to bribes to get goods out of customs or obtain a license or, simply, to make sure your application for anything doesn't accidentally get lost or stay at the bottom of a tall pile for years.
- *speed money* or *grease money:* similar to the "expediting fee," but used for minor transactions throughout most of Asia and elsewhere. Both terms carry the same connotation of lubricating the system to make it work properly and without squealing.
- *dash:* common in anglophone West Africa, used as both noun and verb—e.g., "you'll have to dash him."
- *chai* (tea): common in Anglophone East Africa (note that "tea" also refers to dinner) and parts of Asia.
- *Fanta money* or *Coca-Cola money:* Common in francophone central Africa (Congo, Burundi, Rwanda, etc.).
- *pot de vin:* French for glass of wine—common in North Africa, francophone West Africa and other francophone countries, including parts of Indochina.
- *pourcentage:* French for percentage, normally referring to bribes for large contracts.
- *refresco:* Spanish for "refreshment"—used through most of Latin America.
- *pasalubong:* in the Philippines (but commonly also used to refer to normal gifts to friends and family when returning from a trip).
- *baksheesh:* ubiquitous as a term for "bribe" throughout the Middle East and Central Asia (but also meaning ordinary gifts or normal tips for service).

(continued)

Box 14.2 *(continued)*

Undoubtedly the most sophisticated euphemism is the Italian *tangente,* which replaced the more humble *bustarella* as corruption became an integral component of the political financing system. Taking its inspiration from the circular flow of money and production that characterizes economic activity, the term refers to the portion of money systematically spun straight out of the circular flow by the centrifugal forces of influence and patronage. As noted earlier, the massive corruption scandal that led to the replacement of virtually the entire political class in Italy in the early 1990s and a wholesale change in political system—a bloodless revolution that has not received as much credit as it deserved—was called *tangentopoli,* or "bribe city."

controlled prices up to their market-clearing levels. Others maintained that corruption played a useful redistributive role, transferring resources from wealthy individuals and corporations to those of more modest means, or that it could serve as a tool of national integration by allowing ruling elites to entice or co-opt fractious political, ethnic, or religious groups. Next, it was argued that corruption serves to channel resources to those who can use them most effectively. Finally, some scholars have argued that corruption is a natural stage of development, noting that it was generally widespread in many advanced countries until the early twentieth century, when it was reduced (but not eliminated) through the gradual enactment of public sector reforms.

These arguments fail on several grounds:[3]

- They often focus on the alleged benefits stemming from specific illicit acts and do not consider the systemic impact of corruption. Although a given bribe may have positive results (it certainly does for the recipient), it may also generate negative externalities that degrade the performance of the system as a whole and compromise the economy's long-term dynamic efficiency.
- Many of the effects of corruption only appear beneficial against the background of a failed public sector. The experience of economies such as Singapore and Hong Kong demonstrates that persistent efforts to correct deficiencies in public management yield far greater benefits over time than tolerating corruption to compensate for these deficiencies.
- Corruption encourages people to avoid compliance with all rules, good and bad alike. There is no guarantee that a customs official who takes a bribe today to "expedite" the clearance of badly needed medicines will not take a bribe tomorrow to give clearance to clear illegal narcotics.

Most importantly, the arguments that corruption is not harmful fail the test of common sense. Thus, it is evident that corruption does not channel resources to those who produce most efficiently, but to those who bribe most efficiently and are comfortable with illegal activities. To allege that corruption can help the poor is equivalent to the silly assumption that the rich and powerful are less "well connected" than the poor and the powerless. In civil service, rather than compensating government employees for inadequate salaries, corruption undermines the merit system and compromises morale and professionalism. Corruption is not even an efficient means to cement political loyalties; on the contrary, it breeds public cynicism and resentment toward the political process and those associated with it, and encourages a search for larger bribes from other political forces and the auction of political loyalty to the highest bidder.

A Cautionary Tale

In June 1997, everything looked good in Southeast and East Asia—rapid economic growth, progress in human indicators, social peace, apparent financial stability. There was tolerance of the closed circles of influence and privilege; obliviousness to the mounting (and largely invisible) economic costs from lack of transparency and accountability; and shrugging acceptance of corruption—indeed, even a benevolent view that official theft and private collusion were necessary "lubricants" for the system. These weaknesses were not limited to the government or to lax supervision of the banking system, but included severe problems of corporate governance in the private sector itself, stemming from lack of transparency and absence of strong competitive checks and balances. Merit and competition were wholly secondary to personalistic relations of kinship, bribery, and collusion. And yet, the system had been humming along for many years and the nexus between development and good governance didn't seem to be operative in that part of the world. This was known as the "Asian exception" to the link between public integrity and sustainable economic progress.

Some observers had raised doubts about the sustainability of such a system, but were dismissed as naysayers. A few Cassandras had even predicted collapse, but, like all Cassandras they were ignored. Then, seemingly out of the blue, the Asian financial crisis struck, first in Thailand on July 2, 1997, and then in Indonesia, Korea, the Philippines, and to a lesser extent other Asian countries—with the shock wave spreading through much of the rest of Asia, then Russia and the rest of the world. The worm in the apple was indeed the corruption in the system. The "Asian exception" was no more. It became clear that corruption was indeed a key impediment to sustainable development in Asia, as everywhere else in the world.

The Costs of Corruption

Direct Costs

The direct costs of corruption are both diverse and huge, as the following illustrations show:[4]

- From 1980 to 2000, Indonesia is estimated to have lost $48 billion in corrupt resource transfers abroad, surpassing its entire stock of foreign debt of $40.6 billion.
- In the Italian city of Milano, anti-corruption initiatives in the 1990s reduced the cost of infrastructure outlays by more than one third, allowing the city to increase spending on maintenance, schools, and social services. In Italy as a whole, official corruption in earlier years raised outstanding government debt by as much as 15 percent, or $200 billion.
- If Bangladesh had managed to be as successful as Singapore in reducing its level of corruption, its annual average per capita GDP growth between 1960 and 2000 would have been 1.5 percent higher, leading to a per capita GDP in the year 2000 about 150 percent higher than its actual level and taking at least 30 million Bangladeshis out of poverty.[5]
- When customs officials in Bolivia were allowed to receive a percentage of what they collected, there was a 60 percent increase in customs revenue within one year.
- In New York City, businesses were able to cut $330 million from an annual waste disposal bill of $1.5 billion by ridding the garbage industry of mafia domination. A particular problem was the permeation of regulatory bodies by organized crime.

- It is estimated that as much as $30 billion in aid for Africa has ended up in privately owned foreign bank accounts. This amount is twice the annual gross domestic product of Ghana, Kenya, and Uganda combined.[6]
- The foreign debt of Zaire (now Democratic Republic of Congo) under the dictator Mobutu was equal at the end of the 1980s to the $4 billion estimated private fortune of Mobutu.
- In countries where corruption is endemic, senior enterprise managers spend as much as a third of their time dealing with government officials, as opposed to less than 5 percent of their time in countries where corruption is not a major problem.
- Studies of government procurement in several Asian countries reveal that corruption has caused governments to pay from 20 to 100 percent more for goods and services.

Indirect Costs

Even more damaging can be the indirect costs of corruption, which cannot be measured with precision. Corruption can skew investment decision making to favor large new projects over routine maintenance and rehabilitation, which contributes to lower investment productivity and reduced asset life. At times, public safety is endangered, as when building code violations contribute to widespread structural failure during earthquakes. Morale is eroded and productivity can decline across the civil service. In extreme cases, political stability itself can be threatened. Finally, corruption is especially costly for the poor and the vulnerable—therefore, serious anti-corruption efforts are among the most effective measures to reduce poverty and exclusion. Although these costs may not become apparent for a very long time, the Asian financial crisis showed that in the long-term corruption has a heavy and negative impact on both poverty and economic growth.

Corruption and Economic Growth in Democratic Regimes

A recent study has shown (Drury, Krieckhaus, and Lusztig, 2006) that corruption tends to be less damaging to economic growth in democracies than in unrepresentative regimes—mainly for the plain but strong reason that in a democracy, crooked politicians or public officials can be removed from power. From this point of view, it makes sense to encourage moves toward democracy even in highly corrupt regimes. However, the opposite is probably not true: efforts to reduce corruption in non-democratic regimes are unlikely to lead to improved political governance.

In many countries covered by the above-mentioned study, the correlation between corruption and slower growth is not apparent. However, the analysis comprised a period of only fifteen years—1982 to 1997. It may take much longer for the negative impact on growth to materialize. For example, it took well over twenty-five years for the corruption in the Italian political system, which had been gradually growing from the mid-1960s, to have an adverse impact on the country's economic performance. The Tangentopoli ("Bribe City") scandals of the early 1990s eventually produced a complete cleanout of the political system but without a rapid improvement in the disappointing economic growth record of the country.

In any case, even in democracies where corruption does not appear to have a significant impact on economic growth, its adverse impact on income distribution and poverty remains a reality, by distorting administrative decisions in favor of the richer and better-connected groups. On balance, therefore, one may assess the link between democracy and corruption as follows: In undemocratic regimes, corruption is equally bad for *both* economic growth and poverty; in democratic regimes, corruption is bad mainly for poverty. What the evidence justifies is the general conclusion that the combination of severe corruption and democracy is not sustainable in the long run; persistent corruption will produce stronger and stronger centers of particularistic economic and financial power that, in time, will erode democratic processes. In this sense, the metaphor of corruption as a cancer remains applicable although, in a democracy, it appears to be a much slower-acting cancer.

A Variable Impact

Although corruption is always costly, its impact on the economy and on development is not uniform. Some countries can tolerate relatively high levels of bribery and graft and continue to maintain respectable rates of economic growth, whereas others cannot—depending on three factors. First, a country's natural resource base plays a critical role in its ability to attract investment, allowing corruption to coexist with economic growth for a long time. A second factor is the way in which corruption is practiced—especially its predictability. Where corruption is highly routinized, payoffs are generally known in advance and are concentrated at the top in a "one-stop" fashion. Such an approach reduces transaction costs and adds a measure of predictability to investment decisions, making the country inherently more attractive than other corrupt systems where many different officials can demand unspecified and unanticipated payments, or even countries with honest officials but haphazard application of petty regulations.[7] From the investor's viewpoint, it is the added cost of doing business that matters, and not necessarily the source of that cost. Finally, the extent to which the profits remain in the country and are invested in productive economic activity or flow abroad into foreign bank accounts will also have an impact upon a nation's ability to tolerate relatively high levels of corruption and still enjoy decent rates of economic growth.

On balance, however, countries that tolerate relatively high levels of corruption tend to perform less well economically than they would otherwise. Study after study has demonstrated that corruption is strongly and negatively correlated with the rate of investment, and thus with economic growth. (One of the earliest such studies was Mauro,1995.) Recall once more that the damage done by corruption is often not visible except in the long term. The surface of the administrative and economic apparatus appears intact while, like termites, growing corruption eats away at its foundations until the damage is permanent and irreversible, the administrative apparatus disintegrates, and a thorough rebuilding of public management becomes inevitable.

ETHICS AND INTEGRITY IN THE PUBLIC SECTOR

As discussed in chapter 1, the public service is confronted with difficult challenges and pressures for the twenty-first century. In the traditional mode of public administration, the civil servant was expected to abide strictly by detailed rules of behavior and was held responsible almost only for the *protection* of the state's resources. The requisite behavior was clear and so were the responsibilities. From the 1990s however, there has been an increasing demand for *results,* in part associated with globalization. This demand for results has produced a change in the relationship between the public and private sectors and an increased government reliance on market or quasi-market mechanisms—as chapter 15 describes. In this new environment of orientation to results, the rules of behavior have become hazy. The implicit message of "we don't care how you do it, just do it" is bound to encourage cutting corners and selective compliance with behavioral norms. Government employees may face potential conflicts of interest, in particular from the greater discretionary power that they have to be given in order to make them accountable for results. Moreover, a by-product of globalization has been the increased contacts with the different ethical and cultural norms in other societies, in which certain questionable behaviors and murky relationships are not necessarily prohibited or even frowned upon. In this new context, actions to preserve integrity and ethics in the public service have become even more important.

The General Context

In the last decade, the public administration reforms described in chapter 15 have been accompanied by (and sometimes based on) a questioning of the very notion of "public service" and a mistrust of "bureaucrats." This attitude is not only factually unwarranted, but is also damaging in practice. The complex challenges faced by government in the twenty-first century cannot be met successfully unless the importance of a spirit of public service is recognized and the contribution of good public servants appreciated. In turn, this requires holding firmly to the bedrock values of public service. These core values are common to all countries: public servants are expected to be impartial and equitable in their actions, ensure accountability and effectiveness in the delivery of services, and treat all citizens with responsiveness and respect.

The Politician and the Civil Servant

In representative governance, all public officials, whether elected or not, must be responsible and accountable for how they perform. This means that the integrity of *both* the politician and civil servant must be assured, as both carry a public responsibility, and the distinction between politician and public administrator is not clear cut. The general public does not make such a distinction and holds "the government" responsible for bad services and failures—and rightly so, as most public decisions involve both elected and nonelected officials. This is also true at international and supranational levels. In Europe, for example, citizens often perceive the various European Union's institutions as one single "Brussels" government, making no distinction between the elected members of the European Parliament, the employees and the members of the European Commission, or national public officials meeting in the Council of Europe. International organizations, too, are viewed as a monolith. As a consequence, the public integrity issue necessarily involves all components of a government, and attempts to deal with lapses in conduct should target all types of government officials. In the United Kingdom, for example, the Committee on Standards in Public Life had a mandate to review standards at all levels of government activity.

It is clear that the public cannot accept double standards for politicians and civil servants. However, politicians should be viewed more in the context of their relationship with the civil servants rather than as a separate target for attention, as the nature of their accountability is different. This leaves out of the scope of this book political corruption and the financing of political parties and political campaigns. Political corruption and campaign financing are extremely important issues in many countries, but go much beyond the integrity and effectiveness of public administration itself.[8]

Globalization

One positive development since the late 1990s, as part of the general phenomenon of globalization, is that governments are increasingly watching events elsewhere, including ethical crises and attempts to deal with them. In Australia, for example, problems and public scandals in other countries have motivated an interest in fostering and maintaining appropriate ethical behavior and accountability. In European countries, the same emulative effect can be noticed following the widely publicized procurement scandals that led to the collective resignation of the European Commission in 1999.

Globalization has also increased contacts with public officials in countries with different ethical standards, as well as contacts with business, including foreign or multinational enterprises that may play by different rules of the game. If not addressed, these contacts could lead to a global "lowest ethical common denominator." If addressed constructively, instead, this greater interaction can instead generate pressure to improve standards everywhere. As a major step forward, OECD countries took collective action against corruption by reaching consensus on the need to outlaw the bribery of foreign public officials in international transactions, as provided in the OECD Convention on Combating Bribery of Foreign Public Officials in International Business Transactions (see later in this chapter).

Changing Social Norms

To foster integrity in the public sector, behavioral standards must reflect changing societal norms. This is the case, for example, with measures to eliminate sexual harassment or racial discrimination. What was considered acceptable behavior vis-à-vis female coworkers in the United States as late as the 1970s—"boys will be boys"—is now not only unacceptable but illegal. Or, as Trevor Robinson has noted, a hundred years ago the English bishops condemned homosexuality and favored fox hunting, and currently hold the opposite view on both issues. (Personal communication, 2007.)

Societal norms have never been static. However, paralleling the globalization phenomenon, societal norms are evolving faster than in earlier times—certainly faster than many segments of society are able to absorb. Moreover, religious values and dogmas have increasingly been inserted into the political debate over the last decade. This new major challenge has created new internal tensions in many countries. Illustrations include the "culture wars" in the United States concerning gay marriage and stem cell research; the tension in Turkey between the secular foundation of the state and the resurgence of religious feeling; and, in Europe, the contradiction between a general ethos (or rhetoric) of tolerance and the difficulties of integrating some Muslim immigrant groups into the host society. It is only to be expected that such dilemmas will affect the public servants as much as anyone else.

Public Sector Values

Are Public Service Values Universal?

It is frequently argued, especially in East Asia, the Middle East and parts of Latin America, that international comparison of public service ethics are inappropriate because public ethics are part of the overall value system, which is country and culture specific. For example, giving and accepting gifts is a normal way of doing business in some countries and highly problematic in others; nepotism is viewed as dishonest in some countries but as a perfectly natural practice to "help your own" in others.

Economic differences are also relevant. As discussed in chapter 7, badly inadequate civil service salaries are frequently associated with public corruption. In general, however, differences in public values between countries do not result from any single factor, but from the *interaction* of many different elements, including historical and cultural specificity, level of economic development, strength of civil society, and accepted governance norms.

Nevertheless, despite the real differences among countries there is a convergence of views on what is seen as good and proper behavior of government employees. Certain fundamental values closely associated with good governance and a professional civil service are accepted everywhere: the political values of freedom and justice and the administrative values of legality, personal integrity, efficiency, and impartiality. Of course, these values are weighted differently in each system and articulated in diverse ways in the day-to-day activity of public officials, and in some countries they are only given lip service.

Codes of Conduct for Government Employees

It is impossible and unfair to demand "ethical behavior" from public servants unless they are clearly told the basic principles and standards they are expected to apply to their work and the boundaries between acceptable and unacceptable behavior. A clear, concise, and well-publicized statement of core ethical principles and standards for public employees is necessary to create a shared understanding across government and within the broader community. Such statements are usually referred to as codes of conduct. By itself, like all laws a code of conduct is useless if it conflicts with basic societal norms and/or is not enforced. However, a code of conduct can make a useful contribution to fostering public service integrity when the institutional context is favorable.

Figure 14.1 shows the public service values most often mentioned in developed countries. Impartiality, legality, and integrity rank at the top. All these values should be balanced against one another, especially when they occasionally conflict (e.g., loyalty to the organization versus transparency of public information). Most of these values are self-explanatory. Others are briefly discussed in the next section.

Impartiality and Integrity

In addition to nondiscrimination on ethnic, religion, gender, or economic grounds, the main aspect of impartiality is political neutrality (i.e., nonpartisanship). Civil servants, while loyal to their political leadership, are expected to behave in a manner that does not favor or damage any specific political party or faction. Indeed, as discussed in chapter 8, government employees are subject in their personal political activity to limits that are not applicable to persons in private employment.

While integrity is fundamental and is expected in all sectors of society, it takes on a particular meaning in the public service, as it calls for the ability to hold a public trust and to put the common good ahead of any private or individual self-interest. Typically, governments integrate the standard of "honesty" in the recruitment process of civil servants through background checks, tests, or other ways.

Loyalty

In a democratic context, loyalty to the political leadership and administrative superiors is a requirement for good public service. It is the elected political leadership that represents the people, not a civil servant. Obviously, loyalty must stop at illegality. But loyalty also reaches its limit when obeying an instruction or not reporting a problem could seriously jeopardize a public interest or would require an unethical act (even if not illegal). The loyalty principle is also challenged when public servants are asked to be accountable to the citizen. In theory, there is no conflict between serving a government and serving the clients: users get what they are entitled to, as determined by government policy. But in practice, "responsiveness" and "service to citizens" require public

Figure 14.1 **Most Frequently Mentioned Public Service Values in Developed Countries, 2000**

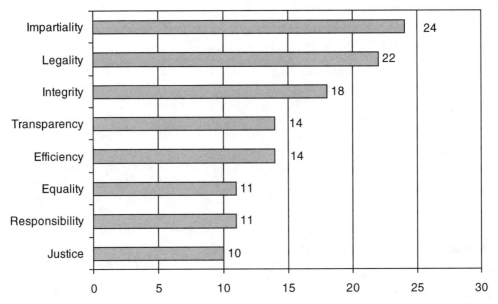

Source: "Building Public Trust: Ethics Measures in OECD Countries." OECD Public Managment Policy Brief No. 7, 2000.

servants to act in their day-to-day activities in a manner which may occasionally conflict with their loyalty to administrative superiors.

Continuity

Civil servants are expected to ensure stability of services to the public. Aspects of continuity are that they cannot desert their office and can only have such outside professional activities as do not conflict with performance of their tasks. (For example, under Article 101 of the Japanese National Public Service Ethics Law of 1999, civil servants have an "obligation to give *undivided* attention to duty.") Another aspect of continuity is that when leaving their position, public officials should not hide or remove any information concerning their past activity, in order to ensure a smooth transition for their successor.

Transparency vs. Discretion

As discussed in detail in chapter 13, government has traditionally been reluctant to release information. Sometimes, there are good reasons. But secrecy also works as a way to hide misconduct. Official transparency is thus one of the most effective ways to promote integrity and prevent corruption. However, because openness leads to extensive control exercised by the citizens and even more by the media, the obligation of openness must be balanced by the value of discretion. This means that public officials should be given clear guidelines about what information they are entitled to provide, how, and to whom. It is the duty of the state to define clearly what "public information" is and to guarantee access to it. In this respect, Article 100 of the Japanese National

Public Service Ethics Law of 1999 prohibits divulging any secret that may have come to employees' knowledge in the performance of their duties. Other countries have similar provisions, as do the major international organizations.

Responsibility and Accountability

Public officials must feel personally responsible and accountable for their decisions and actions. It is essential to develop a good sense of responsibility to the job, to the organization, and especially to the public interest. In this sense, while mobility of civil servants is good for their efficiency and career progression, it should not be so frequent as to weaken their sense of responsibility to the agency for which they are working at any given time. (Among other things, excessively frequent changes in position can be an incentive for corruption.)

Virtually all developed countries, and many developing countries, have explicit provisions similar to that in the Canadian Conflict of Interest and Post-Employment Code for Public Office Holders: "Public office holders, in fulfilling their official duties and responsibilities, shall make decisions in the public interest and with regard to the merits of each case." This naturally requires that the public officials have a clear sense of what is "in the public interest." Views of what public interest exactly means vary in different countries. In any case, employees are expected to arrange their private affairs—to go back to the Canadian example—"in a manner that will prevent real, potential or apparent conflicts of interest from arising, but if such a conflict does arise between the private interests of an employee and the official duties and responsibilities of that employee, the conflict shall be resolved in favor of the public interest." But responsibility alone is insufficient. Accountability—responsibility plus consequences—is the key. When mistakes are made, one often hears from politicians or high-level civil servants statements that they "accept responsibility." Such statements are useless unless accompanied by swift and predictable consequences.

MANAGING FOR INTEGRITY IN A CHANGING PUBLIC SECTOR

As mentioned, a major challenge to public ethics has emerged from the adoption of the many public management reforms discussed in this book—see especially chapter 15. Public managers face a substantially different environment in countries which introduced contestability for public functions and privatized or outsourced a number of functions previously performed by public servants. This does not imply that these reforms have necessarily had a negative impact on integrity in the public service. In the discussion that follows, the intention is to underline the linkage between these reforms and the risk to the ethical framework, with the ensuing need to take realistic complementary action to prevent an unintended weakening of public integrity.

Letting the Managers Manage: The Impact of Delegation

As chapter 10 discussed, it is impossible to hold managers responsible for results unless they have sufficient autonomy and discretionary authority in the use of resources—including employees—that are needed to produce those results. Significant efficiency gains have been achieved in many countries by giving additional powers to managers. Central regulations and control have been reduced, providing flexibility to administer people and resources creatively in ways that are tailored to achieve the outcomes sought by government. In most developed and some developing countries, both the central departments and the line agencies today enjoy far more autonomy than in the past.

Concerns have been expressed that without efforts to maintain good "professional socialization"—that is, the inculcation of public service values—the public sector ethos and the coherence of government action could be jeopardized by these developments. The issue is whether these valued should be developed by and for each government agency or by the government as a whole. On the one hand, the applicable public service values depend partly on the organization's mission and objectives. For example, the ethical issues relevant to an employee of an intelligence agency will be significantly different from those relevant to someone working in the social security department. On the other hand, there is a need to ensure an overall coherent public service ethos, to prevent fragmentation. Thus, even where individual agencies are allowed to design their own agency-specific codes of conduct, they must do so in the context of central guidelines. This is necessary even in countries that have pushed public management innovations the farthest. In New Zealand, for example, there is both an overall Public Service Code of Conduct as well as departmental codes to fit the operational requirements and circumstances of the different departments.

A corollary of giving greater managerial autonomy is the need to reduce detailed rules (as in the United States "Reinventing Government" initiative launched in the mid-1990s) and to introduce goal-oriented provisions on the performance that various units are expected to achieve. The greater freedom of action implied by the principle of "letting the managers manage" allows at the same time more space for irregularities and new opportunities for corruption. Some government officials may simply be confused about how to operate when detailed regulations and rules have been reduced, without an equally clear and reliable specification of performance indicators. Beyond this transitional problem, however, a single-minded stress on "results" inevitably places the manager under pressure to sidestep ethical standards or procedural norms. (See chapter 10.)

This dilemma requires the creation of a new institutional environment in which public servants can be made accountable for the use of their greater discretionary powers while continuing to adhere to the values-based framework. The right balance between delegation and accountability is of central importance in achieving a well-performing and professional public service with integrity. As central regulations and controls are reduced, the role of values and the public interest concepts that they reflect becomes increasingly significant, both as a guide for behavior and as the common reference point and unifying thread for the public service. Mechanisms for safeguarding these values need to be strengthened to protect the public interest in new and current situations, lest the greater service efficiency be paid for by a reduction of integrity. In any event, as stressed in chapter 10, introducing accountability for results does not permit reducing the basic fiduciary duty to protect the public's money in the first place. You do need to hold on to the baby when throwing out the bathwater.

The Impact of Reduced Resources and "Restructuring"

Most governments have faced significant pressure to reduce public expenditure in the 1990s, after the massive expansion in state responsibilities in the previous decades. Measures for more efficient use of resources have included lower budgets and reductions in the size of the public sector workforce. In countries where government overstaffing was substantial and the downsizing focused on the weak-performing employees, staff reductions did not adversely affect public service efficiency. In other countries, where the workforce was appropriate at the start, downsizing required already fully-occupied employees to carry a heavier workload without additional compensation. This can have a negative impact on public servants' morale, and the apparent resulting increases in "productivity" may be accompanied by lower service quality, and short-term improvements may be followed by long-term deterioration of services.

Similar problems might result from inadequate incentives. For example, when "caps" are set on the salaries of senior executive staff, as in the United States, the logic of the senior executive service itself is negated. (See chapter 8.) Additionally, when resources are reduced at the same time as better results are demanded, pressures are generated to cut corners or to bypass due process. Finally, training is often the first activity to be curtailed, with adverse implications for the long-term productivity of the government workforce. It is therefore important to introduce new quality assurance mechanisms at the same time as the government workforce is reduced and budgets are cut.

Public service restructuring also risks affecting the overall state and management of ethics and conduct. Restructuring often includes changes in familiar legal and administrative forms of organization, which generates uncertainty as to which new values should be applied in the new entities, or how to adapt the traditional values to a new environment. In some cases, the organization may have to evolve from a public to a private system of ethics—with more attention to the bottom line and less worry about norms of due process. In any event, a sensible restructuring plan cannot neglect the implications for integrity, incentives and behavior of the employees.

The New Public/Private Sector Interface

The evolution of the public administration has included closer contacts with the private sector. Of course, private companies are also concerned with fostering ethical behavior. Nevertheless, the evidence shows that the closer public/private relationships have created new opportunities for wrongdoing in a number of areas. In France, for example, the decentralization process of the 1990s removed traditional (and inefficient) ex-ante controls and constraints on local government, but did not at the same time provide stronger ex-post oversight. Not surprisingly, this opened the door to several damaging instances of public-private collusion at local government level and has weakened to some extent the credibility of the necessary decentralization process.

The increased involvement of public servants in commercial operations with the private sector also opens up risk in areas such as build-operate-transfer contracts and the management of privatization (see chapter 11 for a discussion of outsourcing). Problems have also arisen about privatization and cross-border transactions, as in Poland; about tax and customs revenues, as in Greece; and in the award of public contracts, allocation of subsidies, and licensing and levying fees, as in Germany. However, it is in the area of information and communication technology (ICT), where outsourcing has been especially extensive, that the most useful lessons can be learned. In Norway, the ICT investments of a number of large government agencies have raised issues of relaxed controls and low accountability, as well as poor articulation of oversight responsibilities among the different levels of government.

The increasing interaction between the public and private sectors should not be discouraged but does call for closer attention on public service values and for requiring external partners to respect those same values. The consequences of a failure to do so were brought home dramatically by the Asian financial crisis of 1997–1999, which was in large measure caused by the degradation of public-private cooperation into collusion and closed circles of influence and privilege. And the critical need for close public oversight of privately executed projects finds no better illustration than the incompetence and corruption embedded in Boston's "Big Dig" project—see Box 14.3.

One central aspect of the new public/private interface is the evolution of employment practices. Traditionally, public servants trade off the higher salaries of the private sector for the security of tenure and the social status associated with government service. The clarity of this trade-off has been blurred in many countries. Security of employment has been weakened by the

BOX 14.3

Boston's "Big Dig"

The elevated Century Artery through downtown Boston, opened in 1959 with a daily capacity of 75,000 vehicles, began in the 1970s to experience traffic problems. These problems progressively became worse, causing (among other things) an accident rate four times the national average and cutting off vital North End neighborhoods and the Boston waterfront from the rest of downtown, thus limiting their participation in the city's growth. Moreover, except for going all the way around the metropolitan area, all north-south traffic to and from the rest of the state and the country had to go through this obligatory bottleneck on I-93. The proposed solution was construction of a mega-project—the Central Artery/Tunnel project (CAT), dubbed "The Big Dig"—essentially replacing the elevated roadway with a 3.5-mile-long tunnel under the center of the city. The solution was a sound response to a real problem—on paper. In real life, incompetence and corruption soon stepped in.

The project, for which the autonomous Massachusetts Turnpike Authority was responsible, involved a consortium of international and national contractors led by Bechtel Corporation, thus associating the largest engineering firm in America with the most expensive highway project in the country. Ground was broken in 1991 and the final ramp downtown opened on January 13, 2006—seven years after the target date and at six times the cost (initially estimated at $2.5 billion in 1985). In addition to the direct costs, the fifteen years of construction and resulting mess in downtown traffic severely strained the economy and quality of life in and around Boston. This, however, was not the end of this dismal situation. Engineer Jack K. Lemley, hired by the Turnpike Authority to investigate the phenomenal cost overruns, noted in March 2006 that there were hundreds of leaks riddling the tunnels and wrote to Authority chairman Matthew J. Amorello that he could not vouch for the safety of the I-93 portion of the Central Artery. He also alleged that new information had surfaced challenging the safety of the project, including more than forty flawed tunnel-wall sections and water-damaged fireproofing, but was denied access to records pertaining to these problems. Massachusetts Attorney General Thomas Reilly cited poor oversight and shoddy work as the factors responsible for the problems. These concerns were tragically confirmed when Boston resident Milena Del Valle was crushed to death when a 3-ton concrete ceiling panel in the tunnel connector fell on the car in which she was a passenger. The ensuing investigation found structural design flaws, including the fact that bolts used to secure the panels were not strong enough to support panel weight for a sustained period—flaws which the Laborers and Iron Workers unions, among others, had pointed out for years.

Governor Mitt Romney sought to remove Mr. Amorello from his $205,000-

(continued)

Box 14.3 *(continued)*

a-year post overseeing the project. In May 2006, an indictment was returned by a federal grand jury, charging six employees of Aggregate Industries NE, Inc., the largest asphalt and concrete supply company in New England, with conspiring to defraud the United States by submitting false records to the Central Artery Tunnel Project and mailing fraudulent invoices to general contractors. The Big Dig was finally completed in late 2007, but more is to come to the surface.

Source: The Boston Globe, various issues, 2005, 2006, 2007.

greater use of fixed-term contracts and, as mentioned earlier, respect for civil servants has given way to mistrust. Also, lateral recruitment from the private sector has taken place with greater frequency, requiring a corresponding increase in compensation in order to be effective. These developments may have positive effects with respect to improving management or applying some private sector innovations. However, there are also concerns that the murkier distinction between public and private employment may contribute to diluting standards in public administration, as result-orientation and monetary performance indicators override public sector values and norms of due process.

Finally, the closer relationship between public agencies and private companies naturally raises the civil servants' propensity to leave government for employment in the private sector. Of course, there is nothing wrong with this, provided that government recruitment and training policies are sufficiently efficient and flexible to prevent a reduction in the overall skill level of the government workforce. However, legitimate concerns are raised about the risk that civil servants may use privileged government information to seek private employment. (Areas of particular sensitivity are tax administration and public procurement.) Once again, the point we wish to make is not that an otherwise healthy development toward public-private initiatives should be stopped, but to insist that the necessary complementary measures must be put in place to prevent the problems that such development might generate.

Most countries have responded to this concern—normally applicable to senior staff levels only—by imposing post-employment restrictions on public servants (e.g., Canada, France, Germany, Ireland, Japan, Korea, Norway, Poland, Sweden, and many others). In France, for example, the law prohibits cumulating public employment with any other private or public employment, with very narrowly defined exceptions.

In the United States, regrettably, the regulations on conflict of interest are much too weak, and weakly enforced at that, to preclude collusion between senior government employees and private companies doing business with the government. Outright bribery is sometimes the result—for example, see the case of Darleen Druyun described in Box 9.8. But even when the behavior is not technically illegal, the extraordinary weakness of U.S. conflict-of-interest rules routinely allows conduct that is patently unethical. The case of former congressman Billy Tauzin taking, immediately after retirement, a high-paying job in an industry that he oversaw as a congressman (summarized in Box 9.7) is an egregious example, but unfortunately is not an exception—the ethical bar having been lowered since the late 1990s to a low level not seen since the 1920s.

Figure 14.2 shows the relative frequency of different measures used in developed countries to promote both individual motivation and ethical behavior.

Figure 14.2 **Measures Used in Developed Countries to Promote an Ethical Public Environment**

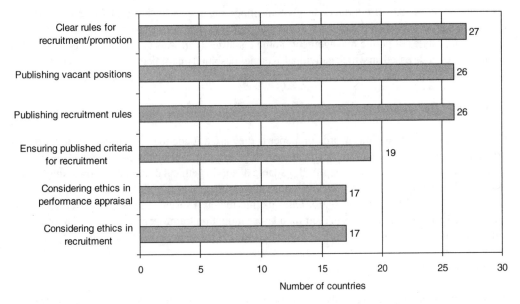

Source: "Building Public Trust: Ethics Measures in OECD Countries." OECD Public Managment Policy Brief No. 7, 2000.

Building an Institutional Infrastructure for Public Service Ethics

Corruption prevention and enforcement must be supported by a sound "ethics infrastructure," the principal building blocks of which are summarized here. In reality, the components of an ethics infrastructure are the foundations of good public administration in general. They are worth recapitulating here, to underline that anti-corruption measures taken in an institutional vacuum are unlikely to be effective. Note that while the ethical infrastructure has been formulated by and for developed countries, it also provides an important set of signposts toward which reform in developing countries can proceed.

Political Commitment

In the absence of sustained political commitment, efforts to encourage ethical behavior in the public administration will be in vain. Successful attempts to improve public sector ethics in OECD countries have been sponsored from the highest political levels: for example, a comprehensive anti-corruption strategy and program were elaborated in Korea in the late 1990s following a direct instruction from newly elected President Kim Dae Jung.

An Assertive Civil Society

Ethics is everybody's responsibility. Individual citizens need to take the trouble of bringing to light instances of misbehavior by government officials. An assertive media is essential in this respect—through its reporting, it can act as watchdog over the actions of public officials. (On the role of civil society in combating corruption, see OECD, 2002.)

Codes of Conduct

As noted earlier, codes of conduct can play an important role in fostering ethics, particularly in countries that have reduced the number of rules applying to public servants and have adopted more "managerial" styles of public management. Some countries (e.g., Australia) chose to enact a broad public service code based on which individual agencies designed a complementary code to reflect their particular objectives and mission. In other countries, codes of conduct are all agency-specific.

Professional Socialization

Codes of conduct remain only words on paper if they are not adequately communicated through processes by which public servants learn, adopt, and practice ethical standards. Training is important to raise ethics awareness and develop skills capable of solving ethical dilemmas; good managers are essential. For example, ethics issues now constitute an integral part of the initial training of future public managers in Belgium; all senior entrants into the civil service in the United Kingdom are required to focus on ethics issues in their mandatory induction training; and in the Czech Republic, ethics are integrated as a special module in both induction and in-service training.

Coordinating Entities

The existence of a coordinating body to promote or oversee public ethics does not absolve managers of their first-line responsibility for ensuring ethical conduct within their jurisdiction, but it can help substantially. An ethics coordinating entity can take various forms—parliamentary committees, central agencies, or specially created bodies—and may assume various roles:

- "general promoter," for example, the role of Norway's Ministry of Labor and Government Administration;
- "counselor and advisor," as the U.S. Office of Government Ethics and the Canadian Office of Values and Ethics for the public service;
- "watchdog" role, as performed by a standing oversight committee such as the Committee on Standards in Public Life in the United Kingdom; and
- "investigator," as France's permanent anti-corruption investigation commission or the New South Wales Independent Commission Against Corruption in Australia.

Supportive Public Service Conditions

The high standards of ethical conduct expected of public officials are one side of the coin. The other side is a set of decent working and living conditions, including sufficient job security, opportunities for promotion and career development, adequate remuneration, and social appreciation. Fair and impartial human resources management policies can ensure that selection and promotion processes in the public sector are based on professional requirements and principles of nondiscrimination and that extraneous factors such as partisan political considerations are ruled out (see chapter 7 for a discussion of government wage policies). If public servants are underpaid, overworked, and insecure, they are more vulnerable to corruption. Indeed, when compensation is insufficient even for basic family subsistence, as in a number of developing countries, widespread bribery is a virtual certainty. Employees cannot be expected to choose personal integrity over the survival of their spouse and children.

Effective Legal Framework

In the overall ethics infrastructure, while supportive employment conditions are the carrot, the legal framework provides the stick. Laws and regulations define the basic standards of behavior for public servants and enforce them through investigation and prosecution. In reviewing its legal framework, a country must check that existing criminal codes and civil service laws, conflict of interest statutes, and other regulations that apply to public servants are clear and consistent. In particular, asset declaration laws—which oblige politicians and senior public officials to declare publicly their assets and financial interests—have proven especially effective in curbing abuses and collusion.

Robust Accountability Mechanisms

Accountability mechanisms should encourage ethical behavior by making unethical activities hard to commit and easy to detect. Guidelines for government activities are needed to check that results have been achieved and due process has been observed. These include internal administrative procedures (e.g., requirements that activities or requests be recorded in writing); comprehensive processes such as audits and evaluations of an agency's performance; whistle-blowing protection, which encourages public servants to expose wrongdoing and refuse to do something inappropriate; and mechanisms external to the executive branch (e.g., oversight by legislative or parliamentary committees).

Naturally, public accountability must not be limited to the executive branch and should encompass the legislature as well as the judiciary. In the United States, regrettably, this has not been the case. The influence of lobbyists on legislators has increased enormously, as shown most obviously by the ratio of lobbyists to legislators. As of end-2004, there were five lobbyists for each member of Congress, with more than ten lobbyists per legislator in New York, Florida, Illinois, Colorado, and Ohio (see Table 14.1). Evidently, the "market" for influence peddling is large and has been expanding. Nor has a moralizing influence been exercised by the scandalously ineffective ethics committees established in the House of Representatives and the Senate—as Box 14.4 illustrates. The inescapable conclusion is that congressional ethics cannot improve substantially unless a separate and *independent* mechanism is established to look into allegations of legislative misconduct. In turn, ethics in the executive branch are likely to remain weak in the absence of an ethical congress with the credibility to exercise robust oversight. Moral laxity in one branch of government provides an alibi for moral laxity in the other. (Thankfully, the integrity of the judiciary has remained high.)

Unfortunately, in January 2007 the Senate once again rejected decisively a proposal to establish an independent office to investigate ethics complaints against senators. On the positive side, both the Senate and the House of Representatives approved major new rules to, among other things, ban lawmakers from accepting free gifts, meals, and travel from lobbyists and require lobbyists to reveal the small donations collected from clients and "bundled" into large political donations—thus evading the limits on individual political contributions. More importantly, the new rules prohibit former members of Congress from any lobbying for at least two years after they leave office. Finally, the new rules require members of Congress to attach their names to special interest bills and "earmarks"—a major step toward curtailing the scandalous explosion of "pork barrel" spending since the beginning of the century—see chapter 6 and Box 6.6.

FIGHTING CORRUPTION

Historically, concern about corruption has run in cycles, in which revelations of official abuses prompted anti-corruption campaigns and administrative measures that subsequently faded from

Table 14.1

Ratio of Lobbyists to Legislators in the United States, 2004

State	Total Lobbyists	Total Legislators	Number of Lobbyists per Legislator
New York	3,842	212	18
Florida	2,041	160	13
Illinois	2,161	177	12
Colorado	1,054	100	11
Ohio	1,280	132	10
Arizona	800	90	9
California	1,032	120	9
Michigan	1,258	148	9
New Mexico	848	112	8
Texas	1,460	181	8
Massachusetts	1,439	200	7
Montana	1,090	150	7
Nebraska	350	49	7
Virginia	946	140	7
Georgia	1,336	236	6
Minnesota	1,200	201	6
Rhode Island	659	113	6
Washington	952	147	6
Wisconsin	817	132	6
Indiana	700	150	5
Kentucky	640	138	5
Missouri	1,065	197	5
New Jersey	582	120	5
Wyoming	417	90	5
Alabama	565	140	4
Delaware	226	62	4
Hawaii	286	76	4
Iowa	601	150	4
Louisiana	523	144	4
Maryland	755	188	4
Oregon	390	90	4
Tennessee	542	132	4
Utah	423	104	4
Arkansas	354	135	3
Connecticut	482	187	3
Idaho	309	105	3
Kansas	574	165	3
North Carolina	541	170	3
Oklahoma	440	149	3
South Carolina	491	170	3
South Dakota	308	105	3
West Virginia	423	134	3
Alaska	140	60	2
Mississippi	402	174	2
North Dakota	272	141	2
Pennsylvania	579	253	2
Vermont	383	180	2
Maine	168	186	1
New Hampshire	178	424	< 0.5
Nevada	Don't Track	63	N/A
	38,324	7,382	5

Source: Center for Public Integrity (2006), available at www.publicintegrity.org.

BOX 14.4

"Ethics" in the U.S. Congress

In 2006, two issues finally came to a boil and brought home the corruption problems in the Congress and the weakness of its internal accountability mechanisms: the umbilical cord between lobbyists and legislators (identified mainly with the name of Jack Abramoff, but pervasive) and the scandal involving Representative Mark Foley and underage pages.

The Lobbyists and the Lobbied. A report by Public Citizen, a nonprofit public interest organization, documented that since 1998, lobbyists' contributions to members of Congress amounted to over $100 million (www.citizen.org). Many of the top congressional recipients served on appropriations committees that allocate federal funds. Lobbyist contributions increased from $17.8 million in the 2000 election campaign to $33.9 million in 2004. The contributions of the top fifty lobbyists averaged more than $200,000, or $25,890 per year, with thirty-six members of Congress (twenty-one Republicans and fifteen Democrats) accepting upwards of a half-million dollars from lobbyists since 1998—including former Senate majority leader Tom Daschle (D-SD), former House majority leader Tom DeLay (R-TX), and former Senator Rick Santorum (R-PA).

The top three industries paying the most lobbyist fees are finance, defense, and education. The following are only a few among the myriad illustrations:

• In January 2004, a group of lobbyists met with then-House Majority Leader DeLay at the restaurant owned by convicted felon lobbyist Jack Abramoff, reportedly to discuss ways to increase contributions to Republican lawmakers.

• Kenneth Kies, former chief of staff of the Joint Committee on Taxation from 1995 to 1998, contributed almost $300,000 to preserve the "synfuel" tax credit, through which $1 billion to $4 billion per year were paid to companies who sprayed coal with diesel fuel or other substances and thereby claimed a tax credit for creating a "synthetic" fuel. The firms for which Kies worked took in nearly $2.4 million in lobbying fees from the Council for Energy Independence and nearly $5.4 million from General Electric since 1998. The top recipient of Kies' contributions is Rep. Jim McCrery (R-LA), who intervened with the IRS and the Treasury on behalf of "synfuel" makers.

• In 1996, lobbyists Denny and Sandra Miller hosted two fundraisers for Senator Ted Stevens (R-AK), the "King of Pork," raising $160,000. Miller was one of two lobbyists who helped negotiate language that called for $30 billion in military spending to lease air refueling tankers from Boeing, one of his clients. (The tanker deal did not go through, and it would have cost the government more to lease the planes than an outright purchase—see Box 9.8.).

(continued)

Box 14.4 *(continued)*

• Four lobbyists were convicted of felonies in 2005 and 2006: Jack Abramoff; Tony Rudy, former deputy chief of staff to Tom DeLay; Michael Scanlon, DeLay's former spokesman; and Neil Volz, former chief of staff to Rep. Bob Ney (R-OH).

The *Page Scandal* does not involve trading favors, but shows the reflexive habit of congressional leaderships to protect colleagues and to cover up events embarrassing to their party. Representative Mark Foley (D-FL) was the focus of an investigation by the House Ethics Committee (officially the Committee on Standards of Official Conduct), stemming from his improper conduct involving current and former teenage House pages. The Committee, under new leadership, promised a thorough investigation, which had the potential to begin restoring the ruined reputation of the congressional ethics mechanisms. Incredibly, however, while the committee found that congressional leaders had covered up Foley's behavior for years, it recommended no action whatsoever—not even a letter of reprimand.

view until the next round of scandals provided further impetus for reform. The desire to reduce or eliminate corruption has been at the core of many innovations for good governance. The major public administration reforms of the late nineteenth and early twentieth centuries discussed in previous chapters—such as the introduction of a meritocratic civil service system, professional management of government departments, or the creation of formal budget, procurement, and audit processes—had their roots in the desire to avoid the earlier practices of blatant graft and political patronage.

Evolution of an International Consensus

The United States was a pioneer in global anti-corruption efforts, with the 1977 Foreign Corrupt Practices Act that prohibited American corporations from bribing foreign government officials. However, without concomitant action by other countries, the act could not be truly effective. Also, U.S. corporations complained, with some justification, that the Act placed them at a disadvantage vis-à-vis other countries' companies. Moreover, at the time, official corruption was frequently viewed as either inevitable or as a lubricant for economic activity.

In the late 1980s and early 1990s, a variety of analytical findings came together to underscore the importance of effective institutions in fostering growth and the pernicious impact that weak governance and corruption can have upon economic growth and development. In parallel, a national and international consensus gradually evolved on the need to combat official corruption, as the chronology in Box 14.5 shows.

A Global Approach

The general rule for reducing corruption is *to raise the expected cost of a corrupt action and lower the benefit expected from it.* The expected cost is the severity (and swiftness) of the penalty multiplied by the probability of getting caught; thus, raising the cost of corruption requires robust and uniform enforcement of the penalties. The expected benefit is the amount of gain from the

BOX 14.5

Milestones in International Anti-Corruption Legislation

Among the many international measures enacted since the end of the Cold War to combat public corruption, the following are most notable:

- In 1992, the World Bank produced the first policy document on "governance and development."
- In 1994, the Organization of American States (OAS) pledged to outlaw cross-border bribery and the "illicit enrichment" of officials in the hemisphere.
- In 1996, the taboo on mentioning and tackling corruption was lifted by former World Bank President James D. Wolfensohn's speech on the "cancer of corruption."
- In 1996, twenty-one member-states of the OAS signed the Caracas Convention, calling for collective action in preventive measures and international cooperation, transnational bribery, illicit enrichment, and extradition. (However, the Caracas Convention was ratified only by Bolivia, Costa Rica, Ecuador, Mexico, Paraguay, Peru, and Venezuela.)
- In May 1996, the OECD approved a resolution encouraging its member-states to end the tax deductibility of foreign bribes and "commissions" paid by their national corporations.
- In December 1996, the United Nations General Assembly passed the Declaration Against Corruption and Bribery in International Commercial Transactions.
- In 1997, the OECD approved recommendations for criminalizing transnational bribery, enacting stricter accounting requirements and external audit controls and tighter public procurement.
- In September 1997, the World Bank introduced a formal anti-corruption policy, and the regional development banks—the Asian Development Bank, African Development Bank, and Inter-American Development Bank followed suit shortly thereafter.
- In 1999, an OECD convention entered in force making the bribery of foreign officials a criminal offense on a par with the bribery of local government officials in the country where the corporation is based.
- In 2000, the International Chamber of Commerce approved tighter rules of conduct that prohibit bribes and recommended adoption of these rules by its member associations and corporations around the world.
- In December 2005, the UN Convention Against Corruption entered into force.
- In September 2006, all international development and financial institutions reached an unprecedented agreement on a Framework for Preventing and Combating Fraud and Corruption—standardizing the definition of corruption, improving coherence of their investigative procedures, sharing information, and assuring that enforcement actions taken by one institution are supported by all others.

corrupt action multiplied by the probability of obtaining it; thus, lowering the benefit from corruption requires effective prevention by reducing the opportunities for corruption.

However, in the current context of globalization this rule cannot be applied successfully on an isolated national basis. The pervasive trans-border nature of much official corruption calls for more than national government action—it requires a global approach grounded on international cooperation and centered on four basic objectives:

- Supporting competitive markets and efficient, effective, accountable, and transparent public administration;
- Supporting promising anti-corruption efforts on a case-by-case basis;
- Ensuring that all projects and programs financed with public moneys receive adequate scrutiny—or at least are fully transparent before legislative approval—and adhere to financial and ethical standards; and
- Vigorously pursuing the "supply side" of corruption—that is, bribes and influence peddling done by large corporations and their pressure on public officials.

As part of this approach, one must also confront the role of the "facilitating intermediaries" (i.e., mainly the banks through which the illicit gains are channeled and which all too often get off scot-free).[9]

The Experience in Developed Countries

All developed countries have criminalized diverse forms of corruption as well as certain other violations of public integrity, as Figure 14.3 shows.

The Main Directions

Echoing the international consensus on corruption, developed countries' experience suggests that corruption prevention should rely on a combination of mechanisms rather than any one single measure.[10] Mechanisms reported as most effective include law enforcement and independent investigation techniques, preventive management methods and financial controls, transparency mechanisms (e.g., declarations of assets, open administration, public exposure), raising the awareness and the skills of officials, and adequate remuneration of public officials. It is also very important to assure that the anti-corruption measures do not result in paralyzing the administration, but achieve a reasonable combination of anti-corruption and efficiency, avoiding "the pursuit of absolute integrity," as warned by Anechiarico and Jacobs (1999).

Targeting Financial Improprieties. Most initiatives target the openings for financial impropriety, mainly through requiring asset registers, listing of corrupt firms, asset declaration systems, registers of political lobbyists, and so on. Corruption prevention is more complex than just passing laws or establishing new anti-corruption institutions. To be coherent, measures must be integrated into the existing environment. Switzerland, for example, has improved the effectiveness of existing general provisions such as criminal, taxation, and competition law. (In Switzerland, the legally protected secrecy of banking transactions does not extend to transactions linked to criminal or terrorist activities.) Germany has introduced risk analysis to identify the areas of the public sector most susceptible to corruption.

Transparency Mechanisms. These mechanisms fall into three principal groups: (1) measures that guarantee the openness of systems and the standardization of public processes; (2) measures that

Figure 14.3 **Forms of Official Misconduct Criminalized by Developed Countries**

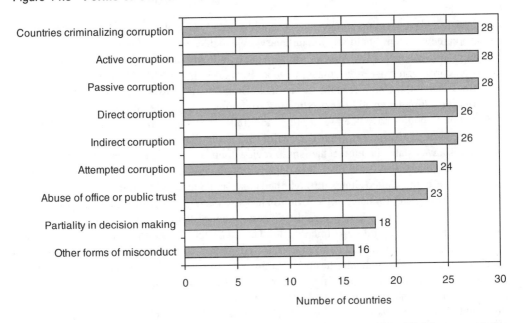

Source: "Building Public Trust: Ethics Measures in OECD Countries." OECD Public Managment Policy Brief No. 7, 2000.

provide access to or scrutiny of public sector processes; and (3) measures that facilitate reporting or exposure of wrongdoing. A recent innovation is the creation of monitoring bodies with special responsibility for administering transparency legislation: Greece established a special parliamentary committee; Italy established the office of "guarantor of legality and transparency"; and, reflecting a growing scrutiny of the financing of political parties, Belgium established a parliamentary commission to oversee the transparency of election campaign funding, and the United States Federal Elections Commissions monitors compliance with political financing rules.

Citizens' Responsibility. It is a bad mistake to conceive of anti-corruption as exclusively a governmental challenge. As in every area of governance and public management, active support and participation by civil society are needed for successful anti-corruption efforts as well. We have examined this topic at some length in chapter 12. Suffice it here to recall that it is impossible for a public official to receive a bribe unless a bribe is given. In a weak and uncertain governance climate, the initiator of the bribe can be the public official using the power to approve or deny, or the private parties to obtain privileges to which they are not entitled. Even when the corrupt transaction is initiated by the public official and the citizens and private firms are the victim, it behooves them to consider the implications of acceding to the bribe demand—not only in order to foster public integrity, but *in their own interests.* Bribes are like potato chips—you cannot eat just one. If satisfied, the first bribe demand will be followed by others. The best single example is in the tax audit area: if taxpayers give in to a tax auditor's first demand for a bribe, they are signaling their ability and willingness to pay bribes and can most certainly expect the same auditor at their door for years to come.[11] It is much better to take one's lumps and pay the additional tax and penalty, if one is legally assessed.

Institutions for Anti-Corruption

Investigation and prosecution of misconduct should normally take place through a well-functioning law enforcement system (including the judiciary) able to detect and sanction wrongdoing. But the legislature also has a role for detecting misconduct, and permanent parliamentary investigative bodies on corruption exist in Germany, Greece, Ireland, Italy, Mexico, Poland, and Sweden. In Belgium, Ireland, the Czech Republic, Germany, Hungary, Italy, Korea, and Mexico, provisions also exist for setting up an ad hoc investigating committee at any time. In some countries, special anti-corruption bodies have been set up (e.g., the Italian Special Commission for the Prevention and Repression of Corruption). On the healthy principle that integrity begins at home, some legislatures have established a mechanism to review their own ethics (e.g., in Sweden through a parliamentary oversight committee, or in Japan through deliberative councils in both houses of parliament, or in the United States through the House and Senate ethics committees).

Investigative power for detecting corruption has also been given to the traditional control bodies within ministries or agencies (e.g., the General Finance Inspectorate in Italy or the Inspectors-General in each federal department of the United States). In addition, some countries have specialized units within the police to investigate corruption (France, Belgium), while in Italy a specialized "anti-mafia" judiciary has been set up to coordinate all activities to combat organized crime. Until the 1990s, these activities did not lead to much more than the murder of some courageous judges. In the last decade, however, after the connections between organized crime and the political elite were finally severed by the bloodless political revolution that ensued from the Tangentopoli scandals, these activities have met with signal success.

To be effective, internal controls need to be combined with independent external controls. One approach is to create independent ethics agencies, such as the U.S. Office of Government Ethics, for oversight of ethics in the executive branch. A majority of countries rely on other mechanisms. Figure 14.4 shows the types and frequency of use of these different institutions in developed countries.

The Approach in Developing Countries

Most of the anti-corruption measures adopted in developed countries are potentially applicable to developing countries as well—taking into account the different level of development and the much more limited administrative capacity. In keeping with the general rule of anti-corruption stated earlier, three principles apply with special force in developing countries:

- Effective anti-corruption cannot be achieved in isolation, but must go through concrete improvements in specific systems or practices of public management—among which budgeting processes, personnel administration, and judicial systems rank at the top.
- Since it is impossible for a public official to receive a bribe unless a bribe is given, the "supplier" of corruption (local as well as foreign) needs to be pursued with as much vigor as the corrupted.
- In dealing with the openings for corruption—the prevention aspect—streamlining and clarification of the regulatory framework ranks at the top in most developing countries.

Along these lines, the generally effective approaches to anti-corruption follow the example of the Hong Kong Independent Commission Against Corruption, which was highly successful under its former head Bertrand de Speville, and in a few years during the 1990s turned Hong Kong from one

Figure 14.4 **Institutions Performing Independent Scrutiny over the Administration**

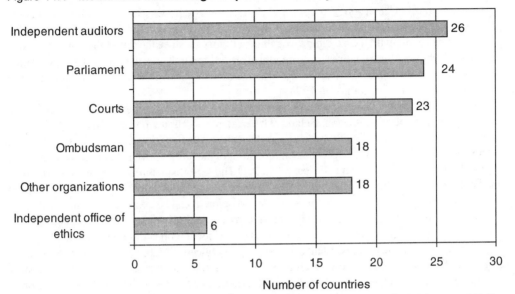

Source: "Building Public Trust: Ethics Measures in OECD Countries." OECD Public Managment Policy Brief No. 7, 2000.

of the most corrupt administrations to one of the most honest—second in Asia only to Singapore. The Hong Kong approach emphasized three concurrent efforts—awareness-raising, prevention, and enforcement. Like the three legs of a stool, each of the three efforts is necessary, none alone is sufficient in the long run. Prevention and enforcement cannot succeed if corruption is viewed as normal or inevitable; awareness and strict enforcement cannot be effective if the opportunities for corruption are too many and too easy; and limiting opportunities for corruption combined with awareness may be equally ineffective if enforcement is lax or nonexistent.[12]

This model of "awareness/prevention/enforcement" needs to be adapted and expanded in most developing countries into six major avenues of reform and intervention:

- find the facts;
- disseminate the knowledge;
- prevent through streamlining of the regulatory framework;
- strengthen enforcement;
- build the accountability institutions; and
- improve public sector management.

Cause for Optimism

As emphasized at the beginning of this chapter, it is very difficult to combat corruption in any country, and success generally requires a considerable coordinated effort over a long period of time. The international experience during the last decade, since the consolidation of the global consensus against corruption, is mixed but on balance positive. As a very broad generalization, Latin America has seen some decrease in official corruption alongside its democratization movement and the decentralization measures. So have a number of African countries—such as Senegal, Uganda, Tanzania, Mozambique, and Botswana—while backsliding has occurred in other countries, primarily Cameroon, Ethiopia, and Zimbabwe, and hopes for a major improvement in public integrity in Kenya and Nigeria are yet to materialize. Asia also shows a mixed picture, but positive on balance—with marked improvements in Indonesia since the fall of the Suharto regime and particularly with the first direct Presidential election, and in Korea with the full consolidation of democracy, more than making up for governance deterioration in the Philippines after the end of the presidency of Fidel Ramos in 1998.

There has been moderate anti-corruption progress in most transition countries, with a sharp turn for the worse in some (e.g., Algeria, Belarus, Uzbekistan, and Turkmenistan) and a "redistribution of corruption" in others (mainly Russia and, to some extent, Ukraine). In general, eastern and central Europe have done better in this respect than the countries of the former Soviet Union, with central Asia in particular in worse shape than in the early 1990s.[13] The sectoral picture shows the most improvement in customs. Customs is the public function where the incidence of corruption has always been among the highest, and there is still a long way to go before it can be considered relatively "clean" in most countries. However, the improvement in many countries has been real and significant, and is proof that reforms can be effective even in areas where corruption is most entrenched.[14]

Aside from the predictable persistent corruption in tax collection, public works, and procurement, an outstanding problem area in most countries is law enforcement and the judiciary—not only damaging for public integrity, but for the overall efficiency of the economy, as contract enforcement, business closures, and so on depend crucially on a well-functioning judiciary. Most often, the problem is with the police and the courts—from a combination of inadequate compensation and lack of accountability for the exercise of their substantial discretionary powers. Occasionally, the core governance problem is found instead in the prosecutorial function. In Bulgaria, for example, after the fall of the communist regime the understandable desire to get away from politically motivated prosecutions gave rise to a reform creating a wholly independent office of prosecutor-general, with total authority over initiating or not initiating prosecutions and practically impossible to remove during his term of office. However, in a wonderful example of the law of unintended consequences and of the dangers of a blinkered focus on a public-private dichotomy, in the country's weak governance environment of the time, the appointment of the prosecutor-general could be heavily influenced by organized crime interests, which would naturally be protected after the individual's appointment. Political capture was replaced by private capture.

But let's conclude with two examples of very rapid progress in anti-corruption from two very different places. Singapore was commonly known in the 1950s as one of the most corrupt places on earth—with most government services for sale; police, judges, and legislators for rent; and ad hoc laws available for private drafting at a reasonable market price. In just a few years, Singapore became a model of administrative integrity and has remained so ever since, through a combination of extremely generous incentives for honest behavior of public officials and ferocious enforcement of the rules, with harsh penalties for illicit actions. Of course, an outcome achieved by an authoritarian government in a city-state at the crossroads of international commerce cannot easily be replicated elsewhere. And yet, consider Atlanta, Georgia. At the turn of the century, the city was not only in deep fiscal trouble, but was seen as hopelessly corrupt. Just five years later, not only had the fiscal deficit turned into a small surplus, but a major improvement in public integrity was underway, with an ethics plan in place and implemented.[15] As stressed throughout this book, sustainability is key—the Singapore success in minimizing corruption was in part due to the political continuity of the Lee Kwan Yew government (whatever else may be said of this government). In Atlanta, the fiscal progress and initial anti-corruption success are yet to be consolidated. The initial results are promising, however, and—once again—demonstrate how "deep-seated" habits of noncompliance and lack of integrity can change rapidly if the rules are vigorously enforced and the incentive framework is rotated toward honesty rather than public theft.

GENERAL DIRECTIONS OF IMPROVEMENT

There is a broad consensus and plenty of evidence from all countries that in the long term, official corruption—defined as abuse of public power for private gain—is bad for public sector effectiveness, bad for the economy, bad for society, and especially damaging for the poor and minorities. Although concrete anti-corruption measures must be identified in the context of the specific country concerned, the listing of some of the costs of corruption indicates at the same time the major areas in which improvements are needed. (Of course, these directions of improvement are general and purely indicative, and each would in itself entail a difficult and multi-pronged reform effort.)

- Reduced rate of economic growth, from stolen sums taken out of the country—a direction of improvement is to strengthen cooperation with international organizations and banks.
- Higher cost of infrastructure, due to bribery—a direction of improvement is better project design and oversight.
- Greater government spending, due to corruption in procurement—a direction of improvement is enforcing procurement rules and providing better appeal mechanisms
- Lower government revenue from siphoning-off revenue into private pockets—a direction of improvement is reforming the tax collection and customs offices.
- Costlier public services, from "grease money" demanded by employees—a direction of improvement is opening opportunities for feedback from the public, along with adequate compensation of government employees.
- Lower effectiveness of aid to poor countries—a direction of improvement is better aid management by the host government combined with cooperation agreements to rule out the dysfunctional forms of inter-donor competition.
- Skewing public investment decisions in favor of large projects—a direction of improvement is the strengthening of project appraisal procedures and the implementation of a sound investment programming process.
- Endangering public safety and the environment by violations of construction or health codes and environmental regulations—a direction of improvement is to strengthen enforcement of the regulations combined with an improvement in the efficiency and integrity of the police and the judiciary.

Improving public integrity requires efforts along three complementary directions:

- Foster awareness, including programs to encourage civil servants' integrity and the formulation of codes of ethical conduct, thus keeping corruption disreputable and setting clear boundaries for acceptable individual behavior.
- Prevent corruption by minimizing opportunities for bribery and abuse of official position, particularly through simplification and clarification of the regulatory framework.
- Aggressive and uniform enforcement.

Anti-corruption activities are part and parcel of the good governance agenda and, as such, any improvement needs to be addressed in the context of the specific reforms in each individual area of public administration outlined earlier in this book. The general rule is, in each area, to reduce through prevention the expected gain from corruption, and increase through enforcement its expected cost (i.e., the probability of being caught combined with the severity of the penalty). Certain other broad considerations, however, are relevant to efforts at improving the ethical climate and reducing corruption, in both developed and developing countries:

- Expose and penalize misbehavior at the top of an organization or of the political system, rather than just catching a few "small fish" for public relations purposes.
- Require asset disclosure and public exposure as powerful means of disciplining corrupt behavior even without criminal prosecutions, and also provide important information to the public in the exercise of its political choices.
- Encourage good management—a climate of trust combined with effective oversight by the responsible manager provides the enabling environment for integrity.
- Focus as much on the private corruptor as on the public official corrupted.
- Recall that, as in law enforcement in general, the swiftness and certainty of punishment are more effective than severe punishments with an extremely low probability of being imposed within a realistic time period.
- Introduce ethics criteria in state employee recruitment and promotion. Explicit consideration of the ethics dimension will winnow out some high-risk candidates.
- Not only protect whistle-blowers but reward them, while at the same time putting in place safeguards against destructive gossip and the creation of a witch-hunt climate.
- Put in place specialized anti-corruption agencies, but only if they are supported from the top, genuinely independent (especially from the regular police), and accompanied by complementary measures on regulatory simplification, legislation, personnel procedures, and judicial efficiency.

QUESTIONS FOR DISCUSSION

1. "Corruption in government cannot be swept away for good without a strong, competent, and honest leader to do so." Discuss.
2. Pick one of the two following statements and make a credible argument for it:
   a. "Public corruption is most likely to flourish in situations of weak governance and loose accountability. Therefore, the overall approach to reducing corruption is to improve the country's governance and accountability mechanisms."
   b. "Public corruption exists because it pays. Therefore, the best approach to reducing corruption is a frontal assault on crooked officials and civil servants, with strong enforcement and severe penalties for corrupt behavior."
3. What are the main forms of corruption and how do they differ from one another?
4. Does it really "take two to tango"?
5. Is corruption equally damaging to economic growth regardless of the type of political regime?
6. If circumstances in a country happen to be such that official corruption is not having any negative effect on economic growth, except for a moral argument is there any compelling reason to make a major effort against it?
7. Has globalization, on balance, contributed to increasing corruption around the world or to decreasing it?
8. Pick one of the two following statements and make a credible argument for it:
   a. "Codes of conduct for government employees are pious statements that do nothing to foster public integrity."

b. "Without a clear code of conduct, government employees cannot be expected to maintain public integrity."

9. "All the international agreements and treaties in the world will not eliminate or reduce public corruption. They will merely lead to the creation of new cutouts and intermediaries, and different channels for the same amount and type of corruption." Discuss.

10. All things considered, do you personally believe that official corruption will diminish during your lifetime, either in your country or internationally?

NOTES

1. Quoted in de Silva (1993, p. 49).
2. See Pope (1996, p. 1).
3. Klitgaard (1998, p. 32).
4. Sources of the following illustrations are various magazines and international reports. Only one is the author's personal finding.
5. Extrapolated from a 1960–1985 comparison made by Shang-Jin Wei, 1999.
6. Pedersen (1996).
7. As an unusual case in point, in the mid-1980s the anteroom of the office of the Director of Customs in Mogadishu (Somalia) sported a table taped to the wall with the *typed* list of "informal payments" expected for clearances and other import transactions. As distasteful as it may be, such a practice at least made it clear to all comers exactly how much they would have to pay in bribes and to whom. To that extent, it was less damaging to the functioning of the economy than opaque and unpredictable bribery.
8. This is why the OECD Anti-Bribery Treaty discussed later in this chapter does not cover "political" corruption.
9. A healthy warning to the international banks was provided in 2006 with the heavy penalties imposed on the Riggs Bank for facilitating the corrupt transactions of Chile's former dictator Augusto Pinochet and "parking" the proceeds of his thefts of the country's resources.
10. OECD (1999).
11. We owe this example to Fuat Andic (personal communication).
12. There are major exceptions. "Stroke-of-the-pen" reforms abolishing key controls (e.g., on prices and exchange rates) can instantly eliminate a major opportunity for corruption. For example, unifying dual exchange rates removes all possibilities to obtain foreign exchange at the official rate only to sell it on the black market at a higher rate—the single quickest and most effective form of corruption. Or, as argued later in this paper, there are times when enforcement is clearly the most urgent priority. Beyond the immediate impact, however, concerted action on all three fronts is necessary if official corruption is to be reduced across the board in a sustainable manner.
13. See the World Bank's "Anticorruption in Transition: Who Is Succeeding and Why?" www.worldbank. org/eca/act3.
14. See World Bank (2005).
15. *The Economist,* August 27, 2005.

PART IV

ADMINISTRATIVE REFORM: EXPERIENCE AND PROSPECTS

CHAPTER 15

Public Administration Reform in Developed Countries

> We know exactly what to do, but we don't know how to win the next
> elections after we've done it.
> —*Jean-Claude Juncker, Prime Minister of Luxembourg, 2005*

WHAT TO EXPECT

Two broad phases of administrative reform in developed countries may be identified from the mid-1970s through the late 1990s: A phase of measures to control government spending followed by a phase of reforms to improve services and relations with citizens. Since then, a third phase has begun, consisting of consolidation and correction to counter the negative effects of past reforms—such as administrative fragmentation and ethical tensions—but without losing the progress made in efficiency and responsiveness. This third phase is ongoing and will continue for the foreseeable future.

Between the end of World War II and the 1970s, governments became too expensive, too big, and too intrusive. The mid-1970s to the late 1980s consequently witnessed budget reductions, public sector downsizing, and privatization. These reforms for "smaller/cheaper government" took place in response to fiscal necessity and thus under strong direction and control from the center of government, particularly the ministry of finance. From the late 1980s to the late 1990s, after fiscal deficits had been reduced in most countries, the goal became "better government." This meant improvements in service delivery, higher-quality regulation, devolution of responsibilities to lower levels of government closer to the citizens, better access to information, and greater transparency.

Despite the broad identification of reform phases, the reform initiatives were driven in each country primarily by domestic concerns tied to specific historical and cultural realities, and their shape, speed, and success were unique to each country. Indeed, both phases of reform had to take place at the same time in a few countries that did not begin to change until after the 1980s, such as Finland, which in the early 1990s had to adapt suddenly to the major repercussions of the collapse of the Soviet Union, its major economic partner. Italy, too, after its extensive cleanup of the political system in the early 1990s, had to implement substantial reductions of the public deficit (which permitted the country to enter the Euro area) at the same time as it was attempting to modernize government activities. Approaches differed as well. Some countries tried to achieve rapid fundamental changes in the roles and functioning of government. Others adopted an incremental approach, to improve the running of government or to stretch major changes over a longer period.

451

There were successes and failures in both groups. However, all had the same objective: adapting government to contemporary technological and globalization changes in order to improve cost-effectiveness of public services and preserve national competitiveness.

THE FIRST PHASE: CHEAPER GOVERNMENT

Controlling Government Expenditure

By the late 1970s, in most developed countries members of the OECD, government had become both overextended and unaffordable. The high level of government expenditure had generated large fiscal deficits, crowding out private investment and jeopardizing economic growth without even improving public services. Steps were taken to reduce and control public expenditure, with substantial success. Most countries reduced their fiscal deficit considerably and, by the end of the century, nine countries (Australia, Canada, Denmark, Finland, Iceland, Ireland, Norway, Sweden, and the United States) were even generating overall fiscal surpluses, while several other countries (e.g., Italy) achieved a "primary surplus," which is a budget surplus excluding interest on the government debt. (The primary balance gives a better picture of current developments, as interest on debt is a reflection of past fiscal problems rather than current ones—see chapter 6.)

For sustained economic growth and financial stability over the long term, fiscal discipline had to be maintained, particularly in view of the globalization of international financial markets. More than ever, governments had to compete with one another for foreign investment, and in order to be competitive they needed low inflation and stable exchange rates, which in turn required fiscal discipline. In Europe, a major influence on national fiscal discipline was exercised by the rules of the European Union, particularly those concerning the requirements for membership in the Euro area, primarily the rule limiting the budget deficit, under penalty of large fines. Although these rules define the levels of both the permissible fiscal deficit (3 percent of GDP) and of government debt (60 percent of GDP), in practice the deficit ceiling is a far more important target.

Obviously, reducing government expenditure meant either that government had to withdraw from certain areas of intervention (i.e., do less) or function more efficiently (i.e., do the same at less cost), or a combination of both. A few OECD countries (New Zealand and, less radically, Australia) went as far as to reexamine systematically the roles and functions of government, but most countries only devised ways of reshaping the traditional roles of the public sector. Among other things, they rationalized organizations that used to perform similar tasks; reallocated services within government organizations; and devolved central responsibilities to subnational governments (see chapter 5).

That said, with few exceptions, most of the essential features—generous pensions, universal medical care, and so on—of the social protection system (the so-called "social state") were not questioned in most developed countries, but were modified in order to ensure their survival: they were "mended, not ended." For example, Germany reformed its public health system successfully to keep health expenditures under control while preserving universal coverage. Moreover, countries with limited social protection provisions managed to achieve public savings in other areas, particularly military expenditure, which was significantly reduced in the 1990s (see chapter 1).

Downsizing

Among the various aspects of the containment of the public sector, downsizing and staff cutbacks have the most direct human implications (see chapter 7). Programs to reduce overall numbers of employees began in most developed countries in the 1980s and early 1990s, in connection with privatization and restructuring of certain public agencies. (In countries like Japan or Korea where government employment was very low to start with, there was naturally no need for deliberate staff reductions.)

In most cases, the reduction in staff was achieved by natural attrition and without outright dismissals. Long-established legislation in most continental European countries, as well as in Japan and Korea, prohibit the dismissal of civil servants for financial reasons. In other OECD countries, strict rules and agreements with labor unions also limit the ability of governments to dismiss employees. In the Netherlands, for example, a collective agreement between the central government and the labor unions obliges the government to look for suitable vacancies for the redundant employee during an eighteen-month period. Moreover, redundancy programs apply to very few categories of Dutch civil servants—generally those with more than thirty-four years of service, who can benefit from favorable conditions of separation from government employment. Like the Netherlands, Sweden makes the agency responsible for ensuring an effective redundancy process, thus limiting top-down attempts by the central government to reduce the number of staff.

These practices are explained by the general public consensus that government should guarantee job protection to its employees. (Job security is also protected for private sector employees.) The high weight to job security in European and Asian developed countries—as opposed to the North American premium on job flexibility—is in some measure a reaction to the historical experience of national instability and popular unrest. It is critical to understand that government labor practices are related to broader social choices which, in turn, flow largely from the particular experience of the country in question. None of these practices is better or worse than another—they are simply different. The only requirement for the policy maker and the public is to recognize clearly the cost of these choices and, if possible, act to alleviate it.

Although downsizing measures have been generally successful in containing the size of the government workforce, it is difficult to assess their impact. First, the term "public employee" is defined differently in different countries and data on public employment are difficult to compare. Also, some countries shifted personnel from central government to subnational government or to public enterprises. Second, downsizing programs have varied a lot from country to country—sometimes cuts were made across the board, at other times they focused on specific sectors (Box 15.1).

More Efficient Government

In general, in developed countries the size of government employment in relation to either the labor force or population has decreased in the last fifteen or so years. Even eschewing forced early retirements or outright layoffs, natural attrition from deaths, normal retirement, and resignations, combined with recruitment freezes and voluntary early retirement programs, have had some success in gradually reducing the size of the government workforce. Naturally, this approach took longer than outright dismissals or involuntary early retirement, but it also entailed a much lower cost in terms of human dislocation and social unrest and was thus more sustainable.

Reviewing the Modalities of Government Intervention

In times of fiscal stringency, social services and benefits can be maintained only through improving their efficiency and lowering unit costs. A major aspect of this has been the streamlining of regulations and administrative procedures to ease the burden on business and the citizens.[1] Most OECD countries now assess the potential impact of new regulations more thoroughly before is-

BOX 15.1

Downsizing in Developed Countries: Selected Experiences

In *Canada,* a program-by-program review identified the programs and services to be closed, and thus the staff positions to be eliminated. About 45,000 employees were removed from public service over a three-year period (1995–1998) as a result. Priority was given to ensuring employment security and minimizing instances of involuntary separation.

In *Finland,* the goal was to maintain or reduce personnel levels as part of an overall strict budget policy. Starting in 1997, each agency was instructed to set staff size within the overall budget limit. As a result, government employment declined sharply in only seven years, from 212,000 in 1989 to 120,000 in 1996. However, only 9,000 of this decline was attributable to staff cuts; the remainder was due mainly to the conversion of government agencies into public enterprises or private companies. Thus, while government employment declined substantially, overall *public* employment fell only marginally.

In *Mexico,* from the early 1980s, the government had made it a policy to limit employment growth as part of its efforts to modernize government, restructure the central public administration, and divest and privatize public-sector enterprises. The central government staff was reduced significantly through layoffs but mainly transfer of services from state agencies to lower levels of government and to public enterprises. As in Finland, public-sector employment was reduced by much less than central government employment. In 1994, severe fiscal problems led to setting new limits on public expenditures, which also included programs to reduce, rationalize, and modernize the public service to increase cost-effectiveness. The target was a reduction by about 10,000 positions (3 percent of the workforce), which included vacancies, thus limiting the number of involuntary layoffs.

suing them, and then monitor their impact. While in the mid-1990s fewer than half of the OECD countries did regulatory impact analysis, as of 2006 only Belgium, the Czech Republic, Greece, Japan, and Luxembourg had failed to adopt the practice.

Governments have also paid greater attention to the efficiency of the public enterprises, and effective corporate governance of public enterprises has acquired new importance. Privatized activities are by definition outside the public sector (although the choice of activities to be privatized and the manner of their privatization are central issues), but the corporate governance of public enterprises has acquired new importance. Corporatization of public enterprises is meant to balance the public interest with the advantages of autonomy for the enterprise, but has succeeded in producing more efficient enterprises *only* when accompanied by measures to make markets more competitive. (The Japanese government has been taking steps to abolish, consolidate, or streamline public corporations. Among other changes, a number of financial institutions were merged and the major issue of the misuse of the post office [Japan Post] savings as a giant piggybank for politicians was finally resolved in 2007 by privatizing the entity.)[2]

Governments have also increasingly contracted out activities to the private sector. In France, for example, where the contractual approach between the public and private sectors is well developed, the practice of *concessions de service public* ("public service concessions") has been in place for a century, especially in water supply. What is new in recent years is the extent to which countries have been prepared to outsource more complex and more central government activities such as information technology, education, and even, in some countries, prison management. A number of countries (such as the United States) have made it obligatory for government entities to explicitly consider external options for many services. (See chapter 11 for a discussion of outsourcing.)

In keeping with the analysis in chapter 11, the OECD experience with contracting out confirms the need for several preconditions, including the existence of a competitive market among suppliers, open and verifiable procurement procedures, and the availability in government of solid technical and legal skills in contract management. These preconditions, along with the high transition costs involved in outsourcing, set practical limits on contracting out complex activities, lest the potential benefits of contracting out dissipate and the costs turn out to be much higher.

Improving Public Management

The two main interrelated areas where efficiency improvements have been sought are personnel management and performance contracting. (The following should therefore be read in conjunction with the more extensive discussion of these topics in chapters 8 and 10.)

Personnel Management

It is often assumed that increasing the effectiveness of public sector organizations always requires more flexible personnel management. This assumption is debatable. Although about half of the developed countries have injected elements of flexibility in government employment contracts, continental Europe and Japan have retained the traditional career civil service system with job security and have fostered greater effectiveness by increasing the weight given to merit in recruitment and promotion decisions, and by greater emphasis to delegation of authority, training, and labor mobility.

OECD countries that have implemented personnel reforms in recent years have focused mainly on giving more responsibilities to managers for improving the performance of their staff. In a few cases, the government agency head was made personally responsible for recruitment and dismissal, as in New Zealand. Much more often, the authority given to managers has been accompanied by new guarantees to protect civil servants in their new working environment. The new system that Switzerland introduced in 2001 gives a greater role to public employee unions, and a similar trend is observed in Nordic countries. Indeed, the elimination of legal protections is typically accompanied by a stronger role of public employee unions. Also, labor practices can be subject to oversight by a public service commission, which sets broad guidelines for personnel management throughout the government while giving line managers much more autonomy to negotiate specific arrangements and make individual personnel decisions. Box 15.2 contains some illustrations.

Some countries now also recruit senior officials on the basis of fixed-term contracts. This has been the case for many years in New Zealand, where all senior civil servants have been placed under fixed-term contracts with precise performance targets. Fixed-term contracts have also been used for certain senior executives in Australia (at the federal level), in Sweden, and more recently

BOX 15.2

Illustrations of Civil Service Reforms in Developed Countries

Italy has been moving since 1993 toward a uniform treatment for public and private sector employees. The terms of employment and pay of civil servants, which used to be set by administrative law, are now covered by contracts under the general labor law. Also, the duties of politicians are more clearly separated from those of public managers, and managers are now paid partly on the basis of performance. Public managers have fixed-term, two- to seven-year contracts and are no longer appointed for life, as in the old system. In practice, however, the fixed-term contracts are routinely renewed.

Korea is introducing an open personnel system (OPS) throughout government. Under the former closed personnel system, vacancies in the higher grades (director level and above) were filled mostly through promotion within the government, and much importance was placed on job security, to the detriment of competition among individual employees. The OPS brought the element of competition into the civil service and made administrative services more transparent. More than one in five top positions in central government agencies (excluding those related to public security such as the National Intelligence Service and public prosecutors) have been open to outside candidates. Professionals from the private sector, especially in law, accounting, and construction, are encouraged to join the public service under contracts defining favorable terms of employment, including salaries. This flexibility is also intended to promote more varied personnel management practices among the different ministries and agencies and to develop the capability to tailor those practices more closely to their programmatic needs.

In *Switzerland,* the civil servant status established in 1927 was abolished in 2001. The focus since then has been on a "cultural change" in the federal government, aligning the new recruitment process with private sector recruitment practices. One aspect of this change is a shift in the onus of employee protection from formal laws to stronger participation by personnel representatives and collective bargaining.

In *Japan,* an important evolution has been the opportunity to recruit from the private labor market. The report of the 1999 Council on the Public Service Personnel System recommended mid-career recruitment from outside the government as a concrete measure to promote openness, diversity, and flexibility in the civil service. The process remains in its infancy, however.

in Italy, Korea, and the United Kingdom. The contract can be renewed, but renewal is contingent on meeting specific "performance" targets (with all the advantages, risk, and complications that this practice entails—see chapter 10). However, other countries that have initiated human resource management reforms have chosen to retain indefinite-duration contracts except for very specific jobs. This is the case of Canada and the Netherlands.

The new style of performance-oriented personnel administration makes itself felt primarily through new classification systems. The classification system must be flexible enough to promote the career goals of public employees while at the same time addressing the needs of the organization, for which the focus is naturally on positions rather than on individuals. In New Zealand, the United Kingdom, and Finland, each government agency is free to use its own job classification.

Devolved personnel practices and increased flexibility can present risks for public service homogeneity and for equity between agencies and among individual employees. To address these risks, several countries, including Australia, have kept the terms of employment essentially the same for all agencies. Nonetheless, whatever the choices have been, most countries have provided for some added flexibility in personnel management. France, for example, did not change its job classification systems but introduced special allowances (*nouvelles bonifications indiciaires*) to address the incentive needs of specific categories of employees (e.g., nurses) that could not be taken into account within the traditional homogeneous and rigid pay system.

Introducing flexibility in personnel management is a costly investment, profitable only over the medium term, and generates internal tensions as well as problems with the labor unions, which generally view these new forms of management as giving too much discretion to middle-rank managers. Mobility is two-edged as well. Mobility within the government improves the skills and broadens the experience of government employees, but an open structure also encourages mobility of the best people *out* of the government—which certainly doesn't help improve administrative effectiveness.

Performance Contracting

"Performance" has been a mantra of bureaucracy for years, although in most countries the government was performance oriented only in rhetoric and not in fact. A stronger performance orientation within government is indeed important and calls for (among other things) a shift from traditional compliance-based controls to result-oriented accountability. Stronger performance orientation can be fostered in various ways that do not require formal contracts. Nevertheless, performance-based contracts can be a useful vehicle for clarifying objectives and stimulating results, while leaving the day-to-day decisions to the managers themselves. By the commonly accepted definition, performance contracting is the range of management instruments used to define responsibilities and expectations between the parties to achieve mutually agreed results. Yet there are considerable differences among the uses and forms of quasi-contractual arrangements and the degrees to which parties are bound by the agreements—see Box 15.3.

Although performance contracting is rated well by the countries themselves—particularly for the greater clarity it brings to agency objectives—at least four important criteria must be must be met:

- As a management tool, performance contracting should be tailored to the needs of each division within the organization.
- The contract modalities should be flexible enough to be linked to other management processes such as strategic planning and the assessment of the individual performance of senior managers.
- Contracts should provide a framework for strengthening accountability for results as part and parcel of the devolution of management authority.
- Contracts must be specific enough to be an instrument for accountability but avoid the excessive detail that will both hamper managerial initiative and generate unnecessary red tape and reporting requirements.

BOX 15.3

Modalities of Performance Contracting in Developed Countries

Seven broad types of performance contracting are used in OECD countries:

- *Framework agreements,* covering overarching strategies and priorities for a department, made between a minister and a chief executive (e.g., framework documents for "Next Step" agencies in the United Kingdom and letters of allocation in Norway).
- *Budget contracts and resource agreements,* setting budget levels between the central budget office or finance ministry and the chief executive of a department or agency (e.g., Danish budget contracts, which originally offered multiyear budget guarantees).
- *Organizational performance agreements* between a minister and a chief executive or between a chief executive and senior managers, breaking down overall strategic goals into program elements and setting specific process and output targets in exchange for increased operational autonomy (e.g., the French tax administration and U.S. performance-based organizations). These agreements are also used by the management of state-owned enterprises in many countries.
- *Chief executive performance agreements* between ministers and chief executives, often to complement organizational performance agreements, or between senior management and staff at various levels (such as those used in agencies in Australia, Denmark, New Zealand, Norway, and the United Kingdom).
- *Funder-provider agreements,* which clarify responsibilities by separating the role of the funder from that of the provider of the services. Purchaser-provider agreements based on a purchase-provider model can be found in Australia (on a limited basis) and New Zealand.
- *Intergovernmental performance contracts and partnership agreements,* which are often linked to the devolution of programs or of funding from national to subnational government. They provide state and local governments with funding in exchange for specified levels and quality of service. Such contracts are more common in education, health care, and labor market services, where the national government retains formal responsibility for service provision but allows programs to be implemented by local authorities. Such partnership agreements between levels of government can be found in Canada, France, Germany, Norway, Spain, Sweden, and Switzerland, among others.
- *Customer service agreements.* These statements of service standards specify the quality and level of services to be expected by clients and, in some cases, the avenues of redress and compensation if services fail to meet the standards. Customer service agreements can be found Australia, Belgium, Denmark, France, Italy, the United Kingdom, and the United States.

THE SECOND PHASE: BETTER GOVERNMENT

The second phase of administrative reform in developed countries has been triggered primarily by public pressure for improved social services and administrative responsiveness. In some countries (e.g., Italy and Greece, among others), citizens had become thoroughly fed up with being treated as a nuisance by state employees whose salaries their taxes were paying. At bottom, therefore, the citizens' reaction consisted of a simple demand that public servants begin to act as . . . servants of the public, rather than as superior beings who may grant or withhold favors from the citizens as they felt like. This public pressure was strengthened by the developments in technology and communication, with the citizens better informed of service standards and the behavior expected from government employees, and also better able to pursue alternative service delivery options (see chapter 11 on exit and voice).

Moving Closer to the Citizen

This broad subject was discussed in some detail in chapters 12 and 13, to which the reader is referred for context and a fuller discussion. We mention here only two illustrations of the movement toward greater transparency, participation, and external accountability that have occurred in developed countries in recent years.

The United States and most other developed countries have moved a long way toward e-government by facilitating issue of licenses and payment of taxes through the internet (which has also reduced substantially the cost of tax collection), among other things. Many countries have initiated so-called "one-stop shops"—central entry points into the public administration for citizens dealing with specific matters, mostly business and investment. In Italy, for example, a one-stop shop at the local level now grants authorization for new industrial plants, unifying the forty different procedures involving many government agencies that were previously necessary.

A good way to track the recent regulatory improvements in the business area is to peruse the changes in the ranking of different countries in the annual *Doing Business* survey started by the World Bank in 2004 and now in its third year (www.doingbusiness.org). The *Doing Business* survey contains a wealth of data on the procedures required in some 190 countries to set up a new business, hire and terminate employees, collect debts, and so on. Even more detailed, although limited to the countries of Eastern Europe and the former Soviet Union, is the Business Environment and Enterprise Performance Survey (BEEPS), developed jointly by the World Bank and the European Bank for Reconstruction and Development, surveying over 4,000 firms in twenty-two countries on a wide range of interactions between firms and the state (see info.worldbank.org/governance/beeps/).

Decentralizing Responsibilities

Decentralization is often encouraged as the best way to bring government closer to the citizens. In the United Kingdom, for instance, in the 1970s and 1980s most local services were performed by nonelected central government organizations ("quasi nongovernmental organizations" or *quangos*) rather than by elected local governments—diluting both representativeness and accountability. In reaction, local governments underwent reorganization in the 1990s to offer the taxpayers better value for their money.

In traditionally centralized governments such as France or Spain, the decentralization that occurred earlier during the 1980s was seen as a fundamental ingredient of democratic governance.

This has also been true, more recently, of countries that became new members of the European Union (i.e., the Czech Republic, Hungary, Poland, Bulgaria, and Romania). Even in countries where subnational government has historically enjoyed high autonomy, its responsibilities have further expanded. In the United States, for example, the National Performance Review of the 1990s endorsed greater "empowerment" of states and localities as a way of unraveling complex federal program requirements and allowing program managers, front-line workers, and community leaders to adapt requirements to local conditions and demand.

As discussed at length in chapter 5, the experience of all countries shows that, in order to be effective, decentralization of responsibilities to lower levels of government must be accompanied by a decentralization of resources to perform the new tasks. Another important aspect of effective devolution is the need for new accountability mechanisms and robust ex-post controls (e.g., the regional courts of account in France) in order to protect against the risk that local officials may abuse the new discretionary authority they have been given. In any event, recall that decentralization is not a panacea, and should only be pursued on the basis of careful scrutiny of its costs and benefits in economic, social, and political terms.

Matching Greater Management Autonomy with Enhanced Accountability

As noted, enhanced accountability, both political and financial, is the requisite counterpart of providing more freedom and flexibility to managers. Devolution of discretionary authority to line managers without any accompanying measure to strengthen their accountability carries risks. Politically, it may also cloud or reduce the responsibility of ministers, and thus public accountability overall. It is the minister, as the appointed representative of the elected executive branch of government, who is ultimately responsible to the legislature.

A key issue is the ability of oversight bodies, such as parliamentary committees and audit institutions, to adjust to the new flexibility and autonomy of public managers, and their preparedness to focus on the larger strategic issues. It is evident from the actual experience of developed countries that many legislators and auditors have yet to make this adjustment. It has proven very challenging, for example, to add a new focus on outputs and outcomes to the traditional legislative oversight of finances and compliance. Legislatures and audit bodies are often hampered by inadequacy of resources and staff, and the management reforms have brought this old problem into sharper relief.

A related issue is the need to exercise adequate control over activities and practices of semi-autonomous public units that are deliberately placed at arm's length from the government. For example, moving the responsibility for important services from the central government to semi-autonomous entities may risk increasing political patronage.

On the financial side, experience has shown that, when giving more discretion to managers to administer their budget, traditional ex-ante controls, instructions, and accounting procedures may no longer be effective or appropriate. Several countries have replaced them with robust ex-post controls completed by spot checks with significant penalties for malfeasance.

Some have argued that the trend to delegate authority with sharper ex-post controls requires the introduction in government of accrual accounting (accounting on commercial accounting principles) and accrual budgeting (see chapter 6). This may be appropriate in those few countries where circumstances and capacity permit, and the benefits warrant the costs. However, it is not necessary—as a regular dialogue on results can provide genuine accountability—nor is it desirable in countries where accounting systems and capacity are weak. In fact, while accrual accounting has been introduced, or is being considered, in most developed countries, accrual *budgeting* has been adopted in only a handful of countries. (In addition, one should keep in mind that accrual accounting has been introduced in countries where a number of prerequisites were in place, primarily data availability and substantial accounting capacity within government. These prerequisites are normally present in developed countries but not in developing countries.)

THE SCOPE OF THE REFORMS

The speed and scope of reforms have varied among developed countries, but it is possible to identify three broad orientations—each reflecting a different attitude toward change, although all with the same goal of more responsive public service to the citizens with fiscal sustainability.

Private Sector Orientation

This orientation has primarily characterized reforms in "Anglo-Saxon" countries. Introducing greater competition and supplier choice has been attractive from the point of view of both greater efficiency and improvements in quality. One of the traditional criticisms of the public sector was its lack of creativity and adaptability compared with the private sector. This led to the conclusion that administrative performance could be improved by exposing public service to market discipline. Common reforms have included breaking up public monopolies (through privatization or other means) and introducing market-type mechanisms (more competition, better pricing, delegated decision making, monetary incentives, or deregulation).

Among private-like management techniques, the use of internal "markets" has been applied to particular sectors (e.g., the health sector in the United Kingdom). These initiatives have led to uneven results. Despite some signal successes (e.g., in New Zealand's weather forecasting services), introducing market-type practices in government has generally not yielded the expected benefits of greater efficiency, more choice, lower price, and better quality, nor have these practices been suitable for achieving the broader public aims. In many cases, pseudo-markets have entailed the worst of both worlds—the inefficiencies of traditional public monopoly and the disadvantages of private monopolies.

Improving Existing Models

The Nordic countries have focused instead on making better use of local governments, to which many tasks were devolved, and of the flexibility of the strong autonomous agencies that were central to the implementation of the performance systems. For example, Sweden enacted substantial decentralization of responsibilities to both local authorities and line agencies—within an overall public sector that remains quite large. These countries have chosen to achieve a modest reduction in scope and improvement in efficiency within a still-major welfare commitment of government to the citizens.

Ad Hoc Orientation

Continental European countries, as well as Japan and Korea, have generally gone for an ad hoc approach to administrative reform. As mentioned earlier, some of the key characteristics of traditional bureaucracies were maintained—including in personnel management—while major changes were introduced in other areas of public administration. These "reform menus" have varied from country to country, and the only generalization is that in all such countries the reform process has been incremental. Some of the most promising across-the-board initiatives are in the areas of transparency in government, and in the use of information and communication technology to improve service quality and convenience for the public (as discussed in chapter 12).

COMMON ISSUES

Regardless of the differences in speed and scope of reforms, a number of common issues have emerged in the experience of all developed countries. The two most general and obvious ones have been that reform invariably turned out to carry costs as well as benefits and that good implementation is key, thus entailing the need to create the proper incentive framework for those responsible for implementation. A discussion of other common issues follows.

Performance Measurement

The subject was examined at length in chapter 10. Briefly, rewarding performance is a very good thing in principle, but is difficult to apply in practice. In particular, measuring individual productivity for the nonmarket products of government activity is highly problematic. Few, if any, of the attempts to provide performance-based annual bonuses for civil servants have successfully raised employee efficiency on a lasting basis. In some cases, they have become mere salary supplements. In other cases, they have had a negative impact on the morale of civil servants with no perceptible influence on motivation and productivity. Many developed countries have therefore abandoned special monetary rewards for individual performance and have moved instead to rewarding team performance at the level of work teams or organizational units, as well as to using nonmonetary forms of recognition. We are only referring here to the practice of annual bonuses. Merit has been and remains a key consideration for individual promotion and career development of government employees in most countries. In that sense, merit is of course linked to higher salaries

Program Evaluation

Also problematic has been the practice of program evaluation—an in-depth assessment of results that goes beyond mere performance indicators and seeks to identify cause-effect relationships and the reasons for a particular level of performance. Evaluation is important because, in principle, it can provide a good alternative to traditional controls in a context of devolved management: if an organization continuously evaluates itself, control ceases to be exceptional and loses any inquisitional character. In Australia, for example, all departments have been required since 1987 to evaluate each of their programs every three to five years. When the evaluations are both competent and independent, such periodic assessments have proven beneficial. However, as the experience of Canada and the United States suggests, such evaluations are of limited use for annual budgeting decisions and expenditure control. Mechanisms to provide for a robust dialogue on the previous year's results as part of the discussions leading to the budget allocation for the subsequent year have proven more effective and much less costly. A few hours of tough questioning by competent civil servants familiar with the sector at hand can yield much more information and underpin stronger accountability for results than volumes of output and outcome indicators.

Ethical Tensions and Fragmentation of Government Action

Developed countries' governments have learned to be alert to the implications of making major changes in a period of uncertainty and instability, as these can create new opportunities for corruption (see chapter 14). Delegating procurement decisions and outsourcing create new partnerships between the public and the private sectors, but also removes traditional controls. Only a strong tradition of public integrity allied with the commitment to sustain an ethical infrastructure can prevent the risk of increasing corruption.

Fragmentation and confusion of government intervention have also emerged as significant risks when giving more autonomy to managers or to lower levels of government. Similarly, the extensive use of the private sector in public service delivery, sometimes in competition with government agencies, has led in some countries to confusion about who is in charge of what. Citizens have faced new difficulties in finding their way in the complexity created by multiplicity of service providers. This has been a recent problem in the social sectors in the United Kingdom, for instance. And in the United States, the prescription drug reimbursement system put in place in 2004 has forced older people to choose among a bewildering variety of drug coverage plans.

Low Morale and Reform Fatigue

Low morale and reform fatigue are only to be expected when civil servants are required to do more with less, or to constantly adapt to change, while at the same time their job security is threatened. The potential negative implications of decentralized personnel management for staff morale have typically been underestimated, weakening the prospects for real reform, which requires the active cooperation of the employees. This is why Australia, Canada, the Nordic countries, and the Netherlands have maintained mechanisms to preserve the cohesion of their civil service through close involvement of employee unions in the reform process (e.g., Netherlands and the Nordic countries) or the maintenance of central systems of job classification (e.g., in Australia).

Looking Ahead

The challenge to governments in the ongoing third phase of public administration reform is to move away from both dogma and adhockery and toward more strategic reform—grounded on a common vision and implemented through genuine communication to and participation by the public. A common vision serves to unify political leaders, senior civil servants, front-line employees, service users and the public at large. Good implementation of changes requires candid communication of the rationale for the change, and its expected costs as well as anticipated benefits; an identification of the probable "winners" and "losers" from the change; a reasonable definition of how the prospective "losers" will be compensated; and the introduction of appropriate incentives (not necessarily monetary) for cooperating with the change. As in all politics, to be successful a reform strategy needs, among other things, to maximize the number of potential supporters and minimize the number of potential opponents. This must be accomplished honestly, gradually building trust with the various stakeholders as forecasts are met and promises are kept. "Spin" will not do. The next and final chapter will address the broad question of the approach to public management reform in the years to come.

QUESTIONS FOR DISCUSSION

1. Is a severe fiscal crisis always necessary to spur major administrative reforms? If so, will the reform invariably consist of expenditure savings through privatizations, cuts in government employment, and the like?
2. In continental Europe, the response to the fiscal difficulties of the 1980s was to effect gradual

adjustments across the board within the same general model of government. In other developed countries, such as New Zealand, the United Kingdom, and Australia, the response was to attempt a major reformulation of the role of the state. Which response was more appropriate?

3. With reference to the question 2, which response was more successful? In terms of what?

4. Are there areas of public administration where the reform focus and effort were similar in all developed countries? (Hint: Think of the difference between efficient and inefficient government intervention.)

5. If you are asked to do more with less and in a shorter time, what do you think will be the likely consequences for your efficiency, quality of activity, and integrity of process? Would your answer differ if you were more closely monitored? What if you were at the same time granted more autonomy and flexibility of action?

6. If the first phase of administrative reform in developed countries was triggered by fiscal crisis, what factor spurred the second phase of reform, toward better and more responsive government?

7. Is it a coincidence that, albeit with several exceptions and in different manners, public administration reforms took place more or less during the same period of time?

8. In the context of administrative reform in developed countries, pick one of the two following Italian proverbs and make a credible argument for it:

a. "He who goes slow goes safe and goes far."

b. "He who goes slow never arrives."

NOTES

This section relies largely on Frédéric Bouder's chapter in Schiavo-Campo and Sundaram (2000), as well as Boston (1998); Ives (1995); Jensen (1998); Premfors (1998); Rhodes (1998); OECD (1995, 1996b, 1997a); and the OECD Public Management web site: www.oecd.org/puma. The synthesis and assessments, of course, are our own.

1. Moreover, complex and opaque regulations are a prime source of corruption, as discussed in chapter 14, and regulatory streamlining is the single most effective means of combating corruption.

2. The privatization of Japan's Post Office resulted from reforms decided under Prime Minister Koizumi, and began in October 2007. Japan Post serves as the only banking facility for Japanese in rural areas, and has assets equivalent to more that $3 *trillion,* with 400 million individual accounts and almost 25,000 branches throughout the country. Its privatization will make it the world's largest bank by far, with Citigroup a distant second (see *China Post,* October 2, 2007).

CHAPTER 16

The Way Forward: Progress, Not Fashion

We must take from an experience only the wisdom that is in it, and stop there; lest we be like the cat that sits down on a hot stove-lid. She will never sit down on a hot stove-lid again—and that is well; but also she will never sit down on a cold one anymore.
—Mark Twain, Following the Equator

Acquire new things while reflecting over the old.
—Confucius

It hardly matters whether a cat is black or white as long as it catches mice.
—Deng Xiaoping

WHAT TO EXPECT

The previous chapters described the main principles, systems, and issues in the different areas of public management, and attempted to look at the various aspects of major issues while offering a balanced account of the advantages and disadvantages of different practices. Each chapter also concluded with a brief set of suggestions for directions of reform and priorities in the various areas. This concluding chapter sets out our personal point of view on the approach to be taken in our interdependent world to improve the administration of the state without losing sight of its fundamentals—a point of view that is summed up in the three quotations at the start of the chapter. We hope this final chapter will trigger for the reader a reflection on the future of public administration—this essential bridge between decisions and achievements, between intentions and results, between rhetoric and reality, between a government and the people it is supposed to serve and to whom it is accountable.

THE NEVER-ENDING STRUGGLE AGAINST FASHION[1]

Reinventing Government?

The expression "reinventing government" was first introduced about fifteen years ago (Osborne and Gaebler, 1992; see also Kamensky, 1996 and Nathan, 1995). Leaving aside the breathtaking ambition and lack of realism of the expression, it is intended to connote a major change in direction of administrative culture and government activity, rather than tinkering at the margin—or, in the language of management consultants, reengineering rather than retooling. Basically, the reinventing-government movement has purported to make government work better and cost less by changing the culture of government and its processes. This would be done by decentralizing authority, flattening organizational structures, increasing managers' involvement in and control of their workplaces, and focusing more on the needs of their customers—the citizens—by improving both the timeliness and the quality of response. Osborne and Gaebler argued for nothing less than a transformation to an entrepreneurial public administration to meet the opportunities and problems of a "postindustrial, knowledge-based global economy."

The vision of the reinventing government movement was brought down to earth and made more practical through the U.S. National Performance Review (NPR). According to then-Vice President Al Gore, who led the exercise, the twin missions of the National Performance Review were not only to make the federal government work better and cost less, but also to close the "trust deficit" by proving to people that their tax dollars would be respected (National Performance Review, 1993). The federal payroll was reduced by about 100,000 employees (on a net basis, after accounting for the hiring of more consultants); hundreds of thousands of pages of unnecessary regulations were eliminated through the Review; and important management principles were introduced into the practice of government. Discounting the hype and exaggeration, the NPR did have notable accomplishments. Unfortunately, as recounted in the previous chapters, whatever trust was restored through the 1990s has vanished in the first years of this century with the explosion in budget "earmarks," unwarranted subsidies to privileged sectors such as energy and agribusiness, abandonment of any pretense at fiscal responsibility, introduction of new open-ended entitlements such as a prescription drug subsidy without any cost-control mechanism, and the utter lack of respect for the taxpayers' money shown by wasteful and questionable expenditure on an unprecedented scale.

Technocratic Delusions and the New Public Management

Every now and then, scholars or practitioners frustrated with the messy nature of human society set off on a renewed quest for the Holy Grail of technical solutions to complex social and political problems. In the last century this has happened at least twice: once with the "technocracy" movement of the 1920 and 1930s,[2] and later with the "New Public Management" that began with the radical New Zealand reforms of the late 1980s and early 1990s.[3]

Ambitious as the "reinventing government" movement was, it was explicitly geared to the problems of a developed, complex, mature administrative apparatus. The NPM, or at least many of its advocates, started in the same context but went way beyond and pretended to be relevant everywhere, regardless of realities on the ground—totally different countries such as Mongolia, Iceland, Nigeria, Haiti, Yemen, Canada, Argentina, Iraq—all were seen as potential candidates for NPM solutions.

At its core, starting from the assumption that private administration is invariably superior to public management, the NPM paradigm advocates the transfer to the private sector of as many public sector activities as possible, through privatization and outsourcing and, when this is manifestly impossible, adopting private business practices for the management of public activity—including extensive internal contracting. The oversimplification of reality and the justified reaction against the view that all social problems require government intervention gave the NPM a lot of seductive appeal and propelled it to the "cutting edge" of "dynamic thinking" on how to manage the "business of government." (It also helped that many of the New Zealand reforms did work pretty well . . . in New Zealand—see Schick [1996].) In the ensuing swoon, many forgot to test the NPM assumptions and to give its prescriptions a good old-fashioned reality check—it would have taken too much homework and caused unsettling doubts, compared with the comforting two-dimensional certainties of the one-size-fits-all, full-speed-ahead, damn-the-torpedoes "new paradigm."

It has taken a long while, but there is a now a broad consensus that many of the NPM claims have not stood the test of actual experience. More than a decade ago, the many weaknesses and problems of the "new public management" were well described by Donald Savoie (1995), who—reacting partly to the anti-Weberian stance of the NPM—warned that it could easily make matters worse rather than better. Much of his indictment has been confirmed by actual experience, and is worth quoting at some length:[4]

> The new public management is basically flawed. By its very nature, the public administration field does not lend itself to Big Answers because private sector management practices very rarely apply to government operations. . . . Public administration operates in a political environment that is always on the lookout for "errors" and that exhibits an extremely low tolerance for mistakes . . . in business it does not matter if you get it wrong 10 percent of the time as long as you turn a profit at the end of the year. In government, it does not much matter if you get it right 90 percent of the time because the focus will be on the 10 percent of the time you get it wrong.
>
> The new public management has yet to deal head on with accountability in government. . . . There is also a world of difference between citizens and clients. . . . Clients can turn to the market to defend their interests or walk away. . . . Citizens on the other hand . . . hold politicians accountable through the requirements of political institutions and through exposure via the media. Politicians, meanwhile, hold public servants accountable through the application of centrally prescribed rules and regulations.
>
> The success of the business executive is much easier to assess than that of the government manager. There is also much less fuss over due process in the private sector than in government.
>
> The new public management gives short shrift to these considerations: it simply ignores them. Rather than tangle with these fundamental issues, the disciples of the new public management employ a new highly value-laden lexicon to disarm would-be questioners . . . reinventing, reengineering, empowering.
>
> If the problem with bureaucracy is one of insensitivity . . . we all too often forget that one person's red tape is another's due process. The solution lies in fixing our political institutions.
>
> The new public management has been with us for over ten years and it has very little to show for itself. To be sure, management consultants have profited extensively.
>
> The basic premise is that private sector management practices are superior to those found in government. . . . The implication is that public service has no intrinsic value. It also belittles the noble side of the public service profession: public servants became public servants because they wanted to serve their country. If they had wanted to become entrepreneurs, they would have joined the private sector or started their own businesses. . . . But the real damage . . . is that . . . we have been diverted from confronting substantial issues of governance and public administration.
>
> The new public management has also overlooked important problems . . . The policy side of government and the ability of bureaucracy to be innovative and self-questioning needed more fixing than did the machine or production-like agencies. The new public management has very little to offer on policy. Instead . . . it speaks to the need for more "doers" and fewer "thinkers."

The new public management . . . may well be making matters worse, given its call for decentralized and empowered machinery of government . . . [that] will make it more difficult to promote coherence in government policy and . . . for the political leadership to secure the necessary information to focus on the broad picture.

Improvements in administration are also necessary. The solution, however, lies not in searching for the Big Answer: government will not be reinvented nor are we finally about to get it right. . . . Improvements in the administration of government will be made: . . . full use of new information technology to strengthen their capacity to provide services . . . new partnership with other government departments to coordinate services.

Innovative thinking in government did not start with the new public management movement. Yet, one senses that anything significant taking place to strengthen the public sector tends to be attributed to the new public management by its advocates. . . . However, improvements are the results of new circumstances, whether it is a tighter budget, new development in computer technology or old-fashioned common sense.

The point to bear in mind is that the solutions that work are practical, rooted in the public and legal realities of government. They should not be expected to represent anything more than gradual and incremental improvements to public administration.

Of Babies and Bathwater: Rebalancing the Argument

Some Things Were Made Better

Savoie was generally right. And yet, consider that in many developed countries in the late 1970s, public administration was a sick old man—insulated from all drafts of change; his ills covered up by an blanket of public spending; demanding that every dollar be accounted for and never asking if anything was achieved by it; barking out petty instructions; squinting at public service through the mechanical application of obsolete regulations; unresponsive to his political masters; and served by persons contemptuous of the citizenry whose taxes were paying their salary.

In retrospect, it was a good thing that the cold shower of the fiscal crisis was followed by a new and robust ideological challenge to shake up old habits, assumptions, and, especially, attitudes. In this dialectical sense, there is an argument that the attackers of the status quo rendered a signal service, whether they championed "reinventing government," "six-sigma quality," "empowering the doers," "renewing public management," or some other catchy slogan.

Moreover, as described in the previous chapter, a number of concrete and important improvements were in fact introduced into public administration in developed countries. As we have seen, some changes went too far and were counterproductive. Also counterproductive were others introduced for dogmatic reasons and without the requisite prior analysis and consideration of their implications. In particular, many of the changes produced nothing but massive transaction costs and squeezed innovation and ethics out of the public service by creating a strict command-and-control system—a new "auditocracy," in the term of Michael Keaney, a professor at Mercuria Business School in Finland: "Whatever innovation occurs now most often involves conjuring results that adhere to the excruciatingly dull plans that are now integrated to the endless cycle of audit."[5]

This is why developed countries are now in a third phase of reform, to consolidate the good changes and correct or discard the bad ones. (To stay with the Hegelian tone, the objective of this third phase is to produce a synthesis of the good parts of the old thesis and the good parts of the new antithesis.) In any case, although serious damage was caused in many cases by dogmatic or ill-designed changes, the damage is neither fatal nor permanent—one hopes—as the administrative system, fabric of governance, and civil society are strong and resilient enough in developed countries to bounce back and correct the excesses.

Some Things Were Made Much Worse

Not so in developing countries. Allen Schick (Schick, 1998) outlined a decade ago some of the reasons why NPM-style reforms are unsuitable to developing countries. Nonetheless, both international donors and the consulting industry have pushed one or another of these reforms in the intervening years, causing serious problems in some countries and a blizzard of red tape in others.

As stressed throughout this book, public administration reforms have a heavy institutional component; depend on adequate local capacity for their implementation; their costs and benefits are unevenly distributed across individuals and groups in society; and their feasibility is heavily affected by the governance context.

First, in developed countries a large part of the important institutional rules governing administrative behavior and society's response is composed of formal, explicit, visible rules. In developing countries, instead, informal rules and customary norms are predominant, and these norms are rarely visible to the outsider (McFerson, 2007). Second, developed countries enjoy substantial capacity in terms of complexity of organizations, flows of information, availability of money, and professional talent. Developing countries, by definition, have weak organizations, inadequate exchange of relevant information, and scarcity of both financial resources and skilled personnel. Third, as a broad generalization, developed countries are more homogeneous economically, socially, and ethnically—while in developing countries heterogeneity is the norm and the interests of different groups must be an explicit consideration in all major administrative decisions. Finally, most developed countries have evolved governmental legitimacy and representativeness, while in many developing countries—with their comparatively recent independence—political accountability remains shaky and civil society weak.

Is it conceivable that a complex administrative practice of a developed country can be transplanted "as is" to a poor country with extremely low capacity, dominated by customs invisible to outsiders, with many transactions running on personal favors and frequent bribery, weak rule of law and accountability, and the ever-present risk of communal violence just under the surface? Is it reasonable to treat—say—Yemen as the equivalent of Iceland, except a lot warmer and populated by tribal Arabs? Is it acceptable to push management flexibility and annual "performance" bonuses in a civil service critically dependent on a delicate balance between contending ethnic groups, where every exercise of management discretion triggers suspicion and conflict? Is it sensible to strip basic government functions of the few skilled and competent administrators and reallocate them to building institutional skyscrapers on sand? Is it permissible to push for outsourcing when the only private supplier firms in the country are owned by relatives of the minister in charge? Is it defensible to replace rudimentary but functioning padlocks protecting public financial resources with complicated budgeting systems focused on ex-post results and leaving the front door wide open for theft and misallocations?

Well, no. Actual experience shows that such "reforms," at best, have been dead on arrival or caused a great deal of commotion and waste of resources to no good effect, or, at worst, had unpredictable and counterproductive consequences—which were of course borne not by those making the recommendations but by the people of the host country, who could hardly afford the loss. Indeed, the contemporary history of interaction between outsiders and the people in poor countries in the public management field has been a repetitive illustration of the old saw that the road to hell is paved with good intentions. As Mark Twain put it: "It ain't what you don't know that gets you into trouble. It's what you know for sure that just ain't so."

The Iron Triangle of Technical Assistance for Public Management Reform

In international assistance to institutional development—particularly in public management—an "iron triangle" has been at work, joining the international consulting industry with the aid organizations financing their services and with the officials of the country receiving the advice.[6] The consulting firms have a general propensity to advocate "state of the art" administrative systems rather than simple improvements that are appropriate to the country's realities and easily implemented. Understandably, too, their commercial interest leads them to look to the next contracts and produce a bias toward recommending the kind of complex systems that can only be implemented with their continuing involvement. The staff in the aid organizations (whether international organizations like the World Bank, the regional development banks and the European Union, or bilateral donor agencies) have an equally understandable tendency to rely on large international consulting firms—a tendency that is reinforced by a desire to be associated with the "modern" and, in most cases, by their lack of the specialized technical competence that is critical in order to tell the wheat from the chaff. The officials in developing countries have little choice but to accept and try to implement the external advice. In time, all concerned become invested in the "reform," both economically and emotionally, and the triangle becomes self-perpetuating.

There is nothing necessarily conspiratorial or sinister about this dynamic. Indeed, in many cases, perhaps most, the consulting firms provide advice on public administration reform that they believe to be appropriate to the circumstances; the aid agency staff finance it because they believe it to be consistent with the overall reform priorities; and the local officials accept it because they believe it is in the interest of their country's development, or wish for reasons of national pride to import "the latest thing." But the damage is still done. When the "reform" is badly implemented or fails to produce positive results, everyone then blames the extremely limited local capacity—with nary a thought to the more plausible explanation that the capacity problems were caused by the overambitious reforms themselves, and rarely an acknowledgement of the grave professional failure to take the capacity realities into account in the first place.

However, in too many cases the consultant-government official-funding agency dynamic is far less benevolent. Some consulting firms and individual consultants push complex management models on poor countries in full knowledge that they are counterproductive and only to assure their continued profitable association with the "reform"; country officials cooperate only to gain bureaucratic influence or, in many cases, to receive kickbacks and other favors; and aid agency staff often lack the intestinal fortitude to resist the pressure to conform to "best practice," or are too lazy to do the homework needed to identify good consulting firms and *monitor* their consultants' advice closely. A heavy whiff of corruption and incompetence hangs over the technical assistance iron triangle, masked by the seductive aroma of reform fashion. In rich countries, this is disagreeable; in poor developing countries, with millions of human beings living on less than one dollar a day and deprived of the most basic government services, it is disgraceful.

This is an extraordinarily difficult dynamic to resist, owing to the strength and convergence of the interests involved. Eventually, the pendulum of fashion may swing back. In the long interim, it may be possible to reduce the incidence of overambitious and overly complex public management "reforms," and alleviate some of their worst effects by creating contestability mechanisms. For example:

- Consulting firms and consultants may be systematically chosen for their familiarity with different modalities of public administration and experience with a variety of countries in order to help lessen somewhat the risk of copycat advice.

- A "kick-the-tires" pool of specialists could be placed on call to take a hard look at major innovations being suggested in individual cases and give their candid views.[7]
- The internal quality assurance mechanisms existing in the major international organizations could systematically include *independent* outsiders.
- Foreign consultants should be routinely handcuffed to knowledgeable local persons who can explain to them the facts of local life.
- A developing country could itself declare a "reform timeout" and in the meantime seek independent assistance to analyze the actual benefits and costs that have been brought about by each of the major reforms attempted during the previous years, and then correct, reverse, or accelerate each reform as the concrete evidence suggests.

We say this with little hope. As of this writing, the juggernaut of mindless NPM-style "reform" has slowed but is still moving along in many poor countries. Most observers and participants now agree on the waste and damage it has caused and continues to cause, but none seem to have the power to stop it.[8]

Principled Pragmatism: A New-Old Paradigm

This book should have made clear that centrally planned, command-based practices of public administration are inefficient and discriminatory—and are thus unsustainable—and that *unmanaged* outsourcing and privatization carry heavy costs for large groups of people and are not equitable—and are thus also unsustainable. There are no pots of gold under either of the opposite ends of the rainbow, only lumps of old coal. The problem at both ends has been the same: an approach to public sector management that is formulaic, often ideological, and occasionally theological.

By contrast, our central theme has been the need to approach public administration in a pragmatic way—the way of political economy. This approach calls for careful consideration of the costs as well as the benefits of *each* proposed administrative change. It also calls for recognition that the costs and benefits of reform are unevenly distributed, and thus that any reform requires complementary measures to assure a measure of social consensus and to be effectively implemented. However, pragmatism devoid of conceptual underpinnings degrades into opportunism and ad-hockery. Yes, you are likely to trip and fall if you either look backward or up to the clouds; but looking straight ahead is no help if you don't know where you're going. The pragmatic approach must therefore be anchored on the bedrock of the fundamental political concepts built through the centuries and valid in all countries—albeit in the different variants befitting their diverse cultures and circumstances. Thus grounded, principled pragmatism in administrative reform can be both efficient and equitable, and meet the requirements of good economics as well as good politics. The strategic and operational elements of the approach we suggest are elaborated in the rest of this chapter.

IMPLEMENTATION: THE MISSING LINK

Cosmetic and Real Reform

Originally contrasted to "revolution" and denoting an improvement in the workings of the existing system rather than a replacement of the system itself, the word "reform" has acquired shamanistic status through misuse and overuse. All changes, however trivial or irrelevant, are now elevated by being labeled "reforms," and new policies typically carry the "reform" tag even when they constitute a throwback to earlier inefficiency, discrimination, or favoritism. It would be far better to rely on more modest and accurate terms such as "improvement" or "correction" and reserve the use of "reform" only to the truly major and infrequent changes. Having broken a lance for semantic precision, however, it is not constructive to insist on words other than those in current use, and we also use the term "reform." What does matter is that the change, however it is labeled, must be effectively implemented. Just as law without enforcement is no law at all, "reform" without implementation is no reform.

This obvious point must be underlined because it is so often disregarded. Genuine reform must address convincingly and realistically the questions of how the reform is to be executed: by whom, when, with what resources, by which incentives, and through what process of careful and sensitive management of change. Often, a great deal of attention is paid to the cosmetic and public relations appearance of a proposed change and little or none to how the change is going to be implemented. Little wonder that public managers and civil servants faced with an unending stream of "new initiatives" often react by nodding in apparent agreement with their political masters and then do nothing to implement the initiatives or, if they are sufficiently irritated, quietly sabotage them. Effective monitoring and enforcement mechanisms take time, resources, and genuine commitment at several levels of government to become operational. Yet, two tendencies often converge in practice to preclude effective changes. The first tendency is the temptation of politicians (and, for developing countries, aid donors) to declare a problem solved and move to the next item on the agenda. (Thus, for example, the presidential authorization in the United States to build a 700-mile fence to keep out illegal Mexican immigrants was publicized in 2006 as a partial solution to the problem of illegal immigration even though no money was provided to build it.) The other tendency is the habit of control-minded elites to try to affect behavioral change by decree. (Military and other authoritarian regimes are particularly prone to this illusion.) There is overwhelming evidence that such change, if any, is purely transitory. The issue of implementation capacity stands right, left, and center of the administrative reform agenda.

Capacity: The Central Concern

Unlike first-stage "stroke of the pen" policy reforms (e.g., price decontrol or exchange-rate devaluation), most public administration changes are second-stage "affirmative reforms," which require careful and consistent efforts over time. Adequate implementation capacity is therefore a must. However, the required capacity need not preexist in its entirety. It can grow apace with reform implementation itself, provided that the administrative reform design explicitly includes such a capacity-building component and is carefully sequenced to assure that its reach does not exceed its implementation grasp. In any event, a comprehensive understanding of "capacity" is necessary.

"Capacity building" is among the most misused terms in the literature and is too often narrowly understood as simply training of employees. As discussed in chapter 8, however, when undertaken in isolation, training has been only a recipe for wasting resources on a vast scale. To begin with, *"capacity" is inherently relative*—and mainly in terms of the complexity of the tasks the system is asked to perform. While institutional innovation and progress should stretch capacity to some extent, they cannot get too far ahead of it, on penalty of failure. Also, as and when administrative reforms do require additional capacity, assistance to help build it must be a core ingredient of the reform itself.[9] Regrettably, as we have seen, experience over the past fifty years shows a troublesome supply-driven dynamic at work, with "cutting edge" reformers and management consultants pushing complex new administrative practices onto a simpler but reasonably well-functioning system and thus *creating* capacity constraints where none may have existed. (Scott Adams' cartoon *Dilbert* has a "consultick" character, who gives the sort of advice that cannot be implemented without him, burrows into the client's wallet and sucks the cash, and never leaves.)

The components of an entity's "capacity" go well beyond employees' skills and include the institutions (in the contemporary meaning of the term, i.e., the formal and informal rules and incentives governing the behavior of individuals in that entity); the organization which enforces/implements those rules (institutions and organizations are often confused); the information needed within the organization; and finally the stock and quality of resources in the organization, including human capital. Thus, "capacity building" should comprise activities to support, in sequence, the following goals.

Institutional Development

Institutional development consists of improvements in the mandate, incentives, and the other basic "rules of the game"—the impact of which translates into a decrease in transaction costs. In countries where habits of interagency cooperation are not well rooted, a top institutional development priority is to establish and enforce new rules encouraging and requiring systematic dialogue and cooperation between the various agencies of government. As discussed later, strengthening the internal administrative linkages is the core of the "capacity-building" challenge.

Organizational Development

The organizational architecture must be adapted to fit with the evolving institutional framework. After the appropriate institutional changes have been decided, it is normally necessary to take a fresh look at the organizational structure of the agency concerned to make sure it is consistent with the new rules.

Information and Communications Development

The improvement in the flow of relevant information, and the attendant decrease in the cost of acquiring it, is a key component of capacity building. It is usually identified with information and communication technology (ICT) innovations, but should not be strictly limited to ICT. For example, the physical configuration of offices can be very important in facilitating or obstructing the easy flow of communication among employees.

Financial and Human Resource Development

After the institutional and organizational review and decisions on appropriate informatization, sufficient financial resources must be provided to each agency to perform the responsibilities assigned to it. Finally, of course, guidance and support are also required for human capital development, through training and other forms of knowledge transfer. As stressed in chapter 8, training programs should be designed as a corollary of the institutional, organizational, and information changes and initiated only after these changes have been put in place, or at least on a coordinated basis.

MANAGING CONSTRUCTIVE ADMINISTRATIVE CHANGE

Main Conditions for Successful Administrative Reform

In addition to the existence of sufficient implementation capacity, for administrative reform in any country to be successful, international experience has shown that several conditions must be met, among which the following merit special attention.

"Ownership"

Not surprisingly, the first condition for successful public management reform is genuine commitment to the reform by the government as a whole if systemic issues are to be addressed, or by a major player in government if the strategy begins with reforms in an individual sector or administrative function. In either case, support from the highest political levels is necessary. Fact-finding and cost-containment measures have less-stringent ownership requirements, but without active involvement at the appropriate level, the returns to these measures will be minimal because of lack of follow-up. Beyond fact finding and cost containment, administrative changes simply cannot be implemented in sustainable fashion on the basis of the main stakeholders' benign neglect, let alone over their opposition. Unfortunately but understandably, it has usually taken a financial or other crisis to generate genuine commitment to the necessary change.

Vision

Notwithstanding the last point, a coherent long-term and public vision is mandatory, even if actual changes must be postponed to a politically propitious time. Government should flesh out in concrete detail the goal of an efficient and responsive administration providing an enabling environment for the private sector while protecting important public interests. Rhetoric alone will not be sufficient: to the extent possible, targets should be precise (not necessarily quantitative), the intended criteria explicit, and timetables reasonably specific. Without a coherent and specific vision of the public administration as it should become, pragmatism becomes ad-hockery, support dissipates, and haphazard reform actions come to a stop. But, however fine, *the vision of a few cannot be a living guide for the actions of the many*. The process of involving the relevant stakeholders in defining a vision of the role and behavior of government organizations is crucial to the practical value of the vision as a policy guide.

Selectivity

Among other things, a clear long-term vision permits selectivity. Selectivity is inevitable because it is obviously unrealistic to try to reform the administrative system all at once. Within a coherent vision, interventions should be focused on those sectors or functions that are important, amenable to significant improvement in a reasonable time, and likely to generate demonstration effects or positive pressures for public management improvements elsewhere. Thus, selectivity does not mean picking winners and losers, focusing on partial solutions to systemic problems, or ring-fencing privileged enclaves. *Selectivity is a criterion for optimal sequencing,* by strengthening in turn different institutional linkages, in the context of the clear long-term vision mentioned earlier.

Sensitivity

This criterion primarily entails an understanding of the situation of those affected and of social constraints. It is sometimes the case that the country's own policy makers and high government officials are out of touch with administrative realities, and officials in the capital are frequently oblivious of the state of public services in local areas. It is essential, therefore, to identify those who do know such realities firsthand and listen to them. A public management reform rests on sand if it is elaborated without consulting those who have relevant information as well as those whose cooperation will be needed to implement it.

Stamina

The long gestation of public administration reforms requires stamina and patience. With their heavy institutional content, such reforms call for a long-term investment of imagination and resources, and for willingness of the government to stay the course. Too often, complex reforms are undertaken on the cheap, thus guaranteeing their failure regardless of how well targeted and designed they may otherwise be. But the need for a coherent and agreed long-term vision emerges here once again: Staying the course makes sense only if the course is the right one.

Some Strategic Pointers

Notwithstanding the importance of a long-term vision for administrative reform, it is the dynamic question of *how* to get there that has suffered the worst disregard in practice, because it is so murky and difficult. It is not surprising that, when faced with the size of the gap between reform goals and institutional realities in many countries, reasonable people shy away from any involvement in government reform efforts. Still, common sense and growing international experience point to various ways to begin to bridge this gap, including the following.

Look at Governance First

Time and effort should not be wasted in attempts to improve public administration in countries where the governance situation makes it impossible. History shows that entrenched rapacious regimes lacking all accountability to the population—Burma (Myanmar), Turkmenistan (until the death of dictator Saparmurat Niyazov in December 2006), and North Korea are the clearest current examples—are by definition uninterested in more efficient public management. Their goal is personal enrichment and power—and continuation of the opportunity to plunder the country. Indeed, for such regimes, public administration reform entails only a risk of losing control.

It is therefore a mistake to assume that *all* governments are interested in improving the economic conditions of civil servants and the efficiency of public management. On the contrary, for a patrimonial unrepresentative regime, an underpaid, de-skilled, ineffective public administration is an asset: it keeps public employees dependent for their survival on the regime's handouts, impels their corruption, precludes their "exit," and turns them into reluctant accomplices. In these kleptocracies, while there might be conceivable reasons for certain other kinds of external involvement, assistance to improve government administration is a wasteful delusion. The first question of would-be reformers must be whether the nature of the regime in power is such as to preclude any realistic chance of improvement.

In the large majority of other countries, where the political and governance landscape is not so bleak, reform is possible—although it is never easy, simple or quick even under the most favorable country conditions.

Fact Finding: An Obligatory Starting Point

Lasting improvements in government performance are politically delicate, of long gestation, and difficult to implement. Nevertheless, in most cases governments can initiate factual and analytical work even when the probability of actual reforms is a long way off. This fact-finding and analytical work is an obvious prerequisite to eventual sensible reform and a nonconfrontational first stage of the change process. Governments are not always aware of problems in their own administrations until the facts are uncovered and, usually, the "bare facts" make the direction of improvement painfully obvious. Even when the timing is not propitious for actual change, governments are often amenable to functional reviews of government organizations, assessments of procedures, improvements of information systems, pilot surveys of user opinions, and the like. Bringing basic facts to the attention of the public can also by itself generate the public pressure that is usually necessary to support difficult reforms. A good example in developing countries is the conduct of a census of public employees, which brings to light the problem of "ghost" employees and other irregularities.

The Torto-Hare Approach

The strategic challenge of sustainable reform is to identify the areas where it is feasible to move very fast and the areas where it is essential to slowly build a solid institutional foundation. To use the metaphor of road traffic, "torto-hare" was the slogan (*tarta-lepre* in Italian, combining tortoise [*tartaruga*] and hare [*lepre*]) coined by the Italian traffic police in the 1960s to describe optimal driver behavior: drive fast or slow, depending on the circumstances. The worst approach to driving in erratic traffic and poor visibility is to go on cruise control, whether at high or at low speed.

In this perspective, the dichotomy often presented between "big bang" reforms and "gradualism" is false. The premise of the big-bang (or "shock therapy") approach is that partial reforms will have no effect in the absence of simultaneous rapid reforms in complementary areas. This is true. The premise of the gradualist approach is that there is only so much change a society can stand at any one time, and the attempt to do too much will end up in a failure to accomplish anything. This is also true. However, although both premises are valid, stretching them to their logical extremes leads to untenable prescriptions. At one extreme, an attempt at shock therapy by reforming everything at once is utterly unrealistic and risks causing extreme damage in a plural society with centrifugal tendencies;[10] at the other extreme, the "fundamentalist" interpretation of gradualism becomes a justification for perpetual tinkering around the edges without any actual progress. The obvious alternative to such ideological approaches is in the middle: administrative reform should move as fast as possible when circumstances permit, and as slowly as necessary when accountability needs to catch up, absorptive capacity to grow, or public consensus to be built. "Torto-hare" should be the motto of the successful reformer.

Testing for Readiness

Following the initial stimulus for administrative reform (which, as noted, has typically come from fiscal crisis), it is important to test where and how the administrative system can respond adequately. Among the various practical ways to test the system readiness, three have had practical success. First, some specific action, no matter how modest, can be enacted as a trigger of significant involvement. If it proves impossible to take easy initial steps, the harder ones to follow will not have much chance of success. Furthermore, to do so will flush out at an early stage the reform opponents. Second, a "transparency window" can be opened up to expose some problems of personnel management or administrative apparatus to public scrutiny and to begin building public support for improvement therein. Third, the best single test of government readiness and commitment is the familiar one of putting your money where your mouth is: a reform initiative cannot be taken seriously if it is not supported by sufficient financial and human resources.

More generally, it is society's readiness that is at issue, not the government's. As the old saw has it, in a democracy people get the government they deserve. But in many authoritarian regimes, too, the administrative culture reflects to an extent the norms of society at large. The behavior of public organizations is determined in part by the expectations of the public. Thus, information, dissemination of "good practices," and other ways to create public demand for reform and raise general expectations of good government are needed to buttress executive efforts to improve administrative efficiency.

Operational Approaches

Grounded on the positive and negative lessons of international experience in improving public management in developing countries, four interrelated operational approaches can be suggested: strengthening intra-system linkages; fostering the creation of "efficient nuclei"; providing space for hope; and turning the incentive framework toward change.

Strengthening Internal Linkages: The Essence of Capacity Building

In many developing countries and in most transition economies, the absence of systematic lines of interagency communication and the lack of incentives to share information (which is often viewed as a personal asset) result in fragmented policy formulation and atomized decision making. Both horizontal coordination between agencies of central government and vertical coordination between central and subnational government entities are typically weak. The challenge is how to improve communication and reduce the cost of information within the public sector.

Picking targets for institutional development is a hazardous exercise: it is difficult to decide whether to strengthen one government agency or another, and the outcome of bureaucratic "turf" disputes is uncertain. The guiding operational criterion for sustainable improvement should therefore be to strengthen the linkages among central government ministries, and between them and subnational government entities. (The physical analogy is to reinforcing the brain synapses rather than attempting to build up any one area of the brain.) Doing so has important advantages: it does not prejudge the appropriate transition path for the system as a whole; entails a direct reduction in transaction costs, by facilitating the flow of information; and is most likely to have positive implications for transparency and accountability. However, positive interaction among government agencies cannot be encouraged by mere rhetoric, but by providing relevant specific incentives for greater information exchange and cooperation. This point leads to the second approach suggested here.

Efficiency Nuclei vs. Enclaves

Action to strengthen interorganizational linkages facilitates the spread of new rules and efficient practices but does not in itself do so. There must also exist dynamic agents of change that can generate the positive "messages" to be transmitted throughout the system by the improved communication channels. These agents, which we call "efficiency nuclei," must be deliberately created to perform a few key selected public functions.

A guiding criterion for selecting these key functions is precisely their contribution to maximizing the linkages within the public sector. By analogy with Albert Hirschman's "unbalanced growth" approach of 50 years ago (Hirschman, 1958), efficiency nuclei should be created largely on the basis of their potential for spreading new institutions and organizational practices throughout the public management system.

An efficiency nucleus should also meet the following practical standards:

- Be small and deliberately meritocratic, both in the initial selection of staff and in the evaluation of staff performance.
- Have flexible and simple procedures.
- Provide sufficient compensation for its staff (this may require fixed-term contracts to permit adequate incentives without compromising eventual decisions on an affordable civil service compensation structure).
- Have adequate material and financial resources.
- Rely on local talent, with external advisers used only when demonstrably necessary.
- Be a transitional arrangement, with a clear sunset clause and advance specification of the procedures to eventually reassign its staff to the relevant government agencies.
- Operate not only to perform specific tasks but also a teaching-by-doing function, in cooperation with other agencies.

The efficiency nucleus approach is applicable in a variety of administrative areas. An illustration can be given in the area of procurement. As discussed in chapter 9, delegating the procurement function to line ministries is risky in the absence of capacity at the center to formulate sound procurement standards and rules, and to make sure they are applied. However, the spending agencies also need advice and assistance in this area, to avoid generating an atmosphere of mistrust and the ensuing micromanagement from the top that compromises both the efficiency and the integrity of the procurement process. In too many countries, corruption problems in procurement have been addressed in ways that produced reluctance to take decisions and inordinate procurement delays. By the efficiency nucleus approach, a small group would be created within the central unit responsible for procurement standards and oversight, to provide assistance to the spending agencies in the flexible implementation of the procurement procedures. This would at the same time improve the implementation of the procedures, strengthen the agencies' capacity to carry out their own procurement, and facilitate timely purchasing decisions. The relationship between the central unit and the ministries' procurement offices would encompass not just oversight and control but also cooperation and mutual assistance, and would therefore encourage informal exchanges of information and advice as and when needed.

The efficiency nucleus approach should not be confused with the creation of enclaves that "ring-fence" segments of the public administration in order to improve them in isolation from the remainder of the system. Institutional enclaves have rarely worked. There are two basic differences between an efficiency nucleus and an enclave. First, an efficiency nucleus aims at spreading institutional improvements throughout the system, rather than building a fortress of modernity within it. Second, efficiency nuclei should be encouraged to emerge within an existing organization and reform it from the inside—a benign mutation rather than an external threat. By contrast, enclaves either ignore or bypass the existing organizations. Understandably, the organizations being bypassed refuse to wither away and actively resist and subvert the reform process. Worse, the enclave approach shuts out the *people* in the existing organizations and gives them no hope of participating in the reform process, thus guaranteeing their opposition. The eventual outcome is extreme administrative duality, with the enclave eventually disintegrating and leaving behind only a dilapidated and demoralized administrative apparatus.

The Role of Hope

This last point leads to an unquantifiable but critical requirement for successful improvements in public management. The design of administrative reforms should incorporate a *potential* benefit for all individuals in the system, allowing them the hope of becoming part of the new institutions and the opportunity of turning themselves from potential reform losers to reform winners. The individual employee's probability of access to the new system may be low, but so long as the possibility does exist, people can still be motivated into supporting the reform by the prospect of improving their chances through cooperation and personal effort. A key proviso is that there must be absolute confidence in the equality of opportunity of access to the new system—however low the probability may be for any one individual.

There should be no illusion that incorporating the role of hope in public administration reform programs will remove resistance to the reform. It can, however, turn some opponents into supporters and, at the margin, spell the difference between success and failure. Also, fairly administered training-for-access programs can have the important demonstration effect that employees are rewarded for effort and performance rather than for political or ideological loyalty. In any event, while removing or relocating determined obstructionists is unavoidable, it is wrong and counterproductive to look at everyone in the "old guard" as useless or as an adversary.

Turning Incentives Around: Internal Adjustment

In every field of human activity, the need to provide individual incentives is recognized and acted upon. It is a peculiarity of public management reform that those pushing the people in the administration to implement certain changes rarely ask themselves the key question: "What's in it for them?" Managing the transition to a better functioning system must include giving administrative units and their employees positive incentives to reform, then placing the burden on them to prove they have earned those incentives. The usual tendency to resist a proposed reform must be turned into a positive tendency to cooperate with it.

A possible approach to turning the incentives in the right direction could consist of the following. The formulation of a coherent administrative reform program would identify the adjustment required for and by each administrative unit. On that basis, appropriate performance criteria would be defined (in participatory manner), which if met would render the unit eligible for favorable consideration. Such favorable consideration could include allowing the managers to apply a new and higher salary scale to their employees; exempting them from general recruitment freezes; giving greater budgetary allocations; or a combination of these and other incentives—all of which should be consistent with the goals of the administrative reform program.

For such an approach to succeed, it is essential to have an autonomous and credible mechanism of evaluation of organizational performance. In Japan, for example, good results have been obtained by having outside agencies initiate and arbitrate reform, giving discretion to administrative entities in pursuing broad reform goals and recognizing the importance of psychological motivation. In developing countries, international participation may be necessary for the credibility of the approach.

SOME CONCLUDING MESSAGES

Our view of the basic components of an approach to effective and sustainable public management is recapitulated in the following checklist.

Consider Risks and Costs as well as Benefits of Reform

It is critical to assess realistically both the expected benefits and the anticipated costs of embarking on major changes in this complex area. The risks of both action and inaction must be considered.

If a part of the public management machinery is performing reasonably well, "innovations" may well make things worse. Conversely, when new and demonstrably better ways of doing things emerge, they should be embraced. As it is said, "if it ain't broke, don't fix it"; but neither should one miss good opportunities to improve it.

Keep Honesty First

At the top of the list of risks of reforms is their implication for administrative integrity—because the fundamental requirement of public administration is to protect the public's resources.

Don't Look for Quick Fixes

Reforms in public administration have a heavy institutional content, and there is no such thing as rapid institutional change. Also, government administration is by definition influenced by political considerations, which are not amenable to purely technical solutions and require a period of gestation and acclimatization, as well as the building of consensus.

Do Look for Quick Wins

It is always advisable, in order to keep the momentum of reform going and give it credibility, to identify and implement some concrete improvement—no matter how small—but visible and well publicized.

Exceed on the Side of Openness

Suspicion is the first natural reaction to proposals for change. It will only be heightened—and resistance to the change maximized—in the absence of honest and effective communications.

Look to the Web

The internet—YouTube, the blogs, camera phones, and online political mobilization organizations—are having a remarkable impact not only on popular culture, but on politics as well (e.g., the wide circulation of certain videos made the difference in several political races in the 2006 elections in the United States). Indeed, the internet may even have the potential of undoing some of the heavy damage that has been done by television to the quality of political discourse and to the citizens' attention span. The internet has already simplified administrative transactions enormously. It may perhaps do the same for public administration reforms, by exposing in real time their faults and absurdities while reinforcing their innovative and vital elements.

Get the Basics Right

This message applies mainly to developing countries, where complex public management tools should not even be considered unless and until the basic machinery functions reasonably well. This is not a prescription for standing pat, but a condition for progress itself—as premature introduction of these tools dooms them to failure—"shortcuts turn into dead ends" (Schick, 1998, p. 131). This principle, among other things, also implies that external donors should contribute to public administration reform in developing countries, but should not drive it. It is only when the government of the country is in the driver's seat, setting the reform agenda and being responsible for it, that there is a chance of sustainable improvements in the country's public management.

Adapt, Not Adopt

Mechanical imitation of "models" developed elsewhere is always unwise.[11] "Adaptation is not imitation," said Gandhi. Improvements in public management must certainly take into account the advances and mistakes made by other countries, but must also rest on a solid basis of country-specific analysis.

And so, in keeping with the spirit of the three quotations at the start of the chapter, the best conclusion for this book is a simple piece of advice:

When you hear "best practice," call the police.

NOTES

1. It may be of interest to the reader that the French word for fashion, *mode*, is the same as the statistical measure of the most frequent value of a variable. Indeed, the only attribute of passing fashion is that it is adopted by the largest single number of individuals. As the group's interests change, so does the mode. The root is from the Latin word *modus,* which is also shared with "model" and "modern." Not incidentally, and in addition to the undertone of groupthink, all these terms carry the same basic meaning of impermanence.

2. The technocratic movement began in 1919 and some adherents are still active today. It is almost entirely of American inspiration, but some of the ideas have been recently picked up in Scandinavia. In essence, technocracy views all established economic, political, and administrative systems as obsolete fossils and aims at replacing them with a scientific system driven by selected educated elites. The movement has several interesting and provocative ideas, which are however negated by the illusion that there exist purely technical solutions to the problems of organized human society (for a skeptical view, see Rivers, 1993).

3. See Schick (1996) for a clear summary of the New Zealand reforms. These came shortly after the major changes brought to public administration in Britain by Margaret Thatcher and were followed in short order by similar reforms in Australia, Iceland, and a few other countries.

4. Reproduced by permission. For an opposing view, see Borins (1995).

5. Letter to the Editor, "Britain's self-defeating 'auditocracy,'" *Financial Times*, August 24, 2004.

6. In the United States, the expression "iron triangle" refers to the three-way trading of favors between an outside interest group, the relevant congressional committee, and the bureaucrats in the executive agency concerned. The interest group (usually an industry lobby) provides political financing to the key congressmen, who in return engineer legislation favorable to the group and provide budgetary support and protection for the bureaucrats concerned, who close the triangle by ensuring implementation of the favorable legislation and "friendly" oversight of the group's activities. Almost half a century ago, President Eisenhower famously warned of the emergence of a "military-industrial" complex. Since then, the reciprocal trading of special favors has become much more complex and pervasive and has accelerated tremendously in the first years of this century—especially through the scandalous budget "earmarking" mechanism described in chapter 6. (Of course, similar iron triangles can be found in many other countries, but these problems have become more corrosive in the United States than in most other developed countries.)

7. These groups could be regional, financed by international organizations, and with a firewall between their members and the consulting industry (e.g., they could never work on assignment for the same countries, either for aid agencies or for consulting firms).

8. The word "juggernaut" is an English mispronunciation of the Hindu God Jagannath—an avatar of Krishna—whose huge and extremely heavy chariot cannot be stopped by any force once it is finally pushed in motion by a crowd of believers during his festival in the city of Puri in the Indian state of Orissa.

9. Concerning technical assistance to developing countries, the International Monetary Fund recommends an ex ante agreement with the country's government on an exit strategy for expatriate advice (Diamond et al., 2005). The exit strategy recommendation is made in connection with computerization of accounting, but it is generally valid for all external technical assistance. While in the poorest developing countries short-term and targeted technical assistance will continue to be necessary in the foreseeable future, a clear timetable for ending reliance on resident expatriate experts is necessary if permanent dependence is to be avoided.

10. The major exception, we are reminded by Constantine Michalopoulos, is a spiral of severe economic and financial instability fueled by expectations, which can only be arrested by a rapid and comprehensive crackdown across a broad macroeconomic front.

11. See note 1 above.

References

Adam, Thomas, ed. 2004. *Philanthropy, Patronage, and Civil Society: Experiences from Germany, Great Britain, and North America.* Bloomington: Indiana University Press.

Agranoff, Robert, and Michael McGuire. 1998. "The Intergovernmental Context of Local Economic Development." *State and Local Government Review,* vol. 30, no. 3, pp. 150–164.

Allen, Hubert. 1999. "Changing Conceptions of Local Governance in Public Administration and Development and Its Predecessors." Paper presented at the Public Administration and Development Jubilee Conference, Oxford, United Kingdom.

Allen, Richard, S. Schiavo-Campo, and T.C. Garrity. 2004. *Assessing and Reforming Public Financial Management.* Washington, DC: World Bank.

Allen, Woody. 1986. *Without Feathers.* New York: Ballantine Books.

Anechiarico, Frank, and James B. Jacobs. 1996. *The Pursuit of Absolute Integrity: How Corruption Control Makes Government Ineffective.* Chicago: University of Chicago Press.

Andic, Fuat, and Suphan Andic. 1996. *The Last of the Ottoman Grandes: The Life and Political Testament of Ali Pasha.* Istanbul: Isis Press.

Andrisani, Paul J., Simon Hakim, E.S. Savas, eds. 2006. *The New Public Management: Lessons from Innovating Governors and Mayors.* Norwell, MA: Kluwer.

Armstrong, Michael. 2006. *A Handbook of Human Resource Management Practice.* 9th ed. London: Kogan Page.

Arrow, Kenneth, and T. Scitovsky, eds. 1969. *Readings in Welfare Economics.* London: Allen and Unwin.

Arrowsmith, Sue, and Keith Hartley, eds. 2002. *Public Procurement.* Northampton, MA: Edward Edgar Publishing Limited.

Ashworth, Kenneth. 2001. *Caught Between the Dog and the Fireplug or How to Survive Public Service.* Washington, DC: Georgetown University Press.

Asian Development Bank. 1999a. Papers presented at the Asian Mayors Forum, Colombo, Sri Lanka, June 28–30, 1999.

———. 1999b. *Development and Management of Cities.* Manila, Philippines.

———. 1998a. *Anticorruption: Policies and Strategies.*

———. 1998b. *Key Themes and Priorities for Governance and Capacity Building in the Asian and Pacific Region.*

———. 1998c. *Indonesia's Decentralization Process.* (Mimeo).

———. 1997. *Development and Management of Megacities.* Manila, Philippines: Asian Development Bank.

———. 1997. *Governance: Promoting Sound Development Management.*

———. 1995. "Megacity Management in the Asian and Pacific Region: Policy Issues and Innovative Approaches," Proceedings of the Regional Seminar on Megacities Management in Asia and the Pacific. Manila.

Asian Productivity Organization. 1998. *Productivity and Quality Improvement in Civil Service.* Tokyo: Asian Productivity Organization.

Bahl, Roy W. 1999. "Implementation Rules for Fiscal Decentralization." *Public Budgeting and Finance,* vol. 19, no. 2, pp. 59–75.

Bamberger, Michael. 1986. "The Role of Community Participation in Development Planning and Project Management." Paper presented at the International Workshop of the Economic Development Institute of the World Bank, Washington, DC, September 21–24.

Barrett, Katherine, and Richard Greene. 1994. "The State of the Cities." *Financial World,* February.

Bellavita, Christopher. 1990. *How Public Organizations Work.* New York: Praeger.

Beschel, Robert, and Nicholas Manning. 2000. "Central Mechanisms for Policy Formulation and Coordination" in *To Serve and to Preserve,* ed. S. Schiavo-Campo and P.S. Sundaram. Manila, Philippines: Asian Development Bank.

Bird, Richard. 1971. "Wagner's Law of Expanding State Activity." *Public Finance,* vol. 26, pp. 1–26.

Bjornlund, Lydia D. and Lydia Bjomlund. 1996. *Media Relations for Local Governments.* London: Intermediate Technology Publications.

Borins, Sanford. 1995. "The New Public Management Is Here to Stay." *Canadian Public Administration,* vol. 38, no. 1, pp. 122–132.

Boston, Jonathan. 1998. "Public Sector Management, Electoral Reform and the Future of the Contract State in New Zealand." *Australian Journal of Public Administration,* vol. 57, no. 4, pp. 32–44.

Bourdieu, Pierre. 1986. "The Forms of Capital." In *Handbook of Theory and Research for the Sociology of Education,* ed. J.G. Richards. Westport, CT: Greenwood Press.

Brint, Steven. 1984. "New Class and Cumulative Trend Explanations of the Liberal Political Attitudes of Professionals." *American Journal of Sociology,* vol. 90, no. 1, pp. 30–71.

Broadnax, Walter. 2000. *Diversity and Affirmative Action in Public Service.* Boulder, CO: Westview Press.

Brzoska, Michael. 1999. "Military Conversion: The Balance Sheet." *Journal of Peace Research,* vol. 36, no. 2, pp. 131–140.

Bunye, Ignacio R. 1999. *Metropolitanization: The Metro Manila Experience.* Paper presented at the Asian Mayors Forum, Colombo, Sri Lanka.

Burki, Shahid Javed, Guillermo E. Perry, and William R. Dillinger. 1999. *Beyond the Center: Decentralizing the State.* Washington, DC: World Bank.

Burton, Ralph Joseph. 1951. "The Central Machinery of Government: Its Role and Functioning." *Public Administration Review,* vol. 11, no. 4, pp. 287–297.

Caiden, Naomi. 1996. *Public Budgeting and Financial Administration in Developing Countries.* Greenwich, CT: Jai Press.

Campos J. Edgardo, and Sanjay Pradhan. 1998. *Building Blocks Towards a More Effective Public Sector.* Washington, DC: World Bank Economic Development Institute.

Cernea, Michael. 1992. "The Building Blocks of Participation: Testing Bottom-up Planning." Working Paper No. 166. Washington, DC: World Bank.

Cheema, Shabbir G., and Dennis A. Rondinelli, eds. 1983. "Decentralization and Development: Conclusions and Directions." In *Decentralization and Development: Policy Implementation in Developing Countries.* Thousand Oaks, CA: Sage.

Chew, L.K.H., and A.C.Y. Teo. 1991. "Human Resource Practice in Singapore: A Survey of Local Firms and MNCs." *Asia Pacific HRM,* Autumn, pp. 430–438.

Cigler, Beverly A. 1989. "Trends Affecting Local Administrators." In *Handbook of Public Administration,* ed. James L. Perry. San Francisco, CA: Jossey-Bass.

Coase, Ronald. 1960. "The Problem of Social Cost." *Journal of Law and Economics,* vol. 3, no. 1, pp. 1–44.

Cohler, Anne M., Basia Carolyn Miller, and Harold S. Stone, eds. 1989. *Cambridge Texts in the History of Political Thought.* Cambridge, England: Cambridge University Press.

Coleman, James C. 1998. "Social Capital in the Creation of Human Capital." *American Journal of Sociology,* vol. 94, pp. S95–S120.

———. 1990. *Foundations of Social Theory.* Cambridge, MA: Harvard University Press.

Commonwealth Secretariat. 1998a. *A Profile of the Public Service of Singapore.* London.

———. 1998b. *Improved Public Service Delivery.*

———. 1997a. *A Profile of the Public Service of Zimbabwe.*

———. 1997b. *Improving Policy Management in the Public Service.*

———. 1996. *Current Good Practices and New Developments in Public Service Management.*

———. 1995a. *A Profile of Public Service of the United Kingdom.* London.

———. 1995b. *A Profile of the Public Service of New Zealand.*

———. 1994. *A Profile of the Public Service of Canada.*

Cooper, Phillip J. 1989. "Legal Tools for Accomplishing Administrative Responsibilities." In *Handbook of Public Administration,* ed. James L. Perry. San Francisco, CA: Jossey-Bass.

Cooper, Phillip J., and Chester A. Newland, eds. 1997. *Handbook of Public Law and Administration.* San Francisco, CA: Jossey-Bass.

Corrigan, Paul, Mike Hayes, and Paul Joyce. 1999. *Managing in the Local Government.* San Francisco, CA: Jossey-Bass.

Dahl, Robert A. 1998. *On Democracy.* New Haven, CT: Yale University Press.

———. 1989. *Democracy and Its Critics.* New Haven, CT: Yale University Press.

Davey, Kenneth. 1999. *Local Government Reform in Central and Eastern Europe.* Paper presented at the Public Administration and Development Jubilee Conference, Oxford, United Kingdom.

———. 1993. *Elements of Urban Management.* Washington, DC: World Bank.

Davis, Richard and Diana Marie Owen. 1998. *New Media and American Politics.* New York: Oxford University Press.

deBlij, H.J., and Peter O. Muller. 2005. *Geography Realms, Regions, and Concepts.* 12th ed. New York: John Wiley & Sons.

Del Duca, Louis. 1996. *Annotations to the Model Procurement Code for State and Local Governments, With Analytical Summary of State Enactments.* Chicago, IL: American Bar Association.

de Silva, K.M. 1993. *Problems of Governance.* New Delhi: Center for Policy Research.

de Soto, Hernando. 1989. *The Other Path.* New York: Harper and Row.

Diamond, Jack et al. 2005. *IMF Technical Assistance Evaluation.* Washington, DC: International Monetary Fund.

Dillinger, William. 1993. *Decentralization and its Implications for Urban Service Delivery.* Washington, DC: World Bank.

Donahue, John. 1989. *The Privatization Decision.* New York: Basic Books.

Drury, A. Cooper, Jonathan Krieckhaus, and Michael Lusztig. 2006. "Corruption, Democracy, and Economic Growth." *International Political Science Review*, vol. 27, no. 2, pp. 121–136.

DuBois, W.E.B. 1903. *The Souls of Black Folk.* Chicago: A.C. McClurg & Co.

Dunn, John. 2006. *Democracy: A History.* New York: Atlantic Monthly Press.

Dutton, William H., ed. 1996. *Information and Communication Technologies: Vision and Realities.* New York: Oxford University Press.

Economic and Social Commission for Asia and the Pacific. 1993. *The Control and Management of Government Expenditure: Issues and Experience in Asian Countries.* Development Paper No. 13, Bangkok.

Edwards, Mike. 2000. "Time to Put the NGO House in Order." *Financial Times,* June 6.

Endriga, Jose. 1996. "Decentralization: Concept and Strategy for Local Development." In *Redrawing the Lines: Service Commissions and the Delegation of Personnel Management. Managing the Public Service: Strategies for Improvement Series No. 2,* ed. Nick Manning and Charles Polidano. London: Commonwealth Secretariat.

Federation des Experts Comptables Europeens. 1991. *Performance Measurement in Public Sector Management.* London: Chartered Institute of Public Finance and Accountancy.

Ferroni, Marco. 2001. *Regional Public Goods in Official Development Assistance.* Occasional Paper 11, Washington, DC: Inter-American Development Bank.

Fesler, James, and Donald Kettl. 1991. *The Politics of the Administrative Process.* Chatham, NJ: Chatham House.

Finer, Herman. 1949. *Theory and Practice of Modern Government.* New York: Henry Holt and Company.

Fiszbein, Ariel and Pamela Loweden. 1999. *Working Together for a Change: Government, Business and Civic Partnerships for Poverty Reduction in Latin America and Caribbean.* Washington, DC: World Bank.

France, Government of. 1992. *About French Administration.* Paris: La Documentation française.

Friedman, Thomas L. 2005. *The World Is Flat: A Brief History of the Twenty-first Century.* New York: Farrar, Straus and Giroux.

Gaant, Jesse Edward Jr., and Veronica Davis Gerald. 2002. *The Ultimate Gullah Cookbook.* Beaufort, SC: Sands Publishing.

Gidman, Philip. 1994. "Public-Private Partnership in Urban Infrastructure Services." Urban Management Working Papers Series. Washington, DC: World Bank.

Girishankar, Navin. 1999. "Reforming Institutions for Service Delivery." World Bank Policy Research Working Paper No. 2039. Washington, DC: World Bank.

———, and Migara de Silva. 1998. *Strategic Management for Government Agencies.* Discussion Paper No. 386. Washington, DC: World Bank.

Glaser, John S. 1994. *The United Way Scandal: An Insider's Account of What Went Wrong and Why.* New York: Wiley.

Gregory, W.H. 1989. *The Defense Procurement Mess.* Lanham, MD: Lexington Books.

Grindle, Richard C., and Kneale T. Marshall. 1977. *Manpower Planning Models.* New York: North-Holland Publications.

Gruber, Jonathan. 2004. *Public Finance and Public Policy.* Cambridge, MA: Worth Publishers.

Gwilliam, Kenneth M. and Ajay Kumar. 2002. "Road Funds Revisited: A Preliminary Appraisal of the Effectiveness of 'Second Generation' Road Funds." TWU Series. Washington, DC: World Bank.

Hailey, John. 1999. *Ladybirds, Missionaries, and NGOs.* Toronto: Commonwealth Association for Public Administration and Management (CAPAM).

Hanifan, Lydia J. 1916. "The Rural School Community Center." *Annals of the American Academy of Political and Social Science,* vol. 67, no. 1, pp. 130–138.

Hauck Walsh, Annemarie, and James Leighland. 1989. "Designing and Managing the Procurement Process." In *Handbook of Public Administration,* ed. James L. Perry. San Francisco, CA: Jossey-Bass.

Heald, David. 1995. "An Evaluation of French Concession Accounting." *The European Accounting Review,* vol. 4, pp. 325–349.

Heller, Peter and Alan Tait. 1983. "Government Employment and Pay: Some International Comparisons." Occasional Papers No. 24. Washington, DC: International Monetary Fund.

Heeks, Richard. 1996. *Reinventing Government in the Information Age.* London: Routledge.

Herz, John H. 1959. *International Politics in the Atomic Age.* New York: Columbia University Press.

Hino, Toshiko. 1999. *NGO-World Bank Partnerships: A Tale of Two Projects.* Washington, DC: World Bank.

Hirschman, Albert O., 1970. *Exit, Voice and Loyalty: Responses to Decline of Firms, Organizations and States.* Cambridge, MA: Harvard University Press.

———. 1958. *The Strategy of Economic Development.* New Haven, CT and London: Yale University Press.

Hochschild, Adam. 1999. *King Leopold's Ghost.* Cambridge, MA: Houghton-Mifflin.

Hood, Christopher C. 1976. *The Limits of Administration.* New York: John Wiley & Sons.

Hondale, Beth, Beverly Cigler, and James Costa. 2004. *Fiscal Health for Local Governments.* San Diego, CA: Elsevier Academic Press.

Huascar, Javier Eguino Lijeron. 1996. *Decentralization, Local Governments and Markets.* The Hague, Netherlands: Institute for Social Studies.

Hughes, Anthony. 1998. *A Different Kind of Voyage.* Pacific Studies Series. Office of Pacific Operations. Manila, Philippines: Asian Development Bank.

Hyden, Goran. 1999. "Governance in the 21st Century: Restoring Legitimacy to Public Authority." *African Journal of Public Administration and Management,* vol. 11, no. 1.

India, Government of. 1997. *Report of the Fifth Central Pay Commission.* New Delhi: Ministry of Finance.

———. 1998. *Report of the Commission on Administrative Law.* New Delhi: Department of Administrative Reforms and Public Grievances.

Ingraham, Patricia. 1993. "Of Pigs in Pokes and Policy Diffusion: Another Look at Pay-for Perfomance." *Public Administration Review,* vol. 53, no. 4, pp. 348–356.

Ives, Denis. 1995. "Human Resource Management in the Australian Public Service: Challenges and Opportunities." *Public Administration and Development,* vol. 15, pp. 319–334.

Jensen, Lotte. 1998. "Interpreting New Public Management: The Case of Denmark." *Australian Journal of Public Administration,* vol. 57, no. 4, pp. 55–66.

Jones, Philip. 1999. "Rent Seeking and Defense Expenditure." *Defense and Peace Economics,* vol. 10, no. 1.

Kamensky, J. 1996. "What 'Reinventing' the Federal Government Means." *Rego Magazine* [online]; available at govinfo.library.unt.edu/npr/rego/regular/meaning.htm.

Kaul, Inge, Isabelle Grunberg, and Marc A. Stern, eds. 1999. *Global Public Goods.* New York: Oxford University Press.

Keillor, Garrison. 1986. *Lake Wobegon.* New York: Penguin Books.

Kellough, J. Edward, and Haoran Lu. 1993. "The Paradox of Merit Pay in the Public Sector: Persistence of a Problematic Procedure." *Review of Public Personnel Administration,* vol. 13, no. 2, pp. 45–64.

Klein, Michael, and Bita Hadjimichael. 2003. *The Private Sector in Development.* Washington, DC: World Bank.

Klingner, Donald E., and John Nalbandian. 1998. *Public Personnel Management: Contexts and Strategies.* 4th ed. Upper Saddle River, NJ: Prentice Hall.

Klitgaard, Robert. 1998. *Controlling Corruption.* Berkeley, CA: University of California Press.

Knapman, Bruce, and Cedric Saldanha. 1999. *Reforms in the Pacific.* Manila, Philippines: Asian Development Bank.

———. 1998. *A Different Kind of Voyage.* Manila, Philippines: Asian Development Bank.

Kongstad, Per. 1974. "Growth Poles and Urbanization: A Critique of Perroux and Friedmann." *Antipode,* vol. 6, no. 2.

Kopits, George, and Steven A. Symansky. 1998. "Fiscal Policy Rules." *IMF Occasional Papers,* no. 162. Washington, DC: International Monetary Fund.

Kraay, Aart and Caroline Van Rijckeghem. 1995. "Employment and Wages in the Public Sector." Working Paper No. 95/70. Washington, DC: International Monetary Fund.

Laking, Robert G. 1996. *Good Practice in Public Sector Management.* Internal memorandum. Washington, DC: World Bank.

Lambla, Kenneth. 1998. "Abstraction and Theosophy: Social Housing in Rotterdam." *Architronic,* vol. 7, no. 2.

Latham, Richard. 1978. *The Illustrated Pepys.* London: Bell and Lyman.

Leigland, James. 1996. "Privatization of Public Enterprise in Asia: Current Patterns and Emerging Issues." In *Public Budgeting and Financial Administration in Developing Countries,* ed. Naomi Caiden. Greenwich, CT: Jai Press, 1996.

Lindauer, David L. 1981. "Public Sector Wages and Employment in Africa." Studies in Employment and Rural Development, No. 68. Washington, DC: World Bank.

———, and Barbara Nunberg. eds. 1994. *Rehabilitating Government: Pay and Employment in Africa.* Washington, DC: World Bank.

Lovrich, Nicholas. 1989. "Managing Poor Performers." In *Handbook of Public Administration,* ed. James L. Perry. San Francisco: Jossey-Bass.

Manning, Nick. 1999. "Making the Cabinet Work: Institutional Arrangements for Strategic Decision-making in Government." Mimeo. Washington, DC: World Bank.

Mauro, Paolo. 1995. "Corruption and Growth." *Quarterly Journal of Economics,* vol. 110, no. 3 (August), pp. 681–712.

McCarney, Patricia, ed. 1999. "Considerations of Governance in Global and Local Perspective." Paper presented at the Jubilee Conference of Public Administration and Development, Oxford, United Kingdom.

———. 1996. *Changing Nature of Local Government in Developing Countries.* University of Toronto: Center for Urban and Community Studies.

McFerson, Hazel M. 2007. "Transplants as Legal Colonization." In *Encyclopedia of Law and Society: American and Global Perspectives,* ed. David S. Clark. Thousand Oaks, CA: Sage.

———. 2002. *Mixed Blessing: The Impact of American Colonial Policy on Society and Politics in the Philippines.* Westport, CT: Greenwood Press.

———. 1996. "Rethinking Ethnic Conflict: Somalia and Fiji." *American Behavioral Scientist,* vol. 40, no. 1, pp. 18–32.

———. 1979. "Plural Society in the U.S. Virgin Islands." *Journal of Plural Societies,* vol. 10, no. 1 (Spring).

Michels, Robert. 1998. *Political Parties: A Sociological Study of the Oligarchical Tendencies of Modern Democracy.* New York: The Free Press.

Milkovich, G., and A. Wigdor. 1991. *Pay for Performance: Evaluating Performance Appraisal and Merit Pay.* Washington, DC: National Academy Press.

Miller, Karen. 2005. *Public Sector Reform: Governance in South Africa.* Hampshire: UK: Aldershot.

Mills, C. Wright. 1956. *The Power Elite.* New York: Oxford University Press.

Molyneux, Maxine, 2002. *Gender and the Silences of Social Capital.* World Bank Poverty Net Library, http://poverty2.forumone.com/library/view/14249.

Montesquieu, Charles de Secondat. 1748. *The Spirit of the Laws.* Reprinted in *Cambridge Texts in the History of Political Thought,* ed. Anne M. Cohler, Basia Carolyn Miller, Harold Samuel Stone. Cambridge University Press, 1989. Available at www.ou.edu/cas/psc/bookmontesquieu.htm.

Musgrave, Richard, and Peggy Musgrave. 1989. *Public Finance in Theory and Practice,* 5th ed. New York: McGraw-Hill.

Nalbandian, John. 1989. "The Contemporary Role of City Managers." *American Review of Public Administration,* vol. 19, no. 4, pp. 261–278.

Naim, Moises. 2006. *Illicit: How Smugglers, Traffickers, and Copycats Are Hijacking the Global Economy.* New York: Anchor.

———. 2007. "Democracy's Dangerous Impostors." *Washington Post,* April 21.

Nathan, R.P. 1995. "Reinventing Government: What Does It Mean?" *Public Administration Review,* vol. 55, no. 2, p. 213.

National Performance Review. 1993. *Creating a Government That Works Better & Costs Less: Report of the National Performance Review,* Washington, DC: U.S. Government Printing Office.

Nellis, John, and Mary Shirley. 1996. *Public Enterprise Reform.* Washington, DC: World Bank.

North, Douglass C. 1991. "Institutions." *Journal of Economic Perspectives,* vol. 5, no. 1, pp. 97–112.

Nunberg, Barbara. 1995. *The State after Communism.* Washington, DC: World Bank.

Nye, Joseph K. 2004. *Power in the Global Information Age: From Realism to Globalization.* Oxford: Routledge.

Nyerere, Julius K. 1962. *Ujaama: The Basis of African Socialism.* Dar es Salaam: Tanzania Government Printer.

Oakerson, Ronald J. 1989. "Governance Structures for Enhancing Accountability and Responsiveness." In *Handbook of Public Administration,* ed. James L. Perry. San Francisco: Jossey-Bass.

Oates, Wallace E. 1972. *Fiscal Federalism.* New York: Harcourt Brace Jovanovich.

O'Leary, Rosemary, and Charles R. Wise. 1991. "Public Managers, Judges, and Legislators: Redefining the 'New Partnership.'" *Public Administration Review,* vol. 51, July/August, pp. 316–327.

Organization for Economic Cooperation and Development (OECD). 2005. *Evaluating Public Participation in Policy-Making.* Paris: OECD.

———. 2002. *Anti-Corruption Measures in Southeastern Europe: Civil Society Involvement.*

———. 2001. *Citizens as Partners: OECD Handbook on Information, Consultation and Participation in Policy-Making.*

———. 1999. *Public Sector Corruption, an International Survey of Prevention Measures.*

———. 1997a. *Issues in Developments and Public Management.*

———. 1997b. *Managing Across Levels of Government.*

———. 1997c. *Report on Regulatory Reform.*

———. 1997d. *Contracting Out Government Services: Best-Practice Guidelines and Case Studies.*

———. 1997e. *Contracting Out Government Services: Best-Practice Guidelines and Case Studies.*

———. 1997f. *Issues and Developments in Public Management: Survey 1996–1997.*

———. 1997g. *Consultation and Communications: Integrating Multiple Interests into Policy.*

———. 1996a. *Integrating People Management into Public Service Reform.*

———. 1996b. *Ministerial Symposium on the Future of Public Services.*

———. 1995. *Governance in Transition, Public Management Reforms in OECD Countries.*

———. 1992. *Public Management.*

Osborne, David, and Gaebler, Ted. 1992. *Reinventing Government: How the Entrepreneurial Spirit Is Transforming the Public Sector.* Reading, MA: Addison-Wesley.

Oszlak, Oscar. 1999. "Building Capacities for Governance in Argentina." Paper presented at the World Conference on Governance, Manila, Philippines.

O'Toole, Barry J. 2006. *The Ideal of Public Service: Reflections on the Higher Civil Service in Britain.* London: Routledge.

Pareto, Vilfredo. 1935. *The Mind and Society: A Treatise on General Sociology.* New York: Harcourt Brace Jananovich. Reprint, 1963; New York: Dover Publications.

Patten, Thomas H. Jr. 1971. *Manpower Planning and the Development of Human Resources.* New York: John Wiley.

Paul, Samuel. 1995. *Strengthening Public Accountability: New Approaches and Mechanisms.* Bangalore, India: Public Affairs Centre.

Pedersen, P.E. 1996. "The Search for the Smoking Gun." *Euromoney,* vol. 49 (September).

Perroux, Francois. 1949. *Concept of a Growth Pole.* Available at www.applet-magic.com/poles.htm.

Perry, James L., ed. 1989. *Handbook of Public Administration.* San Francisco: Jossey-Bass.

Perry, Tod, with Marc Zenner. 1999. "Pay for Performance? Government Regulation and the Structure of Compensation Contracts." Arizona Finance Symposium, Phoenix. April.

Pertierra, Raul, and Eduardo F. Ugarte. 2002. "American Rule in the Muslim South and the Philippine Hinterlands." In *Mixed Blessing: The Impact of the American Colonial Experience on Politics and Society in the Philippines,* ed. Hazel M. McFerson. Westport, CT: Greenwood Press.

Peters, Guy B. 1996. *The Future of Public Administration: Four Emerging Models.* Lawrence: Kansas University Press.

Petrei, Humberto. 1998. *Budget and Control: Reforming the Public Sector in Latin America.* Washington, DC: Johns Hopkins University Press.

———. 1987. *El Gasto Público Social y sus Efectos Distributivos: Un Examen Comparativo de Cinco Paises de América Latina.* Program ECIEL, Rio de Janeiro.

Polidano, Charles. 1999. "The New Public Management in Developing Countries." Paper presented at the 3rd International Research Symposium on Public Management, Birmingham, United Kingdom.

Pope, Jeremy, ed. 1996. *National Integrity Systems: The Transparency International Sourcebook.* Berlin: Transparency International.

Powers, Vicki J. 1998. "Benchmarking in Hong Kong: Mass Transit Railway Excels in Worldwide Industry Study." *Benchmarking in Action,* issue 11. Houston: American Productivity and Quality Center. (Internet edition.)

Premchand, A. 2000. *Control of Public Money: The Fiscal Machinery in Developing Countries.* Delhi: Oxford University Press.

———. 1993. *Public Expenditure Management.* Washington, DC: International Monetary Fund.

———. 1983. *Government Budgeting and Expenditure Control.* Washington, DC: International Monetary Fund.

——— and S. Schiavo-Campo. 2004. *Public Expenditure Management at Subnational Government Level.* Washington, DC: World Bank.

Premfors, Rune. 1998. "Reshaping the Democratic State: Swedish Experience in a Comparative Perspective." *Public Administration,* vol. 76, no. 1, p. 143.

Prud'homme, Remy. 1994. *On the Dangers of Decentralization.* Washington, DC: World Bank.

Putnam, Robert D. 2000. *Bowling Alone: The Collapse and Revival of American Community.* New York: Simon and Schuster.

———. Robert Leonardi and Raffaella Nanetti. 1993 *Making Democracy Work: Civic Traditions in Modern Italy.* Princeton, NJ: Princeton University Press.

Rawls, John. 1972. *A Theory of Justice.* Oxford: Clarendon Press.

Rehfuss, John. 1993. *Designing an Effective Bidding and Monitoring System to Minimize Problems in Competitive Contracting.* Available at www.reason.org/htg03.pdf.

Rhodes, R.A.W. 1998. "Different Roads to Unfamiliar Places: U.K. Experience in Comparative Perspective." *Australian Journal of Public Administration,* vol. 57, no. 4 (December), pp. 19–31.

Riccuci, Norma M. 1997. "Constitutions, Statutes, Regulations and Labor Relations: Dispute Resolution in a Complex Authority Mix." In *Handbook of Public Law and Administration,* ed. Cooper and Newland. San Francisco, CA: Jossey-Bass.

Riley, Thomas. 1993. *Fundamentals of Document Examination for Laboratory Personnel.* Quantico, VA: Federal Bureau of Investigation.

Rivers, Theodore John. 1993. *Contra Technologiam.* Lanham, MD: University Press of America.

Robinson, Mark and Gordon White. 1997. *Civil Society and Social Provision.* London: United Nations University/Wider Research for Action Series.

Rondinelli, Dennis and Shabir Cheema, eds. 1983. *Decentralization and Development: Policy Implications in Developing Countries.* Thousand Oaks, CA: Sage Publications.

Rosenbloom, David H., and Suzanne Piotrowski. 2003. "Outsourcing the Constitution and Administrative Law Norms." *American Review of Public Administration,* vol. 33, no. 1 (March), pp. 103–121.

Sachs, Jeffrey, and John Williamson. 1985. *External Debt and Macroeconomic Performance in Latin America and East Asia.* Washington, DC: *Brookings Papers on Economic Activity,* no. 2.

Saltzstein, G.H. 1989. "Black Mayors and Police Policies." *Journal of Politics,* vol. 51, no. 3, pp. 525–544.

Savoie, Donald. 1995. "What Is Wrong with the New Public Management?" *Canadian Public Administration,* vol. 38, no. 1, pp. 112–121.

Schartum, Dag Wiese. 1998. "Access to Government-Held Information." *Journal of Information, Law and Technology,* vol. 1.

Schiavo-Campo, Salvatore. 2005. "Building Country Capacity for Monitoring and Evaluation in the Public Sector." OED Working Paper Series, no. 13 (June).

———. 2003. "Financing and Aid Management Arrangements in Post-Conflict Situations." *Social Development Papers,* no. 6 (June).

———, ed. 2000. *Governance, Corruption and Financial Management.* Manila, Philippines: Asian Development Bank.

———. 1998. "Government Employment and Pay: The Global and Regional Evidence." *Public Administration and Development,* vol. 18 (December), pp. 457–478.

———. 1996. "Reforming the Civil Service," *Finance and Development,* vol. 33, no. 3 (September), pp. 10–13.

———. 1994. "Institutional Change and the Public Sector in Transitional Economies." Discussion Paper No. 241. Washington, DC: World Bank.

———. 1978. *International Economics.* Boston: Winthrop.

———, and P.S. Sundaram. 2000. *To Serve and to Preserve.* Manila, Philippines: Asian Development Bank.

———, and Daniel Tommasi. 1999. *Managing Government Expenditure.* Manila, Philippines: Asian Development Bank.

———, and Hans W. Singer. 1970. *Perspectives of Economic Development.* Boston, MA: Houghton-Mifflin.

Schick, Allen. 1998. "Why Developing Countries Should Not Try New Zealand Reform." *World Bank Research Observer,* vol. 13, no. 1 (February): pp. 123–131.

———. 1996. "The Spirit of Reform: Managing the New Zealand State Sector in a Time of Change." Report prepared for the SSC and Treasury, August 1996. Available at www.ssc.govt.nz/Documents/Schick_report.pdf.

Self, Peter. 1972. *Administrative Theories and Politics: An Inquiry into the Structure and Processes of Modern Government.* London: Allen and Unwin.

Shah, Anwar. 2007. *Budgeting in Africa.* Washington, DC: World Bank.

———. 1998. "Balance, Accountability, and Responsiveness." Policy Research Working Paper, no. 2021. Washington, DC: World Bank.

Shand, David. 1998. "The Role of Performance Indicators in Public Expenditure Management." IMF Working Papers. Washington, DC: International Monetary Fund.

Sherman, Stanley N. 1987. *Contract Management.* Maryland: Wordcrafters Publications.

Sims, Ronald R. 1993. "Evaluating Public Sector Training Programs." *Public Personnel Management,* vol. 22.

Sivaramakrishnan, K.C., and Leslie Green. 1986. *Metropolitan Management: The Asian Experience.* New York: Oxford University Press.

Smith, B.C. 1985. *Decentralization: The Territorial Dimension of the State.* London: Allen and Unwin.

Starling, Grover. 1998. *Managing the Public Sector.* Philadelphia: Harcourt Brace College.

Stigler, George. 1971. "The Theory of Economic Regulation." *Bell Journal of Economics,* vol. 2, pp. 3–21.

Stiglitz, Joseph. 1996. "Some Lessons from the East Asian Miracle." *World Bank Research Observer,* vol. 11, no. 2, pp. 151–177.

———. 1989. "Markets, Market Failures, and Development." *American Economic Review,* vol. 79, no. 2, pp. 197–203.

Stockholm International Peace Research Institute. 2006. *Year Book 2006: Armaments, Disarmaments, and International Security.* Stockholm: SIPRI.

Sullivan, Louis H. 1896. "The Tall Office Building Artistically Considered." *Lippincott's Magazine,* March. Available at www.njit.edu/v2/Library/archlib/pub-domain/sullivan-1896-tall-bldg.html.

Svara, James. 1999. "Shifting Boundary Between Elected Officials and City Managers in Large Council Manager Cities." *Public Administration Review,* vol. 59, no. 1, pp. 44–53.

———. 1994. *Facilitative Leadership in Local Government.* San Francisco, CA: Jossey-Bass.

Tanzi, Vito. 1997. "Corruption: Arm's Length Relationships and Markets." In *The Economics of Organized Crime,* ed. G. Fiorentini and Sam Peltzman. Cambridge, UK: Cambridge University Press.

———, and L. Schuknect. 1997. *Public Spending in the 20th Century: A Global Perspective.* New York: Cambridge University Press.

Tendler, Judith. 1997. *Good Government in the Tropics.* Baltimore, MD: Johns Hopkins.

Ter-Minassian, Teresa, 1997, ed. *Fiscal Federalism in Theory and Practice.* Washington, DC: International Monetary Fund.

Thomas, John C. 1995. *Public Participation in Public Decisions: New Skills and Strategies for Public Managers.* San Francisco: Jossey-Bass.

Ulrich, Dave, Robert E. Quinn, and Kim S. Caneron. 1989. "Designing Effective Organizational Systems." In *Handbook of Public Administration,* ed. James L. Perry. San Francisco, CA: Jossey-Bass.

United Kingdom Government. 1997. *Your Right to Know.* London: Stationery Office.

United Nations. 1996. "Local Governance." Report of the United Nations Global Forum on Innovative Policies and Practices in Local Governance in Sweden.

———. 1993. "Metropolitan Governance." Summary Report of the World Conference in Tokyo.

———. 1961. *Handbook of Public Administration.* New York: United Nations.

Van Zyl, Johan et al. 1995. "Decentralized Rural Development and Enhanced Community Participation: A Case Study from Northeast Brazil." Policy Research Working Paper No. 1498. Washington, DC: World Bank.

Veblen, Thorstein. 1914. *The Instinct of Workmanship and the State of Industrial Arts.* New York: MacMillan. (See also his original article "The Instinct of Workmanship and the Irksomeness of Labor," *American Journal of Sociology,* vol. 4, 1898–99.)

Weber, Max. 1930. *The Protestant Ethic and the Spirit of Capitalism.* Trans. Talcott Parsons. Introduction by Anthony Giddens. Reissued 1985, London: Unwin Paperbacks.

Webster, R. Douglas. 2002. *Implementing Decentralization in Thailand: The Road Forward.* Washington, DC: World Bank.

———. 2001. "On the Edge: Shaping the Future of Peri-Urban East Asia." Washington, DC: World Bank. Mimeo.

Wei, Shang-Jin. 1999. "Corruption in Economic Development: Beneficial Grease, Minor Annoyance, or Major Obstacle?" Policy Research Working Paper No. 2048. Washington, DC: World Bank.

Weisskopf, Thomas E. 2004. *Affirmative Action in the United States and India: A Comparative Perspective.* London: Routledge.

Wheare, K.C. 1966. *Modern Constitution.* London: Oxford University Press.

Wildavsky, Aaron. 1993. *National Budgeting for Economic and Monetary Union.* Leiden: Nijhoff.

Wilson, J.Q. 1989. *Bureaucracy: What Government Agencies Do and Why They Do It.* New York: Basic Books.

Wise, Charles R. 1990. "Public Service Configurations and Public Organization Design in the Post-Privatization Era." *Public Administration Review,* vol. 50, no. 2, pp. 141–155.

Woolcock, Michael, and Deepa Narayan. 2000. "Social Capital: Implications for Development Theory, Research, and Policy." *The World Bank Observer,* vol. 15, no. 2.

World Bank. 2006. *Doing Business in 2005: Understanding Regulation.* Washington, DC: World Bank.

———. 2005. *Customs Modernization Handbook.*

———. 2004. *Doing Business in 2004: Understanding Regulation.* Washington, DC: World Bank (www.doingbusiness.org/Main/DoingBusiness2004.aspx).

———. 1997a. *Helping Countries Combat Corruption.*

———. 1997b. *The State in a Changing World* (World Development Report).

———. 1996. *Government that Works: Reforming the Public Sector.* Bangladesh: University Press Limited, Dhaka.

———. 1995. *Procurement of Goods: Standard Bidding Documents.*

Zietlow, Guenter. 2004. "Road Funds in Latin America." Senior Road Executives Programme, Road Financing and Road Fund Management, April 26–30, University of Birmingham (UK).

Recommended Websites

ON PUBLIC MANAGEMENT IN DEVELOPED COUNTRIES

The Public Management service (PUMA) of the Organization of Economic Cooperation and Development (OECD) has a website with extensive and up-to-date information. It is by far the best single source of information in this respect. See www.oecd.org/puma.

ON DEVELOPING COUNTRIES

The United Nations Public Administration Network has the most comprehensive website: see www.unpan.org.

Important information on public administration in developing countries is also found at the websites of the World Bank (www.worldbank.org) and of the regional developments banks (www.adb. org, for the Asian Development Bank; www.afdb.org for the African Development Bank; www. iadb.org for the Inter-American Development Bank; and www.ebrd.org for the European Bank for Reconstruction and Development). None of these sites are particularly friendly or easy to navigate, but contain a wealth of information and are well worth the effort.

ON BRITISH COMMONWEALTH COUNTRIES

For public administration issues in former British colonies, now member countries of the British Commonwealth, see Commonwealth Secretariat, www.thecommonwealth.org.

For recent research, activities, and events, see also the Commonwealth Association for Public Administration and Management, www.capam.org.

The Centre for Aid & Public Expenditure at the United Kingdom's Overseas Development Institute promotes discussion and research on core questions of aid policy, aid management, and public finance systems in developing countries: www.odi.org.uk/PPPG/cape.

The Birmingham University Graduate School of Public Administration is an excellent source of analyses of specific issues and relevant references. A listing of abstracts of articles can be obtained through enquiries@grc.bham.ac.uk.

ON THE UNITED STATES

For the *mandate and organization* of U.S. federal departments and regulatory agencies, see the respective websites of each agency (usda.gov for the Department of Agriculture, doi.gov for the Department of Interior, ustreas.gov for the Treasury Department, etc.).

For *information on legislation,* the GovTrack.us website tracks existing legislation and regulations, voting records of members of Congress, and so on. While is it much more difficult to find accurate and timely information on legislation that is about to be voted on, the Library of Congress has been publishing proposed bills online at thomas.loc.gov, as does a new nonprofit website called readthebill.org.

For studies of *efficiency and effectiveness* of government programs, see the General Accountability Office (GAO—formerly the General Accounting Office), www.gao.gov. Perusing GAP studies is also an invaluable learning experience for those interested in independent and rigorous evaluation of government activities.

For *specific issues,* the Congressional Research Service is excellent: www.opencrs.com.

For *state-level administration,* see the National Governors' Association website: www.nga.org.

For *municipal administration,* see the National League of Cities website: www.nlc.org.

ON SPECIFIC TOPICS

On *aid management and public finance in developing countries,* the Centre for Aid & Public Expenditure at the United Kingdom's Overseas Development Institute promotes discussion and research: www.odi.org.uk/PPPG/cape.

For international data on *government revenue and expenditure,* the best source is the International Monetary Fund's Government Financial Statistics (www.imf.org).

On *economic regulations,* a good source is the annual *Doing Business* survey carried out by the World Bank for some 190 countries beginning in 2004. The information must be treated with caution, because country realities may differ substantially from what is reported by the country expert(s) consulted through the survey, but *Doing Business* is still a useful first cut: www.doingbusiness.org. More detailed and more grounded on primary business sources is the Business Enterprise Environment Performance Survey (BEEPS) of over 4,000 firms, conducted jointly by the European Bank for Reconstruction and Development and the World Bank (info.worldbank.org/governance/beeps/). Unfortunately, that survey covers only the twenty-two countries of Eastern Europe and the former USSR.

On *military expenditure* around the world, see primarily the Stockholm International Peace Research Institute at www.SIPRI.org.

On *governance indicators,* there is an abundance of material, some excellent, some confusing, some badly misleading. The researcher will have to carefully evaluate the validity of all those indicators. The most comprehensive sources are the World Bank governance website (info.world-bank.org/governance) and the United Nations Development Program indicators (www.undp.org). See also Governance Indicators for 1996–2002, by Daniel Kaufmann, Aart Kraay and Massimo Mastruzzi: www.ssrn.com/abstract=405841.

Specifically on *transparency and anti-corruption,* the best-known source is Transparency International (www.transparency.org). However, the international ratings are sometimes questionable and in any case systematically lag behind country realities—as they depend entirely on perceptions of corruption rather than objective indicators.

On *external audit* and related issues, see the International Organization of Supreme Audit Institutions (www.intosai.org).

For *major articles and/or surveys on specific topics,* see mainly the newsweekly The Economist—www.economist.com (subscription is needed).

For a variety of international information, see the CIA's *The World Factbook* (www.cia.gov/cia/publications/factbook).

Index

Performance management *(continued)*
  reform, pragmatic approach to, 477–78, 479
  reforms, negative impact of, 182–83, 429–30, 461, 463, 468
  reforms, positive outcomes of, 461, 478–79
  regulatory conflicts, 57
  retrenchment, 180–81, 183, 195–96, 429–30
  rewarding good performance, 186, 188–93, 295, 305–6
  ten commandments of performance, 307–11
  training programs, applied to, 217, 224, 243*b*, 244, 244*b*
  training programs, evaluation of, 218, 219
  transparency, 237, 341*b*, 386, 387, 389*b*, 393
  unions, views of, 213, 457
  voice, promotion of, 81*b*, 234, 237, 304, 315, 320
  zero-based budgeting, 36, 231
  See also Codes of conduct; United States, performance management in; Wage and incentive policy
Personnel, importance of, 176–77
Personnel, information technology and, 407, 408
Personnel administration
  auditors, 147, 148, 351–52
  employee feedback, 84, 342, 343, 354, 446
  improving, 237–39
  information officers, 387–88, 393, 412
  information technology providers, 399–400
  organizational arrangements, 206–7, 208*b*, 238
  overview, 198–99
  questions for discussion, 239–40
  See also Appointments; Elite civil service; Job classification; Job transfers; Ombudsmen; Penalties and sanctions; Performance management; Personnel development; Promotions and advancement; Recruitment; Retrenchment; Rights and obligations of employees; Size of government; United States, personnel administration in; Wage and incentive policy
Personnel development
  as motivation factor, 191, 196, 215
  capacity building, 217–18, 472, 473
  community participation, 348, 364, 369, 370*b*
  elite civil service in developed countries, 242–44, 243*b*, 244*b*, 245*b*
  elite civil service in developing countries, 225, 242, 244–45, 246*b*, 406*b*
  ethical behavior, 221, 242, 258*t*, 434
  evaluation of needs, 218–19, 239
  expenditure reductions, factor in, 196, 430, 432
  information technology initiatives, 403*b*, 406*b*
  international dimension, 224–26, 239, 244–45
  limitations, 215–16, 217–18, 472
  organizational arrangements for training, 219–22, 223*b*, 239, 243, 244*b*

Personnel development *(continued)*
  procurement, framework for, 258*t*
  procurement, subnational, 265, 276, 277
  procurement in the U.S., 274, 275, 276, 277
  public information officers, 387
  questions for discussion, 239–40
  skill gaps, 188, 218, 219, 220, 222, 239
  types, 216–17
Person-related vs goal-related appraisals, 302, 304*t*
Peru, 105*b*, 226, 371
Philippines
  budget transparency, 405, 406*b*
  citizen participation, 361–62, 363*b*, 365, 366, 367
  civil society, 371, 372
  corruption, 11, 419*b*, 421, 444
  media, 396
  NGOs, 366, 378
  ombudsman office, 350
  outsourcing, 331
  personnel management, 199, 208*b*, 221, 305
  pork-barrel spending, 106, 107*b*, 160–61*b*
  subnational government, 101, 110, 111–12, 114, 115, 118*b*
Physical approach to subnational territories, 95–96
Physical capital, 358–59, 380
Physical output performance indicators, 269
PIP (public investment programs), 144–45, 155, 162, 165–67
Poland
  anti-corruption initiatives, 432, 442
  corruption, 430
  procurement practices, 255*b*, 287
  reforms, 83, 195, 255*b*, 440
Policy making. *See* Central government
Political decentralization, 99
Political environment, 7–9, 94–95, 101
  See also Colonies, former
Political fundamentals. *See* Genesis of government
Political neutrality
  as public service value, 210, 426, 427*f*
  developing countries, 193*b*, 242
  job transfers, risks of, 192, 193*b*, 238
  legal framework, 210, 231, 274
  NGOs, 375, 376, 377, 378
  United States, 231, 234–35, 236–37*b*, 237
Pork-barrel spending in the Philippines, 106, 107*b*, 160–61*b*
Pork-barrel spending, U.S.
  diversity of projects, 138, 160*b*
  dual budgeting, 166
  information technology initiatives, 409, 410–11*b*
  rules limiting, 159, 435
  subnational government, impact on, 106, 159, 160*b*
  transparency, lack of, 154, 160*b*, 161
Presidential government system, definition of, 43
Prisons, privatization of, 331*b*